The Strategy of Defeat
at the Little Big Horn

ALSO BY FREDERIC C. WAGNER III

Participants in the Battle of the Little Big Horn:
A Biographical Dictionary of Sioux, Cheyenne and
United States Military Personnel (McFarland, 2011)

The Strategy of Defeat at the Little Big Horn

A Military and Timing Analysis of the Battle

FREDERIC C. WAGNER III

McFarland & Company, Inc., Publishers

Jefferson, North Carolina

All photographs were taken by the author unless otherwise indicated.

LIBRARY OF CONGRESS CATALOGUING-IN-PUBLICATION DATA

Wagner, Frederic C., 1940–
The strategy of defeat at the Little Big Horn : a military and timing
analysis of the battle / Frederic C. Wagner III.
p.   cm.
Includes bibliographical references and index.

ISBN 978-0-7864-7954-2 (softcover : acid free paper) ∞
ISBN 978-1-4766-1881-4 (ebook)

1. Little Bighorn, Battle of the, Mont., 1876—Chronology.
2. United States. Army. Cavalry Regiment, 7th.   3. Command
of troops—Case studies.   I. Title.

E83.876.W233 2014   973.8'2—dc23   2014038532

BRITISH LIBRARY CATALOGUING DATA ARE AVAILABLE

Cover image: *Custer's Last Command* © Richard Luce
(from the collection of Francis X. Young and the artist)

Printed in the United States of America

*McFarland & Company, Inc., Publishers
Box 611, Jefferson, North Carolina 28640
www.mcfarlandpub.com*

To my wife, Lisa,
with whom all things are possible,
and whose love, understanding and patience
made this book not only possible,
but necessary.

Table of Contents

ACKNOWLEDGMENTS

In any work of this nature, one needs the help of others, and in any work of this nature, when one is married, the principal assistant is generally one's spouse, if for no other reason than simple forbearance. In my case, my wife Lisa has been everything anyone could ask for: a cheerleader, an assistant, a listener, and most of all a young woman full of understanding, love, encouragement, and enthusiasm. Without her, nothing I have ever done about the Little Big Horn would have seen the light of day—nothing. If custom did not dictate otherwise, her name would appear above mine, in larger letters, on the book's cover. When you read this work, remember who drove it home; if you need to blame someone, blame me; if you want to spread credit, think of my lovely wife.

While my wife is my driving force, my daughter—Dori Eldridge—made the book possible by her incredible map-work. Dori had never tackled the difficulty of maps and contour lines, symbols and insets, but her brilliant abilities as a photographer and her adeptness at "Photoshopping" (Dori could turn a rock into Saturn with its rings) made my ideas a reality.

Those come from all over the place and many came from five friends I meet up with on the battlefield, every odd-numbered year. They are unusual men because we all met on the Internet, then got together and have been hard-and-fast buddies ever since. We have lived and re-lived this battle hundreds of times, and we agree and disagree, then re-agree, then have a beer. Next to my wife, they are my inspiration ... and my dear friends: (alphabetically, so I do not have to buy the next several rounds) Frank Bodden, Gary Lemery, Scott Nelson, Michael Olson, and Michael "Max" Reeve.

When it comes to haunting the battlefield, most take a back seat to two marvelous people who have encouraged me and who have provided all sorts of data, much of it supporting various contentions as to horse speeds, distances and routes, and therefore form a core in my work on the timing studies in this book: Steve Andrews, a former Marine and Vietnam veteran, and Terry Craft, a marvelous woman who raises horses in Kansas. They have ridden the fields themselves and have provided me with many great photographs, as well as GPS mapping to confirm—or deny—a number of my suspicions. Without Steve and Terry, much of what I have done would have been mere guesswork; with them, it has become certainty.

Another long-time Little Big Horn "passionista" is Diane Merkel, who, over the years, has always been supportive of my work. It was Diane who spurred me on to publish my various works, so whatever I do needs to be accompanied by the notation "It was Diane's idea." Without Diane's encouragement this would have never been published.

The same thanks go to Bill Rini with whom I started all my timing business—unfortunately Bill went his own direction, though as I think about it now, our differences make for very good debate ... again, over that ubiquitous beer—and Stephen Kryzk for opening my eyes to the reality of a more accurate tally of Native Americans living during the mid–1860s. His exhaustive work seems much more realistic than the hypothesizing provided by long-distance "guessti-mates" so many people back then relied on, many of which only served personal needs, much as today. Stephen's insistence upon me giving proper credit to Kingsley M. Bray for having done most of the grunt-work is indicative of a friend's humility. There are also many intangibles that go into an endeavor of this sort, especially regarding the Native Americans. Those intangibles lead one to conclusions and feelings of various kinds, a sort of insightful understanding of things out of one's normal ken. It allows a person to understand how others may act. Mary Lou Backus provided me with just such an emotional understanding through her marvelous writings on the American Indian. Without people like Mary Lou we can never appreciate properly those who have seemed alien to us. From the aspect of the warriors in this historic event, this book would have been highly stilted without her help.

Dale Kosman, one of the most avid and knowledgeable aficionados of *anything* to do with the Little Big Horn—including riding the trails in full woolen uniform in the stifling heat of summer—has patiently and consistently given me permission to use his remarkable photograph of my so-called, "3,411," the terrain feature I believe Custer stood on as he viewed the beginning of Markus Reno's skirmish line fight. Dale took the picture from the valley floor and its clarity leaves me with no doubt 3,411 was Custer's perch. Aside from his friendship and his ever-present smile, I thank Dale for his kindness. The same can be said of Michael Donohue, a summertime park ranger and the chairman of the Temple College Art Department. Mike is another man who never stops smiling, never stops laughing ... even when the laughter is at his own expense ... and is always there to help. The site of Marc Kellog's body has been a controversy over the years and even its present marker location on the battlefield irks many. Mike solved that riddle for me and because it came from him, I know it is true.

I would be remiss if I did not include a very heart-felt thanks to the fine artist, Richard Luce, who painted the magnificent picture gracing the cover of this book. Richard's work is not only beautifully detailed; it borders on the spectacular for its grand, sweeping depictions of battle. I own a print of this beauty, but whenever I want to see the real thing I head to the home of a dear friend, Frank Young, a brother of my sister-in-law, who bought the original—unfamiliar though he may have been with the battle—simply because of its grandness. My thanks go to both Richard and Frank; I feel privileged to be a part of this painting.

Gregory Shelton of the United States Naval Observatory provided me with data helping me form opinions and develop the time/motion studies. Without that data we would be less certain of everything, and along with the accounts of two officers with Custer and the U.S.N.O.'s data, I became convinced of the time standard the Seventh Cavalry utilized.

I met Don Horn several years ago, having heard the name but knowing little about the man. Since then, Don and I have become friends and he has provided me with pictures and notes, letters and books ... we battle ideas and we bore each other with stories. At least, I bore Don with mine; his are way too good to bore anyone. He is a link to the last of those who knew the characters in the "play." His knowledge is invaluable and I have been graced by his friendship.

Anything I do, as well, needs to mention the help and the research of Dr. Richard Allan Fox, Jr., and his brother Dennis. It was Professor Fox' book, *Archaeology, History, and Custer's Last Battle* that drove me on this mission. No one has ever done it better, and while my timeline was done independently of Fox' conclusions, one can only imagine how delighted I was when his scenarios were the only ones fitting completely with testimonies, Indian accounts, and reasonable expectations. Richard Fox found the answers.

Then there is Billy Markland, to my way of thinking the finest researcher of anything to do with the Indian-fighting army of the old American West. I have never met Billy, but we have spoken on the phone and e-mailed one another with trivia and "greatness." Billy's generosity has fed my curiosity without bounds and I rely on him like few others.

John Duquette, a retired U.S. Army armor officer, has provided me with the beautiful movement charts contained in this volume, pictorials helping to show how formations were put together and where American army soldiers fought and remained when the dust and smoke had cleared. John has put up with my constant changing, my constant demands, and, as is typical of a professional soldier, done so without a gripe (that I know of). The most long-suffering of all my soldier friends, however, is the implacable Will Bender who actually sat through and claimed to have enjoyed critiquing my chapter on the valley fighting, as well as being the only person I entrusted my time charts to critique. Will's service in the Army's elite Special Forces is cause enough for me to salute my friend. Is there a Nobel Prize for Patience?

Another unwitting contributor I must heartily thank is Mike Powell who contributed some marvelous information on shell casings found between Weir Peaks and the Reno entrenchment area—probably left by Lieutenant Edward Settle Godfrey's K Company during the pullback from "The Peaks." Mike's heads-up "confirmed"—as best we are able to use that word—my theory where Godfrey set up his skirmish line covering the retrograde. The same thanks go to Justin Schwend who was kind enough to take my friends and me all around the Rosebud valley area, including places normally inaccessible to a bunch of fellows unfamiliar with some of the more obscure historical places. Justin and his lovely wife Cassandra topped off our day with a marvelous barbecue, all done by Cassandra. Justin also provided me with some keen insight on horse speeds and the terminology one should be using. A careful reader will note his clever input.

Sometimes I wondered what anyone would think if they saw my handsome nephew—Richard Camilli—and me, wandering along the high school track, suddenly bursting into a full run, crouched over, then dropping flat to the ground; sometimes crawling, sometimes jogging hunched over ... two lunatics trying to compute speeds and distances and times ... without getting ourselves *too* dirty or worn out. We seldom come across freer spirits than Richard ... or nicer people, for that matter.

And last but certainly not least, my heartfelt thanks go out to a severe critic, an absolutely brilliant individual named Richard L. MacLeod, referred to by many as simply "Dark Cloud." Richard's irascible writings, his brilliant Web-based commentaries, his sharp wit, and his driving determination to get things right, to portray people honestly, to treat history properly, have driven me to what I hope to be a semblance of excellence. He issued the challenge I hope I have met. It is hard sometimes for a man my age to admit he has found a new teacher, but it became very easy when I realized whom I was dealing with in "DC." I will also never forget his kindness when he found out about an illness I subsequently overcame. I looked forward to his "letters" of support, his wit, his charm. Richard MacLeod is an uncompromising champion of excellence and I only hope this work will be worth his smile.

My thanks to them all; their signatures are on every page.

PREFACE

"It is wiser, I believe, to arrive at theory by way of the evidence rather the other way around, like so many revisionists today. It is more rewarding, in any case, to assemble the facts first and, in the process of arranging them in narrative form, to discover a theory or a historical generalization emerging of its own accord."—Barbara Tuchman

On June 25 and 26, 1876, in the wilds of a vast and largely unexplored land tract called the Montana Territory, the United States Army suffered a staggering defeat at the hands of a huge Native American force of Sioux, Cheyenne, and Arapaho warriors. In the more than 137 years since, every aspect of the battle has come under scrutiny, most generating some sort of controversy and disagreement. The only thing we know for certain is one of America's dashing Civil War heroes, Lieutenant Colonel—brevet Major General—George Armstrong Custer, was killed on that sunny, hot, dry, dust-riddled day, though even how he died, who killed him, where he received his fatal wounds, and every other permutation of that event is questioned.

This book—like so many before it—is designed to try to clear some of that dust, but *unlike* so many coming before, does so from two aspects, often talked about but seldom achieved. The first aspect encompasses the military designs of the battle and how they succeeded or failed. The second revolves around my belief the events of the Little Big Horn can only be understood properly by defining the times of day they occurred and then combining those times with the military exigencies of a battle—*any* battle—and placing those time-exigencies in a chronological order squaring with distances, terrain, and field conditions.

As one can see already, this is a military analysis more than a historical recital. For history, I might suggest James Willert's brilliant, day-by-day account, *Little Big Horn Diary*. It is a thrilling book and it is quoted often within these pages. We can add to that, Dr. John S. Gray's *Custer's Last Cam-*

paign, for Dr. Gray was the only person—until now—to attempt a time-motion study of the battle. But it is my belief, however, that Dr. Gray's work is compromised by factors other than objectivity, rendering his entire battle analysis problematic at best. Gray's failures though are mitigated by his riveting account of events leading up to June 25. For the more advanced students of the battle, I may suggest turning to the *sine qua non* of Little Big Horn research, *Archaeology, History, and Custer's Last Battle* by Dr. Richard Allan Fox, Jr. Armed with these three volumes, one can become a Little Big Horn scholar, indeed.

In this work, the reader should be forewarned, not all the battle's events are covered, for some add little to our understanding of tactics and military actions. Major Marcus Reno's retreat from the valley is merely mentioned, glossed over, for we learn nothing from a panicked rout—other than to avoid one! Events of June 26 are not discussed either: the 26th was a siege, highlighted by feats of bravery, bravery runs, and sniping. It adds nothing to our analysis and many other books have covered the day's events, maybe none better than Bruce Liddic's *Vanishing Victory*.

The approach used in *The Strategy of Defeat* is unique. I attempt neither to criticize nor laud the ideas used in the strategic conceptualization of this summer campaign, nor do I attempt to criticize Custer's tactics, even though they failed—all of that is reserved for Monday mornings. As with all military operations, the battle of the Little Big Horn met so many imponderables, so many things that could go wrong, so many unknowns ... and ultimately, so many people who were bent on preventing someone else from forcing his will and ability on them. The critique here is not on Custer's faulty tactics—*if* they were faulty ... and there is sufficient reason to doubt that—but on the factors forcing him to choose those tactics. It was the breakdown of all available knowledge, all available intelligence, all known experiences, all similar approaches—and all of these leading to the final mystery—that mark our continuing fascination with the Little Big Horn, yet we have never been quite able to put our finger on just that problem ... until now ... hopefully.

❧ *Reading the Timelines* ❧

The time-motion study developed for this work took form over a period of close to five years ... most days and many times into the early morning hours of the next. It was developed using topographical maps, ground photographs, aerial photographs and maps, data from the United States Naval Observatory, measured distances, recognized and scientifically carried-out archaeological findings, speeds, artifactual findings, on-the-ground observations, the kindness of friends who provided important data, and—*the major key to the theories contained herein*—the side-by-side narratives of some 200 participants and eye-witnesses, both red and white. The original master document from which the individual lettered Timelines in this book are taken consists of 530 line-entries—3,360 separate records—almost every one of which is documented or "sourced" by the narratives of these participants. Some of the entries—of necessity—are documented by well-known historians and writers (though by design these have been limited—after all, they were not there), while a few others carry the notation, "Simulation." The simulations are not just made-up entries, however. They are the result of a natural flow, a natural progression one would expect to come about from a particular event. For example, other events and testimony dictate Custer was moving down Reno Creek at a fairly high rate of speed. An entry reads, "Main column (Custer/Reno) reaches the confluence of No-Name and Reno creeks. Custer is moving with his five companies abreast—left to right—E, F, L, I, C. Reno is in a column-of-fours, Company A in the center." This entry is commensurate with a column moving rapidly and we have first-hand accounts supporting that conclusion and the formations. Also, we can figure an approximate location and time because of an assumed speed of advance based on these same accounts. A following entry reads, "Command is passing the morass." We know Custer and his troops had to have gone by this terrain feature because we know his route of march, narratives indicating the command entered an area called "the flats," then coming across a deserted tepee a short time later. So while we have no specific *participant attribution* to any event involving these columns passing a morass, in the source notes referring to this entry, we use "Simulation." The simulated entry provides a continuous flow for Custer's movement down Reno Creek and is a logical consequence or progression stemming from the preceding event. It should also be understood we are making no

claim for the definitive here ... much of this is not known as fact. We play the percentages, probabilities and possibilities, supported by as much participant narrative as we could muster. We do not know with certainty what happened here, but we can use the accounts left us to arrive at likely conclusions, and while we make certain assumptions, those assumptions fit the participants' accounts. This book is written that way, with that in mind.

In order to understand fully the issues of time, time zones, and timing, some specifics need to be addressed first. These deal with the development of the driving force of this book, the timelines: "driving force," because without an understanding of the time various events took place, the battle of the Little Big Horn cannot be understood properly, and those failing to realize this are doomed to read a recitation of events without understanding why and how these events transpired. Furthermore, without knowledge of the times—as close to specificity as possible ... or plausible—neither the historian nor the student will ever be able to grasp the tactics employed and properly assess the success, the failure, or the reasoning behind why the tactics were chosen by a particular commander. This lack of understanding can also lead to the unjust condemnation of actions and people. For the historical event of the Little Big Horn, time rules all. And there are too many impressions extant, formed not by fact, but by the opinions of others.

To determine how I reached my conclusions for many of the times contained in the 25 time/motion/speed charts—the Timelines, as they are called—it is necessary to review methodology. To begin with, I identified and developed a series of 37 topics containing some 5,500 line-item events—almost 33,500 separate records—pertaining to the battle. I titled these topics "Incident Reports." For example, among these reports was one called "Times." Included in "Times" were any references by participants to specific times of day, e.g., 3:15 p.m. or noon; and any relative times or references leading to timing events, i.e., "about 15 minutes," "we galloped," "we moved rapidly," etc. The "galloped" and "rapidly" references were then carried over into a separate Incident Report labeled "Speeds." Combined, these two reports alone yielded some 500 line items. (All of these line-item entries were taken from more than 850 pages of excerpted narratives, accounts, writings, and testimonies of some 225 battle participants or contemporaries, on both sides of the fight.)

To determine the accuracy of these reported times and speeds (speeds were used because of their relationship in creating time-events), they were categorized by specific events, i.e., crossing the divide, crossing at Ford A, the battle's first firing, etc.; and then line-items, by name, were compared side by side. Outrageous anomalies were discarded, but only if an attempt to place them in some semblance of context failed. Once a subjective but reasonable test was failed, then discarded they were. Surprisingly, the anomalies proved quite scarce, the most egregious being a 2:00 p.m. Reno-Custer separation time given us by Lieutenant George D. Wallace. More than 40 specific and relative time references rendered Wallace's recollection virtually impossible to accept or substantiate, so its specificity was discarded as an error, yet its relativity considered in some form of retention, i.e., maybe Wallace misread his watch and meant 1:00 p.m. not 2:00 ... on the hour, not some unknown minute between the hour. During all the confusion and the hectic goings-on just prior to the opening salvos of the battle, that was a very possible and plausible error, and in light of other statements Wallace made, there is both motive and logic for this action.

There are some elements of the Timelines needing clarification. First off, there is the layout. Each Timeline shows the local sun time, included simply because we can determine a "noon" reference in Native American accounts, giving us a comparison to the actual watch-time on which the troops operated. As the reader will see, there is a 57-minute difference. (With data from the U.S. Naval Observatory in Washington, D.C., and accounts from two of the officers in Custer's command, I have determined this watch-time to be that used by the column's commanding general, Alfred H. Terry, at his headquarters in St. Paul, Minnesota.) We then have the event referred to; the speed of advance connected to that event (if appropriate); and the distance traveled (also if appropriate). The last column on the right is labeled "Notes," its numbers corresponding to "Timeline Notes" following the Timelines showing where or how the data were determined. This is where one will find the note "Simulation."

The first few Timelines the reader will encounter are pretty straightforward, but beginning with Timeline D, some entries are shaded in light gray. These are included to show attendant significant actions in other areas of the field. This is strictly for comparison and to show where and when those other actions were transpiring while we focus on a specific event.

In Timeline F, the reader will encounter entries in the "Speed" and "Distance Traveled" columns that are "boxed." Those entries indicate the culmination of an event from one significant place discussed in the text to another, and the average speed of that movement. In addition, there are three "double-boxed" entries, all reading, "Sighted 500 yards downstream from Reno Hill," and all pertaining to Lieutenant Charles A. Varnum, Custer's Chief of Scouts on this expedition. This was a highly significant event leading to several

other controversial events, hence the double boxes. The only other feature that may cause question is found in several entries in the "Speed" column, and those are the speeds in parentheses, used to show the reader the speed about to be commenced.

There is also some repetition from one timeline to another, but again, that is to keep specific events or actions flowing in a continuous manner and to re-acquaint the reader with lapsed specifics. Rather than maintain a long, continuous and possibly confusing timeline needing to be referred to constantly, I have chosen to use the 25 individual charts to explain specific events or groups of individuals, e.g., messengers, scouts, etc.

The reader will also encounter a few space-saving abbreviations such as MTC (Medicine Tail Coulee), LBH (obviously, Little Big Horn), and—in the Timeline Notes—the most prominent, RCOI, for the Reno Court of Inquiry, a judicial proceeding held in January and February 1879, in an attempt to clear or damn Major Marcus A. Reno. When the RCOI abbreviation is in italics, it refers to the book of the same name; when in Roman, it merely refers to the event. One other little oddity the reader may notice is the spelling of the last name of the Arikara interpreter Fred Gerard. Throughout Little Big Horn literature, Gerard's name is spelled variously, Gerard or Girard. Girard-with-an-i is the English-American way of spelling the name; with an e it is the original French-Canadian spelling which Gerard apparently used and which I use in this book.

Another issue needing to be addressed is the discrepancy between actual terrain and terrain measured on a flat-surfaced map. This turned out to be easier than I imagined at first, simply because *time ruled all!* For example, if the map distance showed Captain Fred Benteen traveled seven miles between noon and 2:00 p.m. we compute that speed at 3.5 miles per hour. The distance Benteen traveled, however, would be somewhat greater because of the constant up-and-down over the hills and valleys he encountered. That would mean his speed was actually greater as well, but overall, irrelevant, because other events dictated when he began, and when and where he wound up at 2:00 p.m. *Nothing is made up, contrived, or jerry-rigged for convenience; everything is driven by accounts of those who were there!* It is merely a matter of degree; e.g., does "gallop" mean eight miles per hour or 15 miles per hour? Speed, therefore, would become the least relevant constituent in the analysis, everything else dictating that particular facet of the timeline.

The most distinctive feature of this time-motion study—and therefore one certain to generate the most controversy—is the timing of the Custer fight itself. This has never been done before and is unique to this study; in fact, it has never even been attempted ... at least formally, in print. Surprisingly, using the methodology employed with all the other events, its development was relatively easy. By segregating various Native American accounts to determine actions and "whereabouts," then coupling those data with distances and reasonable speeds, and using accounts from men farther upstream as they pertained to sounds and silences downstream, I was able to determine fair beginning-ending times. Indians left few references regarding time—valid or not—but those that were left us were extremely helpful, and when combined with other data gave a surprisingly clear picture of how the fight unfolded.

In the end, I attempted to plug in the many battle scenarios other writers and historians have conjectured. Incredible as it may seem, only one fit my time template ... but I will let the reader make that determination as to which one it was.

Context is extremely important to any work of this nature. The key is being able to place every example, every event, and every action within a specific framework pertaining to a single element, event, unit of time, or unit of organization. For example, M Company: performing a specific operation; advancing on a skirmish line in the valley, or a portion advancing through the woods, etc. All the examples brought up in this work are within a much broader context involving multiple organizations, multiple events, and multiple times, all of which may be interpreted in various ways, and which may be confused with one another because of the broader context. For instance, A, G, and M companies; the valley fight; retreat *to* the timber; fighting *in* the timber; retreat *from* the timber; dismount, mount, dismount, mount, etc. All of those examples could pertain to almost any event within that broader context, but to be accurate, they cannot; they must pertain to a single, specific context and therefore more valid in determining an actual event. The reason this sounds so complicated or difficult is because at any given point in the event there were four or more military units acting independently, yet all calling—in one fashion or another—upon another. And we are not even considering the interaction with the warriors and those various permutations. It is imperative to remember that *when dealing with context, one must fit theory into context, and not attempt to fit context into theory!* This is the most common error writers, historians, and students have made.

Once all the data were collected, line-item entries for each event were compared and an "event-time" arrived at. Again surprisingly, most of these times were easy to compute ... and there were some exceptions, obviously, but they were dealt with as succeeding events unfolded; it became relatively easy to interpolate, commentary about speeds helping immensely because those commentaries added the needed perspective.

Above everything, the battle of the Little Big Horn was a military operation and must always be viewed as such. These men were professional soldiers. Eleven of the 27 assigned officers were West Point graduates and two others had military academy experience, one at West Point, the other at Annapolis. Still others were Civil War veterans, and none of the battle's officers wound up leaving the service prematurely, at least of his own volition. The same can be said for many of the non-commissioned officers—the sergeants and corporals—a number of whom were career cavalrymen, many having served, as well, in the Civil War, and in 1876, the Seventh Cavalry was perceived as the finest cavalry regiment in the U.S. Army. Of the 576 enlisted personnel at the battle, only nine had seen less than six months of military service and six of those men were relegated to pack train duty. While the quality of training was a far cry from that of today, young men were more attuned to and more likely to have ridden a horse and fired a rifle or carbine—the main components of a cavalryman—than men of today would be in driving a tank or firing a rocket launcher prior to military service.

It is imperative readers understand these events as being military in nature, both in design and in execution. If we do not understand that, then all is lost in any effort to find the truth or appreciate the motives and actions of these men. Without that understanding too many pernicious theories, uninformed opinions, and silly fantasies of glory and adventure emerge, only muddying the smooth, logical flow of events eventually leading to the breakdown in discipline and the defeat and partial destruction of a military unit. As with all military operations a certain anxiety was present at the start of the battle, and this anxiety—or adrenalin-filled apprehension, something only natural considering the circumstances—demanded speed and surprise, otherwise it was believed the foe might slip away rendering the entire campaign a senseless and costly exercise, as well as a political embarrassment for an administration already saddled with scorching corruption.

As we cut away through the mists of time, our time-motion analysis reveals the military exigency expressed by the battle's many participants, be they uniformed or not. Many believe George Custer and his regiment walked to the battle. Some believe Marcus Reno, once across the Little Big Horn River, waited 30–40 minutes before commencing his assault, and still others believe Custer himself sat in Medicine Tail Coulee for some 45 minutes while the battle raged on in the valley and Indians were moving around rapidly, chopping up the regiment. (Much of this has been inserted in latter years to make up for a lack of understanding of the time events took place or the amount of time from start to finish. It became easier to say people had to wait in order to make sense of times left us in many participant accounts.) While there is credibility to narratives claiming Custer sat for 15–20 minutes on a ridge at the northern extreme of the field—similar attributions lacking in the other instances—there is a sound military explanation for this action (also lacking in the others). And Custer was hardly idle during this brief, later hiatus, as you will discover. Of course when we look at the Little Big Horn through the filters of the military, we strip away some of the personal, antagonistic drama, the preconceptions and prejudices too many people revel in; we eliminate the scapegoats, the excuses, the personal hatreds and animosities, and we see the battle for what it really was, we see the men for what they really were, and we can judge the commanders and officers for what they did, not for who they liked or disliked. It was history ... but it was more. It taught lessons; lessons pertinent today. And we see mistakes. Reader, mark this well: *mistakes*; not stupidity; not rashness; not glory-seeking ... simply, mistakes.

One final thing ... we ask a multitude of questions throughout this volume, some of which we purposely do not answer. Sometimes the reader must do this himself, he must involve his own thought process. We want this to be a book where the reader can also make his *own* decisions and not just parrot mine; where the student of history can attempt to delve into the mind of a formidable American soldier and possibly answer—for himself—why George Custer did what he did that fateful day. *We* cannot answer those questions ... maybe *you* can.

Without the proper understanding of "why," it becomes impossible to see this seminal event in American history as anything more than a bungled battle between rash, glory-hungry soldiers and two or three iconic Indians and their legions of followers. The battle of the Little Big Horn was anything but.

1

Drums Along the Rosebud

There are very few events in American history continuing to generate the interest and rancor we see with a study of the battle of the Little Big Horn. Any discussion centers around its most famous progenitor, Lieutenant Colonel George Armstrong Custer, and from there, conversations branch off to culpability—if one does not blame the whole debacle on Custer—the forks leading to his senior lieutenants, Major Marcus Albert Reno and Captain Frederick William Benteen. In reality, the entire event usually degenerates into a disagreement of personalities and even with so many proclaiming forbearance we see favorites played in virtually any study ever written.

It is fruitless to go into the specific opprobria heaped upon each officer, but it is worthwhile from the very beginning of this book to make the point none of those individuals deserve all the blame or all the credit for what occurred. If the battle were studied from the perspective of what it really was—a military operation—and its attendant events placed within their proper context and timing—the primary elements of focus in this study—we reach conclusions quite contrary to the norm, and because of the one hundred thirty-seven years of fossilizing cement, conclusions likely to be greeted with eminent skepticism. If the reader wishes to learn and understand, then he should continue on; if not, he should put this book aside and continue to play his favorites, however astray they may lead him.

For all intents and purposes, the historic event of the Little Big Horn began three days before the battle—June 22, 1876—when George Custer was handed his written orders, departed the aegis of the department commander, Brigadier General Alfred H. Terry, and moved with his entire regiment—the first time in its ten-year history it had ever operated as a full, integral command—and proceeded up the valley of the Rosebud Creek in the territory of Montana. Everything prior to the twenty-second was prelude and has been written about quite effectively by authors and historians

James Willert, John S. Gray, Edgar I. Stewart, and many others. Those events were straightforward and ultimately led to Custer's move along the Rosebud, a move precipitated by the belief the campaign's quarry—the Sioux and Cheyenne winter roamers—was located in the valley of the Little Big Horn River. Custer's orders, however, were not quite as straightforward:

Camp at Mouth of Rosebud River
Montana Territory, June 22, 1876
Lieut. Col. Custer, 7th Cavalry

Colonel:

The brigadier general commanding directs that as soon as your regiment can be made ready for the march, you will proceed up the Rosebud in pursuit of the Indians whose trail was discovered by Major Reno a few days since. It is, of course, impossible to give you any definite instructions in regard to this movement, and were it not impossible to do so, the Department Commander places too much confidence in your zeal, energy, and ability to wish to impose upon you precise orders which might hamper your action when nearly in contact with the enemy. He will, however, indicate to you his own views of what your action should be, and he desires that you should conform to them unless you should see sufficient reason for departing from them. He thinks you should proceed up the Rosebud until you ascertain definitely the direction in which the trail above spoken of leads. Should it be found (as it appears almost certain that it will be found) to turn towards the Little Horn, he thinks that you should still proceed southward, perhaps as far as the headwaters of the Tongue, and then turn towards the Little Horn, feeling constantly, however, to your left, so as to preclude the possibility of escape of the Indians to the south or southeast by passing around your left flank. The column of Colonel Gibbon is now in motion for the mouth of the Big Horn. As soon as it reaches that point it will cross the Yellowstone and move up at least as far as the forks of the Big and Little Horns. Of course its future movements must be controlled by circumstances as they arise, but it is hoped that the Indians, if upon the Little Horn, may be so nearly enclosed by the two columns that their escape will be impossible.

The Department Commander desires that on your way up the Rosebud you should thoroughly examine the upper part of Tullock's Creek, and that you should endeavor to send a scout through to Colonel Gibbon's column, with information of the result of your examination. The lower part of the creek will be examined by a detachment from Colonel Gibbon's command. The supply steamer will be pushed up the Big Horn as far as the forks if the river is found to be navigable for that distance, and the Department Commander, who will accompany the column of Colonel Gibbon, desires you report to him there not later than the expiration of the time for which your troops are rationed, unless in the meantime you receive further orders.

Very respectfully, Your obedient servant,
[Signed] E. W. Smith, Captain, 18th Inf.,
Acting Assistant Adjutant General[1]

As one can see, Custer was given a certain element of discretion, discretion many students of the battle claim as *carte blanche* to do whatever he chose. In addition, these same people point out this was not an "order," per se, but merely a "letter of instructions." Those arguments are both specious and fatuous and point out a palpable lack of understanding of how military commands are issued and carried out. A general officer's wishes are tantamount to an order and anyone taking a cavalier attitude with those wishes puts his career in serious jeopardy. Terry included the phrases, "impossible to give you any definite instructions in regard to this movement," "[does not wish] to impose upon you precise orders which might hamper your action when nearly in contact with the enemy," and the delimitation "[Terry] desires that you should conform to them [Terry's views] *unless you should see sufficient reason for departing from them*" [emphasis added]. This, however, is not as clear-cut as it might appear. It takes some studying, but a closer look reveals this leeway pertains only to actions "which might hamper [Custer's] action when nearly in contact with the enemy." It says nothing of ignoring Terry's wishes to ensure Tullock's Creek was properly scouted or of ensuring the upper reaches of the Rosebud valley were free of hostiles. Actions precipitating a premature battle were neither addressed, nor were they included in any of the allowances Terry granted. While there were any number of pre-contact assumptions, i.e., Custer would be the attacking force; an expressed desire Colonel John Gibbon's infantry would participate, etc., it was clear Terry, Gibbon, and Custer were united in their concern the great Indian get-together would disperse too quickly, scattering tribes to the winds. By cutting too early to the Little Big Horn valley, Custer failed to ensure the preclusion of "the possibility of escape of the Indians to the south or southeast by [their] passing around [his] left flank." Despite the growing evidence of a great gathering west of the Rosebud–Little Big Horn divide, there was no assurance more Indians were not to Custer's south and left. Continuing to move up the Rosebud valley, "feeling constantly ... left," would have eliminated or mitigated that possibility. (It is interesting to note here more Indians joined the huge encampment after the battle ended. For example, the "Old Man

Chief" Little Wolf, a Northern *Suhtai* [a Cheyenne branch], had left the Red Cloud Agency in Nebraska to join the Sioux. Depending on whom we wish to believe, this band consisted of a mere seven lodges or, "Little Wolf, 'with 1,000 of his people, including two hundred warriors' departed Red Cloud Agency for the northwest,"[2] and trailed soldiers to the Little Big Horn area, arriving after the first day's fighting ended. In this case, "seven lodges" is much closer to the truth, the other estimate reflecting the hyperbolic ravings surrounding the event.)

Terry's instructions went on:

Should it be found (as it appears almost certain that it will be found) to turn towards the Little Horn, [Terry] thinks that you should still proceed southward, perhaps as far as the headwaters of the Tongue, and then turn towards the Little Horn, feeling constantly, however, to your left.

This wording caps immediately the discretion Custer has been given, relegating that discretion to contact with enemy forces.

In an article appearing in *Blue & Gray* magazine, former Custer Battlefield park superintendent, Neil Mangum, emphasized,

If the trail veered west to the Little Big Horn as expected, Custer was to ignore it and continue south up the Rosebud before turning west and descending the Little Big Horn—unless he saw sufficient reasons to change the orders. The rationale for not directly following the Indian trail across to the Little Big Horn was to minimize the possibility of detection, and reduce the chances of "scattering" the enemy. Indians were notorious for scattering into small bands and melting into the countryside to avoid major confrontations and to elude pursuers, much the way partisan rangers, such as those under John Singleton Mosby, had done during the Civil War. Terry expressed to Custer the necessity of preventing the Indians' escape by advancing far enough south before turning west. Custer's positioning on the headwaters of the Little Big Horn River would enable him to intercept fleeing warriors, give battle, or at least drive them north, down the valley, into Gibbon's column marching up the Little Big Horn.[3]

Furthermore, Fred Dustin brought out this point emphatically in his work, *The Custer Tragedy,* when he wrote,

Terry ... had quickly grasped the situation and reasoned thus; that there were enough Indians in the band already located to make a hard battle possible, and that to make it successful a concerted movement would be necessary. For Custer alone or Gibbon alone to strike them would mean a scattering at the best, with a possibility of disaster, for it was more than possible that this already large band of warriors had been reinforced by hundreds of others.[4]

Warfare is unlike any other profession. If mistakes are made in the corporate world, the worst that happens generally is money is lost. Seldom do corporate errors lead to the loss of human life. That is not the case in the military. Training errors can result in the loss of equipment or in some personal embarrassment, but mistakes in combat almost always lead to the death of soldiers. When an officer issues orders, he does so for specific reasons and to accomplish a specific goal. Generally, such orders carry the full weight of military legality. Whether we couch these "orders" in terms laymen understand as "instructions" or "guidelines," they maintain the force of the officer's will. When this officer holds flag rank, i.e., a general or admiral, the importance of compliance becomes even more paramount. In today's army, the flouting or ignoring of such "wishes" is tantamount to a career-ending decision and one does so at such risk. For George Custer to have invoked his "escape clause" at the point he did and under such circumstances as then existed, was for him to run similar risk. We will discuss this in more detail in the chapter on Tullock's Creek.

On June 21, Terry wrote a report to his commander, General Phil Sheridan, outlining his plan to accompany Gibbon and his Montana column to the confluence of the Little Big Horn and Big Horn rivers, while sending Custer up the Rosebud, across to the headwaters of the Little Big Horn, and down that river. This would be a quasi-pincer movement and while this may seem to seal Terry's thinking process—and intent—as being a single idea in a fixed, linear fashion, there was another consideration. Some time after the disaster, Captain Robert Patterson Hughes, Terry's aide-de-camp and brother-in-law, blamed Custer for Terry's forced move out of the Tullock's Creek valley and into the brutal badlands separating Tullock's from the Big Horn River. Terry had attached a scout named George Herendeen to Custer's column for the specific intention of checking out Tullock's valley. Had Custer complied and Herendeen found that valley free of hostiles, Hughes felt Terry would have simply moved up Tullock's, and then made the easy move toward the Indian village, backtracking a route Gibbon's Captain Edward Ball had scouted previously (April 26–May 1). Terry would have been in position to assist in the battle, especially since it was believed the Indians were camped farther up the Little Big Horn valley than where they were found.[5] Again, while Hughes' supposition was far from apodictic and was issued when everyone was running for cover from the battle's fallout, Custer's failure to scout Tullock's Creek took away an option from his commander, an almost inexcusable military gaffe.

The fact remains, there are enough military opinions—mine included—Custer exceeded his authority and warped and prematurely usurped the discretion he was allowed. Therefore, it was this decision to disobey the spirit—if not the letter—of his orders dictating Custer's tactics at the Little

Big Horn, and we must judge those tactics with this in mind. It would be extremely difficult *to justify these same tactics* were the Seventh Cavalry coming *down* the Little Big Horn valley—as Terry anticipated—instead of *into* the valley via Reno Creek. Custer's tactics on June 25 were born of an illegitimate conjugation and regardless of how sound they might have been on the battlefield it is always with this lack of validity in mind they need to be considered. Given the aftermath of June 25, one wonders what the consequences would have been had Custer survived and managed to eke out even a Pyrrhic victory. To be fair, much of the resultant opprobrium may have stemmed from everyone's desire to distance themselves from the responsibility of failure—and cost—but nonetheless, it is a speculator's nirvana.

The summer campaign of 1876 started long before the summer. The plan called for three independent columns to converge on a general area where the recalcitrant Sioux and Cheyenne were believed to be gathering—possibly somewhere in the Powder River country of eastern Montana. On March 1, Brigadier General George Crook, at the head of some 1,100 troops, plus scouts and reporters, departed Fort Fetterman in the Wyoming Territory. On the seventeenth, part of Crook's column under the command of Colonel Joseph J. Reynolds attacked the 110-lodge Cheyenne village of Old Bear located on the Powder River. Reynolds won a Pyrrhic victory of sorts, only to retire in a modicum of disarray, a feat that earned him a court-martial. By the twenty-sixth, Crook had returned to Fetterman, where he camped out until May 29.

On April 3, in a furious snowstorm, Colonel John Gibbon left Fort Ellis near Bozeman in the Montana Territory, eventually joining with other elements of his Montana column: 431 uniformed personnel of Gibbon's own Seventh Infantry and elements of the Second Cavalry commanded by Major James Sanks Brisbin. Gibbon's thrust was eastward along the Yellowstone River and he was under the command of General Terry, who also commanded the Dakota column leaving Fort Abraham Lincoln, just outside of Bismarck in the Dakota Territory. It was this latter column that contained the 738-man Seventh Cavalry along with some 321 infantrymen, plus a vast wagon train and dozens of scouts. Terry's objective was to march west, establish supply depots, and link up with Gibbon, hopefully keeping the Sioux below the Yellowstone. Terry and Custer departed Fort Lincoln on May 17.

June 22 was the thirty-seventh day of the campaign for Terry, Custer, and the Seventh Cavalry, a campaign of frustration and extreme physical exertion, a campaign laced with harsh weather, difficult terrain, and a maddeningly exasperating and elusive quarry. Other than some small war parties and a pair of semi-ignored sightings by Lieutenant James H. Bradley, Gibbon's chief-of-scouts, the hostile Sioux and Cheyenne were nowhere to be seen. It was not until shortly before Custer began his trek up the Rosebud when it was determined the Indians were most likely somewhere in the valley of the Little Big Horn River. Even at that, the commanders' thinking was faulty, for rather than the upper valley the camp was soon discovered toward its lower end. To make matters even more problematic it was believed operations would have to affect a measure of surprise otherwise the tribes would scatter rendering the campaign's entire strategy an abject failure, and it was known the Indians were aware of the presence of soldiers in the territory. The irony, however, was the Sioux had overlooked the Seventh Cavalry completely.

In addition to George Herendeen, prior to departing, Terry had assigned six Crow scouts and the famous scout-guide, Mitch Boyer, to Custer's command. Then after the regiment had paraded in front of Terry and Gibbon and was beginning its fateful march toward the Rosebud, Gibbon claimed he yelled after Custer, "Now, don't be greedy Custer, as there are Indians enough for all of us!"[6] Custer's response indicated he could take care of the campaign's entire objective, though to be fair, that may be open to some interpretation. A year after the battle, Gibbon wrote,

> The bugles sounded the "boots and saddles," and Custer, after starting the advance, rode up and joined us [Terry and Gibbon]. Together we sat on our horses and witnessed the approach of the command as it threaded its way through the rank sagebrush which covered the valley. First came a band of buglers sounding a march, and as they came opposite to General Terry they wheeled out of the column as at review, continuing to play as the command passed along. The regiment presented a fine appearance, and as the various companies passed us we had a good opportunity to note the number of fine horses in the ranks, many of them being part-blooded horses from Kentucky, and I was told there was not a sore-backed horse among them. General Custer appeared to be in good spirits, chatted freely with us, and was evidently proud of the appearance of his command. The pack-mules, in a compact body, followed the regiment; behind them came a rear-guard, and as that approached Custer shook hands with us and bade us good-bye. As he turned to leave us, I made some pleasant remark, warning him against being greedy, and with a gay wave of his hand he called back, "No, I will not," and rode off after his command. Little did we think we had seen him for the last time, or imagine under what circumstances we should next see that command, now mounting the bluffs in the distance with its little guidons gaily fluttering in the breeze.[7]

At 12:40 p.m. the Seventh reached the broad mouth of the Rosebud, described by G Company lieutenant, George "Nick" Wallace—the regiment's official "itinerist"—as a narrow creek, about three or four feet wide and three inches deep! The valley it ran through was wide, high bluffs to the west and sage-covered hills to the east, the narrow creek snaking through the eastern flats. The day was rainy and the column stopped almost as soon as leaving to re-tie packs the five hung-over civilian packers failed to secure properly. Arikara (Ree) scouts—led by Bob-tail Bull and Soldier—were sent out ahead of the column, though they remained remarkably close for fear of marauding Sioux. Even this march proved arduous, however, for the meandering creek forced the column to cross and re-cross constantly, causing more problems with the pack mules as they struggled through the foliage-hidden creek bed.

Six days earlier, Major Marcus Reno—leading a six-company scout spearheaded by Boyer—had, against orders, entered the Rosebud valley following a discovered trail. At the time, Reno was admonished by Terry (though ironically, Reno had saved Terry the embarrassment of seeing formulated plans go awry because of overlooked intelligence) and pilloried by Custer, who worried Reno's actions had not only alerted the hostiles but that Indian scouts were monitoring the regiment's movements. As they continued south, the terrain became more difficult and at 4:00 p.m. Custer ordered camp near the base of a steep bluff, some twelve miles from where they started and ten miles up the Rosebud. The rain had stopped and wood, water, and grass were in adequate supply, making the site comfortable.

Comfortable, but not cheery. Custer ordered an officers' call and there was a flare-up between him and Fred Benteen—not unusual considering their relationship. After that, however, Custer became conciliatory and in an unusual gesture sought suggestions. He told his officers the Indian Office in Washington estimated they would encounter some 3,000 Indians, 850 of whom would be warriors. (This would tie-in perfectly with the size of the campsites they would encounter in their march up the Rosebud, further leading to the hubris that would eventually kill so many.) Custer, however—more of a pragmatist than the paper-pushers in Washington—added another five hundred warriors to the bucket-list, figuring the agencies would lose that number during the summer hunting months. Even "[t]his figure was an underestimate, for General Sheridan's attempts to control the agency Indians with heavy garrisons would drive out exceptionally large numbers of summer roamers. That was what Custer did *not* know."[8]

After some "house-keeping" instructions—synchronizing of watches; no more trumpet calls; stable guards ordered to wake the troops at 3:00 a.m., ready to march at 5:00— Custer told his troop commanders they would have great volition, saying the only thing to come out of his headquarters would be

> when to move out of and when to go into camp. All other details, such as reveille, stables, watering, halting, grazing, etc., on the march would be left to the judgment and discretion of the troop commanders; they were to *keep within supporting distance* of each other, not to get ahead of the scouts, or very far to the rear of the column[9] [emphasis added for later reference].

Lieutenant Edward Settle Godfrey, the commander of K Company, claimed Custer showed a lack of self-confidence at the meeting, "His manner and tone, usually brusque and aggressive, or somewhat rasping, was on this occasion conciliating and subdued."[10] After making the necessary preparations, Godfrey walked over to the bivouac area for the scouts and met up with Mitch Boyer, the Ree scout Bloody Knife (Custer's favorite Indian scout), and the Crow Half Yellow Face. Boyer—apparently at the suggestion of the Crow—asked Godfrey if he had ever fought these Sioux. Godfrey replied,

> "Yes." ... Then [Boyer] asked, "Well, how many do you expect to find?" I answered, "It is said we may find between one thousand and fifteen hundred." "Well, do you think we can whip that many?" "Oh, yes, I guess so." After he had interpreted our conversation, he said to me with a good deal of emphasis, "Well, I can tell you we are going to have a ----- big fight."[11]

We get an intimation of Custer's failure to comprehend what he would be facing when, on the following day—June 23—around 7:40 a.m., as the column was passing through the first abandoned Indian camp—a camp Lieutenant Bradley had seen on May 27—Custer remarked to his chief-of-scouts, Lieutenant Charles Albert Varnum, "Here's where Reno made the mistake of his life. He had six troops of cavalry and rations enough for a number of days. He'd have made a name for himself if he'd pushed on after them."[12] By 10:20 a.m., they were passing through the second abandoned campsite and by 1:30 p.m. crossing Greenleaf Creek, they reached another (the Cheyenne warrior Wooden Leg, claimed this area was their fourth camp[13]). Between 2:30 and 3:00 p.m. the command reached a point where the valley narrowed, its sides bordered by steep, rocky hills covered with pine. This area marked the limit of Reno's scout up the valley, and then, at about 4:30 p.m. Custer ordered the regiment into camp, choosing a serene spot, with pleasant summer aromas of wild roses, plum, and crabapple. Ash and elder trees covered the creek banks, replacing the by-now familiar willow and cottonwood. To the west rose rugged, pine-covered bluffs; to the east, less rugged cliffs of sandstone topped with pine. And while the signs were abundant, nary an Indian was in sight, only adding to the mystery and foreboding.

At 5:00 a.m. of the twenty-fourth, thirty minutes after five of Custer's Crow scouts departed for upstream, the Seventh Cavalry was on the march again. Two hours later— about 7:00 a.m.—Custer told Herendeen to prepare to take scout Charlie Reynolds and reconnoiter Tullock's Creek, but Herendeen told him it was too early yet, that the gap leading to the creek's headwaters was still farther ahead. Boyer concurred. At 10:30 a.m., the column passed Lame Deer Creek in the vicinity where Boyer had turned back on the seventeenth. Now, four of the Crows reported back, telling of another abandoned Sioux campsite at East Muddy Creek. As the command continued south, Herendeen spotted an Indian trail diverging up Lame Deer and he followed it, but as it continued to diverge, he turned back. By 1:00 p.m. Herendeen had overtaken the column, reporting his find to Custer who immediately ordered a halt.

The East Muddy vicinity proved to be where the fifth Sioux camp had been located and it was here the Indian trail became "more than a mile wide."[14] While the troops made coffee and prepared a meal, scouts were sent out, some to summon Varnum from his advance. When the lieutenant reported, Custer instructed him to check out Herendeen's diverging trail. Varnum protested his scouts could not have missed any such trail, but regardless, he went out to check, returning some two hours and twelve additional miles later. (Varnum claimed Custer told him it was Lieutenant Godfrey who reported the diverging trail.[15] It was also at this time Custer assigned K Company lieutenant, Luther "Luke" Hare, to assist Varnum.)

> Lame Deer Creek joins Rosebud Creek.... Near the junction of the two streams, the crossing of Lame Deer is mandatory. Rosebud Creek skirts the high banks on the left bank, making travel on the right bank more accessible due to the opening up of the valley on that side.
>
> The vast Indian trail heading up Rosebud Creek all but obliterated any good crossing of Lame Deer Creek. Therefore, if any of the bands of Lakota traveling near the end of the vast assemblage wanted to cross Lame Deer Creek, they most likely would have turned and headed up Lame Deer Creek a short distance, crossed the creek, and instead of following the creek back down to the Rosebud, would have cut across country picking up the main trail again farther on.
>
> [T]he deviant travois trail left Rosebud Creek, traveled southeast up Lame Deer Creek about 0.7 miles from the Rosebud, crossed the creek, thence skirting bluffs to the south eventually wound its way back to the trail again. This deviation most assuredly followed the "short cut," or tribal road for a short distance before rejoining the main trail.[16]

Author and retired U.S. Army sergeant major, Thomas M. Heski, believes a possible reason for this pause was Custer wanted to wait for Varnum's return, and certainly, while one can believe Heski, the reason itself would seem a bit flimsy.[17] Custer's personality dictated against a four-hour halt just to see what one of his officers could find on some subsidiary trail. Besides, Heski's Lame Deer Creek description would almost lead one to believe the Crows could have told Custer what Varnum told him upon his return to the command. Still, that, and Custer's need to think things through, could have provided the impetus for the halt. Varnum was to report Herendeen's trail did in fact, diverge, but eventually re-joined the main trail farther upstream. He also reported signs becoming fresher by the mile, indicating an immense force of Indians. Shortly thereafter—about 4:00 p.m.—the fifth Crow scout (White Swan) returned, reporting a fresh camp at the forks of the Rosebud, but still no sighting of Indians.

By 5:00 p.m. the Seventh Cavalry was on the march again, continuing its move, slowly, up the creek. We do not know what Custer thought or was thinking at this time for even if he told some confidante, those he trusted most all died with him. Charles Kuhlman, however, thought the Crows' report was reason "to put Custer on the alert."[18] In *Legend into History*, Kuhlman wrote,

> What the Crows reported during the second halt brought him [Custer] up sharply; for here was something wholly unexpected, something that might call for action different from what was contemplated in his orders. The Crows had been over the trail made, evidently, only a day or two before by the large body of Indians coming from the agencies to join the camps of the Little Big Horn. They had not followed the Indian trail down the Tongue, i.e., the course taken by the rest during their spring wanderings, but had crossed over to the Rosebud a little above the site of the Sundance lodge, where ... the troops struck it soon after resuming the march at 5 o'clock.[19]

This changed everything, but despite Kuhlman's understanding we do not know who else recognized its significance, though according to Lieutenant Godfrey, no one did.

During his earlier scout into this area, as Reno had waited, Mitch Boyer led the Rees farther up the Rosebud and purportedly reached this particular camp where Sitting Bull held a Sundance ceremony (it was abandoned June 8). When Custer's column reached the site, Godfrey noted, "We passed through one much larger than any of the others,"[20] but the significance of this seemed to be lost on the soldiers. Up to this point the size of the winter roamers' campsites had remained fairly constant over the three-week period they spent traveling from the Tongue River. Thus, Custer and his men appeared to have had a false sense of the hostiles' size, even as late as the evening before the battle: the *summer* roamers had not yet joined—or so it seemed.

Boyer may have had other thoughts. James Willert brought up an extremely interesting point by suggesting Boyer figured the *village* sites were up to several weeks old, but the *trails between those sites* were much newer, maybe only a single week. This made sense, for Lieutenant Bradley first saw the Sioux on the lower Rosebud on May 27, twenty-eight days before Custer would leave the valley for Davis Creek and the Little Big Horn, the inference being the village of about four hundred lodges had been joined more recently by other bands of Indians moving *after* the main body.[21] The trails themselves were huge, almost belying the size of the village sites. Edgar Stewart wrote that Reno reported finding "a great Indian trail more than half-a-mile wide made by thousands of trailing lodgepoles."[22] Apparently, it got worse; the farther up the valley, the wider the trail became, until it was "more than a mile wide, the earth so furrowed by thousands of travois poles that it resembled a plowed field."[23] There was more: "The assemblage was a straggling one, since the hostiles did not move in 'Indian file' but in a wide, irregular column, each family traveling by itself, and the group was spread out probably one mile wide and over three miles in length."[24] When Custer passed by several days later, the whole regiment had a chance to see for itself.

> [E]veryone noted puzzling changes in the Indian trail.... Instead of a single heavy trail with old campsites a day's journey apart, there were now multiple trails in various directions and small scattered campsites, some growing fresher and fresher. These were, in fact, converging trails left by summer roamers coming out to join the winter roamers.[25]

Boyer was not the only one to catch the significance of the trail. Lieutenant Varnum wrote, "We struck not only the trail of the Indians but the entire valley of the Rosebud appeared to have been a camp, where they had moved along as the grass was grazed off."[26] Yet it appeared most everyone assumed these camps were simply consecutive locations of one village and not separate villages, all ultimately moving in the same southerly direction. Reno worried about this, but he was one of the few who did.

> The trail in some places was at least three hundred yards in width and deeply worn. The scouts said that it had been made by about fifteen hundred lodges, and since there were doubtless other trails, they agreed that it proved that enormous numbers of Sioux, Cheyennes, and Arapahoes had left the agencies to join Sitting Bull. But the officers, misled by the report that there were only five to eight hundred warriors in the hostile bands, missed the significance of the trail entirely and persisted in believing that these large camps—they were from ⅓ to ½ a mile in diameter—were a succession of camps of a single band, rather than what they were, the single camp of several large bands together.[27]

Sixteen years after the battle, Edward Godfrey wrote the same thing:

On June 24th [the Custer column] passed a great many camping-places, all appearing to be of nearly the same strength. One would naturally suppose these were the successive camping-places of the same village, when in fact they were the continuous camps of the several bands.[28]

Despite the myopia of most, there can be little doubt his scouts informed Custer of the overriding importance of these signs, none whatsoever.

After resuming the march at around 5:00 p.m. the column crossed to the left bank of the creek and moving very slowly, Custer began sending out flankers to check for diverging trails, again worried about the "village" breaking up. "'He said he wanted to get the whole village and nothing must leave the trail without his knowing it,'"[29] but only *con-verging* trails were found. Charles Kuhlman emphasized his point:

We have found no direct evidence that anyone in the command knew that the fresh trail and campsites were made by a second body of Indians after those whose trail they had been following had left the Rosebud. It would seem that had such an important fact been known, Wallace would have mentioned it in his report.[30]

Kuhlman was not the only historian who recognized and wrote about this colossal blunder. In his seminal work, *The Custer Tragedy*, written in 1936, Fred Dustin wrote,

As nearly as ascertainable, there had been a considerable aug-mentation of numbers by large parties from the eastward. It was the fresh trail of these bands that the Crow and Ree scouts had observed, and their passage over the other recent trails has led many to believe that the whole immense body of hostiles was only a day or two ahead of Custer's command, whereas they had, in the greater part, crossed the divide a week before, and had

been in camp on the Little Big Horn, some miles above where Custer found them, for several days. It would seem that the Dakota and their allies were unaware of the close presence of the command until the morning of the 25th when the Ree and Crow scouts saw the six Sioux at the Crow's Nest.[31]

Willert also believed the Indians' intelligence mecha-nism failed them regarding the presence of the regiment.

This poor reconnaissance on the part of the hostiles was a usual habit with them—contrary to the popular notion—for they were not as reconnaissance-minded as some writers would have us believe. Indeed, their carelessness ... could have brought them defeat at Little Big Horn, had not their numbers compensated, for Custer, Terry and Gibbon were able to advance ... almost to the hostiles' village limits without detection.[32]

At 6:30 p.m. the command reached a gap in the western hills leading to the headwaters of Tullock's Creek, and Heren-deen now told Custer he should be off to scout the region, but Custer made no response and the column continued mov-ing forward. No trails went in the direction of Tullock's, and neither did Herendeen.

But Custer—Herendeen recalled—only looked at him, said not a word, and finally the civilian scout reined back to once again take his place in the moving column. Herendeen was unable to fathom Custer's curious behavior at this junction, but Custer's reason should have been obvious—the hostiles *trail* continued up the Rosebud Valley, but *where did it lead*?[33]

Should Custer's reason have been obvious or had other decisions been made already? (Where Charles Kuhlman saw gold, it seems others saw merely pyrite.) Then, just before sundown Custer ordered another bivouac, this one at a sharp bend of the Rosebud. The final act had begun.

2

THE BUSBY BEND

REFERENCES:
Timeline A—June 24—To the Busby Camp and Varnum's Departure, 5:00 a.m.–9:20 p.m.

Had Custer already made his decision to attack as soon as he could get within range of the village regardless of orders and without support from Terry and Gibbon? And if he had, when did he make it precisely? This is mere speculation and the evidence is circumstantial at best, yet there was this four-hour layover from 1:00 to 5:00 p.m. on the 24th and accounts we have make no mention of Custer moving out of his tent despite the constant hither and yon of scouts. Why stop? Just to wait for Varnum? The trails were growing fresher by the hour and while no one had seen a single hostile, even the newest recruits had to know the Sioux were within a day's ride—two at the most. (A paucity of sightings was not quite the case with the Indians, however. Remember that group of Cheyenne? Old Little Wolf's band that had left the Red Cloud Agency in Nebraska? Well apparently, some time during the afternoon of the 24th, two warriors—Big Crow and Black White Man—spotted the soldiers' camp, but what they did with the information rivaled Custer's languor regarding the importance of scouting Tullock's valley. We know Little Wolf did not make the great camp until after the Custer fighting of the 25th and if he had somehow gotten word of the soldiers' presence to the Sioux, no one thought much of it.)

Not long after Custer's sundown halt at the Busby bend, Varnum and his scouts would be ordered to continue to follow the vast trail. As darkness closed in, several scouts returned to report the Sioux had swung west and crossed the divide to the lower Little Big Horn. ("Lower" was a relative term here. We know now it was too early to indicate the Indians were heading in any specific direction; the crossing point on the divide would bring the recalcitrants to the lower part of the Little Big Horn River rather than the upper, but *direction* of march was not determined as yet.) In itself, this

was a surprise, for while Terry's plan was flexible, John Gray felt a Sioux encampment on the lower Little Big Horn was the one situation the plan could least accommodate. Custer's instructions were clear: scout the upper reaches of the Rosebud, then cross to the upper Little Big Horn, move north down that river, and drive the Sioux into the blocking point Terry was to reach on the 26th. This being only the 24th, however, Terry would be a good 30 miles from his objective position. Regardless of the decisions Custer had reached—if any—his choices now were to continue south along the Rosebud, possibly risking detection—according to Gray, though not Neil Mangum—and losing track of the village, or to leave the Busby camp at night in an attempt to cross the Rosebud-Little Big Horn divide, hiding out for a day while Terry moved into the Little Big Horn valley. If this would be the plan, it meant Custer's scouts could keep track of the hostiles and Custer would still have the element of surprise, still attack from above, and still block escape routes to the east.

> Custer could follow Terry's recommendation by marching up the Rosebud tomorrow [the 25th] and starting down the Little Big Horn the next day, thus preserving the timing. Even if these marches were made at night, however, he would leave a trail as readable as a poster, and discovery would warn the village to flee and scatter. He would also lose track of the village and at best have to search for it again; at worst it could escape undetected back to the Rosebud and eastward or down the Bighorn and attack Terry's weaker force on the march.[1]

While one hates to cry sophistry with such a fine academician as Gray, he is clearly rationalizing assumptions and equally clearly cutting Custer a lot of slack here, for as we have seen, no one thought to warn the Sioux of Custer's approach even though they claimed—*post bellum*—to have seen a regiment of cavalry a day's ride away. On June 17, many of these same Sioux and Cheyenne had whipped George Crook's Wyoming column to a standstill farther up the Rosebud, and prior to that fight the Indians had been aware of Crook's column, but had lost touch with Gibbon's, thinking he was still moving eastward down the Yellowstone. They had no idea Gibbon had returned to the Rosebud and they were completely unaware of Reno's earlier movements (note the dates!), Terry's presence, and now Custer's proximity. This argument may seem frivolous and fraught with a soothsayer's sapience, but it is no more so than ignoring the signs made by a patently readable trail discovered and reported some two to three dozen miles from the largest assemblage of Indians in the history—then and now—of North America.

Some writers throw diversions into the mix, but the fact remains Custer was bound and determined to seek out and attack this village, one way or the other, with Terry or without, and based on the objectives of the campaign and the location of the Indians, we cannot fault the man for assuming this role. Only later, when assessing the judiciousness of some of his decisions, can we begin laying blame, or, rather, learning lessons.

Time was now becoming critical, however, for if the village was heading downstream rather than up—an assumption, right or wrong, built on sand—it also meant *Terry* was likely to meet the hostiles sooner rather than later. Another issue roiling the water here was, did the Crows report the Sioux actually *moving* downstream or was it that the tracks were so fresh they just assumed the village had to be lower rather than higher up the valley? All we know for sure is the trail was so fresh it became obvious the Sioux had to be located on the *lower* Little Big Horn—again, *location rather than direction*—and had not yet gone to its upper reaches. Still, no other answers are available; no questions ever asked.

When the scouts returned to the Busby bivouac, Custer went over to their camp and spoke with them for some little time. (Varnum said five Crows were at this meeting; Half Yellow Face—their leader—was still out somewhere.) When the meeting was over, Custer instructed Varnum to leave at 9:00 p.m. and take his scouts with him, while the rest of the command would move at 11:00. Those who had been with the general at the Washita (Indian Territory: Oklahoma) fight in November 1868, would have recognized the pattern. If Custer had not arrived at any final decision regarding his direction of march—and that seems problematic—the news from the scouts had to have been the clincher. "The unexpected news brought by the Crows that the Sioux were probably on the lower, rather than the upper, reaches of the Little Big Horn posed a serious problem that demanded a weighty decision from Custer."[2] *"Weighty"*? Why? The fear Terry and Gibbon might get first crack?

At around 9:20 p.m. Varnum and his entourage of 15 men[3] left the camp for a promontory known as the Crow's Nest—something of a misnomer—some 11 to 12 miles away. As soon as Varnum departed, Custer called his officers together to inform them of the Indians' probable location and

that he wanted a night march to cross the divide so as not to be seen. (It was now fully dark—very dark; nautical twilight ended at 9:22 p.m.—and not everyone was able to locate the general's tent.) Custer's initial idea was to lay low on the 25th and then make another night march, this time to the village, and attack on the morning of the 26th. "Reno wrote in his July 5th report, Custer notified the assembly it was necessary to cross the divide at night as 'it would be impossible to do so in the daytime without discovering our march to the Indians.'"[4] Custer said, "beyond a doubt the village was in the valley of the Little Big Horn."[5] Second Lieutenant Winfield Scott Edgerly (Company D) said, "[T]he Indian's village has been located in the valley of the Little Big Horn and the object (of the night march) being to cross the divide between the Rosebud and the Little Big Horn before daylight."[6] And Custer "told the officers they would have the fight of their lives."[7] Frederic Francis Gerard, the interpreter for the Rees, had told Custer he could expect to find 2,500 to 3,000 warriors, but either Custer chose to ignore the warning or he was confident the numbers did not matter. (Before leaving Fort Lincoln, Gerard told Terry there would be as many as 4,000 warriors if all those who had left the reservations united.[8])

Shortly after the conference broke up, the troops were roused for the march. At 11:00 (possibly as late as 11:30 p.m. according to Godfrey), the Seventh Cavalry began its march into history. At 11:48 p.m. the crescent (12 percent) moon set, and what little illumination one gets from such an astronomical event, ended: the light had been turned off.

We pause now for a moment to confront one of the primary aims of this study, the issue of "time." Without understanding when specific events occurred the entire battle and the actions of its participants become distorted and lead to those forks of dissension we mentioned earlier. If we can accurately place individuals at critical points during the action, we can make better judgments as to their performance and how they handled their responsibilities. To date only one serious study of "time" has been produced, that by Dr. John S. Gray in his book, *Custer's Last Campaign.* Gray's study, however, is flawed from the outset and as one studies it the only conclusion we can draw is its author formed his timeline around personal preconceptions, attempting to fit context into his personal theories rather than the other way around. Furthermore, Gray anticipated criticism by pre-emptive scoffing at possible detractors claiming there was "no evidence of any discrepancy between official and local sun times" and that the "result is so obvious as to be embarrassing."[9] Well, it is not.

The first issue in any time study is determining the time standard. In 1876, there was neither a standard as there is today, nor was there any daylight savings time. The United States only standardized its time zones in 1883, after the Prime Meridian Conference held in Washington, D.C., when new "time zones" were based on Greenwich (England) Mean Time. Prior to that, each town or city established its own time by whatever measure it could devise, some as mundane as a watch in a jewelry store window. At the Little Big Horn, Gray made his case for the regiment's watches being set on local sun time, claiming, if watches were originally set on St. Paul time, they would now be off by more than an hour. "[I]f a watch was carried east or west across 15° longitude, it had to be reset by one hour to read the new local sun time."[10] Gray seemed to make too much of this issue, however, and one can only ask, so what? Why would this prove Terry and Custer had to have reset their watches, especially since any reports needing to be written would be issued to men working and used to being on St. Paul time, including Terry? In 1876, campaigning for weeks and months on end, men may have placed greater reliance on the sun hitting its peak at midday than on the delicate workings of a watch much too susceptible to chill, rain, and dust. To make matters more complicated, John Gibbon's Montana column was an additional 5° farther west and seems to have used Fort Ellis time, which was supposed to have been San Francisco time.

Contrary to Gray, there are a number of historians who believe the column's watches were set on "headquarters" time as used in St. Paul (by a longitudinal measurement, some 57 clock minutes ahead of Little Big Horn time), with others opting for Chicago. Gregory F. Michno writes that Lieutenant George Wallace's watch was set on Chicago time, close to one and one-half hours later than the Montana noonday sun.[11] Tom Heski wrote, "the times carried on various watches throughout the command were set on Department of Dakota, St. Paul Time, and this time was used and consulted regardless of the discrepancy."[12] We agree. Yet Vern Smalley writes that when Custer ordered the June 24, Busby bivouac, it was 7:45 p.m. nearly sunset, and this "time" or "hour" was noted by Wallace and verified by Godfrey as "nearly sundown," thus proving Wallace's watch was set on local time because "nearly sundown" in St. Paul would have been 6:30 p.m.,[13] local time. Smalley's observation, however—like Gray's—presupposes Wallace actually consulted his watch for the precise time rather than simply noting the hour based on field experience and casually recording the time, i.e., knowing the sun set "around" quarter to eight at this time of year. (And in St. Paul, *it did*, give or take some few minutes: 8:03 p.m. Remember, they had been on the march for 39 days, moving constantly

west, very much attuned to and adjusting to time variances. Theoretically, a 7:53 p.m. sunset in the "central zone" would be quite close to a 7:53 p.m. sunset in the "mountain zone." Godfrey never used a specific time, only referring to the halt as being "about sundown." In addition, Heski writes that around 7:00 p.m. in June, the sun is behind the Wolf Mountains, creating shadows in the valley. If there are no clouds, you can still see objects until about 10:00 p.m.[14]; but there *were* clouds on the night of June 24.

The participants themselves appeared ambivalent about specific times. This is rather striking, for it was a military operation after all, yet the "time of day" seems to have played little role if any, was of minor concern at best, and was only cursorily noted by many of those who fought the battle. Even Wallace—who was supposed to keep track of what went on— paid little heed to the times of day events transpired. Former G Company private, Theodore W. Goldin, wrote, "In regard to that night march on the 24th of June, I will say that I have talked with officers and men, and found that none of them had a clear recollection as to time, from that time until many hours later, in fact after Reno's retreat to the bluffs."[15] There were very few accurate times recorded and we have more definitive readings from Indians who noticed the sun directly overhead than we do from soldiers or civilians who constantly state, it was *"about"* two o'clock, or it took place *"between"* 3:00 and 4:00. No one seemed to care other than the regimental sergeant major and company first sergeants responsible for reveille and getting the men ready to move. We see more of this with Lieutenant Varnum's comments over the years, comments pertaining to more than one incident:

> Any statement I may make in regard to time would be a guess on my part.... I have very little to base an opinion of time upon unless I connect it with somebody else's statement.... I base my opinion a good deal on other people's opinions compared with my own as to time.[16]

We must also wonder about the quality of timepieces carried by these men and what affect the constant dust and varying weather conditions had on them. The interpreter, Fred Gerard, was reputed to have had a very fine watch, newly cleaned and repaired just prior to leaving Fort Lincoln. Some of his times might be more accurate than others, especially when comparisons are made, though we run into the issue of why Gerard would pop out his watch while charging down the valley or dodging bullets behind a tree.

While we can assume Gray had his reasons for choosing local sun as his time standard rather than headquarters time, it would appear he chose as well to ignore the two references we have from military participants regarding that standard. The only mention of watches being set came at the officers' call on June 22, when Lieutenant Godfrey said, "We compared watches to get the official time."[17] At the Reno Court of Inquiry held in Chicago in January and February 1879, Godfrey testified:

Q: "What time was daylight in that section of the country at that time of year?"
A: "We did not have the local time, our watches were not changed."[18]

Sounds pretty clear and George Wallace confirmed it at the same inquiry:

Q: "Are you sure the time of your watch was the true time of day when you looked at it, or may it have been an hour or more slow or fast?"
A: "I am not sure about that. It may have been fast or it may have been slow. I never have claimed that it was the local time of the place."[19]

In addition, over the years we have accounts from at least seven enlisted personnel, scout Herendeen, interpreter Gerard, Doctor Henry Rinaldo Porter (accompanying the Reno column during its attack on the village), and three Indian scouts, all alluding to either the divide crossing time or the beginning of the battle, none of which match up with Gray's opinion of a local sun time standard. (Sergeant Daniel Kanipe and privates Edward Davern, Giovanni Martini, William O. Taylor, Charles Windolph, Thomas Coleman, and Jacob Hetler all referred to events such as nearing the village, crossing the river, or the first firing occurring from 11:00 a.m. to 1:00 p.m. According to Gray's analysis, all these events would have occurred well after 2:00 p.m. even using a local time standard. In addition, Dr. Porter claimed the firing began about 1:30 p.m.—remarkably close to the truth, using St. Paul time—and interpreter Gerard claimed Reno retreated by 2:00 p.m. [a reasonable approximation].) Gray also tended to eschew the accounts of Indians—regardless of the situation—but by ignoring as many as 24 separate references to a battle beginning when the sun was more or less overhead or the mid-day meal was being consumed, he leaves us with the impression of inserting his own square-peg theory into round-hole context (see Appendix D). We will see how this all ties in when we reach the crossing of the Rosebud–Little Big Horn divide.

It is with all this in mind, therefore, that we base our studies of time on the Godfrey and Wallace recollections and unless otherwise noted, all times used in this study are based on Headquarters time used in St. Paul, Minnesota, 57 minutes ahead of local sun time.

As we begin to view the events and the battle through the "eyes" of our timing studies, we can set a base mark for the *specific* issue of time at 5:00 p.m., on June 24 (see *Timeline A*), when Custer ordered the command to resume its march from the East Muddy Creek halt (in this case Lieutenant Wallace verified the time, so there is little reason to doubt he checked his watch after a four-hour rest[20]). As we have seen, the Crow scout White Swan returned reporting the discovery of a fresh camp at the forks of the Rosebud, and Varnum had reported the diverging trail spotted by Herendeen re-linked with the main trail, farther up the Rosebud.

The next reported incident of time was 7:45 p.m. established by Wallace for the halt at the Busby campsite. Looking at the events and what transpired between the two halts, however, we begin now to question Wallace's accuracy. For example, the distance between the East Muddy Creek site and the Busby bend site is approximately 12 miles. That would equate to a rate of march of almost 4½ miles per hour—a rather brisk walk—yet we know the command—in Wallace's words—"passed through several large camps. The trail was fresh now, and the whole valley scratched up by the trailing lodgepoles."[21] George Herendeen said much the same thing, claiming as the command began moving again, the trail was becoming fresher and fresher. "We passed over places where a number of camps had been quite close together, showing that the Indians were traveling very slowly, and only moving for grass."[22] The regiment also moved very slowly and made a number of stops. Godfrey noted:

The march during the day was tedious. We made many long halts so as not to get ahead of the scouts, who seemed to be doing their work thoroughly, giving special attention to the right, toward Tulloch's Creek, the valley of which was in general view from the divide. Once or twice smoke signals were reported in that direction. The weather was dry and had been for some time, consequently the trail was very dusty. The troops were required to march on separate trails so that the dust clouds would not rise so high. The valley was heavily marked with lodge-pole trails and pony tracks, showing that immense herds of ponies had been driven over it.[23]

That hardly sounds like a rate of march of 4.4 miles per hour, so now, was this purported 7:45 p.m. halt remembered as local time or actual St. Paul watch time? (*Time and theory* versus *context!*)

To solve this little conundrum we must factor in the following. In a series of letters and interviews in the early 1900s, Charles Varnum told researcher Walter Mason Camp the command went into camp around dark.[24] In the most revealing comment of all, however, Private Charles Windolph of Benteen's Company H, wrote, "On the third day, we made better than 30 miles and went into camp at sundown. *In late*

June up here in this northwest country, that means around nine o'clock"[25] [emphasis added]. The following day, while ensconced on the hilltop after a terrible beating, M Company private, Daniel Newell, alluded to the Indian firing ending at dark: "About nine o'clock."[26] Benteen himself claimed that on the 24th the regiment stopped frequently and for lengthy stays. When they arrived at what Benteen referred to as "Mud Creek," he was

> loudly called by Col. Keogh, to come where he was, that he had been saving for me a snug nook with beautiful grass in it for me, that I might camp next to him. The reply to this was characteristic of the plains, something like, bully for you Keogh! I'm your man.[27]

Colonel William A. Graham (author of *The Custer Myth,* one of the most definitive books ever written about the whole affair, loaded with first-hand accounts) also quoted Benteen as saying much the same thing:

> Where, on coming into camp I heard the voice of my old friend Col. Myles W. Keogh hailing me, saying, come here "old man, I've kept the nicest spot in the whole camp next to me, for your troop, and I've had to bluff the balance to hold it, but here it is, skip off," so I "skipped," putting my troop in the vale the gallant Irishman had held for me.[28]

It was close to twilight at the time[29] and the I Company commander, a dashing Irishman named Myles Walter Keogh, had a tent-fly for shelter, in Benteen's words, more luxurious than his own accommodations. As they settled down Company A lieutenant Carlo DeRudio was telling one of his incessant stories and Benteen interrupted: he thought they would not be staying at this place very long—he had a "*Pre*"— and they should get as much sleep as they could. A *moment* later—again, Benteen's word—an orderly-trumpeter walked up and told them Custer wanted everyone at his tent, at once. Lieutenant Godfrey: "About sundown we went into camp under the cover of a bluff, so as to hide the command as much as possible. We had marched about 28 miles ... we were to be in readiness to march again at 11:30 p.m."[30] Reno, at the 1879 inquiry said twilight lasted until about 9:00 p.m. or after,[31] and even Wallace claimed "deep twilight" came on about 9:00 or later,[32] just about the time captains Benteen and Keogh were buddying-up. Since local sunset was at 7:53 p.m. and the sun dropped below the western mountains around 7:00, making it appear to be darker than it really was, all these indications point to the command being on headquarters time, not local sun. It is true, there were others who claimed different times: Herendeen alluded to a 4:00 p.m. halt, though the allusion was unclear and he never referred to any reason why he might make such a claim. Lieutenant Win Edgerly, in a letter to his wife Grace, on July 4, 1876, claimed they

went into camp at 5:00 p.m., but Edgerly had also told her they went into camp at 5:00 p.m. on the 22nd, possibly confusing the dates and times.[33] Private William O. Taylor of Company A wrote in his 1917 memoirs that the command stopped about 7:00 p.m. on the 24th,[34] but 41 years had passed as Taylor was wandering through his reminiscences and the cobwebs and hyperbole of time frequently cloud recollections. Taylor was not always the most accurate of chroniclers and his effort, informative and important, contained not just a few errors.[35] While this may appear as a modicum of criticism, Taylor may be excused, for as we noted earlier, at a local time of 7:00 p.m. the sun is behind the mountains to the west, giving one the impression of sundown. This all seems to indicate a local phenomenon, transcribed in terms of "official time," thus indicating the onset of a rather confusing duality, one that Charles Varnum would repeat a little later.

Description of conditions is frequently a clearer indicator of time than distant memories of a specific clock hour, i.e., it is much easier to remember an event occurring at sundown than at 7:45 p.m. or 8:30 p.m., expressly. This also feeds into what Private Goldin alluded to when he claimed "none of them had a clear recollection as to time." We should, therefore, be as comfortable with the descriptive as we are with the explicit, especially when the latter is not as definitive as we might like.

If Nick Wallace used headquarters time, then it was 6:48 p.m. local sun, when Custer halted at Busby, too far away from the recollections of "near sunset" to be correct, despite the slack we cut Private Taylor; but if Wallace had his watch set on local sun, the halt would have been 8:42 p.m., *headquarters* time. Despite the fact this looks awfully suspicious, we know Wallace said he "never ... claimed that it was the local time of the place." On the other hand, if one were to check the United States Naval Observatory database for the actual time of sunset in St. Paul, Minnesota, for June 24, 1876, one would see a clock time of 8:03 p.m. very close to Wallace's 7:45, and virtually a perfect fit for the recollections of Benteen, Godfrey, Varnum, Reno, Windolph, *et al.* As noted, Windolph commented sundown was around 9:00 p.m. and that was when they went into camp. It is therefore, reasonable to assume Wallace in fact never checked his watch, but estimated the time of the halt based on his knowledge of sunset at headquarters, as Windolph implied, "around nine o'clock." This would indicate others might have noted the 7:45 local time halt would have been 8:42 p.m. *on their watches.* And it would also mean the 12-mile distance between the East Muddy Creek halt site and the Busby Bend encampment was covered in some three hours, 42 minutes—a speed of 3.2

miles per hour—a time fitting much more neatly with the descriptions of a slow, halting pace than with a quick walk of almost 4½ miles per hour (*Timeline A*). A two-day march of more than 60 miles, laced with halts, stream crossings, and plenty of dust will exhaust both man and beast, so again, it is not unreasonable to think Mr. Wallace simply took a gander at the sky and grabbed his blankets.

Custer and his scouts had been riding well in front of the troops—the Crows riding back and forth with more and fresher reports—and as darkness was falling, three of them returned to report the Sioux had turned west and crossed the divide at a point that *could* lead to the lower Little Big Horn, though they were unsure which direction the turn took them after that. As his command was settling in, Custer met with the Crows who made a suggestion they ride to a promontory near the Rosebud–Little Big Horn divide, a place familiar to them and from where they could view the Little Big Horn valley once it got light. This way they could give Custer reliable information without having to ride all night and into the valley. The general decided to send the Crows out again, to follow the trail until they could locate the village or they had traveled until noon of the following day. The command would stay put pending the Crows' report, a decision Custer quickly changed. In addition, Custer instructed the peripatetic Varnum to go with them. To keep Varnum company he would send Boyer, scout Charlie Reynolds, and eight or 10 Rees.

> The prospect of an *earlier* awareness as to the hostiles' position—if they should be in the Little Big Horn Valley—now prompted Custer to cancel his earlier plan to stay the night in his present position … and to proceed in a *night march* … toward the divide.[36]

Custer told Varnum to leave around 9:00 p.m. The command would move at 11:00.

More times enter here and some may still be faced with the nagging uncertainty of which standard the troops were using, so let us apply some additional common sense and a little Logic 101. Despite a tough, dust-filled couple of days consumed by more than a 60-mile hike, numerous stream crossings, and formation changes to keep the dust clouds manageable and the line of march as straight as possible, the Seventh Cavalry was coming off a four-hour, mid-day break and was within sniffing distance of an elusive foe. As we can see from *Timeline A*, Custer put his men into camp not long before dusk, probably around 7:45 p.m., *local* time in this instance (8:42 p.m., St. Paul–headquarters-*watch* time), and as the troops were arriving and settling in, Custer spoke with

his scouts and then ordered Varnum out once again. If Varnum's 9:00 p.m. ordered-departure time had also been local, it would give him more than an hour of downtime. Under the circumstances that makes no sense, and if it seems too short a period to get ready, we must remember Varnum had been there several minutes already and did not leave until 9:20 anyway (8:23 p.m., local), some 30 minutes past sunset and quite possibly as much as an hour from the time the advance elements of the regiment—Custer included—had reached the bivouac area. Besides, Custer had all the information he would get that day and there was no need to dally. His decision for a night march bears this out. There was little time lost between Custer's talk with the Crows, his sending off of Varnum, and his call to his officers moments later. Any other scenario slows things down too much for a military operation under these circumstances, and the speed and immediacy of the decision-making processes fits more with the personality of the man making those decisions.

Shortly after Varnum's departure, Custer ordered the officers' call, thereby fulfilling Benteen's "Pre." Lieutenant Godfrey remembered the call occurring about 9:30 p.m. (8:33 local, past the end of civil twilight when it is too dark to read and some 48 minutes after Benteen, *et al.,* settled in for DeRudio's bedtime stories), just about the time he and Luke Hare lay down to take a nap.[37] They had just put weary head to saddle blanket when word reached them of Custer's conference. By now, of course, it was quite dark (there are those western mountains again!) for Godfrey described the difficulty he and Hare had locating Custer's tent, and Benteen never did make the brief conference. (This also indicates, by the way, no campfires had been started, further emphasizing the brevity of the stay at the Busby bend.) Custer informed his officers of his plan for a night march—leaving at 11:00 p.m., about one and one-half hours hence—and finding a place to hide during the following day, laying low the 25th, scouting the area, and finding the actual location of the Indians. He would then make plans for the attack, make a night march toward the village, and attack early in the morning of the 26th.

The meeting was short and sweet. As the others stumbled to Custer's tent, Benteen, anticipating his chief's plans, pulled on his "cavalry boots" and instructed First Sergeant Joseph McCurry to make sure the men tightened their horses' bridles, aparejos, etc., and got ready for a speedy move-out.[38] As Benteen groped his way in the dark, he ran into Keogh who told him of the plans: "tis no use going, *you* were right—we move at 11 o'clock, p.m. Sharp, tonight: all right, then, there's no sleep for your humble again tonight. Second night's loss of sleep."[39]

3

DAVIS CREEK AND THE DIVIDE

REFERENCES:
Timeline B—June 24–June 25—Busby Camp to Halt One; Sunset to Sunrise, 5:10 a.m.

C—June 25—Halt One to Custer's Arrival at the Crow's Nest; 3:41 a.m.–8:35 a.m.

D—The Curtiss Incident; 8:15 a.m.–10:00 a.m.

E—Officers' Call—Crow's Nest to the Divide; 8:35 a.m.–11:45 a.m.

The departure from the Busby camp marks the beginning of the final phase of the "Custer" part of the great campaign. It also marks the beginning of more than 137 years of argument and discord over almost every imaginable aspect of the ensuing 45 hours. Up until the move from the Busby bend, things are pretty cut-and-dried, but from sundown on June 24—when "time" became an issue (in our minds)—until the Sioux and Cheyenne left the scene in the early evening of the 26th, there is nary a moment not in some measure of dispute.

Custer ordered the command to move at 11:00 p.m. (10:03 p.m. local) and according to Fred Benteen, Marcus Reno, George Herendeen, Captain Myles Moylan of Company A, Luke Hare, Carlo DeRudio, and Nick Wallace, the column did just that. (In his January 1877 report, Wallace claimed the move took place at one o'clock in the morning, but at the Reno inquiry in early 1879, he brought his opinion more in line with others, shifting his time to 11:00 p.m.) Since it was pitch-black out, one wonders just how anyone could see to determine the precise time, but some small campfires had been lit apparently, so we will give them the benefit of that particular doubt. Of course it could have been Custer ordered the regiment to move at 11:00, and at 11:00 they did indeed begin to march. Then, if anyone could read a watch in the dark they might also say they departed a little later because they were farther down the column. Ed Godfrey[1] and Fred Gerard said it was closer to 11:30, so with all that firepower it seems reasonable to assume 11-*ish* is pretty close to

the mark,[2] and by 11:30 or 11:45 p.m. the entire command was on the move. Just to turn hair a bit whiter, however, John Gray used a 12:30 a.m., local time, departure (that would be 1:27 a.m., headquarters-watch time), but there appears to be little justification for this and if we are seeking the *absolute* truth—as Gray seemed to want—compromise is hardly the way to go about it. On the other hand, it took an hour and 30 minutes to get the packs across Muddy Creek and Benteen claimed that feat was accomplished by 12:30 a.m. (11:33 p.m., local). What is reasonably certain is the distance covered from the Busby camp to the first halt site was approximately 6.2 to 6.7 miles[3]—depending upon where one wishes to place the jump-off point, the exact halt point, and the less than straight-line route to that halt—and while the night was extremely dark, the Davis Creek valley was broad, generally free of major obstacles (the bottom along the creek had occasional areas of timber, but the command also followed the well-worn Indian trail), and pitched at only a slight incline—a gradual climb from 2,340 feet to 4,000 feet elevation—toward the divide, 11 ½ miles away.

The column must have been quite long and that length could account for a number of discrepancies in accounts regarding the time of arrival at the first halt. A total of 640 men left the Busby camp for the divide; 605 of them soldiers (we have deducted Varnum, his orderly Private Elijah Strode, Boyer, Reynolds, five Crow, and six Ree scouts from these totals, 15 in all). If they traveled in a column-of-twos there would have been close to 300 pairs (given the circumstances that makes more sense than a column-of-fours; besides, this type of formation was standard operating procedure in 1876[4]). At a spacing of 10 feet between riders—nose-to-nose—and assuming the spacing was maintained (highly unlikely), the march unit would have been a minimum of two-thirds of a mile long, and that does not count some 175 pack mules that would have added another 500 feet (if we assume they were tethered four abreast and behaved themselves, also, neither of which are likely). Some students of the campaign claim the pack mules were driven in a column-type formation, similar to the troops, but others say they were just formed into an amorphous mass, shaped by the terrain and the whims of the civilian pack herders (this latter choice seems improbable, however, given the unknown terrain, the fact there were only five civilian packers, and the blackness of the night).

The packs are a continuing problem on this journey. While the Rosebud was a mere creek, the mouth was broad and the stream itself snaked through the valley's eastern flats. When Custer reached it on the 22nd, he had to stop to re-tie the packs. As the troops moved up the Rosebud, they found the hills closed in and the valley became narrower. This forced Custer to cross and re-cross the meandering stream, causing problems with the mules as they struggled through the foliage-hidden creek bed, and when they moved farther up the valley the terrain got even more difficult. Wallace wrote:

> [T]he trail followed the high ground, or second bottom, where the soil was poor, the grass thin, and crowded out by sagebrush and cactus. In the lower part of the valley the soil appeared to be good, the grazing fair, the bottom timbered with large cottonwood. Small willows grew thickly along the banks in many places.[5]

When the command broke camp at five o'clock on the morning of the 23rd, Fred Benteen's H Company—and two others—brought up the rear. Benteen had been assigned as Officer of the Day[6] and as such was in charge of the packs. The command was halted at least once during the day's trek to allow the recalcitrant mules to catch up, and when Custer put the regiment into camp at 4:30, it took until sunset for the last of the pack mules to make it in. Benteen approached the regimental adjutant, First Lieutenant William Winer Cooke, asking him to mention to Custer that Benteen had a solution for the pack-problem, but Cooke, ever cognizant of Custer's disdain for suggestions and a recent emphasis on orders and proper military procedure, declined. The following morning, Benteen, braving any looming wrath, mentioned his idea directly to Custer, and for a change it seems to have fallen on responsive ears, for we no longer hear anything particularly onerous about the packs until Myles Keogh tried moving them across the creek as the command left the Busby camp. Of course, Benteen's solution (one company to the front, one on a side—the stream being on the other—and one in the rear, rather than all three companies herding from behind) had less to do with a mellowing of the mules' dispositions than the actual herding technique, so we can be assured the creatures' stubbornness persisted throughout.

While we do not know the specific configuration the pack train assumed as the column left Busby, we can be certain it was no easy job rallying the mules for a nighttime trek.

Again, what we do know is there was a delay caused by trouble getting the animals across Mud Creek. Benteen wrote:

> We were to move at 11 o'clock that night, at which hour we did move, however, there was an hour and a half consumed [11 p.m.–12:30 a.m.], in getting the pack train across Mud Creek [Rosebud flood plain below confluence of Busby and Rosebud Creek]. Colonel Keogh had charge of the packs [rear guard escort] on that move and the column remained impatient on [the] other bank of the creek while Keogh was superintending crossing the pack train.[7]

He went on, "If it took a minute to cross that pack train over the 'Muddy,' it took two hours."[8] His friend, the flamboyant Keogh, was now in charge of the rear guard and he sought Benteen's advice and assistance, "making the very air sulphurous with blue oaths."[9]

Once the pack crossing was accomplished the column seemed to move with some aplomb, despite the dark. It is not unreasonable therefore, to presuppose a closed-up, spread-out, closing-up, spreading-out column of this size to be at least a mile long, accordioning to as many as three miles in length, less than one-seventh to one-half the distance from the Busby site to the first halt. If that seems far-fetched, numbers prove it to be less so. If we accept an 11:00 p.m. start and a 2:15 a.m. arrival at the first halt—"Halt One"—we can compute the average speed at between 1.9 and 2.1 miles per hour covering the distance of 6.2 to 6.7 miles. That means if it took Keogh one and one-half hours to cross Mud Creek, the head of the column *could* have already marched three miles (it is quite difficult to believe a man of George Custer's temperament would have waited, patiently or otherwise, for almost two hours for mules to cross a stream, especially considering Benteen's travail a couple days earlier).

Meanwhile, the Crow scout, Half Yellow Face, was out front guiding the column and Custer ordered Gerard and his Rees to follow any left-hand tracks, no matter how small, to make sure no Indians had headed off the main trail. Godfrey wrote:

> Because of the dust it was impossible to see any distance, and the rattle of equipments and clattering of the horses' feet made it difficult to hear distinctly beyond our immediate surroundings. We could not see the trail, and we could only follow it by keeping in the dust cloud. The night was very calm, but occasionally a slight breeze would waft the cloud and disconcert our bearings; then we were obliged to halt to catch a sound from those in advance, sometimes whistling or hallooing, and getting a response we would start forward again. Finally troopers were put ahead, away from the noise of our column, and where they could hear the noise of those in front.[10]

Well, we know now Godfrey's K Company was not in the lead, nor was Benteen's H. "[T]he only guide of direction I had for my troop was the pounding of the cups on the saddle

Davis Creek. The bluffs are to the valley's north side. The creek flows along the tree line from left to right, and the Seventh Cavalry would have been moving right to left.

of men in rear of the troop preceding us in the column."[11] Still, despite the difficulties, the column moved quickly at times: "the gait was a trot ... kept up for perhaps eight or 10 miles"[12] (actually, as noted, a little less than seven) and at approximately 2:15 a.m. (1:18 a.m., local), Custer halted the regiment (see *Timeline B*), now sure he would not be able to reach or cross the divide before daylight. Captain Myles Moylan claimed this halt took place at 1:30 a.m. (12:33 a.m., local), while Godfrey, Herendeen,[13] and Reno all said two o'clock (1:03 a.m., local). This is particularly interesting because a number of historians and writers give different times. Greg Michno, for example, uses a time of 2:30,[14] while Vern Smalley—citing several sources—interpolates the various timings into a 2:45 a.m., local (3:42 a.m., watch-time), halt.[15] Smalley includes Lieutenant Hare's comments about an arrival "before daylight" (clearly fitting a 2:00 a.m. arrival as well) and Gerard's 4:00 a.m. arrival. It must be remembered, however, Hare, Gerard, and the Rees had been instructed to scout the column's left to look for trails heading in that di-

rection, so it would stand to reason they arrived at the site somewhat after the main column. Gerard said he rode in front with Custer, but for how long he does not say.[16] Wallace claimed the halt was around daylight, but that makes little sense, especially in light of the other witnesses, the distance traveled, and Benteen's comments about moving along at a trot. Besides, Wallace also said it was too dark to read his watch, making "daylight" a tenuous and rather broad guesstimate.

> We started again at 11 o'clock that night and moved on until about daylight. The horses were stopped again without anything to eat. We moved on again at 8 o'clock or 8:45, having gone about 10 miles during the night.... *I cannot tell the time for I could not see my watch*[17] [emphasis added].

Maybe the best indication of a halt around 2:15 a.m. came from Benteen when he wrote that an hour and one-half after they stopped, "daylight began to peer through."[18] With nautical twilight beginning one hour 26 minutes later, this would fit in as the earliest possible time. It would also justify the approximate two-mile-per-hour speed over the 6.5-mile distance. Anything else would tend to knock logic out of kilter. It would also bring Wallace's "daylight" a little closer to the others.

Again, one wonders just how important these "times" were to Wallace and the official record, much less to men like Hare, Herendeen, Godfrey, and the rest. If it were too dark for Wallace to read his watch when the column halted, why would it not have been too dark to read his watch when the column departed at 11:00 or 11:30 p.m. well after civil twilight ended? There are times we take some of this testimony too close to face value. If Luke Hare said the column arrived "before daylight," it emphasizes he was paying more attention to what was happening around him than to a specific time read from a watch, a time some historians seem intent upon locking in on. It would not be flippant to say Hare's observation meant he did not know the precise time the column arrived at Halt One, but it was certainly before it got light (nautical twilight began at 2:44 a.m., local, a watch time of 3:41 a.m.). While it was still far too dark to read, the first traces of light were appearing in the eastern sky, and by the time Hare had arrived, dismounted, figured out what he was doing or going to do, he may have noticed it was not quite as dark as it had been.

At the Reno Court of Inquiry, Captain Moylan was asked the following question and gave his response:

> Q: Is three o'clock about daylight in that latitude at that time of the year?
> A: Well, between two and three o'clock was about daylight.[19]

That seems to explain Hare, Wallace, and Herendeen and brings them back into some semblance of consistency with Godfrey, Moylan, Benteen, and Reno. The only one still dangling is Gerard and if we hark back to the beginning of the march, we remember Custer's words to his interpreter about following left-hand trails no matter how small. Gerard's late arrival time could be attributed to adherence to those orders.

Civil twilight began at 3:34 a.m., local—still impossible to read—and sunrise not until 4:13 a.m., local, way too late for any sort of initial troop arrival. John Gray used a 3:15 a.m. (local) halt time (equating to a watch time of 4:12 a.m.), figuring the column traveled seven miles at an average speed of 2.55 miles per hour. From some random artifacts found in what is believed to be the general area of that first halt, Gray is off in his distance estimate, but no more than 3/10–8/10 of a mile. What is strange about Gray's figures, however, is his use of local time when transposed to St. Paul time, would indicate a departure of 1:50 a.m. and an arrival of 4:12 a.m. There is hardly justification for either time and if he jerry-rigged them

to coincide with Gerard's observations, then he did himself a disservice because of his insistence the command was on local time. As shown earlier, Gray's departure time from the Busby encampment shows no semblance of reality or continuity with the narratives of those who were there.

From the looks of it, Benteen and Moylan may have been *near* the head of the regiment (Benteen, for his comment about the speed of march; Moylan, for his time of arrival)—though neither unit was the lead company—while Godfrey was farther back. If Moylan were correct about leaving at 11:00 p.m. and halting at 1:30 a.m., the distance would have been covered at a speed of some 2.68 miles per hour, pretty close to Gray's estimate, though obviously the specific times are different and our 11:00 p.m.-to-2:15 a.m. time-frame indicates an even slower pace: some 1.9 to 2.1 miles per hour. It is a shame we could not have heard from Keogh, though there is also some evidence—however fragile—in an allusion by First Sergeant John Ryan of M Company, to the way the packs were strung, that companies C and M were with Keogh.

Some authors have written that Fred Gerard said Half Yellow Face and Bloody Knife told Custer—as the column was assembling at the Busby halt—they would not be able to cross the divide before daylight without being discovered by Sioux scouts. (How Bloody Knife—a Ree, unfamiliar with the territory—would know this, we are as much in the dark as the column was when it moved up Davis Creek.) "Assembling at the Busby halt," however, is not what Gerard said, but like so many other things, this observation has been taken out of context or the "scholarship" has been just plain sloppy. Gerard claimed the column pulled out by 11:30 p.m. and he, Half Yellow Face, and Bloody Knife rode to the front and awaited the general's arrival. When Custer showed up he reiterated his desire for Gerard to make sure he scouted far to the left. We do not know how far the column had moved, but at some point—sooner rather than later—Custer halted and Gerard sent out several Rees to locate the trail. As Custer and Gerard were waiting—according to Gerard—the topic of the hostiles' numbers and the issue of crossing the divide were brought up. Custer asked the two Indians if he could cross before daylight, and they replied no. Then he asked if he crossed the divide *in* daylight could he do so without being discovered and again they replied no.[20] (Reno claimed the Crow leader told Custer of this problem around 2:00 a.m.,[21] which would make some sense since that is close to the time the column halted, but we must always keep in mind many of Reno's times are highly questionable.) While at first blush this does not seem of great consequence, it grows in importance when one combines it with the previous incidents, i.e., the Gibbon comment to Custer on the 22nd, Custer's comment to Varnum regarding Reno and his mistake of not pursuing the Indian trail, and the Herendeen/Tullock's Creek-scout circumstances. *The inability to cross the divide and hole-up for a day was just another reason to precipitate a unilateral advance.*

While the main column was leaving Busby and beginning its move up Davis Creek, Lieutenant Varnum and his scouts were already well in advance, heading toward the hilltop called the Crow's Nest. This is something of a misnomer, for the actual "Crow's Nest" is a "bowl" or pocket-shaped area Crow Indians used when stealing horses. Nothing to the west—the direction of march—can be seen from this pocket and the area itself is behind the promontory overlooking the western views, the objective of the scouts. Despite the terrain the ride proved rugged and it ended in this "bowl," a further climb by foot needed to reach the summit. Just as Custer was arriving at his first halt—2:00 a.m.—Varnum reached the Crow's Nest bowl,[22] four and one-half to five miles farther on. Exhausted from traveling more than 70 miles since the morning of June 24, Varnum collapsed and fell asleep. After all, it was still too dark to see anything from anywhere.

It is interesting to note here not everyone believes Varnum and his scouts reached this particular area. In numerous articles and in both his books, author Vern Smalley makes a case that the Crows leading Varnum's party got lost in the darkness and wound up on the divide rather than in the Crow's Nest.[23] According to Smalley, too embarrassed by their incompetence, the Crows lied over the ensuing years about where they brought the scouting party, eventually convincing everyone it was the Crow's Nest and the Crow's Nest hill. Smalley cites as proof a number of comments made by Varnum about subsequent events and how he physically approached the summit. Supporting Smalley's case is the fact no one knows for certain where on this hill—beyond the ridge itself—the scouts and eventually Custer overlooked the valleys beyond. Historian James Willert wrote,

> A rounded oval hill directly southeast of where the great trail crossed the divide, a half-mile or less from the Camp Marker. This hill is exactly on the divide, and from it about everything of note that could be seen from the higher peak was observable from its summit. A few pine trees are growing on it, and were in 1876, forming a slight screen from observation from the Reno Creek Valley. It was easily ascended, especially from the trail where it crossed the divide, and from the little branch of Davis Creek that had its beginning 40 rods [220 yards or 660 feet] southeast.[24]

Edgar Stewart was more perplexed. "[W]e do not know precisely which hill, but in all probability it was the fourth peak

south of the pass which connects the valley of Davis Creek with that of Sundance or Reno Creek."[25] Willert again:

> Tall grass carpeted the slopes of the divide below the ... [Crow's Nest], and the ravine that marked the headwaters of Davis Creek was cloaked in ... pink and white wild rosebuds.... From the north bank of this tributary, the terrain sloped upward several hundred yards to a stand of pine trees, from which vantage ... certain observations could be made across the brow of the divide toward the Little Horn Valley. The divide was directly west of the slope, and to the south, dipped sharply into a broad ravine which formed the source of the south fork of the tributary known today as Reno Creek.[26]

The debate is rendered somewhat moot, however, by subsequent events, and maybe the best case for either theory is in the view itself.

Varnum and the scouts' ride from the Busby camp to the Crow's Nest took about five and one-half hours in the pitch-black night, a speed of a little over two miles per hour. Slowing things down was the Crows' need to stop a couple of times in the dense undergrowth along the stream so they could have a smoke. This is a reasonable explanation for the slow speed and since it would be dark for several more hours, there appeared to be no reason to hurry. Once at the Crow's Nest, Varnum, Boyer, and White Man Runs Him led the horses into the pocket and while most of the scouts slept—waiting for it to get light enough to ascend the summit—Hairy Moccasin and White Man Runs Him climbed to the top. Shortly after civil twilight (3:34 a.m., local; 4:31 a.m., watch-time) the two Crows spotted indications of a large village (presumably the dim glow of campfires and their smoke against the lightening sky) and scurried back down to tell the others. As light began to blossom in the east, Varnum was at the high ground looking into the valleys, but had trouble seeing because of inflamed eyes from loss of sleep and hard riding in the dust. Also spotted were two tepees along Ash/Sundance/Reno Creek, the remnants of an abandoned village. One of the lodges was partly wrecked or knocked over (we are not told how far away these lodges were, though later evidence points to a distance of some 10 miles west of the divide, so it is rather obvious a telescope or field glasses were used to spot them). Once the sky lightened, Varnum wrote a note describing what he was seeing—or what he was told he was seeing—and handed it to a young Ree named Red Star. Varnum directed Red Star—and another Ree named Bull—to deliver the note to Custer, but like so many other things, this is a documented event rife with discrepancies and opinions. For example, Smalley claimed the two Rees departed at 3:45 a.m., local,[27] while others claim it was shortly after 4:00 a.m. Varnum himself said he dispatched the messengers just past 5:00 and that seems to make the most sense, though this is the

The "Crow's Nest," looking east with Reno Creek and the Little Big Horn to the photographer's rear. This is where Varnum and others slept. The horizontal dirt trail near the top of the photograph indicates the middle ravine where some of the command may have waited during Halt Two.

second instance where the *use of local time interposed itself* into the otherwise orderly chaos. "About five o'clock I wrote a note to the General and sent it off by the Rees, telling him the information I got from the Crows."[28] If the sun rose at 4:13 a.m. (5:10 a.m., headquarters/watch time), lighting the eastern sky (and remember, the heights they were at and the ranges to the east made sunrise appear later than it was), it would still seem too early for a tired, eye-sore man to discern very much in the depths of a hazy, still dark, western sky, backed by black ranges of mountains, fronted by bluffs and intervening rolling hills, 15 miles away. It is a reasonable assumption Varnum would not want to report anything to Custer he was not able to personally verify or at least be reasonably sure about, despite the insistence of the Crows (*Timeline C*).

This incident is a perfect example of the lack of attention paid to watch times. At 4:13 a.m., local time, the sun rose making it light enough to pen a note 45–50 minutes later. It is obvious Varnum paid no attention to his watch—just as he claimed—but guessed at the time based on the lapsed interval between the sun's rise and the writing of the note. Having campaigned for 40 days and having lived on the frontier a lot longer, Varnum would be familiar with the general time of sunrise virtually any place he went. If he used headquarters time (as his five o'clock reference) rather than local sun, it would have been only 4:03 a.m. local when the note was written, too dark to be feasible. Plus, it is extremely difficult to believe Varnum would write the note and then pop out his watch to check the time. This is a good example of the confusing use of both time "regions" in describing events and it illustrates a very conscientious officer's lack of concern with precise times, further indicating how little import was placed on these specifics. Charles Varnum was one of the most reliable sources we have regarding the movements of the regiment, but even his testimony takes some interpretation as he compresses times and events into historical blurs.

The distance from the Crow's Nest hill to where Custer first halted was about four and one-half miles. Under normal circumstances and easy terrain—which this was, especially in daylight—a speedy courier could make the trip in less than 45 minutes. Again, however, historians and writers assign all manner of times and speeds to Red Star's trip, essentially ignoring what the man himself had to say. Because his companion's horse fell lame, Red Star was supposed to have held back, taking some two hours to reach the regiment's camp. Red Star, however, said he urged his horse on[29] because he had the note, and knowing its import it is difficult to believe he would have dogged it. In addition, Red Star was a very young man (18 years old, though some records indicate he may have been as old as 22) and the Rees considered this note-carrying business a prestigious mission; it showed the white soldiers trusted him. When he arrived at Halt One and produced the note, Red Star was greeted enthusiastically and congratulated by his fellow Rees. Since it was getting lighter by the minute and there did not appear to be any intervening danger, one wonders why Red Star was not more readily believed. Authors Jack Pennington[30] and James Willert find credibility in his story and cite as proof the scout's comments about the sun rising over the eastern ridges when he rode into camp; by 6:00 a.m. it would have been well up indeed. If Varnum did dispatch the pair around 5:00, local, and Red Star allowed his beleaguered buddy to languish farther behind, he could easily have reached Custer's command by 6:00 a.m. And Bull could have *walked* it in an hour, horse or no horse.

Shortly after the Rees departed, Varnum and his scouts "saw two Sioux about one mile and a half west, moving down Davis Creek toward the soldiers' camp, and six other Sioux to the northeast over on Tullock Fork."[31] Varnum stated one Indian was riding a pony and leading another on a long lariat, a boy following. As they watched, the chief-of-scouts worried the Indians would turn right and cross the divide at the gap, thus discovering the advancing troops by their breakfast smoke, so he led a small foray to intercept them. Varnum took Boyer, Reynolds, White Swan, and one other Crow to chase the Sioux down and kill them, but as they set out they were called back: the Indians had changed direction. The scouts on the heights watched the two Sioux cross the divide: they changed their course away from the divide, but then changed again, moving in the direction of the gap.

In the meantime, Red Star arrived at the camp, by various accounts, alone, zigzagging his horse to indicate the Sioux camp had been located.[32] *Interesting!* If this was the case, chances are he was not too worried about Bull's flagging nag, thereby lending credibility to his story about hustling back with Varnum's note. White Man Runs Him claimed Custer arrived at the Crow's Nest at 6:00 a.m. and if that was anywhere close to true, Red Star indeed hustled and Custer would have taken only 30 minutes or so to gallop the four-plus miles to the Crow's Nest. Indian timing, interpreted into the white man's tongue, however, is notoriously inaccurate and we would be more comfortable with the Crow's timing had we read something about where the sun was in relation to Custer's arrival, something similar to what Red Star left us. The best guessing would have to involve the use of speeds, distances, and physiology of events. We know the distance involved, we have Red Star's say-so about how he ran the course, so we can plot reasonably it took him 40 minutes to go the four and one-half miles, a speed of slightly under seven miles per hour—a trot—and under the circumstances, i.e., Bull's flagging horse, not unreasonable. It is easy to visualize Red Star holding back somewhat, stopping to see if he could help, and then moving on more rapidly. Such actions would drop his overall rate of speed yet leave intact his impressions of hurrying along.

There is anecdotal evidence Red Star rode into camp and spoke first to Bloody Knife. Isaiah Dorman, the Dakota interpreter, spotted the two Rees talking, and told Private John Burkman—Custer's striker—to wake his chief: something was up. Custer, in turn, had Fred Gerard awakened, and as Red Star sat down to have a cup of coffee with Bloody Knife and some other Rees, Custer, Gerard, and Tom Custer came up to have a little powwow. (Captain Thomas Ward Custer was the commander of C Company and a younger brother of George Custer. He was killed with his brother—and an even younger brother, Boston—during the fighting.) Red Star showed the general the note and told everyone he had seen the Sioux camp.[33] Custer asked if the distance to the Crow's Nest was short and Red Star said it was. Custer then told the gathering they would leave for the Crow's Nest at once. Well, after a short detour.

If the time was now 7:20 a.m., local sun, as Gray would have us believe (that would make it 8:17 a.m., watch time), the natural question would be, would George Custer—and Gerard, for that matter—still be asleep that late? Custer was notorious for driving his men and his ability to survive on little sleep was legendary. One can see him trying to catch some shut-eye after arriving at the first halt, but not remaining asleep until well past 7:00 a.m., well past sun-up, not under these circumstances and not with his quarry almost within shouting distance. If the 7:20 a.m. was St. Paul/watch time, however, it would be only 6:23 a.m., local, a much more reasonable hour to work with. The 7:20 a.m., *watch time,* would also fit in very nicely with Varnum's note-writing at 5:00 a.m., local (5:57 a.m., watch), the distance Red Star had to ride,

Red Star's description of his pace, and the time of his arrival at Halt One.

> The scouts all again pushed out to look for the village, and at 11 o'clock at night Custer had everything packed up and followed the scouts up the right hand fork of the Rosebud.
>
> About daylight we went into camp, made coffee, and soon after it was light the scouts brought Custer word that they had seen the village from the top of the divide that separates the Rosebud from Little [Big Horn].[34]

Here is that allusion to a time immediately after sunrise again: *"soon after it was light."* Even if we grant some leeway here and say Custer spoke to the scouts, ran around the encampment, trotted the distance to the Crow's Nest pocket, gabbed a few moments with Charlie Varnum, then scaled the heights, it must still fit within some semblance of reason and the time parameters set by other witnesses, e.g., Varnum and Red Star, depending on the scenario one wishes to use. John Gray, however, has the *two* messengers arriving at Halt One at 7:20 a.m. (local), which is entirely too late,[35] again, unless one is on St. Paul time, in which case it fits.

So now we have Custer, walking over to where the Rees were camped, having a conversation with Red Star and Bloody Knife—Gerard interpreting—and then hopping on his horse and riding around the encampment, yelling for everyone to be ready to move at 8:00 a.m.—one would naturally think Custer would want his command to follow (again, "8:00 a.m." would fit perfectly if St. Paul/Headquarters time were used). Whether Custer *issued* orders to move or just alerted his command *for* a move remains another matter for debate. Benteen remembered Custer passing him by, but the general saying nothing. Benteen then noticed Reno and Lieutenant Benny Hodgson, "on the other side of a ravine," about to have breakfast and he joined them.[36] Some 30 minutes later, the column began to move: no orders, no trumpets. Red Star, however, said as Custer and his small party—in addition to Red Star, Custer's trumpeter, Henry Voss; his brother, Tom; Fred Gerard; Bloody Knife; Bob-tail Bull; and Little Brave[37]—started out, Custer's trumpeter turned and blew his horn. If this is correct, *why?* We can understand Benteen may not have heard it, but was the trumpet call misunderstood by those who did? Did Custer really want his regiment to move?

Lieutenant Godfrey wrote, "We started promptly at eight o'clock and marched uninterruptedly until 10.30 a.m. when we halted in a ravine ... we had marched about 10 miles."[38] Unfortunately, we have to pick and choose here once again, for while the "eight o'clock" and "10:30 a.m." fit the theory, the "10 miles" does not. At first blush the time-distance calculations would yield a speed of four miles per hour, but Godfrey's "10 miles" is sheer nonsense, almost to the point of farce, rendering his entire recollection problematic. Once again it must be remembered, Halt One was only four and one-half miles from the Crow's Nest and only three and one-half miles from where the trailing end of Halt Two would be a couple hours later. Godfrey's ruminations make little sense and the only reasonable explanation is he—some 15 years later—got his distances confused and combined his movements to end at the divide. Myles Moylan agreed with the departure time of 8:00 a.m., though Luke Hare said between 8:00 and 9:00, and George Wallace first used between 8:00 and 8:45, then at the Reno inquiry, settled on 8:45.[39] (That is an interesting span—8:00 to 8:45—for the man supposed to be keeping the itinerary; one might think his ranges would be a little tighter.) Benteen thought they moved about one and one-half *miles* before halting again, which, of course, is wrong by more than half and when compared to Godfrey's distance makes us wonder if these men were referring to the same events.

As mentioned earlier, author Vern Smalley questioned Custer's appearance at the Crow's Nest. In his books, *Little Bighorn Mysteries* and *More Little Bighorn Mysteries*, Smalley fleshes-in his theory that Custer never went to the Crow's Nest hill, but instead looked over the valleys from a spot on the divide Smalley terms "Varnum's Lookout." There is, however, scant evidence of this being the case. Visiting the area in June 2007, I found the location of the "pocket" where Smalley believes the horses were kept, too small and too wet, an area that does not seem to dry out very easily, and it would never have held 15 horses without jamming them together or breaking an ankle. In addition, while the view from his "Varnum's Lookout" is good, it is nothing compared to that from Crow's Nest hill—some 400 feet higher—and no one could walk away from "Varnum's Lookout" with the certainty of having seen signs of a village 15 miles beyond. And no one would walk away without pointing to the towering hill just behind and saying, *Let's go up there, the view's gotta be better!* Fred Gerard, when asked at the Reno inquiry what the terrain was like approaching the lookout point, replied, "On the side we went up was a little ravine with timber in it and part of the way up there was a spring."[40] Furthermore, Gerard said the heights were "several hundred feet" above the Davis Creek valley floor,[41] something "Varnum's Lookout" is not. Smalley is not a lone wolf here, however, as James Willert also felt Custer never made the "arduous" climb all the way up the Crow's Nest hill, but viewed the valley "from the higher ground rising to the north of Davis Creek ... his party mov[ing] to that position,"[42] a different description from what he alluded to earlier. We will not toss the "Varnum's

The Reno Creek valley from author Vern Smalley's "Varnum's Lookout" at the top of the divide.

Lookout" theory so cavalierly aside, however, for it does pop up again with some validity.

That Custer viewed the Reno Creek and Little Big Horn valleys, we are certain. What he saw or did not see is almost irrelevant, for no plans were devised by, or at that time. There also seems to be no question but that Custer remained at the Crow's Nest hill for more than an hour. Gray has him arriving shortly after 9:00 a.m. and leaving about 10:20, which would be valid were it headquarters/watch time. Smalley has him arriving (at "Varnum's Lookout") at 8:45 a.m. and departing at 10:05, also local time. Willert said he arrived at 9:30 and W. A. Graham had him showing up after 10:00, though neither dared enter the time fracas, instead allowing the reader to remain ambivalent as to which standard was being used. Again, where are all these discrepancies coming from? And how could a man of Custer's temperament have taken almost two hours to ride more than four *easy* miles? Well, the answer is, he didn't—refer to *Timeline E*. Red Star gave him the message, there was a brief discussion, he jumped on his horse,

rode around informing his command he wanted to move, a frenzy of activity ensued, and by eight o'clock the command was ready—and Custer had already run off. Did someone mistake Voss' trumpet call for an order to move? Custer—never the patient man—headed for the Crow's Nest, maybe even chomping at the bit because his regiment could not keep his pace.

(Custer's impatience was legendary. More than one of his officers attested to this as the years went on. On July 9, 1925, Graham wrote letters to Varnum and Edgerly. He asked them about a story of Custer stopping for some 45 minutes after sending a written message to Benteen [as Reno was fighting in the valley]. Varnum knew nothing about it, but he did not believe it would have happened. "Any one who knew Geo. A. Custer would find it hard to believe that he could keep still for five minutes under the circumstances." Edgerly responded that he did not think this was "probable."[43] To further emphasize the point, former Civil War general, Allured Bayard Nettleton, who knew and had fought alongside

George Custer during the war, wrote in the *Philadelphia Times* shortly after the Little Big Horn debacle,

> It must be remembered that in fighting with cavalry, which was Custer's forte, instantaneous quickness of eye—that is lightning-like formation and execution of successive correct judgments on a rapidly-shifting situation—is the first thing, and the second is the power of inspiring the troopers with that impetuous yet intelligent ardor with which a mounted brigade becomes a thunderbolt, and without which it remains a useless mass of horses and riders. These qualities Gen. Custer seemed to me to manifest, throughout the hard fighting of the last year of the war, to a degree that was simply astounding, and in a manner that marked him as one of the few really great commanders developed by the wars of the present century.[44]

"Instantaneous," "quickness," "lightning-like," "rapidly-shifting," "impetuous ... ardor," "thunderbolt?" George Custer did *not* walk to the Crow's Nest! And as we shall soon see, he did not walk down Reno Creek.)

So how long did all this take? (Refer to *Timeline C.*) Once Red Star arrived—6:55 a.m. (*watch* time)—a few more minutes went by for his celebratory welcome. As he was settling in for a cup of coffee, the interpreter, Isaiah Dorman, noticed his presence in the scouts' camp. By now we can say it was around 7:05 a.m. Dorman went to fetch Custer's striker, Private John Burkman—7:08—who in turn roused the general—7:12. It was probably another five to eight minutes—7:20 to 7:25 a.m.—before Custer cleared his head, grabbed Gerard, and hot-footed it to where the scouts had pitched themselves. Another lapse of some 15, 20 minutes, reading Varnum's note, talking, then riding around camp—7:45 a.m.—and Custer is off—7:50 a.m.—a flurry of activity as orders were issued and first sergeants cracked their whips, fires doused, and troops mounted—8:00–8:05 a.m.—then, beginning—8:10–8:15 a.m.—Custer moving at a lope up the valley, maybe between a casual gallop and something faster; or simply put, a brisk pace, at least six miles per hour, the general and his entourage arriving at the "pocket": 8:35 a.m.

The pocket of the Crow's Nest could be seen fairly quickly, especially if one followed the scouts' tracks, hugging the south edge of Davis Creek valley, something the Sioux did *not* do. Varnum saw Custer coming and headed down from the hill, greeting his commander as the horses were being sequestered. Salutes were exchanged, Varnum explained what was going on—what the Crows had seen—and somewhere between 8:50 and nine o'clock, George Custer is looking through an eyeglass at the Little Big Horn valley. He listened, watched, and peered, coming away unconvinced he had seen anything of any magnitude. In an April 14, 1909, letter to Walter Camp, Varnum wrote:

> The command came in vision about this time and we watched it approach the gap where it halted. I rode down towards the col-umn & soon met the Genl. He said, "Well you've had a night of it." I said yes, but I was still able to sit up & notice things. Tom Custer & Calhoun then came up to us & Custer was angry at their leaving the column & ordered them back. I told the Genl. all I had seen, as we rode back towards the Crow nest hill and we climbed the hill together.[45]

Varnum is a little misleading here—or, in discussing the battle with Camp some 33 years after the fact, simply mistaken. While he mentions Lieutenant James Calhoun to Camp, Varnum does not mention him in his memoirs written some few years later. Red Star alluded to Tom Custer being in the group, but not Calhoun, and the senior Custer may not have realized his brother tagged along. (Lieutenant James Calhoun was the Custers' brother-in-law and commander of Company L. He was killed in the Custer fighting.) Once noticed, Junior was peremptorily sent back to the column. It is also very likely what Varnum saw coming up the Davis Creek valley was not the regiment, per se—"The command came in vision"—but the Custer party alone. Even Red Star believed that. In *The Arikara Narrative*, published in 1920 from material gathered around 1912, Red Star claimed Custer left the upper Crow's Nest as the troops arrived at the foot of the hill,[46] meaning the main column was nowhere in sight when Custer arrived at the Crow's Nest pocket. Private Peter Thompson, a C Company trooper, alluded to something similar when he wrote, "Custer rode some distance ahead of us and then, turning to the right [*sic*, left], ascended to the highest point of the hills."[47] Years later—in his memoirs—Varnum wrote, "About 10 o'clock the column was in sight heading for a low spot in the divide where the trail crosses. I rode out to meet the troops, but met General Custer & Tom (his brother). He sent Tom back and rode to the Crow Nest with me."[48] Is this the same thing he told Camp? He "rode out to meet the troops, *but...?*" Instead of the "troops" was it just Custer and those few who rode with him? And why would George send his brother back?

As Custer spends his time atop the Crow's Nest, the column is moseying along, a little confused, and rather leaderless. Ornery pack mules are making things difficult in the rear slowing everything even more; no one is sure what is going on. Who issued the order to move? Where are we going? Just follow Custer's route. Though the distance is not far, the going was slow, certainly not a lot faster—if at all—than the night march. Lieutenant Cooke, Major Reno, Captain Benteen, other officers, all uncertain. Are we doing the right thing? *What did he want us to do?*

By the time Custer was ready to leave the overlook, it was pushing 10 o'clock or a few minutes later. While Godfrey, Hare, Moylan, Wallace, and others said the command arrived

Reno Creek and its valley from atop the Crow's Nest hill. The divide is mid-photograph. Davis Creek runs from left to right along the tree line below the divide. The lead portion of the Seventh Cavalry may have waited in this area at Halt Two.

between 10:00 and 10:30 a.m., there is not a breath of a chance Custer himself would have taken two hours to reach the Crow's Nest, not after a 40-day campaign, a forced night march, and a Type-A personality. That leaves us with a command arriving separately and considerably later than its chief. Red Star's simple comment about Custer leaving to meet the troops lends credence to the officers' statements and calls into question some of Varnum's recollections.

(Another example of slippage in Varnum's late, post-battle reminiscences lies with the story of the Ree half-breed scout, Robert Jackson. Varnum claimed Jackson was one of the Rees with him as the command moved up the Rosebud.[49] In a June 27, 2006, e-mail to me, Vern Smalley wrote,

> Custer allowed the men to write one last letter to home, and a courier took them the next morning. I think that the courier was Bob Jackson. He left on the morning of June 23 and was at the Yellowstone Depot on June 25 in time to be discharged and seen by Private Harvey Fox [D Company] who was known to be at the Y[ellowstone] D[epot].

Private George Glenn [H Company] believed Jackson was sent back from the mouth of the Rosebud camp. Glenn saw him there, but did not recall seeing him later.[50] George Herendeen, the scout, said Jackson was *not* at the Little Big Horn on June 25 or June 26, but back at the Powder River [Yellowstone] Depot.[51] Private Stanislaus Roy [A Company], "always heard that Bob Jackson and Billy Cross never forded at Ford A. No one remembers seeing them in the valley fight or on [the] west side of [the] river at all."[52] And finally, the Ree scout Young Hawk claimed Robert Jackson was in the camp at the mouth of the Powder after the battle, but was not *in* the battle.[53] Jackson enlisted for six months on December 25, 1875, meaning he would have been mustered out, or he would have re-upped on June 25, 1876. That required bureaucracy of sorts and as we see, at this particular time Custer was hardly in the mood for the more mundane tasks of military ceremony.)

A number of things began happening about now. For

one, Sergeant William Curtiss of Captain George W. M. Yates' Company F reported some of his belongings missing, probably lost along the trail, falling off one of the pack mules, or more likely, just forgotten and left behind at the first halt.[54] At the Reno inquiry, Myles Moylan testified, "while at the second halt at the foot of the divide ... a sergeant of one of the companies returned on the trail some miles ... for the purpose of recovering ... some clothing of his that had been lost from a pack mule the night before."[55] Curtiss was sent back with four men (F Company privates James Rooney, William A. Brown, Patrick Bruce, and Sebastian Omling[56]) to retrieve it, eventually finding the pack being rifled by three Cheyenne warriors (*Timeline D*). In all likelihood, these Indians were part of pesky Little Wolf's Red Cloud agency band (two of whom may have been Big Crow and Black White Man, the Indians who had spotted the regiment on the Rosebud the day before). Curtiss and crew ran them off, but they made their way back to spy on the troops at Halt Two, then attempted to warn the village, but could not circle around quickly enough, arriving after most of the action was over.

Of course we can only guess when Curtiss reported this to his company commander, but Moylan tells us Curtiss had already been sent back by the time the command was halted at the foot of the divide—Halt Two. Reason dictates Curtiss discovered the missing pack was left at Halt One, probably shortly after the command first moved out. Halt One lasted some six hours, the troops sleeping, building fires, making coffee, and eating breakfast; Halt Two lasted for some one and one-half hours and the troops never got themselves comfortable. With battle looming on the horizon, it would stand to reason Curtiss might want to make some last-minute adjustments and preparations—who knew where another night out would bring them? So despite the fact Moylan's recollection reflected only hearsay at best—going from Curtiss to Yates to Keogh to Cooke (as the commander of the rear guard early on the 25th, Keogh was of necessity informed)—the incident was in all likelihood reported early in the march from Halt One. The author and historian, Richard Hardorff, claimed it was a five-mile trip back,[57] but this is not accurate as the distance between the two halts was only four and one-half miles and Curtiss did not wait until arriving at Halt Two to tell his commander. The distance would include whatever he had to cover from where he told Yates; then back to Halt One—probably some three-quarters of a mile; and then the return trip of no more than two and one-half miles before he caught up to the slow-moving column. Assuming Curtiss and his troopers trotted back—using a speed of six miles per hour—then took 15 minutes to rout the Indians and police up his belongings, hustling back at a faster gait (eight miles

per hour), the whole affair would have taken a little under three-quarters of an hour. Then—based on speeds and distances—we can see an arrival of the column's van in the Halt Two area at approximately 10 o'clock. This would give Custer an extra few minutes atop the Crow's Nest hill and that would fit very well with reported events.

We can now add a few minutes for the general scurry down from the hilltop; Custer locating his senior officers; another short wait as Yates is making his company dispositions and telling the Curtiss story to Keogh, and then the two of them informing Adjutant Cooke; and finally, Custer being informed at his officers' call (*Timeline E*).

Now we enter another false path in the labyrinth. One version of the story has Tom Custer and Jim Calhoun riding out to tell brother George of Curtiss' findings and being greeted with "*Tom, who in the devil moved these troops forward? My orders were to remain in camp all day and make a night attack on the Indians, but they have discovered us, and are on the run.*"[58] As usual, even this comment is shrouded in controversy. Author Bruce Liddic seems to think Custer simply forgot to countermand his march order, writing, "Gerard also recalled Custer ordered his Adjutant, First Lieutenant William Cooke, to keep the command in camp until he returned."[59] Gerard told Walter Camp much the same thing in his January 22, 1909, and April 3, 1909, interviews, though by then Bill Cooke had morphed into Tom Custer: "Custer now told his brother Tom not to move the command from where it was until further orders."[60] *Or maybe both?* Lieutenant Godfrey, however, claimed to have recalled clearly the general telling people to be ready to move, though that is quite different from an actual order to do so, thus, confusion. In addition to Liddic, others also feel it was merely a simple screw-up, and maybe not by Custer or his "faulty" memory. What is so nettlesome, however, is Varnum is fairly precise in this part of his story and even though he omitted Calhoun in later years, there must have been some basis for including him in his conversations with Camp. Varnum claimed he watched as the regiment approached, then descended into the pocket to greet Custer, and a moment later the other two officers appeared, only to be admonished by George for having *left* the column. The "Tom, who in the devil" quote might seem more embellishment than fact, especially when one considers the timing and situational elements involved, but Varnum's overall credibility and honesty may be just enough to tell us something is amiss here.

The evidence poses a situational, abstract quandary. By late evening of the previous day, Custer knew the Sioux were on the lower Little Big Horn. He ordered a night march, an ultra-difficult maneuver considering the problems he had had with the packs. He marches almost seven miles in the pitch-black of night, over unknown terrain, sometimes at a trot, risking the continuity of the entire regiment and its supply train—not to mention the condition of his animals—finally halting after a trek at an average speed of about two miles per hour, indicating all sorts of stops and starts along the way. And we are now asked to believe that after receiving a report the village has been sighted, Custer himself would take two to two and one-half hours to march four and one-half miles in broad daylight, with nothing to do but whistle along the way. That makes no sense, yet Liddic's idea of a simple screw-up does, especially if Varnum was correct and Custer had sent his brother back to the column, and then, some time later the troops appeared, Custer believing he had countermanded his original order to move. That would give brother Tom a double tongue-lashing—this time alongside brother-in-law Calhoun—but George had a lot on his mind and simple mistakes were easy to make. Liddic is undoubtedly correct and it points out something more about George Custer. If the man told Cooke to hold the command where it was, then rode around camp yelling for everyone to be ready to move at eight, it shows us he was in something of a lather. So it is with this in mind that it is impossible to believe Custer himself led the column and took more than two hours to move from Halt One to the Crow's Nest pocket.

The question now arises, where was this second halt? In June 2007, we visited the area with some friends and Professor Richard A. Fox, Jr., and his brother, Dennis. Dr. Fox pointed out the ravine running alongside the eastern opening of the pocket, suggesting military artifacts had been found there. In his Summer 2007 *Research Review* article, Tom Heski wrote that the halt site was in what he called McDougal Ravine, a ravine where a fellow named Keith McDougal also discovered artifacts. This was one ravine before—east of—Dr. Fox' area. While it seems nice to be able to say a particular ravine was where the troops hid, we have also seen this was a long, extended column, not readily adaptable to a rapid deployment within some hidden area off the main route of advance. Also, we have the comments from various participants:

MOYLAN: the halt was at the foot of the divide.
HARE: the column lay concealed about one-half mile before the divide for about one hour between 10 a.m. and noon.[61]
VARNUM: "The column arrived at the trail-crossing of the divide about 10 a.m."[62]
PRIVATE THEODORE GOLDIN: "About eight o'clock, the command moved out and marched steadily for perhaps two hours, when we found ourselves well-sheltered in the ravine at the base of the divide, halted, and remained concealed for some time."[63]
EDGERLY: The regiment was together at about 10 a.m., some 15 miles from the Indian village. They had been halted and

Custer was "on a hill with the Crow and Ree scouts." When Custer came down, officers' call was sounded.[64]

The so-called McDougal Ravine is a little less than two miles from the divide, a distance hardly confused with a half mile, so it makes some sense the command moved into any easily accessible area off the main route. In addition to the two ravines mentioned above, there is a third housing the headwaters of the creek, between the Crow's Nest and the divide itself. As one heads up the valley in a southwesterly direction nearing the divide, the creek takes a sharp, almost 90-degree turn due south, flowing between the divide and the Crow's Nest precipice. Some one and one-half miles beyond this left dogleg the creek divides into a left and a right fork, each eventually ending (or beginning; remember, we are heading *up*stream) in the steeper reaches of the Wolf Mountains about a mile farther on.

So there is the possibility Halt Two was actually a series of halts—or ravines—extending from McDougal Ravine (to the east) to the area behind the Crow's Nest pocket—and we *know* troops occupied these areas—to within Hare's quarter- to half-mile of the divide (to the west). We also know the column was some three-quarters to eight-tenths of a mile in length, consisting not only of disciplined troops, but the very difficult pack train; it took time for the last man to have left Halt One; and its arrival at Halt Two occurred over a period of time similar to, but probably even longer than the time it took in departing the first halt (the effects of variable cueing). The van was certainly greeted by Custer even while the rear guard was still some 20 or 30 minutes away: a long column—probably of pairs—stretched out, and unsure of exactly where it was headed, moving along at a leisurely and hesitant pace.

While up on the Crow's Nest hill, the general putatively accepted favorite scout Charlie Reynolds' exhortations about a large village being sighted. He also paid some heed to Mitch Boyer's assurances and the Crows' confidence the village was there—and huge—but he was still skeptical, especially of the size (Custer was still thinking 800–1,500 warriors). As he finished viewing the western valleys, Custer descended the hill with his entourage, unconvinced he had seen anything of significance, but rather than settle in, he decided to hold a brief conference to explain what he had not seen and reiterate his feelings the column had not been spotted, despite what Varnum told him about the hostiles spotted from the top of the hill. Officers' call was sounded and the entire group gathered near a small knoll atop which sat a number of troops from C Company. Among them was Private Peter Thompson, one of the lucky few from Tom Custer's command to survive the battle. Thompson wrote everyone was engrossed:

Our company was resting quite close to the place where the officers sat in council. This resting place was on a piece of ground slightly elevated above the officers' position, which for the first time on the expedition gave me an opportunity of seeing the officers all together and of noting their appearances. The most noticeable among them was Captain Benteen.

From the manner of the conversation it would seem as though Custer had discovered something that was of great importance. We could not hear the conversation, but we could see that they were all deeply interested. The younger officers did not seem to take any part in the conversation but paid great attention while Custer and the more experienced officers were seeking to solve some difficult problem.[65]

This particular Thompson story rings true, if for nothing else than for its location. Davis Creek valley is relatively flat, though rising into the mountains. As one heads southwest and approaches the divide the valley broadens. The Crow's Nest promontory and its pocket form a southern corner of the valley and a small, intermittent stream branches off the main creek, emanating from higher ground farther south. This intermittent creek forms the ravine Dr. Fox referred to and passes by the pocket on its way to the main creek. A secondary fork comes out of the pocket, probably from the spring Gerard alluded to in his 1879 testimony. Today there is a four-wheel drive track running the length of the Fox ravine and crossing south into the next valley. As this track swings into Davis Creek valley (heading northward) it bends west and connects with the dirt trail that heads across the divide (passing the Walter Camp marker). As it makes this turn west, it skirts the edge of the Crow's Nest hill between that hill and a small rise at the southern extremity of the valley. This rise is the only one of its kind in the valley's upper reaches and is obviously the spot where Thompson viewed Custer's powwow.[66]

Custer complained to the gathered officers that he could not see any sign of an Indian camp and he expressed doubt anything was there[67] despite the fact the Crow scouts told him they could see a village. Gerard, too, said he could see signs of an encampment. In the Camp interviews Gerard said they went up to the "high mountain peak, which was about 13 miles east of the Little Big Horn" and he could make out a pony herd on the hills and tableland beyond the river. Also, he saw a large dark spot or mass and even spotted dust rising, concluding that horses were being driven. He added by this time it was now "some hours after daylight, and the light was strong and the atmosphere very clear."[68] Custer on the other hand, claimed he could not see the village and told his officers he did not believe the Indians could see it either. Fred Benteen thought otherwise. His experience told him Indians had superior vision and he believed what the Crows said was true,[69] trusting rather the sharp eyes of an Indian even to the binoc-

ulars he always carried. He believed this from years on the Plains, but Benteen said nothing to Custer, because he was not invited to "chip in."[70] Around this same time, Custer was informed of the Curtiss business and we also hear of Mitch Boyer telling George Herendeen he had just spotted some Indians lurking nearby (those pesky Cheyenne who had been rifling Curtiss' pack and who had backtracked to spy on the soldiers, probably our old friends, Big Crow and Black White Man). "Just," is another of those relevant words here, for as Custer was discussing the move, was being told of Curtiss, and was complaining about seeing very little, Boyer and Herendeen looked around and found the Cheyenne pony tracks. This had to have been added to the repertoire Custer was absorbing, further reinforcing a growing cacophony of conviction his command had been spotted.

Custer is reported to have told the Crow scout, Half Yellow Face, "This camp has not seen our army, none of their scouts have seen us ... I want to wait until it is dark and then we will march, we will place our army around the Sioux camp."[71] This brought some sharp disagreement from the Crows—and the Ree, Red Star. White Man Runs Him told Custer he should attack, that the Sioux had spotted his dust and the campfires from Halt One. In an interesting digression, James Willert brought up a point that could have had some bearing on Custer's decision-making:

> To [the Crows], when the *enemy was near-at-hand, attack was the only justified action.* The decision of Gibbon to march against the hostile's [*sic*] village [on May 17] had pleased them, but the abrupt cancellation of the projected assault had confused and *displeased* them.[72]

Furthermore, there was always that scattering issue. Bruce Liddic: "If he waited the warriors would come out to fight him to give the women and children time to escape, then all would scatter."[73] Willert: "If the hostiles' village was ... alerted to the presence of the regiment, it would not be long before the warriors would swarm out to attack, to give their noncombatants opportunity to slip away.... Custer could not afford the risk."[74] The irony of the Little Big Horn is regardless of the worries, the plans, and the preparations, this is precisely what happened. Lieutenant Godfrey recalled the officers felt the same way.

> It is a rare occurrence ... that gives a commander the opportunity to reconnoiter the enemy's position in daylight. This is particularly true if the Indians have a knowledge of the presence of troops.... When following an Indian trail, the "signs" indicate the length of time elapsed since the presence of the Indians. When the "signs" indicate a "hot trail," i.e., near approach, the commander judges his distance, and by a forced march, usually in night time, tries to reach the Indian village at night and make his disposition for a surprise attack at daylight. At all events, his

Looking back toward the Crow's Nest area from the divide. The "pocket" would be behind the bare hill slightly left of center. The small knoll where Private Peter Thompson viewed the officers' call is barely visible to the left of the "bare hill."

attack must be made with celerity, and generally without other knowledge of the numbers of the opposing force ... that discovered or conjectured while following the trail. The dispositions for the attack may be said to be "made in the dark," and successful surprise to depend upon luck. If the advance to the attack be made in daylight, it is next to impossible that a near approach can be made without discovery. In all of our previous experiences, when the immediate presence of the troops was once known to them, the warriors swarmed to the attack [this is what happened to Crook], and resorted to all kinds of ruses to mislead the troops, to delay the advance toward their camp or village while the squaws and children secured what personal effects they could, drove off the pony herd, and by flight put themselves beyond danger, and then scattering, made successful pursuit next to impossible.... In Indian warfare, the rule is "touch and go."[75]

The final straw was probably Curtiss' lost pack. After a quick sit-down with Bloody Knife and some of the Rees (most of whom were dead-set against attacking what they perceived as "*otoe*"—too many—Sioux), and assurances by others they had been spotted, Custer decided to attack, a decision he was

not uncomfortable with and quite possibly, overjoyed by. Lieutenant Edgerly remembered the meeting culminated with Custer telling his officers,

> We would press on as quickly as we could and attack them in the village if possible. The idea was that the Indians would not stand against a whole regiment of cavalry, and that as soon as they learned of our advance they would try to get away from us.[76]

At some point, Custer borrowed Lieutenant DeRudio's Austrian-made field glasses to look for the village again. Luke Hare's statements to Walter Mason Camp bear this out: "Custer had been out ahead with scouts viewing [the] valley of the Little Big Horn.... [The column] lay concealed less than one-half mile from the divide for more than an hour. During this time Custer again went to Crow's Nest to look at Indians."[77] Hare did not actually *see* Custer return, but heard he did. In 1910, he told Camp—possibly by letter—

that Boyer said to Custer, "General I have been with these Indians for 30 years and this is the largest village I have ever heard of."[78] It is possible Hare did not specifically mean the "Crow's Nest" and could have been referring to any high perch from which to see the village.

In a letter dated February 24, 1910, to Charles Varnum, Camp stated,

> Hare says that the regiment halted just east of the divide, only ¼ to ½ mile east of it, just far enough to be out of sight from the direction of the Little Big Horn, in the valley right opposite the Crow's Nest, and remained there from about 10 a.m. to about 11:45 a.m. ... DeRudio said the same thing, and added that while here Gen. Custer went the second time to the Crow's Nest.[79]

Varnum denied there was a second trip to the *Crow's Nest*: "I don't think Custer went a second time to the hill. I am in fact quite if not absolutely sure of it."[80] Varnum, however, was not the only one who may have been a little antsy about Custer's skepticism. Reynolds and Boyer were equally concerned about making sure the general made no mistakes when it came to the village's location and size. Varnum went on:

> Something was said by either Custer or myself about DeRudio having a fine pair of field glasses ... but I am almost certain he did not go back to the hill again. I had no breakfast and was frightfully thirsty and was hunting food and drink after I got with the command, and of course can't swear to what occurred while I was so engaged.[81]

So it appears Varnum may not have been at the officers' call, or if he was, when it broke up, someone—ever anxious to convince Custer he may be riding into a hornet's nest—had convinced the general to take one last look, this time using DeRudio's fine field glasses. There is also a time lag to consider here, especially in light of Custer's impetuous decision-making. After reviewing Private Thompson's comments, we can allow for a 20-minute officers' call, followed by a couple of minutes' discussion about the village. The distance from where Custer held his conference to heights on the divide was about ¾ of a mile, and at a canter or trot it would take only seven or eight minutes to reach it. Add another nine or 10 minutes for viewing and chitchat, then eight more for the return trip, and we are in the vicinity of 11:10 a.m. (*Timeline E*).

Whether or not Custer was convinced of a massive village after viewing the valleys from the divide we do not know, but it was from this point on he could have begun devising his tactical plan. Assignments were now made: seven men from each company were detailed to the packs and Lieutenant Edward Gustave Mathey (M Company) was placed in charge, a task Mathey was not unused to. Benteen, knowing his men were standing by and ready, let Custer know he was set to go, and in turn for being first to report was given the honor of leading the regiment forward. Companies already in the ancillary valleys were turned and the regiment headed toward the divide, much of the command—with the packs—still strung out along the Davis Creek valley. Custer then ordered the troop commanders to mount their men and report when ready. Edgerly said this took only a minute.[82] Dispositions made, the regiment began its final march at 11:45 a.m.

Time has now become paramount. Because of what he knew of the Indians, because of the premise around which the entire campaign was built, two elements in Custer's thinking and planning were crucial: surprise and speed. Surprise may have been compromised already; therefore, speed was of the essence. Always speed.

4

THE FLIP SIDE OF THE COIN

There are times we need to cherry-pick bits and pieces of information fitting our theories to see if they work. This is a dangerous practice for it allows one to fling around all sorts of wild hypotheses based on little or no evidence, stringing out a sometimes obscure tidbit to outrageous and unsupportable conclusions; June 25, 1876, is ripe for such subjectivity. While not all the conflicting accounts are worth ruminating over, many elements are worth the effort—the precise departure time from the Busby encampment, as well as the arrival at Halt One, come to mind for issues involving timing. Leaving Halt One and whether Custer accompanied his command or went ahead separately and much more quickly, are important because the amount of time involved leads directly to other events and the conduct of individuals later in the day; hence, our emphasis on timing, much the opposite of its importance on the day of the battle. To make this study as impartial as possible, we are obligated to present conflicting points, one side of which may not fit our own arguments. In attempting to figure out the puzzle we go back to a number of people for snippets of information and when the testimony of those people conflict, we are obligated to sort out truth from mistaken impressions.

Some of the most sterling-clad accounts over the years came from civilians George Herendeen and Fred Gerard; officers Luke Hare, Charles Varnum, Edward Godfrey, and Win Edgerly; and enlisted personnel such as First Sergeant John Ryan; Sergeant Ferdinand A. Culbertson, a 31-year-old Civil War veteran serving under Moylan; and Private Charles Windolph. Much less reliable sources—other than for stage setting or "color-commentary"—are people like privates William Morris, Peter Thompson, and the most mendacious of all, Theodore Goldin. Others—like Lieutenant Carlo DeRudio—we must weigh carefully, because while DeRudio's "descriptives" are important, they are at times interwoven among palliatives—as we shall see. We would love to throw Fred Benteen's name into the "positive" mix, but Benteen is one of the controversial figures of the fight and as such must be recused from much of the definitive—laudatory comments

mistakenly considered self-serving by those who will hear no reasonable arguments to the contrary. Of course, not everyone would agree with our choices here; there are those whose eyes would glaze over at the mention of Gerard, for one, the historian Fred Dustin being among them. "Dustin had no use for the testimonies of Frederic F. Gerard—questioned the validity of all of them,"[1] but I would take issue with that.

Frederic Francis Gerard was an interpreter for the Arikara scouts and ranks as one of the battle's great enigmas. At 46 years of age, he was one of the oldest men on the campaign, yet his experience as a frontiersman has been questioned by any number of historians. James Willert wrote Gerard was impulsive and an inexperienced Indian fighter,[2] despite his age and adventures. With what has to be one of the most sweeping comments ever made about any individual who had taken part in the Little Big Horn fight, Willert claimed Gerard's report to George Custer about the Indians *not* running became the most significant element in Custer's defeat,[3] an observation we are not prone to argue against. As close scrutiny would have it, Willert's claim turned out to be spot on true, but it was a remarkable claim nonetheless given the questions as to Gerard's precise whereabouts when he made his observations. Suddenly, at one of the most critical decision-making points it was the report of interpreter Gerard that became paramount even over reports of scouts strung out all across the front of the advance.

Born in St. Louis, Missouri, on November 14, 1829, and educated at Xavier College where he spent a full four years, Gerard sought his fortune in the deeper West and traveled up the Missouri with Honoré Picotte in September of 1848. He got a job at Fort Pierre—in what is now South Dakota—with the American Fur Company and in 1855 went to Fort Berthold with Picotte, remaining there for several years. On Christmas Day, 1863, a force reported at some 600 Yankton Sioux belonging to Two Bear's band, attacked the post. Gerard and 17 others held them at bay until some friendly Assiniboine drove them off. While everyone else bailed out, Gerard held the post, by himself, for another 10 days, planting explosives, ready to blow the place up if the Indians returned. From that day forward, he was constantly on the lookout for grouchy Sioux who had threatened to kill him, not the least of whom was Sitting Bull. In fact, when the great Indian medicine chief helped himself to Gerard's black stallion, he made considerable noise of his coup.

On July 6, 1872, Gerard hired on as the post interpreter at Fort Abraham Lincoln. Then, to add to his résumé, in 1873, he wound up saving George Custer's West Point friend, former Confederate States general Thomas L. Rosser, and a surveying party, from being cut off by another hostile party of Indians. Not everyone, however, was thankful for Gerard's presence at Fort Lincoln. Marcus Reno had all sorts of problems with the man and at one point had him fired from his duties at the fort. The bad blood spilled over in some of Reno's comments after the Little Big Horn fight, but whether or not Reno's dislike of Gerard was justified—and one suspects the feeling may have been mutual—it is hard to see Gerard pictured as anything but a competent frontiersman. Although Willert paid him short shrift, Gerard's record belies all this distaste and he was certainly not inexperienced at fighting Indians, as Willert would have us believe. On May 12, 1876—five days before the Dakota column moved—Gerard enlisted for the job as interpreter of Arikara scouts for the Seventh Cavalry.[4]

It is interesting to note, while Gerard had a somewhat inflated opinion of himself and a number of his tales do not seem to coincide precisely with those of people we accept as rubber-stamp trustworthy, General Terry thought rather highly of the man. Having returned to Fort Lincoln in the fall of 1876, Gerard went aboard the steamer "Far West" to pay his respects to the general. In the presence of several officers, Terry said:

> Mr. Gerard, I recall very well certain remarks of yours at the outset of the campaign, and particularly your estimate of the fighting strength of the Indians. Had I known you as well then as I do now, the operations of the campaign would have been conducted on a different plan.[5]

Charles Varnum said he saw the same words written in a letter from Terry to Gerard.[6] Despite some self-aggrandizement, this says an awful lot about Fred Gerard.

When the Seventh Cavalry left Halt One, either George Custer left with the regiment and knew it was following him, or he left in advance and did not realize his command was in the process of moving, despite a general understanding he had ordered an eight o'clock move. Herendeen believed everyone departed at once. In an interview for a newspaper held almost two weeks after the battle, he said, "Soon after it was light the scouts brought Custer word that they had seen the village from the top of the divide." Herendeen claimed the command moved up the creek until it was near its head, and then moved into a ravine for concealment. This was "about three miles from the head of the creek where we then were to the top of the divide where the Indian scouts said the village could be seen." After seeing the command put into the ravine, Custer took "a few orderlies" and galloped forward to see for himself. He was there for about an hour and when he returned he claimed he could see no village. The scouts also told him the regiment had been spotted and word was being sent back to the Sioux village.[7]

In a second article written one and one-half years later, Herendeen said, after leaving the Busby camp on the night of the 24th, the command traveled about 10 miles (actually, six and one-half) and stopped to camp around 2:00 a.m. After the scouts reported to Custer that the Indian camp had been sighted, the command moved forward "at early light." Herendeen went on: "About nine o'clock ... Custer halted his troops and concealed them as well as he could." Custer then took an orderly and headed to the divide, about four miles away (again, mileage variances: in reality, less than one mile from this second halt), where Varnum and Boyer were. Custer was gone about one or one and one-half hours.[8]

Varnum as well throws some confusion into the pot. As we saw in the previous chapter, he wrote, "The column arrived at the trail-crossing of the divide about 10 a.m., and Custer came at once to where I was, I riding out to meet him. We climbed the bluff and the Indians tried to show Custer what they saw."[9] Several years earlier, however—April 14, 1909—Varnum wrote a letter to Walter Camp, stating that after viewing the Little Big Horn valley and then spotting some Sioux, Varnum set out to intercept and kill them.

> After sending off the Rees ... Boyer, Reynolds & two Crows with myself started off dismounted.... After, perhaps, a half mile of hard work through very broken country, where we could see nothing I heard a call like a crow cawing from the hill and we halted ... we started back. I asked Boyer what was the matter but he did not know. On our return we learned that the Sioux had changed their course away from the pass but soon after our return they changed again and crossed the ridge. We could see them as they went down the trail towards the command and could then see a long trail of dust showing Custer was moving but we could not see the column. Before it came in sight the Sioux stopped suddenly, got together & then as suddenly disappeared, one to the right & one to the left, so we knew that the Sioux had discovered our approach.... The command came in vision about this time and we watched it approach the gap where

it halted. I rode down towards the column & soon met the Genl. He said, "Well you've had a night of it." I said yes, but I was still able to sit up & notice things. Tom Custer & Calhoun then came up to us & Custer was angry at their leaving the column & ordered them back. I told the Genl. all I had seen, as we rode back towards the Crow nest hill and we climbed the hill together. Custer listened to Boyer while he gazed long & hard at the valley.[10]

Fred Gerard saw things differently. At the Reno inquiry—1879, mind you, 30 years before Varnum wrote the above—Gerard testified when the command halted in Davis Creek (referring to Halt One), "orders were given to make coffee with small fires, the fires to be put out when the coffee was made, the horses to remain saddled, and we would go into camp after daylight."[11] After coffee was made, Gerard went to sleep, Custer eventually waking him and telling him to take the two scouts that had just come in from Varnum and accompany him to their lookout. Either Cooke or Tom Custer came up to the general—Gerard's back was turned, so he was unsure whom—and asked if the command should be moved. Custer replied, "No, you will remain here until I return."[12] (As we have seen, Custer mounted and rode around the encampment—remember how he ignored Benteen?—telling people to get ready to move.) The party mounted and rode "to the foot of the mountain as far as we could go with our horses and then dismounted and walked to the top of the mountain and there found Lieutenant Varnum, Boyer, and Bloody Knife who had accompanied us."[13] Then there was the following exchange:

Q: "Did you return with General Custer from that place and, if so, were the troops found where General Custer ordered them to remain?"
A: "I returned with General Custer to within 40 or 50 yards of the command. The command had then moved out and come about three miles toward us from where we had left them."
Q: "State any facts or circumstances showing how far and in what direction the troops had changed position and whether or not that change had been made by General Custer's orders."
A: "I was with General Custer during the whole time, from the time he left until he returned, and I am satisfied no orders were sent back to move the command."[14]

When Custer asked his brother who moved the command, Gerard claimed Tom answered, "I don't know, the orders were to march and we marched."[15]

Gerard, unlike some others we depend on, was amazingly consistent over the years. When Camp interviewed him in 1909, he told the same story he had told much earlier. The command went into camp early in the morning of June 25, "in sort of a narrow valley some miles east of the divide."

Custer woke him, mentioning scouts had returned from the "high point," and they should go there. "Custer now told his brother Tom not to move the command from where it was until further orders."[16] He then said they went up to the "high mountain peak, which was about 13 miles east of the Little Big Horn." There they made out a pony herd on the hills and tableland beyond the river. He saw a large dark spot or mass, and dust rising, concluding that horses were being driven. This was "some hours after daylight, and the light was strong and the atmosphere very clear."

When *The Arikara Narrative* was published in 1920 from accounts gathered several years earlier—Gerard had died in January 1913, at 83—his story was unchanged. After the night march of the 24th, the horses stayed saddled, the men sleeping on the ground. Two Ree scouts arrived with a message telling of a very large camp in the Little Big Horn valley. They also said Indians had discovered the command and were on the run. Gerard said he, Custer, the two Rees, and two other scouts went to see and reached Varnum about daybreak. He claimed they could see a "large black mass moving in front and down the Little Big Horn and a dense cloud of dust over all and behind." Custer left the lookout area "at a sharp gait," to rejoin the command. Gerard said about halfway back was when the senior Custer admonished his brother for allowing the troops to move.[17]

So, what have we here? Well, we have a minor sequence of events remembered differently by a number of people, all of whom were there in some particular way. The only person, however, who was side by side with the main character, was Fred Gerard and he never changed his story, though some of the details appear modified a bit. And of all those who accompanied—or *may* have accompanied—Custer from the first halt to the Crow's Nest, only Gerard and Red Star survived the battle. Whether George Custer scolded his brother once or twice is irrelevant; he scolded his brother. The key is one way or another George preceded the regiment to the area of the Crow's Nest and the command arrived as Moylan, Varnum, Hare, *et al.,* related: somewhere between 10:00 and 10:30 a.m., well after its commander. When we have sifted through all the evidence and we wind up with conflicting reports from two of the most reliable witnesses, the only way we can make our decision is to go by logic. Would George Armstrong Custer have taken more than two hours to reach the point where he could view what had been reported to be his goal? Our conclusion is no; *resoundingly, no!* By the time his men arrived at the second halt George Custer had already overlooked the valleys beyond and was ready for the next phase of the operation.

5

PLAN A: TULLOCK'S CREEK

Tullock's Creek. Brigadier General Alfred H. Terry's order to George Custer may be the first time one hears of that small tributary. It may also be the last, yet rather than keep the atlas on the shelf, Tullock's passive role in this affair belied its tactical importance, and the significance of Custer's failure to adhere to Terry's order to scout it can be debated among the annals of bungled opportunities.

Tullock's Creek first creeps into the great summer campaign on the evening of April 24, when Colonel John Gibbon ordered Captain Edward Ball to take two companies of the Second Cavalry (Ball's own H and Lieutenant Charles Roe's F) to scout up the Big Horn River as far as the abandoned site of Fort C. F. Smith. Among other things, Ball was to attempt to contact a Black Hills mining party thought to be in that vicinity. He was ordered to return via Tullock's Creek and with that in mind he was to take scouts Tom LeForgé; the Crow Indian, Jack Rabbit Bull; George Herendeen; and "Muggins" Taylor, all of whom had some knowledge of the territory. At about 5:15 p.m. on April 27, Ball's column began its move through the "hayfields" of old C. F. Smith and after three miles reached the abandoned fort, 75 miles from the mouth of the Big Horn River. At midnight Ball halted, going into camp on Rotten Grass Creek. He broke camp around 9:25 the following morning and at 10:10 a.m. of the 28th, the command reached a small tributary of Rotten Grass, moving up the creek and over high, rolling hills. By 11:00 a.m. Ball had reached the top of a high divide. More marching brought him to Lodge Grass Creek (Indians called it Long Creek) and by 6:00 p.m. he had reached the Little Big Horn. He turned left down the river for about a mile, then camped on the west bank in a grove of cottonwoods. The following day, Ball continued down the Little Big Horn valley, noticing the ravine-cut bluffs on the east side of the river, and soon passed through an area where a large Cheyenne camp had been the preceding summer, just below the mouth of Lodge Tail Creek. By 12:45 p.m. Ball was passing the hills the Seventh Cavalry would eventually fight on. He made a brief camp

on the site later occupied by the vast Indian village, and by 2:30 p.m. was on the move again, fording the river and crossing the Wolf Mountains to reach a dry tributary of Tullock's where he camped for the night. The following day Ball moved down Tullock's, a very crooked stream with rather steep banks, making only about 20 miles because he had to stop to allow his horses to graze.

Where precisely Ball crossed the Little Big Horn is unknown. Some believe tracks purportedly seen on the east side of Sharpshooters' Ridge after the battle belonged to Ball's command. (Sharpshooters' is a large mass overlooking the Little Big Horn valley, a terrain feature prominent in the fighting.) Others, such as Bruce Liddic, use the same "trail" as proof Custer went down the east side of Sharpshooters' rather than Cedar Coulee.[1] Direction, distance, and difficulty of terrain, however, make the Ball theory a little thorny and the "Custer route" explodes because of too much evidence against it.

Ball and Roe returned to Gibbon's command on May 1, via Tullock's Creek valley. Through all this they saw nary a sign of Indians and reported such to Gibbon who then penned the Tullock's complex into Little Big Horn history by sending his telegram to Terry. This also shows the importance of the Tullock's Creek valley in the minds of the commanders, especially since their maps showed no correct course for either the creek or the valley itself, and there were no assurances the Indians were moving east, south, or west—or north, for that matter, to cross the Yellowstone behind Gibbon. By mid–June there was some thought the Sioux may have been camped on Tullock's, as Willert described, "a broad valley, running oblique to the Yellowstone, whose western terminus touched the lower Big Horn River, and whose eastern opening emerged somewhere near the valley of the Rosebud."[2]

So with this in mind it is necessary to look at what Terry expected of his cavalry commander.

The importance of Tullock's Creek is predicated on the

assumption Custer would obey his instructions, thereby inextricably intertwining the man with his mission. Too often these two are separated, elevating Custer to the marbled heights of the martyred and obviating the importance of his orders. This is a mistake, for it lays the groundwork for justifying Custer's disobedience, and Tullock's Creek therefore, becomes shunted aside as just another vague landmark of history. Those who rationalize this justification feel Custer would have had to give George Herendeen specific information to take to Terry regarding the precise whereabouts of the Indian village and what his plan of action would be in dealing with it, neither of which Custer was able to provide when he bypassed the Tullock valley turn-off, and neither of which was expected by Terry. As can be seen from his orders, it was specifically stated Custer, *"should thoroughly examine the upper part of Tullock's Creek, and ... should endeavor to send a scout through to Colonel Gibbon's column, with information of the result of your examination."* We see no requirement to include plans or to have found Indians before sending Terry the information required. The *commanding* general wanted to know if Tullock's was clear.

By tossing aside the importance of scouting this area, we assume it was acceptable for Custer to disobey his orders. While we have seen he was given a certain amount of latitude in the execution of those orders, Custer was given *no* latitude in their interpretation. He was ordered specifically to examine "the upper part of Tullock's Creek" and ordered specifically to "endeavor" to report his findings to Gibbon. He neither examined nor endeavored. He was also directed to continue south, *regardless* of whether the trail would leave the Rosebud environs. The following phrase, "Should it be found (as it appears almost certain that it will be found) to turn towards the Little Horn, [General Terry] thinks that you should still proceed southward," already anticipates and precludes Custer's rationale for following the Indian trail. "[U]nless you should see sufficient reason for departing from [these orders]," would, therefore, not apply here because Custer's reasons have already been preempted, they have been *pre*-considered insufficient. In other words, following the Indian trail just because it might diverge from the Rosebud was not sufficient justification for Custer to do what he did. It was *not* an option. At this point, all Terry knew—and expected to know—was Custer was moving up the Rosebud, following his orders. The forethought in the orders trumps the afterthought of their execution.

By sending Herendeen down the Tullock's Creek valley (he would have reported the valley clear of hostiles), Custer would have doubled Terry's choices. Terry would now have options, a commander's dream. Why would he want to be limited to following one specific route when he could have an alternate? By knowing it was safe, Terry had the option of moving up that valley without fear, still believing Custer was continuing up the Rosebud. (An added bonus would be Tullock's was now "known," whereas the route Terry and Gibbon eventually took was not and was considerably more difficult.) And remember, the thinking when these orders were promulgated, was the Indians were moving *up* the Little Big Horn valley, not down. Maybe Terry would not have opted to move deeper up Tullock's than he had moved already, but that would have been his decision and it is not something someone else should have been making for him. Custer's actions therefore, were the height of presumptuousness. The irony here is if Terry had known Tullock's was clear and had chosen to move up its creek, he would have entered the Little Big Horn area at about the same location as the Indian encampment, and even had Custer decided to cut across as he did, the two columns would have, in all likelihood, been united.

A slight digression here makes this even more interesting. When Marcus Reno was ordered out on June 10, to scout the Powder, Pumpkin, and Tongue rivers, there was no mention in the man's written orders about not proceeding to the Rosebud valley. It has been assumed over the years, Reno was told—verbally—not to go that far. John Gray: "Terry explicitly and positively ordered Reno not to move in the direction of the Rosebud, for fear it would 'flush the covey' prematurely."[3] Yet nothing was in writing[4] and Gray lends no support to his supposition. Upon Reno's return to the main column with the news he *had* gone as far as the Rosebud valley and the Indian trail was seen there, the man was admonished by Terry and pilloried by Custer; and this, despite returning with useful intelligence saving everyone some rather red-faced mortification. Much is made about "pincer" attacks and that this was in essence Terry's plan all along, but because of distances and the difficulty in communicating, those types of operations were frowned upon. Besides, Terry never mentioned anything about a "pincer" attack or any formal plan of having the two columns meet, probably in accordance with Sheridan's diktat about it being absurd to expect cooperation in open and broken country. Still, Terry had to be thinking the two columns might be able to corral the hostiles if one was coming down the Rosebud while the other was moving up.

So, here we have Major Reno disobeying verbal orders and returning with some useful information, and Custer disobeying written orders and never returning. Was either man correct in what he did? Was either justified? As we have tangentially speculated, maybe Custer's comment to Varnum about Reno making "the mistake of his life" yields some sort of clue.

A number of battle students believe the only useful time Herendeen could have been sent down Tullock's Creek was after 9:00 p.m. on the 24th, when Mitch Boyer, along with several Crows, returned with the news the Indians' trail led toward the Little Big Horn. Even this they conclude would have been useless information because Herendeen would never have been able to reach Terry in time for the Gibbon column to do any good. Again, however, these people miss the point. Terry had already made the assumption the Sioux were camped on the Little Big Horn. Among other things, what the general needed was to make sure the hostile village had not backtracked into the Tullock valley, in which case they could have slipped between the two forces. Remember, Captain Ball's scout went into the upper portion of this valley from the Little Big Horn area, and Tullock valley also had an exit into the valley of the Rosebud. Custer's command was already above that egress and had the hostiles so desired— and so scouted—they could have moved below Custer, headed back down the Rosebud, then east, down or across the Yellowstone. At this point in time, the Sioux still believed Gibbon's column was headed downriver, for that was its direction the last time it had been seen.

Once again, a report by Custer that the Indian trail led to the Little Big Horn was not required in Terry's orders; Terry *assumed* that was where the trail led when he wrote the orders. An examination of the upper part of Tullock's Creek was required, but separately it was not deemed necessary to specify the Sioux had moved to the Little Big Horn. Some of the irony here was if Custer had sent Herendeen a few hours earlier when the column passed the entrance to the upper portion of Tullock's Creek, Custer could still have informed Terry about how fresh the trail was and that he suspected the Indians to be near, to be in the valley of the Little Big Horn, probably mid- to low-valley, depending on one's perception of its length, and precisely where—high valley or low valley—the trail may have emptied. By the evening of June 24, Terry had to assume Custer was still moving up the Rosebud and the Indians were doing the same, much more slowly, somewhere in the Little Big Horn valley.

Very often the argument is made that the primary concern of the military commanders remained the fear of the hostiles scattering. There is tremendous and even overwhelming validity to that argument: "Every officer on the frontier knew only too well that Indians shunned pitched battles and were so mobile and elusive as to be frustratingly difficult to corral. Thus the overriding fear was that the village would break up and scatter."[5] There is a modicum of intelligence and common sense we must apply, however, and while this is all fully acceptable and had to be the most important concern

to the officers of this campaign, it had not ought to blind them to everything else, something it did clearly, to the cost of several hundred lives.

The final lead-up to the Little Big Horn can be broken into two related phases, the first beginning on June 24. It becomes a three-day affair (we have to include the 26th, though for this study it is of little military value), because the phases are so closely intertwined, yet no "battle," per se, took place during the first phase. This initial phase encompasses the decision-making process. Was Custer right or was Custer wrong in following the Indians' trail from the Busby halt into the Davis Creek valley? This becomes Phase I. It is a strategic problem eventually answered by Custer's decision not to send Herendeen down Tullock's and it is a clear-cut act of flouting Terry's orders: clear-cut; no discussion, no excuses, no nothing. Custer disobeyed his orders. If Terry had given him leeway *here*, that might be a different matter, but he did not. Anything else is merely the wishful thinking of civilians trying to play soldier—or soldiers trying to play general—and their arguments are based on the vagaries and vicissitudes of civilian justice. By necessity, military jurisprudence is much more reality-based.

So again, in summary, Terry gave Custer the option to deviate from his orders, but only in the event of an *other*, "should you see sufficient reason for departing from them." The orders themselves obviated following the trail as "sufficient reason." Custer failed this strategic test and it is *that* process one must address before we can decide if Custer's tactical plans were sound. If we were to judge his actions as a commander during these two days, there would be no further discussion of how good his battle "tactics" were, because he had already failed the "strategic" exam, the exam that got him there. Furthermore, what would have happened to Custer's command had the Indians continued south, *up* the Little Big Horn valley, rather than turning and moving north, *down* the valley? What justification could Custer present Terry then? Custer would have inserted himself between the hostiles and whatever covering or encircling force Terry envisioned and could have brought to bear, regardless of what route the latter had taken. By making the assumption that by sending someone down Tullock's Creek—and by that, an extension of the cavalry command's scouting the valley's upper reaches— Custer would have been informing Terry only of the obvious and it would have been too late to do anything anyway, we are still ignoring the core of Terry's orders. Pure and simple then, Custer disobeyed those orders. Had he survived, he could have presented no justification for doing what he did, no "sufficient reason for departing from them."

Around 7:00 a.m. on June 24, Custer informed Herendeen to get ready to scout Tullock's, but Herendeen told him it was too early, the gap leading to the creek's headwaters was still farther ahead. This implies Custer still had it in mind to follow his orders, at least as late as early morning of that day. As we have seen, as the day progressed, the command received more and more reports of the trail becoming continuously fresher:

1. 7:10 a.m.—The four Crows report in. They reported fresh tracks, "'but in no great numbers.'"[6] The Crows also told Custer the trail was fresher 10 miles ahead.

2. 7:30 a.m.—The march was resumed. Custer sends the four Crows ahead again.

3. 9:20 a.m.—The Crows, trotting at six miles per hour, reach the abandoned Sioux camp at East Muddy Creek.

4. 9:40 a.m.—The Crows head back to the column after studying the campsite.

5. 10:30 a.m.—Crows report again: abandoned campsite at East Muddy Creek.

6. 1:00 p.m.—Custer orders a halt. Scouts sent out.

7. 4:00 p.m.—Crow courier (White Swan) returns, reports finding a fresh camp at the forks of the Rosebud.

8. 5:00 p.m.—Resume the march up the Rosebud. Custer sends out flankers to check for diverging trails, again worried about the village breaking up. Only *con*verging trails found. This is an important point, for there continues to be absolutely no indication of the Indians breaking up.

9. 6:30 p.m.—The command reaches the gap in the western hills that led to the headwaters of Tullock's Creek. Herendeen told Custer, but the latter only kept moving forward and Herendeen simply remained in the column. No trails went in the direction of Tullock's Creek.

This last point brings up what is possibly the most important issue of the entire 40-day campaign, ultimately leading to the stunning importance of Tullock's Creek. Custer, despite reported as being upset at his orders from Terry, appeared to embrace the Tullock's mission, certainly as late as 7:00 a.m. on the 24th. Herendeen verified that. What happened between then and 6:30 p.m. when Herendeen informed the general it was time to head off for the Tullock valley? Why the change in Custer's thinking? When did that change occur?

It has been almost universally accepted that Custer decided to attack the Sioux and Cheyenne village after returning from his foray to the Crow's Nest and after being told several times by several people his column had been spotted and surprise had been all but lost. His officers agreed, but if this were the case, then why the forced night march, why the disregard for his orders, why run the risk of interposing oneself between the Indians and Terry's column? He *had* to know that was a risk. Benteen certainly did. In a slightly different context, Benteen wrote a letter to former G Company private-turned-National Guard colonel, Theodore Goldin, on February 24, 1892, and brought up the very point: "supposing I had found up that valley what Reno and Custer found lower down the river—how in the name of common sense was Gen'l Custer to get back to where I was in time to keep the troops from being chewed up as it were by the combined reds?"[7] So, was George Custer that cavalier about this campaign? While a number of authors state there were no definitive plans for a "pincer" movement or attack, it is common knowledge Terry wanted his infantry involved.[8] Terry's orders—again, while not *definitive*—allude to such a desire: "it is hoped that the Indians, if upon the Little Horn, may be so nearly enclosed by the two columns that their escape will be impossible."

While we will never fully understand the man, there is enough evidence—circumstantial though it may be—to *suggest* Custer decided—some time earlier, maybe on June 24, or maybe even earlier when he made the Reno comment to Varnum as they passed through the first abandoned village—to attack, regardless of locations, circumstances, and forces available. Maybe Custer's own words began the thought process, a process reaching maturation some time on the 24th, maybe between 7:00 a.m. and 6:30 p.m. quite possibly during the four-hour break in the afternoon. He knew he was close, closer even than Reno had been. Sending Herendeen down Tullock's Creek would have virtually forced him to continue along the Rosebud, adhering to his commander's orders, otherwise, how would he be able to justify his actions to Terry? Custer decided he was now close to running down his quarry, and with the same rationale he used in declining the help of Brisbin's cavalry, he decided he could handle what he thought he was seeing on the ground. *And*—and do not minimize this!—Custer knew he had double Reno's force. If he felt Reno could have "made a name for himself" with just six troops of cavalry, imagine how George Armstrong Custer felt with a full regiment.

6

CROSSING THE DIVIDE

REFERENCES:
Timeline F—Divide Crossing to the Flats; 11:45 a.m.–1:05 p.m.

The anabasis had begun, bringing us to face the one specific time dictating the tone of responsibility, the one time in this entire saga keying all those following, the one used to lay blame, to justify, to support, and to conspire about, and a simple statement by Lieutenant George Wallace drives it. In his official report, titled, "Report of the Chief of Engineers ... Appendix ... Report of Lieutenant George D. Wallace, Seventh Cavalry, Saint Paul, Minn., January 27, 1877," Wallace wrote, "At 12 M., on the 25th, we crossed the divide between the Rosebud and Little Big Horn." He confirmed it tangentially at the Reno inquiry in January 1879, when he testified, "We started out at 11:45, at 12:05 it [the march] halted and the division into battalions was made, it moved on at 12:12. That is the only record of time I have."[1]

Again, it is hard to fathom anyone in the command would think at this time to chronicle for the historical record by yanking out a pocket watch on a remote ridgeline. Did Wallace? Too many men were concerned about too many things, not the least of which was—as Benteen said—a massive trail,

> the main trail of the Indians. There were plenty of them on that trail. We had passed through immense villages the preceding days and it was scarcely worthwhile hunting up any more. We knew there were eight or 10,000 Indians on the trail we were on.[2]

There was also the little issue of their commander's skepticism as to the village's size and location, thereby provoking a fair element of uncertainty—anxiety, nerves. The work-a-day soldier may have had other thoughts as well and we can be reasonably certain watch-time was not among them.

The regiment worked its way into the second halt some time between 10:00 and 10:30 a.m., in all likelihood closer to the latter time. Since Custer watched as it arrived and was on the valley floor in time to greet his brother, we should as-

sume not a lot of time went by between those two events. Then there was the officers' call, a short powwow with the scouts, and the remounting of the regiment—probably a second Custer viewing of the western valleys from the divide itself—but also, as we have seen, Luke Hare saying the halt was for an hour only, shortening the time; and Myles Moylan claiming they stopped at the foot of the divide, shortening the distance. A noon crossing therefore—some two hours after the regiment reached the area—would seem to indicate a lack of immediacy and would be at odds with much of the corollary evidence, at least up to that point; unless we consider the decision to attack was not made until some time around 11:00 a.m.—in which case the time works quite well. We are obligated to accept the truth and there is simply too much evidence arguing against any other theory or time scenario. Through the years, Wallace was adamant about this noon crossing and we have additional corroboration from too many others who were there. At the 1879 inquiry, Captain Thomas Mower McDougall, commander of B Company, testified at about 11:00 a.m. he was ordered "to take charge of the pack train and act as rear guard." This was "on the divide between the Rosebud and the Little Big Horn."[3] McDougall appears to have used the word "on" as a euphemism for "in the proximity of," understanding McDougall received this assignment *prior to* the regiment's crossing the divide and before its further breakdown into battalions (such was the price one paid for being the last to report readiness to General George Custer). In his 1892 *Century Magazine* treatise, Godfrey said the command crossed the divide a little *before* noon.[4] That can hold up under scrutiny, as well. Gustave Mathey, the M Company officer who had been placed in charge of the pack mules, also testified at the Reno inquiry he believed the command started between 11 o'clock and noon,[5] not definitive by any stretch. Officers alone were not the sole echoers of the refrain. The quasi-redoubtable Private Giovanni Martini, a Custer orderly that day and one of Benteen's troopers—a man soon to be anointed into the annals of history—said or wrote shortly before his death on Christmas Eve, 1922, that during the officers' call none of the men were allowed near the officers, and shortly, the regiment was on the move again, crossing the divide about noon.[6] Private Charles Windolph agreed. "It was a little before noon when our troop was formed up.... It was around noon ... when we crossed the divide between the Rosebud and the Little Big Horn."[7] (And Benteen's H Company held the advance.)

Until the last 20 or so years, the number of troops who died at the Little Big Horn was still being debated—and no one will ever know for sure the number of Indians killed, their estimates ranging from 30 to more than 300. One of the few things everyone can agree on is George Custer rode to battle with companies C, E, F, I, and L. These units were accompanied by the headquarters contingent of between 12 and 17 men, varying as time progressed and events unfolded. Their destruction is indisputable, but before anyone goes rejoicing like Diogenes having found an honest man, we must remember this five-company breakdown is as basic to the battle's history as the fact Custer led them that day.

We are equally certain this division of command took place shortly after the regiment crossed the divide and Custer ordered a brief halt. At that halt, he issued orders to Benteen and sent him with companies D, H, and K, off in an oblique to the left of the main column's direction of march. Custer then ordered Major Reno with companies A, G, and M, down the left side of a small creek, while Custer himself moved down the right side with captains Keogh and Yates, and the five companies and regimental headquarters. McDougall's Company B escorted the pack train—reinforced with seven men from each company—which brought up the rear of the Custer column.

From an organizational point of view, nothing the military does is haphazard. That is true today and was true in 1876. When determining officer assignments the army goes by rank and seniority, and next to Custer himself, Major Marcus Reno was the senior officer. As such, Reno would have been assigned to lead one of the battalions. Theoretically, he would be assigned the largest unit of division or would have the most important assignment next to that of the commander. Authority would be delegated then to the captains in descending order of seniority. Benteen, with a date of rank of July 28, 1866,[8] and a Civil War brevet of colonel was the senior captain. Myles Keogh had the same date of rank as Benteen, but Keogh's brevet was one grade lower making him the second-ranking captain; George Yates was third; and Thomas Benton Weir (D Company commander), fourth.[9] Since Custer broke his regiment into four battalions the for-

mal progression, descending, would be Reno, Benteen, Keogh, and Yates.

When the Seventh Cavalry left Fort Abraham Lincoln on May 17, Custer had divided the regiment into two wings (Reno and Benteen) of two battalions (Keogh and Yates; Weir and Captain Thomas Henry French [M Company]), each battalion with three companies. His entire command consisted of some 738 officers and enlisted personnel, two civilians, five quartermaster employees, and 43 Indian scouts: 38 Arikara and five Dakota, for a total of 788 able-bodied men. After dropping off 125 men at the Powder River Depot, losing 11 Ree scouts, one Dakota, then another six men to desertion, sickness, and other detached duties, and picking up two more quartermaster employees, five civilian packers, and six Crow scouts, the command departed for its destiny with 655 men: white, red, and black; uniformed and muftied. Another dilution of the fighting force took place when Custer ordered each company to send seven men (one non-commissioned officer and six privates) to help with the pack train. The names of men from the six companies with Reno and Benteen—plus McDougall's Company B escort—are known. We do not, however, know which men specifically from these units were assigned to the packs. We know the names of two from A Company—possibly; three from G; one from H; and four from K, but none from companies B, D, or M.[10] Whoever they were, they survived, or, if killed, at least we know they died on Reno Hill. The names of the men assigned to the packs from the five destroyed companies are much easier to pinpoint because we know they did not die with Custer. Their numbers are inflated, however, and from the names of the survivors, it seems Company C had eight men with the packs; I Company, nine; L Company, 13; E, nine; and F, 10; the extras in all likelihood, assigned to extra duties such as strikers, orderlies, personal cooks, horse-minders, and the like. There were also stragglers—Company C had five; I Company had one; E, two; and F, one—but again, those names are known and they gave reasons for ultimately showing up with Reno. Few men believed assigned to the packs admitted to anything else or gave legitimate reasons for not being with their commands. Wherever they may have been located, this detachment of soldiers eliminated another hundred men from direct combat or combat support until late on June 25.

On June 22, Custer abolished all wing and battalion assignments, only re-assigning battalions as the command prepared for battle. According to author Bruce Liddic, Custer kept the original Keogh-Yates breakdown when he assigned the companies near the divide, the exception being Keogh lost B to the pack train, leaving him with I and C, Yates retaining E, F, and L.[11] In addition, Liddic keeps Custer and headquarters with Yates' command, considering this consistent with the Fort Lincoln assignments. Another author, Jack Pennington, claimed Keogh commanded companies I and L, while Custer and headquarters rode with Yates and companies C, E, and F.[12] Other writers—John Gray,[13] Greg Michno,[14] and Robert J. Kershaw[15]—believe the breakdown was Yates with E and F, and Keogh with C, I, and L. They also claim Custer, with his headquarters detachment—later in the battle—remained on the ridges with Keogh, while Yates was sent to Medicine Tail Ford.

The combination making the most sense, however—based on the available evidence and military protocol—is Keogh being assigned C, I, and L; and Yates, E and F. The archaeologist, Richard Allan Fox, Jr., believes this was the correct breakdown.[16] Furthermore, Company C sergeant, Daniel A. Kanipe, and Company B first sergeant, James Hill, claimed C was assigned to Keogh.[17] This would fulfill the protocol requirement, never something to be minimized when it came to military etiquette and George Custer. Lieutenant Edgerly would agree. In a letter to his wife Grace, written shortly after the battle, Edgerly wrote Custer "gave Keogh command strictly in accordance with his rank on the morning of the fight."[18]

We have further evidence of the "Keogh, three; Yates, two" breakdown from Myles Moylan at the Reno inquiry:

Q: "State if you knew at the time or as it appeared to you afterward, what officers were placed in command of these different battalions and how many there were."

A: "I know nothing personally of it myself. I afterward ascertained that Major Reno had a battalion, Captain Benteen had one, Captain Keogh had one, and Captain Yates had one. Each of these battalions I have named consisted of three companies, except Captain Yates' which was two companies. Captain McDougall being absent with the pack train accounted for the other."[19]

The most convincing argument, however, comes from the final scene of bodies on the battlefield, fully supporting this breakdown. Again, we will see this a little later.

According to Nick Wallace's recollections, the regiment was crossing the divide by noon and with all the anecdotal corroboration, we accept that as fact. (Many years later Edgerly claimed battalion assignments were made at 10:00 a.m.,[20] though this seems an unlikely hour, clouded by the vagaries of time.) A few minutes and a quarter-mile after crossing, Custer halted the column and went off to the side with his adjutant. The two men dismounted and were seen scribbling with pencil and paper. After several minutes—at one time, Benteen claimed it was 15, but this is too long—Benteen was summoned; he was given his battalion and his orders. He was to, "proceed to a line of bluffs about two miles off, at about an angle of 45 degrees: to send a well mounted officer and 10 men in advance—to pitch into any Indians I could see, and in such case, to notify him [Custer] at once."[21] Other than the "bluffs about two miles off," Benteen was remarkably consistent over the years with his statement of the orders he received. He told the same story to the *New York Herald* in August 1876, testified the same way at the Reno inquiry, and wrote it again in his so-called "first manuscript," probably in late 1890. Ed Godfrey—a company commander in Benteen's battalion—agreed. Years after testifying at the Reno inquiry, Godfrey wrote:

> Benteen's battalion was ordered to the left and front, to a line of high bluffs about three or four miles distant. Benteen was ordered if he saw anything to send word to Custer, but to pitch into anything he came across; if, when he arrived at the high bluffs, he could not see any enemy, he should continue his march to the next line of bluffs and so on, until he could see the Little Big Horn valley.[22]

We have to assume Godfrey knew this from being told by Benteen since no one else heard the orders, but the story has held up over the years and other than the fly-by-night theories of Benteen-haters and the conspiracy artists, the mission rings true. The author Roger Darling presented a slightly different version of the orders when he wrote that Frank Gibson, Benteen's first lieutenant, wrote to George Yates' son in 1915, and explained that if Benteen were to find "any Indians trying to escape up the valley of the Little Big Horn, to intercept them and drive them back in the direction the village was supposed to be."[23] Darling's use of this quote, however, tends to distort the original context, adding fuel to the hallucinations of conspiracy theorists. Gibson wrote,

> Colonel Benteen was not guilty of either treachery or disobedience of orders. His orders were ... to take his battalion to the left ... and if he found any Indians trying to escape up the valley of the Little Big Horn, to intercept them and drive them back in the direction the village was supposed to be. After going some distance and to facilitate the movement as much as possible Benteen ordered me to pick six men on the strongest horses, and to hurry over the hills as quickly as possible to see if there were any Indians trying to get away ... and to send back a man or signal, and said he would get all there was left out of the horses, which were jaded. Should he find nothing he was to pick up the trail again and follow it on.[24]

As an order, this makes perfect tactical sense and despite Benteen's later protestations to the contrary, Custer's desire to ensure the upper valley was clear of Indians rendered the mission valid and necessary. Benteen was also purported to have asked Custer, "Hadn't we better keep the regiment together,

Chart 1. Crossing the Divide: Battalion Organization

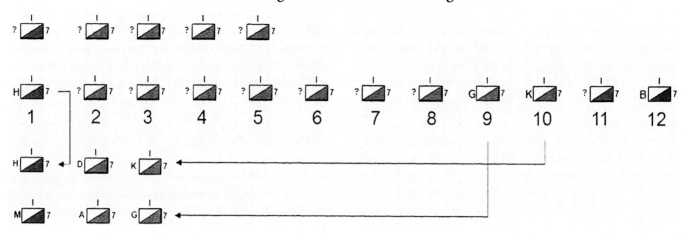

General? If this is as big a camp as they say, we'll need every man we have." Custer was supposed to have responded, "You have your orders."[25] Terse, indeed, defining the relationship between the two men. Years later, this exchange was remembered somewhat differently by Charles Windolph. Windolph's horse was named "Roman Nose" and the H Company first sergeant, Joseph McCurry, wanted to trade horses. His horse, "Tip," was too hard for him to handle and Windolph was an experienced horseman. Windolph was willing, but needed to speak with Benteen. When he sought out the captain, he ran across the officers' conference (prior to crossing the divide). Windolph overheard Charlie Reynolds say, "the

Chart 2. Variable Cueing at the Divide

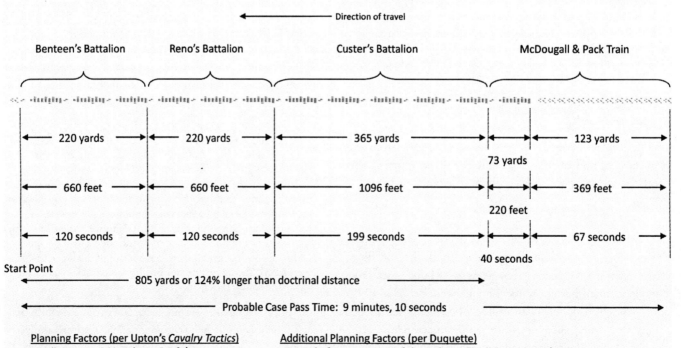

7th U.S. Cavalry Regiment – 12:12 p.m., 25 June 1876
Column of Companies by Fours – Situational Distances
"The Accordion Effect"
(36 Officers, 456 Enlisted = 492 Men)

biggest bunch of Indians he had ever seen." This was when Benteen said, "Hadn't we better keep the regiment together? If that is a big camp we will need every man we have." Custer replied, "You have your orders. Sound to horse."[26] While a small point, this seems to make more sense than someone overhearing a comment while men were off to the side.

According to Wallace, this halt lasted for only seven to nine minutes. We can accept that duration; it is reasonable and there was no need for a longer delay (*Timeline F*). As Benteen called his battalion together and moved off, he passed Reno who asked him where he was going. Benteen told him, to the left, to pitch into anything he came across.[27] Other than that, Benteen knew nothing and whether or not it addled him at the time, he resented his mission more and more as years wore on. His famous glibness and sarcasm did not pop up in the letters he wrote to his wife, but they were prevalent in his testimony at the Reno inquiry. He emphasized there was never an order for him to unite with Reno's command and claimed, "There was no plan at all.... Valley hunting *ad infinitum*."[28] Benteen was adamant about this when asked by the inquiry recorder a little later and he told the court Reno had no right to expect any assistance from him.

> If there had been any plan of battle, enough of that plan would have been communicated to me so that I would have known what to do under certain circumstances. Not having done that I do not believe there was any plan. In General Custer's mind there was a belief that there were no Indians nor any village.[29]

He went on, saying Custer's plan was known only to Custer and not to Reno, "for he must naturally expect his assistance to come from the rear and not from the front."[30] At this point in the day, this far from the village, knowing or believing what Custer knew and believed, Benteen was correct. Custer *did* know, however, he did not want to get caught from behind, *ergo*, Benteen's mission. No plan yet, but the wheels *were* churning. As the indomitable captain moved off to the left, the Reno and Custer columns began their trek toward the Little Big Horn River.

7

BENTEEN'S LEFT OBLIQUE

REFERENCES:
Timeline G—Benteen's Scout; 12:10 p.m.–1:50 p.m.

The importance of time is becoming increasingly apparent. Benteen's ride was not easy and Custer seemed to realize this early on. The captain had gone about a mile when Chief Trumpeter Henry Voss brought word from Custer, "[I]f I found nothing before reaching the first line of bluffs, to go on to the second line with the same instructions."[1] It was 12:18 p.m., and it took Voss only five minutes—at seven to eight miles per hour—to go the ⁶⁄₁₀ of a mile to reach Benteen. Benteen moved another mile when he got additional instructions from the regimental sergeant major, William Sharrow: "[I]f I saw nothing from the second line of bluffs, to go on into the valley, and if there was nothing in the valley, to go on to the next valley."[2] In a February 24, 1892, letter to Theodore Goldin, Benteen said Sharrow instructed him that "if from the furthest line of bluffs which we then saw, I could not see the valley—no particular valley specified—to keep on until I came to a valley (or perhaps the valley) ... to pitch into"[3] anything he came across. Sharrow's journey was tougher than Voss'; at about the time Voss reached Benteen, Custer realized his orders were still not specific enough, so he dispatched the sergeant major. Sharrow put the spurs to his horse and at a 10 mile per hour gait he reached Benteen—now some 1.2 miles away from the main column—at approximately 12:26 p.m.

Custer's orders here are also the generator of some of the anti–Benteen fodder, for a number of critics feel Benteen prevaricated at the Reno inquiry. The following exchange fuels the controversy to this day:

Q: "You acted on your own judgment in returning to the point where you met Major Reno?"
A: "Entirely."[4]
    "My idea was there was more for me to do on the trail. That there was fighting going on or would be going on on the trail, and that I had better go back and help them. I thought I had gone far enough and that I would be needed on the trail."[5]

Q: "Was there any limitation ... in regard to the distance you should go in the direction you were sent?"
A: "No limitations, only as to the valleys."[6]

The intimation here is Custer wanted Benteen to go all the way into the Little Big Horn valley, and because Benteen, on his own hook, cut the scout short, he disobeyed his orders. Either this sworn testimony therefore, was a lie, or anything Benteen said prior to or after the inquiry contradicting the testimony was a lie. Shortly after the battle, however, Benteen wrote a letter to his wife saying he believed he traveled up and down those hills for 10 miles, no valley in sight, and the horses beginning to give out quickly, "as my orders had been fulfilled I struck diagonally for the trail the command had marched on, getting to it just before the Pack train got there."[7] The controversy is fueled by Benteen's contradictory claims that (a) Custer told him to return to the trail if the valley was clear (no valley specified, though certainly *implied*), and (b) Benteen took it upon himself to return, Custer knowing his senior captain would exercise the proper initiative.

This entire purportedly important theme seems irrelevant except to those interested in finding fault with the obstreperous captain. The fact remains, it is extremely difficult to believe George Custer would order the experienced Benteen and three companies of the regiment off on some wild goose chase, up and down difficult slopes and bluffs, and on into an empty valley. It stands to reason if the upper Little Big Horn valley were seen to be clear of recalcitrants—even if that viewing was from some six or eight miles off—Custer would want Benteen to return to the command. The bottom line is Custer sent Benteen off to make sure his flanks were clear and no Indians would either attack from, or escape in that direction. Benteen made this all rather clear in the multi-day letter to Mrs. Benteen. In the beginning of the letter Benteen wrote Custer divided the regiment into three battalions, about 15 miles from the Indian village, though the exact whereabouts was unknown—at least to Custer. Benteen was ordered to go to the left, "for the purpose of hunting for the valley of the river—[I]ndian camp—or anything I could

48

Beginning of Benteen's route from the divide separation (courtesy Terry Craft and Steve Andrews).

find."[8] At the inquiry in 1879, Benteen told the court the ground was rugged and he had to go through defiles and around bluffs. "I went to the second line of bluffs and saw no valley, and I knew the Indians had too much sense to go to any place over such country, that if they had to go to any point in that direction they had a much better way to go."[9] We can see from these statements Benteen's mission—stated or implied—was to clear anything off to the command's left flank as it rode down Reno Creek. Military students—and their ilk—can debate what such a movement is called, but it is immaterial and moot. These officers, despite their differences and their latter-year detractors, were professionals and Benteen knew exactly what had to be done, how to do it, and when to return to the command. And Custer knew it as well, and counted on it.

Custer also instructed Benteen to send a "well-mounted officer" and some six men in advance to scout the bluffs as the rest of his battalion followed, and Benteen did just that, the troops led by his first lieutenant, Francis Marion Gibson, though the difficulty of the terrain allowed Benteen—

mounted on a strong, fast horse—to get ahead of even these outriders. Furthermore, once the easier flatlands leading to the ridges were navigated, the harsh topography forced the battalion to move more to the right of its original angle from the main command. Godfrey brought this out at the inquiry, adding the bluffs were too steep and would fatigue the horses,[10] and they were becoming "jaded by the climbing and descending," many falling behind.[11] Private Windolph also felt the strain. In 1946 he wrote the landscape was rough and rolling and it was not long when they were bearing toward their right, nearer the trail Custer and Reno took. The going was tough. He thought they "covered somewhere around seven or eight miles. That doesn't sound very much, until you take into consideration how hard going it was. I know we were all glad to hit that little valley again."[12] The wear on the horses was beginning to take a toll because of the climbing, the descending, the speed-ups, the slow-downs, the stopping, the starting, a routine more difficult than a steady pace, even one that is accelerated.

We do not know precisely how *far* Benteen rode, but only because of the angle of march and the deviations from it, for we know the route he took in returning to the main trail. Benteen claimed it was some 10 miles[13] before he decided to return, but his estimate was off the mark. From other testimonies and some map work, it appears the battalion turned toward the trail once it reached a small valley with a stream we now call No-Name Creek running its length. That would place Benteen's running distance from the divide separation point at somewhere between three and 4.4 miles, depending on how sharp the angle was cut back (*Timeline G*). Once in the No-Name valley, the distance to the main trail would be lengthened or shortened, again, depending on that original angle. The greater the angle from Custer's track, the greater the distance along No-Name, but regardless, it would never exceed 4.6 miles, straight-line, making the entire trek at between 6.7 and 7.6 miles. Lieutenants Edgerly and Godfrey were a little more equanimous, Edgerly writing to his wife that after going some two to three miles they "found it impracticable to keep to the left" and returned to the main trail.[14] Godfrey thought their return march was about five miles,[15] pretty close to the mark if they took the widest angle away from the divide separation, but somewhat improbable based on testimony and terrain. This would also fit with Edgerly's thinking. Later, Edgerly reiterated the three-mile figure before the turn down No-Name, then, "I judge [Benteen] changed direction about six miles after we started down the valley after going into the hills."[16] (Based on questioning at the Reno inquiry, the "changed direction" comment referred to the left turn into the Reno Creek valley and onto the trail.)

Probably the best study of Benteen's scout was done by Roger Darling in his book, *Benteen's Scout*. In it, Darling included a map modified from the original Quadrangles we have used in most of our studies. Darling's route is reasonable, though based on the testimonies of Godfrey and Edgerly we have concluded Benteen entered the No-Name Creek valley a little below where Darling shows it—the terrain is more

The divide to the first valley in Benteen's scout (courtesy Terry Craft and Steve Andrews).

The second valley on Benteen's scout (courtesy Terry Craft and Steve Andrews).

conducive to a horseman's liking. Regardless, Benteen had to have traveled a map-distance of approximately 4⅛ miles, and considering he probably started off at a solid trot of six miles per hour, by the time he reached No-Name—1:25 p.m.—his speed had dropped to three miles per hour or less. (Note, the distance measurements used to compute Benteen's speeds are from a topographical map and do not account for terrain undulations. The differences between the measurements would result in a greater distance traveled and at a greater speed, though neither would be meaningful and both would still fall within the time parameters used.)

Regardless of the terrain, Godfrey felt they moved rapidly—his company was in the rear and he had to order a trot.[17] Of course it is impossible, as well, to put a finite time on the adventure, but Benteen claimed it took him about one and one-half hours to reach Reno Creek (*Timeline G*).[18] While his distances are generally less than accurate, Benteen's times hold up rather well and there is no dispute among his followers as to their veracity. Windolph thought it took the better part of two hours,[19] but we have no other comments as to duration. If we accept a seven-mile-plus-a-fraction, flat-line distance, and a travel time of one hour 40 minutes, that would equate to an overall speed of some 4.2 miles per hour, rapid indeed, considering the terrain and the fact there had to have been a few pauses to valley-gaze (again, *Timeline G*). Of course some of it could be attributed to a pretty quick move off the start and a faster pace down the No-Name valley— say a quick trot of seven miles per hour—but the whole timeframe is fairly impressive and shows a move of some alacrity. One might expect that from an officer of Benteen's ilk and one would certainly expect it in a military operation. Benteen would have reached Reno Creek and the main trail by 1:50 p.m. in time to see a lone rider approaching and the pack train about a mile back up the creek, two of the key elements in confirming Benteen's overall pace and the time he took to complete his mission.

8

A CHANGE OF PLANS

REFERENCES:
Timeline F—Divide Crossing to the Flats; 11:45 a.m.–1:05 p.m.
G—Benteen's Scout; 12:10 p.m.–1:50 p.m.
*H—Custer/Reno Separation to Reno's Dismount; 1:05
    p.m.–1:36 p.m.*
I—From Separation to 3,411; 1:05 p.m.–1:56 p.m.
Y—Stragglers; 12:42 p.m.–4:30 p.m.

Custer's move down Reno Creek was rapid, surges of speed fused with slowdowns and trotting. The command's mood was almost celebratory, bursts of gunfire intermingled with shouts and peals of laughter. During his valley-hunting soirée, Benteen noted, "The last I saw of the column was the Gray Horse Troop at a dead gallop."[1] He lost sight of the column about 45 minutes after setting out.[2] Win Edgerly lost sight of them after about 10 minutes (clearly a more realistic estimate than Benteen's).[3] He said Benteen moved rapidly[4] and Custer went faster than Benteen's battalion did.[5] Godfrey agreed: "During this march on the left we could see occasionally the battalion under Custer, distinguished by the troop mounted on gray horses, marching at a rapid gait. Two or three times we heard loud cheering and also some few shots."[6] Sergeant Daniel Kanipe, riding with his C Company companions, said, "We went at a gallop,"[7] a consistent claim he made many times: "Custer with his five troops went in a gallop down Mud creek toward the Little Big Horn."[8] M Company trooper, Private William Slaper, wrote, "Throughout the morning we were traveling quite rapidly."[9] Four days after the battle Captain Henry Blanchard Freeman,[10] the commanding officer of H Company, Seventh Infantry, under Gibbon, wrote in his journal, "The whole command moved at a gallop down the valley."[11] Of course Freeman was not there until Gibbon's forces arrived on the 27th, but he did not make it up. Coming so soon after the battle, Freeman's journal entry proved a telling commentary and he had to have been told by officers who were there, men whose psyches were still addled by the immediate events and not yet thinking of the future opprobrium and the colossal attention the fight would eventually engender. Facts flourished on the 29th, not rationalizations, not nit-picking, not second-guessing by inquisitive historians playing one favorite against another and making up their own theories.

Even the scouts agreed. Little Sioux, an Arikara riding near Custer, said the troops moved at full speed,[12] while on a 1919 trip to the battlefield, White Man Runs Him, accompanied by fellow Crow Curley, told General Hugh Scott and Colonel Tim McCoy Custer's column moved down Reno/Ash Creek at a fast trot.[13] Furthermore, this confirmed Edgerly's recollection from the June 24 officers' call about pressing on as quickly as possible, as well as Varnum's comment in a letter to his father that as the regiment rode along the Rosebud, coming across abandoned Indian campsites, "The signs indicated an immense force, and we were in a hurry to take them by surprise."[14]

As the regiment bolted forward, men began dropping behind. This would hardly have been the case had Custer ambled down the creek at the leisurely 3.9- to four-miles per hour pace John Gray[15] and so many others would have us believe. Even catching up, the stragglers would have moved more rapidly than a mere walk. Considering this was a military operation and considering the length of the campaign, the elusiveness of the foe, and the concerns of the planners prior to the final departure from Fort Lincoln, speed was an absolute necessity once this close to the village.

Major General Sir Charles Edward Callwell was a British colonial soldier, trained at the Royal Military College and commissioned into the Royal Artillery in 1878. He fought in the Afghan War of 1880, the first Boer War, and the Turko-Greek War of 1897. In his landmark treatise, *Small Wars,* he wrote:

> Irregular warriors seldom keep a good look out by night, but on the other hand they are generally thoroughly on the alert by day if they imagine the regular troops to be in their proximity. Therefore, if a surprise by day is contemplated it is almost always essential to lead up to it by a rapid march from a distance.

Special troops must in fact as a rule be employed, and the enterprise must be conducted with dash and boldness....

Cavalry, mounted infantry ... are well suited for a surprise by day owing to mobility being so essential for such work.[16]

This describes Custer's situation and it further describes the actions he took. His ultimate failure detracts nothing from his initial strokes and we must view everything from the perspective of a military man.

A sharp, swift military event must follow three principles: *logic*, *simplicity*, and *flow*. A rule of thumb generally accepted for speeds traveled by cavalry at the Little Big Horn is four miles per hour for walking, six miles per hour for a trot, and eight miles per hour when galloping. This is *"The Book."* John Gray adhered to these measurements unbendingly, but reality intrudes when one realizes a horse with rider atop can reach speeds well in excess of 30 miles per hour. At the Little Big Horn one might think that occurred more than once, especially when considering the irritability of the foe. A more realistic assessment of speeds can be found on the "modern-day" Website of Ultimatehorsesite.com, an organization located in Corvallis, Oregon. Paraphrased, we read,

Horses speed varies with their stride length, body build, and other factors, but here is a basic idea of how fast ... horses move at their various gaits: at a walk, roughly three to four mph. A pleasure show horse can go as slow as two mph. Gaited horses— that do not trot—can do a "running walk" as fast as 15 mph. The trot is roughly 8–10 mph. Again, a shorter striding horse could trot slower, and a horse with a long stride could move faster. A canter/lope can be clocked at 10–17 mph. A gallop depends on the horse's condition and athletic ability. Some horses are not built to run fast and may only do a fast canter at their best; however, the gallop is about 30 mph. Thoroughbreds, which are bred for running distance but not speed, have been clocked at over 40 mph. Quarter horses, bred and raced for short distances at speed, can reach 50 mph in short bursts according to the AQHA's website.[17]

Military exigencies suggest clearly these gaits are more realistic than those of a parade-ground manual.[18]

There is the usual vituperation about Custer's speed down Reno Creek and the eyewitness testimonies do little to lower the decibel level of disagreement. One of the more overlooked proofs of a more rapid advance than thought generally is the number of men who fell behind during the 10-mile jaunt. We have already seen the comments from members of Benteen's command on the condition of their horses after the constant climbing and descending, and while Reno's command reported no stragglers, there were a number from Custer's battalions, nine in all, some along the creek, others as the command mounted the bluffs.[19] In addition, Sergeant Kanipe attributed his luck in being sent back as a "messenger" to the trouble his fellow C Company sergeant, George August

Finckle, was having with his horse.[20] What is seldom realized is several Ree scouts fell behind as well: Strikes The Lodge, Rushing Bull, Soldier, Bull, White Eagle, and Red Wolf were all reported to have dropped back, struggling to keep up with the on-rushing troops (*Timeline Y*).

Other than some gun-popping and the laughter of the uninitiated, we know virtually nothing about this move from the divide to the Custer/Reno arrival in the "flats," a terrain feature no more distinguished than a mere widening and leveling out of the creek valley. Prior to reaching these flats, the valley's most unique feature was a morass, a geomorphic landmark thought to be located about seven and one-half miles from the top of the divide. Custer must have by-passed this feature—probably around 12:43 p.m.—never pausing, for it brings not a single mention from anyone in either Reno's or Custer's columns. Just beyond the morass the command reached the upper end of an abandoned Indian encampment, probably the one the young Cheyenne warrior, Wooden Leg, alluded to as the Great Medicine Creek camp, its center being "where the present road crosses a bridge at the fork of the creek."[21] Its eastern end—the end the troops would reach first—was where the Hunkpapa Sioux had camped.

The distance from the morass to the Little Big Horn is four and three-quarters to five miles, depending on river channels and specific points around the swamp. The Indian encampment began about one mile west of the morass and extended for some two to three miles in the direction of the Little Big Horn. Some accounts claim shortly after reaching the abandoned village's eastern extremity, Custer's troops found a single, "lone" tepee containing a dead Cheyenne warrior, and this story of the tepee's location has been perpetuated from almost the first moment writers began chronicling the battle. The problem with the tepee being this close to Benteen's emergence point onto Reno Creek and its historical acceptance over more than 137 years, is it is wrong; it does not tie in, it does not work, and while there *may* have been a tepee standing at the village's eastern end, the troops blew past it and continued their rapid advance down the valley, entering the flats about two miles from the river.

By this time it is 12:57 p.m. and Custer is waving Reno over to his side of the creek.

Time to digress a bit. Once the Seventh Cavalry began its move up Davis Creek and neared the divide, not a single important landmark has been described with absolute certainty and as we have seen this includes the two halts, plus the prominence of the Crow's Nest, *vis-à-vis* the divide. A trip down Reno Creek has already added the morass and now a bogus "lone tepee." What we have determined so far is Custer viewed the massive Indian village from one, and probably two locations. While atop the Crow's Nest Fred Gerard claimed they saw this undulating black mass accompanied by a cloud of dust, indicating the proximity of a large camp. Now, "[t]he camp we had found was the smaller camp (the larger camp was downstream farther), and was on the way to the larger camp and this led us all to believe that the Indians were stampeded."[22] Notice the reference to Indians stampeding, as well as to camps. Bruce Liddic alluded to a secondary village of some 60 lodges, claiming it was Lieutenant Varnum who informed Custer of this and that the village was seen moving in the area of the lone tepee and not the valley of the Little Big Horn.[23] He cited a 1904 book by Charles Brady, *Indian Fights and Fighters*,

> [I]t was thought that about 60 lodges were a few miles up the Little Big Horn above the main village, and in the early morning, when Custer's proximity was discovered, that this small village, knowing that they were but a mouthful for Custer's command, hurriedly picked up and dashed down the valley. It can readily be understood that 60 lodges with the horses and paraphernalia, moving rapidly down the valley, might well create the impression that a very large force was in retreat.[24]

How would this supposed village know "they were but a mouthful for Custer's command?" Fanciful writing, indeed, for there is no supporting evidence for such a village or any sighting of anything even remotely resembling a 60-lodge encampment, least of all in the Varnum writings or reminiscences. We have no Indian references and we have no follow-through as to what would have happened to such a "small" group once it was on the move. The Brady allusion to the regiment being "discovered"—and the Liddic purchase thereof—are also highly problematic, for we have multiple Sioux and Cheyenne sources telling us the first indication of Custer's presence came from individual riders racing through the village only moments before Reno's attack. Anyone two or three miles away from the main camp would have certainly warned the villagers well before the soldiers could have reached the Little Big Horn valley from the proximity of the divide.

The obvious inference here, however, was the soldiers had been spotted and these Indians were on their way to warn the main camp. We will learn more—or *less*—about this village as we continue down Reno Creek, though unfortunately, Varnum says nothing about the sighting in either his testimony at the Reno inquiry, or in his book, *I, Varnum*. At the inquiry, when asked about a village on the right bank of the Little Big Horn, Varnum thought the recorder meant in the area leading up to the river, i.e., along Reno Creek. All Var-

num mentioned was an "old tepee ... and a piece of another tepee," and he said this was a mile from where Reno crossed. That is rather a stretch from a 60-lodge village and there was no reference to another, smaller, running village.[25] Varnum's distance-estimate is also rather telling.

In the trek down Reno Creek, Custer moved along its right—or north side—and Reno moved along its south bank. As we have seen, the first noticeable terrain feature the column approached was the morass—12:43 p.m.—and according to many writers it was shortly after this the command reached the general area of the tepee, some four to four and one-half miles to the east of where Reno crossed the Little Big Horn. When Benteen emerged from No-Name Creek onto Reno Creek, he moved a short distance, came across this morass, and paused to water his horses. Best estimates of the terrain in 1876 put the morass about one-quarter mile west of where No-Name and Reno creeks merge, though there is no water feature at that precise spot today (there is one very near where South Fork enters Reno Creek a little to the west). From there, the historian John Gray estimated it was about three-quarters of a mile to the lone tepee,[26] Roger Darling claiming the distance was closer to 1.4 to 2.4 miles.[27]

Distance, like time, did not seem to ring the memory bell for many of the men associated with the Little Big Horn fight, at least not for the day of the battle. There are, however, numerous examples of wild approximations and when one puts the ruler to the map one sees just how mistaken so many of these estimates really were. For example, Luke Hare claimed he called Custer's attention to some Indians his scouts had spotted and when Custer told him to take the scouts and go forward, they refused, so Custer ordered them dismounted. Hare said this occurred about 200 yards from an Indian tepee and five miles from the river.[28] If correct, that would fit with this so-called eastern lone tepee. Shortly thereafter, however, Adjutant Cooke gave Reno Custer's order to attack and Hare said Reno reached the river in 20 or 25 minutes, and that, if true, would have amounted to a speed close to 15 miles an hour, virtually impossible given the creek needing to be crossed, the terrain features to be moved around, and the testimonies of other men riding with Reno. Yet if the tepee were only two miles from the river and Reno moved at a brisk trot—as was reported by numerous participants—20 minutes would work perfectly, especially since the distance is measured in a straight-line and Reno had to turn left, cross the creek, turn right, all the while going around a couple of knolls.

Hare was not the only one who misjudged this distance and therefore, the location; Benteen was equally at fault. In the July 4 letter to his wife, he wrote that after reaching the main trail they rode six or seven miles and came upon "a burning tepee—in which was the body of an Indian on a scaffold, arrayed gorgeously."[29] The distance was actually 3.3 miles, so at least Benteen, in relative terms, was more accurate than Hare. Benteen said much the same thing at the Reno court, adding that in another mile he ran into a sergeant with a message for the packs, and then in a little more than another mile, he met Trumpeter Martini with a message from Lieutenant Cooke. All that adds up to nine and one-half miles from the morass, which is impossible, though it does place these objects in some sort of perspective. Edgerly's estimate of three and one-half miles from the "burning tepee" to the river[30] and Godfrey's estimate of four to five miles[31] for the same features were not a lot better. If we ignore the distance estimates, however, and try to figure the tepee's site from terrain descriptions, we come up with a much more accurate location.

One of the things making the more eastern location for this tepee unacceptable is Indian sightings in the valley were becoming more numerous and four and one-half miles was still too far by a long shot, with too many intervening terrain features obstructing views. As Custer's command moved down this subsidiary valley, Lieutenant Varnum was moving along the left side of the creek keeping mostly to the higher ground south of Reno's column, part of the usual array of scouts out front. (This type of formation marked Custer's approach throughout the campaign and was cautious, intelligent, and capable soldiering.) As Varnum neared the Little Big Horn he had a better vantage point from which to see into the valley. "From every hill where I could see the valley I saw Indians mounted."[32] Varnum also claimed he saw the main village and more Indians than he had ever seen before. Failing his advantage of high ground south of the advance and within a mile or two of the river, "[i]t was impossible to get a good view of [the village] unless one got out on the valley floor because of the bends in the river and the timber around on the left bank."[33]

While Gerard is known to have spotted running or fleeing Indians from the vicinity of the tepee, two major concerns arise. Bruce Liddic wrote this abandoned village was two miles long, and if we concede this point—and we do—and the real lone tepee was at its upper end—and we do not—then there are clearly no bluffs in that vicinity from which to view the village. A glance at a topographic map[34] shows the Reno Creek valley wide open from the river, to about four to five miles east of Reno's crossing point—Ford A—at which point the valley narrows. This fits perfectly with Liddic's description, but as one glances toward the north, one sees the land rises gently for several hundred feet, and then suddenly turns into sheer cliffs. There are *no* distinguishable "bluffs"

or "knolls" or "buttes" in the immediate vicinity of this so-called tepee area and a view of the village, 50—or 200—yards from that location is impossible. Even a view into the Little Big Horn valley from any higher ground remotely near this site is problematic at best. In more than one interview, the Crow scout Curley tells us he and three other Crows—along with Mitch Boyer—spent some time peering into that valley through a pair of binoculars from just such a "bluff." Walter Camp wrote, "His means of identifying the locality was a high rocky bluff, from which he, Mitch Bouyer [*sic*] and three other Crow scouts, had been watching the Sioux with field glasses all that forenoon before the arrival of Custer's command."[35] Photographs, a terrain-walk, and the maps show only very steep "bluff" areas—really, cliffs—north of where this tepee was supposed to have been located, so like many of Curley's statements over the years, this one is also suspect. Plus the time element does not work.

The Curley dialogues seemed endless. Camp interviewed him at least four times, all more than 32 years after the battle, and General Hugh L. Scott spoke with him as well—in 1919—four years before Curley died. Like Theodore Goldin, Curley brings us down enough labyrinthine dead-ends to bring a smile even to Dædalus and the Minotaur. None of the other Crow scouts who were subjected to the curiosity of white interlocutors and curiosity-seekers—Goes Ahead, White Man Runs Him, and Hairy Moccasin (Half Yellow Face and White Swan died before the interview processes began in earnest)—ever told of any forenoon soirées up steep bluffs in an attempt to peer into a valley some five miles away. Furthermore, the question arises, why would they waste their time this far from the river and with terrain this difficult to negotiate? The answer is, they did not, but they may have, much closer to the river and with a lot less exertion.

There is almost unanimity in the belief Gerard was with Hare on some bluffs, only it was not bluffs, but a decent-sized knoll, reported to have been between 50 and 200 yards to the right of the tepee.[36] In 1922, shortly before his death, retired army sergeant and former H Company trumpeter, Giovanni Martini said:

> Girard, the interpreter, rode up on this knoll and while looking at the receding clouds of dust in the valley discovered a good-sized party of Indians in flight between the troops and the river. He turned in his saddle and shouted to Custer, "Here are your Indians, running like devils."[37]

Martini's comments came 46 years after the battle and one wonders if the former sergeant's memories tended to run together by that time, but Gerard himself said he could "see the town, the tepees and ponies," and furthermore, he estimated the Sioux to be "about three miles away, on the left in the bottoms."[38] There is no possible way anyone could have seen the Indian village from any bluff near what is considered the traditional lone tepee site and that included Varnum riding on the high bluffs to the south.

A final, definitive coffin nail for the eastern site comes from a rather unlikely source. During one of his many visits to the Little Big Horn battlefield and adjoining areas, Custer historian, collector, and writer, W. Donald Horn, took the occasion to visit a friend named Jack Connor who owned and farmed a considerable acreage along Reno Creek.

> One of the most intriguing stories told me by Jack Connor was his finding of a piece of burnt hide when plowing at the base of his Cactus Knoll. By every account a burial tepee stood near the base of Girard Knoll and it had been set afire before Custer reached it. On April 20, 1981, I received a letter from George Osteen, a well-known local Custer historian, wherein he wrote, *"I recall a trip with Mr. I. J. O'Donnell, who traversed the course of Reno Creek from the divide with John Burkman, Custer's orderly, several times, and John had shown O'Donnell where the tepee stood and on the trip with O'Donnell he pointed it out to me. Mr. J. W. Vaughn, who did the most actual field work with a metal detector, over the area, and I were on a knoll about ¾ of a mile from the river, where lay some charred bits of what might have been hide from a buffalo and we tried to orient this site, to the tepee. It may have been right where it stood."* The finding of the two pieces of burnt hide in approximately the same location by two different people, adds credibility to the possibility that Cactus Knoll is, in reality, Girard Knoll.[39]

Connor himself wrote to Horn—including a sketch-map— and in the undated note, said,

> I have indicated that the distance from our house to the Little Horn Ford is about 1.7 miles and about the same distance from the teepee site I showed you. (Where we picked the cactus flower.) I figure that it is about 2.1 miles from the teepee site to the bog [the morass], at least the bog indicated on some maps, at the confluence of middle fork and the south fork of Reno.
>
> Respecting the other teepee site ... it is about ¼ mile downstream from the bog, left side of creek facing downstream. I am now inclined to doubt that this is the lone teepee site. Wrong side. My own opinion ... is that the teepee was put up near the place I pointed out and that the hill, (for clarity I'll call it Cactus Hill [Gerard's Knoll]) is the knoll that Girard rode up on and made the observation of the Indians running like devils.[40]

There are numerous accounts referring to the burning tepee, though most claim Custer ordered it fired. It also places Benteen in the same location some time later (2:35 p.m.).

Probably the best thing this eastern tepee site has going for it is the fact an Indian warrior named Old She Bear was supposed to have been identified as having been the dead man on the scaffold. It is known Old She Bear was a Lakota warrior, though it was reported a Cheyenne warrior by the same name was killed fighting George Crook—quite a coincidence! The Old She Bear purportedly found in the tepee,

however, was thought to be either a Hunkpapa or a Sans Arc. He was reputedly dressed for death by a Sans Arc named Old Eagle and a Minneconjou warrior named Two Bear (also known as Three Bear; *Mato Numpa*), who was mortally wounded in the Reno Hill environs on June 25. The placement of a death tepee that far east might indicate a warrior from the Hunkpapa tribe, since the Hunkpapa were the last in the Indians' line of march. If he was a Sans Arc—or a Cheyenne—it is more likely he would have been in the western lone tepee, the one we believe to be the true location, for the Sans Arc camped nearest the Cheyenne, who were closest to the river.[41] The eminent Custer scholar, Richard Hardorff, as well, took issue with the Cheyenne/Old She Bear fable. In a March 5, 1913, interview, Two Moon[s], the old Cheyenne chief, explained that the body was the dead daughter of a Sioux chief. Hardorff shook his head on this:

> Two Moons is mistaken in his identification of the deceased, whose name was Little Wolf, known as the brother of Chief Circling Bear, a leader of a Sans Arc band. Little Wolf died in his lodge from a gunshot wound to the abdomen, sustained in the Rosebud fight. This funeral lodge was burned by a squad of soldiers from F Company, which advanced in front of Custer's column.[42]

Another indication Old She Bear or Little Wolf was not the Cheyenne many claim, comes from our knowledge the Cheyenne did not generally bury their dead on scaffolds like the Sioux, but rather placed them in caves, if available, or placed them on the ground out of the way of usual travel, wrapping them in blankets or skins, and covering the bodies with stones.[43] Only rarely and only if nothing else were available, did the Cheyenne place their dead on a platform or on tree branches. When he died, no one thought soldiers would soon be tramping through the area.

Additional proof our knoll—where Gerard saw running "devils"—and the tepee were closer to the river comes from the testimony of the Ree scout, Red Bear. As the Rees moved ahead of the column and reached the tepee, Red Bear said they paused, and then started riding around the structure, striking it with their whips. Custer rode up—1:01 p.m.—and began to chastise his scouts, yelling they had been instructed *not to stop* (again, that emphasis on speed!), but to head straight for the Sioux village. A give-and-take ensued between several of the Rees and the general—1:01 p.m. to 1:05 p.m.— and when it was over the scouts "rode on ... but Red Bear noticed that Custer turned off to the right with his men about 50 yards beyond the lone tepee. Gerard rode on with the scouts here."[44] It is obvious Red Bear was referring to a tepee much closer to the Little Big Horn than four and one-half miles away when he claimed Custer "turned off to the right

... 50 yards beyond." Lieutenant Hare—in the advance—recalled seeing, "40 or 50 [hostiles] between us and the Little Big Horn. They evidently discovered us, because they disappeared at once."[45] That tells us in addition to the Indians in the main valley who were supposed to have been spotted from the Crow's Nest, there were more in the Reno Creek valley—*east* of the river—but closer to it. It does *not* tell us anything about the main village, or a secondary village, or the valley, or the river bluffs Custer was soon to mount. Hare's comment confirms a Gerard sighting, though it tells us nothing more of Indians running away, i.e., the direction they took, if they turned up bluffs or crossed the river, and it does not give us a hint as to the sequencing of these events. Furthermore, since intervening bluffs would have prevented Gerard from seeing the village from the traditional, eastern lone tepee area, his comments about "see[ing] the town" could have come only when he was at a different location, in all likelihood, the Little Big Horn valley itself or possibly *in the approaches to the river.*[46]

So, despite its history, despite everything ever written about it, this traditional lone tepee—if it ever existed, and there is some elusive evidence it might have—is irrelevant and it played no part in the saga, nothing to do with Reno, nothing to do with Custer, nothing to do with orders, sightings, or squabbling Rees, other than the possibility it merely stood there in all its solitude and the Seventh Cavalry passed it by. For all practical purposes, the so-called "eastern lone tepee" never existed.

We return now to Custer's advance down Reno Creek. Within the flats, just east of the confluence of Reno Creek and an intermittent tributary we call North Fork, the ground rises up forming a small hillock or knoll. This rise is about 1,200 yards east of Ford A and presents us with more problems. If we refer to the topographical map again and head about two-thirds of a mile east of the ford, we see what appears to be higher ground rising 20–40 feet above the surrounding area—without being too presumptuous and for want of a better name, we can label this "Middle Knoll"—but if we head a little more easterly we can distinguish what is clearly a larger knoll, rising some 80–100 feet above the flats.[47] A command, moving westerly toward the river—toward hostile forces—entering these flats and seeking a better view of what it would be up against, would come upon this higher knoll first. This rise is precisely 1.7 miles, due east, of Ford A. (This is measured in today's miles. The Little Big Horn River ran farther east in 1876, lopping about two-tenths of a mile off the distance. The land has been heavily farmed,

as well, changing some of the topographical features from when the maps were first platted.) The troops were only a little over two miles from the Little Big Horn now and it was nearing one o'clock (*Timeline F*). (It would be another 10 minutes before Fred Benteen had had his fill of valley hunting and made his turn down No-Name Creek.) George Custer motioned for Major Reno to cross the creek and join him (12:57 p.m.). Some of the Ree scouts, having left the divide area earlier and moving at a rather brisk pace, had reached the finely decorated tepee and were investigating its contents. Nearby, reaching the top of this larger knoll, Fred Gerard and several more scouts—probably all pausing to catch their breath—began peering intently into the expanse almost two miles away. Dust was rising and horses and Indian pony drovers were suddenly seen in the Little Big Horn valley—the quarry was within sight! Custer, not on the knoll but seeing the rising dust, asked the Crow scout, Half Yellow Face, what was all the dust in the distance and the scout reputedly answered, *"The Sioux must be running away!"*[48] George Herendeen told Custer the same thing and Gerard and Hare also chimed in, shouting down from the hilltop, all confirming Half Yellow Face's observation. It is from this knoll Gerard spotted those "Indians ... running like devils," and possibly Indians in the main valley as well as a number of others, dead ahead.

Gerard's own statements suggest—nay, *shriek!*—to us he was closer to the river than the eastern tepee: "When we got within two or three miles of Ford A, we could see a big dust over in the valley of the Little Big Horn, there being a north wind, and this gave the impression that the Indians were fleeing north."[49] Moving onto this larger knoll could confirm the sighting and the impression of "fleeing" Indians. It is also interesting to note that other than at the Crow's Nest, this is the first precise indication of where Gerard himself said he was when he saw fleeing Indians. Lieutenant Hare was among the party on the knoll and this is where he told Custer of the Indians out front—some 40 or 50 of them, sitting on the smaller knoll—Middle Knoll—just before the river and who then disappeared suddenly.[50] (It must be understood all of this was going on simultaneously—these were not independent, time-laden reports; things were on the jump, were happening and beginning to happen quickly.) This is where Custer told Hare to move forward with the Rees, the scouts balking; and Custer arguing with them by the tepee—1:01–1:05 p.m. It is where Hare then grabbed a detail from M Company to scout forward—1:04 p.m. And this is where Custer issued his order to Major Reno to attack the village—1:02–1:05 p.m.

As he rode to the attack down the Little Big Horn valley, Reno believed George Custer, at the head of five companies totaling 224 men, was somewhere behind him, following up in the promised support. Whether or not battle students believe this to be the case, Reno believed it and he made his opinion clear right from the outset of the firestorm of criticism following the debacle. In a series of letters, defenses, and rebuttals written in July and August, 1876, between Reno and Tom Rosser—George Custer's West Point friend—and published in the *New York Herald* and the St. Paul–Minneapolis *Pioneer-Press and Tribune,* Reno claimed his orders were given to him by the regimental adjutant, Lieutenant Cooke, and Cooke specifically mentioned the proffered support: "Custer says to move at as rapid a gait as you think prudent, and to charge afterward, and you will be supported by the whole outfit."[51] Seems fairly clear and nothing more than what Reno had written in his after-action report of July 5, 1876:

> As we approached a deserted village, and in which was standing one tepee, about 11:00 a.m., Custer motioned me to cross to him, which I did, and moved nearer to his column until about 12:30 a.m. [*sic*; p.m.] when Lieutenant Cook [*sic,* Cooke], adjutant, came to me and said the village was only two miles above, and running away; to move forward at as rapid a gait as prudent, and to charge afterward, and that the whole outfit would support me. I think those were his exact words."[52]

(One should ignore Reno's times; they were the most inaccurate of any ever given for these events.)

Two and one-half years after the battle, at the inquiry held in Chicago and insisted upon by Reno as a means of clearing his increasingly besmirched name, the major reiterated his claim of Custer's purported support. The two columns—Reno's three companies and Custer's five—moved nearly parallel down Ash/Reno Creek for some time and at some speed. When they got within sight of the Indian tepee, Custer waved his hat, signaling Reno to cross over to the right bank. The crossing was not that easy and by the time Reno managed to join Custer, his battalion was a little scattered and to his commander's rear. The peripatetic Cooke, constantly riding back and forth with instructions from his semi-dæmonic boss, told the major to move his command to the front, noticing along the way a commotion among the scouts, some of whom were stripping, preparing themselves for battle. Reno reached the head of the column and momentarily Cooke gave him the order from Custer. At the inquiry, Reno was asked a question about this support. "From the manner I received the order I could not conceive of any other manner of being supported except from the rear."[53] He went on: "[I]n my opinion there was no other way to support me."[54]

Lieutenants Benny Hodgson—Reno's acting adjutant

(who was subsequently killed during Reno's retreat from the valley)—and Nick Wallace were with Reno at the time. Wallace claimed the command never halted even after Custer called Reno over to the right bank of the stream (once again, emphasizing the urgency Custer felt in getting down the creek, as well as his concern for surprise). As Reno caught up and the two battalions moved parallel Wallace said they passed a tepee containing a dead body or bodies. Shortly after passing the tepee, Adjutant Cooke came to Reno and said, "the Indians were about two miles and a half ahead and Major Reno was ordered forward as fast as he could go and to charge them and the others would support him."[55] Wallace pointed out these were the last orders he heard issued and said the order was given about this way: "'The Indians are about two miles and a half ahead, on the jump, follow them as fast as you can and charge them wherever you find them and we will support you.'"[56] Furthermore, Wallace stressed the point about Reno being supported as well as stressing that was what he, Wallace, understood to be the case. It was the only order he heard given to Reno.[57]

There was supporting evidence, as well, from the civilian doctor. Henry Porter, positioned at Reno's side,[58] heard Lieutenant Cooke—"right near where they struck the first tepee where the dead Indians were" (the *first* tepee, as opposed to the *second* and broken-down tepee nearby)—tell the major the Indians were just ahead and he was to charge them. Reno asked if he would be supported, "if the general was coming along," and Cooke answered yes, the general would support him.[59] (Can anyone imagine this occurring more than four miles from the river-crossing, intervening knolls blocking views into the main valley? It did not.)

There were a number of sightings of Indians well before the battle began and as the troops got closer to the village more and more warriors appeared; alarm started spreading throughout the hostiles' encampment. The Crow scouts, Half Yellow Face, Curley, and White Man Runs Him—who had moved forward onto the knoll in the flats—reported two Sioux warriors who had spotted the large dust cloud raised by the command. These two Sioux—identified as a Hunkpapa boy named Deeds and a Sans Arc warrior named Lone Dog—rode to the ridgeline leading to Reno Hill and began alarming the village by riding in circles. The Crow scout, Goes Ahead, managed to kill Deeds. (Another version of the story claims the warrior with Deeds was a Hunkpapa known as Brown Back—possibly his father—and they came afoul of the scouts, which was when Deeds was killed. It is widely assumed the only woman known to have fought the troops was Deeds' infuriated sister, Moving Robe Woman—aka, Mary Crawler—who exacted some terrible revenge on the bodies of several men.) What has now become clear is there were a number of Indian parties ranging in size from two to considerably larger, outside the village—hunting, looking for stray horses, tending the pony herds, even heading back to the agencies—and several Indians warned the village of the oncoming soldiers, though not quite yet. What is also becoming clear is the whole episode was moving into an exceptionally fluid stage, in timing, events, distances covered, and movements of people.

No one sat for long. Surprise—in whatever form or permutation it came in—was still of utmost importance and despite earlier trepidations, it appeared a modicum of that element had been achieved. As Custer and Reno separated, Luke Hare and some scouts moved to join Reno, and Tom French, the M Company commander, cut out two or three sets-of-fours to ride advance with Hare—1:04 p.m.[60] Reno moved out smartly—at 1:05, 1:06, 1:07 p.m. Varnum arrived from the southern heights—1:06 p.m.—and reported to Custer as Reno's command was passing the general, lead elements now a little more than one mile from Ford A.[61] As Reno rode off, Varnum approached Custer with the news he had seen a large force of Indians and a large village farther down the valley. This "report was apparently the first intimation—from what Custer considered a responsible source—of the immediate proximity of a large number of hostiles."[62] Custer told his chief of scouts to join the major and they laughingly included Nick Wallace (much to Nick's later relief, we are sure!). Two Crow scouts—Half Yellow Face and White Swan—misunderstanding their orders to move to Custer's lead, inadvertently galloped toward Reno. The regimental adjutant went with Reno's column, and Captain Keogh, who wanted to check the terrain for a crossing of his own battalion, rode the column's wake. At 1:08 p.m. Custer instructed George Yates to send out again one of his sergeants and four or five troopers as an advance scout for the main column.

Riding at "a pretty fast gait, sometimes on a trot and sometimes on a lope," Gerard moved forward as well, and came to the Little Big Horn, skirting what we shall call—for the sake of convenience—"Cooke's Knoll," the third and smallest of the west-east knolls in the flats. "I halted there some little time."[63] Gerard and Reno reached the ford at about the same time, Gerard a little to the major's left, within eight to 10 feet of him. As they approached the water, the distance between them increased somewhat, 12 or 15 feet apart, and Gerard halted near the knoll as Reno continued to move at a fast trot.[64] The Ree scouts scattered, some along the river's slopes, others ahead of Reno and across the river. As Gerard reached the knoll and the river crossing—1:13 to 1:14 p.m.—several Rees who had ridden upstream along the river's high

bank to get a better view by peering north over the treetops, informed him the Sioux were not dismantling their village, but were coming out to meet the soldiers.[65] Gerard knew this news would be contrary to what Custer and his officers were expecting and Gerard was alarmed. Reno was now in the middle of the river—1:16 p.m.—guiding his battalion across its cold, 25–30 foot expanse.

Reno's men hit the water, slowing, thus allowing the trailing elements to close gaps. Reno paused in mid-stream, watching as the troops crossed. At this point Gerard claimed he informed Reno the Indians were not running and were coming out, but Reno forever denied this, saying, "The scout 'had no right to speak to me officially.'"[66] At the 1879 inquiry Reno got rather testy about Gerard and opened the door regarding the latter's comment of the Indians not running. While not directly admitting it, Reno said,

> From the manner in which you ask the question it would seem to indicate that [Gerard] came to me in an official capacity which I would not recognize. Of course if he had any information to convey to me, I should have listened to him, but I would not have believed it.[67]

Gerard could have been mistaken in his recollection and Reno could have been correct, for in his interviews with Walter Mason Camp on January 22, 1909, and April 3, 1909, Gerard made no mention of informing the major. Camp wrote:

> After Gerard got across the river, one of the Indian scouts called out that the Sioux were coming up to meet Reno. Gerard exclaimed, "Hell, Custer ought to know this right away, for he thinks the Indians are running. He ought to know they are preparing to fight. I'll go back and inform him." [H]e went back and met Cooke at the knoll ½ or ¾ mile east of the ford. It was probably 75 or 100 feet high, but right in the mouth of the valley. The trail passed to the right of it. When Cooke saw him coming up he said: "Well, Gerard, what is the matter now?"[68]

Camp puts Gerard across the Little Big Horn when he learns the Sioux are no longer in flight, but this is incorrect and reflects the cobwebs of time, for Gerard did not actually see the Indians coming back toward Reno; his Ree scouts did. Also, the knoll in Camp's writing is what we have euphemistically called "Middle Knoll"; Gerard, however, met Cooke not at that knoll, but at the one adjacent to the river described 30 years earlier at the 1879 inquiry.

By this time they had lost sight of Custer's column. Again at the inquiry, Gerard said the trail Reno followed went to the left around the knoll next to the river and was smaller than the trail that continued straight. The right-hand trail was a lodge-pole trail, "quite a large one,"[69] and it was the one Custer continued to follow until he made his right turn. Reno's swing to the left was about a mile from where the columns separated—in all likelihood in the vicinity of

"Middle Knoll"—and the next "knoll ['Cooke's'] was right on the edge of the river's bank."[70] (Each of these features—the three knolls and a dry gulch Reno followed—is shown clearly on the topographic map of the area.)

Since Gerard got no response from Reno, he stood and watched as the command forded the river—1:16 to 1:20 p.m. (*Timeline H*). Then, believing Custer had to be informed of this turn of events, he began to head back, running into Cooke—1:16 p.m.—who was coming around the knoll toward Reno's column about 75 yards from Ford A.[71] Certain testimony has both Cooke and Myles Keogh accompanying Reno's command, some even saying as far as the middle of the river. This seems unlikely however—much of it being hearsay, especially from Godfrey who was not there—and there is no mention of Keogh by Gerard, who also stated Cooke was headed *toward* Reno, not away from him. Gerard is wrong probably about the direction Cooke was headed, however, for it seems clear from the narratives of A Company sergeant, Ferdinand Culbertson and M Company private, James Wilber, Cooke was already at the knoll and was planning either to cross the river after Reno's last man or head back to Custer. Wilber, as well, did not see Keogh there.[72] If Culbertson saw Cooke at the ford, then we know half of Reno's battalion was in the water or had already crossed. Edgerly told Camp officers who were with Reno told him both Cooke and Keogh actually went to Ford A and *crossed* the river. In Edgerly's mind this was proof Custer intended to cross after Reno and support him in the valley. Plus, Keogh was a battalion commander and that would allow him to leave his command.[73] Edgerly's reasoning is sound and provides us with a glimpse into what troop commanders would have thought should be done. In private correspondence with me, author Don Horn brought out the point that

> the only logical reason why Cooke was still at the crossing site when Girard [*sic*] returned was that he was waiting there for Custer to come on.... Cooke had been waiting for Custer on the east side of the knoll as from there Custer would eventually be able to see him and be more easily guided to the crossing site.[74]

In all likelihood, when Reno swung to the left Keogh continued on toward the river—though never getting into it—probably wanting to check out another crossing for Custer's column and as Edgerly alluded, as the senior battalion commander, Keogh would have believed it was his job to do so. As Gerard made his way back, Cooke asked him where he was headed and Gerard told him of the Indians, estimating they were coming up the valley, about two and one-half miles "away and in very large numbers."[75] The adjutant responded, "All right, I'll go back and report."[76] Gerard returned to the ford, met one scout, and crossed the river immediately. None

of this took very much time as the immediacy of the situation had not dissipated, and if anything, the adrenaline only spurred it forward even more quickly.

What is so intriguing about all this—and so important—is Gerard's information was sheer conjecture. He received his report from some of the Rees, a nervous group of men peering maybe some two-plus miles down-valley and into a burgeoning veil of dust. If, as appears likely, Cooke reported this episode to Custer, it caused the latter to veer off to the right rather than support Reno directly.[77] In all likelihood, Custer felt the Sioux "attack" was simply a delaying action to allow families to grab belongings and head downriver toward a modicum of safety. What was the result?

Marcus Reno expected Custer to support him. He expected direct support, not an end-run designed to draw Indians away from his immediate front or fleeing refugees from the rear. Right or wrong, wishful thinking or righteous indignation, this is what Reno always claimed, though Liddic wrote Reno was left with some question as to the precise meaning of Custer's "supporting" role.[78] It appears, however, the word "support" *was* used when Reno was given his orders. Other enlisted personnel—in all likelihood traveling near the front of the column so they could overhear some of what was said—agreed with the notion of "direct support." In his journal, Sergeant Charles White of M Company wrote while fighting on the skirmish line, he believed that up "to this time we had every minute been expecting reinforcements from the rear."[79] Private Edward Davern (Company F), a Reno orderly, claimed a similar tenor to the orders Reno received: "Gerard comes back and reports the Indian village three miles ahead and moving. The General directs you to take your three companies and drive everything before you."[80] (This would also place Gerard nearer the river where he spotted the running Indians, further supporting the contention of the lone tepee in this area—alongside "Gerard's Knoll"—rather than four and one-half miles to the east.)

Cooke's relayed orders led to a significant misunderstanding, however. In Reno's post-battle discussions, he related his belief these orders led him to understand Custer would be right behind him. Liddic, noting this confusion in Reno's mind as to what "support" meant,[81] went on to write he did not believe Custer told Reno to attack the village, per se, but to harass the Indians, delay them, and stop them: "[Custer] never expected his Major to do any serious fighting."[82] We do not agree with Liddic's premise Reno was not expected to do any "serious" fighting, but one cannot argue with his contention there might have been some question in Reno's mind about the support issue. While they disagreed on the exact wording, Reno and his battalion physician, Doctor

Porter—at the court of inquiry—agreed about Cooke's orders to attack. Furthermore, Liddic felt Reno used a little whitewash at the inquiry by denying he had spoken directly to Custer, and others, including Lieutenant Hare and Sergeant Kanipe of C Company, also remembered Custer speaking with Reno *after* Cooke issued Reno the attack orders. This would have indicated Reno's desire to cover up the fact Custer may have told him to attack the village while Custer himself made an end-run, thereby ruining Reno's excuse for a retreat based on the understanding he was to receive direct support.[83] We will never know for sure, but Gerard's report seems to tip the scales in Reno's favor, regardless of whether or not he communicated with Custer directly, and that communication would have come too early for Custer to make the decision to turn right based on Indians setting up a delaying screen. In fact, there is always the possibility Custer merely told Reno to send out advance scouts—troopers, not Indians—to reconnoiter before crossing the river. Custer had already done that with men from Yates' company and we know from Sergeant White that French ordered his first sergeant to forward a detail with Lieutenant Hare.

Now, while speculation here is both dangerous and problematic, let us for argument's sake and another slight digression, assume Custer supported Reno by following him down the valley. What effect would that have on the battle? Well, for one thing, it would have placed a more dynamic and self-assured commander in the valley, and for another it would have more than doubled the strength of the attacking force. In all likelihood, Reno would have never halted his charge and formed a skirmish line. This may or may not have been a good thing, for there was a serious ravine confronting the major and if he had not stopped, his battalion might have been eaten up by the combination of terrain and Indian ferocity, but with Custer right behind him or to his left, these obstacles could have been overcome conceivably. Also, a larger command would have been strung out more to the left, somewhat thinning the ranks, but also better dealing with the dust-raising issue. (This dust tactic was a ploy to allow the hostiles' non-combatants more time to gather what they could and flee. The huge dust screen hid their movements and also concealed the number of Indians who were starting to come out of the village to face the onslaught—also very sound tactics. The fact Reno could not see much beyond the wall of mayhem fronting him was in all likelihood one of the primary reasons for his dismounting.)

Because of the anticipated size of the village, Custer—

despite breaking the regiment into battalions—meant to keep severe control of his command: basic tactics. Liddic felt Custer never went to Weir Peak (correct), but looked over the valley from the heights of Sharpshooters' Ridge (incorrect), but regardless of where he was when he viewed the scene below, Liddic believed it was clear Custer knew the approximate location of his entire regiment, certainly up to the time of Reno's engagement. Liddic said Custer probably saw the long dust cloud to the south that was both Benteen and the packs and while our timing studies can support Liddic's point—at least to location—it is highly uncertain enough dust was raised to be seen from the vicinity of elevation point 3,411—which is where Custer was—or Sharpshooters' Ridge—which was higher, but where Custer wasn't. Reno's location was obvious and the dust plumes created by the separate commands of captains Benteen and McDougall—if seen—could have given the general an idea of just where they were and how long it would take them to reach a battle position. At the time Custer was viewing the beginning phase of Reno's engagement—1:48 p.m. to 1:56 p.m.—Fred Benteen was turning onto the main trail along Reno Creek and the pack train was no more than a mile above Benteen. While dust plumes are possible certainly, it is less likely any could be seen six to eight miles away, especially since the Reno Creek valley was considerably lower in elevation than where Custer would have been and the packs were strung out, thinning whatever dust they would raise. In addition, Benteen had only turned onto the main trail moments before—1:50 p.m.—and would reach a morass shortly—1:54 p.m.—where he would stop to water. The small No-Name Creek valley he had just moved down had not been trod upon previously and it was unlikely much if any dust would have been raised while traveling its length.

Joe Blummer, an Austrian-born former stagecoach driver and one-time owner of the local Garryowen store near the battlefield, believed Custer could distinguish between the two columns and that was why he would eventually dispatch Trumpeter Martini with Cooke's note. "[I]f Custer had not seen the Benteen column coming, he would not have any way of knowing where Benteen might be."[84] Apparently, Benteen never suspected Custer saw him from there, and for good reason, *viz.*, Benteen had barely made the turn onto Reno Creek (*Timelines G* and *I*). In what could be a very telling comment, Benteen said: "When that order was sent to me by Custer, he couldn't tell within 10 miles of where I might be found from the nature of the order I had received from him,"[85] but if Liddic is correct, Custer knew where his entire command was this far into the event and he knew they were mutually supporting or could be, shortly. At best, however, this is a stretch, and one that would soon reach the breaking point. But we are a little ahead of ourselves here.

As Reno approached the river, it appears Custer may have been somewhat ambivalent concerning his next move. What is impressive (*surprising?*) about Custer's planning, however, is the flexibility his battalion divisions provided him. A lot of modern-day theorists claim one of Custer's most serious mistakes was the dividing of his command, but we take issue with that, especially if we are looking at Sunday's battle on Saturday afternoon instead of Monday morning. It may have been "Plan B," but Custer's actions wound up using Reno's battalion as a direct attack to draw Indians out of the village and tie them down. The hostiles would bite at that, thinking by opposing the attackers, they would be giving their families time to escape. While it seems likely Custer would have preferred to bring maximum force against a disorganized mob, in his mind by going around the village he could still round up or drive through the escapees, effectively neutralizing the warriors' superior numbers. And Benteen's battalion, not only useful for clearing the flanks, turned out to be the regimental reserve, a sound military tactic, planned or fortuitous. Never mind that Benteen was actually performing a useful mission; his titular "reserve" status could be used to help either of the "action" commands, be they united or split. While he did divide his forces, they all had legitimate, complementary, and supporting missions critical to the success of the attack, and his subsequent actions suggest he *assumed* he could call on his battalions and use them as he wished, whenever he desired to do so. His fatal mistake was this assumption proved illusionary.

It should be pointed out Benteen's role as a reserve was not planned, as many historians believe. Benteen had a clear and specific mission, very much as Reno did. The fact Benteen might turn out to be useful as a maneuver battalion to be directed elsewhere was strictly fortuitous and no role as a "reserve," per se, was ever mentioned—or planned. Edward Godfrey was adamant about this. He made an entry in his diary on August 7, 1876, about writing a letter "to the *Army and Navy Journal* correcting the prevailing mistake that Col. Benteen's column at the Battle of the Little Big Horn was a 'Reserve' by design."[86]

Cooke's report of Gerard's interpretation of the scouts' sightings confirmed Custer's worst fear: he had arrived a little too late for complete surprise and the Indians were preparing to scatter. It is therefore a reasonable assumption Custer took this tenuous intelligence as fact and made a split-second decision to head off into the high country east of the river rather than follow Reno down the valley, the promised—and hoped-for—"direct support." The two issues confronting Custer's immediate superior, General Terry, throughout the campaign were the size of the hostile force and the concern that once threatened, the Indians would scatter to the four winds. Gerard claimed to have told Terry before anyone had left Fort Abraham Lincoln, that if all the Indians leaving the reservations united the troopers could meet as many as 4,000 warriors.[87] John Gray, however, chipped in the fact, "size was not what worried Custer; his overriding concern was that the Sioux would break up and scatter."[88] There is no question but that Gray was correct here. Lieutenant Godfrey called Custer "possessed" about this possibility.[89] One should tend to think also, regardless of Custer's scorn for the Indians' numbers, he planned on no cakewalk, for at his meeting the evening prior to the battle, he "told the officers they would have the fight of their lives,"[90] and if we believe it was only the following day when Custer made the decision to attack, we must understand his "fight of their life talk," still, somehow included Terry's and Gibbon's forces, hardly something to be included in a pre-planned end-run.

Edgar Stewart took a different view, believing it was Varnum's report of the larger village that caused Custer to veer off from Reno.[91] Stewart was highly critical of Custer here, writing that as the command was passing the lone tepee,

> there was absolutely nothing to warn Custer of the immediate proximity of several thousand very belligerent Indians, except the repeated warnings of the scouts.... In defiance of even the most rudimentary and elementary rules of warfare, Custer had made no adequate reconnaissance to discover the strength and position of the enemy, but assumed, on the basis of insufficient evidence, that the village was already in flight.[92]

This is a bit unfair, however, and does not consider either the circumstances as Custer understood them, or his concern for a camp that might scatter. Moreover, Stewart's assumption is premature, for even this late in the move down Reno Creek, the village was doing no such thing and it was only after Gerard's report that it became apparent the Indians were now on the alert and moving. Reno's after-action report, as well, supports our contention: "General Custer was fully confident that [the Sioux] were running or he would not have turned from me." Furthermore, Terry agreed.[93] What is interesting here as well is some of those who roundly criticize Custer feel he should have known the Indians would stand and fight to protect their families. It cuts both ways, however. In a Walter Camp interview with Win Edgerly—not dated, but after the turn of the century certainly—Edgerly stated he had conducted interviews with Indians involved in the battle. Apparently, the village had gotten information that Custer was crossing [the] divide, but from precedent expected him to attack at daylight [the] next morning. [They w]ere not anticipating ... he would show up in middle of the day. Hence their ponies were still out grazing and generally unprepared.[94]

Quite a dichotomy here; praise to the surprising winner, an ode to the loser. Of course, those boasts rank right up there in believability with the prenatal ruminations Sitting Bull claimed to have had!

If the Indians who had spotted the soldiers' approach were *not* running into the village, it could only mean they were going to put up a stand just long enough to cover the encampment as it was either somehow dismantled or the refugees simply headed off with the winds. Anything else would be un–Indian-like. As Carl von Clausewitz wrote, "An attack on an army in billets is therefore an attack on a dispersed army ... the keystone for the whole operation is the fact that the enemy is temporarily thrown off balance and demoralized."[95] A retreating, panicking force could be dealt with—confusion was an attacking, charging, organized, and disciplined force's best friend—but a strong covering force, protecting refugees about to bolt or already doing so, was something different. It meant now these refugees had to be dealt with as well—and separately—forcing Custer to improvise on the run because of a lack of precise intelligence and because of the time pressure he felt he was under in fearing the Indians would flee. It also explains Professor Richard Fox' contention—though I would question whether he figured it developed quite this early—that much of Custer's movement on the battlefield was an intelligence gathering mission prior to his anticipated attack,[96] a prescient observation, indeed, and one belying the imprecations of so many other scholars. In reality, this was typical Custer and it flies in the face of those who would damn the man as arrogant and irresponsibly reckless. Like so many other words, "reckless" only works within context. His old Civil War boss, Major General George B. McClellan, called Custer "reckless and gallant, 'undeterred by fatigue, unconscious of fear; but his head was always clear in danger, and he always brought me clear and intelligible reports of what he saw when under the heaviest fire. I became much attached to him.'"[97] And one of those who rode with the man, Captain James H. Kidd of the Sixth Michigan Cavalry, said Custer was

> brave, but not reckless; self-confident, yet modest; ambitious, regulating his conduct at all times by a high sense of honor and duty; eager for laurels, but scorning to wear them unworthily; ready and willing to act, but regardful of human life; quick in emergencies, cool and self-possessed, his courage was of the highest moral type: his perceptions were intuitions.[98]

This description could apply equally to a man who fought his own "Little Big Horn" some 65 years later, *Generalfeldmarschall* Erwin Rommel. While speaking of tank warfare— the descendant of Custer's cavalry—Rommel wrote,

> The majority of fighting men in a swift exhausting tank battle at a given moment always succumb to a need for rest. No army is composed solely of heroes. They will insist for one reason or another that they cannot go on. The commander with his authority must combat these natural phenomena of weariness, and wrench his officers and men out of their apathy. The man in command must be the galvanizer of the battle. He must constantly be on the battlefield, in the front line, to exercise his control.[99]

Sounds a lot like George Custer. The implications are obvious and pertain equally to nineteenth century cavalry warfare as well as twentieth century tank battles. The fact remains that at the Little Big Horn, Custer was presented with a serious dilemma, one of scattering, running Indians, *ergo*, the collapse of an entire campaign. Gerard's report was the harbinger of precisely such a quandary and Custer would now be forced to abandon his solidifying plans in favor of a new approach, one having to be carefully, yet rapidly reconnoitered. It was imperative he knew what was happening beyond his zone of immediacy. What occurred now was one of three fateful— and fatal—decisions Custer made this day: he abandoned his plan of supporting Reno directly and turned his five companies to the right, mounting the eastern ridges of the Little Big Horn River. This move sealed Reno's fate.

Custer's plan, despite the fact he formulated it on the fly, then changed it just as rapidly, was a flexible one. That it did not work is more a tribute to the Indians' sheer brute strength, fighting ability, and numbers—along with poor execution by Custer himself—than to any shortcomings in his tactical *thinking*. By dividing the regiment into three fighting battalions, Custer could send any one of them wherever he wanted, providing he maintained a modicum of control. Liddic's theory maintains he did just that at least as far as Sharpshooters' Ridge, and through notes and messengers, possibly a little beyond. If the Indians had continued to run, abandoning possessions in favor of life, there would have been no need for Custer to take the high ground to Reno Hill and beyond. In fact, it would have been ludicrous for him to have even tried. By supporting Reno directly, Custer would have seen the whole battle as a chase, one battalion following another, at some point Benteen joining the fray with fresh troops. In a fracas of that sort, we could expect the military to prevail somehow, though I would suspect the campaign would have been somewhat less than completely successful, a Pyrrhic victory indeed. Terry would have had his snoot full of activity as well and maybe we would have seen just what Gatling guns could have done to a stampeding horde. Gerard's report that the Indians were not running, but were coming out to meet the advancing columns, pointed out to Custer the hostiles were in fact using a covering force to delay the soldiers so the women, children, and elderly would have time to flee. This was the red flag Custer feared; a "defensive" show of some considerable force would compel him to change plans rapidly.

James Willert and a number of others claimed it was also the sight of some hostiles up on the bluffs that helped Custer decide to veer off Reno's trail and pursue the Indians,[100] but we do not know who these warriors were or where they were precisely when spotted. Sergeant Daniel Kanipe took credit for Custer's move to the high ground and claimed it was he who had spotted about 100 Indians in the vicinity of Reno Hill. Could this have been the same sighting as Lieutenant Hare, only a mistaken location? John Gray, however, made the point Custer veered off to the right after speaking with Cooke rather than because these hundred or so Indians were observed. His reasoning was if the Sioux were not running, Reno's force was too small and he would need some measure of support. By following his scouts, Custer could see the action for himself and find a good route by which to make a flank attack that might help Reno sooner. Gray had a point here—though not a very sharp one—and it appears from later testimony, when Custer watched Reno from the bluff, he felt his major was holding his own. One must remember Gray believed Custer saw Reno in action, while author Jack Pennington wrote that Martini's stories indicated Reno had not yet attacked and Custer viewed a quiet, sleeping village. Walter Camp also felt Custer never saw Reno in action.[101] Gray was correct; Pennington and Camp were not. It is, however, problematic if Custer ever knew the seriousness or extent of Reno's trouble and the timing scenarios tend to corroborate it, though it appears—a little later—he was told Reno had been forced back. It is also important to understand Reno was sent to attack with a specific purpose in mind and regardless of Custer's changed plans, the Reno mission never changed. Custer's subsequent actions proved once he veered to the right he was in no way influenced by any thought of support for Reno; that would have only detracted from the main objective: *the destruction of the Indians' fighting ability.* Reno was the support for Custer, not vice versa. Custer was to be the hammer always, never the anvil.

Even if Marcus Reno had his problems with Gerard, the major was now well aware the Indians were not running, but were either coming out to meet him or brazenly whooping it up down-valley—George Herendeen at least, told Reno the Sioux were not running.[102] While his battalion was still crossing the river—and only moments after Gerard's report—a concerned Reno sent his striker, Private Archibald McIlhargey (Company I), to tell Custer the Sioux were as thick as grass—1:16 p.m. A few minutes later, however—1:19 p.m.—fortified with Gerard's report, Custer had already decided to start down the right bank of the river, veering off from Reno's route. Only a few minutes after he dispatched McIlhargey, a nervous Reno sent another messenger—Private John Edward Mitchell (also Company I)—to Custer.[103] It appears by sending Mitchell back to Custer with the same information he gave McIlhargey, Reno was concerned about the clarity of Custer's orders (supporting Liddic's theory of Reno's confusion). He knew he was to head down the valley and engage the Sioux—that much was clear—but then what? Reno had to be unsure about the meaning of Custer's support.

What makes Reno's uncertainty all the more befuddling is the officers' meeting Custer called on the evening of June 24. At this time Custer had not made the decision to attack the next morning. Quite the contrary; if we accept testimonies at face value and put aside suspicions of a one-man conspiracy, Custer had every intention of holing up for a day, resting his men and horses, and launching an attack on the morning of June 26, in all likelihood, with some cooperation from the Terry/Gibbon column. That would entail directly supporting any mission Custer was to assign Reno, for the objective would have been to drive the Indians into the Terry anvil. If Custer expected Terry to be coming from those lower reaches and the Seventh's commander still planned on attacking on the morning of the 26th, why would he have planned for an end-run? The only plausible explanation would be Custer *had* no plans at his officers' meeting and formulated everything the following day when his intelligence-gathering sources had given him more information. Even the timing of the battalion breakdown on the western side of the divide would tend to confirm this. "[T]he column ... crossed the divide ... and descended towards the Little Big Horn River.... Custer shortly called another halt and this time made battalion assignments."[104] Almost everyone agrees.

Liddic wrote, Custer's 90 degree turn occurred about one-quarter mile from Ford A.[105] He could very well be correct, for Varnum claimed when he re-joined the column after riding down Reno Creek, Reno was passing by Custer as Varnum reported to the general. "That was about a mile from where Major Reno afterwards crossed the Little Big Horn."[106] That would also give us the immediacy needed for the argument about Gerard being on the knoll in the flats when he told Custer the Indians were running. Custer had to have continued on, getting even closer to the river (*Timeline I* would confirm this from the point of view of timing; see the two 1:19 p.m. entries). Liddic felt he followed right on Reno's heels and did "not turn to the right several miles or more from the Ford A, as some battle students claim."[107] Liddic believes this—plus Custer's sending of Cooke and Keogh toward the ford—proves he intended to support Reno directly and not make an end-run along the bluffs. Writer/historian Don Horn agrees.[108] Of course, the Cooke and Keogh crossing of the Little Big Horn is another measure of contention and it is possible Liddic and Horn—and myself—may be wrong here, but again, the reasoning is sound, simply by virtue of how close Custer was on Reno's heels, regardless of how far Cooke and Keogh traveled with the major. *Something* made the man move to the right and it was *not* prior planning.

After the battle, Sergeant Kanipe said Custer turned north immediately upon spotting a group of 100 warriors on the high bluffs to the north. Camp also recorded this, though the figure was 60–75 Indians, north of Reno Hill. Liddic tells us, however, Curley said Custer turned about one and one-quarter miles from Ford A. Curley "further explained that they went to the north fork of Reno Creek, and crossed it, going to the hill, and turned westward along the ridge."[109] Some may agree, but a mile and one-quarter is too far to the east, not close enough to the river, though it ties in certainly with Red Bear's recollection of Custer turning to the right some 50 yards beyond the lone tepee. Besides, you can cross North Fork and still be within Varnum and Liddic's distance parameters (maps show the two creeks join a little more than one-half mile east of today's ford; less, from the 1876 river channel). Curley also contended Custer started out before either Cooke or McIlhargey reached him, his move being precipitated by Kanipe's report of the moving Indians. Gerard, at the Reno inquiry, thought there might have been two reasons why Custer veered off to the right: (1) when he heard the reports of the Indians coming out to meet Reno, he might have changed his plans; and, (2) Custer saw a large trail—larger than the one followed by Reno to Ford A—that swung around the eastern side of the knoll he had seen when riding with Reno (our portentous "Middle Knoll"). Trumpeter Martini reported seeing this same trail and knew it was a lodge trail, meaning women and children. *A large lodge-pole trail?* This is what Liddic had alluded to: a secondary village reported by Varnum when he was at the Crow's Nest.[110] (But did Varnum *see* it or just report what Gerard had seen? Or

neither?) Again, we never hear direct testimony from Varnum. (Lodge-pole trails led to easy river crossings and Custer knew this, so we cannot dismiss the claim arbitrarily, but it still leads to the question, what happened to this smaller camp? Besides, this whole area was where the village was camped several days earlier, so the existence of a smaller, secondary village is sheer conjecture.) The only reasonable explanation is the lodge-pole trail swung around the middle knoll in the flats and then proceeded into the Little Big Horn valley rather than up the bluffs toward Reno Hill—and was created before the 25th of June, or if there is validity in the existence of a small village, very early that same morning. It is this move that would have been seen from the Crow's Nest; however, we are not told where this secondary village was in relation to Reno's river crossing, only that it was seen in the valley. Failing this, it is merely more phantom stuff, for we never again hear of the trail or if this smaller village had gone up-country along the heights, an almost insane assumption; we never discover its ultimate destination, either in Indian testimony or in any commentary by the white participants. In essence then—similar to an eastern lone tepee—it simply did not exist.

Now the question on the table is, who were Kanipe's phantom 100? Could they have been from Wolf Tooth's Cheyenne band of about 50 warriors, or maybe the whole band itself? There were any number of Indian military societies guarding or "patrolling" the bluffs east of the river, but none fit the size-description of Wolf Tooth's band.[111] There is some historical evidence for a group of Indians that may have been as large as 50 riders, but—as we have seen already—in the Reno Creek valley, not on the bluffs leading to Reno Hill. As discussed earlier, when Custer, riding ahead of Reno and the rest of the command, reached the lone tepee, several of his scouts reported a number of Sioux riders set to run away. The confusion comes from the fact most writers accept Gerard's presence and primacy of his observations on the higher ground much farther east, but as we have seen here as well, Gerard's own comments cause a considerable ripple and a pretty solid case for a different location, much closer to the Little Big Horn. Wherever he was, Gerard's agreement with other trusted scouts could easily have imbued Custer with the impression the interpreter's observations were as valid as the scouts.' Furthermore, Custer's order to Reno followed immediately leaving us with the impression Gerard had a hand in this too.

Since Hare put a number on them, 40 to 50 is what we will go with (Private Davern, riding near Hare, estimated 20 or 30 or 40[112]). Regardless, even if these were the Indians who were seen thereafter on the heights east of the river, one must

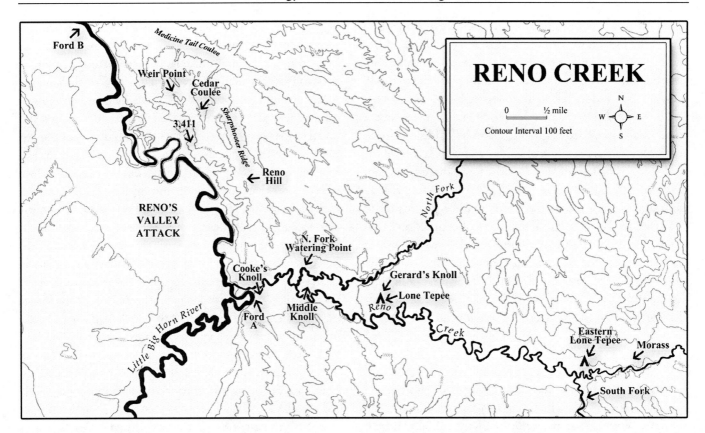

doubt Custer with five troops of cavalry would have chased after a small party that could have been dealt with some time in the future, especially in lieu of the big prize in the valley. This same reasoning is why Custer sent Reno to attack a village and tie down the men-folk, rather than chase and bring to battle a handful of Indians. It is clear the Gerard message—as opposed to the Kanipe sighting—is what caused the right turn and Custer's move up the slopes. Shortly after these Hare, Davern, Gerard, and Herendeen sightings, Custer ordered Reno into the valley while the Yates and Keogh commands would seemingly follow behind.[113] Sergeant Kanipe had nothing to do with it and was in all likelihood parroting the observations of Gerard, Hare, and the others.

Once apprised of the situation in the main valley and figuring Reno could handle matters, Custer veered sharply to the right, in all likelihood with the intention of somehow corralling or charging through the refugees in the lower valley

(rather than engaging in a wild goose chase on the ridges). This maneuver alone would dictate a more intense reconnaissance job, *ergo,* the look out over the edge of the bluffs to view Reno's fight and see what could be seen of the village; the foray to Medicine Tail Coulee ford; and the move farther north, above Last Stand Hill (the purported Ford D reconnaissance). The Indians' determination to provide cover and fight Reno's chargers was the least desirable of the alternatives for George Custer, and one can just imagine the invective greeting Cooke's report. That was the bad news. The good news was when he did see the village from the bluffs, it appeared the intrepid Custer had still caught his adversary by a modicum of surprise and the exodus appeared slow in developing, regardless of the hoopla in the valley. Unfortunately, for George Armstrong Custer and five companies of the Seventh Cavalry, the worst news was still to come.

9

THE LITTLE BIG HORN VALLEY

REFERENCES:
Timeline H—Custer/Reno Separation to Reno's Dismount; 1:05 p.m.–1:36 p.m.
Timeline J—The Valley Fight—Dismount to Retreat; 1:35 p.m.–2:21 p.m.

There is a modicum of evidence Custer spoke to Reno—momentarily—probably instructing him to send out advance riders with Lieutenant Hare to act as a small reconnaissance force. Custer had given Benteen similar instructions and was doing the same thing with several men from Yates' company. Indians had been seen nearby, the terrain was unfamiliar to the troops, and the possibility of an ambush was palpable. Custer was thinking, planning, and devising rapidly.

After receiving his orders Reno moved ahead, approached a small knoll, and swung to the left, re-crossing the narrow stream. He followed a dry, subsidiary creek bed, slowed somewhat to close his ranks as he approached the river, crossed at what we call Ford A, and spent a few brief moments regrouping his command, though there are differences in opinion regarding a stop, per se, depending upon where one was in the formation. This was understandable for Reno began switching from a column-of-fours to a column-of-twos to cross the river; troops slowed, bunching up as they reached the banks; horses plunged into the chilly water, some stopping briefly to gulp a precious mouthful or two, others crowding together, bumping, jostling; commands being shouted, "*Keep moving! No stopping!*"; horses climbing the opposite bank, slipping, falling back; some men dismounting quickly to re-cinch a loose girth or strap, then up again into the saddle; companies intermingling on the west bank as they slowed; then fresh orders for, "*No stopping, keep together, column-of-fours, move out!*" Swiftness, alacrity, haste always uppermost. Once across, they were in a timbered area filled with underbrush and Reno formed his command into a column-of-fours again and proceeded into the Little Big Horn valley. Other forces now began taking over, for the situation was changing rapidly, and messengers were dispatched even as the troops moved on, maintaining order, keeping formation, and increasing speed.

After crossing the river, Reno barely paused to gather his battalion and re-form—1:15 p.m.–1:22 p.m.: cross-to-move-out—*orders*: no stopping, no resting, no drinking water, swiftness paramount; Reno sending word back to Custer, twice: the Indians were not only *not* fleeing as expected, they were moving up the valley to confront his men; he had everything in front of him "and that they were strong."[1] Again, there is a tremendous element of consistency here, backed up by various personalities, both pro- and anti–Reno, civilian/professional, officer and enlisted man alike.

Captain Myles Moylan was a member of the so-called "Custer Clan" and very close to the general. Yet Moylan's testimony in 1879 buttressed Reno's contention about being supported and the fact there was little or no delay in moving into the Little Big Horn valley once Reno received his orders. Benny Hodgson told Moylan Reno's orders were to charge the Indians—they were supposed to be running—and Reno would be supported by Custer's command.[2] When asked a pointed question at the inquiry if a flank attack was considered "support," Moylan hedged a bit, replying it was, in the sense it would draw Indians away from Reno.[3] The business with Hodgson telling Moylan of the "support" is interesting however, because Hodgson was killed within the ensuing two hours and Moylan could have simply elided any reference to support without impugning himself in the eyes of the court. Moylan told the court Reno issued the command to trot, and then reached the river crossing, pausing only slightly to close up the battalion.[4] There is more uniformity here, especially considering the positioning of people within the moving column (Moylan's Company A was second in line behind French's M; First Lieutenant Donald McIntosh's G Company trailed).

Another example of consistent and reasonable testimony by someone who expressed little lost love for the major popped up when Edward Mathey alluded to a comment made by DeRudio about a year after the fight: "If we had not been commanded by a coward we would have been killed."[5] Again however, DeRudio stuck to the facts as he saw them—disguising his own fearfulness—mirroring Reno's testimony. There was no delay at the ford; Reno was the first man in the stream; and as soon as the command cleared the timber on the left bank of the river, Reno formed it in line and began his move toward the village.[6] Despite more peals of derision from the detractors and the uninformed, the anxious and edgy major moved on quickly.

Sergeant Ferdinand Culbertson testified Reno's command left Custer about three-quarters of a mile from the Little Big Horn, near a tepee, and proceeded toward the river at a fast trot. Company M trooper, James Wilber, claimed he was one of the advance scouts assigned to Sergeant White and told to follow Lieutenant Hare. "When John Ryan and 10 men forded [the] river, Cooke sat on [the] bank on his horse. 'We were galloping fast, and just as we got to the river Cooke called out: "For God's sake men, don't run those horses like that; you will need them in a few minutes."'"[7] Culbertson said there was a short, five to eight minute delay in crossing, essentially to close up the column.[8] As the battalion was crossing, Cooke told the men "to close up, that there was hot work ahead of them."[9] French, a few yards behind Reno, directed Sergeant Miles O'Harra[10] to make sure the sets of fours closed up as they hit the river. O'Harra stood in the water to ensure no one stopped, but Private William Ephraim Morris pretended not to hear and let his horse gulp a few precious mouthfuls as O'Harra yelled at him from behind.[11] Many years later, Morris stated categorically "the outfit" did not stop to water the horses,[12] yet we see Morris did. He was probably not the only one.

More evidence of the rapidity of Reno's move came from Doc Porter who thought some men might be galloping as the command followed a heavy trail and then crossed the river. Another *"some,"* stopped and watered their horses—Porter, riding with Reno at the head of the column, being one—as the command passed through. The doctor judged it took 10–15 minutes to reach the ford after Reno received his order (remember Hare's 20 or 25 minutes?) and pulled ahead of Custer,[13] and another five or 10 minutes to cross the ford and form up.[14] The testimonies are consistent.

George Herendeen also supported Reno's version of events to this point. In a statement made in Bozeman, Montana Territory, on January 4, 1878, and published in the *New York Herald,* January 22, 1878, Herendeen claimed Reno started for the river at a gallop. Herendeen's horse fell, but he managed to catch Reno at the ford. As they were crossing the Little Big Horn, he heard some of the Crows yelling the Sioux

were coming. Herendeen spoke the language, understood what they were saying, and told Reno as much. This was a similar report to what Gerard was now telling Cooke—1:16 p.m. Reno waited a few moments until his battalion closed up, then finished crossing and "formed in line of battle on the prairie, just outside some timber [1:21–1:22 p.m.]. The formation was made without halting, and the line kept on moving, first at a trot and then at a gallop."[15] Herendeen said nothing about watering horses or re-cinching saddles, only that the battle formation was made without stopping (yet another indication of the importance of speed and the emphasis passed down from the top, from George Custer).

While Reno followed one of the Indian trails to the ford, the going was not all that easy. In an interview with Walter Camp, some time in October 1909, former private Thomas F. O'Neill of the trailing G Company, said the trail split, moving around a small rise on which some of the Rees were sitting (our Middle Knoll). O'Neill's company went to the left of this terrain feature, down to the river through a small ravine. The other side was strewn with dead logs and timber. It took some time—the definition of "some time" not included—to get through to the valley beyond—"the valley" referring to the dry creek beyond Middle Knoll.[16]

First Sergeant John Ryan of Company M agreed. While some of what Ryan eventually made public came many years after the battle, he has always been considered one of the more reliable sources for information, especially among the enlisted personnel who told their stories. In an article appearing in the Hardin, Montana, *Tribune,* on June 22, 1923, Ryan said as they moved down "through a small valley"—Reno Creek—they saw a few abandoned Indian lodges with the fronts tied up. When the troops reached this point, they could see down the valley and some men saw objects ahead. They were not sure if these objects were Indians or buffaloes. He went on to say this was when Reno received the order to charge the village, though Ryan did not hear the actual order being given.[17] As the troops moved into the river, they encountered "a very strong current, and there was quicksand about three feet deep." After crossing, they made a short halt, dismounted to tighten their saddle girths (again, this is being done by the *lead* company; the trailers did not have that luxury), and then re-mounted.[18]

Finally, there was Charlie Varnum. During the move down Reno Creek, Varnum had been riding ahead of the two commands and to the columns' left, eventually winding up all alone with his orderly, Private Elijah Strode, along the hills above the creek valley. As this valley widened into the flats, he rode down with Strode—his Ree scouts had deserted him along the way—and re-joined the regiment, reporting to

Custer. Varnum moved to go with Reno—after cussing out the Rees—to do whatever scouting remained. Even this close to the Little Big Horn, however, they could not see the village (certainly not from the lower ground), high protruding bluffs, timber, and the bends in the river masking most of the encampment. After leaving Custer, the head of Reno's column soon crossed back to the south side of Reno Creek. Varnum was now at the middle of Reno's column, but was forced off the trail by the speed of the passing troops, finally rejoining the command as some of the men were in the water.[19] By the time Varnum was across the river, one of Reno's companies was already on the west bank. Reno himself was probably across 10–15 minutes after separating from Custer and the entire three-company battalion in a full 15 minutes.[20] Despite the fact Varnum thought there might have been some delay in crossing the river—"in a column of troops getting across there is necessarily some delay, they can't keep closed up in the water"[21]—he did not see anyone stop to water his horse, the column moving too rapidly.[22] Reno reformed his troops without dilly-dallying and began his march downriver—1:22 p.m. He began his move with two companies on line and one in the rear as a reserve, but that plan lasted the whole of some 30 seconds once the major saw what was in front of him.

A column-of-twos was the usual order for marching through rough country; however, while moving down his namesake valley, Reno employed a column-of-fours, switched into a column-of-twos to ford the river, then re-formed his command in a column-of-fours while moving through the timber. Once beyond the timber and brush area, companies A and M were swung left-front into line while moving, Moylan estimating they had gone about one-third of a mile before Reno ordered this formation.[23] At first, Reno moved them to a trot, then a gallop. As the speed increased, Hodgson ordered McIntosh's G to the extreme left, forming as G-A-M, left-to-right.[24]

Varnum and his scouts swung still farther left, but got ahead of and remained well out front and on the far left of the line. Ryan confirmed the M Company position in his Hardin *Tribune* story by telling us between the company's right and the river, there were a lot of bullberry bushes and undergrowth, and Captain French told him to take 10 men and form a skirmish line to guard against Indians in this brush. In all likelihood, Ryan cut out two sets-of-fours and a sergeant for each one and rode the eastern perimeter of the advance, or else he used the same troops he employed when Sergeant White followed Lieutenant Hare to the crossing ford. They moved like that for about one and one-half to two miles until reaching a heavy growth of timber.[25] Liddic agreed with Ryan's depiction of this little scout, though few others

have ever alluded to it.[26] The incident was given additional credence by Herendeen's comments that they could see a large body of Indians ahead, apparently waiting for them, and there were Indians in the timber along the river setting fire to some of the undergrowth.[27]

So, moving down the valley toward the village, we have the scouts ahead and on the far left covering an open flank; the battalion formed as G-A-M, left-to-right; French's M closest to the river, with a detachment numbering from 10–15 men riding along the timbered banks protecting the command's right flank. Solid military tactics, and Reno's sending of French's skirmishers along the river mirrored Custer's penchant for sending out advance troops to reconnoiter in front of the main force. In fact, nothing Reno has done so far warrants even a modicum of criticism. Quite the contrary: his actions are those of a highly competent, able, and confident officer, attuned to the necessity for speed, security, support, and discipline. Based on this and what we know happened less than an hour later, it is not unreasonable to believe Reno's claim he expected Custer to support him from behind, the ensuing trepidation a result of dubiety and the caprice of his commander. The onus of informing his subordinate now falls directly on Custer's shoulders.

The advance down the valley was rapid—10 miles per hour and faster—maybe as much as 12 miles per hour in short, straighter stretches. Gerard said it took only 10 minutes from the time Reno finished crossing the river to the time he dismounted and formed his skirmish line. That is rapid, indeed, for the distance measures variously between 2¼ and 2¾ miles and to cover that distance in 10 minutes would mean the men moved at about 15 miles per hour, a little too fast, especially since Gerard also claimed they did not follow a straight line, but skirted the timber along the meandering stream.[28] DeRudio, too, said Reno moved them to a gallop and the going was not that easy, the valley sandy and full of sagebrush.[29] Varnum agreed with Gerard, stating at the Reno inquiry the troops moved down the valley following the general course of the river and not in a straight line but merely a direct course.[30]

Accurate accounting for distances and times began failing some of the participants about now, adrenaline taking the place of calculated observation. Moylan, for example, said the distance from the crossing to where Reno dismounted was one and one-half miles and they covered it at a gallop in about five minutes, or 10 minutes, or 10 or 15 minutes: "I don't know the exact time."[31] (*We* do; see *Timeline H.*) Dr. Porter was a little more even-keeled, figuring it took between 15–20 minutes—eight to 11 miles per hour—to advance down the valley.[32] Whatever speed it was, Reno never considered the movement a "charge" in the textbook sense,[33] but by the time the third company had moved into line, they were moving at a gallop.[34] DeRudio was equally obfuscatory. Because no trumpet calls were heard[35] and no command to charge was ever given,[36] some considered the movement less than a charge. Nitpicking aside, they hustled down the valley.

It should be noted here, not everyone agreed regarding the alacrity Reno might have shown in this move. Many years after the controversy had settled into a dull roar, the K Company commander, Ed Godfrey, wrote,

> Frankly, I do not believe Custer's command would have been rescued under Reno's leadership. At no time during the battle was his conduct such as to inspire confidence. His faltering advances down the valley, his halting, his falling back to the defensive position in the woods in the old river bed before his command had suffered a single casualty in the ranks; his disorganized, panic retreat to the bluffs with practically no resistance, his conduct up to and during the siege, and until the arrival of General Terry was not such as to inspire confidence or even respect, except for his authority.[37]

In Reno's defense, Godfrey was not present in the valley and while he never seemed to care much for Reno—even then—Godfrey seemed increasingly bitter about him over the ensuing years. The evidence tells us, however, Godfrey was mistaken about "faltering advances down the valley."

Doc Porter became a little less precise in some of his other observations. As speed increased and distance decreased, senses became keener; awareness heightened; immediacy sensitized. Men focused on Indians and obstacles. Dust, dust and smoke; the Indians were ahead, throwing up a screen of dust in front of their village and that was what the men of Marcus Reno's command were heading for. Men flustered; Porter was asked about the dust.

Q: "Was there much dust?"
A: "Some."
Q: "Much or little?"
A: "Quite a good deal."
Q: "Was it not thick?"
A: "Well, yes, so thick at first we could hardly tell what was moving."[38]

Troops in the valley, beginning to move at some speed. Indians and ponies—unknown numbers—retreating in the distance; dust beginning to rise. Soldiers anxious, but confident and joking. Alarms being raised in the village.

One Feather, a Ree scout, said when they began to close on the village, "we saw dust rising high in the middle of the village and the Sioux started toward us."[39]

Sergeant Culbertson (A Company): there was "a very large cloud of dust" in front of the Indian village as the troops moved down the valley.[40] He could see 100–150 Indians—sometimes more—riding back and forth in front of the dust cloud.[41]

Lieutenant DeRudio (A): there was an immense dust cloud in front, and they "could see the shadows of some Indians in that dust." Indians were running around. When Reno halted, the Indians "seemed to be standing, waiting for the command to come up."[42]

Captain Moylan (A): "An immense cloud of dust was seen down the valley."[43] Occasionally they could see figures moving around in openings in the dust. As the command advanced, the dust seemed to recede and numerous mounted Indians could be seen coming out of the dust cloud. The Indians began firing on the troops before the soldiers dismounted.

What did Reno really see as he moved down the valley? We will put it in perspective, based on testimony and comments made by the participants.

What is known so far? Well, we have the battalion line-up. Out front about 50 yards, continuously working their way to the far left of the advancing line are lieutenants Varnum and Hare,[44] their orderlies—privates Elijah Strode and Elihu Clear[45]—along with the scouts, many of whom would run off shortly to look for Sioux ponies. According to Varnum, Nick Wallace and his orderly, Private John Hackett, were with them as well: "We advanced rapidly down the valley, the Indians retiring before us for about a mile, Wallace, Hare and myself riding together."[46] In that same group rode Private Edward Davern, Reno's orderly.[47]

About 40 paces in front of the main line of advancing troops and a little to the right of center was Reno.[48] DeRudio saw him there and Reno was constantly checking the order within his command.[49] Doc Porter was riding just to the major's left, Benny Hodgson on his right.[50] Behind these advance groups, the scout George Herendeen rode on the line with, but about 100 yards to the left of the main body of troops. We have G Company on the left of the line; A in the middle; and M closest to the river, a number of men—we are not quite certain of the exact number, 10, but possibly as many as 15—hugging the brush and timber along the river. Among the men mentioned in different accounts are First Sergeant Ryan and privates James Wilber, Roman Rutten, William E. Morris, and John H. Meier. Morris is mentioned both by himself[51] and by Ryan, while Rutten is mentioned by Wilber.[52] Rutten, however, never claimed this assignment, and instead told Walter Camp,

Approaching Ford A, Rutten's horse, as soon as he smelled Indians, began to act up badly and he could not control him. The only thing he could do was to continually circle him around the three troops. The horse kept this up after passing Ford A and when [he] got down near the skirmish line, the horse lunged ahead of the command and took him considerably nearer the Indians. He therefore circled him around to the right, and came back through the timber and joined [the] command.[53]

We can exclude Rutten therefore, and chalk up the error to Wilber's faulty memory. By taking the narratives of Ryan, White, Morris, and Wilber and shaking them well enough for everything to fall out, we come up with the likelihood of three sets-of-fours consisting of Corporal Scollin and privates Morris, Wilber, Neely, Newell, Klotzbucher, Meier, Thorpe, Galenne, Braun, Gordon, and Turley. We add to that three other NCOs—Ryan, along with White and O'Harra—and we have a reasonable approximation of these seldom-mentioned, but very important skirmishers—15 men in all.

By now, Reno has moved his command to a controlled gallop. Several hundred yards behind, trying to catch up, rode Fred Gerard and Custer's favorite white scout, Charlie Reynolds.[54]

The action described now is from left-to-right. In front of the main line of troops...

Lieutenant Charles Varnum saw "quite a large body of Indians" out front, running away and then running to and fro, back and forth across the valley, trying to raise as much dust as possible. It was impossible to tell how many there were.[55] Suddenly, the Indians stopped and turned. Varnum wondered why, so he looked behind and saw the battalion moving from a column to a line. He figured the Indians wanted to halt and then turn back on the command.[56] When the line began to surge forward, the Indians headed for the camp again, always keeping their distance. The more left and down the valley Varnum moved, the more tepees he saw. The Indians let them come, but never uncovered the village very much.[57] Some shots had been fired before the command was deployed, especially between the scouts and the Indians. He knew Hare fired a few.[58]

Lieutenant Luke Hare was a little in front of the line and 200 yards toward the foothills.[59] As the command continued to move down the valley, the Indians were moving around and stirring up a lot of dust.[60]

Lieutenant Nick Wallace saw lots of dust, but as they moved forward, they could see Indians coming at them.[61] They had moved down the valley about one and one-half to one and three-quarter miles when the first shots came from the Indians.[62]

Private Edward Davern (F) had seen some 20, 30, or 40 Indians a short distance before he reached Ford A.[63] They were upstream from where the skirmish line shortly deployed and on the left side of the valley toward the foothills.[64] Then he saw them down in the bottoms, appearing to be riding in circles, the Indian signal for danger.[65] A mounted skirmish line was thrown out about 200 yards after crossing the river[66] and Davern moved up to ride with Lieutenant Hare about 200 yards in front of the line. The command moved part way at a gallop and Davern saw Indians about 200 yards to the left.[67]

Little Sioux, an Arikara scout, was up ahead of Reno looking for Sioux ponies with several other scouts including One Feather, Strikes Two, Red Star, Boy Chief, and the Dakota scout, Whole Buffalo.[68]

Strikes Two, another Ree, forded the Little Big Horn and overtook a bunch of horses herded by two young Sioux. The Ree scouts followed and soon saw the village. Other Sioux came to help the two herders.[69]

Boy Chief, a scout riding with several others, said there was little firing at this time and the Indian village was just beginning to stir.[70]

So, from the far left of the battalion, there was plenty of dust and a number of Indians moving back and forth. No report yet on the village size. Little or no firing, at least by the troopers. The scouts appear active, several of them beginning to do exactly what they had been instructed to do: run off and steal Sioux ponies.[71]

On, we ride...

Dr. Henry Porter saw only a few Indians, but a great many ponies. The Indians appeared to be driving the horses.[72]

Major Marcus Reno saw 40 or 50 Indians to his front. He described them as decoys. He saw no Indians driving ponies. "Every pony I saw had an Indian on him."[73] There were times Reno could not see the village.[74]

From this it appears the best view of what was happening lower down the valley was from the left side of the command. If Reno could not see the village at times, the implication was at other times he could see some of it. This is indicative of a route following the course of a meandering river. It also points out Reno was not as far to the left as the scouts. He was in the right-center of his advancing line.

We go left again, this time to the main line of men. The situation remains the same...

George Herendeen could see a large body of Indians ahead, apparently waiting for them. There were Indians in the timber along the river and they set fire to the brush. The troops fired on them, but no shots were returned.[75] Out front, Herendeen saw the Indians sitting still on their horses until the troops got nearer.[76]

Private Thomas F. O'Neill (G) spotted Custer's command on the bluffs south of where Reno later fortified. Custer was moving at a trot. By now, Reno's command was about half way down the valley.[77]

Private Henry Petring (G) saw Custer up on the bluffs waving his hat. Other men as well, said Custer was waving his hat.[78]

Captain Moylan (in the center of the line) saw only the Indians turn back on Reno when he was within 500–600 yards of the point of timber where the command halted.[79]

Sergeant Culbertson (A) saw Indians "coming in on our left and front. Most of them would circle off to our left. There were a few shots fired."[80] This was about a half-mile before the skirmish line.

Private William O. Taylor (A) "could distinguish mounted men riding in every direction, some in circles, others passing back and forth."[81] The Indians were gathering their ponies and signaling. Suddenly, the troops spotted puffs of smoke and heard the zing of bullets. Men began to cheer, but Reno yelled for quiet. The river followed a torturous route and its banks were thick with underbrush so the village was completely obscured.[82]

Private John Sivertsen (M) contradicted Taylor's memories of Reno querulousness. Sivertsen remembered as the troops lined up to charge down the valley, they began whooping it up, yelling, *"Hi—yah! Hi—yah!"* Rather than scold them, Reno encouraged them, *"That's right boys!"*[83]

First Sergeant John Ryan (M, on the right of the line, closer to the river than the main body of the company) heard only one shot fired by the time he reached the timber where the command later took shelter. He thought Varnum or one of his scouts on the far left had fired it.[84]

Private William E. Morris (M) felt, "[w]hen the three troops had crossed the river, there were plenty of Indians in view, but they were trekking down the bottom and riding as fast as they could. Command was given, '...*left into line, gallop! Forward guide right!*'"[85] There was a lot of crowding of horses and some became unmanageable.[86] (Remember Roman Rutten?)

From the above, it is obvious most of the activity is being seen on the left side of the command, timber farther ahead obscuring much of the frontal view of the men on the right and closer to the river, but even the G Company troopers were paying more attention to what was happening on the bluffs across the Little Big Horn than to the dust "storm" and

the trouble waiting ahead. Higher-ranking men in the center of the line spoke of the dust and of seeing some Indians, but the size of the opposition was not as clear to them as to the men farther to the left. With only scattered shots—hardly even noticeable—there seemed little thought of danger and the remarks of privates Taylor and Sivertsen about men cheering seem to bear this out. (The other side would agree.) Taylor's comment about the river following a torturous route also indicates the command followed its general course rather than riding down the valley in a straight line.

Crow King, a Hunkpapa Sioux and headman leading about 80 warriors, thought the soldiers began firing only when they were some 400 yards from the village. Furthermore, the Indians delayed, pulling back to give the women and children a chance to get away. Other Indians got their horses and when there were enough, they would attack Reno's command.[87]

Low Dog, a tall, regal-looking 29-year-old Oglala chief, said, "The Indians held their ground to give the women and children time to get out of the way. By this time the herders were driving in the horses."[88]

Sitting Bull, the great Hunkpapa medicine man, said, "Oh, we fell back, but it was not what warriors call a retreat; it was to gain time."[89]

He Dog, a 36-year-old Oglala chief, said as Reno approached, the Hunkpapa went out, mostly on foot. He Dog was in the hills trying to get his horse. Many others were there, as well.[90]

Some who were lagging behind the advancing line of bluecoats were trying to catch up...

Fred Gerard reported nothing as he went down the valley; he was too far behind the troops and they masked his sight lines.

So far, we have covered most of the approximately two and one-half miles down the valley to the dismount area and little if anything more needs to be reported. At this point, it is a solid military operation, carried out exactly as any commander would wish. It becomes dicier from here. Reno began his move at 1:22 p.m.; it is now 1:35.

Reno halts his battalion, primarily because he is nearing a timber field jutting too far into the prairie and he is approaching the dust and smoke, no longer able to make out what is in front of him—it is 1:35 p.m. Fortuitously—or ominously—he sees Indians coming from a creek bed—described by Lieutenant Wallace as a ravine a few hundred yards in front of the river's loop—directly in his shifting line of advance, an advance now facing more northwest than north because of the way the river flowed and the course the command was following.

Major Reno, as they got farther down the valley, began seeing Indians emerging from a ravine out front, some 800–900 yards away.[91] "It was afterward developed that if I had gone 200 or 300 yards further I should have thrown my command into a ditch 10 yards wide and three or four feet deep."[92] He ordered the battalion to dismount. There were many Indians to Reno's front, but he also saw small parties of warriors moving around to the left.[93] Reno said he saw 500–600 Indians, but he also had an idea of how many there could be from what he saw along the trails.[94] He had his officers form a skirmish line and then moved toward Moylan whose company was in the middle. They were there for 15 or 20 minutes, "when word came to me from out of the timber that the Indians were turning our right."[95] Reno left Hodgson on the line with instructions to let him know what was going on there, and Reno took Company G "to the banks of the river."[96]

There seems to be enough testimony about the distance from Reno's crossing point to where he dismounted being covered in 15–20 minutes, an overall speed—considering less than ideal conditions—of eight to 10 miles an hour, not bad and certainly not slow. In fact, if one considers the twists and turns of the river's course, the distance would have been extended, thereby increasing the speed to as much as 12 miles per hour. Reno claimed to have dismounted because he spotted a ravine or coulee disgorging Indians and a quick look at a map confirms the existence of just such an obstacle. In all likelihood, it was the Otter Creek bed—sometimes referred to as Kuhlman's Ravine—a terrain depression that juts out from the river in a *southerly*—then southwesterly—direction, intermittently flooding in extreme conditions. Time and erosion have taken their toll, but the feature is still visible on topographical maps and in some places it reaches a width of 15–40 yards (also fitting Reno's depiction), a gradual, tapering hollow in the prairie's foothills. While distance descriptions of this feature seem to have it beyond the farthest point of advance for the skirmish line, that is highly unlikely—actually, ridiculous—because of the way the Indians left it (from the direction of the village it was a perfect ingress into the path of the on-coming soldiers) and the initial deployment of the line and its advance, both well past the dismount point. Plus, the various artifact fields indicate there were a number of troops—obviously the skirmish line itself—into and beyond it.[97] It appears, as well, these Indians did not plan to be in that coulee, but were coming from the village, masked by the dust, and through the depression. From the soldiers' per-

spective it may have looked as though they had been in the ravine and from the angle it seems the Indians were intent upon pinning Reno's command with its back to the river.

Captain Tom French had no idea why Reno halted and dismounted when he did.[98] (Remember, French moved down the valley on the right side of the line and, as we shall see, was unaware of the position of the ravine concealing Indians.)

As Reno ordered the halt and dismount, he told his officers to form a skirmish line (*Timeline J*). At the same time, he told French to keep the flankers moving into the timber to clear it, as he wanted to sequester his horses there. French then told Ryan, who in turn instructed his sergeants—White and O'Harra—to continue on and clear the woods—1:35 p.m. Once dismounted, in order to face the threat, French swings M Company across the command's rear, from the right of the line to the left, and as he moves into the prairie is now facing west, toward the foothills—1:36 p.m.—and all of it being done in some haste. As Reno organizes the right side of the line—Company A doing much the same as M, but moving between G and M—Benny Hodgson handles the left. Lieutenant McIntosh and Captain Moylan order their horses into the timber—or possibly Reno tells them to do so, we do not know really—but Hodgson and French do no such thing with M Company's horses, both of them recognizing the need for the left flank to maintain its mobility. The excitement and the sense of danger cause several of the troopers' horses to bolt, Rutten's and Private George E. Smith's two of them. (There may have been others, but narratives are confusing and contradictory and bodies found after the battle belie memories. Rutten was lucky; he managed to survive the scare. Smith's head was found on a pole in the village making him considerably less fortunate.)

The skirmish line formed, basically facing west, and as it advanced A Company swung clockwise on G's left, while G pivoted its right on the fulcrum of the timber, both units beginning to move in a more northerly direction. A gap between M and A begins to open as M Company advances straight, more to the west than north—1:40 p.m.

First Sergeant Ryan, riding with his flankers along the timbered banks of the river, said, "When we got to the timber, we rode down an embankment into the timber and dismounted. This was where the channel of the river had changed and was probably 20 feet lower than the level of the prairie."[99] As Ryan's flankers continued on into the woods—in all likelihood, these men remaining mounted—the majority of M Company came up onto the prairie to form part of the skirmish line, some men kneeling, others lying down as they moved along. Ryan re-joined his company sending Sergeant White and a small contingent of men deeper into the

Otter Creek—or its remnants—today. This is the ravine that stopped Reno's mounted advance down the valley. He formed his skirmish line off the photograph to the left.

timber. (As we have already pointed out, it appears the flankers split, and some may have actually gotten into the village.) The company moved through a prairie dog "town."[100] Private James Farley (also known as Turley) could not control his horse and it headed straight for the Indian camp; no one ever saw him alive again. (We will see a different twist on the Farley/Turley saga shortly.) The Indians charged, about 500 coming from the direction of their village.[101] The troops fired volleys into them, hitting several, as Lieutenant Hodgson trooped "the line encouraging the men to keep cool and fire low."[102] When the Indians failed to cut through the troops' skirmish line, they began moving, single file, toward the left of the line. Many rode on the other side of their horses.[103]

The M Company flankers now become a blur simply because they tend to disappear from narratives, yet it is quite possible some of these men advanced farther than anyone and may have even gotten into the village. It appears several of the original group of 10–15 remained together, but either there were "defectors" or Ryan sent only a portion into the

woods. Unfortunately, his memoirs compressed a lot of time and omitted considerable detail. From the looks of it, Ryan himself did not accompany the squad through the timber, but followed the majority of M Company into the prairie and out onto the line. Private Wilber specifically mentioned Ryan's name to Walter Camp, but Ryan makes no reference of it in his memoirs, or in two newspaper articles—the Hardin, Montana, *Tribune,* June 22, 1923; and the Billings, Montana, *Gazette,* June 25, 1923—and according to the Custer historian, Richard Hardorff, Ryan told Camp he accompanied the troops onto the skirmish line and not into the timber.

According to Private William Morris,

Major Reno directed Captain French to send 10 men from the right of his troop to skirmish the woods before directing the number 4's to proceed with the led horses to cover. I was one of the 10 men so detailed. First Sgt. Ryan, in charge of the detail, gave the command—*Double time!* when we were close to the wood, and then—*As skirmishers, march!* We entered the woods, skirmished them to the river, saw no Indians in the woods and immediately returned. When First Sgt. Ryan signaled Major Reno *All right, no Indians in the woods!*, number 4's were then directed to take the horses into the woods, and we rejoined the troop.... M Troop was deployed facing the bench land.... Command was given by Captain French to fire at will, and we proceeded forward toward the bench land.[104]

Not everyone agreed all the command's horses were brought into the timbered area, however, and as the line pivoted, throwing M Company on the left, it appears French kept his horses with his men. Sergeant White's version differed from Morris', White claiming Ryan split the outriders. As the command's right flank rested "in rear of a belt of timber," he claimed 15 men "were at once directed to deploy to the right as mounted skirmishers and to move through the timber. The first sergeant of Co. M directed me to go one way and one of the drunken officers another."[105]

There are inaccuracies in both these accounts. Morris—a somewhat questionable source for veracity despite eventually becoming a New York City judge—wrote the so-called Robert Bruce letters some 50-plus years after the battle and was wrong about leaving the horses in the woods; A and G companies did, M did not, and there are several accounts contradicting him. Sergeant White combined events in his comment about "drunken officers," probably an allusion to reports of Reno being drunk. Tom French was the only M Company officer in the valley fight, the only unit Ryan would have authority in, and while more than one man had a pop or two during this harrowing day, no one was ever proven to be inebriated, Reno included.

Despite the discrepancies, it appears some troopers managed to infiltrate the upper reaches of the Hunkpapa camp, picking their way through the timber on the buffalo and pony trails, heading for the village while trying to clear the woods—1:40 p.m. The "Garryowen Loop," a series of large bends in the river, did not extend very far into the prairie in 1876, and could be bypassed easily by mounted flankers, especially since the loop was dry. This is important to remember because it affects the movement of the right side of the skirmish line and the tactics employed by the Indians. If that "loop" were active, the river would have jutted far out into the prairie changing the entire scope of what actually occurred. By recognizing the loop was dry we can make sense more easily of the testimonies and interviews of the participants. "In the 1930s, Fred Dustin believed that the river's Garryowen Loop had been dry in 1876, only to be naturally refilled with water between 1876 and 1891."[106] Dustin was discredited because maps showed an active loop in 1877, 1878, and 1883,[107] however, an 1877 map cannot prove an 1876 loop active or inactive, and the Little Big Horn River has so many channels emp-

tying and refilling after each hard season, it is impossible to predict its course from one year to the next. (Again, we will see more of this shortly.)

Lieutenant Varnum estimated by the time the command halted, it had covered approximately two miles. He felt 15–20 minutes had elapsed (six- to eight-mph) from the time the crossing at Ford A was complete to the halt and deployment as skirmishers.[108] When the troops dismounted he and Hare rode "in toward the line." The Indian scouts had disappeared and Varnum reported to Moylan—1:37 p.m.[109]

> I saw about the time Major Reno's command dismounted ... as I joined it from the left and front, looking on the bluffs across the river to our right I saw the Gray Horse Company ... moving down along those bluffs.... It was back from the actual edge of the bluffs. The head and the rear of the column were both behind the edge of the bluffs in a sort of hollow and I just happened to catch sight of about the whole of the Gray Horse Company.... I think they were a little farther down than where we struck the bluffs.[110]

Varnum thought the Custer command might be moving at a trot (Custer had a very fast-walking horse and the men usually had to trot to keep up with him[111]), and this would fit with a slowdown as Custer's command approached the head of a coulee and the flatter terrain began to narrow. He described the location where he saw the Gray Horse Troop—1:42 p.m.—as being about one-quarter mile downstream from Reno's final position on the hill,[112] again, fitting with the terrain description. On the prairie, the nearest tepees were about 800 yards from the forming skirmish line and were located in a bend of the river. The bulk of the village was below that. "There must have been quite a solid lot of tepees in that bend."[113] Varnum spotted a large force of Indians to his front and another large force moving around the troops' left flank. The heaviest dust was 800–1,000 yards in front.[114] The land was open prairie, though Varnum learned afterward there were ravines in front of the line.[115]

Lieutenant Hare saw the command stop near the timber, dismounting. It took them 10–15 minutes to go from Ford A to the edge of this timber.[116] Reno began setting up a skirmish line and as Hare looked back downstream he saw only about 50 Indians riding up and down, firing.[117] When the skirmish line was set up, suddenly 400–500 Indians moved out of a coulee in front of the command, firing as they came out.[118] "In [the] valley fight there was a coulee 300–400 yards in advance of the skirmish line (this has all been cut away by erosion of the river) and the Indians were pouring out of it as if concealed there and waiting for the soldiers."[119] He watched the Indians beginning to move to the left and rear.[120] Hare realized if Reno had continued on, "I don't think he would have got a man through." Dismounting when he did was the only thing that saved the command.[121] From here, Hare could see the tops of tepees at the upper end of the village. He thought maybe 400 or 500 tepees were in this area.[122] As he continued assessing the situation, Hare saw the Indians riding "up and back again, back and forth," only 200–300 yards away.[123]

Lieutenant Wallace said when they neared the timber, the command halted and formed into a skirmish line; horses were brought into the timber.[124] "The first I saw of the village was after we were dismounted and were forming the skirmish line…. [T]here was some timber between us and the village."[125] He could see a ravine a few hundred yards in front of an old loop in the river when they halted and Indians were coming out of this ravine.[126] The Indians were thick in front of it,[127] maybe 200–300 when they halted—"something over 200"—numbers constantly increasing until they left the bottoms.[128] Reno halted the command about 150 yards from the river. They then, "advanced to where the creek made a quick bend and the right wing was resting on top of the cut bank with the creek below. The village was across the bend, 75 or 100 yards to the first tepee, but on the same side of the stream we were."[129] The timber anchored the skirmish line's right.[130] The men swung into the open prairie and the line took up a few hundred yards,[131] setting an interval of five yards between each man. Wallace thought 70 or 75 men formed the line.[132]

Private Davern saw Indians moving around to the left, not as a group, but singly when the command halted to form the skirmish line.[133] After the troops halted, Davern came back and saw Major Reno near the woods, firing at Indians. (At the 1879 inquiry, Davern couched this observation with the comment the line had withdrawn to the woods, but he had to be referring to G Company's partial move into the timber.) The Indians were now some 700–800 yards away, but he could not tell how many warriors there were because of the dust. The troops began firing very quickly.[134]

Dr. Porter did not remember any firing until the men were dismounting and at this time he thought the Indians were between 800–900 yards away as the troops began deploying into their skirmish line.[135] The Indians were riding around and around, coming closer, and the firing became more intense. When the line was formed there may have been 50 Indians out front and now about 75–100 fighting the troops. He saw "a good many down the river," but he could not judge the number.[136] As the command dismounted, Porter went looking for his orderly. He moved behind the skirmish line, a little way from the timber and watched as some horses were led into the woods. He met Gerard and a couple of others, stayed with them for a minute or two—paying attention to the fight in front—then rode into the timber, staying there until the retreat.[137]

By the time Reno reached the point where he dismounted, the battalion configuration had changed and the line was formed differently than the march downstream. Theodore Goldin of Company G—one of the more colorful dissemblers connected with the battle and the post–1876 shenanigans—claimed, "In forming his line, Reno brought 'A' Troop on his right, 'M' Troop in the center and 'G' Troop on the left … the Indian scouts on the extreme left."[138] Like so much of Goldin's fantasies, this was never the case.

Fred Dustin, who corresponded with Goldin, said when Reno deployed the skirmish line, French (M) was on the left, Moylan (A) in the center, and "Tosh" McIntosh's G was on the right, suggesting some sort of a "wheel" or "pivot" maneuver as Reno approached the area. (Dustin was correct.) In an "interview" with Walter Camp—probably done by written correspondence between 1910 and 1914—the former G Company private, Henry Petring, verified G's position as being on the right of the line when a detachment of the company was sent into the timber to guard the horses against infiltrating Indians.[139] In a similar "interview" with Camp, former corporal Stanislaus Roy of Company A agreed: Company G on the right, then A in the middle, and M on the left.[140] Roy also agreed with the G-A-M, left-to-right move down the valley,[141] as did Varnum. As Reno ordered his command to dismount, the skirmish line formed with M on the left, A in the center, and G's right anchored on the timber's edge.[142]

As the lines began to advance—A Company swinging clockwise into the prairie, the gap between M and A widening—Reno got word Indians were beginning to infiltrate the woods. He was quick to recognize the threat to his right flank—not to mention the threat to the horses being moved there—and he ordered a number of G Company men off the line, leading them into the woods to confront the threat—1:47 p.m. (In all likelihood, this threat was coming not from Indians from the main village—it was still a little early in the battle for mass infiltration by foot from that area—but from a small, separate encampment located across the river, Indians who had come out of the Spotted Tail Agency in northwestern Nebraska.) At the same time, Reno instructed Benny Hodgson to keep him posted as to what was happening on the prairie.

We now have Adjutant Hodgson controlling events on the prairie and M Company advancing westward—1:40 p.m.—clearing the Otter Creek bed, their horses being held behind them. Indians are whooping it up, but pose no serious threat to the troops north or west—yet. Most Indians are on foot, some shooting sporadically from the prone, others scrambling toward the foothills to get their mounts. The soldiers on the skirmish lines, while advancing, are doing very much the same thing: kneeling, firing, reloading; laying down, firing, reloading; getting up, moving, firing, reloading.

As M Company moves west, it begins to swing clockwise toward the north, the gap between M and A widening. Sergeant Culbertson of A Company, not seeing anyone from M because of the dust and smoke and the fact M is more to his left and rear thereby increasing the gap between the companies, believes he is now the left flank of the skirmish line.[143]

In a November 29, 1908, letter to Walter Camp, John Ryan wrote, "You must recollect that Reno had two different lines of skirmishers."[144] While it is uncertain what Ryan was alluding to—the break in the line or two separate positions of the same line (from the wording and the context, it seems improbable he was talking about separate positions and in all likelihood was referring to distinct M Company and A-G lines)—Ryan was very specific about two skirmish lines. He emphasized his stance by maintaining M Company "was on the extreme left of the line, and Lieut. Hodgson ... was very near to me on the skirmish line ... I heard him pass the remark to the men to keep cool and not to get excited, and fire low."[145] Most writers interpret Ryan's comment to mean the second line—also alluded to by Nick Wallace—was the forward-most advance of a single, unified line. This interpretation is wrong.

Young Hawk, another of the Ree scouts, said, "The soldiers and the scouts dismounted, the horses were held in groups behind the line." The senior Arikara scout, Bob-tail Bull, was on the far left of the line, nearest the foothills as the troops swung in that direction.[146]

Private Daniel J. Newell (M) said, "Major Reno must have seen that we couldn't possibly go any farther and soon the order came to dismount and fight on foot. We threw a skirmish line across the valley, each number four standing behind and holding the horses. Today there is a railway station, Garryowen, right where our line crossed the valley."[147]

Red Bear, an Arikara scout riding with his comrades, said when they reached the proximity of the Sioux camp and dismounted, the firing began. He claimed the Sioux were lying down: "At this time no one was riding around on horseback."[148]

George Herendeen watched as the command halted and began to dismount to form a skirmish line, advancing as horses were placed in the timber.[149] A short time after the troops formed the line, firing became very heavy and Indians started working around the troops' left and into their rear.[150] The soldiers continued to fire rapidly. Herendeen moved to the rear of the line and waited in a small swale where Charlie Reynolds and Fred Gerard joined him, and the three of them

fired at one Indian, their shots falling short, probably 700–900 yards away.[151] Herendeen figured they were there six or seven minutes.[152] After the three men fired at the Indian, they moved their horses into the timber. He estimated the time at 15 minutes from when the skirmish line deployed to when it moved into the timber,[153] but he later changed that by telling Walter Camp the skirmish line was in place for only about five minutes or less.[154]

Fred Gerard and *Charlie Reynolds* dismounted after going down the valley, the troops ahead of them. They tied their mounts to some brush and came out behind the men, right near where the developing line rested at the timber.[155] By this time, the command was already forming a skirmish line and horses were being led into the woods, the right of the line resting on those woods.[156] When Gerard dismounted, he was 40–75 yards behind the troops and, "Not more than four rounds had been fired before they saw Custer's command dashing along the hills one mile to their rear."[157] (The use of the word "rear" would indicate Gerard and Reynolds had their backs to the river, as Custer was riding along the bluffs. This would be another indication Reno was pivoting his command on G Company and swinging it into the valley.) The two men were in the edge of the timber and after they fired a few long-range shots, they started up the embankment leading from the tree line to the flat plain above.[158] Reynolds asked Gerard if he had any whiskey.[159] They now joined Herendeen, Doc Porter, and the Ree scout, Bloody Knife, in a small swale some 45–50 yards from the timber.[160] Gerard noted the left of the line had become the right, G Company anchored on what Gerard called "the brow of the hill," referring to a dried river channel in front of a substantial stand of timber and brush.[161] The party could not see down the valley because the timber extended into the prairie and obscured the panorama ahead of them. In front of the skirmish line Gerard could see out some 1,200–1,500 yards, the river bend obscuring any further view,[162] but he estimated the Indians to be about 1,000 yards from the left flank of the line, in front of, but "not directly in a line with it."[163] More Indians kept coming. They fired at the red men, sighting at 800, 1,000, and 1,200 yards, all rounds falling short.[164] "The Indians were to the front and to the left, going up the valley. First I saw one, then three or four, and beyond that probably 40 or 50 coming up the valley." The first group was about 800 to 1,000 yards away, the next about 1,200–1,500 yards distant.[165] The Indians kept getting closer to the troops, however, coming within 200–250 yards of the skirmish line.[166]

Standing Bear, a young Minneconjou warrior who had just scrambled back from the bluffs on the east side of the Little Big Horn—where he had seen the Custer column rising

The "brow," looking south in the direction Reno's command retreated.

up along the hills—watched as Indians charged close to the soldiers. He could hear and see nothing but Indians, "voices all over and everyone was saying something. It seemed that all the people's voices were on top of the village."[167]

Private William Morris heard Reno direct French to send 10 men to skirmish the woods to avoid ambush. Morris was again one of the 10,[168] and after clearing the woods to the river he returned to his unit. One company was formed up "as skirmishers facing down the bottom,"[169] while "'M' Troop was deployed facing the bench land."[170] About 20 yards away there was a small mound and behind the mound were Bloody Knife, interpreter Isaiah Dorman, Reynolds, doctors Porter and DeWolf, about 15 Rees (*way too many!*), and some others.[171] Captain French told his troopers to fire at will and they continued to move toward the western bench land.

Private James Wilber continued on through the timber with fellow private John Meier and maybe others. Eventually, they got into the first tepees of the village, Private Roman Rutten going in the farthest.[172] (Wilber's tale may have been true, but if so, Roman Rutten was not part of it.)

Some historians question the veracity of this village-adventure, but more than one Indian verified the little sortie. Kill Eagle, a Blackfeet Sioux, was interrogated on September 17, 1876, his story carried in the *New York Herald* on September 24. The warrior claimed some troops worked their way into the southern end of the village, setting fire to several tepees.[173] This was corroborated by the Minneconjou warrior, Red Horse, in a report made by Colonel William Henry Wood, post commander at the Cheyenne River Agency, on February 27, 1877: "The women and children fled immediately down Greasy Grass Creek a little way and crossed over. The troops set fire to the lodges"[174]; and further alluded to by the Northern Cheyenne shaman White Bull (also known as Ice Bear or simply, Ice) and the Cheyenne warrior Soldier Wolf. In an interview conducted by George Bird Grinnell on the Northern Cheyenne Indian Reservation in Montana in 1895, White Bull—through an interpreter—claimed, "Reno charged the camp from below [*sic,* above] and got in among the lodges of Sitting Bull's camp, some of which he burned."[175] Then in 1898, Grinnell interviewed Soldier Wolf and Tall

Bull—two more Northern Cheyenne—and heard a similar refrain.[176] A possible answer may be found in an obscure entry made by Lieutenant Godfrey in his diary on July 15, 1876, less than three weeks after the fighting. Godfrey mentioned having seen a map drawn by Sergeant Charles Becker of C Company, Seventeenth Infantry, under the supervision of Lieutenant Edward Maguire, General Terry's engineer officer. Godfrey wrote Becker

> showed me where there had been camped, or supposed, the Arapahoes. It was on three sides of a square the fourth side being filled in by the lodges of the chiefs. It was cut out of the woods and seems was not seen by any one else and in it were the bodies of three (3) whites.[177]

In a footnote to this entry, Edgar I. Stewart wrote, "[a] contingent of Arapahoes is said to have been in the hostile Indian camp. A clearing in the timber is supposed to have been occupied by their tepees, probably because the Sioux were suspicious that the Arapahoes were spies for the soldiers."[178] There were only five Arapaho warriors at the battle, which means they had five or fewer lodges if they had any family members with them. In a 1928 interview, the old Cheyenne warrior, Young Two Moons, told Stanley Vestal (aka, Walter S. Campbell) there were six Arapaho and they had no tepees.[179] That would mean they had made wickiups for themselves, but if these lodges—in whatever form—were indeed in some timber and the small encampment was closed by Sioux lodges rather than by trees, it is quite possible these were the Sioux tepees alluded to by Wilber, Kill Eagle, Red Horse, Ice, Soldier Wolf, and Tall Bull.

The battle begins to rage...

Private Edward D. Pigford (M) fired only four or five shots while he was on the skirmish line. He did not know precisely how long they were on the line, but it lasted for a very short time.[180]

Private Roman Rutten (M) had great difficulty controlling his horse, the animal continuously trying to run in circles until Rutten finally managed to dismount.[181]

Captain Moylan felt as many as 400 Indians were within 500 yards of the command when Reno halted, maybe even as little as 200 yards away.[182] If Reno had continued his charge, "and gone far enough, he would have been there yet."[183] From the skirmish line's right to the river was probably 150–200 yards, the first 30 timbered, the balance being trees here and there: "In the timber was some heavy undergrowth."[184] There were lodges closer in to the timber, maybe less than 500 yards away and not more than 300 yards from the extreme right of Moylan's command.[185] They were "scattered"—as a group—

but in the main part of the village farther downstream, the lodges were much closer together, "compact."[186] (These "scattered" lodges were probably the ones the M Company flankers set afire, possibly the Arapaho "dwellings.") Moylan felt Reno could do little damage to the village, especially in the timber, for the ground there was much lower than the ground the village stood on and he would wind up overshooting the tepees. The lodges were more in the open ground. Once the command halted Reno deployed the battalion as skirmishers and the horse holders brought the horses into the woods.[187] From there, the timber bent down toward the river. Orders were issued to advance the line and the troops moved about 100 yards.[188] The firing became very heavy and Moylan said his troops fired most of their ammunition and he had to send men back to the horses to get more.[189] After about 10 minutes Reno got a report Indians were coming up along the left bank to threaten the horses. He withdrew the greater portion of G and went into the woods—1:49 p.m. This left a gap between Moylan's right and the edge of the timber and the captain moved his troops wider apart to cover that gap.[190] Moylan believed they remained there for "30 minutes or longer, probably 25 or 30 minutes," with quite heavy firing.[191] (1:35–2:08 p.m. see *Timeline J.*)

Lieutenant DeRudio thought the distance from the fording to the dismount was about two and one-half miles and the command covered it in 12 or 15 minutes (10–13 miles per hour).[192] The order was given to dismount and fight on foot and DeRudio said he was surprised at how orderly it was because of the recruits and the green horses.[193] "I thought at the time he halted and said, 'Good for you.' I saw that we would have been butchered if we had gone 500 yards further,"[194] for there was a coulee 300–400 yards in front of the skirmish line and it was full of Indians.[195] The Indians were now 500–600 yards from the line,[196] and as soon as the command deployed, they began moving closer and to the left.[197] The skirmish line advanced 75–100 yards, yet the troopers' carbines were not able to reach the Indians, but some of the Indians' fire reached the troops.[198] After eight or 10 rounds, the men had to use their knives to extract spent cartridges from their carbines.[199] Indians were filtering out of the dust in groups of three to five[200] and DeRudio saw some 100–150 Indians, total, but in these small groups.[201] Some even came within 200–300 yards of the line's front.[202] Soon, the Indians were to the front, left, and rear. The only side the troops were not receiving fire from was the right. The line remained there for about 10 or 12 minutes—maybe even less[203]—and DeRudio felt the men could not have fired more than 30 or 40 rounds per man while on the line.[204] Finally, Nick Wallace called DeRudio's attention to some Indians entering the timber. DeRudio took five or six A Company men from the right of the line and moved into a small path in the woods to counter the threat—1:47 p.m. He went down a bank, then into an opening where there were some tent poles and some meat drying, and then saw some Indians through the trees.[205] Lodges had been there, but no longer.[206] Company A was now next to the woods on the skirmish line's right, most of Company G having been called into the timber.[207]

Sergeant Culbertson heard no trooper firing until after they halted and formed the skirmish line.[208] The line extended 200–250 yards, maybe a little more,[209] and Culbertson was on its far left. As the command halted, Culbertson saw about 200–250 Indians to the front, riding back and forth, then moving to the troops' left. They were 500–600 yards to the troopers' front when Reno halted.[210]

Corporal Stanislaus Roy (A) figured the command dismounted about 200 yards in advance of the timber, and then moved to a point of the timber.[211] He thought he was on the skirmish line a full 20–30 minutes,[212] firing about 20 rounds.[213]

Private Taylor (A) heard the command, *"Halt! ... Prepare to fight on foot."*[214] As the troops dismounted to form the skirmish line, Taylor led his horses into the timber, thereby missing most of the fight on the line.[215] As he waited in the timber, shots whistled through the underbrush.[216] He said the led horses were under the command of Lieutenant Hare.[217]

Private O'Neill (G) moved to the skirmish line, but there was no hard fighting. They were there for less than 20 minutes.[218] The men were in good spirits, laughing and joking, while the Sioux were riding around, kicking up a lot of dust, but staying pretty much out of range.[219]

Private Theodore Goldin[220] (G) rode up to the command, but it was not yet in action. When he reached Reno—with a note from Custer [*!*] he claimed—there were a few Indians showing to the front, but they soon began to flank the command and move to its rear.[221] Reno was near Moylan and Hodgson.

The situation has become extremely fluid and bullets are flying, albeit from great distances, few if any hitting much other than sagebrush or an occasional prairie dog mound. We have seen Reno moved his command near and along the circuitous river rather than straight down the valley. In some mind-sets this is not fully understood. We think generally of a straight-line run, but that is not the case and the initial angle of the dismounting troops had to be somewhat off from the advance of the skirmish line, a point of timber dictating a pivot across the rear with G Company as the fulcrum. This brought M Company—less the men who had been sent to

skirmish the timber—around to the left side of the skirmish line. In addition, because of the threat to the west—where the Indian ponies were—M Company angled off the line making it a shallow " ⌃ " [chevron] rather than a straight line. As the skirmishers advanced, M moved more west than north, while A and G tried to keep close, also moving west, then bending that angle to the northwest. Normally, we think of the line as straight and between 250–450 yards in length, but neither is the case, as can be seen by some of the testimony, i.e., Culbertson's claim to have been on the far left of the skirmishers when we know his company was the center unit, thus indicating a significant split between A and M. In addition, Lieutenant Edward Maguire, General Terry's engineer officer who made a survey of the battlefield four days after the fighting, estimated the length of the line at its farthest from the woods at about 8/10 of a mile—*some 1,400 yards*![222]—though he added this was not intended to be a definitive measurement. Furthermore, artifacts found in that vicinity bear him out within a few yards, and while Private Charles Windolph was with Benteen's command and not involved in the valley fight, he wrote that over the years he had been told by those who were there, as Reno threw out a skirmish line, it covered the valley almost from river to foothills: "Reno now had his three troops and scouts thrown out in skirmish line, covering possibly the full width of the narrow valley."[223]

This is really interesting stuff here. As noted earlier, it appears not all the horses had been brought into the timber, and if this is the case, it explains a lot about the soldiers extending the skirmish line as far as engineer Maguire's 8/10 of a mile. Because the scouts were originally on the left, it indicates the troops who kept their horses were M Company men and this mobility allowed them to move much farther away from the woods than generally thought. It also explains the fact so many spent cartridges were found so far away, substantiating Maguire's findings.[224] There is additional corroboration from the unlikeliest of sources, a young 13-year-old Oglala warrior named Black Elk. In a 1931 interview with John G. Neihardt, Black Elk said,

> When I got to the timber the soldiers were shooting above us.... We got under the brush little by little and we crossed the flat ... I was underneath in the brush and I did not quite notice what happened above me.... [W]e heard that Crazy Horse was coming.... A little above us I could hear the hoofs of the soldiers' horses that went down into the brush. Then after a little while they went back up again and I followed after them.[225]

The fighting had been going on for quite a few minutes, especially for Black Elk to get so far into the advanced elements of Indians and his descriptions already have troops on a skirmish line. The allusion, therefore, to "soldiers' horses that went down into the brush" could only be of retreating men heading into the timber. The only soldiers fitting that description would be M Company men coming back from almost a mile across the prairie. There is more, though probably tenuous at best. In 1930, Walter Campbell interviewed the Minneconjou, White Bull. In describing the Reno fighting, the former warrior said, in effect, "Some of the white soldiers would shoot from the saddle. When the soldiers shot and moved the Sioux back a little, and then they set up a flag.... When they got off and set their flag the Indians were about to chase them, and then the soldiers took their run."[226] It is not so much in what White Bull recounted; it is in the events sequencing of his narration that lead us to wonder about horses on the skirmish line.

There is another incident we should mention that could have also referred—however obliquely—to the M Company horses being held in the company's rear. If we back up a bit, we remember poor Private Farley/Turley and his uncontrollable horse bolting into the village. John Ryan told the story in an article appearing in the *Montana Tribune*, June 22, 1923, linking it to Reno's arrival to form the skirmish line. While Ryan's remembrances may be less fact than mirage due to the mists of time, they cannot be dismissed so readily, especially since no one else ever commented on Farley's fateful ride and it has always been assumed Sergeant O'Harra was the first man killed. Corroboration is an important element and we do not have it here. There have been a couple of other explanations for Farley's demise, namely, killed in the timber and killed during Reno's retreat, yet neither of those make sense if we consider Farley's horse bolted *into* the village. What would make sense, is once ordered off the line the troops of M Company would have mounted, all the while the area was choked with dust and gun smoke, Indians whooping it up and threatening the troops' rear, confusion beginning to reign, gunfire crackling, and the immediacy of the troops' semi-panic felt by skittish horses. The mayhem could have easily caused Farley's horse to lose its head and run in the wrong direction, toward the village. From that far away from perceived safety, Farley would not have jumped from his panicked horse to run on foot, especially with Indians closing in. Far-fetched?

The clincher, however, came from the M Company troopers themselves, Private John Sivertsen among them. Not only did Sivertsen correspond with Walter Camp, he also left behind a written narrative, and while like so many other similar chroniclers Sivertsen was hardly definitive, he did say, "The Indians were shooting at us *from all sides*. Then we went into a clump of timber.... *When we dismounted in the timber*

I gave my horse to Number Four, who held it with his own and two others" [all emphasis added].[227] With Indians shooting "from all sides," this is a clear reference to the pullback from the skirmish line, not the original dismounting. William Slaper's narrative—as we shall see momentarily—alludes to this as well, and we have heard already from Daniel Newell.

As would be expected, distance and Indian strength estimates vary, but not by much considering the movement of men from position to position and the constant movement and arrival of Indians. It seems the initial Indian force was not very great, maybe around 50 or so (Gerard, Doc Porter, Lieutenant Hare), but this grew exponentially as moments went by: Culbertson, 200–250; Wallace, 200–300; Hare, 400–500 rising from the coulee; Porter, "a great many downriver"; Moylan, 400; Reno, 500–600; Ryan, 500; all fairly consistent, especially considering the circumstances and the locations of the witnesses. (We tend to reject Hare's contention of *hundreds* of Indians rising from that coulee, however. It would have been too early entirely for those kinds of numbers to advance that far from the village.)

Even the distances are consistent. Gerard, Herendeen, and Porter, all behind the skirmish line, estimated the Indians at between 800–1,000 yards away, getting closer all the time. Hare and Moylan, who were much closer, figured 200–400 yards (Hare) and 200–500 yards (Moylan). Even in this instance Hare was closer than Moylan, initially. DeRudio figured 500–600 yards, but he was behind his commander.

There was also considerable agreement the firing became rather heavy and there was unanimity among those who mentioned it, that the Indians were seeking to turn the troops' left flank.

Despite Captain French's questioning of why Reno halted his command, others seemed to think it was not a bad idea, especially considering the circumstances and not discounting the fact there was still plenty of dust to contend with. What was beyond that dust? What was beyond the trees jutting into the valley and masking much of the village? How big were those parties of Indians Varnum, Hare, Porter, and Gerard alluded to coming from downriver?

Soon, things began to get more dicey. Varnum, now in the timber—1:51 p.m.—finally finds Reno—1:57 p.m.—the major telling him to go back and find out what is cooking on the prairie—1:58 p.m. Moylan heads to the edge of the woods and signals for someone to get Reno. Hodgson, having already left the prairie to look for the major, reports mounted Indians are beginning to threaten M Company's left and rear. Reno instructs him to signal Moylan to start pulling his men back to the edge of the timber—2:07 p.m. Reno, as well, comes out, and Moylan tells him it's getting hot out there. Reno concurs and orders him to pull the lines back to the edge of the timber and take up positions in a dried-up river channel well below the level of the prairie.

M Company, beginning to feel pressure from its left, is forced to bend back—2:09 p.m. Somehow, either by word of mouth, by trumpet, or by sight—or quite possibly, simply by virtue of the building pressure—M begins pulling back. It does so by turning right and filling the gap between the village and whatever Indians are fronting it and the A–G skirmish line. M's troops mount and ride for dear life, as witnessed by the Ree scout, Red Bear—2:11 p.m.

Myles Moylan and Fred Gerard claimed the skirmish line pivoted right when it moved back to the dry channel, or "brow" as Gerard would refer to it. This movement and these testimonies would only make sense if M Company were out front beyond the limit companies A and G reached. If the line were contiguous, a right pivot would have brought the troops into the teeth of the Indians to their front, i.e., they would be pivoting *into* the oncoming Indians. It would only make sense to swing right if M were out front—and had its horses—because it could move between unmounted Indians to the north and the rest of the soldiers to M's south and east. There would be a gap created by the A-G line and the Indians to its front: the warriors would not expose *their* flank by being that close to A and G while M was farther advanced and on the Indians' right. This move would place M on the right flank of the brow, which is precisely where it wound up. If M Company had been adjacent to A on a straight, unbroken line the troops would have had to swing backward to avoid the oncoming warriors.

Fred Dustin quoted a Goldin letter, "When the line wheeled to the cover of the edge of the timber, French and Moylan 'about faced,' so that French was then on the *right* of the line, Moylan still in the center, and McIntosh was *then* on the left."[228] This makes little sense, for as Petring said, a part of McIntosh's company had been pulled off the skirmish line shortly after it was formed. They would have been scattered within the timber and to pinpoint their position as being on the left would be an error. Otherwise, Dustin was correct: in the fallback to the timber, French took the battalion's right flank, Moylan the left. In his 1879 inquiry testimony, Moylan himself spoke of this configuration, stating, "About half of M Company had to face to the left again in order to change front in the direction of the hills, as the attack was being made from that direction."[229]

❧

Major Reno had been initially with Moylan on the skirmish line. He thought they were there for 15 or 20 minutes "when word came to me from out of the timber that the Indians were turning our right"[230]—1:47 p.m. Reno left Hodgson with instructions to let him know what was going on, and the major moved Company G "to the banks of the river"[231]—1:49 p.m. When he got there Reno could see many "scattering" tepees. He also felt the Indians were using the woods, sheltering themselves and creeping up on his men. He rode back out to the skirmish line where Hodgson told him the Indians were moving beyond the troops' left flank. Reno ordered him to bring the skirmish line in along the edge of the timber[232]—2:07 p.m.

Doc Porter did not see the village until he went into the timber. He turned his attention to the fight for a few minutes then led his own horse into the woods. "I hadn't been there but a few minutes before the men came in on my right and on my left, and in a few minutes I heard that a man was shot." Porter went to look for him and while he was looking he saw Reno mounted, "and I heard him tell someone that we had to get out of there, that we had to charge the Indians."[233] Finally, he saw the village through a little opening in the woods, the nearest tepees being about one-quarter mile away (could these be the ones our intrepid M Company raiders got into, the same ones seen by Myles Moylan?) and the village extending downriver more than a mile. He estimated there were about 1,000 lodges from what he could see,[234] but he saw no Indians in the timber.[235]

Lieutenant Varnum saw heavy firing from the Indians when the troops were on the skirmish line. He also saw the difficulty the troops were faced with. "[T]he whole valley seemed to be covered with them. How many Indians that dust covered it is impossible to estimate. That dust, more or less, covered the main force of the Indians."[236] When he had been on the skirmish line for 10 or 15 minutes, Varnum heard someone say Company G was going to charge part of the village down through the woods. He was still mounted and decided to go into the woods to join the "charge"—1:50 p.m.

> When I had been on the line 10 or 15 minutes I heard someone say that "G" Company was going to charge a portion of the village down through the woods, or something to that effect. I heard some of the men calling out, "G Company is going to charge!" I was on my horse and I rode down into the timber to go with the company that was going to charge the village.[237]

Varnum rode into a glade within the timber—1:51 p.m.— and saw the stream, figuring part of the village was across the river and that was what they were going to attack. He heard no orders, but saw Reno with G Company men, helping to deploy it as the troops moved through the woods—1:57

p.m.—G being on the downstream side of the glade. Reno asked Varnum if he had just come from the skirmish line and Varnum replied in the affirmative[238]—1:58 p.m. It was tough going and Varnum was "delayed by the narrow intricate paths in the first edge of the timber." Reno asked him to go back and check on the line, then report to him.[239] As Varnum turned back—2:00 p.m.—and rode through the glade he met Benny Hodgson—2:03 p.m. He asked Hodgson if he had come from the line and Hodgson said yes. Varnum told him Reno wanted to know how things were going. The two officers remained together for about a minute—2:03–2:04 p.m.—Hodgson thinking his horse was shot.[240] Varnum went to the line, but when he reached the end of the woods he saw the men had fallen back to the edge of the timber[241]—2:09 p.m.

Lieutenant Wallace watched as the skirmishers advanced, the horses in the woods, the line's right flank resting on the timber.[242] He saw Reno go into the timber with McIntosh and men of G Company.[243] The rest of the command advanced until the right of the line hit the loop of the stream, then they halted.[244] Shortly after this, Wallace looked back, but did not see Custer. He asked Moylan if they should send a message to the general and the two officers asked the scout, Billy Jackson, if he would be willing to take a note to Custer. Jackson said he would never make it through. Suddenly Wallace spotted Indians moving to the soldiers' rear.[245] Because the timber concealed much of the village, Wallace could not judge its physical dimensions. He could not estimate numbers except he "saw plenty of Indians,"[246] and he noticed instead of pressing the command's front, they were moving around the left flank. After being in line "some time," it was reported the Indians were across the Little Big Horn and trying to get at the troopers' horses. This was when G Company was taken off the line and moved into the timber.[247] It was clearly after setting up his skirmishers Reno took the men into the woods,[248] because Wallace saw Reno on the line for a few minutes, then saw him go into the timber. While he heard Reno's voice, Wallace did not see the major again until they arrived on Reno Hill.[249] The troops were now beginning to run low on ammunition. Wallace said much of it had been used and he knew one company had to withdraw some of its men to retrieve more from the saddlebags. This was done before pulling back to the timber.[250] He also said both Moylan and Varnum told him they had to take half their company and head back for ammunition.[251] The situation was becoming more precarious because Indians had been seen across the stream and within 50 yards of the troops in the timber as well as in the soldiers' rear.[252] Soon the Indians were getting into the timber—one end of the woods was only about 100 yards

from the village[253]—and the troops were beginning to receive fire from across the river.[254]

Wooden Leg was a young Cheyenne warrior who had gone for a swim with his brother, then fell asleep, when suddenly he heard firing up the valley. After preparing himself, he rode through the huge Indian village. When he arrived at the Hunkpapa camp the air was full of dust. He could not see where to go, so he followed other Indians. "I was led out around and far beyond the Hunkpapa camp circle. Many hundreds of Indians on horseback were dashing to and fro in front of a body of soldiers. The soldiers were on the level valley ground and were shooting with rifles."[255] He got beyond and behind the troops.

Lieutenant Hare felt the pressure. There was a force of 200 or so Indians constantly riding to the skirmish line's front, 200–250 yards away—scattered as usual—but many of those who came out of the ravine were now heading around the line's left flank.[256] Hare remembered seeing Reno only once, about 50 yards distant, moving from the "park" back out to the skirmish line.[257] Hare also noticed it might be about 600 yards to the first tepee.[258]

Private Davern went with Hare into the timber, into the so-called glade, and saw some of the village tepees from there. They were about a thousand yards away.[259] He saw eight or 10, scattered, rather than thick.[260] He tied his horse with the G Company horses. When he was in the woods, Davern heard heavy firing on the skirmish line and said to Lieutenant Hare, "Can't be possible that the Indians are driving us."[261] Davern did not see the skirmish line break up on the plains, but he next saw it at the edge of the timber.[262]

Fred Gerard thought the firing on the skirmish line lasted only about five[263] or 10 minutes[264] before the troopers began pulling back. He saw a soldier hit and told him to ride into the timber, the doctor was there. As the Sioux began passing to the line's left and rear, "the men soon broke from the line and went into the woods.... The men ran into the timber pell mell, and all resistance to the Sioux ceased."[265] He described the pullback as the left flank (M Company) now becoming the right, making it seem as though the troops pivoted into the Indians' advance—in front of itself—rather than behind.[266] The troops moved into the dry riverbed channel and faced the prairie on the cut-bank. "The men were almost six feet apart along the brow of a hill below which was a belt of timber."[267] The general firing into the timber was now coming from the south and the northwest, but the "brow" or "bench" leading up to the level of the prairie protected the troops from the west.[268] Gerard and Reynolds had returned to the timber where they saw Varnum. They moved to the extreme right and stayed there four or five minutes.

Gerard fired maybe seven shots when they heard the order, *"Men! To your horses!"*[269]

George Herendeen had gone into the timber. When he came back out, he found himself separated from Gerard and Reynolds. Herendeen now saw Indians circling around the hills and coming closer in the valley, moving to the troops' left and rear.[270] He took about five minutes going into the timber, tying up his horse, and getting back out.[271] He could not see the troops because of the way he was facing, but he saw Indians getting into the woods. The soldiers began falling back into the timber, Herendeen claiming he was one of the last to reach it.[272] As he went back into the woods firing at the Indians—about seven or eight shots—he discovered all the horses were gone except his. He had tied up his horse somewhere between the glade—which was between the village and the horse—and the prairie.[273] When he reached the glade he saw a company drawn up in line—in close order—facing the stream.[274] He could still hear the skirmish line firing.[275] Finally, Herendeen sat down in a buffalo trail and waited for the Indians to get closer. The skirmish line stopped firing shortly after this.[276] The soldiers fired for about 15 minutes and were deployed for only about 20 minutes before the general retreat began.[277]

First Sergeant Ryan heard the order to fall back to the timber; Indians began closing in on the rear. This was when Sergeant Miles O'Harra was mortally wounded.[278]

Private William Slaper (M) also recalled O'Harra was shot on the line. Finally, word came to them to pull back into the timber. "We got back there about as quickly as we knew how. In this excitement, some of the horse holders released their animals before the riders arrived, and consequently they were 'placed afoot' which made it exceedingly critical for them."[279]

Private William Morris (M) was trying to rejoin his company after the adventure through the timber. M Company was advancing toward the benchland to the west and the Indians began coming at them from their right as well.[280] When the company was within 400 yards of the Indians, French ordered them to lie down and fire.[281] The firing was very heavy on both sides and Morris figured they were there about 15 minutes.[282]

Private Pigford (M) saw Sergeant Miles O'Harra wounded on the skirmish line about 40–50 yards from the timber.[283]

Captain Moylan saw the Indians moving to the left of the skirmish line and he went to the edge of the brow of the dry river channel and called for Reno to come see what was happening. Reno came up, looked, and ordered the line withdrawn to the woods[284]—2:07 p.m. The companies made a right flanking movement to get to the edge of the brow.[285]

Moylan said there were Indians on the right side of the river as well, and men were moved to cover the bluffs on the other side of the stream.[286] Not less than 200 Indians had turned the left flank before it was withdrawn and others had gone through the foothills to come up on the left. They had closed to within 500–600 yards and were scattering all over the bottoms.[287]

Private Taylor (A) thought "it ... but a very few moments after we had taken the horses into the timber before the men came ... back for them."[288] Suddenly, the troops came rushing into the woods looking for their horses. Taylor felt they remained in the woods not over 15–20 minutes.[289]

Private Goldin (G) thought from the time the skirmish line deployed to the time the men moved into the timber was not more than 15 or 20 minutes.[290]

Private O'Neill and whatever G Company men remained in the prairie spotted the Sioux trying to turn the left flank, moving about half way to the hills to the left. The soldiers then moved back to the woods, firing behind a small rise in the ground between the timber and the plain.[291]

Red Bear, the Ree scout, thought there was a lot of dust and smoke and it was very hard to see. As the Sioux moved farther to the soldiers' left, he began moving to the timber, trying to follow Little Brave. Suddenly, "he saw 10 soldiers on horseback in full retreat toward the timber. At this point there was a deep cut and the horses of the soldiers fell into it and he heard the soldiers calling out, 'Whoa, whoa.'"[292]

Lieutenant DeRudio, in the timber, began to see Indians infiltrating the woods, maybe as many as 30 or 40.[293] The command remaining on the prairie also began to move into the forest.[294] DeRudio wanted to get to the north side of the woodland and was facing in the direction of the village. Less than two minutes into the timber, he reached a spot and stopped, waiting there about five or six minutes[295]—1:49 p.m. As he looked up toward the bluffs on the east side of the river, he saw Custer, Lieutenant Cooke, and one other man, mounted, and watching the fight in the valley—1:53 p.m. DeRudio thought they were a thousand yards away.[296] He said this was about four to six minutes before Reno retreated.[297] After 10 minutes in the woods, his company's trumpeter (Private David McVeigh, who was serving as DeRudio's orderly) brought his horse and told DeRudio they were leaving.[298] The men near DeRudio got their horses and mounted, but there were no trumpet calls, no orders shouted that DeRudio could hear. He saw a guidon "on the bank of the creek" and told one of the men to get it. The soldier said it was too hot and rode on. The men seemed to be in a panic, "Because they would not obey my orders to stay there."[299] DeRudio decided to get the guidon himself. He did not have to go back more than 40 feet and he crawled up the bank, retrieved it and saw 20–40 Indians coming. The Indians fired at him, but scattered.[300] As he retreated down the path, the Indians reached the place where the guidon had been and fired on him again.[301] DeRudio met Lieutenant Hodgson who said he thought his horse had been hit.[302]

Private Daniel Newell mounted up and as M Company was waiting for orders, he claimed to have heard Captain French say to Reno, "What are we going to do now?"[303]

First Sergeant Ryan said, "There is nothing to do but mount your men and cut your way out. Another 15 minutes and there won't be a man left."[304]

Major Reno: "Mount your horses and follow me."[305]

We give the last word to the intrepid *Lieutenant Varnum* who spotted Moylan, but could not see all the men. Moylan said his horses were beyond the left flank of the line and the Indians were circling into the timber from his left, trying to cut them off. Varnum went back in an attempt to bring the horses up[306]—2:12 p.m. He had no trouble reaching them and saw no Indians there[307]—2:15 p.m. He rode back into the glade and called for A Company men to grab their horses and follow him—on foot—2:16 p.m. Others followed as well—2:17 p.m. They moved up behind Moylan—2:19 p.m. Varnum dismounted and went to the line. Moylan yelled he was running short of ammo and ordered every other man back to the horses to get more.[308] Varnum then went to the right of the line—on the brow—where he met Gerard and Reynolds and had a drink: booze[309]—2:21 p.m. They spoke and Varnum stayed with them for one to four minutes[310] and was with them when the command prepared to leave.[311] By now the heaviest force of Indians was to the right: "The largest body of the Indians were nearest the village,"[312] 300–400 yards from the line. There were probably 300–400 of them in Reno's immediate front when the troops were on the brow of the hill, "and there may have been a great many more."[313] Varnum "was on the line and heard some of the men yelling, *They are going to charge!*" He went for his horse and mounted.[314] He did not hear any trumpet calls. Even though he saw no Indians there, a lot of bullets were beginning to come in from the rear, though he was not sure whether the rounds came from up on the bluffs or from inside the woods.[315]

It is obvious the situation has deteriorated, almost to the point of Reno having lost control. Has it, however, deteriorated to the point where the three companies must try to leave the field?

In assessing this, we must look at a number of factors:

(1) terrain; (2) the enemy force; (3) the mission; (4) our own force; and (5) time. Each has its own variations and subsections. Terrain, for example: what is it like; how big is it; is it defensible? The "enemy force" is easy: how big is it and what are its intentions? The mission is more difficult: have we fulfilled it; can we fulfill it; is it necessary to fulfill it; what are the costs in fulfilling it or failing to fulfill it? Our own force: [see, "the enemy force"]. Time: what are the consequences of time, and do we have any? There is no specific order for these factors, though mission is primary if it is still possible to fulfill. If not, then the primary mission becomes survival so we can re-assess and try to accomplish the original mission by other means or in another way.

In this situation we have a fairly good idea of the Indian strength and it can be measured with the simple word, hundreds; many hundreds, and possibly even a thousand. Reno rode away from Custer with 170 men—total—and promptly began losing scouts along the way, some even before he crossed the Little Big Horn. By the time he ordered the dismount, the command was left with 153 effectives, including two doctors, two interpreters, and several scouts—and Reno. (Reno thought his command consisted of about 120 soldiers and 25 scouts.[316] He had no way of knowing exact figures, for he had been given the assignment less than two hours earlier and had no time for the niceties of a head-count.) If we strip away the scouts, interpreters, and doctors we are left with 138 uniformed personnel, including 11 officers. Since there were seven enlisted men assigned as orderlies and as doctors' aides, we are now left with 120 fighting men in the three line companies. To make matters more problematic, one man in four was assigned as a horse-holder, meaning they were placed in the timber with their charges—or, in M Company's case, behind the advancing troops—and thus rendered ineffective as an offensive force. That left 90 men to man the skirmish line. This proved to be a shortcoming with a cavalry command, and based on the terrain obstacles and the dust-raising tactics of the Indians masking their numbers and intentions, it was a situation more forced on Reno than one of his own doing.

How about the terrain? Was Reno's battalion capable of holding the timber? To answer this properly, some insight from participants and contemporaries is needed. In order of seniority (Note: those marked with an asterisk, *, were not in the valley fight):

*Colonel John Gibbon, commander of the Montana column, testified at the Reno Court of Inquiry some of the timber in Reno's woods was of considerable size.[317] The timber "was just above where the stream cuts into the second bench a considerable way," leaving the bank almost as high as the

ceiling in the inquiry room.[318] (Unfortunately, we do not know how high that was.) There was no timber around the bend. Inside the timber there was a wide-open space, maybe 50 yards wide, with evidence of an old Indian camp. "[T]here was another open glade looking toward the prairie to the left and rear of the position."[319] The bluffs were back from the stream opposite Reno's timber position. Gibbon did not think those bluffs could have commanded much of the woods because they were too long a rifle shot away. On the right bank, "there was very little of what you would call timber. There was brush-wood and small trees, very thick and tangled in some places, with a good deal of fallen and dead timber among it."[320]

Captain Frederick Benteen was asked if he could have joined Reno in the timber. His response was, he could have tried. He also said he would not have tried if he did not have the packs and if he had tried, his "losses would have been very much greater than they were." Benteen felt the seven companies—including the packs—would have been wiped out.[321] He saw the timber on June 28 and he told the Reno court the beginning of the village was 600–800 yards from the woods. Benteen thought the timber could have been held for five to six hours and early the next morning they would have all been killed.[322] In a rather telling exchange, Benteen was asked if he had joined Reno in the timber, would not that threat have helped Custer. He replied, "It would not have made a particle of difference."[323]

Captain Thomas French had no idea why Reno halted and dismounted when he did, neither did he know why Reno ran for the hills. "When he started to that hill he had told me, not one minute before, that he was going to fight—this was in reply to a question of mine."[324] By this comment one can make the assumption French thought the woods defensible—certainly for a while.

Captain Myles Moylan told the inquiry court, "From the timber Major Reno could not have done any damage to the village or anyone in it. The ground was so much lower than that on which the village stood that he would overshoot the village"[325]; and, if they had remained in the timber, Moylan said the command would have been "annihilated."[326] Despite this, in answer to the recorder's—Lieutenant Jesse Lee—question, "If General Custer in passing there and seeing such deployment, would he expect that command would retreat in 30 or 40 minutes?" Moylan replied, "No, sir, he would expect it would hold its position."[327] (An interesting question by Lee: it appears he accepted a 30–40 minute timeframe as necessary for all this action. See *Timeline J*.)

First Lieutenant Edward Settle Godfrey wrote, he and Lieutenant Hare went down into the valley on June 28, to examine Reno's position in the timber. After listening to Hare's explanations, Godfrey told him Reno could and should have held his position. Hare did not agree.[328]

First Lieutenant Edward A. Maguire, Engineering Officer for General Terry, testified at the inquiry the timber was 150 yards wide by Reno's skirmish line.[329] Trees on the river's right bank were sparser than the foliage in Reno's timber, agreeing with Colonel Gibbon's assessment.[330]

Lieutenant Carlo DeRudio thought the timber could have been held as long as the command had ammunition. He also felt if the ammunition had been used judiciously, it would have lasted for three or four hours.[331] Many years after the battle, DeRudio felt the same way. He was interviewed by Walter Camp on February 2, 1910, the interview prompting Camp to write,

> Reno should have held to the timber. [DeRudio] Says there they would have had reasonable shelter, and Indians would never have come into the brush to fight, and Reno could easily have stood them off and held a thousand of them there who went down to fight Custer.[332]

("Indians would never have come into the brush to fight," *eh?* It seems someone had forgotten about the 30 or 40 Indians DeRudio had seen infiltrating the woods when he first entered, or the 20–40 who had chased after him when he retrieved his guidon. Which parts of DeRudio's stories are we to believe?)

The timber area was vaguely horseshoe-shaped on a dry creek, rather like an opening parenthesis. The bottom was 25 yards wide and thickly wooded. Thick undergrowth and large cottonwood trees lined the riverbanks. The bank was 10–12 feet high—to the prairie—and few places to go down except on pony or buffalo paths.[333] The underbrush was so thick you could not get through unless there was a trail.[334]

Lieutenant Charles Varnum was asked at the inquiry if there was any place in the bottoms where a good defense could have been organized. He said he did not know and did not even know how large the woods were. Varnum felt there were not enough troops to hold the timber,[335] but he also believed the edge of the woods was an excellent defensive position. It was the rear—the part along the river—that was of concern.[336]

> Any body of men placed near an Indian village like that is certainly threatening to the village. It certainly created a diversion to the extent of the number of Indians necessary to keep us in the woods.... I don't think the entire force of the village was attacking us in the woods. I don't think the entire force of the Indians was ever attacking us because after we got on the hill we could see parties of Indians a long way off.[337]

Varnum described the timber as being very heavy along the edge of the second bench; dense underbrush, little paths into it made by animals, then the glade with grass, small trees along the river's banks. He thought it might have been 100 yards from the right of the skirmish line to the river.[338]

Lieutenant Nick Wallace felt if Reno had remained in the timber every man would have been killed.[339] Reno's timber grew in a former bed of the river and the trees were young, none as big as a man's body, and there was thick undergrowth. The body of timber was crescent-shaped on a bank four or five feet high. It was only 25 yards wide, offering no real protection; the command could not have remained there.[340] The prairie was four to five feet higher than where the timber grew.[341]

Lieutenant Hare thought if the Indians had charged the woods, the command would not have lasted more than a few minutes, but Indians did not fight that way. [Usually! The men of M Company would have disagreed, however, after their experience on the prairie skirmish line.] "I think we could have stood them off about 30 minutes by using the ammunition judiciously."[342] He added if they had stayed in the timber much longer—even 20 minutes—they would have been shut in and would not be able to get out. "I think all hope of support from General Custer had vanished."[343] As a slight hedger, Hare added at the end he did not think it was absolutely necessary to charge out of the woods at that time.[344] There was very little large timber there; it was mostly underbrush.

> The basin or park was about 200 yards wide and the north bank 400–500 yards long where it runs into the river. There is a cut bank downstream and there is a bend on the other side continuing to where the river makes this cut bank, in this there is a little park containing about 10 acres of ground.[345]

The prairie was five or six feet above the level of the "park" and ran around the "park."[346]

First Sergeant John Ryan looked toward the river as he mounted and saw Indians coming from that direction—"completing the circle"—riding through the brush and laying flat on their saddles. He mentioned this to French, but the captain mistook the riders for Custer's men. The Indians were firing at the troops from all sides. Ryan told French, "The best thing that we can do is to cut right through them…. In my opinion, if Reno had remained in the timber a short time longer not a man would have made his escape as the Indians outnumbered us 10 to one."[347]

Private Goldin described Reno's timber as "a forest … of good sized cottonwoods, in which there was sagebrush, bullberry thickets and considerable rank grass."[348]

Fred Gerard felt with enough ammo and provisions, the timber could have been held.[349] He felt Reno could have made a splendid defense in the woods.[350] The timber was in a bottom formed by the river. Its left edge was 12 or 13 feet lower than the plain.[351]

George Herendeen did not think the Indians could have gotten the troops out of the timber at all if the soldiers had enough provisions and water.[352] He believed Reno could have easily held the timber, despite what might be as many as 1,800 lodges and 3,500 warriors.[353]

What does the timber area look like today?

The position was in something of a shallow horseshoe-shaped dry loop of the river with brush and trees beginning on the channel's side opposite the valley. It was on a slight plateau—though below the general prairie—and when the skirmish line withdrew the men pulled back into an old river channel. The channel bank on the prairie side was what Fred Gerard referred to as the "brow," and it was against this "brow" the troopers formed yet another skirmish line.

The active river on its north and east sides and this dry channel on its west and south sides surrounded the whole sunken plateau containing the timber and underbrush. It was also considerably larger than reported. The area between the river channels—active and dry—was an irregularly shaped oval, much wider on the north or village side than on the south or retreat side where it tear-dropped off. It is approximately 775 yards long at its longest axis and 235 yards wide from the prairie edge of the brow—around the middle of the new skirmish line—to today's flowing river. The northern end is as wide as 420 yards, but is of no real concern to us other than as the safe haven for infiltrating Indians (as described by Black Elk). Few if any troops reached that area, or if they had, remained there, including those men from M Company who managed to get into the village, and it is doubtful that was the route they would have taken. The southern end of the timber tapers almost to a point. It should also be noted the river's channel has changed dramatically over the years, but little at this exact spot, probably due to the depth of the channeling and the nearness of the bluffs. What today is called the "Garryowen Loop," was considerably less prominent in 1876 and did not interject itself—actively—between Reno's timber and the village. There were no reports of troops crossing water to get into the Indians' encampment, though again, that route is problematic. This is important to understand, especially when visualizing the movement of the A-G skirmish line.

When Reno rode down the valley, M Company had 46 enlisted personnel, G Company had 35, and A Company, 39. As the horse-holders moved into the woods—or behind their company—the units were depleted by some 25 percent, giving

Chart 3. Reno in the Valley (1)—After Crossing the Little Big Horn River

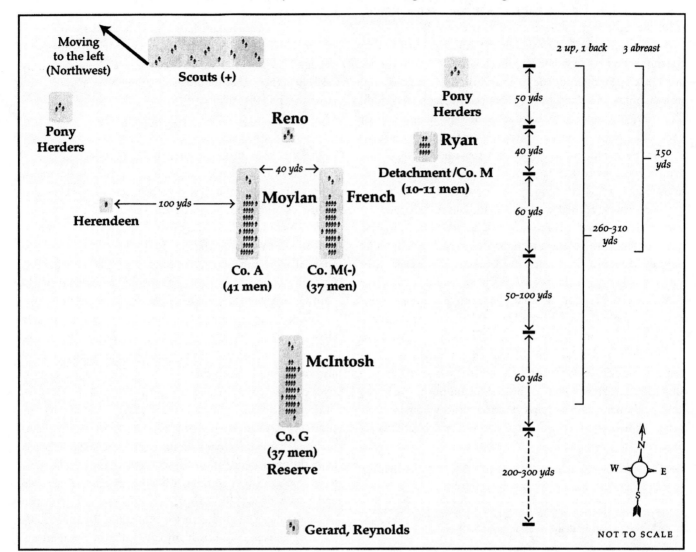

M, 34; G, 26; and A, 29, all within one or two men. Then, most of G was pulled off the line and brought into the timber by Reno, but we do not know the exact number of men either yanked off or remaining on the prairie floor. What we do know is 10 of G's men—including Private John J. McGinniss whose horse bolted into the village—were left behind in the woods when Reno retreated. We can, therefore, make an educated guess these men were part of the contingent brought into the timber and dispersed. Added to G's horse-holders, that totals 19 troopers, leaving the company with only 16 men, and some of that number was in all likelihood part of the timber group. For argument's sake, however, we will use 16 as the number for the skirmish line, bringing the total on the prairie floor to a maximum of 79. It should be noted here—as a word of caution—four men from M Company also remained in the timber when Reno retreated: sergeants

White and Carey; Trumpeter Weaver; and Private Sivertsen. We know from the Morris and Sivertsen accounts they both fought on the prairie, Morris coming out after skirmishing the timber. Since Wilber and Meier were not among those left behind, we may assume as well, they managed to fight on the prairie, keeping the total—at least academically—at 79.

If the normal five-yard interval were maintained, a 79-man skirmish line would be approximately 400 yards long, considerably shorter than Lieutenant Maguire's 8/10 of a mile estimate (1,400 ± yards). Maguire's distance measurement, however, clearly indicated there had to be multiple skirmish lines—as we heard from First Sergeant Ryan—rather than one long, contiguous line, and this would fit with the M Company advance toward the foothills rather than the village proper. Nick Wallace's testimony in 1879 seemed to dispute Maguire's findings, Wallace claiming only 75 men manned

Chart 4. Reno in the Valley (2)—Participants' Locations

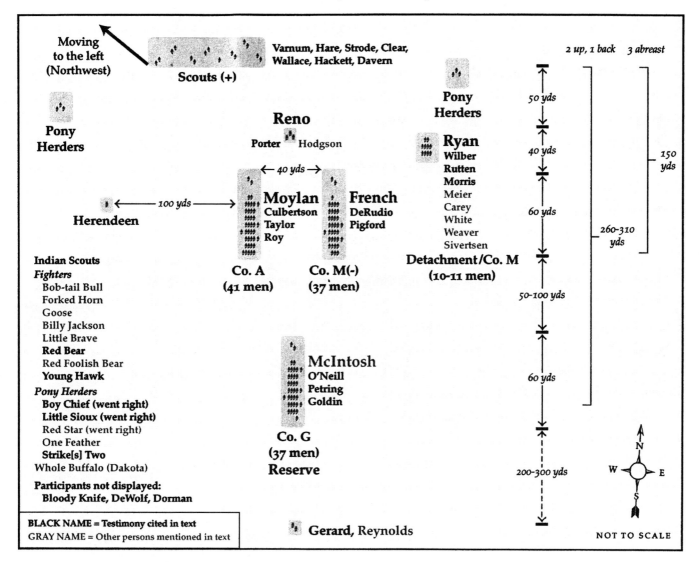

Moving to the left (Northwest)

Scouts (+)

Varnum, Hare, Strode, Clear, Wallace, Hackett, Davern

Pony Herders

Pony Herders

2 up, 1 back   *3 abreast*

Reno

Porter   Hodgson

← 40 yds →

← 100 yds →

Herendeen

Moylan
Culbertson
Taylor
Roy

Co. A
(41 men)

French
DeRudio
Pigford

Co. M(-)
(37 men)

Ryan
Wilber
Rutten
Morris
Meier
Carey
White
Weaver
Sivertsen

Detachment/Co. M
(10-11 men)

50 yds
40 yds
60 yds
50-100 yds
60 yds

150 yds

260-310 yds

Indian Scouts
Fighters
  Bob-tail Bull
  Forked Horn
  Goose
  Billy Jackson
  Little Brave
  Red Bear
  Red Foolish Bear
  Young Hawk
Pony Herders
  Boy Chief (went right)
  Little Sioux (went right)
  Red Star (went right)
  One Feather
  Strike[s] Two
  Whole Buffalo (Dakota)
Participants not displayed:
  Bloody Knife, DeWolf, Dorman

McIntosh
O'Neill
Petring
Goldin

Co. G
(37 men)
Reserve

200-300 yds

N
W — E
S

BLACK NAME = Testimony cited in text
GRAY NAME = Other persons mentioned in text

Gerard, Reynolds

NOT TO SCALE

---

the line (close!) and its length took up only a few hundred yards (375 at normal interval). Wallace, however, was the only remaining G Company officer on the prairie, and hanging out near the timber where the remainder of his command was, may have been unaware of the M Company separation, not as eye-rolling an assumption as one might think, especially considering the noise, the dust and smoke, and the ever-increasing number of Indians, not a situation to be taken too cavalierly. One would suspect Wallace to pay more attention to the threat than to the whereabouts of another company. There was some corroboration of Wallace's assertion from Fred Gerard when he claimed the foothills were about 1,000–1,200 yards from the line's left extreme[354] (the distance from the edge of the timber to the beginning of the foothills in that locale is approximately 1,500 yards), but Gerard too, was all over the place, behind the A-G line, in a swale, and in

and out and back in the timber again, remaining there even after the retreat. Another particularly important clue to a rift line, however, is Sergeant Culbertson's testimony of his being on the extreme left. As noted earlier, Culbertson was a member of A Company and that unit was positively identified as the middle unit. This would indicate the Company M portion of the line was not within immediate sight, certainly not in the direction Culbertson was moving. Engineering and artifacts are pretty empirical, so Maguire's distance, other first-hand testimony, and the location of physical findings would connote movement, rather than mendacity or error. It would also argue for a longer time element for the skirmish line, further throwing some cherished theories to the wind. In addition, both Moylan and Gerard said the companies made this right flanking movement to get to the edge of the brow. That would only make sense if M Company were extended far out

Chart 5. Reno in the Valley (3)—Moving into Line

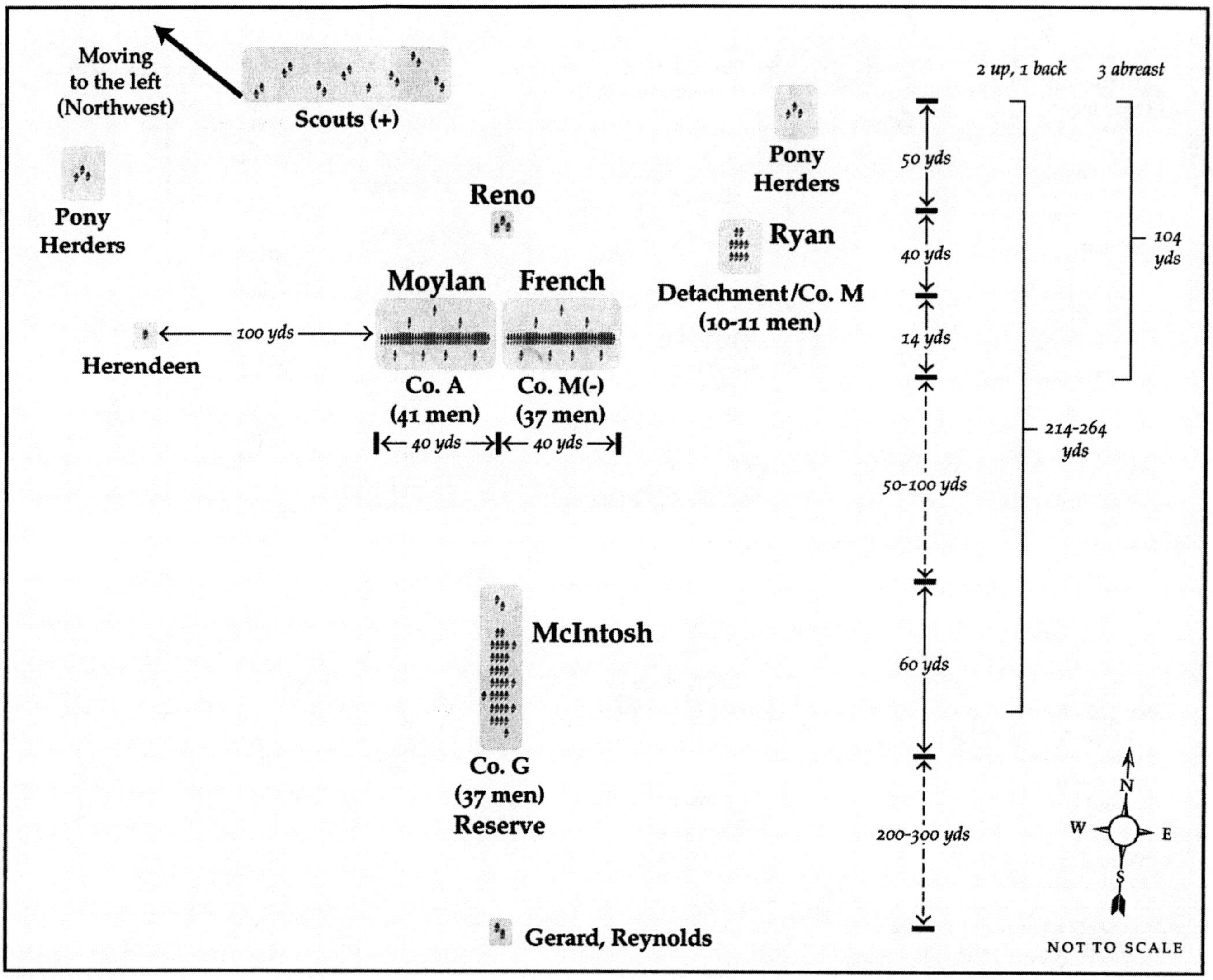

in the prairie, otherwise it would have simply backed up and swung in the way it had come, especially being under that type of pressure. By being 1,400 yards out, the shortest way back to the timber would have been to the front and right—where M wound up being positioned on the brow—not to its left and rear. We have therefore another of the big discrepancies for this event, a discrepancy of time ranging from a duration of as little as 10 minutes or less (Gerard and DeRudio), to as long as 30 minutes (Moylan, Wallace, Culbertson, and Corporal Roy).

The artifact field in the old dry channel brow was extensive, but only for some 270 yards, indicating a 54-man line were the proper interval maintained. Regardless of whether Wallace's 75-man line or our 79-man line is correct, interval was not maintained and men began to bunch as pressure mounted and they were withdrawn. Again, as noted earlier,

Gerard thought the men on the brow were no more than six feet apart (150–158 yards), versus the textbook solution of 15 feet (375–395 yards). The distance along the dry creek bed from the right flank of the brow line to the river was 235 yards (considerably more than Varnum's estimate of 100), which was almost as long as the skirmish line itself (or much longer if we use Gerard's measurement). The distance along the channel from the left flank of the line to the active river was much greater, some 420 yards. This latter area was especially troubling, for it was the troops' left flank the Indians had been concentrating on and it was along this axis any breakout to safety would have to occur. It was an impossible situation to maintain and if the line had been spread from one end of the dry channel to the other, the distance between men would have been some 35–40 feet, completely unacceptable in any sort of defense, fluid or otherwise.

Chart 6. Reno in the Valley (4)—Battalion on Line

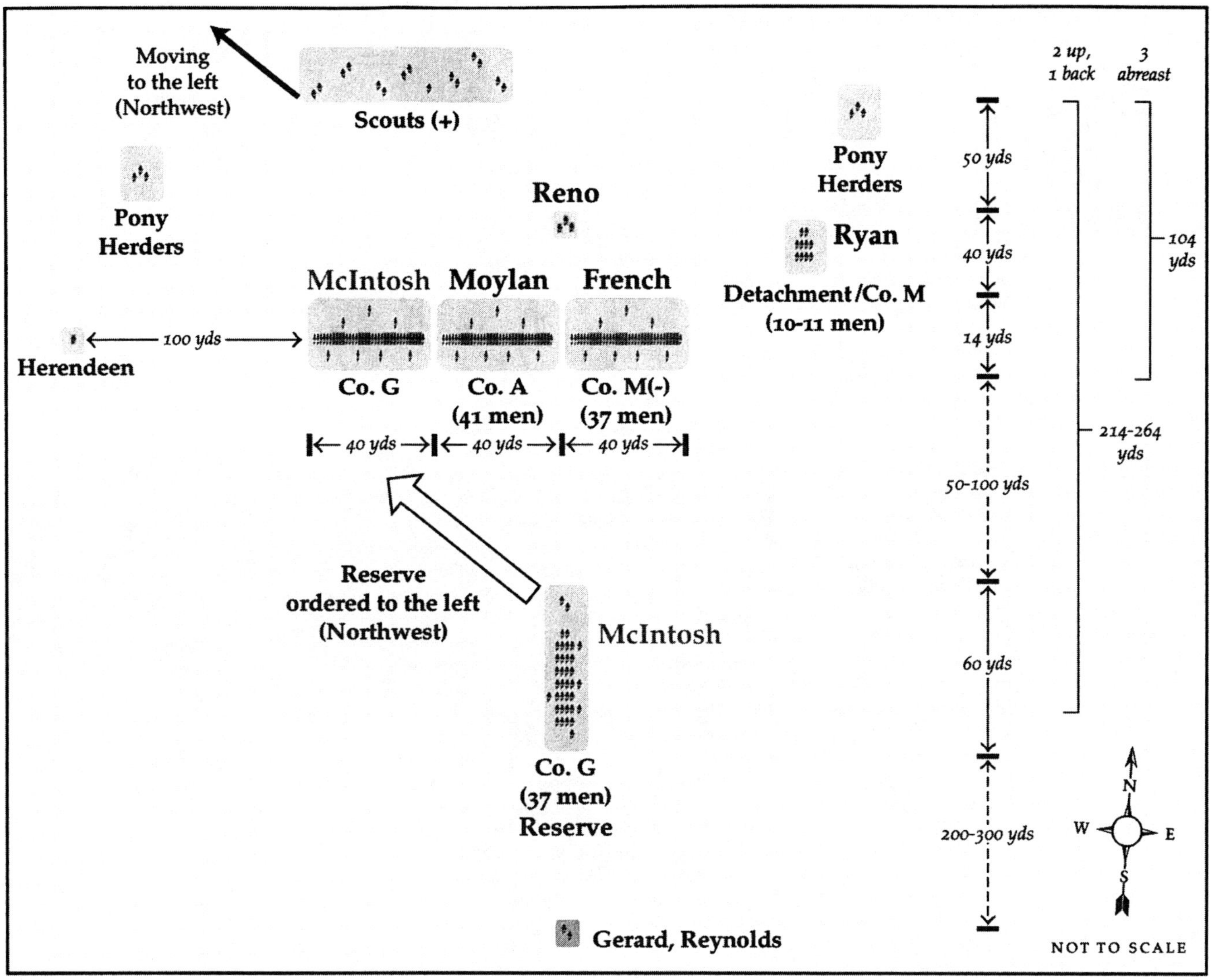

Moving to the left (Northwest)

Scouts (+)

Reno

Pony Herders

Pony Herders

2 up, 1 back   *3 abreast*

50 yds

Ryan

Detachment/Co. M (10-11 men)

40 yds

104 yds

McIntosh **Moylan** **French**

Herendeen ← 100 yds →

14 yds

Co. G **Co. A (41 men)** **Co. M(-) (37 men)**

214-264 yds

|← 40 yds →|← 40 yds →|← 40 yds →|

50-100 yds

Reserve ordered to the left (Northwest)

McIntosh

60 yds

Co. G (37 men) Reserve

200-300 yds

N
W   E
S

Gerard, Reynolds

NOT TO SCALE

In a complete repudiation of the one-on-one frontiersman tactics espoused by Gerard and Herendeen, and the seemingly twee testimony of lieutenants Godfrey and DeRudio, the great Prussian military thinker, Carl von Clausewitz, wrote about defending forests:

> It is in the interest of the defender, even more than of the attacker, to command an unimpeded view, partly because he is the weaker of the two, and partly because the natural advantages of his position lead him to develop his plans later than the attacker.... If [the defender] took up a position in the middle of the forest, both of course would be equally blind; but this equality would be detrimental to his interests....
>
> Impenetrable forests ... where one must keep to the roads traversing them—do present opportunities for indirect defense ... one can initiate a battle when conditions are favorable....
>
> No matter how impenetrable a forest, however, its direct defense is still a risky matter ... and no forest is so impassable that small units cannot infiltrate it in hundreds of places ... a general breakthrough is sure to follow.[355]

And while it did not pertain to forests, per se, Napoléon too, did not much care for "fortifications," claiming the side that stays within is beaten. Varnum was correct in his assessment of the brow—if properly manned—affording a good defensive position, but that was not the case here, and his observation about the rear was quite prescient.

Another serious issue in defending a densely timbered area is fields of fire, especially when the defender is outnumbered as Reno's command was. Major General Sir Charles Callwell wrote in *Small Wars*:

> Should mounted troops, unsupported by infantry, come upon a hostile gathering on ground where charging is impracticable, they have no option except to dismount and to act on foot. On ground where there is a good field of view there is no objection to cavalry doing this; but it is most dangerous when there is any fear of a sudden rush of determined foeman directed either against the dismounted troopers or the horseholders, and

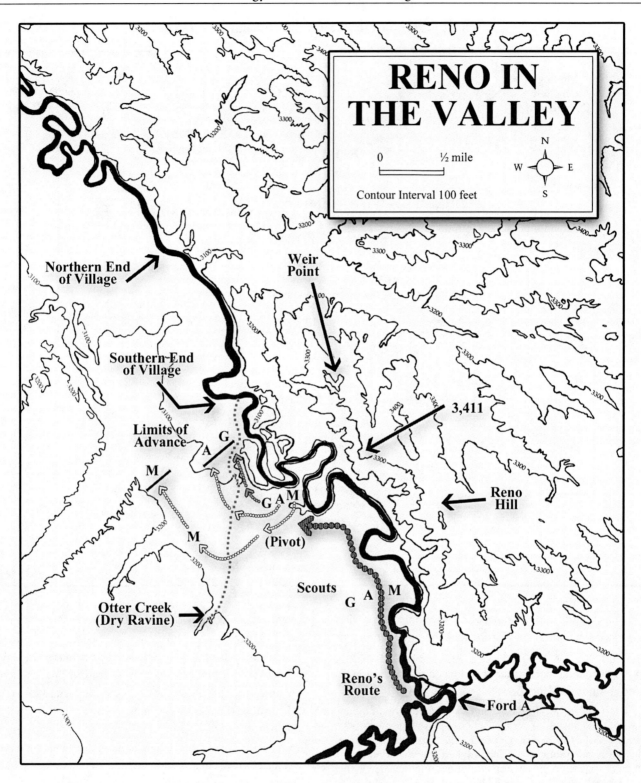

under these conditions mounted rifles always have an awkward task.[356]

This was the case with Reno's men in the timber. While the preponderance of force was located on the brow, other men struggled in the brush, many held to the buffalo trails leading hither and yon. Within the timber, there were no proper fields of fire, no areas where interlocking and enfilading carbine fire could maintain a proper defense and withstand Callwell's "sudden rush." Other, much-needed troops kept the horses in the glade, unable to contribute to any action and strapped with the possibility of being hit by infiltrators. With an inability to cover the entire area, the new line's rear was in peril from easy ingress from the right and increasing danger from across the river behind. There was enough brush and timber on the east bank of the Little Big Horn to cover warriors fording the river, and not enough troops to prevent such a crossing. Infiltration was a major concern and at the 1879 inquiry there was ample expression of just such fear. There were reports Indians were beginning to set fire to the timber, a common enough ploy, and even if that had not happened prior to the retreat, it was to occur shortly after the troops left for the bluffs, threatening the 20 men left behind.[357] And we have not even mentioned the continuing and increasing threat from the left, the direction the command needed to go if it was to reach safety.

The debate about whether or not Marcus Reno could have held the timber position for any length of time will continue for however long there is a debate about the battle of the Little Big Horn—it is one of the key elements in the entire saga—but it is clear from the size of the area, the size of Reno's force, and the size of the Indians itching to make a point, the men of this battalion would have been doomed had Reno chosen to stay. Author Donald W. Moore agreed when he wrote, "The 'timber' was not a defensible position and would

have been fatal to Reno and his men."[358] Civilians, used to civilian ways of fighting, thought they could hold out, but even they were circumspect. If only, if only, but "if only" did not exist. Only one officer we know of—who was in that predicament—agreed, also "if only." Another one, many jaded years later, concurred.

Yes, Reno could have stayed for a few minutes longer, but what would that have gained? It would not have helped Custer and it certainly would not have brought Benteen, not without the packs, and by that time who knows what would have happened? Reno did not have the provisions and companies A and M, at least, had used a great deal of their ammunition. (Ryan, as well, alluded to a shortage of ammunition in M Company.[359]) Reno's method of retreat is a different issue, but its genesis stems from the very make-up of the area he was trying to defend. The type of woods prohibited proper command and control and Reno was quickly losing that control. Was that his fault? Commanders bear ultimate responsibility—it is part of the definition. There is, however, a certain thing called circumstance and over the æons it has claimed its share of victims.

10

3,411 AND RETREAT

REFERENCES:

Timeline I—From Separation to 3,411; 1:05 p.m.–1:56 p.m.
J—The Valley Fight: Dismount to Retreat; 1:35 p.m.–2:21 p.m.
K—Scouts; 11:30 a.m.–4:35 p.m.
N—Messengers; 12:12 p.m.–2:41 p.m.
O—Benteen: Reno Creek to Reno Hill; 1:50 p.m.–3:07 p.m.

It is a documented fact Custer looked out over the valley of the Little Big Horn when he approached the area of Reno's dismount. As we have seen, people—more than one—saw him. Part of his command was seen as well. No one disputes that. Many battle students, however, claim Custer made a trip to the heights of Weir Point/Peaks, while a smaller group believes he was not at Weir, but viewed the valley from Sharpshooters' Ridge. There is justification for both, and both sides claim reason and testimony as their ally. The problem is, if one carefully studies the handmaidens each side claim as their own—and we apply a map and a ruler to the conundrum—neither location is correct. That statement alone brushes aside more than 135 years of an on-going wrangle.

The testimony given at the Reno inquiry was sworn testimony and if we consider "duty-honor-country" as the time-honored standards of our military, then this indeed must be accepted as reasonable truth. The inquiry was conducted only two and one-half years from the date of the battle—so memories were still sharp—and in addition to officers, several others—enlisted men, scouts, interpreters, and civilians—testified. Colonel John Gibbon, the commander of the Montana column, was also called, as were a couple of other campaign participants. While many students eschew this inquiry claiming it was nothing more than a wild-eyed conspiracy designed to whitewash the actions of Marcus Reno and Fred Benteen, shield a sloppy military, and protect the reputation of a damaged regiment, this opinion is fatuous and becomes an excuse used to prop up theories of malfeasance and the white feather.

Much of the fascination of the Reno Court comes from the context of the entire questioning, the attitude developed by the recorder (the titular prosecutor)—First Lieutenant Jesse Lee—toward the witnesses, as well as a similar attitude by Lyman Gilbert, Reno's counsel. A great deal of historical inquisitiveness is lost or not satisfied when one realizes much testimony was not allowed by the court officers because it did not pertain to Reno directly—the only person being inquired about—but was directed at or about the deceased Custer. The personalities of various participants became clear as the questioning moved on and answers given. Benteen came across as acerbic, witty, smart, sarcastic, bored, and an exceptionally professional soldier, while not quite as willing to volunteer as much information as many today would have liked—and he is condemned for it by some. Dr. Henry Porter's testimony proved he was a lot less observant than some experts claim. Lieutenants Varnum, Hare, Godfrey, Edgerly, and Wallace exhibited military professionalism, even as Wallace appeared clearly sympathetic to Reno's plight. Myles Moylan—a "Custer Clans-man," and a man whose bravery during the latter part of the battle was questioned—was fair to Reno while also trying to be fair to events. Carlo DeRudio was not the buffoon many make him out to be and that falls much more in line with the man's personal history prior to the battle. In fact, much of DeRudio's testimony allows us to form a ratiocinate basis for what transpired during Reno's battle in the bottoms and the sightings of Custer's command on the bluffs. DeRudio was not kind to Reno—though not directly combative—and anyone assuming he was involved in any sort of conspiracy has either not read the transcript or is much too in love with his own sclerotic theories. While DeRudio engaged in some dissembling—either to watch Reno squirm or because his own memory was a bit faulty, or maybe just to explain away a queasy stomach during the battle—his sighting of Custer is of major import. Trumpeter Giovanni Martini's testimony—changing over the years—is much more lucid at this inquiry, and contrary to the beliefs of conspiracy theory advocates, confirms much of what others agreed or testified to.

As we have seen already, there were a number of sightings of Custer's command after Reno crossed the Little Big Horn. What is notable, is no one but DeRudio saw Custer standing stationary on the bluffs watching the battle below—1:53 p.m. This is important, for it marks DeRudio as being the sole witness of Custer spending some time viewing the fight in the valley, assessing the situation—and by logical extension—planning his next move. Another witness—Private Henry Petring of G Company—claimed to have seen Custer on the bluffs waving his hat, though Petring did not say Custer was stopped when he waved and Petring claimed Reno's command was still heading down the valley, not yet stopped and deployed. (A close look at the timing would argue against Custer stopping en route; *Timeline I*.) Other men, as well, said Custer waved his hat,[1] as did DeRudio, but this was at least several minutes after Reno halted, probably around 1:44 p.m. as Custer's command headed toward the top of Cedar Coulee.

DeRudio's timeline had Reno's men on a skirmish line in the prairie for 10–12 minutes,[2] a specious claim leading us away from the truth. As we saw in the previous chapter, Reno's troops fell back to the timber as the pressure was becoming untenable. Another 10 minutes elapsed when the company's trumpeter brought DeRudio his horse and told him they were leaving.[3] While in the timber, DeRudio claimed to have spotted Custer and Adjutant Cooke—along with one other person he could not identify—on the bluffs across the river, about 1,000 yards away.[4] Throughout the years—and at the Reno inquiry—this distance estimate has brought yawns and guffaws, and not a modicum of derision.

> Counsel Lyman Gilbert ... had difficulty believing ... DeRudio when [he] claimed he could recognize Custer and his party from a 1,000 yards away by their particular mode of dress, even while silhouetted on the edge of a bluff. General High L. Scott also doubted the authenticity of DeRudio's sighting.[5]

But be that as it may, when silhouetted against a bright June sky and the only forms visible, it is possible to identify well-known figures. One can also ask the reasonable questions, (1) who else would it be? and (2) why would DeRudio make it up? To stretch the imagination even further, the actual distance was probably closer to a full mile! (There are some who believe Reno's timber was located in the so-called "Garryowen Loop," basing their argument on a handful of artifacts discovered by an avocational historian and archaeologist, Jesse W. Vaughn, using a metal detector. This defies reason, however, for it would increase DeRudio's sighting distance by more than one-half mile.)

DeRudio went on to testify, about two minutes after entering the woods he reached a place where he stayed some five to six minutes. This is when he spotted Custer. Four to five minutes later, Reno began his movement out of the timber.[6] All told, DeRudio judged the time to be 20–30 minutes from the deployment as skirmishers in the prairie, to the time the command left the woods,[7] something of an understatement, though we may accept a retreat beginning some 10–12 minutes after the command entered the timber[8] (*Timeline J* and *O*; DeRudio's timing here would be consistent with other's testimony and it would protect his own claims). Charles Varnum estimated the command held the woods for 10–15 minutes.[9] George Herendeen estimated the skirmish line held for 15 minutes and it was a total of only 20 minutes from deployment to retreat,[10] rather tight. Fred Gerard said 10 minutes on the skirmish line on the prairie and 10 minutes on the new skirmish line at the edge of the cut-bank surrounding the timber. After those 20 minutes the order was given to leave the woods.[11] Gerard, too, understated the total time. (For equanimity's sake, it should be noted again, neither Gerard nor DeRudio were Reno's biggest champions; less time in action and defense equaled more time flustered.)

Unfortunately, we do not know DeRudio's precise location in the timber, but we can make a reasonable guess he was closer to its south side than its north, despite where he said he wanted to go. The south side was where his Company A was positioned and where DeRudio described the guidon incident. Because of the way the river looped, his line of sight to the east would be relatively unobstructed except for taller underbrush and smaller-trunked trees. That would help since it seems apparent DeRudio was rather hunkered-down. If he were to turn more to his left, the larger trees and their higher canopies would be a hindrance because of the way the river looped back toward the timber. DeRudio's line of sight therefore, would be much clearer in the direction of Reno Hill than if he were to look toward Weir Peaks farther downstream.

> Q: State whether you saw the column of General Custer, or any portion of it, at any time after Major Reno parted from him at the abandoned tepee, if so, where and what effect did what you saw have on you.
> A: I did not see any part of the column of General Custer. The only observation I made was while I was in the woods. General Custer, Lieutenant Cooke and another man I could not recognize came to the highest point on the bluff and waved their hats and made motions like they were cheering, and pretty soon disappeared. I judge by that that probably his column was behind the bluffs.
> Q: Where was that?
> A: It was on the highest point on the right bank of the creek, just below where Dr. DeWolf was killed.
> Q: Did you see the place generally known as the point Captain Weir went to?
> A: Yes...

Q: Was General Custer on that point?

A: No, on one nearer the river and the highest point on that side. Where I saw General Custer the river comes right under the bluff. The bluff comes in very narrow there, hardly wide enough for a horse to stand on.[12]

This is one of the more remarkable exchanges of the entire proceeding (the third man DeRudio alluded to was in all likelihood Tom Custer, since he was thought to have been traveling as the general's titular aide). Not only does DeRudio expressly rule out Weir Peaks, but he describes Custer's position with reference to the bluffs meeting the river and the point where Dr. DeWolf was slain. In addition, he thought this spot was about 500–600 yards downstream from Reno's position on the hill,[13] and was quite insistent it was the highest point. He emphasized going there with Benteen on June 27.[14]

This description is not Weir Peaks. If we look at the topographical maps[15] of the battlefield and measure a 600 yard distance downriver from "Reno's position on the hill"—not far from where DeWolf was killed—we strike a high area along the modern-day service road.[16] Weir Peaks is another three-quarters of a mile farther downstream. On the map, this "high area" shows as "3,411" feet in elevation; Weir shows an elevation marker at "3,413" feet, its contour lines topping out at some 3,440 feet. In addition, the bluffs leading to the river from that "high area" are precipitous and end at the river's edge, fitting DeRudio's description perfectly. Weir Peaks are set back, not only from the beginning of the bluffs, but the bluffs themselves end on a wide, flat area as broad as 2,000 feet from the bluffs' base to the river.

We need to trace this back a little. Custer surprised Reno by not following directly behind. As we have seen, when Cooke informed the general the Indians were not running, Custer swung off to the right. Warriors down the valley were obviously setting up a screen to give their families time to evacuate and if that proved successful, the entire campaign would have gone up in the dust cloud being raised downriver. As he swung to the right once beyond the lone tepee—1:19 p.m.—Custer watered his horses for about five minutes at a small creek called North Fork—1:20–1:26 p.m. Once past the watering place, the command moved in a diagonal line for about 300 yards up onto the bluffs—1:26–1:27 p.m.— noticed finally by some of Reno's men in the valley. Martini claimed Custer, moving very fast, then swung the column a little to the right, going another 400–500 yards[17]—1:27–1:29 p.m. The command continued to gallop, at times no longer visible to Reno's battalion in the valley. Martini said he rode within six feet of Custer's right rear, and as Custer led he swung his battalions more inland, obviously seeking the eas-

iest and fastest route up the hills, the tail wagging the dog. Another survivor, Sergeant Daniel Kanipe, confirmed the speed the command was moving. Kanipe said Custer's men went at a trot and a gallop all the way up the bluffs and when they saw Reno's command in action, began yelling, urging their horses on at a breakneck speed in a wild run. Theodore Goldin too, alluded to this. In an exchange of letters between Goldin and William A. Graham in 1922, Goldin said he recalled no halt by the Custer column as it climbed the hills. The command merely slowed as Custer galloped over to the bluffs to view the valley.[18]

Despite the fact Custer's horse brought him well out in front of his troops, many men actually got ahead of him and the general had to caution them: *"Hold your horses, boys; there are Indians enough down there for all of us."*[19] This—and the troops' momentum—took a couple of minutes (*Timeline I* and *J*). There is also the distinct possibility Custer, trailed by Cooke and brother Tom, rode closer to the bluffs, while he directed Keogh and Yates to move along the easier, inland route. That, however, is incidental.

As they neared Reno Hill—1:38 p.m.—Martini said there was "a kind of big bend on the hill. [Custer] turned these hills and went on top of the ridge. All at once we looked on the bottom and saw the Indian village.... We could see only children and dogs and ponies around the village. No Indians at all."[20] As one crests Reno Hill, the bluffs veer sharply to the left: Martini's "big bend." In that area it is difficult to see very far downstream into the valley—the trees interfere— and Martini's reference to seeing only children in all likelihood referred to the wide area of flats extending to the river from the base of the Weir Peaks bluffs. Indians from the Spotted Tail Agency were believed to have set up camp on these flats east of the river and it is highly probable as their warriors heard the sound of gunfire and learned of Reno's coming down the valley, they bolted for the river to confront the threat.[21] Evidence for the existence of this satellite village comes from the reports of Lieutenant Oscar F. Long of the Fifth Infantry who interviewed Sioux scouts during an 1878 trip to the battlefield.

Lieutenant Long's informants reported that a small, disaffected band from the Spotted Tail Agency, Nebraska, arrived on the Little Bighorn after the main camp was established. This small group had about 20 men of fighting age and established its camp on the east side of the river near the upper end of the main camp.[22]

All that were left in the Spotted Tail camp for Custer's oncoming troops to see were children, women, and yapping hounds. In addition, Martini said there was no dust and he reiterated they "could see the dogs and children around the

3,411 as seen from the Little Big Horn valley floor. This is DeRudio's "highest point" (courtesy Dale Kosman).

tepees."[23] This fits perfectly with the Spotted Tail area, and why would any dust be there? It was on the opposite side of the river from Reno and the main village, the opposite side from where the main force of warriors would be gathering; the village was tiny, 20–30 lodges; and the warriors would be afoot, running for the river's edge, hardly conditions to raise much dust. One must also remember anything Martini contended to have seen—or not seen—had to have been for a fleeting moment. Despite his later claims, there is no reason for George Custer to have included this orderly in any group of people he may have taken to the edge of the bluffs. (There is a modicum of credence given to the notion an orderly may have been one of the three. In the questionnaire Graham asked Goldin to fill out, the former private stated Custer's color sergeant—Robert Hughes of K Company—accompanied Custer to the bluff's edge.[24] Of course, if this were true one could also ask why DeRudio never reported seeing a flag with the three riders.) George Custer saw Reno's men in action; it is beyond comprehension if Martini were one of the

three seen by DeRudio, he could have missed the dust rising in the middle of the valley and the fighting beginning in that same area.

Martini's comment about "no dust" and seeing only "children and dogs" has confused people for years, no one picking up the significance of the Spotted Tail camp, but at no point in the entire sequence from the time Reno and Custer approached the Little Big Horn River to the time the firing began, were the Indians unaware of the proximity of the Seventh Cavalry. A number of Indians were in the hills on the right bank of the river hunting for roots and herbs; Indians were running down the valley—some herding ponies—the alarm had been sounded; and people were scurrying to and fro. Greg Michno, in his book, *Lakota Noon*, cites numerous examples of Indians hearing or being warned.

Moving Robe [up Shoulder Blade Creek, moving toward the village]: "Already turning out to be a hot and sultry day." Warrior warning that soldiers were only a few miles away.[25]

Antelope [alongside the LBH]: Bathing in the river with

friends from the Minneconjou camp. "It was sometime past the middle of the forenoon when two Lakota boys came running ... shouting, 'Soldiers are coming!'"[26]

Black Elk [alongside the LBH, moving into the village]: At the river near the Hunkpapa camp when he heard the alarm. Criers said soldiers had been spotted at "lone tepee."[27]

Eagle Elk [in the village, heading north]: An Oglala, crossing the Hunkpapa camp when he heard shooting towards the river.[28]

White Bull [north of the village, heading in]: After breakfast—probably at least an hour past eight a.m.—he was north of the camp on the west side of the river, 125 yards from the bank. "It was turning out to be a hot, lazy, almost windless day ... the trails were dusty." He heard the alarm and "climbed a slight hill; across the long flat to the south he could see the soldiers approaching."[29]

Standing Bear [on the east side of the river, heading into the hills near Weir Point]: Awoke late in the morning. "When the sun was overhead ... decided to go down to the river to swim." Upon returning, he put on a shirt and braided his hair and was eating with his grandmother when there was a commotion outside. He learned that an Oglala named Black Bear had been east of the river up near the divide looking for horses when he spotted the soldiers. He came back to warn the camp. He ran downstream (north), then cut to the river, crossed it, and climbed up a "prominent hilltop called Black Butte." He peered south—upstream—seeing soldiers. The troops were spread out, coming down the slope to the river. "Standing Bear stood and watched for a time.... The soldiers crossed the river and were coming down the flat toward the Hunkpapa camp." He was in the middle of a large cactus bed. As he looked up again, "he saw more soldiers to the south and east, on the same side of the river as he [Custer]."[30]

Beard [in the village, moving northeast toward river]: "[T]housands of Lakota fighting men." Slept late that morning. The sun was high overhead as he walked to the river for a swim. Went back and had lunch. Finishing, he went to Muskrat Creek [Medicine Tail Coulee] where he joined his brother herding horses. He heard yelling back in the camp—soldiers coming—"and decided to climb the bluffs along the east bank ... for a better look."[31]

Colonel William A. Graham also found Martini's comments about the napping village perplexing.

> But from the ridge evidently he did not see the Indians or Reno's command. I assume that the timber below hid them from view. But he did see the village, and this, I think, was his first view of it. It was, apparently, deserted by its fighting men. What more natural, then, that he should cheer and shout to his men, "We've got 'em this time!" and dash for a ford, that he might cross and attack in the rear, and on the way send the "hurry-up" message to Benteen.[32]

James Willert's view of Martini's testimony was somewhat different, though he arrived at a similar conclusion. He felt Custer saw Reno hotly engaged (though Willert believed Custer viewed the scene from Weir Point). As Custer scanned the valley, he realized he had achieved a modicum of surprise, and

so crowded were the lodges that only occasionally could movement be observed—and, curiously, this appeared *passive*. Martini said that "children and some dogs" were visible, squaws were moving about. The firing from up the valley was heavy, so sounds from the village downriver were almost nil. Smoke from cooking fires within the camp were visible, but in overall impression, the encampment for the most part appeared quiet and almost somnolent. The young Crow, Curley, recalled: "When we looked down to the camp, we noticed there were not many around and Mitch Boyer said he thought the Indians were out campaigning somewhere."[33]

Quite a rationalization! Part of Martini's problem, however—other than a language issue, as he was from Italy and in the United States for only three years—may have stemmed from the fact *he* did not overlook the valley; Custer, Cooke, and one other did, common sense telling us it was not Martini, hardly a member of the Custer brain-trust. If we can believe the Varnum, Gerard, and DeRudio sightings, Custer saw the beginning of the engagement, and it did not include sleeping dogs. Also, any doubt Custer did not see Reno in action has to be put to rest simply by reading the comments of the Crow scouts accompanying the general. White Man Runs Him said, "Custer and his brother [DeRudio's third person?] went to the right of us and halted on a small hill. His troops were moving forward below him. Custer turned around as he reached the top of the hill and waved his hat," fitting in with what DeRudio claimed; also, Sharpshooters' Ridge is not "a small hill." He also said Custer "did not leave that place until Reno had started fighting."[34] Goes Ahead: Custer "rode to the edge of the high bank [note "bank," not "ridge"] and looked over to the place where Reno's men were"; Hairy Moccasin: "we could see the village and could see Reno fighting"; and Curley: "Custer made a brief survey of the situation and turned and rode to his command ... just saw Reno going down the valley but did not see him come back [i.e., retreating]."[35]

By the time Custer reached the high ground 600 yards downriver from Reno's entrenchment area—1:48 p.m.—the village was well astir. How long he was watching the festivities, we do not know, for DeRudio only glanced up, taking note of the three riders (*Timeline K*). Custer had to have been watching for several minutes—eight to 10 is not unreasonable: 1:48–1:56 p.m.—for Varnum had seen the Gray Horse Troop—riding in the "middle" of the five companies—shortly after Reno ordered his command to dismount. If Custer was leading the pack, then let his companies move past him as Kanipe reported, he had to have seen Reno form the skirmish line—or at least begin fighting it. Assuming Custer left within three minutes of DeRudio seeing him that could have been as much as eight minutes of viewing time (*Timeline J*).

View of the Little Big Horn valley from atop 3,411. The photograph was taken from the top of the peak seen in the previous picture. Reno's skirmish line could be seen in the flats just to the right of center and the timber he eventually retreated to—and from—can be seen just above the river water in the right upper quadrant of the photograph.

Another indication the map elevation marker, 3,411, was the spot where Custer watched the action comes from Martini when he claimed they could see the river from the top of the ridge,[36] something you could not see from Sharpshooters' Ridge. When asked how far they had traveled from the watering point to where they saw the village, Martini replied, "About an hour and a half [*sic?*] after we left the watering place till we got to that place."[37] This makes less sense than Martini's "sleeping village" conundrum. Assuming the "hour and a half" to be a typo—or a gaffe—and what Martini really said—or meant—was "a *mile* and a half," that puts the column approaching DeRudio's high ridge and still well before the twin Weir Peaks. Once past the halt at this point, Martini went on: "We went more to the right from that ridge and went down to a ravine that went to the river. At the same time General Custer passed that high place on the ridge and a little below it he told his adjutant to send an order back to

Captain Benteen."[38] Notice Martini did not say Custer went *up* to "that high place," but passed it by, then, when "a little below it," he spoke to Lieutenant Cooke. This particular bypassed "high place" now appears to be Sharpshooters' Ridge.

We find more evidence DeRudio's sighting was not Weir Peaks by again comparing Martini's testimony to the topo maps. The head of Cedar Coulee—that "ravine" Martini referred to—is close to one-half mile upstream from—or before—Weir Peaks and its attendant "loaf." The coulee head would be reached well before the command reached Weir. Martini said the place where Custer viewed the valley was the highest point and it was *500 yards from the head of the coulee.*[39] The place DeRudio saw Custer was almost exactly 500 yards upstream from the head of the coulee. (Weir Peaks is downstream and much farther away than 500 yards.) If we take Martini's "500 yards" from near the head of the coulee and back it upstream, then take DeRudio's "500–600 yards" from Reno Hill and bring it downstream, they intersect precisely at 3,411 on the map.

In addition, this ties in with a description by Theodore Goldin:

> As a matter of fact, the Custer column passed over the ground where Reno made his first halt (on the bluffs) as well as where he made his final stand. They passed to the left and along the base of that high bluff, and on down to where they entered the ravine.[40]

This was consistent with a stance Goldin had taken several years earlier in his letter exchange with Graham. In a 41-question letter Graham sent him, one of the questions asked was "With reference to Reno's position on the hill ... how far down the river was this high point?" meaning where Custer overlooked the valley. Goldin's response was, "My recollection is that it was just a few hundred yards below the point where Reno's line was finally formed."[41] While Goldin indicates no halt, his description of the route makes it clear neither the command nor Custer moved onto Sharpshooters' Ridge.

At the Reno inquiry Martini was asked who Custer was with "on the hill." This was after he was asked about "that high place," the context of the question now referring to Weir Peaks. Martini's response was Custer was riding with his brother Tom and his nephew.[42] Again, there is confusion in his testimony and it has to do with the way some of the questions were worded and Martini's understanding of English, plus the lack of place names and the constantly changing terrain, one "high place" after a "high point," one "hill" after a "ridge" after a "bluff." The "high point" here refers to Weir Peaks, but Martini understood "the hill" and that was where the command was riding, i.e., up to what eventually became known as Reno Hill. (With brother Tom and nephew Harry Armstrong Reed as riding companions, it appears younger brother Boston had not yet caught up with the column.)

At first blush it appears safe to assume this particular "high place on the ridge" is now Weir Point, especially as Martini went on, stating the command "went more to the right from that ridge and went down to a ravine that went to the river."[43] This "more to the right," however, refers to the area between the bluff—3,411—overlooking the river and Sharpshooters' Ridge: if one stands on this bluff where we believe Custer watched the valley fighting, but looks downstream rather than west, the troops would have traveled to the right of the viewer. The ravine would have to be Cedar Coulee—the first, only, and easily accessible ravine from the bluffs—Martini (and everyone else) being unaware Cedar Coulee would not go to the river directly, but would instead empty into Medicine Tail Coulee. Furthermore, he may have understood Custer to say something like, "We'll take this

ravine to the river," and took the phrase in its most literal sense. It gets really interesting here because Martini is now asked if Custer went to "the high place on the ridge"—in this contextual instance, a clear referral to Weir Point—and he replied, No, only the Indian scouts did.[44] (Notice the plural, "scouts.") *This statement would also exclude Martini from a similar trip!*

As the command approached the head of Cedar Coulee, George Custer or Adjutant Cooke—or even Tom Custer—had either stopped the column or slowed its pace, though Martini claimed Custer did not stop, but Cooke did, to write a message.[45] (Remember, according to both Martini and Fred Gerard—who had seen it in the general vicinity Varnum mentioned—the column had been moving quite rapidly.) Once at the head of the coulee, Custer instructed Cooke to send an orderly calling up Benteen and the pack train—2:00 p.m. Cooke hastily penciled the note—again, Cooke was taking no chances, already recognizing the language issue—and handed it to Martini with instructions to find Benteen, give him the note, and return if possible. In his 1879 testimony, Martini was specific: the note was handed to him near the head of the coulee.[46] (This story gained several permutations as time wore on, with Martini getting closer and closer to the penultimate action, always a little more involved than a mere orderly; one can assume the embellishments of time and one's personal sense of history took their historical toll.) Cooke also told him to backtrack on their trail and to hurry. (Taken in conjunction with the speed Custer had been moving, that simple little word, "hurry," is important for what follows.) Again, these locations make eminent sense, despite Martini's statements years later when he had everyone convinced he was given the note some 600 yards from Ford B. If Custer had just viewed the scenes in the valley, i.e., the on-going battle, part of the village, etc., why would he wait until he got within a stone's throw of the Little Big Horn—some three or more miles from where he first saw the village—before he sent back a note? Would it not make more sense to send the note as soon as he reached his command, 500–600 yards away?

Fortified with the note, Martini rode back these 500–600 yards to the same ridge where Custer had seen the village—2:06 p.m. (*It is hardly believable he would have ridden up to Weir Peaks or Sharpshooters' Ridge!*) He looked into the bottom—*but he did not stop* (again, ruling out Weir Peaks)—and saw Reno's command engaged in the prairie.[47] At the inquiry Martini was asked, "Was his line deployed in skirmish form?" and the trumpeter replied, "Yes, sir,"[48] but he did not see Reno in the timber.[49]

If we are to believe Martini to this point—and in his

1879 deposition there is little to doubt—then his testimony throws DeRudio's positioning or veracity—into some question. There are a couple of nexuses here. The first is Varnum and where he was when he saw the Gray Horse Troop; the final is Martini's view when he was heading back to Benteen. Both of those form the points for everything in between. If Martini was correct and the command had been galloping since watering their horses, Custer could not have reached that point on the ridge and have been watching for very long. The distance traveled was only about two miles and could have been done in well under 20 minutes, fitting with Varnum's observations, his location, and Reno's movements, i.e., the two columns had been moving in fairly close tandem. DeRudio claimed Reno's command withdrew into the timber the same time as DeRudio himself,[50] and this is where the dissembling begins. Based on the testimony of others, it appears DeRudio *had to have gone into the timber well before the valley skirmish line collapsed*, and he had to have remained there considerably longer than he admitted. Varnum's observations occurred a few minutes after the line in the prairie was setting up. Therefore, it is unlikely Custer would have been on that bluff during this period, otherwise Varnum would have noticed since both events occurred within the same general area.

We have to give Custer a few moments to direct his column toward Cedar Coulee—at 1:44 p.m.—and then to come to the high point on the ridge—1:48 p.m.—where he was spotted—1:53 p.m.—by DeRudio; the timing here works fine. While much of Martini's latter-year commentary must be taken as the rumblings of the mists of time, there are comments that fit and clarify some of the tenebrous testimony of 1879. For example, in his 1908 and 1910 interviews with Walter Camp, Martini said Custer never left his command to wave his hat and when he was on the high point, his whole command was with him, sitting on their horses. "As soon as the command left this high point everybody passed out of sight from Reno's position and went down the hollow toward Dry Creek [Medicine Tail Coulee]."[51] In his discussion with Camp, Martini described once more the sight from "the high ridge," deviating somewhat from his 1879 account and adding a little more detail:

> Then Custer halted command on the high ridge about 10 minutes, and officers looked at village through glasses. Saw children and dogs playing among the tepees but no warriors or horses except few loose ponies grazing around. There was then a discussion among the officers as to where the warriors might be and someone suggested that they might be buffalo hunting.[52]

"Buffalo hunting." That *used* to be Boyer's comment. Notice, as well, the command was now halted. A further note of cau-

tion is necessary here. We have this dichotomy of a perception of a massive village, yet we see as well what Reno's men had to say regarding the *initial* numbers they faced: not that many, and it may be this observation that lulled Custer and his officers into a false sense of having caught the Indians "napping," the full weight of what they were up against not being manifested until much later.

In the 1910 interview, Martini said Custer halted on Weir hill, but could only see about one-third of the village.[53] That does not fit the description of what can be seen from Weir "hill" and we can rule it out simply as mistaken fantasy. Camp wrote,

> Martin says whole column passed over the high ridge from which they could plainly see village and children and dogs in it. Martin says he was with Custer after he passed the high ground and left him just as the command started down a ravine to get off the bluff, somewhat to the right of highest ground and about 1,000 feet from it.[54]

"Ridge" and "bluff" do not sound like Weir Peaks, and "bluff" does not sound like Sharpshooters' Ridge, the large hill set back from the "bluffs." Also, notice the comment about Martini being with Custer *after* he passed "the high ground," and then (Martini) *left* him (Custer) *just* as the command started down the ravine. Cedar Coulee—the ravine in point—is reached before the Weir complex (two peaks and a "loaf"). The head of Cedar is to the right of the bluffs where Custer, Cooke, and one other viewed the valley, and the 1,000 feet comment is a reasonable description of the distance traveled from the viewing point on the bluffs to the coulee head. In the same conversations, Martini begins to obfuscate by suddenly describing the note incident as occurring a half-mile down the ravine, going on, that halfway down the dry creek they came into full view of the village. *Sheer fantasy!* There is no ravine in the entire area where one could have seen the full village and the allusion could only refer to Medicine Tail Coulee, putting Martini considerably closer to the river. This is merely a little self-congratulatory backslapping by Martini. Despite all this, the clincher comes with the Camp notation: after Martini had left with the message, he traveled

> 500–600 yards or perhaps three-quarters of a mile, "I got on same ridge from which Genl. Custer saw the village the first time and on looking down on the bottom I saw Major Reno and his command engaged already...." Thinks that from the time he saw Reno he was 15 or 20 minutes getting up [river] to Benteen.[55]

"[F]ifteen or 20 minutes getting up to Benteen" from 3,411—across Reno Hill and down the hillsides toward the flats—is rather fast for a man whose horse—unbeknownst to him—had just been hit by enemy fire. The total distance from where Martini was given the note to where he met Benteen was something in the range of 2.7 miles and if we allow for a 39–minute jaunt (in the timeline, we record Martini's trip as four minutes from the head of Cedar Coulee to 3,411, then an additional 35 minutes to the junction with Benteen at 2:41 p.m., the trip interrupted by a brief encounter with the younger Custer brother, Boston, at 2:19 p.m.), we come up with a pace of some 4.2 miles per hour, only a brisk walk in total, but not bad for a man on a wounded horse (*Timeline N*).

Martini continued by saying he got back on the trail *before* he got to the hill where the command had halted. That makes sense only if he was given the message at or near the head of Cedar Coulee, traveled back the few hundred yards, and then reached the high ridge. If Custer had gone to Weir, Martini would have been either *before* the Peaks or parallel to the complex (parallel, at this point, could be anywhere in a 360° circle, excluding the trail), but it would be parallel and not *after,* again ruling out Weir from this description. Also, Martini was obviously wrong about the column *always* moving, though it is apparent Custer was now in an even greater sweat to get to the lower end of the village. The column had to have stopped or slowed to a crawl in Cedar Coulee, and to Martini's credit, he brought up that point in the Camp interviews some 30 years after the Reno court.

While this may be begging the point, it was surely not Martini accompanying Custer and Cooke to the high ridge. Custer may have wanted an orderly nearby, but an orderly would not have been one of two people important enough to take along to view a battle. While DeRudio's wishful "timing" at the Reno inquiry would seem to indicate Custer watched as Reno pulled into the timber and the skirmish line Martini alluded to at the inquiry was the line on Gerard's brow, this is not the case. Martini could not have seen troops on the brow—it was too far along the channel and the trees would have intervened. As we have seen, it was more than 400 yards from where the dry channel left the active river to where the left flank of Company A began and Martini could not have seen that. Bruce Liddic agreed, though for different reasons.[56] Liddic felt Custer would not have reached Medicine Tail Coulee by the time Martini had gotten back to the place where Custer looked over the valley. Liddic is absolutely correct here. Martini's testimony therefore—having seen Reno's troops on a skirmish line—can be considered accurate.

We now have to digress a bit, for we are not finished with either Weir Peaks or Sharpshooters' Ridge.

So far, we have been looking at this mainly from the perspectives of Lieutenant Carlo DeRudio and Private Giovanni Martini, two men who have had their share of detractors over the years. What about George Custer? Well, the biggest thing on Custer's mind had to be his fear of the village breaking up and scattering. This fear was further reinforced by Fred Gerard's report that rather than a complete surprise attack or a helter-skelter chase down the valley—one the soldiers were likely to win—the command was going to have to deal with the Sioux coming out to meet Reno. To Custer, this action by the warriors was indicative of only one thing: a screen to mask the scattering; the Indians were buying time for their families to head for the hills. Custer needed to prevent this. From the moment he veered right, his main weapon became speed, so he spent a few minutes watering his horses to prepare for the run, then headed uphill, deviating his route for ease of travel, and moving as rapidly as the terrain would allow. (This is supported by testimony, once by an eyewitness—Gerard—and twice by participants—Martini and Kanipe.) Custer did not slow down and he reached the high ground of Reno Hill, then beyond. So far, there is no need to look into the valley because he knows the village is still farther downstream and he knows Reno has not yet attacked, or is only in the process of doing so. (These are not assumptions. One could see the massive dust cloud *in front* of the village—an obvious conclusion—and while hearing a pop or two, one could understand the significance of a lack of gunfire, both events testified to by several men riding with Reno. Besides, Adjutant Cooke had been to the river crossing and had a good idea of the village's locale—even his orders to Reno indicated that. Plus, the fact Martini saw no dust, further indicates he was not with Custer at the bluff's edge.)

By the time he passed the high ground of the Reno Hill area, Custer was looking at the beginning of the descending coulee system circuitously (and, at first blush, fortuitously) draining into the Little Big Horn and he directed his command to slow, to pass him—or it had already done so by its sheer momentum—and to head into what becomes known as Cedar Coulee. He tells his battalion commanders—the seasoned captains, Keogh and Yates—to give their horses a short break while he heads to the high ridge on the bluffs to assess the situation below. The command slows, stops, and Custer takes Cooke and one other, probably brother Tom.

At this point, we have no idea what these three men first—or last—saw, but we can hazard a pretty good guess they observed Reno's command extending a skirmish line into the prairie. Not a lot more. How would Custer have felt? Probably pretty good; Reno was doing his job. Custer may have been oblivious to the danger developing on Reno's left flank—because it was still too early, there were few mounted warriors, and there was too much rising dust and smoke—but the skirmish line was moving in the right direction(s) and the Sioux were keeping their distance, mostly on foot. True, the charge into the village had stalled, but Reno was dealing with the Indians in front of him—*maybe most of the Indians Custer thought he would have to face!*—and Reno's men appeared aggressive in their movements. It was not necessary to get into the village to create the needed havoc; nearness was sufficient. What little else Custer could see of the village was somnambulant—some women, children, and dogs (quite possibly, as he gained the heights, some scattering turnip-diggers on the river's east side, not what one might expect to see in a prepared, alerted camp)—and whatever warriors were not out hunting were sure to be kept busy by Reno. Now Custer could face the only dilemma still confronting him: a village preparing to scatter.

While this ridgeline where Custer viewed the valley was high, it did not afford him a good look at the camp's lower end. It is quite possible he noticed the twin peaks a little farther downstream, but they were steep, difficult to mount, and too far off his route of advance. With his men waiting in the coulee, scaling Weir Peaks was a waste of time, something he was not willing to do. The complex was just another unnecessary stopping point, and besides, the ridge on which he did stop was as close as he could get to where he heard the firing from the valley and from where he could view Reno's progress. In order to see properly what was downstream, Custer needed to *go* downstream and he needed to go there fast. From a strictly military perspective—always keeping the mission and military instinct in mind—it was more important to get closer to the objective of preventing the dissolution of the village and the scattering of its inhabitants than it was in finding another nearby view that might still not tell him everything he needed to know. There were no percentages in taking that chance. He could seek high ground downriver and at the same time be much closer to his enemy, thereby restricting or preventing escape. As it was an hour and 30 minutes earlier, speed was the most essential thing.

There is a strong lesson to be learned here. Whenever one looks at military operations—past or future—three informal elements should be kept in mind: logic, simplicity, and flow. Without these fundamentals, the event probably did not happen, or if it did, it failed. Combat is generally fairly simple—emotions funnel it in that direction. Once the bullets begin to fly plans are often forgotten, changed, or laid aside and events unfold in a logical sequence, accounting for firepower, numbers, psychology, discipline—and fear. One of the great tactical theorists of the early twentieth century,

the Imperial German Army's General Wilhelm Balck, wrote, "Bullets quickly write new tactics."[57] This is especially true in fast, sharp, mobile, and quick-moving actions. Sometimes these elements overlap, but rather than being exclusionary, the overlap acts as confirmation. If an event or an action is not logical, in all likelihood, it did not happen. If the explanation of an event proves to be too difficult, it probably did not happen that way, and we must adhere to the rule of Ockham's Razor: *lex parsimoniæ*: actuality must not be multiplied beyond that which is necessary. If an event does not flow from other events or in a contiguous manner, or it is too roundabout, it probably did not happen.

Custer's move from where he watered his horses to his arrival beyond Reno Hill is a case in point. Because of what he believed was happening—a covering force of Indians hiding the beginnings of the village dispersal—he was in a big rush: *logical*. He moved his command at a very rapid pace: *logical*. He swerved to take advantage of the terrain: *flow*. From there, he moved in the most direct route, given the vagaries of terrain: *flow*. He directed his command as close to the action as possible, detouring slightly from his route of march in order to assess what was happening to a part of his regiment and to see what he could of his enemy: *logical, simple*, and in the *flow* of movement. When he finished viewing the valley he made a determination what to do next, i.e., get to the lower end of the village and re-assess. His command was pointed in that direction: *flow*. What would a side-trip to Weir Peaks have accomplished? He would have seen more of what he had already seen—redundant; counter-flow, a difficult maneuver, especially on horseback; time-wasting. A move there made no sense. It would violate all three principles: logic, because he has already seen Reno fighting; simplicity because of the difficulty and the diversion; and flow, because it would detour him from where he needed to go—it was a waste of time. Given the mobility of both sides and the speed needed to accomplish his goals, a direct flow and a simple plan were best suited to Custer's aims. With the ferocity of the Indians and what they had at stake on this day, nothing else makes the slightest sense; Custer would know this.

The problem with any theory of Custer viewing the valley from atop Sharpshooters' Ridge is a matter of distance—therefore, flow. DeRudio has come under hyperbolic criticism for his claim of having seen Custer and Cooke on the bluffs some *1,000* yards away. If those individuals had been on Sharpshooters' Ridge, it would have added an additional 250–300 yards. Silhouetted against a bright blue sky, we can deal with three figures at a thousand yards (in reality, closer to 1,400), but adding another 300 begins to push against the periphery of whimsy. The natural inclination of a commander to head toward high ground or a prominent landmark when approaching from a distance dissipates as one gets closer and sees those heights as being too far afield from the action, or too far off the route he might want to take. It is also more important to view action from "closer" than from "higher." It is this same closer-versus-higher rationale that prompted a commander of Custer's ilk to approach Ford B instead of viewing the goings-on in the valley only from the heights of the Luce/Nye-Cartwright ridge complex. We must always keep in mind as well, that ease of terrain and a direct route make for the speediest going and if speed is what we are interested in—fitting the Custer profile—the only time we climb hills is if they are in our way and easily negotiable and a detour around them might prove to be too long, or if they can bring us some immediate advantage no other option affords. The heights of Sharpshooters' Ridge fit neither criterion, especially if the commander is interested in getting a close-up look at the gunfire he hears in the valley. The option of Weir Peaks is even worse, for it is steeper, farther from the sound of gunfire, and diminishes the commander's command and control ability because he is forced to move farther from his troops. In a highly fluid situation such as this, control is critical and while this particular time frame represented only the opening salvo of the fight, reconnaissance was far from complete, enemy strength was still unknown, and Indians had been sighted on the right bank of the river. (It was the loss of this control—the inability of each battalion to support the others—prompting Benteen's criticism of Custer after the debacle was over. We shall see more of this later.) The closer one kept to his troops, the less one had to fear of losing control. According to Trumpeter Martini, those troops were in Cedar Coulee. A jaunt to the peaks of Weir would have separated Custer from his men by some 500, difficult yards. At least at Sharpshooters', the command would have been closer and the going was not as tough. Sharpshooters' Ridge bends the principle of "flow"; the Weir complex snaps it.

It is along these lines of logic, simplicity, and flow that we now lay our theories.

As we have seen, DeRudio claimed he saw Custer five to six minutes before Reno retreated and he estimated it took only five to six minutes for the command to begin getting across the Little Big Horn in its retreat.[58] This is palpably false. While there is little or no reason to doubt DeRudio's sighting, there is considerable reason to doubt the surrounds of his timing. If we go back to our timeline and compare the theoreticals to the Reno inquiry testimony, we see DeRudio spent considerably more time in the timber than he let on—the "surrounds"—giving Custer plenty of time to get down a very difficult Cedar Coulee, then into Medicine Tail Coulee,

and up onto Luce Ridge. If Cedar had been wide enough for a column-of-fours (*doubtful*) and had been free of low-growing junipers (*doubtful*), Custer could have made Ford B in 25–30 minutes from the top of the coulee without spreading out his command to unacceptable lengths, something a commander would not want to see happen at this point in the battle. (DeRudio told the court Custer could have reached the ford in 20 minutes from where he had seen him.[59]) We would need to add 10–15 minutes to account for the difficult going, however, and then tack on a few minute's halt once atop Luce Ridge (*Timeline K*). Still, he covered the 3¼ miles in under an hour and had plenty time to view the lower Little Big Horn valley before being screened by covering fire from Keogh, thus accounting for volley firing heard some 44 minutes after Reno's retreat began and some 62 minutes after Custer started his move down Cedar. If Custer had been able to move more quickly, the volley firing could then have come from Calhoun Hill, but this is less likely. The artifact fields on both Luce and Nye-Cartwright indicate enough activity to justify volleys having been fired there and the time references from men atop Reno Hill further attest to these ridges as being the only possible locations. This scenario would also eliminate some of the stress caused by a literal interpretation of DeRudio's testimony.

If the Indians left the valley scene some little while after Reno's men got to the top of the hill—warriors were milling around, watching Benteen for awhile—then it stands to reason Custer was not confronted initially by any large number of Indians as he approached Ford B. At the Reno inquiry, Benteen said he thought there were about 900 Indians in the bottoms—about one mile away—circling around, when he arrived on the hill[60]—2:57 p.m. He thought the Indians remained there no longer than one-half to three-quarters of an hour,[61] before heading downstream. Others agreed. Our work shows the full force of Indians confronting Reno was still in the valley, mopping up, whooping it up, and searching for white stragglers and strugglers—at 3:02 p.m.—as Benteen's men were arriving on the hilltop. They would not have readily left in the face of this additional threat. The first indication of Indians leaving came around the time of the volley firing—3:07 p.m.—and this was in all likelihood Crazy Horse and his followers.[62] By 3:17 p.m. it had become apparent greater numbers of Indians were leaving and by 3:37 p.m. there was no longer any doubt the majority had departed for downstream. DeRudio confirmed part of Benteen's comments when he said soon after Reno's command left the woods and reached the hill, firing began on the other side of the village,[63] but it was a few minutes after the command reached the top of the hill[64] and it was after the heavy firing began down-

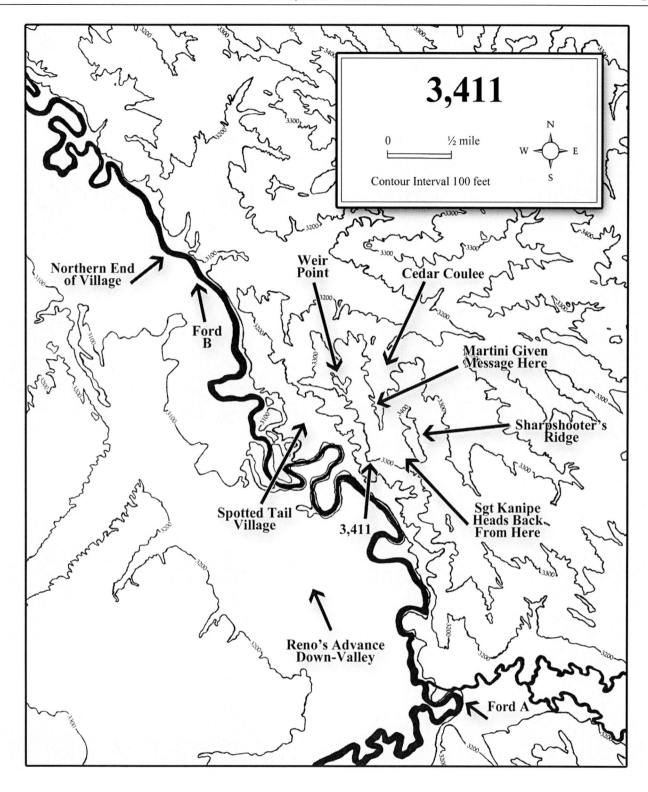

stream when the Indians left Reno.[65] He even clarified this a short time later when he testified Reno was not on the hill for 10 minutes when the firing started farther down the river.[66] "I heard immense volleys of firing and more than half the Indians around Major Reno left. Part of them went on the highest bluffs and part went down the river. Some of them picketed their ponies under the bluffs and lay down flat, watching Major Reno."[67] Reno's orderly, Edward Davern, gave us additional confirmation when he claimed shortly after he reached the hilltop—3:03 p.m.—he heard firing, volleys from downstream, though not very distinct, and most of Reno's command was already on the hill.[68]

So it appears evident Custer was nearing or had already arrived at the Medicine Tail ford as the larger body of Reno's men reached and was consolidating the hilltop. Custer's movements would have been, on and off, at a high rate of speed—despite and because of the obstacles in the path he had chosen—but that is reasonable and consistent with his actions to that point, and even if his movements were slowed by a few minutes it would still tie in with the claims of many that firing downstream began shortly after Reno's men reached the hill.

This was the prelude to the first volley firing heard and based on the archaeological evidence, the initial volleys would have had to have been fired on Luce Ridge, in all likelihood by Myles Keogh's battalion.

11

A List of Messengers

REFERENCES:
Timeline N—Messengers; 12:12 p.m.–2:41 p.m.

As Custer's rapidly moving command approached the easternmost swale area of Reno Hill, it turned sharply to the left and headed toward the bluffs and the looming mass of Sharpshooters' Ridge ahead and to the right. As the lead elements neared 3,411, Sergeant Daniel Kanipe was sent back to Captain McDougall with a verbal message to speed along the pack train. Or so Kanipe claimed.[1]

It was also around this time men began falling behind, their horses—or their personal wherewithal—beginning to play out. An entire set-of-fours from C Company dropped behind and never made the battlefield (eventually cozying-up on Reno Hill), rather a startling coincidence, especially since three of the men had been in the service only nine months.[2] Another C Company trooper, Private Morris Farrar had also fallen behind, though Farrar's lagging seems to have been legitimate. It appears his horse may have been the first to break down and did so along Reno Creek, possibly even planting the seed in the imagination of Farrier Fitzgerald, which of course, led to thoughts of imitation by the rookies. The Australian Farrar was a seasoned soldier and a veteran of the Civil War and it seems unlikely he would have pulled any of the straggling shenanigans. As the minutes wore on, Company E would lose privates William Shields and William Reese; F Company, Private John W. Sweeney; and I Company, Private Gustave Korn.

Kanipe, however, was of a different stripe. A well-regarded junior sergeant (he had been in the service less than four years, and went on to marry his deceased first sergeant's widow, Missouri Ann Wycoff Bobo, less than a year after the battle), Kanipe professed to being given a verbal message from Tom Custer, his mission to head back and tell Captain McDougall and Lieutenant Mathey to hurry the packs. While at first blush this sounds credible one wonders why Tom or anyone else would have needed to send a message at this junc-

ture of the adventure to speed the packs. Hardly a shot had been heard; Custer had not even viewed Reno's progress from the bluffs; and 607 soldiers knew precisely where the packs were, enough dust rising from their trail to indicate they were hustling right along. (A good estimate of the time Kanipe left the command would be around 1:47 p.m. shortly before George Custer reached 3,411. The packs would have been a little more than one mile above the confluence of Reno and No-Name creeks, just before Benteen's command made its left turn onto the main trail.) Furthermore, it was not until after the battle was over and the tally of dead fairly well known before Kanipe revealed who it was exactly who sent him back. We can also add the fact previous messengers—Chief Trumpeter Voss and Sergeant Major Sharrow—were instructed to return to the command, and the last known messenger to be dispatched, Trumpeter Martini, admitted to being given similar orders, with only a single caveat: if he was able to do so. Kanipe never admitted to any such request. Quite possibly the most damning evidence against him, however, comes from a previously unexplored study of the event's timing (*Timeline N*).

If Kanipe's tale were true, it is not unreasonable to assume Tom Custer would have sent him back as the five companies were galloping past the southwestern shoulder of Sharpshooters' Ridge, maybe a minute or so before Custer reached 3,411; this would indicate a departure time of 1:47 p.m. Based on a study of numerous other factors yet to occur but all tied in, Kanipe would have reached Benteen about 2:39 p.m. some 52 minutes after receiving his "orders." Despite Benteen's poor distance estimates, we can reasonably assume the two men met about one-half mile west of the lone tepee, an overland travel distance of 2.6 miles for Kanipe. Those 52 minutes of travel time would equate to a speed of three miles per hour, 25 percent slower than the cavalry manual's speed for a walk. If the Custers were so all-fired anxious to move the packs along, then it appears they failed to convey their eagerness to Kanipe. Unless, of course, our good sergeant somehow *malingered*?

Kanipe's defenders—and they are legion—cite the fact he would have never known Custer's entire command would have been wiped out, but that argument is specious at best. Kanipe would not have needed to know the Custer boys would die; at the time, he told no one who sent him and it continued that way until some time after the results were tabulated. It was only then Kanipe revealed it had been Tom who sent him back to hurry the trains, and poor Tom was dead (convenient choice, too, since George was surrounded by orderlies, one of whom—Martini—survived). In addition, while the so-called message was for the packs, both Mc-Dougall and Mathey stated they never received any such notification from any such messenger, nor did they see Kanipe until the hilltop imbroglio. And if the Custers had survived, it would have been easy enough for Kanipe to claim his horse broke down and he was just doing his duty as any good NCO might to help bring up the packs as he saw fit; hardly conclusive evidence, but enough to raise the specter of doubt in an event with almost as many such specters as participants.

The last messenger we know of became eventually the most famous: Trumpeter Private Giovanni Martini, also remembered as John Martin, the man who carried Adjutant Cooke's written note to Benteen.

Custer had seen all he needed to see at 3,411. Reno was doing his job, albeit slowed somewhat in the process, as the hostiles were putting up a good show. As Custer viewed the valley he could see many Indians heading toward the pony herds to the west, but many of those fronting the major were only on foot and were giving way as Reno's skirmish lines continued to advance, his men appearing invigorated and moving with aplomb. There were few mounted warriors, certainly nothing that could not be handled. After several minutes of viewing, Custer, Cooke, and the third man DeRudio reported seeing, broke away from the bluff's edge and headed toward the command, now closing up and slowly moving into Cedar Coulee. As they approached the head of the coulee, George Custer instructed Cooke to send a messenger back to Benteen to hurry him along and to speed the packs while he was at it. Orderly Martini was the natural choice. There was a slight problem, however; one of language: Martini was an emigrant from Italy who had been in this country only three years and his English was faulty, at best. Cooke solved the problem by writing a note and handing it to him with instructions to return to the command if possible. Things were beginning to pop and Indians had been sighted on the high hills around them: few, but still.

The note read, "Benteen, Come on. Big village. Be quick. Bring packs. W. W. Cooke. P. S., Bring pacs [sic]."[3]

As simple as its wording may appear, this note has been driving battle students crazy since its writing. The note was simple, however, its meaning just as simple: Custer wanted Benteen; he wanted him to move quickly; and he wanted him to bring the packs. While some would place hidden implication or intention in the note, e.g., Benteen was supposed to "support" Reno, it is impossible to say and the best interpretation is always the simplest. What did the note say? That is what the note meant. Custer wanted Benteen. Was Benteen to exercise his judgment once he arrived at the scene of the action—as Custer might expect and as Benteen alluded to in a different context? One would think so. Another interesting aspect of the note is the use of the phrase, "Be quick," rather than, "Come quick." While the difference appears meaningless the word "be" implies Benteen should simply hurry to the scene, whereas the use of the word, "come," might imply something more ominous and infer Benteen hurry to the initiator of the order.

Martini was given the note somewhere near the top of Cedar Coulee, though in later years flights of imagination brought him closer to the danger of the final action. In 1879 he testified, "We went more to the right from that ridge and went down to a ravine that went to the river. At the same time General Custer passed that high place on the ridge or a little below it he told his adjutant to send an order back to Captain Benteen."[4] Then Martini claimed he rode back some 500–600 yards—maybe ¾ of a mile (1,300 yards)—and went on the same ridge where Custer had seen the village. He paused momentarily and looked into the valley—but did not stop—and saw Reno's command engaged.[5] This distance would put him in the coulee, but fairly close to its head, not mid-way down or 600 yards from the river as he claimed in later years.[6] Martini started back at approximately 2:02 p.m. and somewhere during his ride along the command's trail—probably just as he reached 3,411—2:06 p.m.—and slowed to peer at the action down below, his horse was hit in the rump by Indian fire, in all likelihood emanating from the handful of warriors who had made their way to the east side of the river. Martini did not even notice, but the wound began to slow his horse.

From the point of view of a casual student of the battle, the wounding of Martini's horse appears to be just another meaningless incident. The implication, however, is considerably farther reaching than at first thought. Martini was given the note below the head of the coulee. That indicates Custer's command was already in the ravine, ready to move forward, or possibly already wending its way slowly down. The scouts—Boyer, White Man Runs Him, Goes Ahead, and Hairy Moccasin—were perched atop Weir Peaks, adjacent to Cedar Coulee. As Custer began to move forward, Boyer joined him in Cedar Coulee, and the three Crows, waiting a few minutes longer, began to head north, downriver, along the bluffs—2:12 p.m. The timeframe for Martini is somewhere between 2:02 p.m.—when he began his trip back—and 2:10 p.m.—when he reached Reno Hill. In all likelihood his horse was wounded somewhere within this eight-minute window. Since Weir Peaks was still occupied by the three Crows, there had to have been hostiles on or near the top of the bluffs on the river's east side, somewhere south of Weir but north of 3,411. As the Crows proceeded north additional Indians occupied those peaks, but their concentration was minimal[7]—probably less than two dozen on the entire east side. It had to be the Indians between Weir and 3,411 that wounded Martini's horse and shortly thereafter—between 2:38 p.m. and 2:46 p.m.—killed Doctor James DeWolf and Private Elihu Clear. The significance of all this is multifold. First of all, Indians in this locale would tend to confirm the location of Reno's timber area, rather than another area farther north. That small forest is easily seen and easily fired into from these bluffs, though with little accuracy. If a location farther downstream were used, there would be no reason for Indians to be this far south. Secondly, the paucity of Indian artifacts and ammunition found in the Weir Peaks area confirms a lack of massive Indian activity, contrary to some

Indian accounts and the beliefs of many battle students, i.e., that Crazy Horse and a portion of his band crossed the river and scaled these heights in pursuit of Reno's command. Third, it confirms the narrative of Crow scout, Goes Ahead, when he talks about circumnavigating Weir Peaks as the three scouts returned to Reno Hill from a downriver trek along the bluffs.[8] Any Indian presence in that vicinity—however small—would act as a deterrent, especially if the Crows were moving back along the heights as they claimed. That leads to other determinants, as we shall see in the chapter on scouts.

When he reached Benteen, Martini had managed to cover some 2.7 miles in 39 minutes, a travel time of 4.2 miles per hour. Along the way, he encountered the younger Custer, Boston—2:19 p.m.—who had been driving his horse to catch up to the column. (Early in the advance, Boston had moved back to the pack train to change horses and had been struggling to catch up to his brothers. He would eventually overtake them on Luce Ridge, dying alongside both on Custer/Last Stand Hill.) While they paused only momentarily to exchange information, it was enough to slow Martini's overall gait, yet 4.2 miles per hour with a wounded horse was not unrespectable, especially when compared with Sergeant Kanipe's weak-kneed effort.

12

INTO THE TUNNEL

REFERENCES:
Timeline I—From Separation to 3,411; 1:05 p.m.–1:56 p.m.
K—Scouts; 11:30 a.m.–4:35 p.m.
M—Boston Custer; 12:04 p.m.–2:42 p.m.
N—Messengers; 12:12 p.m.–2:41 p.m.

It is time to head into the unknown—the truly unknown! Up until now, we have been able to piece together various events based on eyewitness testimony of participants, however contradictory some of it may have been. Once Trumpeter Martini left the command with Lieutenant Cooke's note, however, we have no more reliable *military* or civilian witnesses to the events that were to unfold downstream, culminating in the deaths of 210 men, including George Custer.

As we have seen, a few moments after crossing the Rosebud-Little Big Horn divide Custer split his regiment into four separate battalions. After sending Benteen off to the left to scout the ridges and to peer into the upper Little Big Horn valley to see if any Indian encampments were up that way, the remainder of the regiment proceeded rapidly down Reno Creek for about 10 miles, Custer's battalions moving along the right bank, Reno's along the left. As emphasized, this move was done in some haste, in a belief the regiment had been seen by Indian scouts, thereby forfeiting surprise, with the attendant fear the village would scatter. At some point down the trail the command came to an area used as an Indian campground. By now, the small valley was widening and about two miles farther on it opened into its widest extreme, the flats. Once into this area, Custer called Reno's command over to the right bank and when Reno caught up, the two columns moved parallel for a few moments, Custer formulating orders for his second-in-command. It was in this area where the so-called lone tepee was found; where Interpreter Gerard mounted a knoll and saw Indians hastily herding some of their ponies downstream, Gerard yelling out, "There go your Indians, running like devils"; and it was where Adjutant Cooke issued Reno orders to head down the Little

Big Horn valley and attack the village, assuring the major he would be supported "by the whole outfit." From this point it was only about a mile and one-half to where Reno would cross the river.

As Reno went forward, Custer followed, then suddenly veered off to the right as Reno was either crossing the river or re-forming on the left bank, Custer's impetus being a report from Gerard, via Adjutant Cooke, that the Indians were not running but had turned and were heading back upstream to meet Reno's advance. This report dictated to Custer the still hoped-for surprise was either not to be or was only partially successful and the Indians were setting up a defensive screen to hide the village and allow the families to make a getaway. The only way Custer could prevent such an event was to swing right, follow the high country to get at the Indians from behind, cutting off their escape route and forcing them back toward the village and the euphemistic Reno "anvil." As is consistent with a military operation and common sense, everything was being done in some haste.

Once he received his attack orders Reno moved out smartly. The trail he followed went to the left and was smaller than the trail splitting off to the right, a larger, lodge-pole trail. After separating from Custer, Reno's command came to a small knoll near the river, and went around it, losing sight of Custer's column. It was a little more than a mile from where they separated, and the "knoll was right on the edge of the river's bank."[1] While near this knoll Gerard spoke to Cooke. As Gerard made for the river crossing, several Arikara scouts off to his left called his attention to the fact the Indians were coming up the river, no longer running away. Gerard paused, notified Reno of this development, got no response, and watched as part of the command forded the river. Believing Custer should know of this turn of events, Gerard rode back and spotted Cooke coming around the knoll—so *he* said; we don't: we believe Cooke was already heading that way—toward Reno's column. They met about 75 yards from Ford A.[2] Cooke asked him where he was headed and Gerard told him of the Indians. Cooke responded, "All right, I'll go back and report."[3] At this point, Gerard could not see Custer's column.

At the Reno Court of Inquiry, no one reported having seen Custer once the split was made, no one saw him veer off to the right; however, in an interview with Walter Mason Camp—probably conducted in October 1909—former private Thomas F. O'Neill, a G Company trooper riding in the Reno battalion (G Company was the rear unit of Reno's column, thereby lending some credibility to O'Neill's assertion), claimed Custer got to within 300–400 yards of the river before turning to the right.[4] If this were true then Custer seems to have turned up a small ravine containing an intermittent stream flowing into Reno Creek. This would have been closer to the Little Big Horn than traditionally thought and would have precluded Custer watering his horses in what is now called North Fork. At the inquiry however, Trumpeter Martini testified Custer did not go near the river—once again, no definition of "near" provided—but watered his command for about five minutes at a little creek. Based on times and distances, Martini's depiction can be interpreted as some 800 yards from the river and it seems more correct than O'Neill's. And remember, knolls intruded in sight lines and Reno's battalion was moving at a considerable clip. Custer's watering halt was for less than 10 minutes[5] (*Timeline I*)—1:20–1:26 p.m.—and from there, the command moved in a straight line for approximately 300 yards, again moving very quickly.[6] Custer then shifted a little to the right, going another 400–500 yards[7] before straightening out on smoother, higher ground. If we look at a topographical map, a measurement of the approximate distances described by Martini brings us out to comparatively level, rising terrain making traveling a lot easier than moving even farther inland or riding along the bluffs.[8] This route leads to the highest terrain south of the Benteen-Reno Hill complex and would also explain the sundry sightings of Custer's column by Reno's troops as they headed down the Little Big Horn valley. The undulating terrain and the column's movement to the east of intervening rises explains the fact Custer's command was not always seen from the valley. This route would also keep Custer himself—riding ahead and off to the left of his five companies—within periodic sighting distance of the valley, yet still close enough to be able to control his moving columns. If he issued any command at all, it was for Cooke and the battalion commanders, Keogh and Yates, to key in on a prominent terrain feature in the general direction Custer wanted to go, a feature rising above everything in the area: Sharpshooters' Ridge. One can almost hear his command: *"Head toward that high ground, Cookie! I'm gonna ride the bluffs!"* Once cresting the high ground Custer could get a much clearer view of the valley and direct his battalions accordingly.

In typical Custer fashion the man rode well ahead of his troops. His horse was faster than most and he had the luxury of switching between two—maybe even a third—meaning the animals were considerably more rested than the horses of his soldiers. As he rode along the bluffs—watching Reno dismount to form a skirmish line—Custer could have seen the lay of the terrain and he signaled for his command to move between the bluffs and the large hill, and head in the direction of sloping ground leading into a coulee, the ground now aiding and even dictating the direction of movement. This would have placed the five companies between two significant promontories south of Medicine Tail Coulee: Sharpshooters' Ridge—which he reached first—and the Weir Peaks complex. Beyond Sharpshooters' and just as he would have reached Weir, a coulee formed, one appearing to head in the direction he wanted to go.

On September 18, 1908, while retracing the movements of the Seventh Cavalry, Walter Camp interviewed Curley, the Crow scout who accompanied Custer part of the way. According to Curley, Custer moved

> directly across the country, on the crest of a long ridge, running to the bluffs and coming out at a point about 500 feet north of the Reno corral. From here Custer passed along the crest of the bluffs for fully ¾ mile, in full view of the river and of the valley over across it. Custer hurried his men, going at a gallop most of the time. Reno and his command were plainly seen by Custer's whole command while marching this ¾ mile.[9]

Camp assumed the column used Cedar Coulee as the ingress route to Medicine Tail, but Curley did not say it directly. In fact, he alluded to

> some distance south of these [the Weir peaks] there is a high ridge running parallel with the river, but not so high as the peaks. Custer's command passed into the valley of a tributary of just behind this ridge and the peaks and went down it, going in a direction directly north and coming out into the bed of Reno Creek [Medicine Tail Coulee] about a mile from its mouth at Ford B.[10]

While the word "behind" appears to indicate the opposite side, i.e., the east side of Sharpshooters' Ridge, this is not the case, for there is no "valley of a tributary" on that side of Sharpshooters,' and "behind" could be just as easily considered the west side of the ridge, especially when one looks at Sharpshooters' position, *vis-à-vis* the head of Cedar Coulee. We could also interpret the comment, "just behind this ridge and the peaks," as "between the two" prominences.

On August 24, 1919, several years after the Camp dialogue, General Hugh L. Scott interviewed Curley, White

Man Runs Him, and the Minneconjou, Feather Earring, who was also at the battle. Scott wrote,

> Custer turned around as he reached the top of the ridge and waved his hat, and his men at the bottom of the hill waved their hats and shouted. Custer kept on going on the ridge and the men followed him.... We galloped our horses and moved fast after Custer and his men. Custer went to a point on the ridge and then turned to the right and followed a coulee down in a northerly direction.[11]

In this case, the phrase "turned to the right" can also be deceiving. If, however, we see Custer at "a point on the ridge" being the topographical high point of 3,411 and Custer viewing the Reno fight, a turn "to the right" would be a turn off his right shoulder toward Cedar Coulee.

In 1910, Camp interviewed Carlo DeRudio. While not specifically pointing out a trail, DeRudio alluded to the fact Custer's command was in a column-of-fours, but in one or two small, narrow places, changed to a column-of-twos.[12] This could have been a reference to Cedar Coulee, the only place narrow enough to require such a move. Lieutenant Win Edgerly of Company D, was quoted in the *Leavenworth Times* from a statement he made at Fort Yates on August 18, 1881:

> I mounted the troop and followed [Captain Thomas Weir]. After going a few hundred yards I swung off to the right with the troop and went into a little valley which must have been the one followed by Custer and his men, or nearly parallel to it, and moved right towards the great body of Indians, whom we had already seen from the highest point.[13]

After going down the "valley," Tom Weir—still on the bluff—motioned for Edgerly to swing his command back to where he—Weir—was. This is considered Weir Peaks.

To be fair, however, in the early 1900s, Camp interviewed Edgerly—probably by letter—and Camp wrote, "When Weir and Edgerly went out from Reno did they not see Custer's trail. Does not recall seeing it anywhere.... Edgerly soon turned to right into a little valley *which must have been the one followed by Custer and his men, or nearly parallel to it.*"[14] [The emphasis was Camp's quoting of Edgerly's comment from the *Leavenworth Times*.] While Edgerly's admission of not seeing the trail is rather disconcerting, it should be remembered Custer's precise route this far back from the killing fields was not the uppermost thought in anyone's mind at that point in time. Reno's command had become a mess, an awful lot of rather irate Indians were still spitting fire less than a mile away, and there was one hullabaloo happening to the north. Volleys of firing had been heard in that direction, no one had any clear orders, and all the supplies and a lot more men were still some distance away. If he were to be followed, no one needed a trail to tell anyone where Custer was. Edgerly himself had no specific instruc-

tions and his boss was now hotfooting it along the bluffs toward what must have seemed like Armageddon. Edgerly headed for a natural route north: Cedar Coulee. So had Custer.

From the view at 3,411, the situation was simple. Custer saw Reno fighting in the valley. Reno was doing what his commander wanted him to do: hold the attention, tie down, and draw the warriors to him. Reno was succeeding. So far, intelligence estimates of the Indian strength appeared accurate. It was also obvious Custer was correct: the Indian resistance was a screening action to provide time for the escape of the families. Custer needed to head that off, but he had to know the extent of the exodus, both in numbers and distance. Therefore he needed to go north in the direction the so-called refugees were moving. He also needed the rest of his command for it now seemed obvious he had found the entire complement of his search, the entire contingent of Sioux and Cheyenne recalcitrants. Finally, he needed to find a river crossing that would bring him below the farthest elements of the escapees. Cedar Coulee appeared to be the first leg of that journey.

Nowadays we look at Cedar Coulee and debate the efficacy of moving a column-of-fours down its narrow, juniper-laden course, and posit the assertion Custer could not possibly have moved through its narrow confines. The problem with this contention however, is multi-fold. First and foremost, Custer would not have known of the coulee's difficult route and once in he would not have turned back. Second, we have no assurance the juniper bushes were there in 1876, or of their proliferation if they were, and the entrance into the coulee was very inviting and wide enough for his command. Third, we know for certain, march formations were changed regularly as necessity and terrain dictated. Reno changed his front from a column-of-fours to a column-of-twos as he crossed the Little Big Horn at Ford A, then back to a column-of-fours once on the river's left bank; the men were well attuned and well prepared for such maneuvers. Custer's "command was in a squadron formation (company front) of column-of-twos, moving at a trot and gallop all the way up the bluff."[15] This was a 50-foot frontage of 10 horses across, about 20 horses per column, 200 feet deep.[16] After dismounting in the valley, Lieutenant Varnum spotted the Gray Horse Troop *only*, moving north on the bluffs. That would indicate Custer's column had already changed its formation as the route narrowed between the edge of the bluffs and the looming mass of Sharpshooters' Ridge. As for the vegetation, James Willert—in a discussion of Curley's meanderings—had the young Crow scout returning to the column from a lookout point ahead, which was in a "sage-brush ravine [moving] in a direction which bore 'away from the valley.'"[17] That is Cedar Coulee, clearly, and it tells us the coulee had at least some bushes; a large number of them could have dictated movement. Custer would have slowed and re-formed or he could have swung his column up along the coulee's banks, or both. Neither is an unreasonable assumption and both could have occurred, each slowing the column's movement and causing events to fit even more snugly into the time-scheme of volley firing heard later atop Reno Hill.

So the route down Cedar Coulee proved more difficult than anticipated. Its overall length, from head to its confluence with Medicine Tail Coulee is some 1¼ miles, a good 15–20-minute walk under the best of circumstances. These men were not walking, however, and by the time Custer reached the head of the column from his trip to 3,411, the command's advance elements were a good ways down, but now having stopped, had also bunched up. In order to keep going with any semblance of order it is not unreasonable to assume Custer changed his formation once again, from a column-of-fours to a column-of-twos and may have even ordered his troops up the coulee's slopes to avoid the numerous bushes. Based on DeRudio's sighting of the men atop 3,411, we can give Custer some eight minutes of viewing time— 1:48–1:56 p.m.—and consider that reasonable, especially with all that was going on and all Custer needed to see. That would mean he left the heights at approximately 1:56 p.m. (as plotted), and at a quick trot reached the head of the coulee in four minutes. This is when he instructed Cooke to send a message back to Benteen (*Timeline K* and *N*).

Complicating the move down Cedar was the fact there were hostiles on the east side of the river, though not in any great numbers—at least not initially. We can account for at least 22—16 Sioux and four Cheyenne, by name; along with two other unknown Cheyenne alluded to in sundry narratives—and while we know one of the Sioux (a Sans Arc named Elk Stands Alone) and a Cheyenne (Whirlwind) were killed, indicating they were there during the Reno entanglement, or later on the 25th, or (less likely) during the 26th, but certainly after Custer had gone through—that still leaves a minimum of 18–20 warriors watching Custer's column make its way north.[18] In all likelihood some of these Indians were near Weir Peaks, as Custer headed toward Medicine Tail Coulee. It is also likely some of them re-crossed the Little Big Horn and alerted warriors who were not engaged in the valley fighting. Custer's presence was an additional surprise and one even less welcome than the first. This was now thrust, counter-thrust, thrust again.

By 2:05 p.m. Custer had reached the head of his command after instructing Cooke to send the message. After a difficult trip down the coulee, possibly switching formations and climbing coulee banks, Custer reached the bottom by 2:25 p.m., a trip of some 20 minutes. After a brief slowing and bunching up to allow the column's tail end to close, Custer opened the cylinders once again, turning left into Medicine Tail and heading in the direction of the Little Big Horn River.

None of this went unobserved. As noted, a number of Indians had made their way across the river and had seen Custer's column. One of these was a Hunkpapa named Iron Cedar, who broke for the bluffs, climbed down, swam the river and sought out the war chief, Gall. By this time, Gall was either fretting about the safety of his family or well aware of what had befallen them. After finding Gall, the two men bolted for the river, crossed and scaled the bluffs just in time to see Custer make his turn into Medicine Tail[19] (also, *Timeline K*). If Iron Cedar was on the river's right bank he would have seen Custer's approach at about 1:42 p.m., just as the column had crossed Reno Hill. In all likelihood, Iron Cedar was atop Weir Peaks, the obvious high point east of the river and just below the advancing troops, and he would not have stayed there long.

As Custer's scouts reined in and began milling about (this would have included the Crows—White Man Runs Him, Hairy Moccasin, Goes Ahead, and Curley—as well as Mitch Boyer; and according to some anecdotal evidence the Ree scout, Black Fox[20]), Iron Cedar would have turned on his heels and headed toward the village to warn of this new threat. That feat could have been accomplished in under 10 minutes—including the river swim, 1:42–1:51 p.m.—and once across he would begin his search for Gall. By now, with the village in wholesale panic, that was probably not an easy task, but by 2:10 p.m., the two men were back in the river crossing to its right bank. Weir Point was no longer an option, suddenly occupied by three of the Crows (the peripatetic lad Curley was already hot-footing it back south with Black Fox, both of them beyond Reno Hill and immediate danger). We can give the two Hunkpapa several more minutes, but by 2:23—right about the time Reno's men bolted from the timber—they were atop some bluffs watching Custer's column approach the mouth of Cedar Coulee. In all likelihood as well, the two Sioux came perilously close to the three Crow scouts who, having been released by Boyer, were wending their way north along the line of bluffs fronting the Little Big Horn. All this signaled imminent danger to Gall and Iron Cedar, and after watching for a few minutes, they began to make their way back to the village, reaching it by 2:39.

At about 2:32—and well into Medicine Tail Coulee heading toward the river—Custer spotted an easy slope off

Medicine Tail Coulee, looking toward the Little Big Horn River (trees in the background). Photograph was taken about 100 yards west of the turn out of Cedar Coulee (courtesy W. Donald Horn).

to his right leading to the top of a series of high ridges. Knowing he must cross these hills to get farther north and figuring he could see the valley more clearly, Custer swung his command to the right and mounted the ridge (notice how simple all this is and how easily one action flows from another, none requiring vast divergences from plans or routes). At 2:39 p.m. Custer and his lead elements reached the top of Luce Ridge and because of the easier terrain, the remainder of the two battalions was right on his tail. He stopped and looked around, peering down the valley and seeing the mass, northward exodus of hundreds upon hundreds of Indians—maybe even thousands. A moment or two later, shouts arose signaling a lone rider galloping at full tilt. It was younger brother Boston arriving—2:42 p.m. (*Timeline M*)—and bringing with him news of Reno's withdrawal and Benteen's arrival on Reno Creek. While the news about Reno was troubling, Boston had seen only the very early stages of the retreat, and neither the full extent of the debacle was known, nor was Reno's retreat route, a fact of prime significance and with never before discussed implications.

Common sense dictates Reno would retreat back *up* the valley and it probably never occurred to George Custer his major might have been forced early across the river, thereby interjecting his broken command between Custer and the expected arrival of Benteen's battalion. This is not as far-fetched as it may seem for up-valley was the route Reno knew and others believed it as well. Private Daniel Newell said,

> Our first idea on retreating to the river was to get back to the place where we had forded, but the Indians hidden in the timber and whom we had passed in our charge down the valley were busy by now and had cut us off there. So there was nothing to do but cut through the line between us and the river.[21]

The cutting off of this avenue of retreat was apparent even to the Indians. Foolish Elk, one of the more reliable Indian eyewitnesses, was riding with Crazy Horse that day and made the allusion to just such a movement in a September 22, 1908, interview with Walter Camp: "The soldiers retreated across the river at the nearest point they could reach and seemed to be in too much of a hurry to take their back track to the ford where they had come into the valley."[22]

Had Custer realized the implications of such an event, it is conceivable he would have broken off his advance and the outcome of the battle would have turned in a very different direction. Furthermore, Custer's decision to move north tells us Reno's plight was of little concern. What is extremely interesting, however, is the fact Custer absorbed the information about Benteen's arrival on the trail and based on his own calculations of how long it took him to go from the morass to the ridge he was on currently, Custer could have figured Benteen would be in this exact spot in about one to 1¼ hours, or *at about 4:00 p.m.* That would mean Custer would have to head toward the ford just west of where they were sitting, assess the situation from up close, and if it was necessary—as it appeared it might be—to continue heading north, find a crossing point, and situate himself in such a position his following minions would be able to see him, re-join him, and proceed to the assault. Soon, we will see just how precisely Custer judged and adhered to these calculations, to this schedule.

Boston Custer is an interesting sidebar to this whole entanglement. Very little has been written about him and most historians and battle students pay him short-shrift, sticking him automatically as an add-on, reaching the main column in either Cedar or Medicine Tail Coulee. In all likelihood, neither is true. What is known is Boston started out with the packs, but only to get himself a fresh horse and it is unclear where he joined them or where they were when he left. He spent the rest of the trip trying to catch up to his brothers (*Timeline M*), with only a passing reference by men of Benteen's command as he galloped by them while they were watering at the morass, and then the courtesy of an "aside" from Martini as they exchanged information just south of Reno Hill. When George Custer halted the column approximately one-quarter mile west of the divide, the pack train was still gathering on the east side. Assuming Boston went back at this time to exchange horses—which turns out to be the only reasonable time he could have done it—then he would have been able to catch the main command not much before it reached Luce Ridge. Unfortunately—like so many other events—we have little left behind telling us very much and while Boston's ride appears to be nothing more than another morsel of Little Big Horn minutiæ, it is important in that Boston would have been the only one who could have told his older brothers about Reno's plight. One of the few references we have connecting Boston to the packs comes from a February 26, 1909, letter written by Tom McDougall to Walter Camp in which McDougall remembers speaking with the younger Custer.[23] This probably occurred shortly after the lead of the regiment crossed the divide and halted for the battalion breakdown

and Boston rode back to the packs, exchanging horses and then starting out again as the whole train began to move. One can add to this the comments made to Walter Camp by former A Company trumpeter, William G. Hardy. Camp wrote, "Hardy says Boss Custer was with the five cos when Reno separated, and Boss said he was going to where the fighting would be. Haddon had Boss Custer's extra pony. Boss had two Indian ponies."[24] Hardy made no distinction, however, as to which Custer-Reno separation he was referring to: the one at the divide or the one in the flats near the lone tepee. As we shall see momentarily, however, it appears Hardy was referring to the separation at the divide. Also, there was no "Haddon" in the Seventh Cavalry, but that could have been a combination of faulty memory and innumerable unknown aliases within the regiment. In addition, the comment about "going to where the fighting would be," indicates nothing more than a possible reference to going with a maneuver battalion as opposed to remaining with the rear guard or packs.

The next Boston sighting we have comes at approximately 1:50 p.m. as Benteen's battalion was reaching Reno Creek and approaching the morass. A lone rider was seen galloping toward them and Lieutenant Edgerly recalled Boston "had stayed back with the pack train and was now hurrying up to join the general's immediate command. He gave me a cheery salutation as he passed, and with a smile on his face, rode to his death."[25] This covers a distance of some 8⅛ miles from slightly east of the divide and by 1:50 in the afternoon, Boston had been trotting at a speed of only 5.3 to possibly seven miles per hour, not very fast. Realizing he was not gaining on the main command, he opened up and when he passed Benteen's column, he was at a gallop. Even with George Custer's slowdowns and halts, Boston's galloping would have had to continue almost unabated for him to make up the distance and reach his brother any place before the killing grounds. The Edgerly sighting should be considered definitive and would eliminate any possibility of Boston reaching his brothers near the lone tepee in time for the Custer-Reno separation.

We can assume, therefore, Boston had to have been moving at a rate of 12 miles per hour down the remaining third of Reno Creek, also halting at or near the same spot his brother watered, then following the shod trail, moving up the slopes toward Reno Hill and running into Martini at about 2:19 p.m. After exchanging information—"*Your brother's ahead*"; "*Benteen's down yonder ... and do you know your horse has been shot?*"—Boston moved on, crossing Reno Hill at 2:24 p.m. Reno began his retreat at 2:23 p.m. and since Boston was passing over 3,411 at 2:26 (a not unreasonable speed of 13 miles per hour), he had to have seen mounted troopers running from the Indians.

While it would take a mounted column of 200-plus men a fair amount of time to negotiate the difficulties of Cedar Coulee in any semblance of military order (in this case some 20 minutes), the younger Custer was under no such constraint and he would have been able to navigate through its blockages fairly easily—maintaining a decent rate of speed of 8.4 miles per hour—in about eight minutes. Therefore, he would have made the turn into Medicine Tail Coulee at 2:35 p.m. increasing speed down the coulee's broad expanses, and finally arriving behind his brothers at Luce Ridge at 2:42 p.m. Anything before or later than this would be highly unlikely and the speeds used to compute any other scenario would have to be too fast entirely or ludicrously slow.

13

FORD B: ATTACK OR RECONNAISSANCE

REFERENCES:
Timeline R—From 3,411 to Ford B and Volley Firing; 1:38 p.m.–3:07 p.m.
W—Warriors; 1:02 p.m.–5:17 p.m.

Once atop Luce Ridge, Custer's precise route and objective become even greater enigmas; route and events have always been in question, starting from the first hours after the discovery of the debacle. Beyond Luce and Nye-Cartwright ridges, Custer's trail becomes clearer, and of course we know where his command wound up, though whether or not he went farther, then backtracked, is still not immutable fact. Even the shrewdest of immediate observers was befuddled. At the end of the July 4 letter to his wife, Benteen wrote, "The latest and probably correct account of the battle is that none of Custer's command got into the village at all."[1] Benteen's opinion had changed, probably during a hiatus in the writing of the letter, for a little earlier in the same correspondence, he stated, "I am of the opinion that nearly—if not all of the five companies got into the village—but were driven out immediately."[2] His opinion changed again, in all likelihood the result of constant discussions and theorizing, for at the inquiry in February 1879, Benteen admitted at first he thought Custer had gone down to Ford B, but by the time of the inquiry he had changed his mind, feeling Custer never went there. From his testimony it seems he believed Custer cut straight across Luce and Nye-Cartwright ridges.[3] This opinion now remained consistent throughout Benteen's remaining years and in a January 16, 1892, letter to Goldin, Benteen agreed with Ed Godfrey's theory of Custer's route.[4] Unlike Benteen's testimony at the Reno inquiry, Godfrey said he thought Custer had attempted to cross at Ford B, though he found no evidence of specific fighting.[5] Reno's defense counsel brought up the point the shod horse tracks seen at the ford might have been made when Indians drove captured army horses across the river[6] and while conceivable, it must be remembered the Indian activity after the Custer command had been destroyed could very easily have obliterated any tracks west or south of the Luce/Nye-Cartwright complex as the hostiles rode toward the Benteen and Reno battalions.

Confusion in 1886 was no different than it was 10 years earlier or 137 years later. As Godfrey walked the field with an old antagonist, Gall, the soldier asked the warrior about Custer's route.

> On the battle-field in 1886, Chief Gall indicated Custer's route to me, and it then flashed upon me that I myself had seen Custer's trail. On June 28, while we were burying the dead, I asked Major Reno's permission to go on the high ridge east or back of the field to look for tracks of shod horses to ascertain if some of the command might not have escaped. When I reached the ridge I saw this trail, and wondered who could have made it.[7]

In notes for his 1892 article, Godfrey continued that he

> dismissed the thought that it had been made by Custer's column, because it did not accord with the theory with which we were then filled, that Custer had attempted to cross at the ford, and this trail was too far back and showed no indication of leading toward the ford.... The ford theory arose from the fact that we found there numerous tracks of shod horses.[8]

It should also be noted here that while our timing studies indicate Gall would have seen Custer's column enter Medicine Tail Coulee—2:25 p.m.—Gall and Iron Cedar would have departed the bluffs at 2:29 p.m. prior to Custer beginning his move up to Luce Ridge—2:32 p.m. The two warriors would not have reached the village until about 2:39 p.m. the same time Custer reached the top of Luce. The next thing we can assume of Gall is his gathering of warriors and his heading for the nearest crossing—Ford B—not reaching it until about 3:09, a couple minutes after Custer's departure from the same area (*Timeline R and W*).

It is from the heights of Luce Ridge where a decision would be made to continue north or head toward the river, or both. That tracks were seen going to the killing grounds only indicates troops—some troops—on Luce and Nye-Cartwright moved in that direction. Any tracks going back into Medicine Tail Coulee or down the ridges toward the river could have been obliterated by Indians crossing at Ford B, Indians heading up Medicine Tail, and Indians cutting across both Nye and Luce, all coming from the direction of the Custer battle or the village.

Godfrey's comment—"this trail was too far back"—lends credence to the theory, while Custer *may* have gone—or *did* go—to Ford B, it was more of a reconnaissance than an attempt at crossing. The Seventh's surviving officers could visualize no intent to cross the river with so much of the command so far back. Simply put, it did not make sense to these men. This is further borne out by Benteen's mixed comments cited earlier. The tracks befuddled all and no one really knew, and the paucity of dead cavalry horses on the battlefield indicated they were either run off or captured, meaning the shod tracks found at Ford B could have been either residuals from a cavalry foray or an Indian celebration with captured mounts. The only continuity led across Luce and Nye-Cartwright, then onto Calhoun Hill.

Further insight is garnered from Graham's citing a later edition of Godfrey's article. Godfrey wrote when Reno began to fall back, "Gall started with some of his warriors to cut off Reno's retreat to the bluffs."[9] He stated by this time, Custer had crossed the "dry creek"—Medicine Tail Coulee—"and was marching along and well up the slope of the bluff forming the second ridge back from the river and nearly parallel to it."[10] This certainly seems like a description of the move up Calhoun Hill and then along Battle Ridge, though the timing is questionable. Godfrey went on to write,

> The command was marching in column of fours, and there was some confusion in the ranks, due probably to the unmanageableness of excited horses.... The accepted theory for 10 years after the battle, and still persisted in by some writers, was that Custer's column had turned the high bluffs near the river [*East Ridge, then Luce Ridge to the column's right*], moved down the dry coulee [*Medicine Tail*] and attempted to ford the river near the lowest point of these bluffs.[11]

Godfrey's editorializing—whether it involves Reno's move down the valley or this event—is moot, as well annoying and even misleading. We do not know if Custer's horses were unmanageable or not, and one can be assured by the time Godfrey figured the continuity of the trail included Battle Ridge, the route was marked not by the print of shod horses, but by the blood of dead cavalrymen.

Neither Godfrey nor Benteen, however, had the hindsight of latter-day research or the knowledge of Indian narratives garnered many years after the fighting alluding to the presence of soldiers at the Medicine Tail crossing. In addition, Godfrey never did the timing work and if, in later years, Gall claimed to have been involved in the Reno fighting, it was news to many who were. From the top of the east bank bluffs only a "Winged Gall" could have watched Custer enter Medicine Tail Coulee and then have made it back to help cut off Reno in his retreat. Reno began his retreat at approximately 2:23 p.m. at which time Gall and Iron Cedar were still struggling up bluff faces. By the time Gall got back to his camp, Custer was atop Luce Ridge and the first of Reno's men were reaching their hilltop entrenching area—2:38–2:39 p.m. (*Timeline R*).

While there are some who doubt Custer moved to Ford B the preponderance of evidence shows them to be wrong. In an undated interview with Walter Camp, the Oglala warrior, Shave Elk, claimed once he got his horse he and another Indian crossed the Little Big Horn at Medicine Tail ford and began riding up the coulee when they spotted Custer's column coming toward them.[12] They rode back down Medicine Tail and re-crossed the river, riding through camp and warning of the approach of more soldiers. Custer's column "came down this coulee toward the river and stopped just a little while, but not long and the Indians crossed over and attacked them. There were a few soldiers ahead of the main body."[13] There was firing on both sides and "we chased the soldiers up a long, gradual slope or hill in a direction away from the river and over the ridge where the battle began in good earnest."[14] There is some time compression here, for Custer was not "chased" anywhere and while the battle "began in good earnest," that part of it was yet to come. We can chalk up the hyperbole to either over-exuberance or economy of speech.

Shave Elk was not the only one to be startled when he saw bluecoats coming toward the village. Standing Bear, a Minneconjou warrior, claimed Custer's dust was seen as he approached the village down a dry coulee.[15] In 1907, Standing Bear told Judge Eli Ricker, "Custer came down the ridge across the creek—the second or rear ridge from the river. He made no known attempt to reach the river to cross."[16] In footnote five pertaining to that interview, author Richard Hardorff cleverly points out the discrepancy between this interview and the one done three years later with Camp. There is no issue here however, if Custer merely came to a point on a bluff and made no attempt to cross, even if E Company sat near the ford. Furthermore, Standing Bear claimed the soldiers halted near Ford B,[17] while the Oglala, Flying Hawk said, "Custer came down on the second ridge from the river, and he stopped on the high hill above the Indians."[18] This would seem to indicate the "Custer Bluff" area, the extension of the ridges where First Sergeant Butler's marker is placed currently. Hardorff's description in footnote three appears to agree.

A number of other warrior interviews bear this out. According to a map provided by Camp, Two Eagles, a Cu Brulé Sioux, claimed the troops went down the Luce/Nye-Cartwright complex to Ford B, and not directly across Luce/Nye to Calhoun Hill.[19] Two Eagles also claimed Custer's men were all mounted as they came down the coulee.[20] While seemingly contradictory, the testimony of a Minneconjou named Lights adds additional credence to the contention of a foray toward the river. In the spring of 1909, Lights told Sewell Weston as the troops approached the river near Ford B, they were dismounted. "They got to within a quarter of a mile of 'B' [ford]. That was as near as they ever got to the river."[21] The prominent Cheyenne, Two Moons, a headman in the Kit Fox warrior society and one of the leaders during the fighting, claimed two Cheyenne warriors near Ford B were the first to fire on the advancing Custer column.[22] Waterman, one of the handful of Arapaho warriors there, told Colonel Tim McCoy, "These troops were trying to cross the river and attack the camp, but the Indians drove them back."[23] Brave Wolf, a Northern Cheyenne, told George Bird Grinnell in 1895, Custer's soldiers got near the river, but none crossed.[24] The Northern Cheyenne warrior, Ice, claimed "Custer rode down to the river bank and formed a line of battle and [prepared] to charge."[25] The Hunkpapa woman, Pretty White Buffalo, who apparently reached the ford area in time to see troops there, claimed "[s]he saw the troops come up, dismount ... the rest deploy and advance on the run toward the river. She saw the terrible effect of the withering fire which greeted the approach from the willows on the Indian side of the stream."[26] A little self-serving hyperbole there, but a good description nonetheless.

The famed Cheyenne warrior, American Horse, told Grinnell, after the Reno fighting Indians ran down the river "and saw Custer coming down the hill and almost at the river." American Horse claimed he "was one of the first to meet the troops and the Indians and the soldiers reached the flat about the same time." Custer "was down on the river bottom at the river's bank." The troops fought there "for some little time," then "gave way and were driven up the hill."[27] Another Cheyenne warrior, the so-called Contrary, Brave Wolf, claimed an officer was killed "where Custer made his first stand—nearest the river.... One company started to run when Custer was near the river and the rest [of the battalion] fired on them and made them come back. This was the Bay Horse Company, probably Keogh's."[28] (Yates' F Company also rode light bays.[29]) In addition to all this, one of the most definitive statements came from another Northern Cheyenne warrior named White Shield. In a 1908 interview with Grinnell, White Shield said, "When the Gray Horse Company got pretty close to the river, they dismounted, and all the soldiers back as far as I could see stopped and dismounted also."[30] Too much evidence: Custer went to Ford B.

Over the years, it has been statements like these that have driven researchers mad, but when put in proper perspective, they all agree within the same loose parameters we have seen with the commentary of white troopers in the Reno command. With Custer and his five companies sitting atop Luce Ridge it is very easy to picture the troops peering into the Little Big Horn valley a little more than a mile away. From there Custer could see the full expanse of the village or at least see it extended below the ford, and according to Wooden Leg,

> The Cheyenne location was about two miles north from the present railroad station at Garryowen, Montana. We were near the mouth of a small creek flowing from the southwestward into the river. Across the river east of us and a little upstream from us was a broad coulee, or little valley, having now the name Medicine Tail coulee.[31]

That could preclude a crossing at this point. Custer would also see the mass, down-valley exodus of people, but would still not be able to know how far this flight extended or how many people were already *where?* Maybe a closer look—with no intention of crossing—would clear things up; thus, the move to Ford B.

There also remains the possibility—not strong, but plausible—Custer's foray was a feint aimed at taking pressure off Reno. Based on our timing we see Boston Custer crossed the 3,411 ridge in time to see the beginning of Reno's retreat—2:26 p.m. We also see Boston reached the head of the command as it neared the summit of Luce—2:42 p.m. There is no credible evidence of the younger Custer reaching his brothers before that and the only indication to the contrary come from the minds and pens of writers. Unfortunately they offer neither credible timing nor anecdotal evidence for their positions and without that we cannot make the assumption Boston reached the column either in Cedar Coulee or Medicine Tail Coulee. Once atop Luce Ridge, it is possible George may have been able to see enough, convincing him to move farther north. The drawbacks to that idea, however, are he was still a full mile or more from the river and from that distance river bluffs interfered with his sightlines in viewing the full extent of the village; plus the dust raised by fleeing families could have obscured the extent of the exodus. Either of these would have posed sufficient reason for Custer moving closer to the river, and Boston's news of Reno's plight would have added another. There was always the chance—however remote—a perceived peril at an intermediate point would have drawn off sufficient Indians to ease pressure on Reno and at the same time force warriors to a false threat. If Custer underestimated the size of the Indian force (and he did), then a successful feint to draw warriors away from Reno would have caused him little concern. The fact we know Custer moved to Ford B bears no relation to his initial plans of moving farther north directly off the ridge complex.

As we have seen in *Timeline R*, Custer arrived at Luce Ridge at about 2:39 p.m. If we give him 10 minutes to greet brother Boston, listen to his report, discuss briefly the pending situation with his officers, then instruct Myles Keogh to remain back and cover an advance toward the river, we would have headquarters and the Yates battalion beginning their move to the ford at 2:49 p.m. If the testimony of the warriors is anywhere near reasonable—and we should accept it is—then Custer began his move down the ridge, sending Smith's Gray Horse Troop back into the coulee as flank protection, just as the Oglala, Shave Elk, claimed. (Surely it was noticed Indians were beginning to gather on the river's eastern ridges to the south, and like Indians fronting Reno as a screen to protect fleeing families, Custer too, needed a screen; again, solid military tactics.) There is no reason why Custer himself would have to go back into the coulee when his objective was seen more clearly from the height of the ridge as he advanced, and he needed that intelligence.

Despite the efficacy of splitting his battalion in a move toward the ford, however, it must be remembered this is conjecture, and in fact, there is some evidence against a split. In an undated interview with former Second Cavalry lieutenant, Edward J. McClernand who was part of the Terry-Gibbon command and who viewed the battlefield two days after the fighting, "there was a double column-of-fours down Medicine Tail Coulee." This trail turned across into Deep Coulee, then up to its forks, and onto Finley Ridge. McClernand claimed the trail was too regular to be anything but a cavalry trail.[32] A double column-of-fours indicates separate units, i.e., two companies—or possibly two platoons riding abreast. As usual, there is some evidence to the contrary. After hearing of additional troops to the east and downriver, the Ute/ Southern Cheyenne warrior, Yellow Nose, headed that way and crossed the river "where a small stream entered from the east."[33] (This precise location is hard to figure, unless the Medicine Tail Coulee, Deep Coulee, or Deep Ravine ford deltas were wet from the heavy winter run-off.) "Ascending a promontory formed by this gulch and the river," Yellow Nose and the Indians with him saw troops coming toward them. The soldiers were advancing along the crest of a divide running back from the Little Big Horn.[34] This "promontory"

seems like it may be the so-called "Curtis Knoll" forming the southern end of Greasy Grass Ridge and the troops were coming down the Luce Ridge extension, beyond "Butler Ridge" toward "Custer Bluff," the end of the ridge before it drops to the flats leading to Ford B, some 325–350 yards away. The troops were coming at a gallop. If this is all true, we may add Yellow Nose and a few others to the small force of Indians greeting the Yates battalion as it deployed near the ford.

Neither command's speed was overly rapid at this time, Custer moving probably at a rate of some six to eight miles per hour, Smith averaging a bit more to keep parallel. By 2:55 p.m. Custer would have arrived at the bluffs overlooking Medicine Tail ford, and about three minutes later, Smith would be arriving at the low ground immediately in front of his commander, then dismounting all or part of his company to set up skirmishers. By giving Custer credit for solid tactical maneuvering, we can also make sense of the statements of Shave Elk, Flying Hawk, Standing Bear, Two Eagles, Brave Wolf, Waterman, Lights, and the rest. This would also mark the beginning of the "Custer fight," its timing supported tenuously by narratives left us by Good Voiced Elk. In 1909, the 56-year-old Hunkpapa told Walter Camp, "Custer was making direct for the village as though to cross the river and come into the village, when the Indians went over and drove him back. Custer's fight started about ½ hour after Reno's retreat."[35] With Reno's retreat beginning at 2:23 p.m. and Smith arriving at Ford B at 2:58 p.m. Good Voiced Elk's estimate of the timing appears eerily accurate.

(It should be noted here, archaeological findings of Indian cartridge cases in the vicinity of Ford B are virtually meaningless as a tool to assess whether or not Custer's command was at the ford. Soldier narratives mention seeing Indians celebrating in this vicinity—shooting rounds into the air—some little while after the Custer fighting was believed to have ended.)

The question arises now, did Custer intend to cross the river at this point, and attack the village? The answer is an emphatic, *not a chance!*

First of all, no commander worth his salt would move to an attack with 58 percent of his force a mile to the rear. (At this point, we can assume all the stragglers had dropped out and Custer's entire command was some 210-strong. Keogh's battalion consisted of his own I Company, 38 men; Harrington's C Company, also 38 men; and Calhoun's L Company, the largest at 46. Yates had companies E and F, both with 38 troopers; and headquarters, consisting of 12 souls, including Mitch Boyer and three civilians: Boston Custer; nephew Autie Reed; and the newspaperman, Marc Kellogg.) Second, with hundreds of families hot-footing it through the valley below, there had to be clouds of rising dust obscuring everything more than a few hundred feet west of the river. There was no clear picture even from the river bluffs and no prudent commander would ever charge into that chaos. No, Custer was at the ford all right, but he needed further reconnaissance, not some haphazard attack to puncture an under-inflated balloon, one that would bring him across a river into a mostly empty village, not knowing whether to turn left or right, either decision exposing his rear. A further indication Custer never intended to cross at Ford B was the fact that despite some post-battle bravado, there was sharp but only limited resistance from the Indians, probably numbering no more than some two dozen warriors.[36]

Of course there are those who believe in the timeworn theory, dubbed by archaeologist Richard Fox as the "fatalistic" theory[37]: Custer attempted to cross at Ford B, but was foiled by an overwhelming force of Indians lying in ambush. While this approach to the Custer fight has its usual group of adherents, there is less evidence of its viability than even the idea Custer never went to the ford in the first place. First and foremost, the timing precludes such a rout; too much time elapsed—as we shall see—between the arrival at the ford and the end of the fighting, and if Custer had been routed out of the area the battle would have ended much sooner. Second, the overall body placement mitigates against the theory and if there was severe fighting and a wholesale retreat, the fact only two troopers were killed anywhere near the ford—one of whose horse bolted across the river, the man's body found in the village after the battle[38]—also tells us a rout was unlikely. Lastly, if Custer were forced away from this area, why would he then proceed northward, away from his support, rather than back the way he had come? He had Myles Keogh and three companies of cavalry close to a mile in his rear and Keogh could have provided covering fire for a withdrawal back along the high ground, not into a ravine. With a disciplined force of more than 200 cavalrymen Custer was unlikely to be *forced* anywhere, at least by the number of warriors he was faced with in the coulee or ford area. Custer's friend and schoolmate, Tom Rosser, agreed: "Had Custer been repulsed at [Ford B] ... his column would have been driven back upon the line on which he had approached and the proposition [Custer's "repulse"] is too silly to be discussed."[39] (This same logic may be applied to the thinking regarding Reno's retreat route.) Anyone believing Custer went to Ford B to attack the village is bereft of a basic understanding of tactics and pays no credit to Custer either as a soldier or a tactician; while he made mistakes, this was not one of them. So again, the answer here is, no, and George Custer moved north of his own volition, his tactical concept very much the way he would have liked and the opposition easily swatted away.

There is little reason for Custer to have spent more than 10 minutes assessing events from the bluffs above the ford. If he arrived there at 2:55 p.m. by 3:05 he was on his way to an agreed upon rendezvous site north of the Luce/Nye-Cartwright complex Keogh was currently occupying. With Custer on the move and Smith continuing to act as his screen, Keogh needed to keep distance between the commands and encroaching Indians. He solved that problem by ordering his troops to fire on any Indians within range. The time was 3:07 p.m.

Myles Keogh sat back and watched, but it was not just his fellow soldiers on his mind. He also watched as Indians began gathering on the east side of the river farther upstream, the warriors likewise watching as Custer made his way toward the ford and them. As Custer finished his survey and began moving off the bluff, this burgeoning threat drew Keogh's ire and fire, much of it directed at a band of about 50 mounted warriors led by two Cheyenne braves, Wolf Tooth and Big Foot, coming down Medicine Tail from the east. That was unacceptable of course, as it would threaten Custer's rear. Keogh would have also seen the three Crow scouts as they made their way along the bluffs toward Ford B, though we have no idea if he recognized them (we will address the scouts issue in the next chapter). The handful of Sioux and Cheyenne on the east bank—if allowed—would have come down the coulee closest to the river and behind the scouts. While one tends to think the Crows were not uppermost in Keogh's mind, the additional threat to Smith and Custer was.

As we saw earlier, one can make the assumption some of these Indians on the east side of the river fired on Messenger Martini as he made his way toward Benteen, hitting the trumpeter's horse in its rump and indicating the warriors were closer to the troops rather than farther away. From here, some warriors had to have moved north following Custer's progress, otherwise it is hard to imagine Keogh wasting the effort and the ammunition shooting at Indians some 1¼ miles away. While the troops' Model 1873 "Springfield carbine would reach a range of 2,800 yards before the bullet would fall below the minimum of 300 feet per second,"[40] its maximum effective range was much closer to 250 yards. Assuming Keogh sought to either kill or scare whoever he was shooting at, the firing fan seen in the artifact field[41] puts the Indians right smack in Medicine Tail Coulee, right in Algernon Smith's rear—a good enough reason to draw volley fire. This would have chased any riders back up Medicine Tail, and had the coulee been their point of egress—based on that fan—the route indicated other hostiles would have traveled down West

Coulee (the coulee closest to the river and the second coulee west of Cedar) or the ridges on either side of its banks. The fact no attendant bullets show up as artifacts is consistent with shot landing in intermittent waterways and being washed away over decades (or, just as likely, simply that no one ever thought to look there), very much like the problem arising with a lack of artifacts in Deep Ravine. Indians suddenly appearing in the troops' rear would explain the volley firing and would also be consistent with the immediacy such an event seems to suggest.

14

SCOUTS

REFERENCES:
Timeline I—From Separation to 3,411; 1:05 p.m.–1:56 p.m.
K—Scouts; 11:30 a.m.–4:35 p.m.
N—Messengers; 12:12 p.m.–2:41 p.m.
Y—Stragglers; 12:42 p.m.–4:30 p.m.

Pinning down the movements of the various scouts is another difficult task in analyzing the battle. We do not know the precise number used by the regiment and even Charlie Varnum got some of the names confused or just outright wrong. Walter Camp in all his research came up with the names of 44 Arikara and Dakota scouts, including those carried as quartermaster employees.[1] William A. Graham carried 43[2]; Roger L. Williams listed 55, total, including Dakota and Crow[3]; Vern Smalley showed 39[4]; and John Gray, 36.[5] While these numbers are correct in one form or another, none of them properly account for the scouts at the Little Big Horn on June 25, 1876.

By best estimates, 655 men crossed the Rosebud-Little Big Horn divide. Of that number, 607 belonged to the regiment; the rest were civilians acting as scouts and interpreters, enlisted Indian scouts, guides, a reporter, packers, and the so-called quartermaster employees. Discrepancies are found among the Indian scouts and this is understandable, especially considering the vagaries of name. For example, neither Williams nor Graham list Red Foolish Bear and Foolish Bear as separate individuals, but the ultimate researcher, Walter Camp, did, as does Vern Smalley. To make matters worse, Smalley claims Red Foolish Bear crossed the Little Big Horn with Reno, fighting in the valley, while others say the two men are the same and "Foolish Bear" carried messages and was not even present during the fighting. Another problem is some carry Bloody Knife in the same category as a "Ree scout," while others—separating the categories—consider him a "quartermaster employee." Then there is "Curley"—the Crow—versus "Curly"—the Ree—different spelling, and

when one adds the name "Head"—"Curly Head"—different again, but the same Ree.

Taking all of this together and comparing the names to various accounts made over the years one is able to show the following breakdown, *excluding* the term, "Quartermaster Employee":

Interpreters (2)
1. Isaiah Dorman (for the Dakota scouts)—killed during Reno's retreat
2. Fred Gerard (for the Rees)

Guides/Scouts (4)
1. Bloody Knife (a Ree, but carried separately as a QM employee)—killed in Reno's timber
2. Mitch Boyer (attached from Gibbon's command, June 22)—killed with Custer
3. George Herendeen (attached from Gibbon's command, June 22)
4. Charlie Reynolds—killed during Reno's retreat

Civilians (3)
1. Boston Custer (carried as a QM employee)—killed with Custer
2. Marc Kellogg (reporter)—killed with Custer
3. Harry Reed (nephew to the Custer brothers)—killed with Custer

Packers (5)
1. William Alexander
2. Ben Franklin Churchill
3. John Frett
4. Frank Mann—killed on Reno Hill
5. John Wagoner

Crow Scouts (6; all attached from Gibbon's command, June 22)
1. Curley
2. Goes Ahead
3. Hairy Moccasin
4. Half Yellow Face—inadvertently followed Reno's command
5. White Man Runs Him
6. White Swan—inadvertently followed Reno's command

Dakota Scouts (4)
1. Caroo—did not cross the Little Big Horn
2. Matoksha—did not cross the Little Big Horn
3. White Cloud—did not cross the Little Big Horn
4. Whole Buffalo

Arikara (Ree) Scouts (24, not counting Bloody Knife, above)
1. Black Fox—did not cross the Little Big Horn
2. Bob-tail Bull—killed fighting with Reno
3. Boy Chief
4. Bull—did not cross the Little Big Horn
5. Bull Stands In Water—did not cross the Little Big Horn
6. Billy Cross—unclear if he crossed the river; may have been with the pack train
7. Forked Horn
8. Good (or Pretty) Face—accompanied the packs, initially; did not cross the Little Big Horn
9. Goose
10. Billy Jackson
11. Little Brave—killed fighting with Reno
12. Little Sioux
13. One Feather
14. Red Bear
15. Red Foolish Bear
16. Red Star
17. Red Wolf—did not cross the Little Big Horn
18. Rushing Bull—did not cross the Little Big Horn
19. Soldier—did not cross the Little Big Horn
20. Stab—rode initially with Benteen, then left; did not cross the Little Big Horn
21. Strikes The Lodge—did not cross the Little Big Horn
22. Strikes Two
23. White Eagle—did not cross the Little Big Horn
24. Young Hawk

Ree Messengers Along the Rosebud, Not at the Battle (4)
1. Curly Head
2. Foolish Bear
3. Howling Wolf
4. Running Wolf

This gives us a total of 48 sundry personnel accompanying the command, not counting two contract surgeons carried on the regimental rolls, and the four Ree scouts used as messengers.

As we noted earlier, more evidence of Custer's rate of speed down Reno Creek comes in the form of stragglers. Not only did troops begin to fall behind, but several scouts did as well (*Timeline Y*). As we can see in *Timeline K*, the Ree scouts, Soldier, Bull, and White Eagle, dropped back, finally—by 1:05 p.m.—catching up to the command, approaching the regiment's tail-end as Custer stopped for a few minutes at the lone tepee. Varnum, who had been riding out front and to the left, discovered all the scouts who had started out with him had fallen by the wayside and were now intermingled with the lead elements of the command. He

> reported to Genl. Custer two or three times on what I saw, but got at last far to the left front and found I had only Pvt. Strode ... with me. As our paths had diverged to some extent, I was some time rejoining the command and found all my scouts bunched at the head of the column.[6]

Varnum proceeded to "cuss out my Rees, telling Custer they had run away from me while I was out to the front."[7]

Some confusion occurred when Half Yellow Face and White Swan were directed up the bluffs to precede Custer, but misunderstood and wound up ahead of Reno. This left Custer with four Crows and Black Fox—the Ree—as he mounted the bluffs on the Little Big Horn's right bank. By the time the commands separated and were on their way downstream, Custer had the five scouts[8] plus Mitch Boyer; and Reno had Gerard and Dorman; Reynolds, Herendeen, and Bloody Knife; as well as two Crows. In addition, one of the Dakota scouts—Whole Buffalo—followed (or preceded, it is unknown which) Reno, along with 13 Rees, giving him a total of 21 sundries to add to his contingent of 138 troops. On the way down the valley he lost at least six of the scouts.

Custer never expected his scouts to do any of the fighting and he had told the Rees they should be off stealing ponies. These six decided that was a good idea, but as Reno headed downstream, Strikes Two, Red Star, One Feather, Little Sioux, Whole Buffalo, and Boy Chief found Sioux women and children—as well as Sioux ponies—irresistible. While the Rees forever denied they were the guilty parties, someone dispatched Gall's wives and children, all along stealing a number of horses, probably in the range of 28.[9] The pony stealing accounts are fairly consistent, including names of scouts who never crossed the river, descriptions of where the ponies were herded, and even the ravine south of Reno Hill where they were temporarily sequestered until they could be moved—and lost again, being chased by more irate Sioux.

After being captured, the horses were moved across the river onto a flat at the base of the bluffs, then up a shallow ravine to the hilltops. Once there, other straggling Rees entered the picture (*Timeline Y*). These were some who followed Custer's command, but lagged far behind and included Bull Stands In Water, Soldier, White Eagle, Stab, Strikes The Lodge, Bull, and Billy Cross, as well as the three remaining Dakotas, Caroo, Matoksha, and White Cloud. We hear virtually nothing about Pretty (or Good) Face, Red Wolf, and Rushing Bull, although it is accepted Pretty/Good Face spent much of the time with the pack train.

Reno began his move down the Little Big Horn valley at about 1:22 p.m. and we can figure the six scouts broke away from the command no more than six minutes later—1:28. That would fit with the speed they were moving, the fact we know the scouts preceded Reno's command to and after Ford A,[10] and the location of the flats where the scouts herded the horses after re-crossing the river. Those flats are approximately one mile below where Reno began his downstream foray, and after cutting out the ponies they could handle, the flats would have afforded the scouts a perfect crossing, a rally point, and a route up to perceived safety on the bluffs. By 1:40 p.m.—

18 minutes after starting out—the horses could have been herded across the river and up to the hills. At this time, Reno's command has been deployed as skirmishers and Custer is beyond Reno Hill, though he had stragglers and trailers still making their way north.

We can now allude to the fantasy left us by one of C Company's stragglers, Private Peter Thompson, lagging behind somewhere near Reno's entrenching area on the hill, either before or after. Someone fired on the Ree scouts mistaking them for unfriendlies[11] and these fellows had to be stragglers, though possibly the C Company malingerers, Fitzgerald and Brennan. We can figure a timeline of some 15 minutes from that 1:40 p.m. mark, to when the Rees were fired on—about 1:55 p.m.—for Custer was still at 3,411 watching Reno's fight (*Timeline I*) and even the stragglers were beginning to close the gaps. The "sending" of Sergeant Kanipe enters the picture here as well, for as the scouts were milling about trying to control their purloined horses, trying to decide where to put them and what to do next, Strikes Two spotted another soldier—this one with stripes on his sleeves—heading toward them.[12] The only possible fit is Kanipe and this would have occurred about 2:07 p.m. if he were to reach Benteen as claimed.

One of the things so interesting here—especially with this location—is the scouts claimed to sequester these stolen ponies in a nearby ravine. The only such feature in the entire area lies some 250 yards east of elevation marker 3,375 on the topographical map—fitting perfectly with the Rees' accounts—and from this spot several of them made their way to Reno Hill, following Custer's wake. This would not have been until about 2:20 p.m. however, and Custer would have been well down Cedar Coulee by that time. There is also the likelihood Boss Custer and Trumpeter Martini met in this same general area at about this time and it cannot be ruled out it may have been those two—rather than C Company stragglers—who took the pot-shots at the scouts (*Timeline N*).

All of this seems fairly straightforward and we now turn our attention to the Crow scouts, a more difficult and contentious matter.

Many battle students believe the four Crows moved ahead of Custer's command and viewed the valley fighting from atop Weir Peaks, unless of course one is still imbued with the fantasy of Custer himself being at Weir, but we dismiss that as nonsense. Instead, we find it more realistic to rely on the recollections of some of the Crows. According to Hairy Moccasin and Goes Ahead, as Custer reached the area where he was to view the action in the valley—3,411—he instructed the scouts to move north to the high ground looming ahead.[13] Both reasonable and logical. Mitch Boyer and three of the Crows proceeded to do just that. And Curley was not among them! As the party of four moved north, Curley held back and was seen with the Ree, Black Fox.[14] We learn of this from Goes Ahead—who was there—and Boy Chief—who was not—and rather than rely on hearsay, we prefer to accept only what Goes Ahead claimed. Since this is not a trial by jury, however, we must pay some heed to the oral claims of participants, however obtuse; for all we know, Black Fox himself may have told Boy Chief.

In our timing schemes, at a pace of seven to eight miles per hour, Boyer and the Crows would have reached Weir Peaks by 1:53 p.m. covering the distance of 1,350 yards in about seven minutes. From there they would have done what all good scouts do: watch. Arriving at 1:53 would have afforded them the following views: lots of dust and smoke in the valley; Reno's skirmish line advancing; Custer and a couple of friends sitting astride their horses, peering intently into the valley from a high knoll to the south; and a slowing command of more than 200 soldiers moving into the head of a ravine to the rear. We now have an unusual—and it seems lost or overlooked—comment from Goes Ahead and White Man Runs Him. Boyer re-joined Custer from the vicinity of Weir Peaks—2:07 p.m.—rather than from the bluff near Ford B, the so-called Boyer's Bluff.[15] Other than a single comment by Hairy Moccasin during an interview with Walter Camp many years later,[16] there is no other mention of Boyer being with the Crows after everyone departed from Weir. Boyer's re-joining Custer closer to Weir Peaks rather than a mile or more down Indian infested ridges and ravines makes eminent sense. While this will raise eyebrows, certainly, one must then ask, how Boyer could have anticipated Custer's going to Ford B, thereby precipitating the scout's phantom ride along the ridges to meet Custer. It makes no sense, for at the time there was no plan for Custer to go that ford. A group of three Crows would attract little attention—read, *interest!*—from Indians who were clearly not yet galvanized into any sense of organized or mass action, and the Crows may have even been mistaken for fellow–Sioux by lurking hostiles, while Boyer's mode of dress would have marked him as a scout. The three scouts—"released" by Boyer—began to move northward—2:12 p.m.—along those ridges and bluffs—*without* Boyer—a story the three stuck to for the remainder of their lives. It was also a story not deviating a whit from its original telling, making it consistent and believable. And again, other than onc lone allusion by Hairy Moccasin *many* years later, there is no mention of Boyer—or for that matter, Curley—being with them.

Curley's tales varied over the years, reaching the crescendo of a young scout covered in a stolen red Sioux blanket, watching the final throes of the Custer battle from a ridge to the east. Say what you will about the man; he had a sense of legacy. As the years wore on even some of the white veterans expressed doubt about Curley's exploits. Former M Company private, William Slaper wrote, "For 'Curley' I will say that I do not believe he ever got to the Custer forces, but skirmished his way around the outside until a chance presented itself for him to make his escape undetected. I am certain he was not in the fight."[17] Even more accurate might be the reserved comments of his fellow scouts. For example, Goes Ahead related his story in *The Arikara Narrative*, maintaining as Custer swung off from Reno, there was one Ree scout and the four Crows with him.

> Custer rode to the edge of the high bank and looked over to the place where Reno's men were, as though planning the next move. When they had arrived at about the point where Lieutenant Hodgson's headstone was placed later, the three Crow scouts saw the soldiers under Reno dismounting in front of the Dakota camp and thought that the enemy were "too many." Close to where Reno and Benteen later in the day were attacked by the Dakotas, on the ridge of hills above the river, the three Crow scouts were left behind and Custer's command went down the draw toward the lower ford on the run.[18]

At the same time, Goes Ahead was sure Curley was not with them. He indicated Curley and the Ree, Black Fox, rode off together.[19] Furthermore, Goes Ahead claimed the three Crows rode along the bluffs, keeping back out of the sight of the Sioux in the valley—*and along the ridges?*—and reached the end of the bluffs, "just above the lower ford," (Ford B) then dismounted and fired into the Dakota camp, into the circle of tepee tops they could see beyond the trees.[20] In addition to the fact Goes Ahead had excluded Curley from this little foray, he ended his tale by saying, "They heard two volleys fired and saw the soldiers' horses standing back of the line in groups," and then the scouts "rode back along the ridge" and met the Ree scouts and the pack mules.[21] This is significant for a number of reasons, which we shall see soon.

Much less reliable is the testimony of Hairy Moccasin who told Walter Camp in 1911, the four Crows and Boyer accompanied Custer.[22] He claimed, however, Curley left the command at Weir Peaks, and Boyer released the other Crows near the Ford B area. Then they went back along the Medicine Tail and south coulees (probably meaning direction, north-south), and along bluffs past Reno Hill almost to Ford A where they met Benteen. On the way, they met a dismounted soldier who went with them to Benteen.[23] While there is nothing here to call the man a liar, there is no corroborating evidence from Benteen—or anyone else—about

meeting a dismounted soldier with the Crows who directed them to Reno Hill. At a later date, Hairy Moccasin said after heading back, they met Benteen "just" south of where Reno and Benteen later entrenched.[24]

The last of the Crows was White Man Runs Him. Camp interviewed him as well, though the exact date is unknown. In a February 1910, letter to General Charles A. Woodruff, however, Camp wrote, "Benteen met the three Crows on the first rise of the bluffs north of the mouth of Sundance [Reno] Creek. This is 1,600 to 1,800 feet north of Ford A, and about 1⅛ miles ... south of Reno Hill." He added Godfrey was adamant about this, saying there could be no mistake as he himself, rode up to one of them and tried to converse.[25] *Fine!* But we are not done with Mr. Godfrey.

Several years later in a battlefield interview by General Hugh Scott (August 24, 1919), White Man Runs Him said Boyer was the one who told them to go back, but he did not see Curley. He also claimed the "first time we stopped on the bluff [was] when Mitch Boyer left us to go to Custer, and before we returned to Reno those nearest began to run."[26] He added Curley had gone with the Rees and the horses, claiming the Rees said Curley was with them when they reached the mouth of the Rosebud.[27] Colonel Tim McCoy who accompanied Scott during that trip, transcribed the following. (Graham wrote this was the most definitive account by any of the Crows, despite a few "minor details"; McCoy was extremely proficient in sign language.) White Man Runs Him said the Crows went back along the ridge and found Reno's men "entrenched" there, and just about the time Reno attacked the village, Curley met some Rees and together they ran off a large bunch of Sioux ponies, riding away with them. After the battle, White Man Runs Him met some Rees who said Curley went with them to the mouth of the Rosebud.[28]

What we seem to have here is the following: Custer told Boyer and the Crows to head up to the high ground, *viz.,* Weir Peaks. Three of them went with Boyer, but Curley hesitated and went with Black Fox. Once on Weir Peaks, Boyer released the Crows and headed down to Cedar Coulee to rejoin Custer's advancing command and report what he had seen—a larger camp and a longer exodus. The Crows then followed the bluffs toward the river, advancing all the way to the bluffs' end near Ford B. From there they fired on the village and saw Custer's command on the high ground of Luce Ridge. The Crows then backtracked. In the meantime, Curley and Black Fox moved south, beyond Reno Hill toward Reno Creek. The question arises now, however, how far did those three Crows backtrack and who did they first meet, Reno or Benteen?

This is important to establish in that it demonstrates

Curley's whereabouts and how much of his wayward story telling we should believe (see *Timeline K*). We allow for the scouts' arrival at Weir Peaks at 1:53 p.m. and we have also figured Custer left the vicinity of 3,411 at about 1:56. Figuring Curley and Black Fox would not leave the command until Custer and his entourage were pretty much consigned to heading north, we can assume the two scouts turned to go in the opposite direction by 2:00 p.m. If they moved at a trot they would be passing over Reno Hill by 2:05. At 2:07 p.m., Boyer has released the Crows and turned toward Custer in Cedar Coulee, and by 2:12, having watched the fighting in the valley and Custer moving down Cedar, the three Crows head off Weir and begin their trek north, down the bluffs. By 2:28, Curley and Black Fox reach Reno Creek—or better yet, North Fork—where they pause and water their horses. The Crows, meanwhile, reach "Boyer's Bluff" at 2:32 p.m. They stop, dismount (so they claimed), and watch. At about this same time Custer is beginning his move up to Luce Ridge. There are only scattered Sioux and Cheyenne about, so there is no real danger for anyone—other than the possible threat of a band of Cheyenne led by Wolf Tooth and Big Foot, though in all likelihood these warriors were much farther up Medicine Tail Coulee and well behind Custer—and the racket haunting Reno's command farther upstream is nothing more than a distant trémulo. The Crows now begin to shoot at village tepees or any other convenient target they see, their shots falling among the Sans Arc and Minneconjou tepees. They also watch as Custer and Yates—with Smith in the coulee—head toward the ford and shortly they become aware of the volley firing of Keogh's command, some of which may have been aimed at them inadvertently.

In the meantime, Reno has broken from the timber, and Benteen is on his way. At 2:38 p.m. the first men of Reno's routed command begin reaching the hilltop on the east side of the Little Big Horn, long vacated by Curley and Black Fox. Between 2:41 p.m.—when he ran into Martini—and 2:48 p.m.—when he reached the river, Benteen spotted three or four Indians on the bluffs some 400–500 yards off to his right. At first he thought they were hostile, but when he rode toward them he realized they were Crows. They said there was a "big 'pooh poohing' going on." He then saw men on the bluffs and immediately rode there meeting Reno.[29] As for identification, all we know from this is they were Crows, or at least one of them was.

Lieutenant Edgerly left us with a little more. In his 1881, *Leavenworth Times* statement, Edgerly said Benteen's column hurried toward Ford A, but when they came close they spotted the Crow, Half Yellow Face, who beckoned them up the hill. They followed.[30] Lieutenant Godfrey agreed. At the

Reno inquiry, Godfrey said simply, when Benteen's battalion got within "a mile of the bottom" they saw some Crows who directed them to the right,[31] a statement he confirmed years later in his *Century Magazine* article: "There was a short time of uncertainty as to the direction in which we should go, but some Crow scouts came by, driving a small herd of ponies, one of whom said, 'Soldiers,' and motioned for the command to go to the right."[32] It was only years later in an undated interview with Camp that Godfrey got more specific. He said as they got closer to the ford, he met an Indian who he believed was Half Yellow Face (though he admitted it may have been a Ree). Godfrey asked where Custer had gone and the Indian pointed off to the right. The column moved in that direction. "Benteen must have been some distance ahead of his command."[33] This all differs a little, however, from Godfrey's original writings. Several days after the battle, he made the following entry in his diary:

> Some Crow Indian scouts came up over the hills driving a herd of ponies and soon came to us and I asked by signs which way we could go down to the bottom or get to the command. [H]e motioned to go to the right, and I told Col. Benteen so we went that way a short distance and soon came to where Col. Reno with his Cos A, G, & M were.[34]

The Half Yellow Face identification, therefore, came years later and we know for certain five of the Crow scouts did no pony droving that day. While a misidentification of someone we do not know is understandable, it would be less so entirely when it came to the clear distinction between the appearance of a Crow Indian and an Arikara. In a footnote to Godfrey's diary entry, Edgar Stewart wrote, "These were Arikaras. Godfrey's mistake in calling them Crow has been repeated by many subsequent writers."[35] But was it a mistake? Maybe there was a Crow, a single Crow, and the mistake was merely in identifying them all as Crow.

Private Charles Windolph of Benteen's H Company said they passed several Indian scouts—not sure if they were Crow or Ree—driving some Sioux ponies (confirming Godfrey's thoughts), and the scouts yelled, "Soldiers," pointing to the hilltop to the right. Benteen ordered drawn pistols and the command galloped up the bluffs.[36]

Some might be apt to accept Edgerly and Godfrey's statements the "Crow" directing the command toward Reno Hill was Half Yellow Face (who, with White Swan rode off with Reno), but the problem with this recollection is White Swan had been wounded in the valley fighting and Half Yellow Face never left his side. If we consider Reno did not begin his retreat until 2:23 p.m. and the first of his men did not reach the hilltop until 2:38 p.m. it would leave no time for either—or both—Half Yellow Face and White Swan to reach a point slightly north of Reno Creek. Lieutenant Varnum would have agreed with this, for in his various interviews with Camp he claimed he first noticed Half Yellow Face and White Swan on the bluffs right after Reno's retreat, hardly giving them the time to reach Benteen and return.[37] In addition, despite the claim of Camp (in his letter to General Woodruff), we have only an assumption those who met Benteen were the three Crow who had advanced along the bluffs toward Ford B. White Man Runs Him said they went back along the ridge and found Reno's men "entrenched," and Goes Ahead said when they got back they met the Ree scouts and the pack mules, an intimation all were together. The only place that could have been was atop Reno Hill, well after Benteen's arrival.

Hairy Moccasin was the only bogey here, but despite his claim the three went back and met Benteen, we must understand this came from the Camp interview—an intermediary doing the translating—and may be fraught with Camp's penchant for inserting opinion in place of uncertainty. While one hates to call yet another testimony into question, there is the matter of some 40 years of time elapse and the Crows' tendency to exaggeration. Maybe over the years more embellishment fit into the place of less reality. This can be seen in Hairy Moccasin's claim they met a dismounted soldier—and they *probably* did, i.e., Private Peter Thompson—who accompanied them to Benteen—which he *certainly* did not! Thompson, supposedly horseless, advanced in their direction and would have met them only after Reno and Benteen were ensconced on the hilltop.

It is therefore, highly likely Benteen ran into young Curley, Black Fox, and maybe a couple of other Rees, this despite the tenuous identifications by Edgerly and Godfrey. We must understand these Crow scouts had been attached to the regiment only since June 22—three days earlier—and if we are to believe all the attendant testimony of the advance up the Rosebud, the Crow's Nest, and everything else to this point, then it is somewhat far-fetched to think Edgerly and Godfrey could recognize Half Yellow Face by name, especially since they were rarely seen in that short period of time, and why would they even know the scouts' names? Remember, as well, it was not until 1881 when the first "positive" identification occurred and by that time everyone probably knew of everyone else. The timing evidence—the most empirical of all—supports a Curley/Black Fox meeting with Benteen, especially when combined with Windolph's recollections. None of the other Crow scouts were driving ponies that day, yet there is anecdotal evidence of Curley accompanying Rees driving stolen horses toward the Rosebud.

And why does any of this matter? For the simple reason, if true, it calls into question everything Curley as a witness told us about the Custer fight. None of his testimony would be worth a plugged farthing.

15

"Benteen Is Coming!"

REFERENCES:
Timeline G—Benteen's Scout; 11:50 a.m.–1:50 p.m.
L—Reno's Retreat to Benteen's Arrival; 2:11 p.m.–3:05 p.m.
N—Messengers; 12:12 p.m.–2:41 p.m.
O—Benteen: Reno Creek to Reno Hill; 1:50 p.m.–3:07 p.m.
P—The Pack Train; 10:40 a.m.–4:17 p.m.
Q—Benteen's Arrival to the Arrival of the Packs; 2:57 p.m.–4:17 p.m.
T—Calhoun Hill Deployment; 3:14 p.m.–3:37 p.m.
U—Keogh to Custer on Cemetery Ridge; 3:29 p.m.–3:57 p.m.
W—Warriors; 1:02 p.m.–5:17 p.m.

Benteen arrived at the confluence of No-Name and Reno creeks at 1:50 p.m. He had covered a total of approximately 7.1 miles since separating from the main command and he had done so at a rate of some 4.2 miles per hour, not bad considering the terrain. His speed was inflated somewhat because of an estimated seven miles per hour trot after leaving the divide separation and again when he turned down No-Name Creek. Climbing and descending hills and ridges had brought down his average speed considerably (*Timeline G*). By the time Benteen reached Reno Creek, Custer was viewing the fighting in the valley from atop 3,411, and Reno's skirmish line was advancing. Sergeant Kanipe was already heading back, message or not; Boyer and the three Crows were on their way to Weir Peaks; and the Hunkpapa warrior, Iron Cedar, was climbing out of the Little Big Horn River in search of Gall. As Benteen looked around, he spotted the head of the pack train to his right, close to a mile up-creek.

To the right, however, was not where the action was and Benteen turned left, following the shod trail. In about ¼ to ½-mile, the command came upon a large swamp or morass and Benteen stopped to water his thirsty animals. As usual, there is controversy here and this time it revolves around several issues: (1) how long did the battalion water; (2) was gunfire heard; (3) what prompted Captain Tom Weir's impa-

tience, an impatience that saw him in a huff, leading his company out ahead of the others.

At four to five miles from the river, another two to three miles to the village, and intervening bluffs masking sound, it is doubtful any gunfire prompted Weir to move; it was more impatience than anything else. As for the duration of the halt, that again depends on where someone was in the column. After putting all the accounts and testimonies together, it is not unreasonable to compute a watering time of 14 minutes—1:54–2:08 p.m.—a little over the mid-range of the estimates. The beginning of the departure was also shortly after Weir left—2:07 p.m.—meaning only a minute or so. We can therefore compute a time of 2:08 p.m. for Benteen's leaving the morass. The question now arises as to his speed moving down Reno Creek.

The only way to calculate speed is by determining start and finish points, both in distance and in time. We calculated Benteen's arrival at the morass on two indicators. The first is a direct reference from one of his officers, Lieutenant Edward Godfrey. In an entry in his field diary added a few days after the battle, Godfrey wrote, "soon after we passed the old village camp we watered our horses [*sic*; they watered *before* passing the camp]. This was about 2 o'clock p.m."[1] The second involves a combination of known times and distances, reasonable speeds, and other anecdotal but less precise evidence—generalities, in other words. One of the primary axes is the time Custer crossed the divide and separated the Seventh Cavalry into battalions. Another is the end point of Benteen's journey: his arrival on Reno Hill. We know from a number of testimonies this occurred shortly after Reno's beaten troops began arriving on the hilltop (*Timeline L*). We have determined Reno dismounted his command at 1:35 p.m., began moving it into the timber some 32 minutes later—2:07 p.m.—and completed this move at about 2:11 p.m. as the last of M Company's troopers galloped into the brow area. Virtually every shred of evidence we have points to the fact Reno spent only 10–12 minutes in the timber, indicating a retreat time of approximately 2:23. It is impossible to tell with any precision when the first of Reno's routed command began arriving on the hilltop, but a reasonable estimate is not much before 2:38, some 15 minutes after the fiasco began. Lieutenant Varnum stated, a few moments after reaching the top of the bluffs a column was spotted moving downriver toward them. The column arrived 10–15 minutes later.[2] He went on to say, "My statements in regard to time are more or less a guess. In 10 or 15 minutes Colonel Benteen came up."[3] A little later in the Reno inquiry, Varnum was asked, "How long after retiring from the timber did Captain Benteen unite with [Reno]?" Varnum's reply was, "I would say 20 or 25 minutes."[4] While Varnum cautioned more than once about his *specific* times, his *relative* times seem to be accurate.

George Wallace was not quite as definitive, saying soon after reaching the top of the hill it was reported Benteen was coming.[5] We hear from others, as well. Former corporal, George W. Wylie of Weir's D Company, in an October 16, 1910, interview, told Walter Camp he saw the very end of Reno's retreat as the Benteen column was approaching the hilltop.[6] Benteen's first lieutenant, Francis Marion Gibson, told Camp, Benteen reached Reno's area before Reno came up from out of the bottoms.[7] Luke Hare claimed Benteen arrived about 10 minutes after Reno reached the top of the hill.[8] It goes on. In undated correspondence with former private Stanislaus Roy of Moylan's A Company, Camp inserted Benteen arrived 10 minutes after Roy got to the top of bluffs. One could assume Roy told him this or Camp devised it from intimation.[9] Godfrey wrote, "My recollection is that it was about half-past two when we joined Reno" on Reno Hill[10] (maybe a little too early). Martini talked often of the arrival. At the Reno inquiry he told the court recorder they got on the ridge where he had seen Reno fighting and saw Reno's command retreating to the same side of the river they were on. He estimated it took about 45 minutes after meeting Benteen to when they reached Reno on the hilltop and Reno's men were retreating when they reached it.[11] Years later he said they could see Reno's fight in the valley and his men retreating—consistency.[12] Edgerly said when they got to Reno's position on the hill some of the major's men were still struggling their way up the bluffs.[13] And finally, Camp wrote that former K Company private, Patrick Corcoran, told him Benteen reached the bluff before Reno and about an hour before McDougall with the packs.[14] All things considered—and since we have a modicum of actual watch time given us by Godfrey as a guide—we can determine Benteen arrived on Reno Hill in front of his command at approximately 2:57 p.m. the last of his troops galloping up the slopes some eight minutes later at 3:05 (*Timeline O*), variably cued for column length and accordioning.

This is contrary to work done by John Gray. In his 1892 article for *Century Magazine*, Ed Godfrey wrote,

> I remember distinctly looking at my watch at 20 minutes past four, and made a note of it in my memorandum-book, and although I have never satisfactorily been able to recall what particular incident happened at that time, it was some important event before we started down river. It is my impression, however, that it was the arrival of the pack-train.[15]

Gray jumped all over the Godfrey hesitation and claimed it was actually the time Benteen arrived on Reno Hill.[16] (Of course, Gray was using the local sun time, which would have put Benteen's arrival at 5:17 p.m. St. Paul time.) Gray also used a 20-minute watering at the morass (arrival of 2:37) with a departure time of 2:57 p.m.,[17] thereby telling us Benteen took one hour 23 minutes to go approximately 6.3 miles, a speed of 4.6 miles per hour, or slightly above a textbook cavalry *walk*. For an officer of any caliber, involved in a combat situation of any magnitude, that finding amounts to an accusation, not a simple statement of fact. Gray's use of tenuous memory musings as immutable fact muddies his entire thesis and questions his motives and preconceptions. There is little if any foundation for any claim Benteen arrived on Reno Hill anywhere near 4:20 p.m. Godfrey did, however, attempt to revise his 1892 article some 16 years later, but apparently this revision was not printed until Libbie Custer had it published in 1921. In it, Godfrey reiterated, his "recollection is that it was about half-past two when we joined Reno."[18] An extract contained in Graham's *The Custer Myth* also brings up Godfrey's bafflement over the 4:20 notation in his memorandum book. Graham wrote in a footnote, Godfrey, after reading Graham's time analysis, figured the 4:20 was when Benteen's column joined Reno, but this is clearly an error and an error John Gray chose to ignore in his own work, treating it instead as fact. One can only conclude Gray chose this "sudden enlightenment" occurring some 50 years later to the exclusion of sworn testimony only two and one-half years after the battle, to fulfill an agenda or preconceived notion Benteen took his own sweet time in arriving. Godfrey's initial impression of arriving on Reno Hill prior to 3:00 p.m. was, and is, correct and the 4:20 referred either to the arrival of the packs or the arrival on the hill of Herendeen and the men left in the timber.

The corollary to all this is Gray has everything occurring later than it actually did, but by doing that he inadvertently slows Custer's advance down Reno Creek, thereby calling that officer's competence into question, albeit unintentionally. Again, we ask the simple question, *Why would any commander worth his salt walk down Reno Creek when his entire objective lay before him and was in danger of running away?*

And we conclude with the simple answer being, *He didn't!* And neither did Fred Benteen.

We can now answer our own question of how fast Benteen moved from the morass to Reno Hill by examining the data we have. With known start and ending times, known distances, and reasonable speeds, our studies have determined Benteen would have arrived at the morass around 1:54 and departed at 2:08 p.m. 14 minutes watering. At 2:35 he reached a burning tepee: "After leaving the watering place a few miles brought me to a beautifully decorated tepee of buffalo hide, just on trail. I dismounted after riding around the lodge, peeped in, and saw the body of an Indian."[19] That would equate to a speed of some 7½ miles per hour, considerably faster than many believe. Four minutes later, Kanipe approached (*Timeline N*), probably about ½ mile west of the tepee. That meeting was not for more than seconds and hardly even engendered a slowdown. In fact, gunfire could now be heard and Benteen increased his speed to a slow gallop (eight miles per hour). At 2:41 p.m. Martini reached the column (*Timeline N*) with Cooke's note. Benteen showed the note to Tom Weir who made no comment and Benteen stuffed it in his shirt pocket. Within the next seven minutes, Benteen had reached the Little Big Horn—2:48 p.m.—saw clouds of dust and smoke, Indians and some soldiers, and then spotted what he took as Crow scouts on the bluffs above him. These scouts directed him northward up the hillside and nine minutes later—at 2:57 p.m.—Fred Benteen arrived on Reno Hill amidst the debacle of Reno's retreat. By 3:05, his entire battalion had arrived. From the morass to Reno Hill, 6.3 miles, Benteen averaged 7.7 miles per hour, a slow gallop, and hardly something to be condemned for. At 3:07 p.m. many in the now re-united commands heard heavy firing from downstream.

Benteen arrived on Reno Hill hundreds of yards ahead of his men and one can only imagine what he thought when he first reined in. Both Kanipe and Martini had said—or intimated—the battle was well in hand and the troops were having a gay old time of it, though what Benteen saw when he reached the river may have tempered those impressions somewhat; the scene on Reno Hill told him a different story altogether.

As he looked around, Benteen thought Reno's men were in "pretty good order," but "well shaken up," and the men coming up on foot were "pretty well blown." No one was in a line of battle.[20] In response to a question at the 1879 inquiry about whether or not Reno's command was engaged at this time, Benteen replied, "I think the Indians saw me about the

time I saw them, and that checked their pursuit. They came around, probably four or five or more, to the highest point of land there. Maybe they had been there all the time, I don't know about that."[21] The first thing Benteen asked Reno was, where was Custer? He showed Cooke's note to the major who replied, he didn't know.[22] There was more said, however, yet we seldom, if ever, hear of it. Benteen's lieutenant, Frank Gibson, in a letter to George L. Yates (Captain Yates' son) dated April 28, 1915, wrote that Benteen added, "'Well, let us make a junction with him [i.e., Custer] as soon as possible.' This I know, for I heard it."[23] While this may seem to be a trivial point, it emphasizes Benteen's concern for what he was beginning to understand rather than the supposed lack thereof and his reputed nonchalance at Custer's ultimate fate. We find it somewhat comical—and certainly hypocritical—that the usual array of Benteen detractors conveniently overlook this comment.

Charles Windolph said as they reached the "brow of the first set of rolling hills the river valley suddenly opened up below us to our left." About a half-mile away they saw figures galloping on horseback and a lot of shooting. They saw masses of Indians a little farther downstream.[24] Windolph's first view of Reno Hill was of troops forming a skirmish line, while others were making their way up a "narrow coulee that led from the river." Some men were on foot, others on horseback, but overall, Reno's command was "disorganized and downright frightened," with hundreds of Indians in the valley, firing at stragglers. The Indians were perhaps a half-mile away.[25]

As can be expected, others saw things differently. Private Patrick Corcoran of Godfrey's trailing K Company told Walter Camp Benteen reached the bluff before Reno and about an hour before McDougall with the packs,[26] but we can be pretty much assured Marcus Reno was already there and Corcoran's failure to spot him was due more to the fact K Company did not arrive until last (about 3:05 p.m.); the confusion was considerable; volley firing was beginning to rattle from somewhere downstream; and within 25 minutes of Corcoran's arrival, Reno was headed back down the bluff in an attempt to locate his missing adjutant, Benny Hodgson. Corcoran's recollection about the packs, however, was spot-on correct.

As for the men doing the retreating, they felt things had gotten pretty much out of hand. At the inquiry the recorder used the term, "demoralized rout" and asked Lieutenant Varnum if he felt that was the condition of the command during the retreat from the timber. Varnum replied, not at the head, but "[t]he rear I think was."[27] He believed a charge had been started and the first men struck some Indians, others following.

He tried to make the head of the column, yelling for the men to stop, not knowing what was going on.[28] When he reached the front, Varnum said, "This won't do, this won't do. We have got to get into shape."[29] Then he saw Reno and Moylan and knew someone was in charge. At that point, Varnum was asked what his feelings were when he reached the top of the hill. He replied he could only speak for himself.

Q: "Well then speak for yourself."
A: "I felt as though I had been pretty badly licked."[30]

Private Davern felt the command was now demoralized and that was why not everyone could get their horse and get out.[31] And that was while the men were still in the timber, just before the wholesale retreat. Lieutenant Hare testified there was considerable confusion and a pretty fast retreat.[32] When Godfrey arrived with Benteen, "Lieutenant Hare, the second lieutenant of my company, but who had been detached to serve with the scouts, came up and said he was 'damned glad' to see me—that they had had a big fight in the bottom and got whipped like hell."[33] Doctor Henry Porter, as good a judge of men's reactions that day as anyone, testified when the column broke from the woods the rear was in disorder. "[E]very man seemed to be running on his own hook."[34] The first officer Porter saw on the bluffs was Varnum who had his hat off and was yelling, "For God's sake men, don't run. There are a good many officers and men killed and wounded and we have got to go back and get them."[35] (Porter insisted Varnum made this comment while still on the bluffs, not on the hilltop.[36] Of course a frustrated Varnum could have been yelling for order the entire way.) Then, when Porter saw Reno, he asked, "Major, the men were pretty well demoralized, weren't they?" Reno responded, "No, that was a charge, sir." Porter then told the recorder the men were demoralized. "They seemed to think they had been whipped."[37] So despite Reno's rather twee comment, it was pretty clear what the condition was on the hilltop as Benteen approached.

Benteen showed Reno Cooke's note, then assessed the situation and began taking action. After issuing orders deploying his troops—he ordered D Company into a skirmish line, the men standing to horse awaiting orders[38]—Benteen further talked to Reno. At 3:07 p.m. Keogh's firing was heard by a number of men. Benteen always claimed he never heard it, a rather dubious assertion, though it is possible if one were overly consumed with other issues. Varnum heard it, however. A few minutes after Benteen's arrival, he borrowed Nick Wallace's rifle and popped off a few frustrated rounds. As he handed the rifle back, he heard firing downstream. "Jesus Christ, Wallace, hear that? And that?" This was the only firing Varnum heard and he claimed it was not volley firing,

"but a heavy firing, a sort of crash, crash. I heard it only for a few minutes."[39] A few minutes later, after assessing the situation with Reno's men and the need for ammunition, Benteen ordered Hare to head back to the packs and cut out two ammunition mules, telling him to hustle the mules along (*Timeline Q*). Hare had either lost his horse or the animal was incapacitated, so he borrowed Godfrey's and sped off— 3:18 p.m.[40] Nine minutes later—3:27 p.m.—Marcus Reno grabbed the indomitable Sergeant Culbertson[41] and a few good men and headed back down the bluffs to find the body of his fallen adjutant. It was no wonder Godfrey testified at the 1879 hearing, Reno gave Godfrey no orders; Benteen still did. Benteen "seemed to be giving the commands."[42]

In the meantime, the momentum of the valley Indians' fury was waning. Rather than press their attack across the river and up the bluffs, the warriors chose instead to mill around the bottoms, searching for wounded or hidden white men, and posturing for the winded troops on the hilltop. One of the reasons for the dissipation of the attack appears to be Benteen's arrival. As Lieutenant DeRudio stumbled back into the timber after the bulk of Reno's battalion departed, he watched as the Indians followed Reno's command to the crossing. Some of the Indians stopped and began pointing upriver. DeRudio looked and saw troops approaching the upper ford near where Reno crossed; he assumed it was Benteen. As they got closer to the river he saw the troops turn and disappear over a bluff. The Indians watched for about 10 minutes. DeRudio believed the sight of these additional troops is what caused the warriors to stop.[43] Private Davern agreed the red men held back, though he did not mention Benteen as the cause. At the Reno inquiry, Davern testified he crossed the river a little below the rest of the command, the stream being too crowded up above where others were crossing. He was at the rear of the retreating column and when he reached the water he saw Indians firing into men in the river. As he crossed, Davern saw two Indians to the left and up the bluffs, but none of the Indians chasing the troops in the valley crossed the river.[44]

As Benteen's men consolidated their position with Reno's battered command, the Indians remained in force in the valley for as long as 10 minutes after the volley firing downstream, before any appreciable number began leaving. When he first arrived, Godfrey said he saw not less than 600–700 warriors in the bottoms, with a great many moving upstream—*toward* Reno's command, not away in the direction of Custer—and others in the ravines on the right bank. Soon, those moving upstream began heading back down,[45] and according to the Oglala warrior, Flying Hawk, that included Crazy Horse and his band (*Timeline W*).[46] Going up toward Reno Hill, Edgerly estimated 800–1,000 Indians in the bottoms,[47] though Luke Hare claimed at the same inquiry only about 100 Indians—or 150—remained in the valley when Benteen arrived.[48] Of course it took several minutes for Benteen's entire battalion to reach the hilltop, so Hare may have misjudged or compressed the time. Benteen himself always stuck to a number of 800–900 warriors for those first several minutes. It stands to reason therefore, it was Benteen's arrival rather than any early spotting of Custer's men that caused the vast majority of valley fighters to pause in their pursuit of Reno, this in spite of Gall's earlier foray to the east-side bluffs and his trepidatious return to the Hunkpapa circle.

This battle migration of warriors now raises the question of just how many of these Indians wound up in the Custer fight. The only thing we know for certain is not all the Indians who fought Reno also fought Custer. Over the years and through the accounts, interviews, and statements of various participants, we have been able to discover the names of some 106 Indians believed or known to have fought Reno, and 185 who fought Custer specifically.[49] That would represent a multiplier of 1.745—Reno to Custer—and if we applied that to Edgerly's average of 900 and Benteen's equal amount—estimates not much greater than Godfrey's "not less than" 600–700—we would arrive at a figure of 1,571 Indians arrayed against George Custer's five companies: 210 men; odds of 7.48 to one; a figure accepted generally by many historians, but arrived at by different means. We can break this down further by determining the Indians who fought against both commands and then using the same methodology to find how many new warriors joined in the battle against Custer.

By comparing the two "rosters," we find 47 of the 106 Indians we believe fought Reno, also fought Custer. That equals 44.34 percent, or approximately 399 of the estimated 900 Indians in the bottoms. That would mean 1,172 additional warriors went up against the Keogh-Yates battalions, Indians who did not participate in the valley fight. The remaining 500 "Reno" Indians therefore, either stayed behind to watch events on the hilltop—as reported by Davern and DeRudio[50]—or headed back into the village to ensure its safety and watch the fighting downstream. It would also give us a "known" warrior force of some 2,072, not counting those who got into neither fight, or those who accompanied the fleeing families downstream and remaining in Squaw/Chasing Creek to protect them.

(While this method of determining the size of the war-

rior force is not perfect certainly, it fits quite well with the known historical record and its use is not unique to this particular study of the Little Big Horn battle. A variation was used by archaeologists Douglas D. Scott and Richard A. Fox, Jr., and Melissa Connor and Dick Harmon, in determining the number of firearms used by Indians in both the Custer and Reno battles.[51])

It did not take Luke Hare very long to reach the packs. Mathey and McDougall had been driving the trains unmercifully, no longer concerned about dust or mired mules. By 3:09 p.m. the lead mules were approaching the lone tepee area[52] (*Timeline P*) and Mathey slowed things down a bit to close up the stragglers and allow McDougall—who had wasted some 20 minutes hauling a half-dozen creatures out of the morass—to catch up.[53] They stopped briefly to peer inside the smoldering tepee where McDougall said he saw the bodies of three dead Indians.[54] After hanging around for several minutes—Mathey claimed 10–15,[55] but in all likelihood it was several minutes less—Mathey spurred the mules on again. A few minutes later the two officers watched as eight to 10 Rees drove by with some 15 stolen Sioux ponies.[56] One of them—the half-breed scout Walter Mason Camp thought might have been Billy Cross—told Mathey there were too many Sioux to fight.[57] (Cross, like several of the other Rees—including Black Fox who had left the hills with Curley, then left Curley—wound up back on Reno Hill when a half-dozen trailing Sioux warriors got their horses back.) In 1908, after interviewing former G Company corporal, John E. Hammon, Camp wrote Hammon claimed he "met [a] band of Rees going off with drove of Sioux ponies and mules. They passed the pack train as it was going toward Reno, after Knipe [*sic*; Kanipe] had taken message to it. Knipe also speaks of passing them."[58]

Hare must have bellowed to Mathey to cut out two ammo mules and have them hustled up the hills quickly, ahead of the rest of the train: *"Follow me!"* At 3:32 p.m. a refrain of only two minutes or less, Hare sped back to his beleaguered colleagues, and Mathey—now sharply energized and sending the ammo on its way—turned the packs north toward the hilltops. (At this same time, Custer is on his way even farther north to find a river crossing below the fleeing Indians; Lieutenant "Jimmi" Calhoun has deployed his men in skirmish lines along the southern and southwestern crests of the hill to be named for him; and Myles Keogh is configuring the rest of his dispositions, including the sequestering of his horses in a swale just below and to the north of Calhoun Hill [*Timeline T*].)

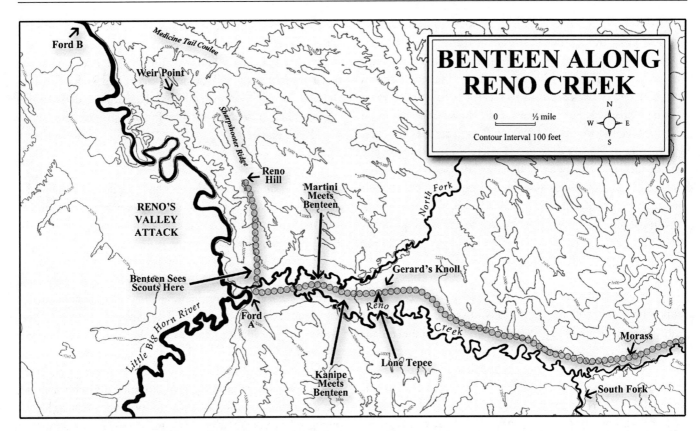

In the meantime, in a rather bizarre move, Reno headed back down the bluffs to retrieve or check on the body of his dead adjutant. Minutes prior to that, however (*Timeline Q*), Captain Tom Weir, Win Edgerly, and the company first sergeant, Michael Martin, were discussing the volley firing heard downstream—3:15 p.m. As the firing had almost ceased, Weir came up to Edgerly and asked him what he would do if Weir went downstream but the other companies would not go. Edgerly replied he would go with his captain. Weir then went off to see Reno—3:17 p.m.

After the fact, Edgerly claimed he did not know if Weir spoke with Reno, but wrote in his diary, "[Weir] told me later ... he hadn't spoken to Reno or Benteen, but rode out on the bluff hoping to see something of Custer's command."[59] Weir also told Edgerly, "he concluded he had better take a look ahead before asking Reno so he mounted and started to the front with only an orderly."[60] As usual, there are those who would disagree with this interpretation of events. Private John Fox, also of D Company, told Walter Camp he heard Weir speaking with Reno just before Weir moved out from Reno Hill.

> Weir remarked, "Custer must be around here somewhere and we ought to go to him." Reno said, "We are surrounded by Indians and we ought to remain here." Weir said, "Well if no one else goes to Custer, I will go." Reno replied, "No you can not go. For if you try to do it you will get killed and your Company with you."[61]

According to Private Fox, Moylan and Benteen overheard this conversation "and talked as though to discourage him." Weir said he was going anyway and Reno did not object.[62] Of course Benteen denied hearing anything of the sort and in that regard one must accept Benteen's word and consider Private Fox mistaken, for no one else supported the private's contention and one wonders why Fox would have even been near enough to overhear the conversation when he should have been paying closer attention to the skirmish line he was deployed on. As Reno was leaving for Hodgson, Weir moved toward his command and without saying a word to Edgerly or anyone else, he and his orderly moved out, heading downstream. Edgerly saw this and mounted the men.[63] Since Weir had often allowed his lieutenant to handle the company, Edgerly thought nothing of Weir's move, and figuring permission had been given, decided to follow.[64]

At this point, one is justified certainly in asking what is going on in this seeming chaos. We have the senior officer heading off to find a body and a senior captain wandering toward the teeth of the enemy, with or without permission, while hundreds of Indians are still milling about across the river, even while their ranks are thinning as more and more warriors moved downstream toward a newer-looming threat.

At 3:43 p.m. as he is approaching Reno Hill from his

mission to the ammunition packs, Hare spotted D Company moving north. (Custer has just arrived at Ford D [*Timeline U*].) Two minutes later, Hare arrived on the hilltop, and most of the Indians who routed Reno's command have left the bottoms (could this situation have been what Hare was alluding to when he spoke of 100–150 Indians in the valley?). It was 3:45 p.m. and George Custer had less than an hour to live.

16

CUSTER MOVES NORTH

REFERENCES:
Timeline S—Ford B to Calhoun Hill; 2:49 p.m.–3:44 p.m.
T—Calhoun Hill Deployment; 3:14 p.m.–3:37 p.m.
W—Warriors; 1:02 p.m.–5:17 p.m.

The resistance at Medicine Tail ford was sharp but scattered and Custer could tell there were not many warriors there. He could also tell there was a mass, panicked exodus from the village, some "refugees" heading toward the western hills, but most heading north down the valley; and he could see he was not at the end of the village, that it extended another several hundred yards downriver—maybe even as much as ¼ to ½ mile. Therefore, crossing here was ridiculous, akin to flailing at air, something he had already surmised. If he were going to corral or destroy these Indians, he would have to go farther downstream—as he had in all likelihood already told Keogh and Yates; but this was risky and Custer had to know it, had to understand it. Circumstances this late in the event should have dictated a modicum of caution and re-thinking, but instead, he opted for risk, sealing himself off from any support.

At 3:05 p.m. his rear protected by Smith's dismounted troopers along the river, Custer descended from the bluff into Deep Coulee, then up its cut-bank and out onto and across the coulee's broad flats toward the upper end of what we later named Finley-Finckle or Calhoun Ridge (*Timeline S*).

> The artifact patterning and distribution gives the impression of soldiers moving up Deep Coulee toward Calhoun Hill.... The expended army cartridge case distribution indicates there was some firing as the movement took place, but it appears light or at least limited in scope. The distribution of Indian caliber bullets also gives the distinct impression that the army movement was under fire.[1]

This move north, linking up with Keogh at 3:22 p.m. on Calhoun Hill (see *Timeline S* and *T*)—a promontory terminus of the Finley-Finckle/Calhoun Ridge-line—was the second fateful—and fatal—decision Custer made this day. It elimi-

nated any possible return to—or help, from—supporting elements of his regiment, and made his orders to Benteen impossible to fulfill. Not only that, but similar to the situation with General Terry and *his* orders/instructions, it eliminated any choice Benteen may have thought he had in fulfilling his orders. Circumstances, instead of Benteen, now dictated his full commitment to Reno, an egregious error. Once beyond Ford B and the flats of Deep Coulee, Custer had put too much distance between himself and any means of support. To make this situation even more untenable, the major ingress route to Custer's rear would become this same ford, meaning Custer cavalierly allowed the gap between himself and his anticipated reinforcements to be filled by his adversary.

Two minutes after Custer began his move away from the ford, Myles Keogh unleashed the first of two volleys aimed at Indians *probably* in Medicine Tail Coulee and Indians *possibly* coming down West Coulee. One Bull and White Bull both stated, "The volleys fired by Custer may have been Custer's men firing at a charge of Indians."[2] Back upriver these volleys were heard clearly—at least by some. This was when Varnum shouted to Wallace about the firing, though Godfrey wrote only after Benteen had reached Reno Hill did they "hear occasional shots, not enough to intimate that a battle was going on. Soon after reaching this point two volleys were heard down the river where Gen. Custer was, but his force was not in sight."[3] (Our Lieutenant Godfrey had some hearing issues, so while there is enough evidence to make us believe these volleys were fired, Godfrey's account may be hearsay.) Even those still trapped in the timber along the river heard it, however. DeRudio said soon after the command left the woods and reached the hill, firing began on the other side of the village. "I heard immense volleys of firing and more than half the Indians around Major Reno left. Part of them went on the highest bluffs and part went down the river. Some of them picketed their ponies under the bluffs and lay down flat, watching Major Reno."[4] (Those going down the

Deep Coulee flats. Custer and the Yates battalion moved up these flats to Calhoun Hill in the upper left. Deep Coulee itself is to the photograph's right, just below the higher ground.

bluffs could have been the Indians on the receiving end of some of the volleys directed at the West Coulee area.) The firing began at least a few minutes after Benteen's command reached the top of the hill,[5] and some several minutes after the heavy firing began downstream most of the Indians left Reno.[6] Overall, the firing lasted about one and one-half hours and then died off with small shots.[7] (This would fit perfectly with our analysis: first volleys fired at 3:07 p.m., running to the battle's end at 4:40 p.m. "The first volley was very plain, then it got farther on and then it died out."[8]

Ten or 15 minutes after Reno left the woods, Fred Gerard—still ensconced in the timber and unable to reach the combined Reno-Benteen commands until late the following day—heard firing in the hills on the right side of the river. Gerard watched as Indians scaled the ravines up to the high ground and he heard continuous firing downstream, both he and DeRudio hearing three or four volleys intermingled among the continuous firing (Indians trailing Smith from Ford B, Smith retaliating). Gerard described the volleys as

being from 50 or 100 guns, a continuous, scattering firing, sometimes only single or four or five shots, seemingly marching downriver. Farther downriver, the firing got much heavier and lasted until dark.[9] After Gerard heard the sound of "scattering shots" on the right bank—what he presumed to be Custer's line of march—it was 15 or 20 or 25 minutes before the firing became general.[10] (Note the continuous equivocation.) The heavier, downstream firing Gerard estimated came from the Custer battlefield lasted about two hours (and based on our time studies, this was a fairly accurate estimate). Following the sound of guns, Gerard calculated the firing from the bluffs off to his right lasted about 20 or 25 minutes.[11] He guessed the heavy firing occurred between 3:00 and 4:00 p.m. "Yes, sir, heavy firing. I know there was a long space of time that there was no firing. I heard a few shots in the bottom, one, two, or three."[12] Gerard said it was about a half hour from the time the heavy firing ceased downriver and the firing began around Reno Hill.[13]

Gerard's testimony here provides us with some of the

Deep Coulee. This was the Indian's main route to Keogh's rear. Others kept their horses here.

most accurate and corroborative information available—fitting in nicely with what troops on the hill said—and it gives us a very nice time reference backing up more general comments of others. It also sets a fine reference for the length of the Custer fighting and the end of the downriver battle.

A minute after Custer departed the high ground for Deep Coulee and beyond—3:05 p.m.—Algernon Smith would have re-mounted E Company and set out after the general—3:06. During these movements, Henry C. Dose, a G Company trumpeter attached to headquarters as an orderly, was killed. Historian Richard Hardorff claimed Dose was found "a short distance above the lower fork of Deep *Ravine*, with arrows shot in his back and sides"[14] [emphasis added], and while the description of the body is accurate, it appears Hardorff is wrong if he claims Dose was killed in Deep Ravine rather than Deep Coulee. Some of this doubt—and Hardorff's data—may arise from the work of Walter

Camp who believed Dose was killed at an elevation point Camp labeled "84" on his battlefield map.[15] "According to Camp's map ... 'elevation 84' rises just south of Deep Ravine, a short distance from the river."[16] That location is too far, however, from the descriptions left us by troopers who saw the body.

Private Henry Petring, Sergeant John Ryan, and Private James Boyle all testified that Dose was found near Ford B. The similarity in names [between Dose and Chief Trumpeter Henry Voss] may have resulted in [George] Glenn's[17] misidentification, as Lieutenant DeRudio had stated that the first body found near the ford was "so disfigured as to be unrecognizable, but from the marks on the pants we knew it was a trumpeter."[18]

Private Boyle told Camp the "body of Trumpeter Dose was found on [the] flat near Ford B between two coulees [Camp's narrative]."[19] (With the exception of First Sergeant Ryan, all these men—including Dose—were G Company troopers.) Hardorff's findings may also have been influenced by former B Company private, Augustus DeVoto. In a letter to Camp, DeVoto wrote, "When we buried Custer's men we found his chief bugler's [sic; trumpeter's] body about a mile away from Custer's battlefield, all alone and stark naked. His body was in a kneeling position and his back was stuck full of arrows."[20] While DeVoto's description of the body was accurate, he was mistaken about the identity. Never mentioning Chief Trumpeter Voss by name, DeVoto had to have been referring to Trumpeter Dose, a seemingly common error in identifying similar names. The "mile away" reference could—and would—place him near Ford B, and since we know from several other accounts Voss was found near George Custer, DeVoto's misidentification was palpable. In addition to all this, as Lieutenant DeRudio went to Ford B after the battle he saw no signs of cavalry fording there, but about 500 yards from the ford, he saw the body of a trumpeter, "lying in the bottom of a little coulee."[21] (Since the distance from the river to the actual mouth of Deep Coulee, where the cut-bank rises to the flats, is approximately 420 yards, this description fits perfectly, especially considering Dose was with Custer atop the edge of the bluffs, almost 350 yards from the river, then descended into the Deep Coulee delta area. See Appendix A.) On June 28, Benteen killed a white horse that was wounded and lying in a pool of mud on the right bank of the river, a little distance below the ford. The trousers of an enlisted man were hanging on the branch of a log stump.[22] George Wallace, as well, saw the horse, but Wallace believed it to be dead already.[23] Trumpeters rode white horses.

Among the "fatalists" there is speculation George Custer was either mortally wounded at Ford B, or badly incapacitated. Subsequent movements of the command, however, render that argument rather flimsy and reflect more a mentality riddled with excuses for the defeat than any semblance of reality. From a military perspective, the loss of a commander such as George Custer—in this location, at this time in the event—would make a move north, farther away from any means of support, utterly preposterous and it is almost inconceivable men the likes of George Yates and Myles Keogh would ever consider such stupidity. Only a commander still convinced he was in complete control, a plan firmly in his mind, would have continued north. That alone obviates Custer's incapacity.

Having said that, there is evidence—tenuous at best—of an officer shot and wounded at the ford. In 1938, the artist/historian, David Humphreys Miller, interviewed a former Oglala warrior named White Cow Bull, who—based on some of his tales—resembled an Indian version of Theodore Goldin. He told Miller a story of visiting a Cheyenne maiden as the fighting broke out.[24] It turned out White Cow Bull claimed to have been all over the battlefield, but at this particular moment he just happened to be at Ford B when Smith's Gray Horse Troop came galloping to the water's edge. After some sharp exchanges of fire, a warrior named Bob-tail Horse shot out of his saddle a soldier mounted on a gray horse. Not to be outdone, White Cow Bull followed suit, only the Oglala's choice was wearing a buckskin jacket (in 100 degree heat, no less), making him a figure of some importance. Of course by the time White Cow Bull, David Humphreys Miller, and author Jack Pennington finished parsing the tale, George Custer lay mortally wounded in the Little Big Horn River, only to be dragged out and hauled even farther away from any succor or support. We can attribute some credence to the story, though prudence—not to mention logic—forces us to substitute the E Company commander, Algernon Smith, for George Custer. This would only deserve to be a footnote except for the fact Smith was the only E Company man not found among the rest of E Company when bodies were identified on June 27–28. It is possible Smith was incapacitated or died before his men took to Deep Ravine, but that coincidence raises the specter of some other possibility such as the Ford B wounding. While most of the statements from White Cow Bull are self-serving and therefore suspect, those of the Northern Cheyenne Contrary, Brave Wolf, are not. Brave Wolf's comments, contained in the June 27, 1877, report of Lieutenant Oscar F. Long, Fifth U.S. Infantry, coupled with those of two other prominent Indians, the Cheyenne, White Bull, and the Minneconjou, Hump, claiming an officer was "killed" "where Custer made his first stand—nearest the river," lend credibility to the theory. In addition, an Oglala brave named Horned Horse also alluded to Custer making a dash to cross the river, but being met by such tremendous fire, he pulled back, losing a couple of men in the water.[25] We will grudgingly concede the point and insert Algernon Smith where the fatalists claim George Custer.

After keeping encroaching warriors at bay, Myles Keogh would have turned his troops northward toward present-day Nye-Cartwright Ridge, reaching it in three to four minutes—3:12 p.m. By this time troops would have been firing at will at anything that moved—and much did. As Custer steered his command away from the ford and toward Calhoun Hill, more Indians began arriving at the river's edge (*Timeline W*), crossing the Little Big Horn, and firing at what they may have perceived to be "fleeing" soldiers. Some of Smith's men were seen to dismount (so Indians claimed[26]), ostensibly to provide additional, stable covering fire as the mounted troopers moved on (this is what *we* would claim) and more and more

Indians crossed the river, the red men always remaining far enough back to ensure fairly ineffective fire by the whites. Contrary to the fatalists the move by Yates' battalion was orderly and well managed. According to the Oglala warrior Lone Bear, when Custer's troops mounted upper Finley Ridge, they did so as a group, none splitting off to head toward the Calhoun Coulee-Deep Ravine areas. They all went to Calhoun Hill.[27] Lights, the Minneconjou, agreed with this; he had crossed the Little Big Horn and worked his way quickly up the depths of Deep Coulee, remaining out of sight as Custer's troops moved up the flats. He claimed to have seen the soldiers move directly to Calhoun Hill, none splitting off to go elsewhere. He was emphatic about it.[28]

By 3:12, Keogh had arrived on Nye-Cartwright and set up a skirmish line to provide additional covering fire. Between 3:14 and 3:17 p.m. Custer and Yates' men began arriving on Calhoun Hill, and while there was no panic certainly, Custer did not walk there; he had to have moved fairly rapidly because of the situation in the valley, and best guess is a speed of about eight miles per hour—a slow gallop—easily attained across the flatter terrain. When Custer arrived on the hilltop, Keogh re-assembled his battalion and began to move there as well. Meanwhile, Smith kept leapfrogging his troops, and between 3:17 and 3:25 p.m. saw the arrival of the last of his company. By 3:22 p.m. Keogh would have covered the distance between Nye-Cartwright and Calhoun Hill—1,500 yards, figuring as well, a slow gallop of eight miles per hour—and Custer's command was once more united (*Timeline T*).

By this time a *final* plan of action had to have coalesced fully in the commander's mind and we should be allotting no more than a few minutes for him to outline the courses of action he wanted his officers to take. It is almost ineluctable fact Custer would have told Keogh and Yates—3:23 p.m.– 3:26 p.m.—he would be heading farther north to find a crossing ford at or below where the fleeing Indians were gathering and he wanted Keogh to hold the high ground to cover Custer's rear, to act as a reserve—and, by the way, to await Benteen's arrival.

It is at this moment we are able to see—and maybe appreciate fully—the events as they unfolded farther upriver. Because Boston Custer had reported Reno's plight, it was known the major was in some sort of trouble—its full extent, never known—but like the arguments of those—including myself—who say, had Custer been in trouble at Ford B he would have retreated the way he had come rather than strike out for unknown country, it is not an unreasonable assumption for Custer to believe Reno had done the same thing, i.e., moved back *up*valley rather than attempting a river crossing and scaling of precipitous bluffs in the teeth and whipping

tail of attacking Indians. It was logical; but logic failed Custer here because of assumptions, assumptions that failed to consider both the number and the temperament of the Indians; assumptions of the invincibility of the Seventh Cavalry; assumptions never considering the *il*logic of panicked retreat and its outcomes. Reno had—quite inadvertently—interjected himself between Custer and the advancing Benteen.

To make matters worse—though it did not seem to be that way at the moment—the warriors were taking their own sweet time in recognizing the threat and taking action to head it off, unintentionally giving the troops a false sense of security. There are all sorts of indications telling us this was the case. The Oglala, Low Dog, said when they found out about the Custer column, "We retreated until our men got all together, and then we charged upon them."[29] The Brulé, Hollow Horn Bear, claimed the Indians were "prepared to fight Custer. They went to Custer as soon as they could recover from the earlier fight with Reno. Some talk had to be indulged in before they went to Custer, which took some time."[30] Pretty White Buffalo, who saw a good deal of the fighting, said, "[Indians] quickly crossed the river, and by hundreds galloped to his rear, out of range at first, but taking advantage of coolie [*sic*] and mound, soon hemming him in constantly narrowing circles."[31] Lights said there was some fighting between Ford B and the troops' move up Finley Ridge, but it was "not very vigorous."[32] Wooden Leg, the young Cheyenne warrior, gave us the best description of how the battle was beginning when he said the soldiers were easy to see because they were silhouetted on the ridges and their horses were with them. The Indians, on the other hand, were crawling in gulches, jumping up and shooting, then crawling on a little farther, movements not quite indicative of hurtling speed as some would like us to believe. "We were lying down in gullies and behind sagebrush hillocks. The shooting at first was at a distance, but we kept creeping in closer all around the ridge."[33]

After a brief hiatus of some three to four minutes for Custer to outline his plan, he took Yates' battalion and moved north—3:27 p.m. Two Eagles saw the commands separate, one of them heading north through what we call today the Keogh Sector.[34] Keogh then deployed his troops and waited— 3:27–3:44 p.m.—Calhoun's L Company atop the high knoll, horses kept in a swale just north of the peak; and Lieutenant Henry Moore Harrington's C Company along the ridge to the north and slightly west of the highest ground occupied by Calhoun. There was no reason to deploy formally Keogh's own I Company—at least initially—though if he did, it had to be just north of the others. Or so we think. It makes sense Custer had instructed Keogh to remain there, await Benteen's

Battle Ridge as seen from the lower portions of Calhoun Hill. It was in this general area that Keogh kept his horses. Last Stand Hill is at the far upper right.

arrival, and then proceed north along the crest of the ridge, all the while keeping an eye out for Custer and Yates, who, from what we have been told by Indian participants, were sitting atop modern-day Cemetery Ridge for several minutes after their reconnaissance to find a northern ford below the fleeing refugees. A logical deduction might conclude Custer told Keogh to follow the ridge and Custer would place himself in such a location as to be seen so the commands could re-unite.

This move north became the final fateful decision Custer made and the one sealing his doom (we will discuss this in more detail a little further on). By abandoning Keogh to the role of rear guard, Custer compounded the mistake he made when he left the environs of Ford B. Indians seeking to cut off troops they had seen sitting atop Calhoun Hill, forded the Little Big Horn at the Deep Ravine ford farther downstream from Ford B, yet still well above the refugees who were gathering in Squaw Creek (and therefore a crossing unacceptable to Custer). Then they made their way up the ravine and

through a gap in the long north-south ridge the southern end of which was occupied by Keogh. Thus, they split Yates and Keogh, linking up with Indians who had crossed at Ford B and had made their way to the east of Keogh's position, effectively surrounding his three companies. Custer returned from his northern trek—where he had finally ascertained the limit of the Indians' retreat—and positioned himself on Cemetery Ridge, awaiting—as planned—Keogh's doomed command.

As a corollary to this final blunder, a gap[35] in Battle Ridge—as a purely military concern—had to have played a major role in Keogh's defeat, though it is never discussed or even mentioned in any of the histories of the battle. Such a gap would have formed a natural frontier for Keogh's boundary and because of its distance from Calhoun Hill the defense of that gap would have forced him to spread his command too thinly—and it *had to be defended!* The gap presented Indians emanating from the head cut of Deep Ravine with a perfect route through the ridgeline and into the troops' thinly spaced perimeter; but we are ahead of ourselves here.

As Custer moved farther north, Indians were on the move as well. While there was still no immediate threat, troops deploying on Calhoun Hill and the general area could see warriors moving up the flats just north of Deep Coulee and there is a strong possibility they saw horsemen crossing the ford and moving into the coulee, disappearing rather quickly from view. "The Indians had crossed the Greasy Grass Creek [Little Big Horn River] above where Custer tried to cross, in great numbers, and cut him off from Reno. They got around behind (east of) him,"[36] claimed Feather Earring. This was of some concern, especially if the flow continued unabated, for hidden movement up that coulee would bring warriors much closer to the barely entrenched troops with no fear of exposure. Plus, no one knew where the coulee flattened out and there was always the concern of Indians appearing suddenly to the soldiers' rear (east). Other Indians dismounted, sequestered their horses in the coulee, and then crossed the flats in front of Greasy Grass Ridge (which parallels the river) moving up Calhoun Coulee on foot. That brought an increased threat to the troops' front as well as their southern flank and rear. The hope had to have been that the numbers were manageable and Calhoun's carbines could keep them far enough away until Benteen arrived (*Timeline W*).

The desultory fighting continued. White Shield told Grinnell Indians did not charge into the troops, but shot at them from behind "the hills."[37] White Bull said they were now in many small bunches,[38] and some Indians—including himself—went up a draw and were seen by the soldiers who fired at them. The troops dismounted, then re-mounted. The soldiers made "four companies and one company was shooting at them in the draw."[39] (Note, this observation would also pertain to the eventual C Company move off Battle Ridge and into Calhoun Coulee.) Thunder Bear, a Yanktonai Sioux, said the Indians dismounted and went into the gullies.[40] Gray Whirlwind, another Yanktonai, said as the Indians forded the river to approach Custer's command they waited in a coulee before attacking.[41] Little Hawk, a Northern Cheyenne, returned from the Reno fighting and went up a small ravine other Indians were using in approaching Custer's troops.[42]

By 3:29 p.m. the lead warriors who had crossed the ford both on foot and horseback and who had moved into Deep Coulee, began reaching Calhoun Coulee, still out of effective range of the cavalry carbines. They now began their slower, more cautious infiltration toward the Calhoun Hill/Battle Ridge complex. Others continued up Deep Coulee into the environs of what we call today, "Henryville." This careful infiltration into Calhoun Coulee was done initially at speeds between five and six miles per hour for some 1,350 yards

(*Timeline W*), bringing warriors within threatening range of the troops. Arrows were soon lofted into the air, wounding or even killing some horses and men, Gall claiming the Indians made a special effort to kill the horse-holders and stampede the horses.[43] (Battlefield markers show the position of several troops who died in this swale area, but it is unknown if they were casualties of this arrow assault or the ensuing panicked rout. If the former, company casualty numbers would need to be recomputed, but we have no way of knowing.) As best can be determined, if the Hunkpapa warrior, Gall, got into the Keogh fighting—and there is some doubt about that, too—then at 3:33 p.m., he would have reached the Henryville area. By 3:34 to 3:37 p.m. warriors in Calhoun Coulee were close enough to pose a serious threat, having covered another 570 yards by crawling and darting, speeds varying between 2½ to 4½ miles per hour.

In the meantime, Custer and Yates were moving north, probably preceded by Mitch Boyer and Yates' F Company scouts to clear the way: advanced "eyes." Moving briskly at some 10 miles per hour, they completed the 2.33 miles from Calhoun Hill to the Squaw/Chasing Creek ford, or from another, smaller ravine just below. In either case, this was what Custer needed: it brought him at or below the fleeing Indians. *Ford D!*

While we know very little about this move from any Indian accounts, archaeology tells us (a) it took place (at least part way), and (b) it did not progress unopposed, though again, the measure of the opposition is transitory at best. In the 1994 Midwest Archaeological Center and University of Nebraska-Lincoln's joint metal detecting survey conducted by doctors Douglas Scott and Peter Bleed, enough spent bullets and cartridge cases from both sides were found, indicating route and activity. Furthermore, Two Moons claimed Custer marched up behind Battle Ridge, riding beyond where the monument is and "down into the valley until we could not see them,"[44] and the artifacts found there would confirm his recollection, even though it was recorded some 37 years later. Richard Fox hung part of his theory of a foray to Ford D on this narrative, and such a move fills in the necessary time lapses we must deal with from the separation on Calhoun Hill to the battle's end, as seen from Weir Peaks and commensurate with additional Indian accounts. To be fair, the evidence is not definitive and while in general agreement with Fox, Scott and Bleed point this out. While stating, "There is clear evidence for combat actions on the northern extension of Custer Ridge [Battle Ridge], in the ravines below the Custer Ridge Extension, and along an extension of Cemetery Ridge adjacent to the old park entrance road,"[45] they add,

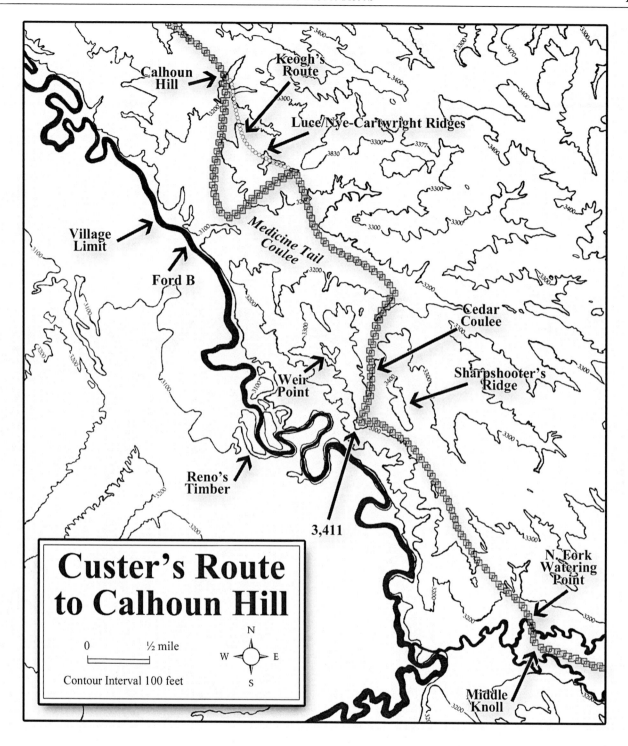

We may reasonably conclude that the left wing and Custer did move north through Last Stand Hill and northwesterly along the Custer Ridge Extension at least a quarter mile. However, Fox's (1993) theory that the command moved west to near the river is not supported by any *archaeological* evidence gathered to date. The presence of scattered Indian caliber bullets on the ridge and in adjacent ravines suggests the soldiers' movements were under fire *by a few warriors*[46] [all emphasis added].

We find additional support for such action in the writings of the Cheyenne tribal historian, John Stands In Timber,

when he told Margot Liberty some Indians had crossed the river and began firing at the troops "from the brush in the river bottom."[47] Such a sortie also forms part of the hypothesis of separation we see based on the marker placements and the reports of June 27th and 28th identifying various bodies and their attendant units; in addition, it gives us a glimpse into Custer's thinking and how he viewed his mission. The 1994 findings, while somewhat open to interpretation, put life into the scanty anecdotes that helped Fox form his thesis, and

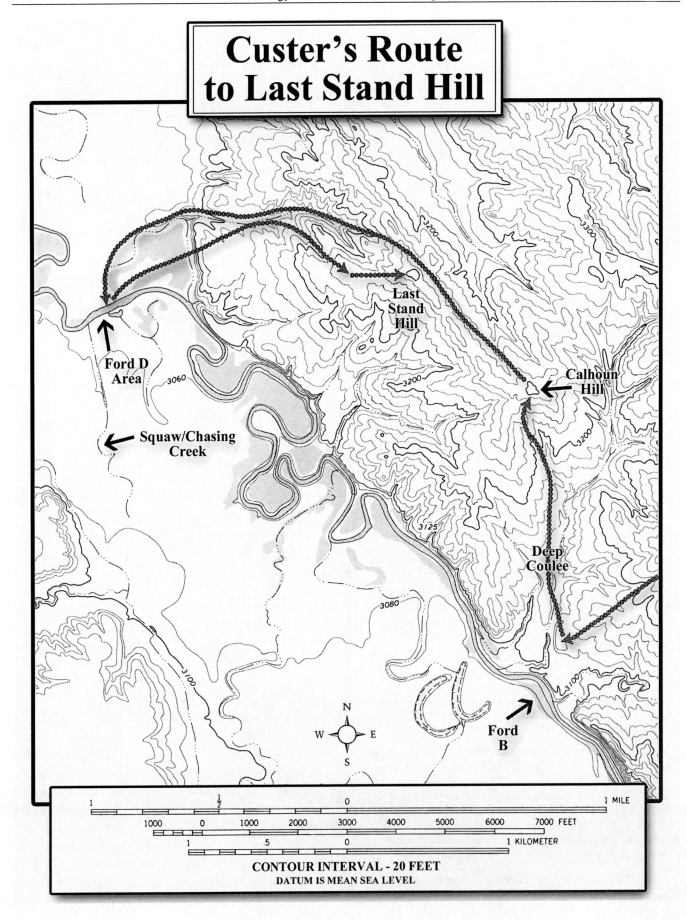

Custer's Route to Last Stand Hill

CONTOUR INTERVAL - 20 FEET

DATUM IS MEAN SEA LEVEL

combined, they are clearly more credible than the void left by fatalists and the less informed.

This, the most northern clash, occurred close to midway between Calhoun Hill and Ford D, and if we measure that distance as 2.33 miles, then the firing occurred almost exactly one mile from Calhoun Hill, in an area referred to today as the Custer Ridge Extension. The object of the troops' fire may have been Indians already having crossed at Ford D and making their way toward the southern fields. Many of these warriors—such as the Hunkpapa, White Hair On Face—would have accompanied the fleeing families[48] to the safety of the dry creek when the Reno firing began. In addition, they could have been part of the Wolf Tooth/Big Foot contingent that had moved north. This group's speed, combined with the troops' halt of several minutes atop Calhoun Hill, would have allowed them to make the slightly greater circumferential distance and arrive at the ridge extension ahead of Custer's command. Regardless of whether they were warriors riding with Wolf Tooth or Indians accompanying the fugitives, the numbers could not have been great—yet. Most of those who had fled with the women and children would have remained with them, and Indians who had fought Reno were only nearing the Ford B vicinity around this time (*Timeline W,* 3:43 p.m.). It was not until another 12 minutes had elapsed before the first rush of Indians from the valley fight were reaching Squaw Creek—3:55 p.m.—and this northern ford.

Despite the additional pin-prick of resistance, Custer would have barely slowed and would have arrived at the ford around 3:42 p.m. about the same time or a minute before warriors fresh from the fighting in the valley began arriving at Ford B: Indian strength was now gaining quickly. The troops *must* have been seen as they approached Squaw/Chasing; there *must* have been screams and shouting and panic among the non-combatant Indians, and any warriors there *had* to have reacted swiftly and violently. In four minutes or less—3:46 p.m.—Custer and his men—having seen what was needed to be seen—were on their way back and it is not impossible to imagine infuriated Indians tailing them—on horseback and afoot, pests to be ignored or swatted away—sniping as they went, yet keeping at a distance until their numbers mounted. Our ubiquitous friends—Wolf Tooth and Big Foot—might have been among them. Flying Hawk said, "Some of the Indians crossed from the place the women fled to and went across at the lower crossing west of Custer Hill."[49] Stands In Timber wrote, "Hanging Wolf was one of the warriors who crossed the river and shot from the brush when Custer came down to the bottom. He said they hit one horse down there, and it bucked off a soldier, but the rest took him along when they retreated north."[50]

Four minutes later—probably about 3:50 p.m.—the *Bismarck Tribune/New York Herald* reporter, Marc Kellogg, mounted on a mule and trailing the rapidly moving troops, was killed.

17

HELL IN A VERY SMALL PLACE

REFERENCES:

Timeline U—Keogh to Custer on Cemetery Ridge; 3:29 p.m.–3:57 p.m.

V—Cemetery Ridge to the End; 3:54 p.m.–4:40 p.m.

W—Warriors; 1:02 p.m.–5:17 p.m.

Myles Keogh had to be growing concerned. Custer had barely departed and Keogh was already seeing increasing numbers of Indians crossing Medicine Tail ford, many of them disappearing into the mouth of the ravine just beyond the crossing some 1,700 to 1,800 yards off. Others had crossed and were moving parallel to the river and entering the wide coulee, both areas to Keogh's westward-facing front. "All the Indians had come out on horseback. Almost all of them dismounted and crept along the gullies afoot after the arrival near the soldiers."[1] None were within reasonable range so the firing had to be sporadic by both sides.

We can assume Custer instructed Keogh to "fortify" the high ground, but it would not have taken much of a military genius to make that decision, and "fortify" would be a malapropism, certainly. There was also a shallow swale area—a depression—to the north and rear of Calhoun's higher ground, and Keogh instructed his commanders to sequester their horses there, hoping they would be safe from both sight and direct fire—at least for the short time Keogh was expected to hold this position (probably no more than 30–40 minutes). In the meantime, Lieutenant Calhoun, recognizing the threat from the higher (easterly) reaches of Deep Coulee, positioned much of his company facing south in the direction of the ridges he and the rest of the Keogh battalion had come from, in essence, to counteract Indian infiltration toward those eastern ridges. Fewer L Company men faced west toward the river and its ford. It appears fairly straightforward Keogh instructed Lieutenant Harrington to string out C Company along the ridgeline to Calhoun's immediate west and north, but we have no indication how Keogh positioned his own company—until he realized the significance of the gap in the ridgeline. "The soldiers now in view were spreading themselves into lines along a ridge. The Indians were on lower ridges in front of them, between them and the river, and were moving on around up a long coulee [Deep Coulee] to get behind the white men." As we have already noted, Wooden Leg claimed the soldiers were easy to see because they—with their horses—were silhouetted on the ridges. The Indians, on the other hand, were crawling in gulches, jumping up and shooting, and then crawling on a little farther.[2] Standing Bear agreed, telling Judge Eli Ricker in 1907, when Custer went up to Calhoun Hill he disposed his forces along the top of the ridge.[3]

There is no way one can make a definitive determination of I Company dispositions with any semblance of certainty and the marble markers positioned along the retreat route offer no help. We can, however, make certain assumptions. It appears the only "organized" force of Indians in the vicinity may have been the elusive Wolf Tooth/Big Foot band, generally thought to be some 50 warriors.[4] We have also been told Wolf Tooth or Big Foot divided this band into two parts, and while it is not unreasonable to have included one part—or the whole band, for that matter—into the volley-firing incident, it is even less unreasonable to assume these Indians trailed Keogh as he left the complex of southern ridges. That being the case, we can figure some of these Cheyenne made their way north and were now located in the upper reaches of Deep Coulee, or even behind the ridge to the east of Calhoun Hill, still out of sight and range of Calhoun's carbines. Some may have headed farther north to confront Custer as he sought his northern ford. If our supposition about Wolf Tooth being in Medicine Tail Coulee is anywhere near correct, then a 10-mile per hour jaunt for some 2,000 yards would place at least a couple dozen warriors to the east, and moving.

By the time Custer left Keogh's battalion, other Indians—mostly Sioux, but some Cheyenne as well[5]—were leaving the mouth of Deep Coulee and were moving at a quick pace of some five to six miles per hour—still afoot—parallel to the Little Big Horn and into the lower reaches of Calhoun Coulee, the broad, flat-*ish*-looking expanse between two ridges and in front of Harrington's company. This move would have been for about 1,350 yards only—within sight of the troops, but still out of effective carbine range.

Some Indian accounts have the fighting occurring quickly, rapidly enveloping the bluecoats in furious charges and brutal, hand-to-hand combat. Others—as we have seen already—claim the severest fighting was slow in developing and they explain how warriors approached the troops and the caution and subterfuge used. It is these latter voices, the ones of reason rather than bravado, we have chosen to hang our theories on, so time being relative it is not unreasonable to assume, given distance and speed—as well as adrenaline and emotion—in some 17 minutes after Custer departed in search of a crossing point, Keogh was coming under greater pressure from Indians who had been using the gullies and washouts of the coulees, the bushes and sagebrush, to creep closer and closer, arching arrows into the air, and threatening the men and horses on the ridges and in the swale. By 3:40 to 3:44 p.m. the situation on the ridge was becoming increasingly untenable. (Custer would have arrived at Ford D. See *Timeline U.*)

No one knows how it began, but it is apparent either Keogh ordered his C Company commander to charge into the coulee to roust out the marauding warriors, or Harrington took it upon himself—in all likelihood at the behest of his first sergeant, Edwin Bobo; but charge he did, and the results were spectacular.

As we saw earlier, the maximum effective range of the troops' carbines was approximately 250 yards. Somewhere between 3:34 and 3:37 p.m. enough Indians were able to get within 100 yards or so of Harrington's command, to pose a substantial threat, and action needed to be taken despite the troops' ability to retaliate now with their longer-range weapons; but while these Indians were moving within range, it was exceedingly difficult to root them out because of the terrain, their numbers, and their swift movements, darting back and forth, ever closer, the lethality of their arrows beginning to take its toll.

Richard Allan Fox, Jr., described the Custer battalion composition in terms analogous to what we have described here, using similar sources.[6] It is with this in mind we have the whole of C Company on the ridge—37 men including Harrington—preparing to move into Calhoun Coulee to disperse the encroaching Indians. Fox makes his point vividly:

C. G. du Bois's organization of the Custer battalion is also at odds with prescriptive expectations of the period. He too called each of the wings "battalions," assigning Companies I and L to one and the cavalrymen of E and F to the other. According to du Bois, C Company at some point divided into two platoons, with one assigned to each "battalion" in order to equalize unit strengths. Tactical prescription, however, did not require equal-strength wings in a battalion. Indeed, in a five-company battalion, one wing could be expected by design to have an additional company. And platoons could be eliminated altogether in under strength companies such as those in the Custer battalion. All in all, there is simply no evidence for tactical divisions smaller than the company.... The du Bois speculation, then, is extremely difficult to justify.[7]

This C Company move is the source of great confusion to some when trying to piece together the flow of the battle. Wooden Leg told us,

After the long time of the slow fighting, about 40 of the soldiers came galloping from the east part of the ridge down toward the river, toward where most of the Cheyennes and many Oglalas were hidden. The Indians ran back to a deep gulch. The soldiers stopped and got off their horses when they arrived at a low ridge where the Indians had been.[8]

Many consider this the charge of E Company off Last Stand Hill, their penultimate move before dying in Deep Ravine. Thomas Marquis footnoted the Wooden Leg comment by writing, "The Indians differ as to the color of the horses ridden by these soldiers, but military students of the case believe this to have been Lieutenant Smith's troop,"[9] i.e., the E Company Gray Horse Troop. These so-called "military students" should know better, however; this would hardly seem accurate for several reasons, not the least of which would be the simple fact no one could be confused as to horse color if an entire company of men mounted on gray or white horses came charging off a hilltop. We can confuse sorrels with bays, but never sorrels with grays. Furthermore, it is almost inconceivable any cavalry unit in the dire straits E Company found itself in that late in the fighting would suddenly halt and dismount in the face of fleeing Indians running from a cavalry charge. When we add to this additional Indian testimony alluding to the stampeding of grays toward the end of the battle, we can conclude there were two separate charges, one preemptive, the other desperate, the latter comprised of a few men on horseback, many more afoot. The Arapaho warrior, Waterman, suggested this by saying when the troops moved back to the hills (compartmentalized: Last Stand Hill, as opposed to the general area of the battlefield), they got off their horses. "Some of the horses got away and came down to the river where they were caught by some of the Indians. These were gray horses and some sorrels."[10] (It should be noted, C Company rode sorrels, while F, I, and L rode standard bays: mahogany bays, blood bays, standard chestnuts, and standard browns, not altogether dissimilar from sorrels and easily confused by Indians who, in 1876, had no clue what a "sorrel"

Calhoun Coulee as seen from Battle Ridge. Lieutenant Harrington charged into the lower ground, then retreated to Finley-Finckle Ridge to the left. In all likelihood, Captain Myles Keogh would have viewed part of the debacle from this point.

was and whose memories of horse colors 45years after the smoke and dust cleared were no more precise than the memories of old bluecoats trying to figure out where they knelt down in the valley.)

In a clear reference to the C Company move, Wooden Leg told Marquis:

> After about an hour and a half of the slow fighting at long distances, the group of 40 soldiers who rode down from the ridge along a broad coulee and toward the river were charged upon by Lame White Man, followed at once by many Cheyennes and Sioux. This place of the first Indian charge and the first sudden great victory is inside of the present fence around the battlefield and at its lower side.[11]

The battlefield reference to a broad coulee clearly places the action inside Calhoun Coulee, posing no further confusion between this 40-man charge and any similar move off Last Stand Hill by the Gray Horse Troop. The description also lends tremendous credence to Wooden Leg's other recollections radiating out to time, movements, and locations.

Harrington did not need to go very far into the coulee to clear the area and assure the Indians' indirect fire would no longer threaten the troops or their horses. In all likelihood, yelling and screaming, pistol in hand, the young lieutenant led his men at a brisk 12 miles per hour, a maximum of 650 yards—probably less—into the broad coulee, Indians scampering hither and yon as fast as their legs could carry them. It is not inconceivable Harrington then ordered his troops to halt and dismount—as Wooden Leg claimed—anchoring the company's flanks on the sides or crests of the two ridges forming the coulee, either in enclaves or a ludicrously thin skirmish line. If this latter were the case, his 36 men would have occupied a line of some 850 yards, either splitting the company or putting a distance of more than 70 feet between men, in either case, a completely untenable position and one recognized as such by a lot of very savvy Indians. This was the beginning of the end.

It is difficult and unfair to focus blame on any one man for the debacle that followed. If Harrington went the 650

The bottom of Calhoun Coulee. Lieutenant Harrington and his C Company troopers charged off the ridge at the top of the photo into the broken terrain of the coulee. The photograph shows clearly the bushes and the folds of terrain that would have masked and hidden Indian movements and numbers. From the top of the ridge, the coulee appears considerably flatter and more inviting, and it is only until a horseman enters the coulee's depths that he discovers the difficulty he has assumed.

yards some discovered bodies seem to indicate,[12] he did so only to clear the area and eliminate the threat. This distance may be a little long, however, and there is additional evidence Harrington traveled only 440–500 yards (not a great discrepancy, especially considering the flight of panicked troops). Archaeologist Fox wrote, "Thomas Marquis, who must have accompanied his Cheyenne informants to the site, estimated that the charge proceeded about 500 yards down a draw."[13] Fox had written previously, "The archaeological evidence begins about 440 yards down the ridge, a distance quite similar to the 500-yard estimate of Marquis."[14] Once committed, a pullback to his start point would have been too risky for Harrington and would have only invited the Indians to return, emboldened. A dismounted skirmish line in the coulee—ridges looming over both flanks—was an unattractive option, and splitting his command to occupy small enclaves was little

better. In any case, once Harrington ordered dismount, his fate was sealed and according to Wooden Leg, the lieutenant did just that.

Lame White Man was probably the principal Cheyenne chief at the Little Big Horn. While known among his tribal members and the Sioux by a seemingly myriad number of names, *viz.,* White Man Cripple, Mad Wolf, Mad Hearted Wolf, Rabid Wolf, Dull Knife; and Bearded Man or Moustache, by the Sioux; he is almost always referred to as Lame White Man. Born around 1839, he was a Southern Cheyenne, though he had been with the northern branch for so long, he and his family were considered part of that subdivision. Most sources consider him the leading Cheyenne chief at the battle, though some dispute the claim—why should Indians be impervious to the wrangling ritual? Wooden Leg, however, stated Lame White Man was the head Cheyenne warrior chief, not Two Moons, while Tall Bull claimed he was one of three Cheyenne head chiefs at the battle, along with White Bull/Ice (not to be confused with the Minneconjou of similar name), and Two Moons.[15] Wooden Leg also claimed Lame White Man was regarded as the most capable warrior chief among the Cheyenne. This was the man Henry Harrington was sent to chase out of Calhoun Coulee.

At any of those distances, Harrington's charge would have taken no more than two minutes—3:44 p.m.–3:46 p.m. (see *Timeline U*)—and by 3:46 p.m. he was directing his NCOs how he wanted their men deployed. Within three additional minutes, the Indians who had run for cover rallied around Lame White Man, and by sheer ferocity and dint of numbers overwhelmed the stunned soldiers. Indians popped up suddenly from everywhere and those who had not received the brunt of the galloping cavalrymen simply surged forward to add their numbers to those who had turned and rallied. In the thick of it was Lame White Man. The Oglala warrior, Respects Nothing, claimed the Indians attacking Harrington's command (not mentioned specifically in his narrative) had reached this point via the Ford B (mouth of Water Rat Creek) route, which makes sense, though it would be unlikely these Indians formed the full complement. He continued:

> The stones in the cemetery [*sic*; a reference to the marble markers] at the southeast, or rather in the line running down toward the river from Calhoun Hill, is where the battle began, and it is plain to see that an effort was made at that point to check the advance of the Indians, and a good many soldiers fell there.[16]

Numerous Indian witnesses supported this view. Northern Cheyenne warriors, Brave Wolf and White Bull/Ice, as well as the Minneconjou, Hump, said, "Calhoun's [*sic*; Harrington's] company, leaving the command and charging down the ridge on the hill where the Indians were, drove them before him, but soon after was surrounded and all [were] killed."[17] He Dog said the fighting began at Finley Ridge.[18] Tall Bull, a Northern Cheyenne, said the beginning of the fight was at the Finley marker and the first volley was from there.[19] Tall Bull was not there however, reaching the area as the soldiers had been forced up the ridge to the right of "Custer's [Calhoun] Coulee," Indians driving them there.[20] Another Northern Cheyenne warrior, Little Wolf, indicated a skirmish line along the map references for the Finley-Finckle Ridge line,[21] though this does not mean necessarily there was an actual skirmish line there, only that troops occupied the position along some or part of its length. Archaeologist Fox found no evidence of a skirmish line along the ridge and any occupation was momentary at best.

In answering [Walter] Camp's queries, Hollow Horn Bear mentioned that the troopers "went" from Calhoun Ridge [Finley-Finckle Ridge] to nearby Calhoun Hill, implying that they did not stop. He also added, metaphorically referring to terror and panic, that they were drunk. Thus, it seems likely that no skirmish line existed there. Certainly, archaeological evidence for significant government firearm use is absent. Ultimately, those soldiers still alive must have traversed the ridge, as Runs The Enemy intimated, en route to Calhoun Hill, seeking safety there with other right-wing units.[22]

Other accounts as well say the troops were driven to that area, and the Brulé, Two Eagles, confirmed it when he told Sewell Weston the fighting on Finley Ridge, Calhoun Hill, and in the Keogh Sector were all moving fights—hardly indicative of skirmish line characteristics—and the only "firm stand made" was on Last Stand Hill.[23] Again, discrepancies reign, though again as well, they appear minor and the differences accounted for by individual locations and a person's definitions of "stand" and "moving." A year after the Two Eagles interview, Lone Bear, an Oglala, told Weston short stands were made on Finley Ridge and Calhoun Hill, but a heavy "stand" was made in the Keogh Sector. Many horses were killed in this vicinity and Lone Bear seemed to think Keogh made a longer stand than the one on Last Stand Hill[24]; body placements discovered by the survivors on June 27 tend to confirm Lone Bear's recollections. Lieutenant Edward McClernand also called attention to the proliferation of dead horses on the ridge.[25]

We can see more of the minor confusion—again, something we must adjust for individual placements and times—in various descriptions of the troops' movements. Lights said most of the soldiers on Finley Ridge, Calhoun Hill, and in the Keogh Sector were mounted. Those on foot either had their horses shot or stampeded.[26] Lone Bear took the exact opposite viewpoint when he told Weston in 1909, from Finley Ridge to Last Stand Hill the troops were dismounted and moving. At times, short "stands" were made,[27] the whole indicative of men being routed and forced from place to place. Two Eagles took a middle ground, saying in the fighting along Finley Ridge and up to Calhoun Hill—this would be C Company solely—some troopers were dismounted while others fought on horseback,[28] probably very close to the truth. Mounted or on foot, the troops were moving, and moving as quickly as they were able.

The attack on C Company had to have been furious, especially considering the Indian accounts of the troops' movements: mounted and dismounted men. One does not give up his mobility in situations such as this without a fight; one does not run on foot from a devastating enemy intent on raising one's scalp. Also, one can imagine the same intensity that greeted troops during Reno's retreat, greeting Harrington's command and causing a panic among overwhelmed men. It is unlikely, however, any of the Indians involved in the valley fighting were engaged in this area as yet. While there is some evidence Crazy Horse and his followers were part of the first wave of warriors to leave the Reno battle, it is doubtful any of this group—seeing soldiers on the ridges to the east and Indians crossing the river in pursuit—crossed at Ford B, choosing instead to head farther downstream to get behind the white men. This being the case, other than the passing Crazy Horse, the first Indians from the valley fighting to arrive at the Medicine Tail ford would not have crossed the river much before 3:43 p.m. a minute or so before Keogh sent C Company into the coulee (*Timeline W*). This does not mean they were not involved in the mayhem atop Finley-Finckle, but it is unlikely they participated in the coulee fighting.

What is also very interesting here is the narrative of both Two Eagles and Lone Bear and their descriptions of the fighting. Notice they make no claim of being or seeing the action in Calhoun Coulee, but begin referring to this phase of the battle once it reached Finley Ridge. Both warriors were known to have participated in the valley fight[29] and their lack of reference to whatever happened in the coulee could mean they reached the battle only as Harrington's men began arriving on the heights of the ridge—3:53 p.m.—or were already there. Lights, on the other hand, while making no reference to any coulee, does say many of the troops were mounted, the only time that having been the case being when Harrington began his charge. The 10 minutes from 3:43 to 3:53 p.m. would have been sufficient for the "Reno" Indians to have crossed the river and reach Finley Ridge. Also, if Gall were in this part of the battle—and remember, there is some question about his presence[30]—he could have been well ensconced in the Henryville area, already firing on Calhoun Hill and keeping the L Company troops busy.

While fighting in the coulee had to have been furious, it seems the troops grasped immediately what they had ridden into and it did not take long for them—or Harrington—to understand they needed to reach support, and fast! This enlightenment came not without cost, however. It is never a good idea to attempt to determine definitive battle theory based on today's marker placement, but we can be reasonably sure of the accuracy of some of the markers in this particular area.

There are three cavalry markers on the coulee ridgeline and another four in the coulee itself, one of them near Finley-Finckle.[31] The markers in the upper reaches of the coulee indicate troops died during the charge, while the others indicate a path of retreat. (We will throw in this caveat: markers and their placement should be used as a guideline only. There are nine markers, total, in Calhoun Coulee, but artifacts have not been found at all these sites, making some placements problematic. Also, there is no allowance for Trumpeter Dose. In addition, there are 19 markers atop Finley-Finckle Ridge, 17 of which are considered non-paired. For a breakdown of the marker placements, see Appendix C, sub-section, "Summary Analysis of Marker Placement.")

Harrington would not have had more than a couple minutes before Indians turned back and launched their assault, so setting 3:49 p.m. as a time when C Company men were scurrying to take up positions and at the same time suddenly meeting the warriors' wrath is not unreasonable. Again, it must be remembered, this was a battle, and we have reached the beginning of its vicious and furious hand-to-hand stage; in a firefight, a single minute is sometimes an interminable period of time. As we have seen from numbers of troops and distances covered, along with the overwhelming numbers of warriors, resistance in the coulee could not have lasted long, and within a four-minute time-frame, Harrington's beleaguered men would have begun to break for Finley-Finckle Ridge: the high ground—3:53 p.m.

Some two minutes before—3:51 p.m.—while the majority of C Company was still in the depression of the coulee, Captain Tom Weir was scaling the heights of Weir Peaks. No one knows what Weir saw—or if he understood what he was seeing: it had to be a jumble of dust and smoke and mounted warriors heading for a shrouded ridgeline.

There was cause for puzzlement, for in all likelihood there was a paucity of gunfire, the Indians' close-in weapons, i.e., hatchets, war clubs, the terrifying knife-sticks, even bows and arrows, doing most of the killing, the troops doing most of the running. Around the same time—3:53 p.m.—Crazy Horse had reached the head-cut of Deep Ravine and was about to mount the final 525 yards up to Battle Ridge and through the gap in the ridgeline, inserting himself between Keogh and Custer's commands. At a speed of 10 miles per hour, it would take the Oglala only two minutes to crest the ridge and bridge the gap, and within another four minutes—3:59 p.m.—trailed by some 200 warriors, to reach the ridgeline just east of Battle Ridge, chopping up part of Company I along the way. Shortly, he would repeat the foray in the opposite direction, finishing the job.

A minute after C Company broke, Custer, having completed his trip from Ford D, was mounting the slope to Cemetery Ridge.

Markers indicate C Company lost seven men before the unit's remnants reached the perceived safety of the higher ground from the coulee floor. This would have brought the command down to 29 enlisted personnel, plus its lieutenant.

The mayhem atop Finley-Finckle Ridge had to have been extraordinary. The archaeological work of 1984 and 1985 found little evidence of firing by troops, despite allowances for foragers, scavengers, and souvenir hunters over the years. A depiction of close-in fighting would tend to confirm this observation, for a carbine would be useless and the troops' revolvers would have been exhausted after six rounds. Six times 30 would equate to only 180 bullets and we can be assured not every man first shot and emptied his revolver on the ridge, then spent precious moments reloading. One can also imagine the fury of the Indians, those on foot harassing the troops up the coulee walls, while others—mounted warriors entering the battle from the valley fighting—dashed across the Deep Coulee flats bringing a wall of galloping horseflesh into the melee. If we add the accumulating dust and smoke, the inability of the troops to gain any semblance of order or organization, then factor in flailing hatchets, war clubs, knife sticks,[32] and knives, Indian gunfire from Greasy Grass Ridge to the immediate west, along with an overabundance of Indians, and we have the makings of a complete rout.

Archaeological evidence suggests troops traversed this ridge quickly, not stopping to set up a defense, and taking a number of casualties as they moved.[33] The bodies of C Company sergeants Finckle and Finley were identified there,[34] and another 10–17 markers show the approximate locations of other C Company men. This being the case, the unit had no more than 18 men remaining by the time it retreated to the heights of Calhoun Hill; 51 percent killed, so far.

The fate of C Company's commander, Lieutenant Henry Moore Harrington, has never been determined; his body—along with those of lieutenants Porter and Sturgis—was never found or identified. We do however, have indications Harrington may have been one of 12 men who perished on Finley Ridge. Little Hawk claimed an officer was shot and fell from his horse, then some soldiers mounted. At the same time, the Ute, Yellow Nose, and a Northern Cheyenne named Contrary Belly made a charge, followed by the "rest" of the Indians.[35] (It is widely believed this was the action where Yellow Nose grabbed a company guidon, and if so, it would have to be that of C Company.) While we take Indian identifica-

tion of white officers with a grain of salt, Harrington was one of the more distinguishable officers because of his white, fringed canvas trousers. Besides George and Tom Custer who were reported to be clad in buckskin pants and blouses, Harrington was the only other person definitively identified as wearing non-regulation pants. Buckskin shirts or blouses seemed to proliferate among the officer ranks, but few wore them that day preferring to roll them on their saddles because of the intense heat.

(Earlier we had discussed the possible wounding of Algernon Smith at Ford B, and his identification as an officer. While Smith could very well have been wearing a buckskin blouse at the time, he was believed to have worn a blue "fireman's" shirt underneath, and blue regulation trousers, though he often preferred to wear shoes with white gaiters rather than boots.[36] These differences alerted Indians to "important" people in the otherwise mundane world of military uniforms.)

Brave Bear, a Southern Cheyenne who had been involved in the fight against Reno, echoed Little Hawk's comments about an officer being killed here. Brave Bear claimed he saw Yellow Nose, with a flag, coming out of a group of dead soldiers. Then eight soldiers started toward the company on the knoll. Behind these soldiers was an officer on horseback. The officer killed a Cheyenne and shot a Sioux before he himself was killed. Brave Bear claims to have captured the officer's horse.[37] If correct, this officer would have been Harrington and this is the only allusion to his being anyplace other than Last Stand Hill. The tale makes sense, especially since Harrington's body was never identified. Richard Hardorff stated the same thing essentially[38]; he also claimed Tom Custer was with his brother, acting as Aide-de-Camp, and Harrington commanded C Company in Tom's absence. All this is correct. Furthermore, Hardorff identifies one of the slain Indians as either Black Bear or Limber Bones (Cheyenne), and notes as well the particular value of Harrington's horse: "Harrington rode a large and powerful horse, described as being very fast,"[39] a prize indeed for any Indian. Brave Bear said,

These three companies turned all their horses loose; that is, the horses that were not shot down [already]. Only one officer stayed on his horse. It did not take long to kill them here. I saw Yellow Nose with a flag coming out [from] among the dead soldiers. Eight soldiers started towards [the] company on [the] knoll. The officer on horse[back] was behind them. [A] Cheyenne charged this officer, [and] this officer shot him in [the] head. [A] Sioux with scalp lock charged at him also, and he shot this Sioux in the breast. Another Indian [then] rode up and shot this officer off his horse. I captured his horse. It was [a] sorrel horse. This officer killed these two Indians. I have been told since [then] Custer was with that one company on [the] knoll.[40]

(It is interesting to note Hardorff, who has provided us with so much brilliant source work, and who—in my opinion—is absolutely correct with his speculations about Harrington and Tom Custer, contradicts himself somewhat in his identification of various Indians involved in the different fights. He identifies this particular dead Cheyenne as either Black Bear or Limber Bones, with the identity of the Sioux unknown. We know of two Black Bears at the camp that day, one referred to earlier as an Oglala thought to be lurking near the divide; but this was not the man involved here. The second was indeed a Cheyenne, but in his work, *Lakota Recollections,* Hardorff speculates Black Bear was possibly an unidentified warrior seen by White Bull and killed in the Reno fight.[41] As for Limber Bones, there was only one identified person of that name, a 20-year-old Cheyenne son of Horse Roads, killed, and later buried in the hills west of the camp.[42] This Limber Bones was believed to have been one of the so-called "suicide" warriors,[43] and was believed to have been killed on the north slope of Last Stand Hill a little later in the battle.[44] As for Custer being on the "knoll," Brave Bear is mistaken, based on his description of where he was when viewing this action, though understandable, some 30 years later.)

Harrington's fall on the Finley-Finckle ridgeline is disputed by retired army master sergeant and author Walt Cross in his book, *Custer's Lost Officer.* Cross argues the lieutenant was indeed shot from his horse, but survived the incident, fighting his way with a knife back onto his mount and thence to temporary safety on Last Stand Hill.[45] This is more fanciful than realistic, however, and while Cross does a yeoman's job bringing the Harrington saga more attention than it ever received before, his work is challenged by his attempts at fitting context into theory rather than the reverse, and is further complicated by the dramatization of his protagonist riding hither and yon on his snorting Bucephalus, firing a brace of pistols at howling Indians while his gallant soldiers maintained a calm, steady fire, ammunition—or the lack of it—always being an issue. No attention is paid to distances, terrain, or the narratives of Indians who helped disassemble this command. While some may consider the Black Bear story problematic, its relating fits with the timing and circumstances of C Company's demise and was not elicited with any goal in mind. Cross quotes both Richard Fox and Gregory Michno to support his contention of the C Company move into Calhoun Coulee, but then he concocts the drama of a still-viable command surviving an overwhelmed L Company atop its hill, a completely new and unsupportable rendition of the battle and a misquoting—or misunderstanding—of both Fox and Michno. So while the Brave Bear story is not

definitive by any stretch, the mere fact the man claimed to have captured an officer's horse lends greater credibility to his reminiscences than the poorly supported fancies of modern-day authors. At least the horse grabbing could have been seen by others; there is nothing supporting Cross' speculations.

Only L Company bodies were identified on Calhoun Hill, which leads one to believe the men of C Company never became a part of the hill's defense. If we assume the marker placement is anywhere near correct, then no more than 18 men—and probably fewer—from C made it across the hilltop and into Keogh's company sector along the eastern side of Battle Ridge, and most of them would perish there.

Fighting on Calhoun Hill became equally intense and Calhoun's skirmish lines were the only organized, textbook defense the troops mounted in this area. Some even believe this was the most difficult area of the fight for the Indians. Artifact placement, marker placement, and archaeology tend to dispute this view however. While there is no question the fighting was intense and furious, much or even most of it conducted on foot, it appears it did not last long and Calhoun's lines collapsed very quickly. There is the allusion again, of a moving battle, not something one might expect of skirmish lines holding a defensive position.

There are 14 markers on Calhoun Hill, though only 11 are considered accurate and unpaired. Yet, with 46 men, Calhoun's company was the largest in Custer's command and if we allot a dozen troops as horse-holders, that still leaves 34 men (including two officers) to fight two skirmish lines. Therefore, one might expect to have found more than 11 bodies atop the hill. While Low Dog claimed soldiers stood their ground and made no attempt to run away,[46] he was an Oglala Sioux and had been in the valley fight, so we do not know when he arrived or if he was speaking about this particular phase of the battle. Even Two Moons claimed few Sioux took part in this fighting.[47] We contrast Low Dog's memories with those of others. As we have seen already, Two Eagles claimed the fighting in this sector was a moving battle, and Lone Bear said there was only a short stand made on Calhoun Hill,[48] a memory confirmed by another Oglala, Red Hawk.[49]

While marker placement in the overall Battle Ridge/Calhoun Hill/Finley-Finckle Ridge sectors seems to indicate panic, Indian testimony isolates that panic to specific areas. Gall claimed Keogh and Calhoun never broke, but fell back step-by-step until reaching the ridge where they died.[50] Lone Bear's narratives tend to bear this out. It is clear, however, with more than half its members killed—including its lieutenant—and with no dead bodies reported atop the hill, C Company men who survived the Finley Ridge melee were in a big rush to get away. That is generally indicative of panicked flight. If we add the 11 L Company markers to those of C, we have no more than 91 troopers remaining and being hemmed in by Indians storming across Calhoun Hill, up Calhoun Coulee and Finley Ridge, Indians having made their way up Deep Coulee and now ensconced on the ridge to the troops' east, and suddenly Crazy Horse bursting across and cutting the escape route to the north. Considering the circumstances and Indian movements, too few men have died here, indicating a serious lack of defensive positioning. While not alluding to panic specifically, Ed Godfrey hinted at it in a letter he wrote to E. S. Paxson on January 16, 1896: "The scene on the left (north and east of Crittenden Hill [Calhoun Hill] or near the point on the map marked 'spring') where the Indians stampeded the 'led horses' of Troops I and L must have been a wild one."[51]

At about 3:54 p.m. Calhoun would have been feverishly shifting his skirmish line in an attempt to cover the retreat of C Company and get the unit's fleeing men through his lines. A minute later, Crazy Horse and some 200 warriors broke across the crest of Battle Ridge, racing toward the ridge to the east, many of them intermingling with Keogh's dismounted troops. By 3:58, the warriors south of the hilltop pulled themselves from cover—some mounted, others on foot—and attacked across Calhoun Hill forcing the wavering skirmish line off the heights and into the I Company men. By 3:59, Crazy Horse has crested the eastern ridge and after a brief pause to gather other Indians led by the Minneconjou, White Bull, heads back into the maelstrom he has just precipitated.

Referring to Appendix C, sub-section "Marker Placement," we see a total of 13 non-paired markers (numbers 169 and 170 appeared to be paired)—numbers 158 through 169, and number 171, coming off the northern end of Calhoun Hill. Markers 158 and 159 are at the northern end of the hill and in all likelihood represent the first troops killed coming off the hilltop. The next five—160 through 164, inclusive—are located coming off the hilltop beyond and north of 158 and 159 and into the swale area between Calhoun Hill and the Keogh Sector: eastern Battle Ridge. This is where the horses were held, and we do not know if these markers represent fleeing troops or men killed by the arching arrows emanating from Calhoun Coulee minutes earlier. In all likelihood, one of these markers represents Private Charles Graham, whose body was identified on a line between Calhoun and Keogh. Graham was the only L Company trooper—other than the officers—identified in this area of the battlefield close to Calhoun Hill. Beyond marker 164, we have a line of six more—165 through 169, then 171—extending

north off Calhoun Hill, two of which—168 and 169—are clumped together (consider 169 and 170 as paired markers representing only one man). It appears all 13 of these markers represent men from companies C and L, as Company I would still be somewhat more north having attempted to cover the gap in Battle Ridge. By now, Keogh's command would have been whittled down to 78 men, and the 43 dead we have counted already—including Harrington and the two officers from L, lieutenants Calhoun and Crittenden—are from companies C and L, leaving those units with a combined strength of only 40 men.

An additional word of caution is required here. While we can discuss these markers, their placement is far from accurate and it should be remembered the numbers we use are only guidelines. The number of markers exceeds the number of deaths; many are paired, though we try to make allowances for those; and the totals along the various fighting routes do not equate precisely to the number of men we know were in the commands.

Once beyond 171, we have a large grouping—172 through 199—most within a defined area where one can consider a stand was made. The marker numbers are deceiving here and in all likelihood represent between 25–33 individuals (depending on one's view of how many escaped to die on Last Stand Hill), one of whom—marker 174—is found along the eastern boundary fence and is believed to represent Company I blacksmith, Private Henry Allen Bailey. Archaeologists Fox and Scott felt Bailey tried to get away and "dashed across the ravines and up the final side slope."[52] There were several eyewitness accounts of a single soldier trying to make a getaway and being intercepted by Cheyenne warriors, and in one account by Crazy Horse himself. The Oglala warrior, Flying Hawk said, "One soldier was running away to the east, but Crazy Horse saw him and jumped on his pony and went after him. He got him about half a mile from the place where the others were lying dead. The smoke was lifted so we could see a little."[53] Possibly a little more credible were the testimonies from several Cheyenne who claimed to have seen the incident. Big Beaver, a 17-year-old Northern Cheyenne, said,

> A soldier got up and mounted his horse (this was one of Keogh's men, or Sorrel Horse Troop), and rode as fast as he could towards the east. This is the lone marker next to the fence to the east of the Keogh position. Two Cheyenne Indians cut him off and killed him. They then scalped him and hung the scalp on the sagebrush. I went over there and got the gun and some other things, and that was the first gun I ever owned.[54]

Wooden Leg's version had the soldier on foot breaking away from the main action. He verified Big Beaver's claim of recovering a weapon as well as the scalp-on-the-sagebrush incident. Two Moons alluded to the incident as if he were one of the assassins, otherwise pretty much keeping to the facts presented by Wooden Leg and Big Beaver. He added, "The authorities say the body was never found. That is partly explained by the fact that some bones of men from which the dogs had eaten the flesh were found in the Indian camp."[55]

Of the other markers in the numerical sequence, two sets are paired—numbers 183 and 199; and 194 and 195; two numbers—182 and 196—represent no markers at all; and one marker—188—has an "A" and "B," each representing a single individual. These 25 markers would represent men from all three of the companies in Keogh's battalion, number 178 representing Keogh himself.

Crazy Horse's arrival across Battle Ridge broke Keogh's back. While some historians believe the fabled warrior rode even farther north to get into the battle, this seems quite unlikely. It is unknown if Eagle Bear—another Oglala—fought with Crazy Horse specifically, but we do know he was involved in the fighting around the Custer column.[56] He claimed, "Many of our warriors rode into a ravine where Custer could not see them but through which he would have to pass to reach our village."[57] (Custer, sitting atop Cemetery Ridge would need to get through Deep Ravine to reach the village directly.) Pretty White Buffalo said she saw Crazy Horse leading Cheyenne warriors up a ravine, followed by Crow King and his Hunkpapa followers.[58] He Dog—the leader of the Soreback band who was known to be with Crazy Horse—told Walter Camp, "at" Keogh is where Crazy Horse charged and cut the soldiers in two,[59] and then, several years later, spoke of the gap in the ridge they broke through, splitting the troops.[60] This description could only be up the reaches from Deep Ravine.

The initial breach of the gap and into Keogh's lines would have occurred around 3:55 to 3:59 p.m. variably cued for the column's length—but this was not a singular event restricted to this time period: at 3:54 p.m. the pack train was spotted approaching Reno Hill, Reno now ordering the command to move forward toward Captain Weir; Custer had just reached the crest of Cemetery Ridge and may have even seen or been aware of the horde of Indian riders coming out of Deep Ravine and heading across Battle Ridge, thereby prompting him to send Yates into the basin area in an attempt to stanch the flow of Indians from traversing that ridge—3:59 p.m. Varnum was starting down the bluffs to bury Hodgson—3:55 p.m. Harrington and C Company were in their

death throes atop Finley-Finckle Ridge; and by 3:57 p.m. Edgerly and D Company, using Cedar Coulee, reached the east side of Weir Point, continuing forward.

From this point on we know very little, other than from what we can discern from stark white markers along a lonely ridgeline. If they are anywhere near accurately placed, men indeed died a frightening and forlorn death, and one not mercifully administered: many of the bone fragments unearthed in 1984 and 1985 come annotated with "blunt forced trauma" (see Appendix C, sub-section, "Markers"). While White Bull claimed Crazy Horse rode east of these particular killing fields, it is clear he did not stay there, but after gathering warriors together charged back among the now-panicking troops to administer the final blows—4:04–4:15 p.m. Richard Fox claims there were no "last stands," and while there may have been no textbook "last stands" formed from deployed skirmish lines, there was clearly a throng gathered around Myles Keogh, though even that compressed group held out for but a few minutes against the overwhelming flood of warriors. Only 10 men from Keogh's battalion[61] were identified north of this sector, meaning the rest—or most—perished with their companies, or within their battalion's area of operation.

Marker placements now begin to confuse things even more. Keogh had 122 troops under his command (there is a question regarding the two orderlies originally assigned to Reno and sent back to Custer with messages—privates McIlhargey and Mitchell—especially since their bodies were identified on Last Stand Hill, but let us for argument's sake say they remained with their assigned unit, Company I). Placements show nine bodies in the Calhoun Coulee environs; 19—17 non-paired, meaning two spurious markers—atop Finley-Finckle Ridge; 14—11 non-paired—on Calhoun Hill; five in the swale area between Calhoun Hill and the lower side of the Keogh Sector along Battle Ridge; five on west Battle Ridge—four non-paired; and 89—81 non-paired—markers in the Keogh Sector. This totals 141 markers (plus two separate stones for Foley and Butler), 127 of which are considered legitimate today. If we allot two of the 127 to Butler and Foley (a bit to the south) and one to either Private David J. O'Connell or Charles Siemon, both of L Company (one of whom also fell outside this perimeter[62]—in Deep Coulee—in what appears to have been a getaway attempt) we are left with 124 markers. Because we know at least 11 troopers from this battalion were identified to the north of these six sectors, at most, 107 men from Keogh's battalion would have been killed within this all-encompassing area. This means there are 17 markers in this area where no bodies

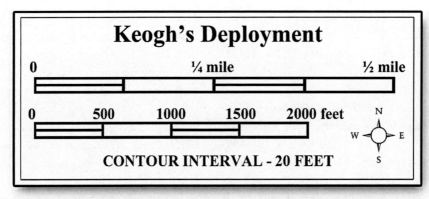

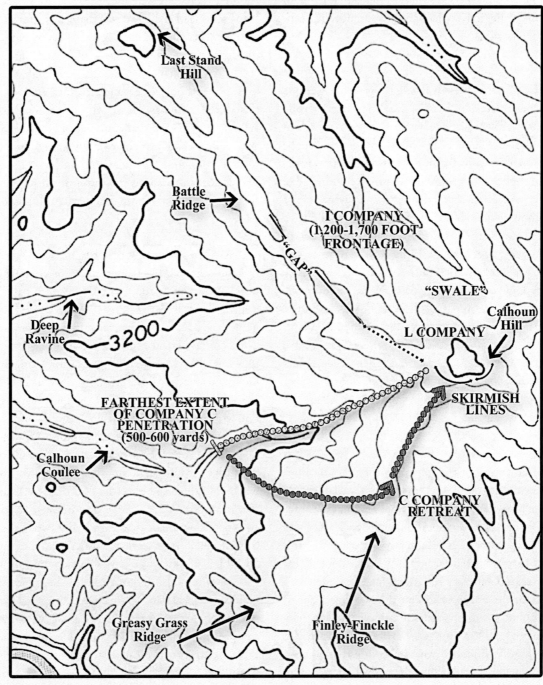

could have been found, exaggerating the count and scope of the battle by 34–36 markers depending on how one accounts for Butler and Foley.

Confusing as it may be, the markers, coupled with some of the Indian accounts, continue to tell the tale. North of the cluster generally associated with Keogh himself, there is only a hodgepodge array to show where men died; no order, neither rhyme nor reason; a finite number without a definitive rationale; a display indicative of panic or sheer madness. Again, while not definitive, one can just imagine from the picture painted by Wooden Leg of the terror striking dismounted troops: hundreds of [Indians] riding here and there all the time, most of them merely changing position, but a few of them racing back and forth in front of soldiers, in daring movements to exhibit bravery."[63]

If we employ an area breakdown of markers in the Keogh Sector only, we can define certain groupings as follows: (1) five markers on west Battle Ridge (numbers 111–115), two of which are considered paired, leaving us with four possible bodies. It is unclear if these were men attempting to escape the maelstrom of the Keogh fighting, or were some of the last to leave the Last Stand Hill area. (2) Five markers on the east side of Battle Ridge at the north end of the Keogh Sector (numbers 116–120), four of which are considered nonspurious. (3) A grouping of five stones (243–247) in the northernmost end of the Keogh Sector, one of which is erroneously marked for Marc Kellogg, three of these five are nonspurious. (4) A group of eight (235–242) just south of these and off the service road to the east. Of these eight, only four are believed to be legitimate. This leaves us with 71 markers constituting the rest of the sector, 26—24 non-spurious— forming the so-called "Keogh grouping"—those gathered around Captain Myles Keogh. Based on 107 men dying in this sector, that would leave only 26 non-spurious markers for the remainder of the ridge between the Keogh grouping and those in the northern sector (and certainly these would represent men assigned to cover the gap in the ridge, men pushed back by the on-rushing warriors, dying where they fell). The total then, for the entire Keogh Sector—not counting the markers on west Battle Ridge (1, above)—should be 61 where today we see 89, an overage of 28 markers. Remember as well, there is that differentiation between "paired" and "grouped." We should also make note, in this northern sector grouping, numbers 201 and 202 are considered paired, but those two, along with Marker 200, appear to be for only one person. Overall, these numbers would seem accurate, providing the 11 escapees into the Last Stand Hill area is equally precise. If this latter number fails the test, it would change the numbers north of the Keogh grouping.

As we alluded to earlier with the Gall accounts, the mélange of markers between Keogh and Custer are indicative of men in panic. Continuing his metaphor beyond Calhoun Hill, Hollow Horn Bear said the soldiers were moving all the time and were drunk.[64] While Gall was a little more charitable, claiming the troops never broke,[65] he also said the soldiers never fought in a line along the ridge.[66] While that comment may seem innocuous by itself, when taken with other comments and the physical presence of markers on the field, it points out no established linear defense was maintained in this sector. That indicates a complete breakdown, ultimately leading to panic. This is reinforced by other accounts. A Minneconjou warrior named Turtle Rib claimed when he reached the scene, soldiers were on foot, engaged in a running fight.[67] Pretty White Buffalo said, "Those who ran away left [their guns] behind."[68] The Minneconjou White Bull claimed the Indians attacked amidst a great deal of dust, driving the soldiers to where the monument is today.[69] Flying Hawk said a lot of the soldiers were killed close-in, with tomahawks and arrows,[70] and in 1908, Two Eagles told Sewell Weston no soldiers tried to escape until the fighting in the Keogh Sector. Then, "eight soldiers" crossed over Battle Ridge, west of Finley Ridge.[71] (We can forgive the "west of Finley" comment as "left of" or "north of," and attribute it to interpretation or lack of directional terminology knowledge.)

No one knows how long the fighting in the Keogh Sector lasted, but indications—common sense coupled with warrior narratives—tell us not very long. We allot some 30 minutes from the time Crazy Horse crested Battle Ridge to a final mop-up—3:55–4:25 p.m. (*Timeline V*). Keogh must have had his hands full and we do not know if he was aware of the gap in the ridge until it was too late. The location of the scattered bodies can represent panic as well as a last-ditch effort to defend that gap—again, *an absolute necessity!*—troops routed by hordes of mounted warriors pouring across, troops pushed back into the lower areas of the ridge by sheer momentum, with Keogh's final location indicating a futile attempt to control both the northern end of the Calhoun debacle as well as his own sector.

We can also figure no one from C Company could have reached the "safety" of Last Stand Hill before 4:05 p.m.— not on foot, anyway—simply by virtue of calculating foot speed and distance, then factoring in weight of uniforms and boots, stamina, ambient temperature, terrain, and the gauntlet that had to be run (see the *Administrative Entry, Timeline V*), all of which would limit speed. And between 3:55 p.m. and 4:25 p.m. George Custer was having his own problems.

18

THE GRAVEYARD WATCH

REFERENCES:
*Timeline U—Keogh to Custer on Cemetery Ridge; 3:29 p.m.–
3:57 p.m.*
V—Cemetery Ridge to the End; 3:54 p.m.–4:40 p.m.
W—Warriors; 1:02 p.m.–5:17 p.m.

Custer's move back from Ford D had to be rapid indeed—probably 12 miles per hour or faster (*Timeline U*). There was no time to waste; things were becoming critical and these Indians were in no mood for bargaining. Besides, it was now pushing four o'clock—3:46 p.m. (just about the time Harrington, more than a mile and one-half away was ordering his command to dismount in Calhoun Coulee)—and Benteen should be approaching the higher ground where he would spot Keogh's troops. Custer had seen all he needed to see; knew the full extent of the village, the full extent of the Indians' retreat; and had found a suitable ford. It was time to position his command where Benteen and Keogh would be able to catch sight of him. He ordered Yates to lead out, to skirt along the river, heading the move back through some flats, and to seek a higher ridge in view of the hogback where he had left Keogh, and he could not have been pleased with what he saw ahead of him: too many mounted warriors crossing the river farther upstream and disappearing from view into a deep ravine.

Despite circumstances, an escape to safety was still not out of the question; it may have been too late for Keogh's men—though Custer would not have known that—but not for Yates' battalion, now some 86 men. Whether Custer still did not recognize the precariousness of his situation, still felt he was in full control and on the offensive, or if it was now a matter of honor, sensing the disaster on the other side of the ridge, we will never know, though actions seem to choose the former. There comes a point when a good commander must cut his losses and pull away, and despite his errors, it remains George Custer was a fine commander. So what happened?

As Richard Fox pointed out, the paucity of ammunition found on the battlefield—regardless of the depredations of souvenir hunters—indicated less gunfire and more close-in fighting with hand weapons, and this lack of firing *noise* may have led Custer to a false sense of security: minimal fighting (read: *firing*), despite all the rising dust and the warriors he was seeing. (This lack of gunfire is supported not only by the archaeological findings of blunt-force trauma, but by eyewitness and first-hand accounts in various permutations: privates William O. Taylor [A Company], John Bailey [B], Edwin Pickard [F], and Lieutenant Richard Thompson [K Company, Sixth Infantry] in his findings after the battle; and the Indians themselves, *viz.*, Iron Hawk, Little Voice, Old Bull, Standing Bear, and Thunder Bear, among others.)

At 3:54 p.m. some eight minutes after leaving Ford D (*Timeline U*), moving parallel along the river, then counterclockwise in a scythe-like swing-back to approach the lower end of Cemetery Ridge from its south side, Custer began the easy ascent to the ridge's crest (*Timeline V*), and from that moment to about 3:59 p.m. he set up his dispositions, no more than a stringing out of his command, probably dismounting Smith's Gray Horse Troop for better fire control. According to the tribal historian, John Stands In Timber, Custer's troops "retreated to the flats below where the superintendent's house is now located. They waited there for about half an hour, while Indians assembled in the vicinity and fired on the soldiers from the ridges north of the flats."[1] At a later date, he added, "But they waited too long. It gave many more warriors a chance to get across and up behind the big ridge where the monument stands, to join Wolf Tooth and the others up there."[2] We question, however, Stands In Timber's use of the word, "retreated," preferring instead to recognize Custer's deliberate movements as a continuation of his offensive mind-set. Our timing analysis of the warriors' movements precludes a massive build-up this early in the event, thereby allowing Custer to maintain options and a channel of withdrawal, were he so inclined. This situation, however, did not last long.

While C Company was being routed, the disintegration

Deep Ravine (along the upper portion of the picture) and the "basin" area where Custer sent Yates to try to stem the tide of Indians moving up to Battle Ridge (toward the photograph's left).

of the I and L commands had not occurred yet, but it appears Custer was coming under pressure of his own—mounting by the minute—as soon as he reached the ridgeline. We must not forget the Wolf Tooth/Big Foot band harassing him on the way to Ford D—alluded to by Stands In Timber and supported by the Scott/Bleed work—plus any number of other Indians now gathering from across the river, and choking off any further northward movement. Crow King said when the troops realized they were surrounded, they dismounted,[3] probably setting up an opportunity for the Two Kettles Sioux warrior, Runs The Enemy, to breach Custer's "line" on the ridge, and run off some of the command's horses. Fox wrote,

> Runs the Enemy's [allusion to, Custer's] "line" probably stood, at least in part, near the modern visitor center, which is on Cemetery Ridge below and some 750 feet west of the Custer Hill apex. On departing the ridge, Runs the Enemy, after capturing some horses, returned to his original position in the Calhoun vicinity, where he helped to destroy the right wing

[Keogh's battalion]. Thus it is clear the left wing [Yates' battalion] had deployed on Cemetery Ridge before the onset of disintegration in the Calhoun and Keogh sectors.[4]

Fox' observations and research tie in perfectly with our timing scenarios developed through other means. Moments before the Runs The Enemy coup, Custer and Yates had to have been watching Crazy Horse's warriors moving up the head-cut of Deep Ravine toward the crest of Battle Ridge. Quickly recognizing the catastrophic consequences of continuing to allow such infiltration, Custer ordered Yates into a shallow basin area commanding the egress route from the ravine about half a mile away. Yates, moving at a slow gallop of about eight miles per hour (allowing for the terrain), arrived there about 4:06 p.m. (*Timeline V*). This additional split proved the penultimate disaster, eliminating any further chance of survival, and it was made all the worse by Yates' inability to plug the bottleneck. (There is very little historical evidence for this move by Yates. Richard Fox alludes to it, but other than

Deep Ravine. The main access route for Indians moving toward Last Stand Hill, and Crazy Horse's route to Battle Ridge. This is where the bodies of 28 soldiers from E Company were reputedly found. In all likelihood, in 1876, the ravine's head-cut was where the bend is seen in this photo, just above mid-photograph. This would make the Yates move to the basin area even more likely, keeping him at a reasonable arm's length from the ravine's egress point.

the John Stands In Timber account we have scant additional information. Probably the only other hint of an F Company presence comes from the archaeology. On a rise above Deep Ravine there is an isolated marker [257] between the ravine and Greasy Grass Ridge. Walter Camp's interviews maintained that the body of Corporal John Briody of F Company had been found there with one leg cut off and placed under his head. The placement of the discovered bones would be consistent with such an event [see Appendix C: Markers: Marker 257]. That at least would indicate some F Company presence, even if only in retreat.)

While standing in this basin area today one might question the efficacy of such a tactical move by Custer, but it must be remembered in 1876 the head-cut of Deep Ravine was 50 yards or more closer to the river, creating a reasonable firing lane between Yates and any warriors arising from the depths of a ravine. Only a huge surge of rapidly moving men would

negate any advantage that distance could have afforded the F Company troopers.

While Custer was maneuvering his two companies toward Cemetery Ridge, Indians were crossing the Little Big Horn at Ford D—3:58 p.m.—gathering, building their numbers to the north of Cemetery Ridge, most mounted, others dismounting. By 4:07–4:08 p.m. having moved a mile to a mile and three-quarters at a 12–14 mile per hour gallop, the warriors had sealed the northern limits of the battlefield,[5] and as Yates reached the basin, the fighting had escalated into a terrible crescendo of death in the Calhoun and Keogh sectors, Calhoun's position in a state of collapse and Keogh—unable to move north—surrounded and fighting for his life (see *Timeline W,* 4:04 p.m.–4:15 p.m.). The deadly deracination had begun.

The pressure building on Custer and Smith now alone atop Cemetery Ridge was beginning to take its toll. Already,

The South Skirmish Line as seen from Last Stand Hill. Deep Ravine is seen off to the left, while the southern edge of Cemetery Ridge can be seen on the far right. The basin area is to the photograph's center-left. It was down this forlorn ridge the remnants of E Company charged, only to be driven to the death trap of Deep Ravine.

Smith had lost a number of his horses, his mobility—cavalry's life-blood. The Indians crossing at Ford D cut off the north (the Scott/Bleed work alludes to that); and more Indians crossing at the Deep Ravine ford have now seen the troops on the ridgeline and have begun moving up the flats, effectively sealing off the south, and completing the surround. As Yates reached the basin area—4:06 p.m.—the gunfire from both directions, as well as Runs The Enemy's foray, are forcing Custer toward the higher ground of Last Stand Hill—4:09 p.m. (refer to *Timeline V*). Soldier Wolf claimed as the Indians started to prevail, the troops "began to give way, retreating slowly, face to the front."[6] He added as the soldiers fell back they came "nearly to where the monument now is. Then they turned and rushed over the top of the hill,"[7] and while we do not know precisely what Soldier Wolf meant by "over top of the hill," an analysis of the marker placements indicates as many as seven men from the Custer/Yates group may have been killed in the Keogh sector. His observations fit in equally

as well with our timing analysis, for we have Custer's lead elements arriving at the hilltop at 4:13 p.m. several minutes after any troops on foot from Keogh's command could have reached the same hilltop.

The Northern Cheyenne, Little Hawk, said not many soldiers were killed in "the charge up the ridge where soldiers and Indians were together,"[8] but casualties were beginning to mount and at least six troops died on Cemetery Ridge as they moved toward higher ground.[9]

> Beginning at the visitor center, and extending down Cemetery Ridge through the national cemetery, maintenance complex, and housing area below, the ground is hopelessly disturbed.... [Author/historian] Michael Moore ... found indirect evidence (in the Custer Battlefield National Monument archives) for six marble markers that were once located at the visitor center site but that allegedly were removed before construction of that facility (1950s).[10]

One of the more interesting things about this Fox observation is no E Company bodies were identified at any location other

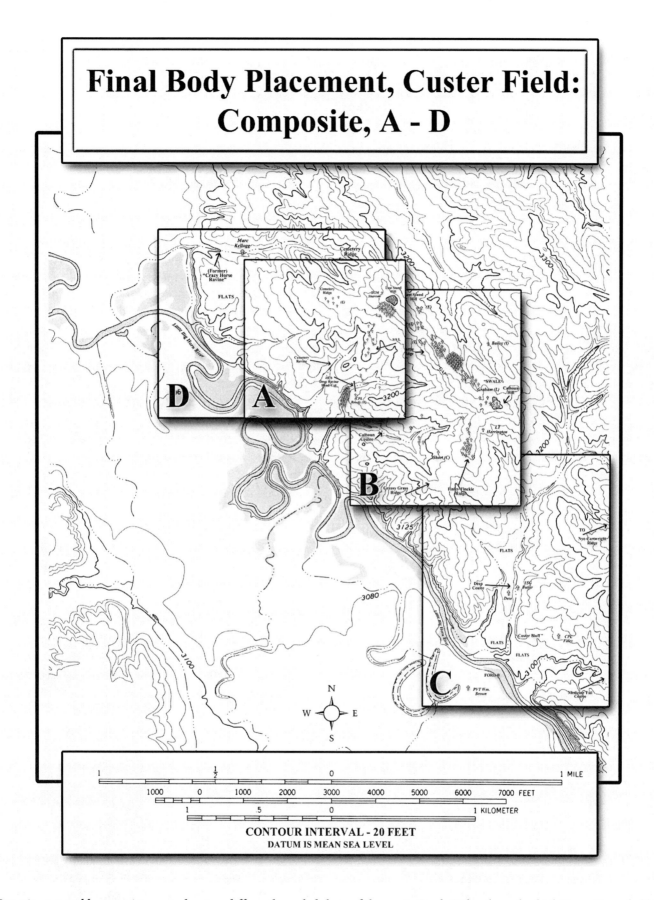

Final Body Placement, Custer Field: Composite, A - D

CONTOUR INTERVAL - 20 FEET
DATUM IS MEAN SEA LEVEL

Opposite, top and bottom: As seen today, two differently angled shots of the gap in Battle Ridge through which Crazy Horse led his warriors, thus breaking Myles Keogh's back. The first was shot from a sharper angle to the ridgeline, but Deep Ravine angles off to the right—unseen—in both photos. Captain Yates moved his F Company into the flat, basin-type area in the right-center of the second.

than Deep Ravine (Lieutenant Smith, of course, is the lone exception). Since we know—or think we do—28 E Company men fell in the ravine, if we add the six from Cemetery Ridge, we have possibly identified the final locations of 34 of the 37 enlisted men of the Gray Horse Troop. This would make perfect sense and in a rather circumstantial manner tend to confirm accounts left us by a number of the warriors who fought there. That would make an assumption of the remaining three men falling on the South Skirmish Line (the ridge extending down from Last Stand Hill) equally valid, especially considering the reports only a small number of bodies were found on that "line": Captain Tom McDougall said there were just a few bodies between the "deep gully" and where Custer lay; he was sure there were less than 12 and might not have been more than six.[11] Lieutenant Richard E. Thompson, K Company, Sixth Infantry, and Terry's Acting Commissary and Subsistence Officer, agreed, telling Walter Camp only nine or 10 men lay between Custer and the gully.[12]

As Custer's troops became more and more embroiled, George Yates, also coming under increasing pressure, began to move back toward his commander and the high ground of Last Stand Hill. In all likelihood, Yates began his move about 4:12 p.m. just before Custer's lead elements reached the highest ground, and we can figure—based on actual distance measurements and the imponderables of Indian pressure and fright—Yates began arriving at the hilltop just as the final remnants of E Company were arriving—4:15 p.m. (*Timeline V*). From this point, for the next 10 minutes, the fighting intensified and the troops remaining from Keogh's command arrived, accentuating the burgeoning disaster. Indians chasing these Keogh fugitives only added to the overall melee, though of necessity and wont, they kept a reasonable distance once confronted by the relatively larger numbers of Custer's left wing. By this time the die had been cast; there was no longer any hope of retreat.

The final act of overrunning Last Stand Hill is veiled in as much mystery as any other part of the maelstrom. Dr. Fox believes there was no "last stand," while others shudder at the thought no such heroic act took place. The truth, however, is hidden in the semantics. If one remembers the movie, *Fort Apache*, starring John Wayne, Henry Fonda, and George O'Brien, one could hearken back to the final battle scene, the small clutch of troops, gallantly commanded by Lieutenant Colonel Owen Thursday and his erstwhile friend Sam Collingwood, as they waited in grim reality for the final rush of Apaches, a rush also shrouded in the battle's dust, mounted warriors swooping across the last cloaked remnants of resistance, a rush leaving only dead and no clear picture of man's final moments. One would suspect those soldiers might have

been George Custer and George Yates, and Hollywood guessed accurately at what no one really knows.

We can surmise then, during those brutal 10 minutes between 4:15 and 4:25, the final desperate attempts at survival coalesced into some sort of gamble, one concluding only a mere 15 minutes later. The intensity of the battle, the increasing dust and smoke, and the fury of the Indians have now combined to make moments seem like minutes. Algernon Smith goes down, and Custer quickly decides on a bold stroke, hopeless though it may seem, of sending the remnants of the Gray Horse Troop under Lieutenant Jack Sturgis, mostly dismounted and fearful men, down the ridgeline to scatter Indians—with what objective in mind we will never know, maybe just to clear a path for the others, a leapfrogging attempt to open a channel to the river. And charge they did, some dying along the way, the rest driven by Indians who were having none of it, into the deep ravine where they were later found.

Waterman said when the troops moved back to the hill they got off their horses. "Some of the horses got away and came down to the river where they were caught by some of the Indians. These were gray horses and some sorrels."[13] Tall Bull: the soldiers made no charges.[14] Two Eagles: the soldiers never made a charge.[15] Lights: the soldiers never made a charge.[16] Hollow Horn Bear: the soldiers never made a charge.[17] Julia Face: the soldiers never charged.[18] Foolish Elk: "Custer" charged the Indians twice.[19] Soldier Wolf: from this point on, everything was confused. The Indians mounted a "grand charge" and nothing could be seen because of all the dust and smoke.[20] Standing Bear: the troops were surrounded when suddenly their horses broke away.[21] John Two Moons: the Indians charged among the soldiers on the hill.[22] Thunder Bear: at the end of the fight the Indians rushed Custer's men on the hill and killed them with clubs and arrows.[23] Little Hawk: "Most of them were killed by Indians hidden behind the little ridge, but there was some charging into these troops by Indians."[24] The Minneconjou, White Bull: the Indians "charged soldiers at close hand. Some soldiers ran. Others shot with pistol, and others shot with rifle. Some beat with rifle as [a] club."[25] Lights: "not very positive about any stand being made at ... [Keogh's stand]. If there was a stand made it was short. The only stand of any great length was at ... [Custer Hill]."[26] Lone Bear: a good "stand" was made at Last Stand Hill, but not as good or as long as the one made in the Keogh Sector.[27] Flying By: no stands were made except the one on Custer Hill.[28] Foolish Elk: the only stand made was near the monument.[29] Turtle Rib: no stand was made except at the end of the long ridge (Last Stand Hill). Here, the bay and gray horses were all mixed together.[30] Two Eagles: the hardest fighting

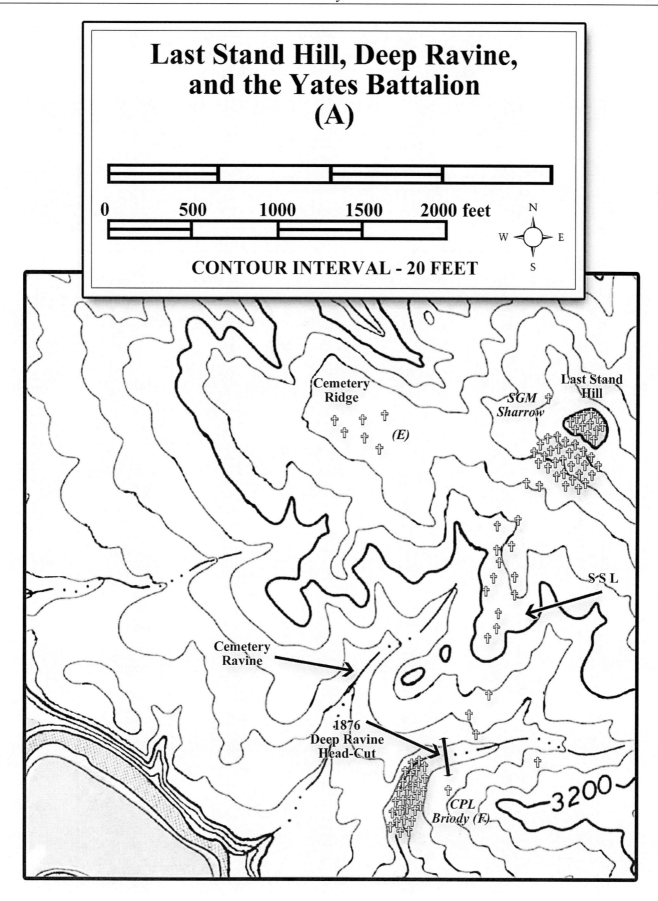

Last Stand Hill, Deep Ravine, and the Yates Battalion (A)

0   500   1000   1500   2000 feet

CONTOUR INTERVAL - 20 FEET

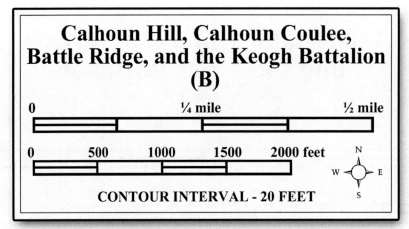

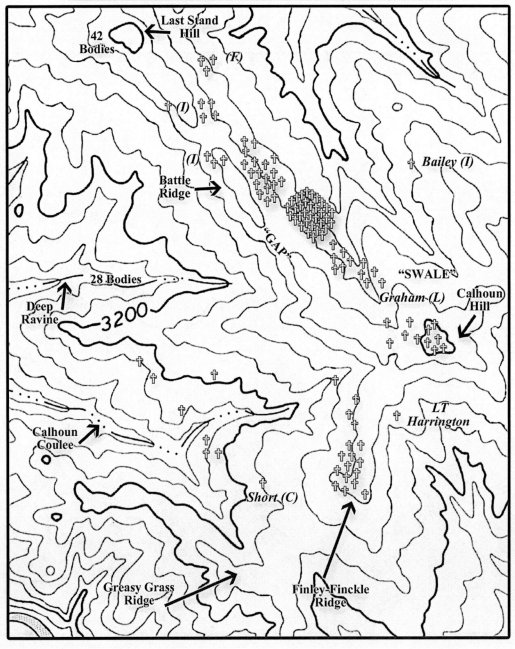

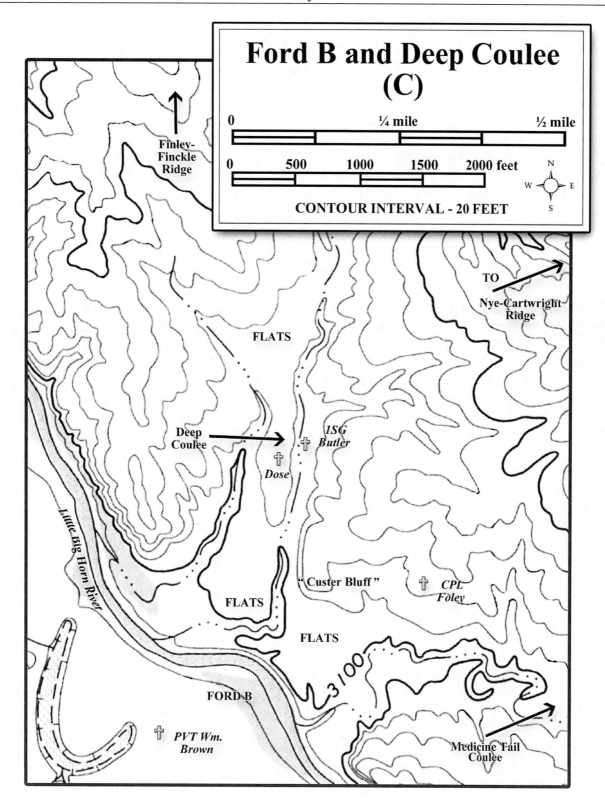

Ford B and Deep Coulee (C)

occurred at Last Stand Hill.[31] Lone Bear: no soldiers were killed on the top of Last Stand Hill because while they made a short stand there, they were forced over the hill.[32]

Oddly, Lone Bear's reference is the second we have seen to soldiers being forced over "the top of the hill." Soldier Wolf alluded to it and we made an assumption he could have been referring to the stragglers from Keogh's command. Another indication of this comes from archaeological work done in 1994. Referring to their artifact markings, Doug Scott and Peter Bleed wrote,

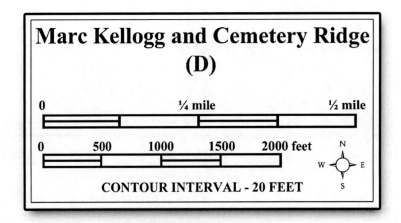

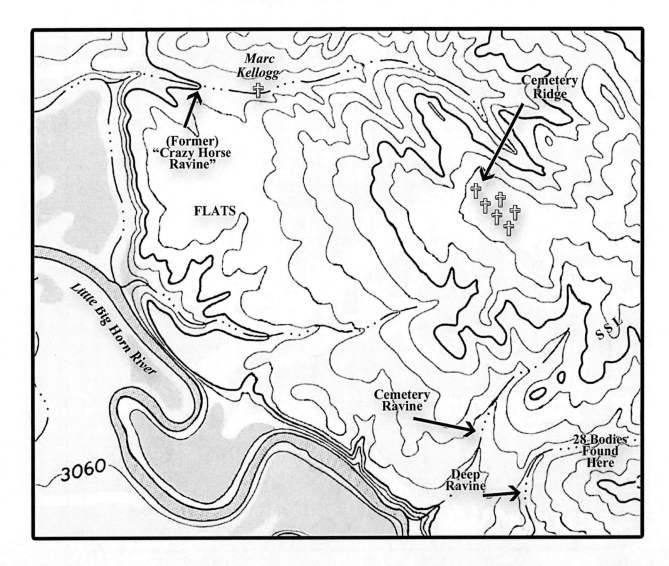

[Cartridge cases] FS8049 matched to FS8050, and FS8091 matched to FS8094. In both situations the matched [Colt revolver] cases were within one or two meters of each other. The clusters of fired cases were situated in a ravine just out of sight of Last Stand Hill [below the Custer Ridge Extension]. This protected situation may be the reason the cases were deposited. To extract fired cases and reload a Colt revolver requires opening the loading gate, revolving the cylinder chamber with the fired case to a position opposite the open gate, manipulating the extractor rod to expel the fired case, reloading the chamber, and finally rotating the cylinder to the next chamber. The process requires time and a location in a protected ravine and out of the line of fire, if the battle was still raging, would seem a likely scenario to fit this find.

Cases FS8049 and FS8050 matched to a Colt case (FS1605) found in Calhoun Coulee below Greasy Grass Ridge in 1984.... The matching case from 1984 was found nearly one mile from the two 1994 case finds.[33]

This firearm identification could indicate at least one of these two men were from C Company, and since no horse remains were identified in this area we may assume the individual arrived by foot. If correct, this position was obtained later in the battle, after 4:05 p.m. and probably closer to 4:15 when the final stragglers of E Company arrived and Yates' F Company began arriving on Last Stand Hill (see *Timeline V*), helping to corroborate Lone Bear and Soldier Wolf's observations. Two C Company men were identified in this general vicinity: privates Ygnatz Stungewitz and Willis B. Wright, though the Wright identification is problematic (see Appendix C: Markers: Marker 199).

Furthermore, while little is made of this, it points out the fury of the Indians and the ferocity of their attack, somewhat sooner—and lasting a little longer—than generally believed. James Willert wrote,

Curiously, there are only two white markers along the north slope beyond Custer's last position. However, on a map, drawn by Captain Benteen after the battle, he indicated that bodies were seen by him down the north slope. He noted on the map: "Ravine off here containing 30 bodies which were not found nor buried."[34]

Obviously, Benteen got his numbers wrong or lumped together too many bodies, too many locations, and too many directions, but not all the markers on Last Stand Hill are placed where men actually fell (it could also mean Benteen's "north slope" referred to the South Skirmish Line coming off the north end of Battle Ridge). In 1881, Win Edgerly said they found the bodies of George Custer, his brother Tom, Adjutant Cooke, along with a few enlisted men and several horses, all on the knoll.[35] A couple years earlier, he included Lieutenant Reily in that grouping and indications are he was correct.[36] George Wallace agreed, telling the Reno court 20–30 men lay near, but not right around Custer.[37] This would clarify Benteen's comments, as well as the accounts of Lone Bear and Soldier Wolf and would indicate troops fell on the northern and eastern sides of the knoll, where no markers are located today. Privates Dennis Lynch (F Com-

pany),[38] August Siefert (K),[39] and Thomas O'Neill (G)[40] variously identified sergeants Hughes and Vickory-Groesbeck, and Chief Trumpeter Voss as being near their commander, observations that would make sense based on assignments and loyalties. There is some evidence as well, Private Edward C. Driscoll of I Company made it this far, only to fall near Custer. That would complete this immediate grouping near the top of the knoll as eight men, including the general.

Shortly before the end, the so-called "suicide boys" struck—4:32–4:36 p.m. (*Timeline W*)—beginning the hand-to-hand fighting. Then Wolf Tooth's warriors charged in. Indians now on Cemetery Ridge charged in among Sturgis' exhausted E Company troopers who had come down the South Skirmish Line from the hilltop, and forced them toward the abyss of Deep Ravine where more Indians were waiting for the final kill. Standing Bear told Walter Camp the troops between Custer Hill and the river got there on foot and were killed in the deep ravine.[41] By 4:36 p.m. George Custer's remaining command atop the knoll was overrun and the Minneconjou warrior, Hump, related, "The Indians and whites were so mixed up that you could hardly tell anything about it."[42] Standing Bear said he saw Indians charging all around him and soon the Indians and soldiers were all mixed together. There were so many guns going off he could not hear anything else. "The voices seemed to be on top of the cloud."[43] A Hunkpapa named Little Buck Elk said the Indians were "as thick as bees at the fight, and that there were so many of them that they could not all take part in it."[44] Two Eagles said the last action occurred as troopers left Last Stand Hill and tried to get away into Deep Ravine; they were all dismounted.[45] Lone Bear claimed the men killed between Last Stand Hill and Deep Ravine were killed in the last stages of the fight and were going from the hill toward the river.[46] Lights said the soldiers killed in the Custer sector were moving from Last Stand Hill toward Deep Ravine and this was at the end of the fight.[47] Tall Bull told Walter Camp, "I was near [Deep Ravine on Camp's map] and heard a big war whoop that soldiers were coming. Soldiers came on foot and ran right through us into deep gully, and this was the last of the fight, and the men were killed in this gully."[48]

Not much of a "last stand." And then there was silence. It was over. The time was 4:40 p.m.

19

Too Late—Reno Follows

REFERENCES:
Timeline K—Scouts; 11:30 a.m.–4:35 p.m.
X—Weir Peaks and Return; 3:10 p.m.–5:30 p.m.

At 3:40 p.m., Lieutenant Winfield Scott Edgerly began moving D Company northward in the direction of his commander and the downstream gunfire (*Timeline X*). No need to gallop; a six-mile per hour pace sufficed as he had Captain Weir always in sight. (At this same time, George Custer was two minutes away from arriving at Ford D; Keogh, Calhoun, and Harrington were feeling first the pinprick, then the sting of arching arrows tumbling onto their commands; and Luke Hare, returning from the pack train, saw Edgerly's men moving north—3:43 p.m.[1]) It is unclear what others thought of Weir's precipitate action and it is even unclear if his action was precipitate. At the Reno inquiry, Benteen told the recorder, "Captain Weir sallied out in a fit of bravado, I think, without orders."[2] This remained a consistent theme with Benteen—"consistency" being a trait of some importance to the man—for a number of years later, he said at the time he and Reno spoke for a bit—Benteen used the phrase, "After a few words with Col. Reno"—and Benteen asked where Weir and D Troop had gone. He was told they had moved, without orders, down the river.[3]

Shortly before Edgerly began his move north, the three Crow scouts skirted the triple prominence to their front,[4] and arrived in the vicinity of the troops on Reno Hill—3:38 p.m. (*Timeline K*). Their physical appearance and apparent solitude seem to cause the troops little alarm, for we hear of no opposition or apprehension with their approach and they soon joined their fellow scouts, the Ree, Red Bear, and the Dakota, White Cloud,[5] among the packs—3:43 p.m. The volley firing heard about 30 minutes earlier has now become a general sound-of-battle, described as such by Fred Gerard and bringing no further comment from any of the troops. At 3:45 p.m. Luke Hare has returned to the command, the ammo mules several hundred yards behind him (*Timeline X*). By this time most

of the Indians who had gathered in the valley had disappeared downstream, leaving only about 100–150 on both sides of the river to keep a wary eye on the soldiers atop the bluffs.[6]

Within minutes, the two mules had reached the hilltop and one of the crates was broken open, ammunition distributed to those who needed it, all the while more stragglers from the valley command were reaching the safety of the heights. Godfrey confirmed the timing of this when he told the Reno court soon after Weir moved out, the ammunition packs arrived.[7] He also claimed the command was put on "readiness" to follow Weir right after the two mules arrived, but it was then decided to wait for the arrival of the rest of the train.[8] We can assume—since Reno had not returned—the initial inclination to advance was Benteen's, only to be countermanded by Reno a couple minutes later.

As the packs moved toward the hilltop troops and herders could see men of Reno's command "slowly climbing up the hill,"[9] other than those still trapped in the timber, the remainder of the troops who fought in the valley. By 3:49 p.m. Weir had approached the southernmost slope of the twin peaks and was beginning his climb; a minute later Edgerly reached the head of Cedar Coulee, also continuing on. In the meantime, Reno, who some 20-plus minutes earlier had grabbed Sergeant Culbertson and several others to hunt for Benny Hodgson's body, returned to the hilltop—3:50 p.m. He spotted D Company heading north, saw the ammo being distributed, and ordered Lieutenant Hare forward to tell Weir to see if he could make contact with Custer:

> I told him [Hare] to go to Captain Weir who, on his own hook, had moved out his company, and tell him to communicate with General Custer if he could and tell him where we were. I knew in what direction to send him because General Custer's trail had been found.[10]

This is quite possibly a disingenuous and self-serving reminiscence. He also ordered Lieutenant Varnum to take some men and shovels and head down the bluffs to bury Hodgson, though where Reno thought Varnum would get entrenching tools is anyone's guess, unless there were some on the ammo mules. Varnum, however, told Reno he had nothing with which to bury Hodgson and he would have to wait for the packs to come up.[11] He waited a few minutes for the leading elements of the train to arrive, then grabbed two spades and headed downhill with four of McDougall's B Company men: Sergeant Benjamin Criswell, Private August DeVoto, and two others. It was now 3:57 p.m. and more packs were arriving, the train strung out far behind.

Shortly after Tom Weir scaled the northernmost peak, Hare set out to contact him—3:52 p.m. At that time, the majority of the packs were about a mile away but within sight, and spurred on by Lieutenant Mathey and Captain McDougall the mules were moving at as rapid a pace as they had all day. McDougall said he saw some black objects on a hill and thought they were Indians. He told his men they would have to charge those people "and get to the command," and he put one platoon in front of the pack train and the other in the rear.[12] Many years later he told Walter Camp he instructed his men, if attacked, the front platoon was to deploy, the troops with the mules were to circle them, shoot them, and use them as a barricade.[13]

What we are seeing on this hilltop is a mixed command—half whipped, half untested—trying to assess its situation, reassert itself, gather its various elements, and continue with its mission, however problematic or uncertain it may have seemed at this juncture. Nothing, however—from the moment George Custer moved the Seventh Cavalry across the divide—to now, indicates these officers and men operated in any fashion other than a military command under competent guidance (an exception would be Reno's retreat from the timber, not so much the act, but the manner in which it was carried out). Based on the vast majority of eyewitness accounts, combined with properly measured distances and reasonable speeds determined as well by sundry accounts, we see no haphazard or irresponsible leadership. From a logical and reasonable study of a given military operation, none of the claims of writers, historians, and so-called battle students questioning and railing against the competency of men like Reno, Benteen, and even George Custer, ring true. Custer made his share of mistakes—and they were mistakes of a dreadful nature—but they were not the errors of an incompetent commander, rather the errors of a gambler, a risk taker, a man who misjudged his enemy and overestimated the ability of his small command. Custer's superiors made many of these same errors, without the immediate horrors and the attendant derision found in the Indian Wars postbellum years.

When properly exhibited and displayed, Benteen's actions were those of a man in complete control, a man who knew what had to be done and how to do it, and it is irresponsible, bizarre, and ludicrous to conclude otherwise. Reno displayed far less competence, but there is no viable, ineluctable proof for claims of drunkenness, and while his method of departure from the valley can be questioned, the fact remains we cannot prove any other method would have improved results other than to satisfy the writers of military textbooks. The fact also remains, by leaving the timber when he did Reno saved his command. We can debate methodology, but any discussion on timing is fatuous at best. Even the Indians themselves have debunked as myth Reno's early departure freeing up hordes of warriors to fight Custer.

At approximately 3:55 p.m. the first of the packs began arriving in the vicinity of Reno Hill, preceded by McDougall and one of his platoons. As Varnum grabbed some shovels, McDougall threw out a skirmish line,[14] and a couple minutes later—4:00 p.m.—the overall move toward Weir Peaks started, Benteen and his H Company leading out, followed by Godfrey's K, then French's M. As he arrived, McDougall spotted the tail end of D Company entering Cedar Coulee almost a mile away. Benteen said at about the time the packs arrived, he noticed one of his companies had begun moving north and he followed with H and K. "I had to get in sight then, of what I had left my valley hunting for."[15] While many detractors would like us to believe Reno and Benteen sat on their haunches while Custer and his five companies perished, Godfrey, in an August 7, 1876, letter to *The Army and Navy Journal*, wrote, as soon as the dispositions were made, "Weir's company was sent to look for Genl. Custer."[16] This is especially cogent since it was written only 43 days after the event, and while Godfrey was no admirer certainly of Reno it tends to confirm Reno's claim Weir was indeed *directed* to proceed north, a claim we are still hesitant to accept fully, especially in light of Edgerly's recollections.

As an aside, it is interesting to recall Godfrey's antipathy toward Reno, especially since much of it was recorded as the campaign progressed. In an August 15, 1876, entry in his field diary (note the closeness in dates between this entry and Godfrey's letter to *The Army and Navy Journal*), Godfrey wrote,

[Second Lieutenant Henry Perrine Walker, G Company, 17th Infantry] says he has been detailed as personal Aid de Camp on the staff of Genl Terry, apparently for the purpose of carrying orders to the Commdg. off. of 7th Cav. Maj. Reno has been playing *"ass"* right along and is so taken up with his own importance that he thinks he can "snip" everybody and comment on the orders he receives from Genl Terry's Hdqurs. and insult his staff, so there is not any one the personal staff on speaking terms.[17]

Reno had recently turned down Godfrey's application to command the leaderless L Company, saying someone from within the company would probably be promoted to fill the vacancy, but when Godfrey re-submitted the application at a later date, Reno approved it. One wonders from whence the animosity arose.

The timing of the command's move north is critical in understanding the relationship of these remaining companies of the regiment to the Custer battalions and when they died. It is also critical when discussing the reputations of the two senior officers—Reno and Benteen—and whether or not they dallied in their efforts to relieve the doomed command. Could this move have saved Custer? As we have seen, with the exception of some odd decisions by Reno—affecting no one but Reno—there was little wasted time from when Benteen arrived on the hilltop to when the move north began. We can question the speed of the actual movement, per se, or the determination of Reno, but it is inane to question the overall actions of the remaining companies and their officers. Lieutenant Hare, who played a significant role in the hilltop events, estimated it took some 45 minutes from the time Benteen arrived to when the command started its northward trek[18] (our studies indicate 3:05 p.m. to 4:00 p.m.—55 minutes—versus Hare's 45). Many years later, he supported this contention through a variation, by telling Walter Camp he believed the move did not start until at least an hour after Reno retreated up the bluffs[19] (this would be from 2:38 p.m. to 4:00 p.m. one hour 22 minutes, versus his earlier, RCOI, "45 minutes" comment). Varnum used an hour and a half from the time Reno began reaching the hilltop to when "the whole thing started."[20] Rather than precise or relative times, Varnum's account of the activity on the hill may be even more descriptive. He wrote his father, telling him, "as soon as we could get into any sort of shape we started along the bluff to try and unite with Custer."[21] Sergeant Culbertson claimed it was a little less than an hour after he heard the firing from downstream when the command started for Weir Peaks,[22] all of these recollections reasonable and fitting within our analysis.

As with everything else, there are conflicting accounts claiming the move north took place somewhat later. These accounts, however, came many years later and quite possibly reflect time's erosion of memory. Godfrey, in his 1892 article, claimed the move began around 5:00 p.m.,[23] a strange entry indeed, especially in light of those he recorded in his field diary when he claimed the command headed downstream right after the packs' arrival.[24] Shortly before his death, Tom McDougall, in a letter to Walter Camp, said the packs were on Reno Hill for one and one-half hours before the whole command started out in search of Custer.[25] Closer to the event, we have Private Edward Davern who felt the move took place between one and two hours after the packs had come up.[26] Trumpeter Martini's testimony at the Reno Inquiry supported Davern as Martini believed the move began about one and one-half hours after the packs' arrival.[27] Even Private Windolph thought it was about 5:00 p.m. when Reno and Benteen ordered the whole command forward, though Windolph hedged by adding it was very hard to "estimate" time under the circumstances.[28] These discrepancies are hard to reconcile and one cannot assume the two enlisted men were referring to the arrival of the ammunition mules because that took place only 12 minutes prior to the general downstream exodus. Specific watch times are also unreliable, especially since so few enlisted men carried watches and as we have noted, conditions were not the best during the 40 days on the campaign trail.

We have weighed our choices, however, and have opted to accept the former for two primary reasons. The first is that Lieutenant Edgerly, who had moved his D Company ahead of the rest, told Camp companies H, K, and M followed him about 30 minutes after D Company departed the hilltop. That would compare to the charted times (see *Timeline X*) of 3:40 p.m. to 4:00 p.m. 20 minutes, versus Edgerly's 30. In turn, Varnum proved to be the most convincing because he tied the command's move—a specific event—into another specific event already linked with previous episodes and times: his return to the hilltop after being recalled before reaching Hodgson's body. Varnum claimed he was gone a total of 20–25 minutes and our work plots that at 3:57 p.m. At 4:09, a messenger reached him, telling him to return, and by the time he reached the hilltop—4:20—"most of the command had started to move on down the stream along the bluffs with the exception, I think, of Captain Moylan's company and possibly some of the others."[29] Since Varnum's foray is tied in with other events, it offers greater relevance to timing than a mere memory of a specific or relative time, regardless who said it or even when it was related: 3:57 p.m.–4:20 p.m.

At this point in the day, the emphasis was less one of speed than of wariness. In addition, "We carried a number of badly wounded men and to move, they had to be carried in blankets…. The command moved down the river along the top of the bluffs, following Custer's trail, which we found."[30] (Particular attention should be paid to Varnum's comment about finding Custer's trail, a point of contention among many historians. Finding it here—at Cedar Coulee—precludes some beliefs of a trail along the east side of Sharpshooters' Ridge.) As alluded to, Varnum saw Moylan's company, the outfit charged with carrying the wounded, and after beginning to move, Moylan sent a man forward to tell Reno he needed help moving these men. Moylan then moved forward himself and spoke with McDougall who sent a platoon back to assist.[31] McDougall confirmed the incident,[32] as did Varnum.[33] In addition, the route had to be peppered with—though at discreet distances—warriors left behind after the valley fighting—quite possibly as many as 150—below and strung out along the bluffs, and probably a little more nervous seeing advancing troops.

While Tom Weir sat atop the northern peak, Win Edgerly continued moving forward.[34] After traveling about one and one-half miles from Reno Hill—beyond the Weir complex—Edgerly saw Weir motion for him to return—4:02 p.m. (*Timeline X*).[35] Several minutes later, Reno's orderly recalled Varnum, and the command was on the move—4:09 p.m. At the same time, Hare reached Weir, telling him of Reno's request to contact Custer, but Weir, watching the dust and smoke-shrouded mayhem some 2¼ to three miles away, is having none of it. By 4:14, Edgerly has moved D from in front of the hill complex up the slopes of the Weir loaf and is beginning to position his troops—4:15–4:18 p.m. A moment later he spotted Benteen, French, and Godfrey approaching from the south. As Edgerly's men hunkered down, they were ordered to begin firing at marauding Indians to their front, again, the remnants of the warriors who had confronted Reno in the valley. According to Sergeant Thomas Harrison, the troops "had stopped back at the south end of this sugarloaf and Edgerly said he would go out to the end of the sugarloaf to look down and see if he could see Custer while they were out there."[36] By 4:20 p.m. Fred Benteen had climbed the northernmost bluff and was standing side by side with Weir. If they could have seen anything in the dusty veil overhanging the Custer fields, they would have seen C Company bodies strewn along Finley-Finckle Ridge; they would have seen Calhoun's stricken command decimated on his hilltop; they would have seen Keogh's last remaining handful of men struggling toward Last Stand Hill; and they would have seen the remnants of companies E and F battling to remain alive amidst a horde of Sioux and Cheyenne warriors bent on their destruction.

Companies H, M, and K arrived about 4:20, and spent the next 15 minutes positioning for a defensive stand. Edgerly described the H Company position as occupying the twin peaks in a file, while D was placed at a right angle on the loaf. French's M Company set up a little to Benteen's rear, while Godfrey's K was positioned adjacent to D, but on a narrow side-spur along the bluffs adjacent to the river and M Company—4:20–4:35 p.m. (*Timeline X*). Godfrey said he stopped his troops "a little below on the hillside." He then went to the top of the hill to see what lay beyond. While he was up there—probably on the loaf—he saw Indians downriver starting back toward them, maybe three or four miles away. The troops were ordered to dismount and Godfrey formed a "skirmish line on the crest of the bluff next to the river about that high point … with M Company which was on the high point."[37] Years later he said,

> Our command did not appear to attract their attention, although there was some commotion observable among those near to our position. We heard occasional shots, most of which seemed to be a great distance off, beyond the large groups on the hill. While watching this group, the conclusion was arrived at that Custer had been repulsed, and the firing we heard was the parting shots of the rear guard.[38]

First Sergeant John Ryan supported Godfrey's contention. "We saw at a distance from a mile and a half to two miles parties, whom we supposed were Indians, riding back and forth and firing scattering shots. We thought they were disposing of Custer's wounded men."[39] Private Windolph described the positioning: "Here we were stretched out all over the hell's half acre, a troop on this hill knob, another in this little valley and over there a third troop. Behind, at a slow walk, came the pack trains, the wounded men and the rear guard."[40]

In the meantime, after a short delay with Moylan to assist with the wounded, Varnum headed downstream to join the men on Weir Point. At about 4:42 p.m. he reached Edgerly's men on the loaf. "That was on the far point of a long range of high bluffs which ran along the right bank of the Little Big Horn. I went on to where his company was dismounted and firing at Indians who seemed to be coming from out on the prairie and turning back."[41] A little later in the testimony he added:

> I went to the position of Captain Weir's company at the far point of the ridge down-stream. At that time his men were firing at pretty long range—I should say 700–800 yards—at Indians here and there. At that time I could see all over the plain where … the Custer battlefield had been, and it was just covered with Indians in all directions, coming back toward us.[42]

Edgerly claimed this firing lasted about three-quarters of an hour and if we look at *Timeline X*, we see the links to other events and how they tie in with his recollection. He deployed his command between 4:15 and 4:18 p.m. ordering his men to fire at will. At 4:53, the firing eased, commensurate with Varnum's account at the Reno court, of slow, long-distance firing[43]; and at 5:04 p.m. Edgerly began his withdrawal from the hilltop.

By 4:43 p.m. George Herendeen, noticing the gunfire slackening from downstream, began his move from the valley timber, bringing with him most of the troops who could not make it out during Reno's retreat. Herendeen's action had to have been aided by the "watcher"-Indians' downstream move brought about by the Benteen advance toward Weir. Around the same time—4:45 p.m.—word began to spread among the Indians on the Custer field that additional soldiers were seen on the high bluffs to the south. Indians in the vicinity of Calhoun Hill now began moving toward Weir Point, joining up with many of those who had stayed behind to monitor the troops on the southern hills—those "watchers." By 4:50, more and more Indians were turning and making their way south toward the entrenched troops, aiming to finish the job George Custer started. Many of them began at a slow gallop, but by the time they were joined by others, speeds would have reached 12–14 miles per hour, especially up the easier draws and coulees (*Timeline X*). Seeing the burgeoning seriousness of the situation, Benteen made his way back quickly to Reno, warning the major the position atop these knolls was untenable—4:51 to 4:57 p.m. Luke Hare recalled hearing Benteen tell Reno the area they had just come from was the best place to make a stand.[44] Reno agreed and dispatched Trumpeter George B. Penwell (K Company) to tell French, Godfrey, and Weir to pull back. By 5:00 p.m. Herendeen and the valley stragglers would be reaching the vicinity of Weir Peaks, only to be caught up—again—with troops about to retreat. Herendeen looked back and saw not only were Indians moving toward them across the hills and coulees to the north, but many were returning up the valley as well.[45]

At 5:03 p.m. the galloping Penwell—having traversed the three-quarters of a mile of open space at 10 miles per hour—is signaling French, and has reached Godfrey's command with the orders to move. Penwell informed Lieutenant Hare—who Godfrey had just instructed to take 10 men to occupy higher ground on the company's right—and Hare notified Godfrey of the change in plans. French yelled over to Edgerly, instructing him to pull back. By 5:04 p.m. the entire command of four companies occupying the Weir complex was on the move—a beginning move of eight to 10 miles per hour—the trains and rear columns turning as Moylan reached Reno who told the captain it would not be necessary to move forward any more as "the whole force of Indians was in front of Captain Weir's command ... and firing at us."[46] As Reno

arrived, Benteen threw French's company—still afoot—at right angles to the river to screen Weir's withdrawal. Benteen instructed French to pull back slowly, but the whole operation did not work out as well as Benteen expected. French fell back much too quickly and Weir's company was high-tailing it as well, so Benteen ordered Godfrey to serve as a blocking force somewhere between the Weir complex and Reno Hill.[47] The fact the Indians did not make the most of their opportunity, plus a staunch defense by Godfrey (noted by Benteen)—"carrying out his instructions more faithfully and in a more soldierly manner"—allowed Benteen enough time to get a defensive line forward as the retrograde began reaching Reno Hill.[48]

As the last of D Company moved off the sugarloaf and into a small draw leading into Cedar Coulee—5:07 p.m.; eight to 10 miles per hour—Edgerly began to grapple with his horse, his orderly, the veteran Sergeant Harrison standing nearby to assist. Meanwhile, bullets were coming closer and closer, and Edgerly claimed as he struggled mounting, Indians got within 15 feet of him and Harrison. The horse kept moving away, so Harrison moved in such a way as to prevent the animal from going any farther. Harrison kept smiling and told Edgerly the Indians were bad marksmen from so close.[49]

At 5:09, Godfrey's company—the last to leave the hill complex—began its move toward Reno Hill. After Hare had come to him with the order to withdraw, Godfrey said,

> I had gone some distance ... when, looking back, I saw French's troop come tearing over the bluffs, and soon after Weir's troop followed in hot haste. Edgerly was near the top of the bluff trying to mount his frantic horse ... he vaulted into his saddle and then joined the troop. The Indians almost immediately followed to the top of the bluff.... They then started down the hillside in pursuit.[50]

As D Company made its way back up Cedar Coulee, the company farrier, Vincent Charley took at least one round in the hips and collapsed off his horse, according to Sergeant Harrison, "near a ravine to the left. Perhaps a one-quarter mile or less from the two peaks"[51]—5:11 p.m. Some historians dispute the location—and Charley's battlefield marker is out of place today—but Corporal George Washington Wylie from D Company, verified Harrison's observation: "This was some distance south of Edgerly peaks [Weir Peaks] (and probably about opposite the ravine on east side of bluffs in which the cedar trees are growing)."[52] In discussing the death, Richard Hardorff wrote that Charley's body was found "some 250 yards south of Weir Point."[53] With 200 Indians hot on their tail, Harrison said Edgerly instructed the wounded man to crawl into a ravine and they would come back for him as soon as Edgerly could get reinforcements. As the two rode

Chart 7. Reno Hill—Night of June 25th

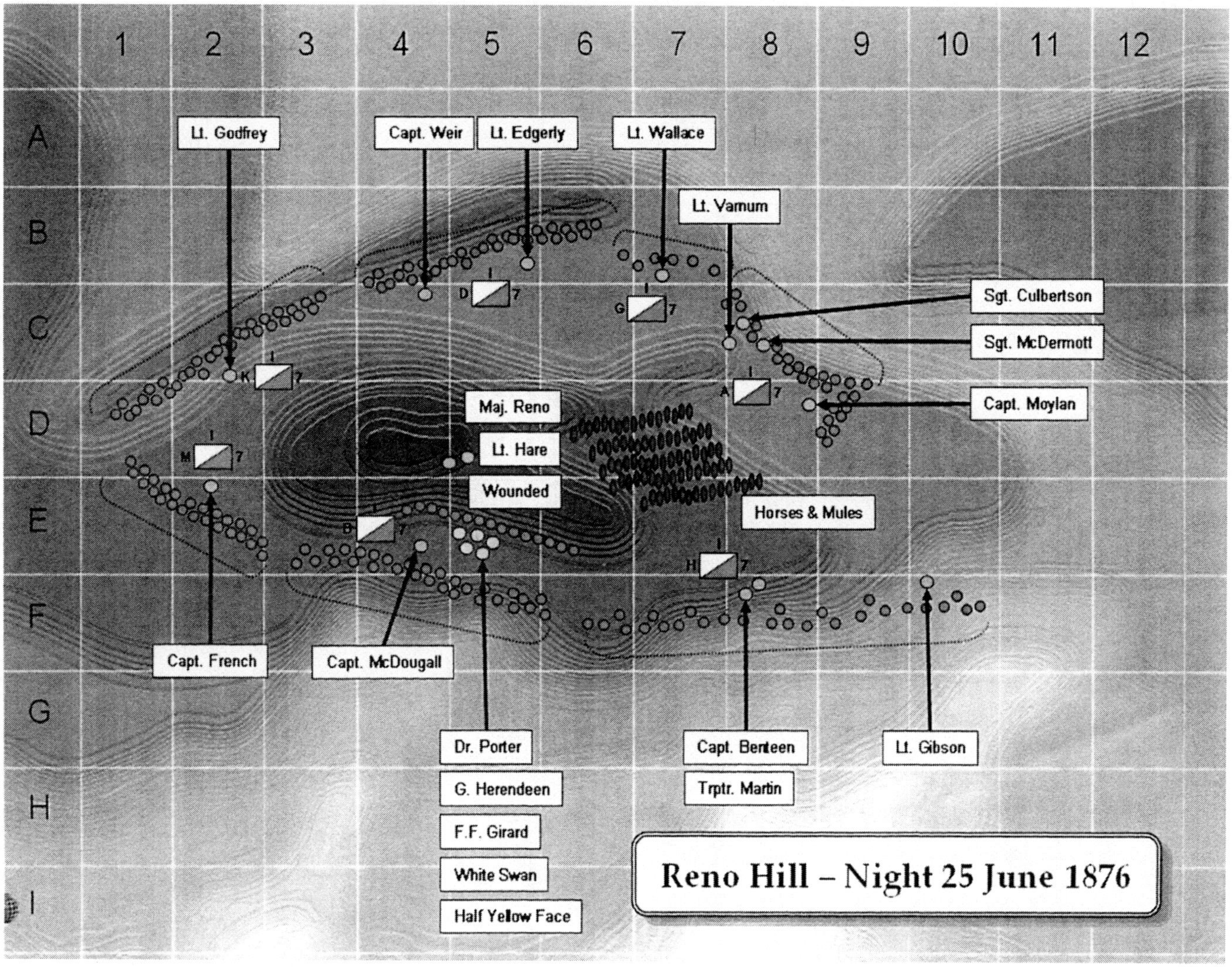

Reno Hill – Night 25 June 1876

on, they glanced back and saw Indians swarming over and finishing off the wounded soldier.[54] Edgerly regretted the incident for the rest of his life, and in the July 4 letter to his wife, he wrote, "He [Capt. Weir] said orders had been given to fall back and we must obey them. That was the one thing I regretted more than any other thing that happened to me, for I had promised that wounded man I would get him out and wasn't able to raise a [finger] for him."[55]

The death of Vincent Charlie was of very little consequence when measured against the casualty totals sustained on other parts of the field. Yet, I cannot escape the thought that the abandonment of this one man presents itself as a pathetic story of trust and betrayal. To those students who condemn Reno for abandoning his wounded and who champion Weir for his quick resolve to go to Custer's aid, I suggest they take another look at Weir's involvement in the abandonment of Vincent Charlie. I find Weir's conduct in that matter deplorable.[56]

Godfrey's skirmish line was set up just south of Sharpshooters' Ridge[57]—5:17 p.m.—and enabled the rest of the struggling command to set up in preparation for receiving K Company. Cartridge cases found there confirm the presence of troops on a small ridgeline leading to the bluff's edge at 3,411. Godfrey sent back his horse-holders leaving him with only 22 or 23 men, but this was enough to delay the onrushing warriors. He complained that he dismounted his men, "for a rally of the retreating two troops. Did they rally? Not much! But left me to hold the sack!" He was also "harassed" by Reno's "*repeated* orders 'to retire at once,'" Reno making no attempt to reinforce him.[58] (Thus, some of Godfrey's animosity?)

Once the troops were back on Reno Hill First Sergeant Ryan said, "great numbers" of Indians advanced and made several charges. The firing became very heavy, rapid, and general, all along the line, ending only after dark.[59] According to Godfrey, the command was set up as follows:

The packs were then unloaded and used for a breastwork, and Moylan's Co was inside of it. Benteen was on the crest of the bluffs on the upper side of the camp. "B" co was on his right lower down and the line continued from left to right, "M," "G," "D," and my Co was interpolated with the last three when I came in from the Skr. line.[60]

Shortly after 2:00 a.m. the following morning, the firing resumed. The battle of the Little Big Horn had another day to go.

20

DESIGNED TO WIN, DOOMED TO FAIL

Custer's dividing his regiment was not the cause of his defeat. In fact, used judiciously, division of command—even in the face of greater numbers: basic military principles dictated concentration in the presence of a superior enemy—had proved to be a rather successful tactic, and one employed with great success by Robert E. Lee during the Peninsula fighting and afterwards.[1] Somewhat lost in this whole donnybrook is the fact Custer caused his own predicament by allowing elements of his command to become separated too widely, thereby forfeiting their ability to provide mutual support. As noted earlier, in his *Century Magazine* article Edward Godfrey claimed as the column began moving up the Rosebud Custer gave great discretion to the troop commanders, but saying they were to keep within supporting distance of each other. In this same article, Godfrey listed three causes for Custer's defeat: the overwhelming number of warriors and their unexpected and surprising cohesion; "Reno's panic rout from the valley"; and the defective extractors of the carbines.[2] Then in his 1908, revised version, Godfrey listed a fourth possible cause: the division of command.[3] He believed dividing the command was not itself a faulty tactic, but he laid the blame on the lack of "*full co-operation* of the separate commands." He felt if,

> Reno made his charge as ordered, or made a bold front even, the Hostiles would have been so engaged in the bottom that Custer's approach from the Northeast would have been such a surprise as to cause the stampede of the village and would have broken the morale of the warriors.[4]

Godfrey then took a different tack by saying, "With the entire command concentrated under Custer's leadership the charge would have been carried *home*, and, I believe, successfully."[5] Yet this responsibility was not Reno's, it was Custer's, and the emphasis on "supporting distance" while moving up the Rosebud seems to have been lost in the June 25 chase euphoria. That can hardly be considered Reno's fault. Godfrey is also taking either a significant amount of literary license or is interjecting an equal amount of biased personal opinion when he accuses Reno of *not* making "his charge as ordered." God-frey was there neither when Reno received those orders, nor was he present when Reno carried them out, and there was not a single individual who claimed to have heard them who ever accused Reno of failing to make "his charge as ordered."

Godfrey's reassessment and addition of the caveat, "concentrated" force, may have arisen from his association with Benteen. In his series of letters with the charlatan Goldin, Benteen wrote, "That is all that I blame Custer for—the scattering, as it were, (two portions of his command, anyway) to the—well, four winds, before he knew anything about the exact or approximate position of the Indian village or the Indians."[6] Benteen's opinion, expressed to Goldin in a February 24, 1892, letter was not new.

Once beyond the lone tepee, Reno's sole mission was to bring the Indians to battle. He was no feint, no diversion, no secondary effort. He was part and parcel of the main attack. Reno was to hit them first; that would tie them down, and Custer would follow up with a second wave, theoretically knifing through the surprised village. When Custer was told there were Indians to Reno's front and they were coming out to confront him, he believed the element of surprise had been compromised and the Indians in the valley were forming a screen to allow the majority to escape. A Washita-type, Sand Creek–type attack was now out of the question. Also, Custer had to know warriors would be accompanying the so-called fugitives and in order for his attack to be successful—to fulfill his mission—he was going to have to do an "end-run" and bag the Indians in the north, their obvious retreat route. Critics may infer anything they want here, but given the campaign's objectives, this was basic common sense and therefore basic tactics. Furthermore, these were tactics that had worked before against these same Indians.

When Custer sent Benteen off to the left, he had several very good reasons. Number one, Benteen would make sure the upper valley was clear, thereby protecting the command's rear. As Benteen said at the Reno inquiry, Custer would know his captain would terminate the mission when he saw fit and return to the main command; he was that type of officer:

bristling with initiative and intelligence, regardless of personal animosities. By sending him to the left, Custer also set up a reserve—fortuitously or not—he could maneuver any way he wanted. And he understood this when he gave Benteen his mission; it was standing operating procedure. Custer employed the same principle with his use of Keogh's battalion. He did it on Luce and Nye-Cartwright ridges and again on Calhoun Hill. While the final consequences were unintended, Custer believed he had not separated his battalions from mutual support, the eventual, boiled-down fatal flaw in his plans. It seems apparent as well Custer saw dust plumes he interpreted to be from both Benteen's battalion (probably wrong) and the packs (certainly correct), so in his mind he believed each of his maneuver elements were capable of supporting the other. Since Reno was moving in the right direction and the village appeared larger than anticipated—all of which Custer saw from 3,411—he sent a message back for Benteen to follow him: Custer. Not help for Reno; at that time, Reno needed no help; but certainly an open-ended request, more fitting to Benteen's personality.

As he viewed Reno's men on the skirmish line, Custer had to be pleased. While his original intentions were Reno's battalion should scythe through or into the village, he had to know this was now unrealistic because of the numbers of Indians coming out to fight. The fact Reno's battle was unfolding somewhat slowly was good, because Reno's men were advancing and the Indians were keeping their distance and backing away when Custer saw them. That equated to time, time for Custer to move farther north to bag—*or destroy*—those who were fleeing.

His plans began to break down, however, when he moved too far north and when Reno was overwhelmed. When Reno's positions were shattered it was not the release of Indians to fight Custer that mattered, it was the insertion of Reno's broken command between Custer and the anticipated arrival of Benteen that caused the mutual support to evaporate. That support was predicated on the continued mobility of each of the battalions: their ability to remain in contact with one another. The sudden break in the action flow, plus the widening gap between the forces (allowing Indians to fill it) is what broke the textbook's rules. Of course, the fact there was an overwhelming number of Indians that could have dealt with any of the army's best plans, makes the whole thing something of a sand-table exercise—rock-drill, in other words!

Custer did not—*could* not, militarily—foresee Reno's defeat; but whether Reno stayed in the woods until he was annihilated (which would have allowed Benteen to reach Custer, exacerbating the disaster) or left 30 minutes later than he did, the results were going to be the same. The only reason we know what we do about this battle is because Reno retreated when he did. Remember, Benteen arrived on the hilltop only a few minutes after Reno's men began reaching it, and if they had remained in the valley for any length of time, Benteen would have joined them there, allowing the Indians to finish what someone else started, regardless of past behavior. *These Indians were going nowhere!*

Simply put, Custer moved too far, too fast, without insuring his battalions were properly supported. He made no contingencies for a breakdown of any of the pieces and he made no contingency for a potential breakdown of the whole. This is easier to write than to do, especially when one is operating on the fly as Custer was. All the more reason to ensure support; all the more reason to exercise some caution; all the more reason to bring maximum force to bear; all the more reason to have utilized a pre-planned envelopment, not one predicated on a secondary whim with virtually no communications. This was standard tactical doctrine, even in 1876. As Carl von Clausewitz wrote,

> An attacker bent on a major decision has no reason whatever to divide his forces. If in fact he does so, it may usually be ascribed to a state of confusion. His columns should advance on no wider a front than will allow them to be brought into action simultaneously. If the enemy is divided … minor diversions are in order—strategic feints, made with the object of maintaining one's advantage. Should the attacker choose to divide his forces for that purpose he would be quite justified in doing so.
>
> The division of the army into several columns, which in any case is indispensable, must be the basis for envelopment in the tactical attack; for envelopment is the most natural form of attack, and should not be disregarded without good cause. But the envelopment must be tactical.[7]

When you add to this a gross underestimation of the enemy, both in size and intent, all you need to add is the expected "unforeseen."

It is all too easy, however, to criticize George Custer and because of the way life, society, and the military are structured, equally easy to slough off a failed mission because he was the commander and bore the responsibility. There were reasons, and because of that, there must be equal and commensurate understanding, otherwise we focus on blame solely and we learn nothing. The rationale behind Custer's continuous moving north was simple. As mentioned previously, the great inherent in this campaign was the Indians' penchant for scattering: fear the winter roamers would not be gathered up and dealt with, and the campaign—already 40 days old—collapsing as an abject flop. This of course would call into question the entire strategy and the abilities of every commander to carry out their assignments. The press—already smattered with the beginnings of "yellow journalism"—

would have a field day with perceived military incompetence, and it would take years to quell the finger pointing. Once Custer stirred the hornet's nest he had to do something about it.

Within the context of his original thinking—even altered because of Gerard's report—Custer's plan would have been sound had he not underestimated the intentions and strengths of his foe and had he kept his subordinates informed and his maneuver elements within mutually supporting distance. In all likelihood he would still not have been able to pull off the victory—alone—but he would have been able certainly to stave off the ignominy of his ultimate defeat, and a more cautious approach—both physically and methodologically—would have allowed Terry and Gibbon time to reach the field, combining forces. This combined force would have put more than 1,000 troops and sundries up against a divided and semi-panicked camp and it would have brought the Gatling guns of lieutenants Low and Kinzie into the battle. Benteen's "support" of Reno—along with the attendant results—helps prove the point.

Calling Custer rash only serves as personal criticism, teaching us nothing. To say the man made too many assumptions would be much closer to the truth and would serve as a platform into "lessons learned," always an important element in military debriefings. The reader should not get the wrong impression here, however. We are not cutting George Custer any slack; the responsibility for the debacle rests solely with him, but we are saying rather than attribute the defeat to personality issues—which would be ludicrously wrong—it is more important to understand the outcome in terms of failed military procedures. As for the others—Reno and Benteen—those who rush to condemn them for Custer's demise unwittingly condemn Custer for incompetence; we cannot have one without the other. Custer made mistakes, but that takes little away from a great soldier. Napoléon made mistakes. Robert E. Lee made mistakes. We can blame Lee for his caution at Gettysburg, just as we can blame Custer for his impatience at the Little Big Horn. One cost a man the war; the other cost the man his life. In the long run of history, which led to the more significant aftermath?

One of the biggest problems we have in analyzing responsibility for the Little Big Horn debacle is in the analysis of perception. In many ways, it is the civilian perception of what military operations should be like and how they work, versus the more pragmatic military, on-the-job control of fear, panic, danger, and maneuver, and all the other variables constituting the prelude to, and the battle itself. As to Custer's

tactical plans, Fred Benteen's deployment to the left was not a wild-goose chase. In light of the situation once Custer made his commitment, the deployment of Benteen's battalion was sound. The deployment of Marcus Reno's battalion was equally sound, and Custer's own movement to the ridges above the river—ostensibly and initially a reconnaissance mission rather than direct support of Reno—could be viewed as sound as well, though conversely, Custer completely failed in keeping his subordinates apprised of what he was going to do. This constant business about Custer's biggest mistake being dividing his command shows a lack of tactical understanding, a lack of military understanding, a lack of understanding of the conditions Custer faced, and a slim knowledge of the workings of a nineteenth-century, Indian-fighting army. Rather than being the root cause of his demise, the division of the regiment actually led to the majority of the command surviving, the mistakes being made well before the tactical phase of the battle unfolded, fortuitous maybe, but success engenders its own "luck." To be fair to the reader, however, Lieutenant General Philip H. Sheridan felt the division was an essential element in the defeat. "There certainly were enough Indians there to defeat the 7th Cavalry, divided as it was into three parts, and to totally annihilate any one of these three detachments in the open field, as was proved in the destruction of one of them."[8] What Sheridan failed to state—at least in conjunction with the above comment—is *no one*, certainly no one in the immediate vicinity of the Montana Territory on June 25, 1876, *knew* the Indians had nearly as many warriors as presented themselves in front of any of Custer's commands, and military hubris being as it was, such "knowledge" would have been rendered virtually irrelevant anyway.

Again, the excuses run hot and heavy, the rationalization of Custer's actions rampant and never considering the man's orders. In an article appearing in the same 1892 edition of *Century Magazine* as Godfrey's article, Brigadier General James B. Fry wrote, "Believing, as he and Sheridan and Terry did, that he was strong enough for victory, if Custer had not attacked, and the Indians had moved away ... Custer would have been condemned, perhaps disgraced."[9] "Perhaps" is the cogent word here and if Fry used it to excuse Custer's action, then he could just as easily have used it to describe a theoretical Indian move from the Little Big Horn into Tullock's Creek valley and beyond. Once again, Terry's orders to his regimental commander were designed to punish Indians, not to assuage the feelings of an embarrassed marplot.

Despite any soundness in these tactical troop dispositions, we must emphasize again, Custer underestimated two things: the size of his enemy and the fact they did not run.

(It appears everyone but the scouts felt the same way.) The issue was Custer had scouts on the ground and these scouts warned him of both circumstances. For sound troop dispositions to be effective a good commander must be able to adapt them not only to changing situations, but to the "fog of war," in this case the times *both* these circumstances had arisen on the prairie. (1) Size: in 1865, a huge military expedition was launched under the command of Brigadier General Patrick Edward Connor. It was designed very much the same way the 1876 expedition was formed, a three-pronged attack, and it failed. One of the columns actually passed between a large Indian camp of some 1,500–2,000 lodges on the Powder River and another even larger on the Little Missouri. Some 18,000 Indians were supposed to have been in the two villages.[10] In 1868, it was estimated there were 50,000 Sioux, including some 8,000 warriors[11]; and (2) determination: the December 21, 1866, Fetterman massacre; the Indians certainly did not run that day. So there *was* precedent for both. Custer failed to allow for either of those contingencies; both had happened before. His tactical dispositions, therefore, while generally sound, were not suitable for the conditions he encountered at the Little Big Horn, not once he allowed his maneuver battalions to fall out of mutual support. His scouts warned him!

(It should be noted here the size of the Sioux nation in the 1860s and 1870s—of which the Lakota were only a part [maybe 50 percent]—is another of those highly contentious and volatile subjects raising the dander of many historians and students of the Little Big Horn battle. With the benefit of modern scholarship, archives, computers, and a more pragmatic, statistical approach to the available historical documents, however, we can make a determination the entire Nation was probably no larger than 25,000 people in 1868. Since some 25–30 percent could be considered adult males, this puts the "warrior" population at about 8,000. These numbers suggest the War Department figures of the times were seriously inflated, despite population growth through the period studied.[12])

Custer's tactics did not work, but it was not because they were not sound. One could make as strong an argument a unified command would have been wiped out just as easily as Custer's divided battalions. While division of command coupled with failure to support can be considered the ultimate error, there was no guarantee of success even if mutual support occurred. These Indians were going nowhere and at the same time, they exhibited surprising cohesion, *à la* Fetterman. And again, harking back to an earlier chapter, this is precisely why Custer's actions must be reviewed in the afterglow of his failure to adhere to Terry's orders of moving all

the way to the headwaters of the Rosebud, then cutting west and descending the Little Big Horn valley. Had he done that, his tactics would have been invariably different and the full force of this prong possibly utilized. Whatever Custer did from the Busby camp on, must be viewed in the light of his orders and whether or not he followed them or did not follow them commensurate with Terry's intent. Custer knew what Terry intended, and everything Custer did with Terry's objectives in mind must be considered in that way. Let us say there was no confusion and Custer was simply given an order to "seek and destroy." Nothing more. Find them and kill them. That may have influenced him to employ different tactics such as not sending Benteen to the left; maybe not splitting his command into four or five battalions, but maybe only two. If one judges Custer's actions outside the parameters of confusing orders from Terry, one is only going to criticize or condone without fully understanding the "whys" of what Custer did. Circumstances can make a general great, but they can also ruin a great general. Judging Custer outside those orders is not fair to the man and teaches us incorrect lessons. Those conclusions would appear to be invalid.

Custer's belief was the Indians would scatter and his actions were based on that premise, at least up until he reached the Luce/Nye-Cartwright/Ford B areas. That was what Indians always did. Here, however, it was not the case and this belief is why Custer headed north. He saw Indians heading down the valley, but he could also see they were consolidating in the area of Chasing Creek. That is why he went back to Cemetery Ridge to await Benteen and Keogh: he thought he had them. They had not scattered, not yet; they had just run. That was different from what he thought when he veered right, leaving Reno alone in the valley. *That was the difference!* Yes, they ran, but no, they did not scatter and Custer recognized this: an unseen nuance, and one that had disastrous effects.

There is another issue needing to be addressed. The key in assessing the veracity of testimony is in determining why someone might lie or say what he did. The only valid reason for a lie is the testimony so proffered would aid in increasing someone's importance or contribution to the historical event, or to protect oneself, some*one* else, or some*thing* else. Otherwise, the testimony given can be considered reasonably accurate—within its surrounding parameters—especially when corroborated by others, even if such corroboration takes the form of mere allusion. There must also be an element of common sense to the testimony, principally, common sense fitting with the milieu, either physical or event-driven.

It is extremely important the reader remembers these men did not go into this battle knowing, believing, or thinking much of what we consider important today was important then. Watch times were incidental; few paid any heed to the way Reno moved down the Little Big Horn; was a gallop eight miles per hour, 10 miles per hour, or 15–20 miles per hour? What did a fast-walking horse mean—in miles-per-hour? Yet ever since the last of the smoke cleared, the last of the dust settled down to earth, our so-called battle students have taken literally every uttered word—especially those confirming or conforming to their opinions and dreams—discarding those they do not want to hear or believe, for those are the ones that may tarnish the gleam of their heroes. In 1927, Edward Godfrey told Frank Anders, his godfather,

> Without mincing words that up to Benteen's death he was the finest type of accomplished cavalry officer that the United States army ever had. He specifically did not except Custer. He said to me, "I was never a Custerite." He said that Benteen was utterly reliable, trustworthy, had a keen sense of humor, a very fine natural sense of distances, areas, number of men in formations, either large or small and that he was especially fine in strategy and tactics. That his ideas of striking distances never failed to hold good. He was especially good at the judging of the capability of man or beast on a campaign, and that he was especially good in the conservation of the troops under his command. Godfrey, in a direct question that I asked him why the Custer-Benteen hatred he made the answer that they were too [*sic*] good cavalrymen in one regiment and that they radically differed in every way as to administration, training, care of men and horses, tactics, strategy and campaigning.[13]

Yet if we added up all the distances Benteen gave us for his march down the Reno Creek valley, we would wind up west of the Little Big Horn River and into the foothills of the Big Horn Mountains. Disingenuous? No, just unimportant, especially at the time and to the men. The importance lies only with those of us seeking the truth, seeking to understand, or more pedantically, seeking inimical "proof" to faulty theory. It is imperative this be understood and the only things of certainty were the mission, the fear, and the fact tomorrow things would never again be the same.

THE TIMELINES

The Notes column (far right) refers the reader to the Notes to the Timelines immediately following Timeline Y.

A. June 24: To the Busby Camp and Varnum's Departure; 5:00 a.m.–9:20 p.m.

Local Sun Time	Command's Watch Time	Event	Speed	Distance Traveled	Notes
June 24					
4:03 AM	5:00 AM	Command departs camp.	Varied		1
6:13 AM	7:10 AM	The four Crows report in. They reported fresh tracks, "'but in no great numbers.'" The Crows also told Custer the trail was fresher 10 miles ahead.			1
6:33 AM	7:30 AM	The march was resumed. Custer sends the four Crows ahead again. The order of march now had Custer and two companies about ½ mile in advance—with C Company in the lead—and companies M and I as the regimental rear-guard.			2
8:23 AM	9:20 AM	The Crows, trotting at six miles per hour, reach the abandoned Sioux camp at East Muddy Creek. This was apparently Sitting Bull's "sundance" camp.	6 MPH		3
8:43 AM	9:40 AM	The Crows head back to the column after studying the campsite.	6 – 7 MPH		4
9:33 AM	10:30 AM	Crows report again: abandoned campsite at East Muddy Creek.			5
12:03 PM	1:00 PM	Custer orders a halt at East Muddy Creek to await Varnum's return. This was the second halt of the day and the 5th Sioux camp, Sitting Bull's "sundance" camp. It was in this camp that Custer's flag blew down, prompting the omens that followed.	2 MPH	16 Miles	6
4:03 PM	5:00 PM	The regiment resumes its march up the Rosebud, across to the narrow, sage-covered left bank of the valley, passing "through several large camps. The trail was now fresh and the whole valley scratched up by trailing lodgepoles." The column moves very slowly and a number of halts were made. The Ree scout, Billy Jackson, said the trail was more than 300 yards wide.		Depart Muddy Creek	7
7:00 PM	8:20 PM	The sun is behind the mountains to the west, creating shadows in the valley and giving one the impression of sundown.			8
7:45 PM	8:42 PM	*Nearly sunset*—Custer orders the command into camp at the Busby Bend. The 7:45 time established by Wallace. Godfrey: "[a]bout sundown." Windolph: "went into camp at sundown. In late June up here in the Northwest country that means around 9 o'clock." Reno said twilight lasted until about 9 o'clock or after; Wallace said "deep twilight" came on about 9 o'clock or after. Varnum said it was nearly dark.	3.2 MPH	12 miles additional from East Muddy Creek halt	9
7:48 PM	8:45 PM	Custer meets with five of his Crow scouts and instructs Varnum to head for the Crow's Nest at 9 PM.			10
7:50 PM	8:47 PM	*Close to twilight*—Benteen settles into a small vale next to Keogh.			11
7:53 PM	8:50 PM	*Sunset*			12
8:23 PM	9:20 PM	Varnum and his scouts leave for the Crow's Nest.			13

B. June 24–25: Busby Camp to Halt One;
Sunset, 8:50 p.m.–Sunrise, 5:10 a.m.

Local Sun Time	Command's Watch Time	Event	Speed	Distance Traveled	Notes
7:53 PM	8:50 PM	*Sunset*			12
8:23 PM	9:20 PM	Varnum and his scouts leave for the Crow's Nest.	4 MPH — 6 MPH		13
8:31 PM	9:28 PM	*Civil twilight* ends -- too dark to read.			12
8: 28 PM — 8:33 PM	9:25 PM — 9:30 PM	Godfrey and Hare settle in when Custer calls his officers together and informs them of his intention to move at 11 PM. The meeting was short and sweet.			14
8:38 PM	9:35 PM	Custer's officers' call ends.			15
9:22 PM	10:19 PM	*Nautical twilight* ends—full darkness begins.			12
10:03 PM	11:00 PM	The command begins leaving the Busby encampment.	4 MPH		16
11:48 PM		*Waxing crescent (about 12% of disk illuminated) moon* sets.			12
11:33 PM	June 25: 12:30 AM	Keogh gets the last of the pack train across Mud Creek.			17
June 25: 1:03 AM — 1:33 AM	2:00 AM — 2:30 AM	Varnum and the Crows reach the area of the Crow's Nest pocket.	2.13 MPH — 2.36 MPH, including halts for smoking	11 miles	18
1:18 AM	2:15 AM	Command begins arriving at Halt 1.	1.9 MPH — 2.1 MPH	6.2 — 6.7 miles	19
2:44 AM	3:41 AM	*Nautical twilight* begins—the end of full darkness.			12
2:48 AM	3:45 AM	Light on the horizon.			20
3:34 AM	4:31 AM	*Civil twilight* begins—reading still impossible.			12
3:50 AM — 4 AM	4:47 AM — 4:57 AM	Varnum awakened and climbing to the Crow's Nest hill.			21
4:13 AM	5:10 AM	*Sunrise*			12

C. June 25: Halt One to Custer's Arrival at the Crow's Nest; 3:41 a.m.–8:35 a.m.

Local Sun Time	Command's Watch Time	Event	Speed	Distance Traveled	Notes
2:44 AM	3:41 AM	*Nautical twilight* begins—the end of full darkness.			12
2:48 AM	3:45 AM	Light on the horizon.			20
3:34 AM	4:31 AM	*Civil twilight* begins—reading still impossible.			12
3:50 AM — 4 AM	4:47 AM — 4:57 AM	Varnum awakened and climbing to the Crow's Nest hill.			21
4:13 AM	5:10 AM	*Sunrise*			12
4:18 AM	5:15 AM	Varnum arrives at top of Crow's Nest; he cannot immediately make out anything in the LBH valley because of swollen eyes.			22
5:00 AM	5:57 AM	Varnum begins to write note.			22
5:03 AM	6:00 AM	Varnum hands note to Red Star with instructions to deliver it to Custer.			22
5:13 AM	6:10 AM	Red Star and Bull reach their horses and set out for Halt 1.			23
5:58 AM	6:55 AM	Red Star arrives at Halt 1. (*LT Wallace verified a 7 AM arrival.*)	6 MPH	4.5 miles	23
6:08 AM	7:05 AM	Isaiah Dorman sees Red Star settling in for a bit of breakfast and seeks out PVT Burkman.			24
6:11 AM	7:08 AM	Dorman tells Burkman of Red Star's arrival from the Crow's Nest.			25
6:15 AM	7:12 AM	Custer awakened.			25
6:23 AM	7:20 AM	Custer meets with Red Star, Bloody Knife, Gerard, and others.			26
6:53 AM	7:50 AM	Custer and party leave for Crow's Nest.	(@ 6 — 8 MPH)		26
7:03 AM	8:00 AM	Varnum says this is the last time he knew anything about the actual "time" of day.			27
7:18 AM	8:15 AM	Regiment leaves Halt 1, McDougall's B Company in the lead. It was a "stop-start" march; unsure of destination; concern about keeping packs up and together.	At 2.3 MPH		28
7:33 AM	8:30 AM	Varnum spots Custer's party—mistaking it for the "regiment"—approaching Halt Two; begins his descent to the "pocket."	6 MPH	4 miles	29
7:38 AM	8:35 AM	Custer arrives at Crow's Nest "pocket."	6 MPH	½ mile	29

D. The Curtiss Incident; 8:15 a.m.–10:00 a.m.

Local Sun Time	Command's Watch Time	Event	Speed	Distance Traveled	Notes
7:18 AM	8:15 AM	Regiment leaves Halt 1, McDougall's B Company in the lead. It was a "stop-start" march; unsure of destination; concern about keeping packs up and together.	At 2.3 MPH		28
7:38 AM	8:35 AM	Curtiss tells Myles Keogh of the missing pack.		Regiment: .75 miles	30
7:39 AM	8:36 AM	CPT Keogh informs CPT Yates of the missing pack. Yates instructs Curtiss to take four men and retrieve the pack.			31
7:40 AM	8:37 AM	Curtiss leaves with four troopers to find pack.	6 MPH		32
7:46 AM	8:43 AM	Curtiss and his men arrive back at Halt One and find Indians rifling through his pack and other stuff left behind.			33
7:47 AM — 7:53 AM	8:44 AM — 8:50 AM	Curtiss' detail runs off the Indians and secures the loose equipment.			33
7:58 AM	8:55 AM	Custer reaches top of Crow's Nest. Among the Rees on the hilltop are Red Star, Bull, and Black Fox.			34
8:01 AM	8:58 AM	Curtiss turns and begins trip back to column.	At 8 MPH		33
8:19 AM	9:16 AM	Curtiss and detail arrive back at the column and notify Yates of their findings.	8 MPH	2.4 miles	33
9:03 AM	10:00 AM	Regiment begins arriving at Halt Two at the base of the divide. Custer and Varnum watch it arrive.	2.3 MPH	3.5 — 4.5 miles	35

E. Officers' Call—Crow's Nest to the Divide; 8:35 a.m.–11:45 a.m.

Local Sun Time	Command's Watch Time	Event	Speed	Distance Traveled	Notes
7:38 AM	8:35 AM	Custer arrives at Crow's Nest "pocket."	6 MPH	½ mile	29
7:58 AM	8:55 AM	Custer reaches top of Crow's Nest. Among the Rees on the hilltop are Red Star, Bull, and Black Fox.			34
9:03 AM	10:00 AM	Regiment begins arriving at Halt Two at the base of the divide. Custer and Varnum watch it arrive.	2.3 MPH	3.5 — 4.5 miles	35
9:08 AM	10:05 AM	Custer starts down the Crow's Nest hill.			29
9:13 AM	10:10 AM	Custer arrives back down in "pocket" where horses are kept.			36
9:18 AM	10:15 AM	After chewing out Tom Custer and Calhoun, GAC calls for an officers' call.			37
9:19 AM	10:16 AM	LT Cooke informs Custer of the Curtiss lost pack incident.			33
9:23 AM	10:20 AM	Officers are all gathered alongside a small knoll occupied by C Company troopers.			38
9:25 AM	10:22 AM	George Herendeen wanders off some 500 or 600 yards up a dry creek and spots what he though might have been a deer or an Indian.			39
9:28 AM	10:25 AM	Boyer sees Herendeen and asks him about what he has seen. Boyer tells him he saw three Indians with three or four loose horses. They moved rapidly off in the direction of the village.			40
9:38 AM	10:35 AM	Boyer tells Custer what he and Herendeen have discovered.			41
9:43 AM	10:40 AM	Officers' call ends; Custer has decided to attack the village immediately, though he is still uncertain of its precise location and its size.			42
9:43 AM — 9:58 AM	10:40 AM — 10:55 AM	Assignments are made and Tom McDougall and B Company are assigned to accompany the pack train, "to take charge of the pack train and act as rear guard." This was "on the divide between the Rosebud and the Little Big Horn."			43
9:53 AM	10:50 AM	Someone—Boyer, Reynolds—convinces Custer to take one more look at the LBH valley using DeRudio's field glasses.			44
9:54 AM	10:51 AM	Custer agrees to go to the divide ridge in another attempt to see the village, and calls for his horse, taking a small party with him to the top of the divide.			45
10:03 AM	11:00 AM	Custer reaches the top of the divide, just 100 yards or so from where the column is to cross.	6 MPH	¾ mile	46
10:13 AM	11:10 AM	Custer spends some time looking into the Reno Creek valley and the LBH valley. Finished, he turns and heads back to his regiment.			47
10:21 AM	11:18 AM	Custer arrives back at Halt Two. Convinced or unconvinced, he orders his command to get ready to move.	6 MPH	¾ mile	48

E. Officers' Call—Crow's Nest to the Divide (cont.)

10:22 AM — 10:47 AM	11:19 AM — 11:44 AM	Command readies to move.			49
10:33 AM	11:30 AM	LT Varnum, PVT Strode, and the Rees lead out, cross the divide, and head to the left front. LT Hare takes the Crows and heads off to the right.	@ 10 MPH, increasing speed		50
10:48 AM	11:45 AM	March resumes.			51

F. Divide Crossing to the Flats; 11:45 a.m.–1:05 p.m.

Local Sun Time	Command's Watch Time	Event	Speed	Distance Traveled	Notes
10:48 AM	11:45 AM	March resumes.			51
10:53 — 11:03 AM	11:50 AM — Noon	Regiment begins crossing the divide just before noon. Main column—in fours and led by H Company—is about ½ mile long.	Trot: @ 6 MPH	**From the divide crossing:**	52
11:03 AM	Noon	Custer halts column, its rear already below the top of the divide.	6 MPH to a halt	½ mile	53
11:03 AM — 11:13 AM	Noon — 12:10 PM	Custer and Cooke go off to the side, break the regiment into battalions, and inform Benteen to move off to the left.			54
11:07 AM	12:04 PM	Boston Custer turns back toward the packs to change horses.	(6 MPH)	(4/10 of a mile)	55
11:11 AM	12:08 PM	Boston Custer reaches the packs, stops, and speaks briefly with CPT McDougall.		4/10 of a mile	56
11:11 AM	12:08 PM	The pack train, driven by LT Mathey and CPT McDougall, having crested the divide, pauses right behind the main column.	Varying		57
11:13 AM	12:10 PM	Benteen breaks off from regiment to scout to the left.	(@ 6 MPH)		58
11:15 AM	12:12 PM	Regiment resumes march, Custer down the creek's right bank, Reno down the left bank.	(@ 10 MPH)		59
11:16 AM	12:13 PM	After traveling some 250 — 300 yards, descending into the Reno Creek valley from the heights of the divide, Custer realizes Benteen will not be able to see into the LBH valley from the first line of ridges. He orders CTMP Voss to ride to Benteen and tell him to continue on to the next ridge.	10 MPH, increasing to 12 MPH, varying down to 6 MPH	.15 miles from separation	60
11:16 AM	12:13 PM	CTMP Voss leaves the column and heads to Benteen.	(7 MPH)	.15 miles from divide separations	61
11:21 AM	12:18 PM	After changing horses and as the packs begin to move, Boston Custer heads for the front of the main column.	6 MPH		56
11:21 AM	12:18 PM	McDougall and the packs begin to move.			57
11:21 AM	12:18 PM	CTMP Voss reaches Benteen with Custer's message: "[I]f I found nothing before reaching the first line of bluffs, to go on to the second line with the same instructions" [Benteen].	7 — 8 MPH	Voss: 6/10 mile from Custer; Benteen: ¾ mile from separation	63
11:21 AM	12:18 PM	Custer's column is advancing between two small knolls and approaching the waters of Reno Creek. He slows to a trot so Voss can catch up, but still concerned that his orders to Benteen are not specific enough, Custer dispatches SGM Sharrow with addition instructions.	10 MPH down to 6 MPH	.83 miles from Voss separation; .97 miles from divide separation	60
11:21 AM	12:18 PM	SGM Sharrow leaves the column and heads to Benteen.	(8 MPH — 10 MPH)	.97 miles from divide separations	64
11:21 AM	12:18 PM	Having just passed the morass, Varnum, Strode, and the Rees have moved down Reno Creek and now begin to swing toward their left, mounting the higher bluffs on the south and west side of the South Fork — Reno Creek confluence. Their speed decreases sharply.	10 MPH — 6 MPH	8 miles from the divide crossing	65
11:22 AM	12:19 PM	Voss turns from Benteen and heads back to main column.	12 MPH		60
11:27 AM	12:24 PM	Custer's column is moving along Reno Creek as CTMP Voss re-joins it.	6 MPH	1.43 miles from divide separation	64
11:27 AM	12:24 PM	Voss reaches the head of Custer's column on the main trail along Reno Creek.	10 — 12 MPH	1 mile	64

F. Divide Crossing to the Flats (cont.)

11:29 AM	12:26 PM	SGM Sharrow reaches Benteen with Custer's additional instructions: "[I]f I saw nothing from the second line of bluffs, to go on into the valley, and if there was nothing in the valley, to go on to the next valley." "[I]f from the furthest line of bluffs which we then saw, I could not see the valley—no particular valley specified—to keep on until I came to a valley (or perhaps the valley)…to pitch into."	Sharrow: 10 MPH; Benteen: 5 — 6 MPH	Sharrow: 1.2 miles; Benteen: 1.95 miles from divide separation	67
11:30 AM	12:27 PM	Sharrow starts back for the main column.	10 — 12 MPH		60
11:41 AM	12:38 PM	Sharrow reaches Reno Creek. The tail-end of Custer's column can be seen far up ahead. Sharrow increases his speed.	12 MPH, increasing to 14 MPH along Reno Creek	1.9 miles from meeting Benteen (3.14 miles from divide separations)	64
11:43 AM — 12:28 PM	12:40 PM — 1:25 PM	Benteen is continuing on, mounting another ridge. Benteen spots the Gray Horse Troop of Custer's column, moving very rapidly: "at a dead gallop."	3 MPH (average speed, 4 MPH)	1 mile ±	68
11:44 AM	12:41 PM	41 minutes from crossing the divide—main column (Custer/Reno) reaches the confluence of No-Name and Reno creeks. Custer is moving with his five companies abreast—left to right—E, F, L, I, C. Reno is in a column-of-fours, A Company in the center.	Average: 10 + MPH, with speeds varying from 6 to bursts of 15 MPH	6.9 miles	69
11:45 AM	12:42 PM	As the commands move down Reno Creek, varying speeds between rapid bursts and slower canters, a number of the Ree scouts begin to fall behind. These include Strikes the Lodge, Rushing Bull, Soldier, Bull, White Eagle, and Red Wolf.	10+ MPH down to as low as 6 MPH		70
11:46 AM	12:43 PM	43 minutes from crossing the divide—Command is passing the morass.	10 MPH	7.3 miles	64
11:48 PM	12:45 PM	The fast pace of the advancing column nows begins to take its toll on some of the troops' horses. C Company trooper Private James Watson begins falling behind.	Declining gait, down to a walk		71
11:50 AM	12:47 PM	47 minutes from crossing the divide—Command reaches confluence of South Fork and Reno creeks.	10 MPH	7.9 miles	64
11:51 AM	12:48 PM	LT Hare, seeing Custer right behind him, increases his speed to move farther ahead.	12 MPH, increasing to 14 MPH		72
11:55 AM	12:52 PM	SGM Sharrow reaches No — Name Creek.	15 MPH	3.4 miles since reaching Reno Creek	64
11:56 AM	12:53 PM	Varnum and Strode — having lost the Rees along the way — reach a high elevation mark ("3405," grid square 13) where they halt, looking into the LBH valley. From this height, they can see up the valley as well as down the valley and part of the Indian encampment.	3.9 MPH since leaving Reno Creek	2.3 miles	73
Noon	12:57 PM	The regiment enters the "flats." Reno is called to the creek's right bank.	Increasing to 12 MPH	9.8 miles from the divide crossing	74
Noon	12:57 PM	Seeing a tepee up ahead, LT Cooke orders a detail from Company F to move out ahead and check it out.	Company F detail moving to 14 MPH		71
Noon	12:57 PM	Varnum and Strode—alone atop the high ground lookout point—watch as the regiment enters the flats. They begin moving toward the flats.	(9 MPH)		75
12:01 PM	12:58 PM	SGM Sharrow catches the main column. Custer sends him ahead immediately to tell LT Hare to report back if he saw any Indians. Before Hare reached the lone tepee SGM Sharrow overtook him in a great rush and told Hare to send back word as soon as he saw Indians. Custer was obviously very anxious.	15 MPH	1.52 miles from No — Name Creek.	72
12:04 PM	1:01 PM	Custer reaches the lone tepee.	8.54 MPH, average, from the divide approach	10.11 miles from the divide crossing	76

F. Divide Crossing to the Flats (cont.)

12:04 PM — 12:08 PM	1:01 PM — 1:05 PM	A slight delay ensues as Custer berates Ree scouts who stopped at the tepee. The Ree scout, One Feather, goes into the tepee while others strike it with their whips. Custer orders the tepee fired.			77
12:04 PM — 12:08 PM	1:01 PM — 1:05 PM	LT Hare and Fred Gerard, sitting atop a knoll, see Indians running in the LBH valley and some 40 to 50 more near a small knoll farther down the creek valley. They yell down to inform Custer, Gerard yelling, "There go your Indians, running like devils!" PVT Davern noticed them as well, estimating 20, 30, or 40.			78
12:05 PM	1:02 PM	Gerard rides off the knoll and joins Reno's column heading toward the LBH River in search of a ford. A number of his Rees preceed him.	7 MPH		79
12:05 PM	1:02 PM	Several scouts, seeing a Hunkpapa youngster named Deeds and another warrior, chase them as they try to signal a warning to the village. The Crow scout, Goes Ahead, kills Deeds.			80
12:05 PM	1:02 PM	Custer instructs LT Cooke to issue orders to Reno to attack the village. Custer also tells Cooke to stay with the major until he crossed the river. Myles Keogh follows Cooke.			81
12:06 PM	1:03 PM	LT Hare, coming off the knoll, is ordered by Custer to take a mounted detail from Reno's battalion and proceed toward the river ahead of Reno to hunt for Indians.			82
12:06 PM	1:03 PM	LT Cooke issues the attack orders to Reno: "Custer says to move at as rapid a gait as you think prudent, and to charge afterward, and you will be supported by the whole outfit." LT Wallace: "The Indians are about two miles and a half ahead, on the jump, follow them as fast as you can and charge them wherever you find them and we will support you." Dr. Porter: Reno asked if he would be supported "if the general was coming along," and Cooke answered yes, the general would support him. PVT Davern: "Gerard comes back and reports the Indian village three miles ahead and moving. The General directs you to take your three companies and drive everything before you."			83
12:07 PM	1:04 PM	LT Hare approaches CPT French for a detail to scout ahead. French orders his first sergeant—John Ryan—to cut out 10 men to accompany Hare.	10 — 12 MPH		84
12:08 PM	1:05 PM	The Ree scouts, Soldier, Bull, and White Eagle—struggling with slower horses—catch up to the rest of the command.			85
12:08 PM	1:05 PM	65 minutes from divide crossing—Reno's command separates from Custer.	8.16 MPH from divide approach	10.3 miles from divide crossing	86

G. Benteen's Scout; 12:10 p.m.–1:50 p.m.

Local Sun Time	Command's Watch Time	Event	Speed	Distance Traveled	Notes
11:13 AM	12:10 PM	Benteen breaks off from regiment to scout to the left.	(@ 6 MPH)		58
11:16 AM	12:13 PM	CTMP Voss leaves the column and heads to Benteen.	(7 MPH)	.15 miles from divide separations	61
11:16 AM	12:13 PM	Benteen's column is moving toward the first line of ridges.	6 MPH	3/10 of a mile from separation	62
11:16 AM	12:13 PM	After traveling some 250 — 300 yards, descending into the Reno Creek valley from the heights of the divide, Custer realizes Benteen will not be able to see into the LBH valley from the first line of ridges. He orders CTMP Voss to ride to Benteen and tell him to continue on to the next ridge.	10 MPH, increasing to 12 MPH, varying down to 6 MPH	.15 miles from separation	60
11:19 AM	12:16 PM	At this time Benteen is still advancing toward the first line of ridges.	6 MPH	6/10 of a mile from separation	62
11:20 AM	12:17 PM	Benteen's men see Custer's columns moving at a high rate of speed.			62
11:21 AM	12:18 PM	CTMP Voss reaches Benteen with Custer's message: "[I]f I found nothing before reaching the first line of bluffs, to go on to the second line with the same instructions" [Benteen].	7 — 8 MPH	Voss: 6/10 mile from Custer; Benteen: ¾ mile from separation	63
11:21 AM	12:18 PM	Custer's column is advancing between two small knolls and approaching the waters of Reno Creek. He slows to a trot so Voss can catch up, but still concerned that his orders to Benteen are not specific enough, Custer dispatches SGM Sharrow with addition instructions.	10 MPH down to 6 MPH	.83 miles from Voss separation; .97 miles from divide separation	60
11:21 AM	12:18 PM	SGM Sharrow leaves the column and heads to Benteen.	(8 MPH — 10 MPH)	.97 miles from divide separations	64
11:22 AM	12:19 PM	Voss turns from Benteen and heads back to main column.	12 MPH		60
11:27 AM	12:24 PM	Benteen's column "came to very high bluffs," and he sends LT Gibson and six men to the top. Gibson came back and reported seeing no Indians, only more bluffs. They begin skirting the steeper bluffs.	6 MPH slowing to 4 MPH	6/10 of a mile additional (1 1/3 miles from separation)	66
11:29 AM	12:26 PM	SGM Sharrow reaches Benteen with Custer's additional instructions: "[I]f I saw nothing from the second line of bluffs, to go on into the valley, and if there was nothing in the valley, to go on to the next valley." "[I]f from the furthest line of bluffs which we then saw, I could not see the valley—no particular valley specified—to keep on until I came to a valley (or perhaps the valley)…to pitch into…."	Sharrow: 10 MPH; Benteen: 5 — 6 MPH	Sharrow: 1.2 miles; Benteen: 1.95 miles from divide separation	67
11:43 AM — 12:28 PM	12:40 PM — 1:25 PM	Benteen is continuing on, mounting another ridge. Benteen spots the Gray Horse Troop of Custer's column, moving very rapidly: "at a dead gallop."	3 MPH (average speed, 4 MPH)	1 mile ±	68
12:04 PM	1:01 PM	Custer reaches the lone tepee.	8.54 MPH, average, from the divide approach	10.11 miles from the divide crossing	76
12:28 PM	1:25 PM	After climbing 3 to 4 ridgelines, Benteen turns his command down No-Name Creek to return to the main trail.	Average speed: 3.3 MPH	4 1/8 miles from separation	109
12:28 PM — 12:53 PM	1:25 PM — 1:50 PM	Benteen's battalion begins its move down No-Name Creek.	@ 7 MPH	(2.9 miles to travel)	109

G. Benteen's Scout (cont.)

12:51 PM — 12:59 PM	1:48 PM — 1:56 PM	Custer and two others—in all likelihood, LT Cooke and CPT Tom Custer—atop elevation point 3,411, watch the action in the valley below.			136
12:53 PM	1:50 PM	Benteen's column reaches the confluence of No-Name Creek and Reno Creek. The packs are seen about one mile up Reno Creek. A single rider—Boston Custer—is seen coming toward them.	Benteen's scout before turning: 4.2 MPH	2.9 miles from turn; 7.1 miles, total	141

H. Custer/Reno Separation to Reno's Dismount;
1:05 p.m.–1:36 p.m.

Local Sun Time	Command's Watch Time	Event	Speed	Distance Traveled	Notes
12:08 PM	1:05 PM	65 minutes from divide crossing—Reno's command separates from Custer.	8.16 MPH from divide approach	10.3 miles from divide crossing	86
12:08 PM — 12:12 PM	1:05 PM — 1:09 PM	Reno moves toward the river. Formation is M, A, G, column-of-fours.	9 MPH	6/10 of a mile from separation	87
12:09 PM	1:06 PM	Varnum and Strode reach Custer, who instructs them to go with Reno. LT Wallace tags along.	9 MPH (Average speed from divide: 7.2 MPH)	1.2 miles from lookout point; 11.5 miles — total — from divide crossing	88
12:10 PM	1:07 PM	Custer has slowed his column to a fast walk to put distance between him and Reno. Reno's command passes by and Custer proceeds toward the river, only 1.6 miles away.	@ 5 MPH	1/6—mile from separation	89
12:11 PM	1:08 PM	Custer instructs CPT Yates to send the NCO and 4 or 5 EM forward to act as an advance scout. These would be the same men Cooke ordered forward moments earlier.			71
12:12 PM — 12:19 PM	1:09 PM — 1:16 PM	Reno skirts Middle Knoll, re-crosses the stream, and takes a dry creek bed to the river. His lead elements reach the LBH.	9 MPH	1.1 miles from separation	90
12:16 PM	1:13 PM	Custer is now 2/3 of a mile from the separation point and 1 mile from the LBH.	@ 5 MPH	2/3 of a mile from separation	91
12:16 PM	1:13 PM	LT Hare and the M Company detail reach the Little Big Horn. Seeing Indians ahead, Reno shouts for the men to wait and re-join their company. Hare crosses the river; the detail waits for Reno and French.	10 — 12 MPH	1½ miles from start	84
12:16 PM — 12:17 PM	1:13 PM — 1:14 PM	Fred Gerard, riding to the left and out front of Reno by eight or ten feet, reaches a small knoll next to the river crossing at Ford A. He halts about 15 — 20 feet from the river's edge.	7 — 8 MPH	1.7 miles from knoll and lone tepee	93
12:18 PM	1:15 PM	Reno, slightly ahead of his command and just behind Gerard, reaches the LBH River.	8 — 10 MPH	1.7 miles, total, from separation	95
12:18 PM	1:15 PM	Gerard is informed by several of his Ree scouts that the Indians are coming back up the valley to confront the troops.			96
12:19 PM	1:16 PM	As Reno enters the river, Gerard informs him of the turn of events. Reno ignores him.		1.7 miles, total, from separation	97
12:19 PM	1:16 PM	Gerard pauses, then turns back and meets LT Cooke. Gerard informs the adjutant of the Sioux moving up the valley. Cooke turns immediately and heads back to Custer.			97
12:19 PM	1:16 PM	Reno begins crossing the LBH at Ford A, formation changing to column-of-twos. SGT O'Harra positioned to keep troops moving. Some pause, briefly, to water.	5 — 7 MPH	1.7 miles, total, from separation	98
12:19 PM	1:16 PM	Herendeen informs Reno of Indians moving up the valley. Reno, thinking Custer is right behind, sends PVT McIlhargey back with a message.			99
12:22 PM	1:19 PM	As Custer is passing alongside Middle Knoll, Cooke intercepts him and informs him of Gerard's report. They are ½ mile from the LBH.	Cooke: 10 MPH; Custer: 5 — 6 MPH	Cooke: 850 yards from previous knoll; Custer: 1 ± mile from separation from Reno	100
12:22 PM	1:19 PM	Custer hears Cooke's report and makes the fatal decision to try to get to the northern end of the village. He swings his command to the right and orders a gallop.	@ 9 — 10 MPH		101
12:23 PM	1:20 PM	The last of Reno's battalion has crossed the LBH. Hearing nothing from Custer, Reno sends his cook, PVT Mitchell, back with another message.	5 — 7 MPH		102
12:24 PM	1:21 PM	Reno pushes his troops on; early river crossers that stopped to re-cinch are now re-mounted.	7 — 8 MPH, speed increasing		104
12:25 PM	1:22 PM	Reno begins his move into and down the LBH valley. Formation has M on the right, A on left, G in reserve. G is then brought into line on the left.	10 — 12 MPH, varying in stretches	.48 miles to the open valley (840 yards)	105

H. Custer/Reno Separation to Reno's Dismount (cont.)

12:25 PM	1:22 PM	CPT French instructs 1SG Ryan to take men and ride in skirmish formation along the river's timbered edge to ferret out any Indians he found there. These men were probably SGTs White and O'Harra; CPL Scollin; and PVTs Newell, Meier, Thorpe, Galenne, Braun, Gordon, Turley, Wilber, Morris, Neely, and Klotzbucher, making it a total of 15 troopers.	10 — 12 MPH		106
12:25 PM	1:22 PM	As Reno begins his move down the valley, a number of Ree scouts move with him on the command's far left. These scouts include Young Hawk, Goose, Red Star, Strikes Two, Little Sioux, Bob-tail Bull, Forked Horn, Red Foolish Bear, Boy Chief, Little Brave, One Feather, Billy Jackson, and Red Bear. Bloody Knife is with them, as well, as is the Dakota scout, Whole Buffalo.	10 — 12 MPH		107
12:26 PM — 12:37 PM	1:23 PM — 1:34 PM	Reno's command moves down the valley rapidly, some troops spotting Custer's command on the bluffs.	12 MPH	½ mile so far	108
12:29 PM — 12:30 PM	1:26 PM — 1:27 PM	Finished watering (5 minutes), Custer's command mounts the bluffs, rapidly, and is seen by some of Reno's troops.	@ 8 MPH	300 yards	110
12:31 PM	1:28 PM	Several Ree scouts including Red Star, Strikes Two, Little Sioux, and Boy Chief break away from the advancing troops to chase three Sioux women and two or three children hiding in the timber-line and trying to make it back to the village. They kill at least two of the women and the children, and then spot some 25 or 30 Sioux ponies. They herd the horses across a ford. They see One Feather and *Pta-a-te (aka* Whole Buffalo, one of the Dakota scouts). Red Bear continued to ride with the troops down the valley.	12 MPH	1 mile from crossing at Ford A.	112
12:38 PM	1:35 PM	Reno orders his command to dismount.		Approximately 2½ miles from Ford A crossing	114
12:38 PM	1:35 PM	1SG Ryan orders several of the M Company flankers to continue through the timbered area to clear it. Some eventually reached the top of the village, quite possibly the Arapaho encampment. Privates Wilber and Meier may have been two of them. Another may have been SGT White. 1SG Ryan re-joins his company, placing one of the sergeants in charge of the skirmishers.	10 — 12 MPH, slowing to 4 — 6 MPH in the timber	2½+ miles	115
12:38 PM	1:35 PM	1SG Ryan orders the other M Company flankers to clear the woods, PVT Morris amongst them. "Ryan, in charge of the detail, gave the command, *Double time!* when we were close to the wood, and then, *As skirmishers, march!* We entered the woods, skirmished them to the river, saw no Indians in the woods and immediately returned."	6 — 8 MPH		116
12:39 PM	1:36 PM	Reno's troops begin deploying.			117

I. From Separation to 3,411; 1:05 p.m.–1:56 p.m.

Local Sun Time	Command's Watch Time	Event	Speed	Distance Traveled	Notes
12:08 PM	1:05 PM	65 minutes from crossing the divide—Reno's command separates from Custer.	8.16 MPH from divide approach	10.3 miles from divide crossing	86
12:09 PM	1:06 PM	Varnum and Strode reach Custer, who instructs them to go with Reno. LT Wallace tags along.	9 MPH (Average speed from divide: 7.2 MPH)	1.2 miles from lookout point; 11.5 miles — total — from divide crossing	88
12:10 PM	1:07 PM	Custer has slowed his column to a fast walk to put distance between him and Reno. Reno's command passes by and Custer proceeds toward the river, only 1.6 miles away.	@ 5 MPH	1/6 mile from separation	89
12:16 PM	1:13 PM	Custer is now 2/3 of a mile from the separation point and 1 mile from the LBH.	@ 5 MPH	2/3 mile from separation	91
12:16 PM	1:13 PM	Some Ree scouts, having trouble with their horses, ride with Custer's column, trying to catch up. These scouts are Soldier, Bull, and White Eagle.			92
12:17 PM	1:14 PM	The Ree scout, Stab—who had been with Benteen's column initially—rides up to Soldier and the others. He rides on ahead, to follow Custer's column up the bluffs.			94
12:17 PM	1:14 PM	Two more C Company troopers—Brennan and Fitzgerald—fall out.			71
12:18 PM	1:15 PM	Gerard is informed by several of his Ree scouts that the Indians are coming back up the valley to confront the troops.			96
12:19 PM	1:16 PM	Gerard pauses, then turns back and meets LT Cooke. Gerard informs the adjutant of the Sioux moving up the valley. Cooke turns immediately and heads back to Custer.			97
12:22 PM	1:19 PM	As Custer is passing alongside Middle Knoll, Cooke intercepts him and informs him of Gerard's report. They are ½ mile from the LBH.	Cooke: 10 MPH; Custer: 5 — 6 MPH	Cooke: 850 yards from previous knoll; Custer: 1 ± mile from separation from Reno	100
12:22 PM	1:19 PM	Custer hears Cooke's report and makes the fatal decision to try to get to the northern end of the village. He swings his command to the right and orders a gallop.	@ 9 — 10 MPH		101
12:23 PM — 12:24 PM	1:20 PM — 1:21 PM	Lead elements of Custer's command reach a small stream—probably North Fork—and pause to water their horses.	9 — 10 MPH	335 yards	103
12:24 PM — 12:29 PM	1:21 PM — 1:26 PM	Custer's command waters its horses.			103
12:26 PM — 12:37 PM	1:23 PM — 1:34 PM	Reno's command moves down the valley rapidly, some troops spotting Custer's command on the bluffs.	12 MPH	½ mile	108
12:27 PM	1:24 PM	The Ree scouts, Soldier, Bull, and White Eagle follow after Custer's command.			94
12:29 PM — 12:30 PM	1:26 PM — 1:27 PM	Finished watering (5 minutes), Custer's command mounts the bluffs, rapidly, and is seen by some of Reno's troops.	@ 8 MPH	300 yards	110
12:30 PM	1:27 PM	Mitch Boyer, the four Crows—and Black Fox it appears, as well—leave Custer's command a couple minutes early to head up the bluffs.	10 MPH		111
12:30 PM — 12:32 PM	1:27 PM — 1:29 PM	Custer's command continues to mount the bluffs and after about 300 yards, swings off on a right angle for another 600 — 700 yards.	8 MPH	670 yards, total, from watering	103
12:37 PM	1:34 PM	Custer's command continues to mount the hills, more inland and out of sight of Reno's men, but with Custer closer to the bluffs.	9 MPH	Another ¾ of a mile	113
12:38 PM	1:35 PM	Reno orders his command to dismount.		Approximately 2½ miles from Ford A crossing	114

I. From Separation to 3,411 (cont.)

12:41 PM	1:38 PM	Custer's command is approaching Reno Hill after picking up speed as the terrain evened out.	9 MPH	1+ miles from watering	113
12:41 PM	1:38 PM	Custer's scouts—Boyer, the four Crows (Goes Ahead, Hairy Moccasin, White Man Runs Him, and Curley), and it appears the Ree, Black Fox, as well—riding slightly ahead of Custer, are crossing over Reno Hill and beginning to slow as they swing left and approach the edge of the bluffs.	10 — 12 MPH, slowing to 7 — 8 MPH	1½ miles from watering	119
12:44 PM	1:41 PM	PVT Peter Thompson of C Company drops out of formation as his horse begins to break down. He is on the northern side of Reno Hill. The rest of the command passes him by.			124
12:44 PM	1:41 PM	As Thompson dismounts to tend to his horse, the F Company advance scouts pass him by.	10 MPH		125
12:45 PM	1:42 PM	Varnum sees Gray Horse Troop on bluffs.		Sighted 500 yards downstream from Reno Hill	126
12:45 PM	1:42 PM	The Hunkpapa warrior, Iron Cedar, on or near Weir Point, sees Custer's column approaching near the bluffs to the south. He turns immediately and heads down the bluffs to warn the village of more soldiers.	(5 MPH)	(2/3 of a mile across the river and into the village)	127
12:47 PM	1:44 PM	Custer cautions his excited troops as they move toward the head of Cedar Coulee. The command begins to slow its pace considerably. "Hold your horses in, boys, there are plenty of them down there for us all."	7 — 8 MPH	1 + miles	128
12:49 PM	1:46 PM	The scouts, now mingling around Custer and watching Reno's command, are told by Custer to proceed to the high ground north—Weir Peaks. Boyer, Goes Ahead, White Man Runs Him, and Hairy Moccasin turn and head toward Weir.			130
12:50 PM	1:47 PM	It is not unreasonable to assume that if SGT Daniel Kanipe was sent back with a message for CPT McDougall and the packs, he would have been sent about this time, from approximately this location: the southwestern shoulder of Sharpshooters' Ridge.			134
12:51 PM	1:48 PM	13 minutes after Reno's dismount—Custer arrives at 3,411. His troops slow even more and head for the depression of Cedar Coulee.			135
12:51 PM — 12:59 PM	1:48 PM — 1:56 PM	Custer and two others—in all likelihood, LT Cooke and CPT Tom Custer—atop elevation point 3,411, watch the action in the valley below.			136
12:52 PM	1:49 PM	LT DeRudio reaches the spot in timber where he is to see Custer.			137
12:55 PM	1:52 PM	Curley and Black Fox mingle just north of Custer as he looks over the valley.			146
12:56 PM	1:53 PM	Boyer and the three Crows—Goes Ahead, Hairy Moccasin, and White Man Runs Him—arrive at Weir Peaks.	7 — 8 MPH	¾ of a mile (1,350 yards)	147
12:56 PM	1:53 PM	DeRudio sees Custer at 3,411.			148
12:59 PM	1:56 PM	Custer leaves 3,411.			152

J. The Valley Fight—Dismount to Retreat; 1:35 p.m.–2:23 p.m.

Local Sun Time	Command's Watch Time	Event	Speed	Distance Traveled	Notes
12:38 PM	1:35 PM	Reno orders his command to dismount.		Approximately 2½ miles from Ford A crossing	114
12:38 PM	1:35 PM	1SG Ryan orders several of the M Company flankers to continue through the timbered area to clear it. Some eventually reached the top of the village, quite possibly the Arapaho encampment. Privates Wilber and Meier may have been two of them. Another may have been SGT White. 1SG Ryan re-joins his company, placing one of the sergeants in charge of the skirmishers.	10 — 12 MPH, slowing to 4 — 6 MPH in the timber	2½+ miles	115
12:38 PM	1:35 PM	1SG Ryan orders the other M Company flankers to clear the woods, PVT Morris amongst them. "Ryan, in charge of the detail, gave the command, *Double time!* when we were close to the wood, and then, *As skirmishers, march!* We entered the woods, skirmished them to the river, saw no Indians in the woods and immediately returned."	6 — 8 MPH		116
12:39 PM	1:36 PM	Reno's troops begin deploying.			117
12:40 PM	1:37 PM	LT Varnum begins joining command from out front.			118
12:41 PM	1:38 PM	Custer's command is approaching Reno Hill after picking up speed as the terrain evened out.	9 MPH	1+ miles from watering	113
12:43 PM	1:40 PM	Five minutes from dismount—Skirmish line is deployed and begins moving forward. A gap forms between M Company and A as M moves toward the western foothills and A begins to swing more to its right.			120
12:43 PM	1:40 PM	Five minutes from dismount—The other half of the M Company skirmishers—at least Meier and Wilber, but probably SGT White as well—have reached the first of the Indian tepees and begin setting them on fire.	4 MPH — 6 MPH	500 — 600 yards (.284 miles) from entering the timber	121
12:43 PM	1:40 PM	A number of the Ree scouts deploy with Reno's troops, almost all of them on the left. Red Bear said the Sioux were lying down, and "no one was riding around on horseback."			122
12:45 PM	1:42 PM	Varnum sees Gray Horse Troop on bluffs.		Sighted 500 yards downstream from Reno Hill	126
12:47 PM	1:44 PM	Custer cautions his excited troops as they move toward the head of Cedar Coulee. The command begins to slow its pace considerably. "Hold your horses in, boys, there are plenty of them down there for us all."	7 — 8 MPH	1 + miles	128
12:48 PM	1:45 PM	Having been split in two, the first group of M Company flankers have rapidly cleared the timber and have returned to their unit. PVT Morris is amongst this group.	6 — 8 MPH	Unknown, but probably 500 — 600 yards and back.	129
12:49 PM	1:46 PM	The M Company flankers who had reached the village were now concerned about being cut off and begin to head back into the timber area.	@ 6 — 8 MPH		131
12:50 PM	1:47 PM	Reno leaves the general area where he is with Moylan and heads into the timber, taking LT McIntosh and a group of G Company troops with him. Moylan is forced to spread his command farther apart to cover the gaps. Hodgson is told to keep Reno informed.			132
12:50 PM	1:47 PM	DeRudio arrives in timber.			133
12:51 PM	1:48 PM	13 minutes from Reno's dismount—Custer arrives at 3,411. His troops slow even more and head for the depression of Cedar Coulee.			135
12:52 PM	1:49 PM	DeRudio reaches the spot in timber where he is to see Custer.			137
12:52 PM	1:49 PM	Reno, with his G Company troops, reaches the timber.			138

J. The Valley Fight—Dismount to Retreat (cont.)

12:53 PM	1:50 PM	Varnum—hearing G Company is going to charge through the timber—leaves skirmish line for woods.			139
12:54 PM	1:51 PM	Varnum enters timber.			145
12:56 PM	1:53 PM	DeRudio sees Custer at 3,411.			148
12:58 PM	1:55 PM	Varnum reaches glade.			145
12:59 PM	1:56 PM	Custer leaves 3,411.			152
12:59 PM	1:56 PM	M Company flankers who fired the tepees have made their way back into the Reno timber area and seek out other troops and their company.	6 MPH	½ mile from the village	153
1 PM	1:57 PM	Varnum reaches Reno.			145
1:01 PM	1:58 PM	Varnum speaks to Reno.			145
1:03 PM	2 PM	Varnum leaves glade.			145
1:06 PM	2:03 PM	Varnum meets Hodgson; they speak briefly.			145
1:07 PM	2:04 PM	Varnum leaves Hodgson.			145
1:10 PM	2:07 PM	Reno and Hodgson reach the edge of the prairie; Moylan explains the situation and points out the Indians turning M Company's flank. Reno orders a pullback to the "brow" at the edge of the timber.			160
1:11 PM	2:08 PM	33 minutes from dismount—Skirmish line begins pulling back.			164
1:12 PM	2:09 PM	CPT French, seeing A Company pulling back, orders his command to mount-up.	2.3 MPH	Route: 1.3 miles from dismount	165
1:12 PM	2:09 PM	Varnum reaches end of timber; sees the line is moving back and is in the process of establishing a skirmish line on the "brow."			145
1:13 PM	2:10 PM	Varnum sees Moylan.			145
1:14 PM	2:11 PM	Last of A Company men reach the "brow," forming a skirmish line with G Company.	Some running, 5 — 6 MPH	250 — 300 yards	170
1:14 PM	2:11 PM	M Company, now fully mounted and harassed on its flank, makes a break for the timber line, supported by A and G's covering fire.	12 MPH	(8/10 of a mile)	171
1:14 PM	2:11 PM	Varnum speaks with Moylan.			145
1:14 PM	2:11 PM	Crazy Horse, followed by a considerable number of his warriors, begins arriving as M Company breaks for the timber.			172
1:15 PM	2:12 PM	Varnum goes for Company A horses.			145
1:18 PM	2: 15 PM	Varnum finds Company A horses in glade.			145

J. The Valley Fight—Dismount to Retreat (cont.)

1:18 PM	2:15 PM	Last of M Company arrives at the "brow" of the timber.	12 MPH	8/10 of a mile	174
1:19 PM	2:16 PM	Varnum tells the Company A horseholders to mount up and follow him.			145
1:20 PM	2:17 PM	Varnum leaves glade with Company A horses.			145
1:22 PM	2:19 PM	Varnum reaches Moylan.			145
1:24 PM	2:21 PM	Varnum spends a minute or two with Gerard and Reynolds. They have a quick drink.			176
1:26 PM	2:23 PM	48 minutes after dismounting—Reno begins retreat.			177

K. Scouts; 11:30 a.m.–4:35 p.m.

Local Sun Time	Command's Watch Time	Event	Speed	Distance Traveled	Notes
10:33 AM	11:30 AM	LT Varnum, PVT Strode, and the Rees lead out, cross the divide, and head to the left front. LT Hare takes the Crows and heads off to the right.	@ 10 MPH, increasing speed		50
11:21 AM	12:18 PM	Having just passed the morass, Varnum, Strode, and the Rees have moved down Reno Creek and now begin to swing toward their left, mounting the higher bluffs on the south and west side of the South Fork — Reno Creek confluence. Their speed decreases sharply.	10 MPH — 6 MPH	8 miles from the divide crossing	65
11:45 AM	12:42 PM	As the commands move down Reno Creek, varying speeds between rapid bursts and slower canters, a number of the Ree scouts begin to fall behind. These include Strikes The Lodge, Rushing Bull, Soldier, Bull, White Eagle, and Red Wolf.	10+ MPH down to as low as 6 MPH		70
11:51 AM	12:48 PM	LT Hare, seeing Custer right behind him, increases his speed to move farther ahead.	12 MPH, increasing to 14 MPH		72
11:56 AM	12:53 PM	Varnum and Strode—having lost the Rees along the way—reach a high elevation mark ("3,405," grid square 13) where they halt, looking into the LBH valley. From this height, they can see up the valley as well as down the valley and part of the Indian encampment.	3.9 MPH since leaving Reno Creek	2.3 miles	73
Noon	12:57 PM	Varnum and Strode—alone atop the high ground lookout point—watch as the regiment enters the flats. They begin moving toward the flats.	(9 MPH)		75
12:04 PM — 12:08 PM	1:01 PM — 1:05 PM	A slight delay ensues as Custer berates Ree scouts who stopped at the lone tepee. The Ree scout, One Feather, goes into the tepee while others strike it with their whips. Custer orders the tepee fired.			77
12:04 PM — 12:08 PM	1:01 PM — 1:05 PM	LT Hare and Fred Gerard, sitting atop a knoll, see Indians running in the LBH valley and some 40 to 50 more near a small knoll farther down the creek valley. They yell down to inform Custer, Gerard yelling, "There go your Indians, running like devils!"			78
12:05 PM	1:02 PM	Gerard rides off the knoll and joins Reno's column heading toward the LBH River in search of a ford. A number of his Rees preceed him.	7 MPH		79
12:05 PM	1:02 PM	Several scouts, seeing a Hunkpapa youngster named Deeds and another warrior, chase them as they try to signal a warning to the village. The Crow scout, Goes Ahead, kills Deeds.			80
12:06 PM	1:03 PM	LT Hare, coming off the knoll, is ordered by Custer to take a mounted detail from Reno's battalion and proceed toward the river ahead of Reno to hunt for Indians.			82
12:07 PM	1:04 PM	LT Hare approaches CPT French for a detail to scout ahead. French orders his first sergeant—John Ryan—to cut out 10 men to accompany Hare.	10 — 12 MPH		84
12:08 PM	1:05 PM	The Ree scouts, Soldier, Bull, and White Eagle—struggling with slower horses—catch up to the rest of the command.			85
12:09 PM	1:06 PM	Varnum and Strode reach Custer, who instructs them to go with Reno. LT Wallace tags along.	9 MPH (Average speed from divide: 7.2 MPH)	1.2 miles from lookout point; 11.5 miles — total — from divide crossing	88

K. Scouts (cont.)

12:16 PM	1:13 PM	Some Ree scouts, having trouble with their horses, ride with Custer's column, trying to catch up. These scouts are Soldier, Bull, and White Eagle.			92
12:16 PM	1:13 PM	LT Hare and the M Company detail reach the Little Big Horn. Seeing Indians ahead, Reno shouts for the men to wait and re-join their company. Hare crosses the river; the detail waits for Reno and French.	10 — 12 MPH	1½ miles from start	84
12:16 PM — 12:17 PM	1:13 PM — 1:14 PM	Fred Gerard, riding to the left and out front of Reno by eight or ten feet, reaches a small knoll next to the river crossing at Ford A. He halts about 15 — 20 feet from the river's edge.	7 — 8 MPH	1.7 miles from knoll and lone tepee	93
12:17 PM	1:14 PM	The Ree scout, Stab—who had been with Benteen's column initially—rides up to Soldier and the others. He rides on ahead, to follow Custer's column up the bluffs.			94
12:18 PM	1:15 PM	Reno, slightly ahead of his command and just behind Gerard, reaches the LBH River.	8 — 10 MPH	1.7 miles, total, from separation	95
12:18 PM	1:15 PM	Gerard is informed by several of his Ree scouts that the Indians are coming back up the valley to confront the troops.			96
12:19 PM	1:16 PM	As Reno enters the river, Gerard informs him of the turn of events. Reno ignores him.		1.7 miles, total, from separation	97
12:19 PM	1:16 PM	Gerard pauses, then turns back and meets LT Cooke. Gerard informs the adjutant of the Sioux moving up the valley. Cooke turns immediately and heads back to Custer.			97
12:19 PM	1:16 PM	Herendeen informs Reno of Indians moving up the valley. Reno, thinking Custer is right behind, sends PVT McIlhargey back with a message.			99
12:22 PM	1:19 PM	As Custer is passing alongside Middle Knoll, Cooke intercepts him and informs him of Gerard's report. They are ½ mile from the LBH.	Cooke: 10 MPH; Custer: 5 — 6 MPH	Cooke: 850 yards from previous knoll; Custer: 1 ± mile from separation from Reno	100
12:25 PM	1:22 PM	As Reno moves down the valley, a number of Ree scouts move with him on the command's far left. These scouts include Young Hawk, Goose, Red Star, Strikes Two, Little Sioux, Bob-tail Bull, Forked Horn, Red Foolish Bear, Boy Chief, Little Brave, One Feather, Billy Jackson, and Red Bear. Bloody Knife is with them, as well, as is the Dakota scout, Whole Buffalo.			107
12:27 PM	1:24 PM	The Ree scouts, Soldier, Bull, and White Eagle follow after Custer's command.			94
12:30 PM	1:27 PM	Mitch Boyer, the four Crows—and Black Fox it appears, as well—leave Custer's command a couple minutes early to head up the bluffs.	10 MPH		111
12:31 PM	1:28 PM	Several Ree scouts including Red Star, Strikes Two, Little Sioux, and Boy Chief break away from the advancing troops to chase three Sioux women and two or three children hiding in the timber-line and trying to make it back to the village. They kill at least two of the women and the children, and then spot some 25 or 30 Sioux ponies. They herd the horses across a ford. They see One Feather and *Pta-a-te (aka* Whole Buffalo, one of the Dakota scouts). Red Bear continued to ride with the troops down the valley.	12 MPH	1 mile from crossing at Ford A.	112

K. Scouts (cont.)

12:41 PM	1:38 PM	Custer's scouts—Boyer, the four Crows (Goes Ahead, Hairy Moccasin, White Man Runs Him, and Curley), and it appears the Ree, Black Fox, as well—riding slightly ahead of Custer, are crossing over Reno Hill and beginning to slow as they swing left and approach the edge of the bluffs.	10 — 12 MPH, slowing to 7 — 8 MPH	1½ miles from watering	119
12:43 PM	1:40 PM	A number of the Ree scouts deploy with Reno's troops, almost all of them on the left. Red Bear said the Sioux were lying down, and "no one was riding around on horseback."			122
12:43 PM (to 1:13 PM)	1:40 PM (to 2:10 PM)	Ree scouts have captured a number of Sioux ponies and have herded them across the LBH and up a small coulee coming off the bluffs. They run into the tail-end of Custer's command and are fired upon by some trailing soldiers who mistake them for Sioux. The scouts now include Rees, Red Star, Strikes Two, Little Sioux, Boy Chief, One Feather, Bull-Stands-In-Water, and the Dakota, Whole Buffalo. (They will meet several others who did not cross the river with Reno, including the Rees, Soldier, Bull, White Eagle, Stab, and Billy Cross; and the Dakotas, White Cloud, *Caroo*, and *Ma-tok-sha*.)	5 MPH, average	1 mile	123
12:49 PM	1:46 PM	The scouts, now mingling around Custer and watching Reno's command, are told by Custer to proceed to the high ground north—Weir Peaks. Boyer, Goes Ahead, White Man Runs Him, and Hairy Moccasin turn and head toward Weir.			130
12:55 PM	1:52 PM	Curley and Black Fox mingle just north of Custer as he looks over the valley.			146
12:56 PM	1:53 PM	Boyer and the three Crows—Goes Ahead, Hairy Moccasin, and White Man Runs Him—arrive at Weir Peaks.	7 — 8 MPH	¾ of a mile (1,350 yards)	147
12:58 PM	1:55 PM	As the leading Rees reach the hills above Reno Hill, they are fired on by some troopers lagging behind Custer's behind. The Ree scout, Stab, is amongst those shot at and he joins others with the stolen ponies.			150
1:03 PM	2:00 PM	Curley and Black Fox turn to head back down to Reno Creek.	(6 MPH)		155
1:05 PM	2:02 PM	Curley and Black Fox pass over 3,411.	6 MPH	250 yards	64
1:08 PM	2:05 PM	Curley and Black Fox are passing over Reno Hill.	6 MPH	An additional 500 yards (.3 miles)	64
1:08 PM (12:56 PM — 1:15 PM)	2:05 PM (1:53 PM — 2:12 PM)	The three Crows continue to watch the fighting in the valley.			157
1:10 PM	2:07 PM	Boyer, seeing Custer's command moving down Cedar Coulee, releases the three Crow scouts and moves off Weir Point, heading for the front of Custer's column in the coulee.			161
1:13 PM	2:10 PM	By now, Ree scouts have captured a number of Sioux ponies—28—and have herded them across the LBH and up a small coulee coming off the bluffs. As they were doing so, they ran into the tail-end of Custer's command and were fired upon by some trailing soldiers who mistook them for Sioux. The scouts now include Rees, Red Star, Strikes Two, Little Sioux, Boy Chief, One Feather, Bull-Stands-In-Water, and the Dakota, Whole Buffalo. Stab has already joined them, and they are soon joined by several others who did not cross the river with Reno, including Rees, Soldier, Bull, White Eagle, Strikes The Lodge, and Billy Cross; and Dakotas, White Cloud, *Caroo*, and *Ma-tok-sha*.			167

K. Scouts (cont.)

1:15 PM	2:12 PM	The three Crow scouts—Goes Ahead, White Man Runs Him, and Hairy Moccasin—begin heading north along the bluffs.	4 MPH — 6 MPH, stopping along the way		173
1:23 PM — 1:33 PM	2:20 PM — 2:30 PM	After hiding some of the Sioux ponies in a ravine to the east of the ridgeline, several Rees head toward Reno Hill. This is where they will see the soldiers in full flight, many scaling the bluffs to reach the hilltop.		To the ravine: 250 yards from high point 3.375; Reno Hill: 900 — 1,250 yards	175
1:26 PM	2:23 PM	48 minutes after dismounting—Reno begins retreat.			177
1:31 PM	2:28 PM	Curley and Black Fox reach Reno Creek. They stop and water their horses.	5 MPH	2.1 miles from leaving the column	64
1:33 PM	2:30 PM	Boy Chief and several other Rees—Little Sioux, Soldier, Stabbed, Strikes The Lodge, and Strikes Two—arrive at Reno Hill where they see Reno's men in full flight, many of the troopers scaling the bluffs, some beginning to reach the hilltop.		900 — 1,250 yards from sequestered horses	184
1:35 PM	2:32 PM	The three Crows—Goes Ahead, Hairy Moccasin, and White Man Runs Him—reach the far end of the bluffs overlooking Ford B.	4 MPH average, stopping and starting	1 1/3 miles from Weir Peaks	186
1:35 PM — 2:13 PM	2:32 PM — 3:10 PM	The three Crows watch as Custer's command mounts the ridges to the north and east, then the Crows fire into the Indian village, their shots falling in the Sans Arc and Minneconjou camps.	Halted on the bluffs		186
1:41 PM	2:38 PM	Billy Cross, Bull, Red Bear, Soldier, Stab, Strikes Two, White Eagle, Red Star, Red Wolf, and Strikes The Lodge head back to the ravine where the stolen ponies are hidden with the intention of driving them back along Reno Creek.	6 MPH		190
1:47 PM	2:44 PM	Several Ree scouts arrive back at the ravine where the stolen horses are sequestered. They begin culling out about 15.		1,100 — 1,300 yards from Reno Hill area	190
1:51 PM	2:48 PM	Benteen reaches the Little Big Horn and has now seen friendly Indians on the bluffs just north of Reno Creek. These scouts direct him toward Reno Hill. It appears they were the young Crow, Curley, and the Ree, Black Fox, and may also have been joined by a couple more Rees with stolen ponies.	7 MPH	1,525 yards from meeting Martini	202
1:52 PM	2:49 PM	Several Rees take about 15 horses from the ravine and head down the hills toward Reno Creek. In all likelihood these are Billy Cross, Bull, Red Bear, Soldier, Stab, Strikes Two, White Eagle, Red Star, Red Wolf, and Strikes the Lodge. They run into both Benteen's command and the pack train. After the packs turned toward the hills, trailing Sioux retrieved their horses and the Rees returned to the hilltop.	(@ 3 — 5 MPH)		190
1:55 PM	2:52 PM	As Benteen's command begins to mount the bluffs and follow their commander, they are passed by several Indian scouts—not sure if they were Crow or Ree—driving some Sioux ponies, and the scouts yelled, "Soldiers," pointing to the hilltop to the right.			207
2:13 PM	3:10 PM	Goes Ahead, Hairy Moccasin, and White Man Runs Him leave the bluffs above Ford B and head back along the way they came. They now begin to move faster.	6 MPH		228
2:15 PM	3:12 PM	Black Fox—identifiable by a white bandana tied around his head—leaves Curley and joins fellow Rees driving stolen Sioux ponies.			230

K. Scouts (cont.)

2:21 PM	3:18 PM	Eight to ten Rees drive about 15 stolen Sioux ponies along Reno Creek and meet the pack train west of the lone tepee. One of them was the half-breed Billy Cross. It appears some of the others were the Ree stragglers, Bull, Red Bear, Soldier, Stab, Strikes Two, and White Eagle, along with Red Star, Red Wolf, and Strikes the Lodge. After the packs turned toward the hills, trailing Sioux retrieved their horses and the Rees returned to the hilltop. These are the same scouts who passed Benteen on his way to Reno Hill.	5 MPH	2 miles from picking up the horses in the ravine	237
2:21 PM	3:18 PM	Black Fox—seen with a white handkerchief tied around his head—leaves the Rees and joins the pack train.			230
2:26 PM	3:23 PM	The three Crows reach a point near Weir Peaks and instead of re-mounting the Weir complex, head over toward Cedar Coulee.	6 MPH	1 1/3 miles from bluffs above Ford B	239
2:41 PM	3:38 PM	The three Crows arrive amidst the confusion on Reno Hill.	6 MPH	1½ miles after turning from Weir Peaks	252
2:46 PM	3:43 PM	The three Crow scouts meet up with the Rees, Red Bear and White Cloud, on Reno Hill, all of them milling around the pack mules.			257
3:33 PM	4:30 PM	Little Sioux and some other Rees head back to the ravine where they had sequestered the stolen Sioux ponies. There they met other stragglers, Boy Chief, Rushing Bull, Caroo, Red Bear, and Strikes Two.			298
(3:38 PM — onwards)	(4:35 PM — onwards)	The Rees—Little Sioux, Soldier, Strikes Two, Boy Chief, Stab, Red Wolf, Bull, One Feather, Strikes the Lodge, and maybe some others—begin herding the captured horses back along Reno Creek toward the Rosebud. They were trailed by a number of Sioux warriors. Billy Cross was reported amongst them (see 3:18 PM).		900 — 1,250 yards	299
(3:38 PM — onwards)	(4:35 PM — onwards)	Red Bear's version of this has the following heading back with the horses: Bull Stands in Water, Rushing Bull, Red Wolf, White Eagle, Red Star, Pretty Face, Red Bear, One Feather, and Whole Buffalo. He also claimed the following stayed behind with the troops: Strikes Two, Stab, Soldier, Boy Chief, Strikes the Lodge, Little Sioux, White Cloud, Caroo, Bull, and Billy Cross (see 3:18 PM).		900 — 1,250 yards	300

L. Reno's Retreat to Benteen's Arrival; 2:11 p.m.–3:05 p.m.

Local Sun Time	Command's Watch Time	Event	Speed	Distance Traveled	Notes
1:14 PM	2:11 PM	Crazy Horse, followed by a considerable number of his warriors, begins arriving as M Company breaks for the timber.			172
1:15 PM	2:12 PM	Varnum goes for Company A horses.			145
1:18 PM	2:15 PM	Varnum finds Company A horses in glade.			145
1:18 PM	2:15 PM	Last of M Company arrives at the "brow" of the timber.	12 MPH	8/10 of a mile	174
1:19 PM	2:16 PM	Varnum tells the Company A horseholders to mount up and follow him.			145
1:20 PM	2:17 PM	Varnum leaves glade with Company A horses.			145
1:22 PM	2:19 PM	Varnum reaches Moylan.			145
1:24 PM	2:21 PM	Varnum spends a minute or two with Gerard and Reynolds. They have a quick drink.			176
1:26 PM	2:23 PM	48 minutes after dismounting—Reno begins retreat.			177
1:28 PM	2:25 PM	Varnum, now mounted, heads out of the woods on the tail of the last of the troops.	12+ MPH		179
1:29 PM	2:26 PM	Boston Custer is passing over 3,411; he looks into the valley briefly and sees Reno's command galloping from the timber, Indians in pursuit.	13 MPH	4/10 of a mile from mid-point of Reno Hill	64
1:33 PM	2:30 PM	Boy Chief and several other Rees—Little Sioux, Soldier, Stabbed, Strikes the Lodge, and Strikes Two—arrive at Reno Hill where they see Reno's men in full flight, many of the troopers scaling the bluffs, some beginning to reach the hilltop.		900 — 1,250 yards from sequestered horses	184
1:38 PM	2:35 PM	Benteen reaches the lone tepee	7.5 MPH	3.4 miles from the morass	187
1:39 PM — 1:49 PM	2:36 PM — 2:46 PM	DeRudio—still in the timber—watches as masses of Indians follow Reno's command to the crossing, fighting all along the way.			188
1:41 PM	2:38 PM	The first of Reno's troops begin reaching the hilltop.	Varying speeds, from 13+ MPH down to a crawl	Variously, 1.14 — 1.38 miles	189
1:42 PM	2:39 PM	Custer reaches the top of Luce Ridge.	6 MPH	½ mile	193
1:45 PM	2:42 PM	Other Indians—primarily Cheyenne like American Horse and Brave Wolf—leave the valley fight and head back to their village.	6 to 8 MPH		198
1:49 PM	2:46 PM	DeRudio watches as Indians continuing harrassing Reno's command at the crossing. Some of the warriors stop and begin pointing upriver. DeRudio looks and sees troops approaching the ford where Reno crossed. He assumes it is Benteen. As the troops get closer to the ford they turn and disappear over a bluff.			188
1:49 PM	2:46 PM	Varnum reaches the hilltop.			201
1:53 PM	2:50 PM	SGT Culbertson reaches the hilltop.			204

L. Reno's Retreat to Benteen's Arrival (cont.)

1:53 PM	2:50 PM	Crazy Horse, now alerted to more troops mounting the bluffs and hearing that there are additional troops farther downstream, begins to gather his warriors to head off Custer's command.			206
2:00 PM	2:57 PM	82 minutes from the time Reno dismounted/112 minutes from the Custer — Reno separation—Benteen arrives on Reno Hill.	8 MPH from meeting the Crows; 7.7 MPH, from the morass	6.3 miles from the morass	211
2:03 PM	3:00 PM	Benteen's troops begin arriving on Reno Hill.			213
2:05 PM	3:02 PM	Indians still in full force in valley. Estimates ranged from 600 to 1,000 or more.			214
2:06 PM	3:03 PM	PVT Davern reaches the hilltop.			215
2:08 PM	3:05 PM	Last of Benteen's command reaches Reno Hill.			216
2:08 PM	3:05 PM	Godfrey estimates 600 to 700 Indians in the valley with more arriving. In addition, he spots quite a number in the ravines on the east side of the LBH. He also sees dust from ther packs and estimates they are some 3 to 4 miles away. In reality, the packs are within 1/2 mile of the lone tepee. Edgerly estimated 800 — 1,000. Benteen used a figure of 900.			218

M. Boston Custer; 12:04 p.m.–2:42 p.m.

Local Sun Time	Command's Watch Time	Event	Speed	Distance Traveled	Notes
11:07 AM	12:04 PM	Boston Custer turns back toward the packs to change horses.	(6 MPH)	(4/10 of a mile)	55
11:11 AM	12:08 PM	Boston Custer reaches the packs, stops, and speaks briefly with CPT McDougall.		4/10 of a mile	56
11:15 AM	12:12 PM	Regiment resumes march, Custer down the creek's right bank, Reno down the left bank.	(@ 10 MPH)		59
11:21 PM	12:18 PM	After changing horses and the packs begin to move, Boston Custer heads for the front of the column, now some distance away and moving more rapidly.	6 MPH		56
12:53 PM	1:50 PM	Boston Custer, beginning to pick up speed, approaches the morass and sees Benteen's command.	5.3 MPH — 7 MPH	8 1/8 miles from east of divide	140
12:53 PM	1:50 PM	Benteen's column reaches the confluence of No-Name Creek and Reno Creek. The packs are seen about one mile up Reno Creek. A single rider—Boston Custer—is seen coming toward them.			141
12:54 PM	1:51 PM	Now at a full gallop, Boston Custer passes Benteen's battalion, waving as he goes by.	12 MPH		144
1:12 PM	2:09 PM	Boston Custer passes the lone tepee.	12 MPH	3½ miles from passing Benteen	64
1:18 PM	2:15 PM	Boston Custer reaches Middle Knoll; turns to the right on Custer's shod trail.	12 MPH	1 mile ± from lone tepee	64
1:19 PM	2:16 PM	Boston Custer reaches North Fork; pauses only briefly to let his horse gulp some water.	12 MPH	335 yards	64
1:22 PM	2:19 PM	Boston Custer meets Martini. They pause for only seconds, Boston pointing the way to Martini and Martini telling Boston where George Custer is. Boston points out Martini's wounded horse.	Martini: 5 MPH; Boston Custer: 13 MPH	Martini: ¾ mile; Boston Custer: ½ mile	169
1:26 PM	2:23 PM	Reno begins retreat.			177
1:27 PM	2:24 PM	Boston Custer is now passing over Reno Hill.	13 MPH	1 mile from Martini meeting	64
1:29 PM	2:26 PM	Boston Custer is passing over 3,411; he looks into the valley briefly and sees Reno's command galloping from the timber, Indians in pursuit.	13 MPH	4/10 of a mile from mid-point of Reno Hill	64
1:35 PM	2:32 PM	Riding hard down MTC, Custer begins to move up the slopes to Luce Ridge.	10 MPH	9/10 mile (2+ miles, total, from top of Cedar Coulee)	185
1:38 PM	2:35 PM	Boston Custer turns into Medicine Tail Coulee. He increases his speed.	10 MPH, average	1¾ miles from Reno Hill	64
1:45 PM	2:42 PM	Boston Custer reaches the top of Luce Ridge. He informs his brothers of all he has seen, including the fact that Benteen is on the main trail.	12 MPH	1.4 miles	64

N. Messengers; 12:13 p.m.–2:41 p.m.

Local Sun Time	Command's Watch Time	Event	Speed	Distance Traveled	Notes
11:16 AM	12:13 PM	After traveling some 250 — 300 yards, descending into the Reno Creek valley from the heights of the divide, Custer realizes Benteen will not be able to see into the LBH valley from the first line of ridges. He orders CTMP Voss to ride to Benteen and tell him to continue on to the next ridge.	10 MPH, increasing to 12 MPH, varying down to 6 MPH	.15 miles from separation	60
11:16 AM	12:13 PM	CTMP Voss leaves the column and heads to Benteen.	(7 MPH)	.15 miles from divide separations	61
11:21 AM	12:18 PM	CTMP Voss reaches Benteen with Custer's message: "[I]f I found nothing before reaching the first line of bluffs, to go on to the second line with the same instructions" [Benteen].	7 — 8 MPH	Voss: 6/10 mile from Custer; Benteen: ½ mile from separation	63
11:21 AM	12:18 PM	Custer's column is advancing between two small knolls and approaching the waters of Reno Creek. He slows to a trot so Voss can catch up, but still concerned that his orders to Benteen are not specific enough, Custer dispatches SGM Sharrow with addition instructions.	10 MPH down to 6 MPH	.83 miles from Voss separation; .97 miles from divide separation	60
11:21 AM	12:18 PM	SGM Sharrow leaves the column and heads to Benteen.	(8 MPH — 10 MPH)	.97 miles from divide separations	64
11:22 AM	12:19 PM	Voss turns from Benteen and heads back to main column.	12 MPH		60
11:27 AM	12:24 PM	Custer's column is moving along Reno Creek as CTMP Voss re-joins it.	6 MPH	1.43 miles from divide separation	64
11:27 AM	12:24 PM	Voss reaches the head of Custer's column on the main trail along Reno Creek.	10 — 12 MPH	1 mile	64
11:29 AM	12:26 PM	SGM Sharrow reaches Benteen with Custer's additional instructions: "[I]f I saw nothing from the second line of bluffs, to go on into the valley, and if there was nothing in the valley, to go on to the next valley." "[I]f from the furthest line of bluffs which we then saw, I could not see the valley—no particular valley specified—to keep on until I came to a valley (or perhaps the valley)…to pitch into…."	Sharrow: 10 MPH; Benteen: 5 — 6 MPH	Sharrow: 1.2 miles; Benteen: 1.95 miles from divide separation	67
11:30 AM	12:27 PM	Sharrow starts back for the main column.	10 — 12 MPH		60
11:41 AM	12:38 PM	Sharrow reaches Reno Creek. The tail-end of Custer's column can be seen far up ahead. Sharrow increases his speed.	12 MPH, increasing to 14 MPH along Reno Creek	1.9 miles from meeting Benteen (3.14 miles from divide separations)	64
11:55 AM	12:52 PM	SGM Sharrow reaches No-Name Creek.	15 MPH	3.4 miles since reaching Reno Creek	64
12:01 PM	12:58 PM	SGM Sharrow catches the main column. Custer sends him ahead immediately to tell LT Hare to report back if he saw any Indians. Before Hare reached the lone tepee SGM Sharrow overtook him in a great rush and told Hare to send back word as soon as he saw Indians. Custer was obviously very anxious.	15 MPH	1.52 miles from No — Name Creek.	72
12:22 PM	1:19 PM	As Custer is passing alongside Middle Knoll, Cooke intercepts him and informs him of Gerard's report. They are ¾ mile from the LBH.	Cooke: 10 MPH; Custer: 5 — 6 MPH	Cooke: 850 yards from previous knoll; Custer: 1 ± mile from separation from Reno	100
12:22 PM	1:19 PM	Custer hears Cooke's report and makes the fatal decision to try to get to the northern end of the village. He swings his command to the right and orders a gallop.	@ 9 — 10 MPH		101
12:50 PM	1:47 PM	It is not unreasonable to assume that if SGT Daniel Kanipe was sent back with a message for CPT McDougall and the packs, he would have been sent about this time, from approximately this location: the southwestern shoulder of Sharpshooters' Ridge.			134

N. Messengers (cont.)

12:51 PM	1:48 PM	Custer arrives at 3,411. His troops slow even more and head for the depression of Cedar Coulee.			135
1:03 PM	2:00 PM	Custer arrives at top of Cedar Coulee; instructs Cooke to send messenger.	6 MPH	675 yards from "3,411" (4/10 of a mile)	154
1:04 PM	2:01 PM	Cooke writes note; hands it to Martini. He was instructed to bring it to Benteen and also told to come back to the command if there was no danger, otherwise he was to stay with his company: "Benteen, Come on. Big village. Be quick. Bring packs. W. W. Cooke. P. S., Bring pacs [sic]."			156
1:05 PM	2:02 PM	Martini heads back.			156
1:09 PM	2:06 PM	Martini reaches 3,411; sees Reno's troops fighting on the skirmish line in the valley. He continues on without pausing.	Now, 6 — 7 MPH	675 yards from near the head of Cedar Coulee	158
1:10 PM	2:07 PM	Kanipe, walking slowly, is seen by the Rees who are still milling around the hilltops with the captured Sioux ponies.	3 MPH	1 mile	159
1:13 PM	2:10 PM	Martini, in the vicinity of Reno Hill, sees stragglers from C Company. He does not stop but begins to slow. His horse has been wounded, but he is unaware of it.	6 MPH down to 5 MPH		169
1:22 PM	2:19 PM	Boston Custer meets Martini. They pause for only seconds, Boston pointing the way to Martini and Martini telling Boston where George Custer is. Boston points out Martini's wounded horse.	Martini: 5 MPH; Boston Custer: 13 MPH	Martini: ½ mile; Boston Custer: ¾ mile	169
1:38 PM	2:35 PM	Benteen reaches the lone tepee. Slows down a bit and rides around the burning structure. He does not stop and continues on, increasing his speed.	7.5 MPH	3.4 miles from the morass	187
1:41 PM	2:38 PM	The first of Reno's troops begin reaching the hilltop.	Varying speeds, from 13+ MPH down to a crawl	Variously, 1.14 — 1.38 miles	189
1:42 PM	2:39 PM	Kanipe reaches Benteen.	3 MPH	2.6 miles	191
1:42 PM	2:39 PM	SGT Kanipe reins up next to Benteen, but again, Benteen does not halt and directs Kanipe to the rear in the direction of the pack train.	Benteen: 5 MPH, up to 8 MPH	(¾ mile west of the lone tepee)	192
1:44 PM	2:41 PM	Martini reaches Benteen in the "flats," less than one mile from the Little Big Horn.	Down to a 4.2 MPH, average	2.7 miles from just below the head of Cedar Coulee	196
1:44 PM	2:41 PM	Benteen halts momentarily to read the message from Cooke. He shows it to Tom Weir and Win Edgerly who have caught up. Benteen now continues toward the river.	8 MPH	(1/3 mile from meeting Kanipe)	197

O. Benteen: Reno Creek to Reno Hill; 1:50 p.m.–3:05 p.m.

Local Sun Time	Command's Watch Time	Event	Speed	Distance Traveled	Notes
12:53 PM	1:50 PM	Benteen's column reaches the confluence of No-Name Creek and Reno Creek. The packs are seen about one mile up Reno Creek. A single rider—Boston Custer—is seen coming toward them.	Benteen's scout before turning: 4.2 MPH	2.9 miles from turn; 7.1 miles, total	141
12:53 PM	1:50 PM	The head of the pack train reaches a point about 1 mile above No-Name Creek.	4.01 MPH	6.25 miles from the divide	142
12:54 PM	1:51 PM	Now at a full gallop, Boston Custer passes Benteen's battalion, waving as he goes by.	12 MPH		144
12:57 PM	1:54 PM	Benteen's battalion begins arriving at the morass.	6 MPH	¼ to ½ of a mile from the turn	149
12:57 PM (to 1:11 PM)	1:54 PM (to 2:08 PM)	Benteen orders a halt to begin watering his horses.			149
12:59 PM	1:56 PM	The last of Benteen's battaltion arrives at the morass.	7 MPH	725 feet from the head of the column	151
1:10 PM	2:07 PM	CPT Weir, impatient at the long watering delay, moves his D Company forward without Benteen's permission. Godfrey said, "Weir became a little impatient at the delay of watering and started off with his troop, taking the advance, whereas his place in column was second. The rest of the battalion moved out very soon afterward and soon caught up with him."	@ 7 MPH		162
1:11 PM	2:08 PM	Benteen's column begins leaving the morass.	@ 7 — 9 MPH to start, catching up with Weir		163
1:13 PM	2:10 PM	Lead mules of the packs begin reaching the morass. Mathey orders the men to push on without stopping.	3.8 MPH	1.25 miles additional	166
1:38 PM	2:35 PM	Benteen reaches the lone tepee. Slows down a bit and rides around the burning structure. He stops momentarily and peers in, then continues on, increasing his speed.	7.5 MPH	3.4 miles from the morass	187
1:42 PM	2:39 PM	Kanipe reaches Benteen.	3 MPH	2.6 miles	191
1:42 PM	2:39 PM	SGT Kanipe reins up next to Benteen, but again, Benteen does not halt and directs Kanipe to the rear in the direction of the pack train.	Benteen: 5 MPH, up to 8 MPH	(½ mile west of the lone tepee)	192
1:43 PM	2:40 PM	Hearing occasional firing only, LT Godfrey concluded the fight was over and they would have little to do but congratulate the others and help destroy the plunder. As the firing became more distinct, however, the command began to increase its speed.	6 MPH, moving up to 7 and then 8 MPH		195
1:44 PM	2:41 PM	Martini reaches Benteen in the "flats," less than one mile from the LBH.	Down to a 4.2 MPH, average	2.7 miles from just below the head of Cedar Coulee	196
1:44 PM	2:41 PM	Benteen halts momentarily to read the message from Cooke. He shows it to Tom Weir and Win Edgerly who have caught up. Benteen now continues toward the river.	8 MPH	.83 miles west of the lone tepee (1/3 mile from meeting Kanipe)	197
1:51 PM	2:48 PM	Benteen reaches the Little Big Horn and has now seen friendly Indians on the bluffs just north of Reno Creek. These scouts direct him toward Reno Hill. It appears they were the young Crow, Curley, and the Ree, Black Fox, and may also have been joined by a couple more Rees with stolen ponies.	7 MPH	1,525 yards from meeting Martini	202

O. Benteen: Reno Creek to Reno Hill (cont.)

1:52 PM	2:49 PM	Several Rees take about 15 horses from the ravine and head down the hills toward Reno Creek. In all likelihood these are, Billy Cross, Bull, Red Bear, Soldier, Stab, Strikes Two, White Eagle, Red Star, Red Wolf, and Strikes the Lodge. They run into both Benteen's command and the pack train. After the packs turned toward the hills, trailing Sioux retrieved their horses and the Rees returned to the hilltop.	(@ 3 — 5 MPH)		190
1:55 PM	2:52 PM	As Benteen's command begins to mount the bluffs and follow their commander, they are passed by several Indian scouts—not sure if they were Crow or Ree—driving some Sioux ponies, and the scouts yelled, "Soldiers," pointing to the hilltop to the right.			207
2:00 PM	2:57 PM	82 minutes from the time Reno dismounted/112 minutes from the Custer — Reno separation—Benteen arrives on Reno Hill.	8 MPH from meeting the Crows; 7.7 MPH, from the morass	6.3 miles from the morass	211
2:03 PM	3:00 PM	Benteen's troops begin arriving on Reno Hill.			213
2:08 PM	3:05 PM	Last of Benteen's command reaches Reno Hill.			216

P. The Pack Train; 10:40 a.m.–4:17 p.m.

Local Sun Time	Command's Watch Time	Event	Speed	Distance Traveled	Notes
9:43 AM — 9:58 AM	10:40 AM — 10:55 AM	Assignments are made and Tom McDougall and B Company are assigned to accompany the pack train, "to take charge of the pack train and act as rear guard." This was "on the divide between the Rosebud and the Little Big Horn."			43
10:53 AM — 11:03 AM	11:50 AM — Noon	Regiment begins crossing the divide just before noon. Main column—in fours and led by H Company—is about ¼ mile long.	Trot: @ 6 MPH		52
11:07 AM	12:04 PM	Boston Custer turns back toward the packs to change horses.	(6 MPH)	(4/10 of a mile)	55
11:11 AM	12:08 PM	Boston Custer reaches the packs, stops, and speaks briefly with CPT McDougall.		4/10 of a mile	56
11:11 AM	12:08 PM	The pack train, driven by LT Mathey and CPT McDougall, having crested the divide, pauses right behind the main column.	Varying		57
11:21 AM	12:18 PM	McDougall and the packs begin to move.			57
12:53 PM	1:50 PM	The head of the pack train reaches a point about 1 mile above No-Name Creek.	4.01 MPH	6.25 miles from the divide	142
1:13 PM	2:10 PM	Lead mules of the packs begin reaching the morass. Mathey orders the men to push on without stopping.	3.8 MPH	1.25 miles additional	166
1:15 PM	2:12 PM	McDougall arrives at the morass as the pack mules continue to be driven on. Five or six of the mules are stuck, however, and McDougall orders his men to extricate them.	3.95 MPH	7.5 miles from the divide	57
1:30 PM	2:27 PM	McDougall's troops get the last of the stuck mules out of the morass and push them on.	6 to 8 MPH		57
1:31 PM	2:28 PM	Lead elements of the pack train begin reaching the opening to the "flats."	3.5 MPH	1 to 1 1/3 miles from the morass	182
1:42 PM	2:39 PM	According to Kanipe, the packs would now be about two miles east of Benteen's command. This would put them some 3.2 miles east of the LBH River. Not a bad guess by Kanipe.			191
1:48 PM	2:45 PM	Mathey continues to drive the pack train and is now less than 1½ miles east of the lone/burning tepee, fairly well confirming Kanipe's observation.	3.5 MPH	> 2 miles from the morass	199
1:48 PM	2:45 PM	McDougall with the recalcitrant mules catches up to the rear of the main body of the train, which is continuing to string out further.	6 to 8 MPH	< 2 miles from the morass	200
2:00 PM	2:57 PM	Benteen arrives on Reno Hill.			211
2:12 PM	3:09 PM	Lead mules of the pack train begin arriving in the vicinity of the lone tepee and Gerard's Knoll. Mathey slows down so the train can close up. McDougall rides up to meet him. The tepee was smoldering and McDougall stops to peer inside where he sees three dead Indians.	3.5 MPH down to 2 to 3 MPH	1.4 miles from last report; 3.4 miles from morass	225
2:17 PM	3:14 PM	Mathey starts the train moving again.	3 to 4 MPH		231
2:21 PM	3:18 PM	McDougall and Mathey watch as 8 to 10 Rees drive about 15 captured Sioux ponies past them. One of them—a half-breed, possibly Billy Cross—tells Mathey there are too many Sioux to fight.		¼ of a mile west of the burning tepee	236

P. The Pack Train (cont.)

2:21 PM	3:18 PM	LT Hare is sent to get ammo mules from the pack train. LT Godfrey lends Hare his horse.			238
2:21 PM	3:18 PM	Eight to ten Rees drive about 15 stolen Sioux ponies along Reno Creek and meet the pack train west of the lone tepee. One of them was the half-breed, Billy Cross. It appears some of the others were the Ree stragglers, Bull, Red Bear, Soldier, Stab, Strikes Two, and White Eagle, along with Red Star, Red Wolf, and Strikes the Lodge. After the packs turned toward the hills, trailing Sioux retrieved their horses and the Rees returned to the hilltop. These are the same scouts who passed Benteen on his way to Reno Hill.	5 MPH	2 miles from picking up the horses in the ravine	237
2:21 PM	3:18 PM	Black Fox—seen with a white handkerchief tied around his head—leaves the Rees and joins the pack train.			230
2:26 PM	3:23 PM	Company B, now in advance of the packs, meets a Crow scout—in all likelihood, Curley—who explains in sign - language that "much soldiers down."			240
2:32 PM	3:29 PM	Mathey and the lead mules are in the Middle Knoll area when LT Hare approaches. Mathey halts the train.	3.5 MPH	1 ± mile from area of Gerard's Knoll	244
2:33 PM	3:30 PM	LT Hare reaches the packs and Mathey cuts out two ammo mules.	10 MPH	2 miles from Reno Hill	245
2:34 PM	3:31 PM	Mathey—listening to Hare—orders two ammo mules cut out of the train to follow Hare.			244
2:35 PM	3:32 PM	Hare begins the trip back to Reno Hill.	(10 MPH)		245
2:35 PM	3:32 PM	The ammo mules follow right behind Hare, but at a slower pace.	(7 MPH)		244
2:35 PM	3:32 PM	Mathey starts the pack train forward, following Hare's lead up the bluffs.	3.5 to 4 MPH		247
2:35 PM	3:32 PM	Pistols drawn, CPT McDougall places one platoon of B Company behind the pack train, and one platoon ahead, and moves forward toward the men on the hilltop.	8 MPH		248
2:48 PM	3:45 PM	Hare reaches Reno Hill. The ammo mules are a couple hundred yards behind him.		2 miles	261
2:51 PM	3:48 PM	CPT McDougall and one platoon of his B Company approach and begin arriving at Reno Hill.	8 MPH	2 miles	248
2:55 PM	3:52 PM	Lead elements of the pack train are less than 1 mile from Reno Hill.	4 — 6 MPH		64
2:58 PM — 3:20 PM	3:55 PM — 4:17 PM	Pack train begins arriving on Reno Hill. Benteen's timing would have put the arrival of the first mules at about 4:15 PM.	2 2/3 to 4 MPH (3.51 MPH from divide crossing)	2 miles from meeting Hare; 12.7 miles from divide crossing	281
3:20 PM	4:17 PM	The last of the pack train arrives on Reno Hill.			290

Q. Benteen's Arrival to the Arrival of the Packs; 2:57 p.m.–4:17 p.m.

Local Sun Time	Command's Watch Time	Event	Speed	Distance Traveled	Notes
2:00 PM	2:57 PM	82 minutes from the time Reno dismounted/112 minutes from the Custer — Reno separation—Benteen arrives on Reno Hill.	8 MPH from meeting the Crows; 7.7 MPH, from the morass	6.3 miles from the morass	211
2:03 PM	3:00 PM	Benteen's troops begin arriving on Reno Hill.			213
2:05 PM	3:02 PM	Indians still in full force in valley. Estimates ranged from 600 to 1,000 or more.			215
2:06 PM	3:03 PM	PVT Davern reaches the hilltop.			215
2:08 PM	3:05 PM	Last of Benteen's command reaches Reno Hill.			216
2:08 PM	3:05 PM	Benteen directs his companies to form a dismounted skirmish line along the bluffs.			217
2:08 PM	3:05 PM	Godfrey estimates 600 to 700 Indians in the valley with more arriving. In addition, he spots quite a number in the ravines on the east side of the LBH. He also sees dust from ther packs and estimates they are some 3 to 4 miles away. In reality, the packs are within 1/2 mile of the lone tepee. Edgerly estimated 800 — 1,000. Benteen used a figure of 900.			218
2:10 PM	3:07 PM	On Reno Hill, heavy or volley firing is heard from downstream. Loud firing continues for several minutes.			222
2:10 PM	3:07 PM	Herendeen, still in Reno's timber, hears heavy firing from downstream. It lasted about an hour.			223
2:13 PM	3:10 PM	As Benteen orders his men to consolidate the hilltop and set up a skirmish line, LT Edgerly sees they are still coming under some fire from Indians hidden on the hilltops and behind rocks and bushes. He also sees a number of Reno's wounded. Benteen orders the Indians to be driven away.			227
2:15 PM	3:12 PM	A number of troops from Benteen's battalion head for the marauding Indians atop the hills to drive them away.			229
2:18 PM	3:15 PM	CPT Weir discusses the situation and the firing heard downstream with his lieutenant, Win Edgerly. Edgerly assures him he would follow if Weir were to head north.			232
2:20 PM	3:17 PM	Edgerly discusses the situation with the D Company first sergeant, 1SG Michael Martin. They agree that the command should go toward the sound of the firing.			229
2:20 PM	3:17 PM	More Indians begin leaving the valley and heading downstream.			234
2:20 PM	3:17 PM	CPT Weir decides to discuss the situation with MAJ Reno.			235
2:21 PM	3:18 PM	LT Hare is sent to get ammo mules from the pack train. LT Godfrey lends Hare his horse.	10 MPH		238
2:23 PM	3:20 PM	Benteen's troops who had chased the Indians from the hilltop return and stand-to-horse.			229

Q. Benteen's Arrival to the Arrival of the Packs (cont.)

2:26 PM — 2:30 PM	3:23 PM — 3:27 PM	CPT Weir is with MAJ Reno and CPT Benteen. Whether or not Weir seeks permission to move downstream has never been satisfactorily established, but he leaves the meeting and goes to get his striker. Edgerly claimed, "He told me later that he hadn't spoken to Reno or Benteen, but rode out on the bluff hoping to see something of Custer's command." PVT Fox heard Weir speaking with Reno just before Weir moved out from Reno Hill. "Weir remarked, 'Custer must be around here somewhere and we ought to go to him.' Reno said 'We are surrounded by Indians and we ought to remain here.' Weir said, 'Well if no one else goes to Custer, I will go.' Reno replied, 'No you can not go. For if you try to do it you will get killed and your Company with you.'" Moylan and Benteen overheard this conversation "and talked as though to discourage him."			241
2:30 PM	3:27 PM	Weir turns and leaves, and taking his striker only with him, starts to head downstream.			242
2:30 PM	3:27 PM	At Weir turns and leaves, Reno takes SGT Culbertson and several men and heads down the bluffs to find LT Hodgson's body.			243
2:38 PM	3:35 PM	CPT Tom Weir takes his orderly and starts downstream.	6 MPH		250
2:40 PM	3:37 PM	More and more Indians involved in the valley fighting begin to leave, heading downstream to the sound of the volley firing.	Various speeds		251
2:41 PM	3:38 PM	The three Crows arrive amidst the confusion on Reno Hill.	6 MPH	1¼ miles after turning from Weir Peaks	252
2:43 PM	3:40 PM	Edgerly begins moving D Company downstream.	6 MPH		250
2:46 PM	3:43 PM	Hare is approaching Reno Hill after cutting out a couple of ammo mules. He sees Edgerly and Company D heading downstream.	10 MPH		255
2:46 PM	3:43 PM	The three Crow scouts meet up with the Rees, Red Bear and White Cloud, on Reno Hill, all of them milling around the pack mules.			257
2:47 PM	3:44 PM	Keogh sends C Company into Calhoun Coulee to relieve pressure from Indians infiltrating up the coulee.			258
2:47 PM	3:44 PM	This was the beginning of the general firing heard by Fred Gerard after the "scattering" shots many described as volleys.			259
2:48 PM	3:45 PM	Hare reaches Reno Hill. The ammo mules are a couple hundred yards behind him.		2 miles	261
2:48 PM	3:45 PM	Most of the Indians are now out of the valley, only about 100 — 150 remaining on both sides of the river.			262
2:51 PM	3:48 PM	The two ammo mules reach Reno Hill and one of them is stripped immediately, the boxes broken into and ammo distributed.	5 — 7 MPH	2 miles	265
2:51 PM	3:48 PM	CPT McDougall and one platoon of his B Company approach and begin arriving at Reno Hill.	8 MPH	2 miles	248
2:51 PM	3:48 PM	More stragglers from Reno's command reach the hilltop.			266
2:52 PM	3:49 PM	CPT Weir reaches Weir Peaks and heads up its slope.	6 MPH	1½ miles	268
2:53 PM	3:50 PM	Edgerly and D Company reach the head of Cedar Coulee and begin descending it.	6 MPH slowing to 4 MPH	9/10 mile	269

Q. Benteen's Arrival to the Arrival of the Packs (cont.)

2:53 PM	3:50 PM	Reno returns from searching for Hodgson's body. He sees D Company moving north and orders Hare to tell Weir to try to make contact with Custer. At the same time, Reno orders Varnum to take the shovels from the ammo mules and some men and go down the bluffs to bury Hodgson.			270
2:54 PM	3:51 PM	CPT Weir reaches the top of the northern-most peak.			271
2:55 PM	3:52 PM	LT Hare leaves for Weir Point to tell CPT Weir to try to contact Custer.	6 MPH		272
2:55 PM	3:52 PM	Lead elements of the main pack train are less than 1 mile from Reno Hill.	4 — 5 MPH		64
2:57 PM	3:54 PM	Packs seen several hundred yards off; Reno orders the command to begin moving north.			274
2:58 PM — 3:20 PM	3:55 PM — 4:17 PM	Pack train begins arriving on Reno Hill. Benteen's timing would have put the arrival of the first mules at about 4:15 PM.	2 2/3 to 4 MPH	2 miles from meeting Hare	281
3:00 PM	3:57 PM	Varnum, securing spades from the packs, heads down the bluffs to bury Hodgson.			276
3:00 PM	3:57 PM	LT Edgerly and D Company, using Cedar Coulee, reach the east side of Weir Point.	3 MPH	3/10 additional miles	268
3:03 PM	4:00 PM	The general move toward Weir Peaks begins, Benteen's command leading out. Godfrey first claimed he was 3rd in line, the told Camp the order of march was M, K, H; Wallace said H, then K led. Edgerly said H, K, and M.	5 — 7 MPH		280
3:03 PM	4:00 PM	As he arrives on Reno Hill, Tom McDougall sees the tail-end of Edgerly's troops in Cedar Coulee.			282
3:05 PM	4:02 PM	D Company reaches its farthest point in advance of Weir Peaks. Edgerly stops his troops and sees CPT Weir motioning for him to return and come to the high ground. He begins turning his troops toward Weir.	3 to 4 MPH	1.6 miles, total, from Reno Hill	283
3:12 PM	4:09 PM	An orderly from Reno reaches Varnum mid-way down the bluffs and tells him to return to the command. They are moving downstream.	A cautious crawl		285
3:12 PM	4:09 PM	Hare, climbing the steep peaks, reaches CPT Weir and tells him of Reno's request that he try to contact Custer.	5 — 6 MPH	1½ + miles	286
3:17 PM	4:14 PM	LT Edgerly and D Company have moved back up Cedar Coulee and climbed the slopes of the Weir loaf to get in position.	5 MPH	1 mile	287
3:17 PM	4:14 PM	Benteen, French, and Godfrey approach Weir Point, the command stretched out behind them.	Now, 4 MPH	1½ miles	288
3:18 PM	4:15 PM	Edgerly sees Benteen, French, and Godfrey nearing Weir Point.			288
3:18 PM — 3:21 PM	4:15 PM — 4:18 PM	Edgerly spreads out his troops along the north side of the "sugarloaf" of Weir Point.			289
3:20 PM	4:17 PM	The last of the pack train arrives on Reno Hill.			290

R. The Approach to 3,411 and Ford B; 1:38 p.m.–3:07 p.m.

Local Sun Time	Command's Watch Time	Event	Speed	Distance Traveled	Notes
12:41 PM	1:38 PM	Custer's command is approaching Reno Hill after picking up speed as the terrain evened out.	9 MPH	1+ miles from watering	113
12:41 PM	1:38 PM	Custer's scouts—Boyer, the four Crows (Goes Ahead, Hairy Moccasin, White Man Runs Him, and Curley), and it appears the Ree, Black Fox, as well—riding slightly ahead of Custer, are crossing over Reno Hill and beginning to slow as they swing left and approach the edge of the bluffs.	10 — 12 MPH, slowing to 7 — 8 MPH	1½ miles from watering	119
12:44 PM	1:41 PM	PVT Peter Thompson of C Company drops out of formation as his horse begins to break down. He is on the northern side of Reno Hill. The rest of the command passes him by.			124
12:44 PM	1:41 PM	As Thompson dismounts to tend to his horse, the F Company advance scouts pass him by.	10 MPH		125
12:45 PM	1:42 PM	Varnum sees Gray Horse Troop on bluffs.		Sighted 500 yards downstream from Reno Hill	126
12:47 PM	1:44 PM	Custer cautions his excited troops as they move toward the head of Cedar Coulee. The command begins to slow its pace considerably. "Hold your horses in, boys, there are plenty of them down there for us all."	7 — 8 MPH	1 + miles	128
12:49 PM	1:46 PM	The scouts, now mingling around Custer and watching Reno's command, are told by Custer to proceed to the high ground north—Weir Peaks. Boyer, Goes Ahead, White Man Runs Him, and Hairy Moccasin turn and head toward Weir.			130
12:50 PM	1:47 PM	It is not unreasonable to assume that if SGT Daniel Kanipe was sent back with a message for CPT McDougall and the packs, he would have been sent about this time, from approximately this location: the southwestern shoulder of Sharpshooters' Ridge.			134
12:51 PM	1:48 PM	Custer arrives at 3,411. His troops slow even more and head for the depression of Cedar Coulee.			135
12:51 PM — 12:59 PM	1:48 PM — 1:56 PM	Custer and two others—in all likelihood, LT Cooke and CPT Tom Custer—atop elevation point 3,411, watch the action in the valley below.			136
12:55 PM	1:52 PM	Curley and Black Fox mingle just north of Custer as he looks over the valley.			146
12:56 PM	1:53 PM	Boyer and the three Crows—Goes Ahead, Hairy Moccasin, and White Man Runs Him—arrive at Weir Peaks.	7 — 8 MPH	¾ of a mile (1,350 yards)	147
12:56 PM	1:53 PM	DeRudio sees Custer at 3,411.			148
12:57 PM	1:54 PM	Benteen's battalion begins arriving at the morass.			149
12:59 PM	1:56 PM	Custer leaves 3,411.			152
1:03 PM	2:00 PM	Custer arrives at top of Cedar Coulee; instructs Cooke to send messenger.	6 MPH	675 yards from "3,411" (4/10 of a mile)	154
1:03 PM	2:00 PM	Curley and Black Fox turn to head back down to Reno Creek.	(6 MPH)		155
1:04 PM	2:01 PM	Cooke writes note; hands it to Martini. He was instructed to bring it to Benteen and also told to come back to the command if there was no danger, otherwise he was to stay with his company: "Benteen, Come on. Big village. Be quick. Bring packs. W. W. Cooke. P. S., Bring pacs [sic]."			156

R. The Approach to 3,411 and Ford B (cont.)

1:05 PM	2:02 PM	Martini heads back.			156
1:08 PM	2:05 PM	Custer reaches the head of his column; begins move down Cedar Coulee. He slows because of the terrain and the fact he wants to keep his command closed up for fear of marauding Indians.	@ 2½ to 4 MPH		64
1:08 PM (12:56 PM — 1:15 PM)	2:05 PM (1:53 PM — 2:12 PM)	The three Crows continue to watch the fighting in the valley.			157
1:10 PM	2:07 PM	Boyer, seeing Custer's command moving down Cedar Coulee, releases the three Crow scouts and moves off Weir Point, heading for the front of Custer's column in the coulee.			161
1:13 PM	2:10 PM	Gall and Iron Cedar head off to swim the LBH and climb the bluffs to watch for the soldiers on the east bank.			168
1:15 PM	2:12 PM	The three Crow scouts—Goes Ahead, White Man Runs Him, and Hairy Moccasin—begin heading north along the bluffs.	4 MPH — 6 MPH, stopping along the way		173
1:26 PM	2:23 PM	Reno begins retreat.			177
1:28 PM	2:25 PM	After tough going down Cedar Coulee and its slopes, Custer reaches Medicine Tail Coulee and heads toward the LBH River and the village.	3 + MPH average, increasing to 8, then 10 MPH	1+ mile	180
1:29 PM	2:26 PM	Gall and Iron Cedar watch as Custer turns into MTC.			181
1:35 PM	2:32 PM	Riding hard down MTC, Custer begins to move up the slopes to Luce Ridge.	10 MPH	9/10 mile (2+ miles, total, from top of Cedar Coulee)	185
1:35 PM	2:32 PM	The three Crows—Goes Ahead, Hairy Moccasin, and White Man Runs Him—reach the far end of the bluffs overlooking Ford B.	4 MPH average, stopping and starting	1 1/3 miles from Weir Peaks	186
1:35 PM — 2:13 PM	2:32 PM — 3:10 PM	The three Crows watch as Custer's command mounts the ridges to the north and east, then the Crows fire into the Indian village, their shots falling in the Sans Arc and Minneconjou camps.	Halted on the bluffs		186
1:41 PM	2:38 PM	Reno's troops begin reaching the hilltop.			189
1:42 PM	2:39 PM	Custer reaches the top of Luce Ridge.	6 MPH	½ mile	193
1:42 PM — 1:57 PM	2:39 PM — 2:54 PM	Gall rallies some warriors and begins to move toward Ford B. They are all mounted.	(8 MPH)	Various	194
1:45 PM	2:42 PM	Boston Custer reaches the top of Luce Ridge. He informs his brothers of all he has seen, including the fact that Benteen is on the main trail.	12 MPH	1.4 miles	64
1:45 PM — 1:52 PM	2:42 PM — 2:49 PM	Custer, Keogh, and Yates assess Boston Custer's information about Benteen. Custer decides he has between 1½ – 1¾ hours before Benteen arrives, so he needs to hurry his reconnaissance and position himself where he can meet Benteen.			64
1:52 PM	2:49 PM	After viewing the LBH valley and the hills to the north, Custer drops off Keogh with instructions to deploy his battalion and protect Custer's rear, then heads toward the river with HQ and Yates' battalion.	@ 6 MPH moving to 8 MPH		203
1:53 PM	2:50 PM	Algernon Smith and Company E break off and head into MTC.	8 MPH		205
1:56 PM	2:53 PM	Cheyenne warriors American Horse and Brave Wolf, having left the Reno fighting, reach the Ford B area of the Cheyenne village.	8 — 10 MPH	1½ miles	208

R. The Approach to 3,411 and Ford B (cont.)

1:58 PM	2:55 PM	Custer and Yates arrive at the bluff overlooking Ford B.	8 MPH	6/10 mile	210
2:01 PM	2:58 PM	LT Algernon Smith arrives at Ford B and proceeds to the river's edge, deploying his troops and dismounting some of his men. He sets up a screening force covering the troops on the ridge above him. There is also some evidence from Indian interviews that a soldier wearing buckskin was wounded at this time. That could have been Smith.	8 MPH	1 mile	212
2:08 PM	3:05 PM	His rear protected by Smith's Gray Horse Troop at the ford, Custer moves across "Custer's Bluff" and into Deep Coulee, then the "flats" beyond, heading for the northern ridgeline later named Finley — Finckle Ridge.	8 MPH		219
2:09 PM	3:06 PM	Trailed by sharp, sniping fire, Smith—his company fully remounted—begins moving away from Ford B. He heads for the Finley Ridge area and Calhoun Hill. Yates protects his rear.	8 MPH		220
2:10 PM	3:07 PM	Keogh spots Indians coming down North MTC—in all likelihood Wolf Tooth and Big Foot—plus Indians along West Coulee's ridges, and orders his troops to open fire.			221

S. Ford B to Calhoun Hill; 2:49 p.m.–3:44 p.m.

Local Sun Time	Command's Watch Time	Event	Speed	Distance Traveled	Notes
1:52 PM	2:49 PM	After viewing the LBH valley and the hills to the north, Custer drops off Keogh with instructions to deploy his battalion and protect Custer's rear, then heads toward the river with HQ and Yates' battalion.	@ 6 MPH moving to 8 MPH		203
1:53 PM	2:50 PM	Algernon Smith and Company E break off and head into MTC.	8 MPH		205
1:55 PM	2:52 PM	The Oglala warrior, Shave Elk, and several others begin to move up MTC. They see Smith's command and immediately turn around to head back to Ford B.			301
1:56 PM	2:53 PM	Cheyenne warriors American Horse and Brave Wolf, having left the Reno fighting, reach the Ford B area of the Cheyenne village.	8 — 10 MPH	1½ miles	208
1:58 PM	2:55 PM	Custer and Yates arrive at the bluff overlooking Ford B.	6 MPH	6/10 mile	210
1:58 PM	2:55 PM	As Yates' F Company pulls up, PVT William Brown's horse bolts and runs down the bluff, across the flats and into the river. Brown is dragged off by Indians and killed.			302
2:00 PM	2:57 PM	Benteen arrives on Reno Hill.			211
2:01 PM	2:58 PM	LT Algernon Smith arrives at Ford B and proceeds to the river's edge, deploying his troops and dismounting some of his men. He sets up a screening force covering the troops on the ridge above him. (*There is some evidence from Indian interviews that a soldier wearing buckskin was wounded at this time. That could have been Smith.*)	8 MPH	1 mile	212
2:08 PM	3:05 PM	His rear protected by Smith's Gray Horse Troop at the ford, Custer moves across "Custer's Bluff" and into Deep Coulee, then the "flats" beyond, heading for the northern ridgeline later named Finley-Finckle Ridge and Calhoun Hill.	6 MPH		219
2:09 PM	3:06 PM	Trailed by sharp, sniping fire, Smith—his company fully remounted—begins moving away from Ford B. He heads for the Finley Ridge area and Calhoun Hill. Yates protects his rear.	8 MPH		220
2:10 PM	3:07 PM	As Custer enters Deep Coulee, TMP Dose is killed.	Increasing to 8 MPH	Between 150 and 500 yards from Ford B	303
2:10 PM	3:07 PM	Keogh spots Indians coming down North MTC (the Wolf Tooth and Big Foot band), plus Indians along West Coulee's ridges and orders his troops to open fire.			221
2:12 PM	3:09 PM	Keogh, seeing Custer and Smith pulling out, orders his troops to head for Nye — Cartwright Ridge. His troops continue to fire at the harassing Wolf Tooth band.			64
2:12 PM	3:09 PM	Gall arrives in the vicinity of Ford B; sees Smith's command (E Company) pulling back through the Deep Coulee flats toward the Finley — Finckle Ridge and Calhoun Hill area.	6 MPH	1½ miles	304
2:15 PM	3:12 PM	Some of Smith's troops begin to dismount on the Deep Coulee "flats" to provide stable covering fire for the withdrawing horsemen.	Dismount; 6 — 8 MPH for the horsemen		305
2:15 PM	3:12 PM	Keogh arrives on Nye — Cartwright Ridge.	8 MPH	¼ mile	64
2:15 PM — 2:20 PM	3:12 PM — 3:17 PM	Keogh, on Nye — Cartwright, sets up a mounted skirmish line and continues to fire at encroaching Indians.			306
2:16 PM — 2:18 PM	3:13 PM — 3:15 PM	Some Indians—initially three Cheyenne and four Sioux warriors—cross the LBH and continue to harass Smith's men; this is the beginning of the Indian movement across Medicine Tail Ford. Wolf Tooth and Big Foot continue to engage Keogh's troops, albeit from a distance.			307

S. Ford B to Calhoun Hill (cont.)

2:17 PM — 2:20 PM	3:14 PM — 3:17 PM	Custer and Yates, with Smith's E Company following to cover the move, begin arriving on Calhoun Hill to re-unite with Keogh.	8 MPH		308
2:18 PM	3:15 PM	Custer orders forward immediately the F Company advance scouts to reconnoiter for a river ford.	10 MPH		64
2:18 PM	3:15 PM	Keogh begins his move toward Calhoun Hill from Nye — Cartwright.	6 — 8 MPH		64
Starting @ 2:18 PM and continuing	Starting @ 3:15 PM and continuing	More Indians arrive at Medicine Tail Ford and begin crossing. Some on horseback ride up Deep Coulee for as far as 1 mile; others dismount and begin making their way on foot toward the Calhoun Coulee area.	10 — 12 MPH	650 yards to 1 mile	309
2:20 PM	3:17 PM — 3:25 PM	Smith begins arriving on Calhoun Hill.	6 to 8 MPH	1 to 1.1 miles from Ford B	310
2:21 PM	3:18 PM	Lead Indians on horseback—crossing at Ford B—dismount in Deep Coulee and begin infiltrating up the cut-bank, into the flats, and across toward Calhoun Coulee. Others continue to ride up the coulee toward Henryville.	12 MPH (mounted); 5 — 6 MPH on foot	.38 of a mile (670 yards) to 1 mile	311
2:22 PM and continuing	3:19 PM and continuing	Indians, mostly on foot and out of range of the cavalry carbines, make their way toward Greasy Grass Ridge and Calhoun Coulee.	5 — 6 MPH	¾ mile (1,350 yards)	312
2:23 PM	3:20 PM	Wolf Tooth sees Keogh's movements and begins mounting and crossing the ridges, heading toward Calhoun Hill.	10 MPH		313
2:25 PM	3:22 PM	Keogh arrives on Calhoun Hill.	8 MPH	.86 of a mile (1,500 yards) from Nye — Cartwright	64
2:26 PM — 2:29 PM	3:23 PM — 3:26 PM	Custer, Keogh, Yates, and Cooke discuss their dispositions and the situation they see in the valley. Custer asks Boyer if there is a ford farther downstream, a ford beyond where they see the refugees gathering. Boyer assures him he will be able to find one farther north.			64
2:28 PM	3:25 PM	The last of Smith's Company E troops arrive on Calhoun Hill. These were the men who had dismounted and formed a rear guard for the leading horsemen.	Varying speeds; some men re-mounted, others—on foot—still firing at encroaching Indians		314
2:30 PM	3:27 PM	Part of Wolf Tooth's band reach upper Deep Coulee and the Henryville area. They sequester their horses in the ravine and begin infiltrating toward Calhoun Hill.	10 MPH	1.14 miles (2,000 yards)	315
2:30 PM	3:27 PM	Custer takes HQ and the Yates battalion and heads north in search of a crossing point.	10 MPH		316
2:33 PM	3:27 PM	L Company men take up skirmish line positions.			317
2:30 PM — 2:47 PM	3:27 PM — 3:44 PM	Keogh deploys his battalion, moving his horses into the swale area behind Calhoun Hill.			318

T. Calhoun Hill Deployment; 3:14 p.m.–3:37 p.m.

Local Sun Time	Command's Watch Time	Event	Speed	Distance Traveled	Notes
2:17 PM — 2:20 PM	3:14 PM — 3:17 PM	Custer and Yates, with Smith's E Company following to cover the move, begin arriving on Calhoun Hill to re-unite with Keogh.	8 MPH		308
2:18 PM	3:15 PM	Custer orders forward immediately the F Company advance scouts to reconnoiter for a river ford.	10 MPH		64
2:18 PM	3:15 PM	Keogh begins his move toward Calhoun Hill from Nye — Cartwright.	6 — 8 MPH		64
Starting @ 2:18 PM and continuing	Starting @ 3:15 PM and continuing	More Indians arrive at Medicine Tail Ford and begin crossing. Some on horseback ride up Deep Coulee for as far as 1 mile; others dismount and begin making their way on foot toward the Calhoun Coulee area.	10 — 12 MPH	650 yards to 1 mile	309
2:20 PM — 2:28 PM	3:17 PM — 3:25 PM	Smith begins arriving on Calhoun Hill.	6 to 8 MPH	1 to 1.1 miles from Ford B	310
2:21 PM	3:18 PM	Lead Indians on horseback—crossing at Ford B—dismount in Deep Coulee and begin infiltrating up the cut-bank, into the flats, and across toward Calhoun Coulee. Others continue to ride up the coulee toward Henryville.	12 MPH (mounted); 5 — 6 MPH on foot	.38 of a mile (670 yards) to 1 mile	311
2:22 PM and continuing	3:19 PM and continuing	Indians, mostly on foot and out of range of the cavalry carbines, make their way toward Greasy Grass Ridge and Calhoun Coulee.	5 — 6 MPH	¾ mile (1,350 yards)	312
2:23 PM	3:20 PM	Wolf Tooth sees Keogh's movements and begins mounting and crossing the ridges, heading toward Calhoun Hill.	10 MPH		313
2:25 PM	3:22 PM	Keogh arrives on Calhoun Hill.	8 MPH	.86 of a mile (1,500 yards) from Nye — Cartwright	64
2:26 PM — 2:29 PM	3:23 PM — 3:26 PM	Custer, Keogh, Yates, and Cooke discuss their dispositions and the situation they see in the valley. Custer asks Boyer if there is a ford farther downstream, a ford beyond where they see the refugees gathering. Boyer assures him he will be able to find one farther north.			64
2:28 PM	3:25 PM	The last of Smith's Company E troops arrive on Calhoun Hill. These were the men who had dismounted and formed a rear guard for the leading horsemen.	Varying speeds; some men re-mounted, others—on foot—still firing at encroaching Indians		314
2:30 PM	3:27 PM	Part of Wolf Tooth's band reach upper Deep Coulee and the Henryville area. They sequester their horses in the ravine and begin infiltrating toward Calhoun Hill.	10 MPH	1.14 miles (2,000 yards)	315
2:30 PM	3:27 PM	Custer takes HQ and the Yates battalion and heads north in search of a crossing point.	10 MPH		316
2:33 PM	3:27 PM	L Company men take up skirmish line positions.			317
2:30 PM — 2:47 PM	3:27 PM — 3:44 PM	Keogh deploys his battalion, moving his horses into the swale area behind Calhoun Hill.			318
2:32 PM	3:29 PM	Lead Indians on foot from Deep Coulee, begin reaching Calhoun Coulee, still out of effective range of the cavalry carbines atop Calhoun Hill and Battle Ridge. They begin their slower infiltration toward Calhoun Hill/Battle Ridge. Others continue up Deep Coulee into what is now called "Henryville."	5 — 6 MPH	¾ mile (1,350 yards) up Deep Coulee	319

T. Calhoun Hill Deployment (cont.)

2:36 PM	3:33 PM	Gall, with more warriors, reaches the Henryville area.	3 MPH	1 2/10 miles from Ford B crossing	249
2:37 PM — 2:40 PM	3:34 PM — 3:37 PM	Lead Indians, infiltrating on foot, begin reaching a point within 100 yards of Battle Ridge/Calhoun Hill. Their arching arrows begin to threaten the troops and held horses in the swale and along the ridge.	2½ to 4½ MPH	570 yards into Calhoun Coulee (now, 1.1 miles from Ford B)	320

U. Keogh to Custer on Cemetery Ridge; 3:27 p.m.–3:58 p.m.

Local Sun Time	Command's Watch Time	Event	Speed	Distance Traveled	Notes
2:28 PM — 2:46 PM	3:25 PM — 3:43 PM	Many Indians who left the Reno battlefield begin arriving at Ford B. Some continue on toward Ford D. Others—who did not get into the valley fight—are arriving, as well.	8 — 10 MPH	3.42 miles from Reno's retreat crossing	256
2:30 PM	3:27 PM	Custer takes HQ and the Yates battalion and heads north in search of a crossing point.	10 MPH		316
2:33 PM	3:27 PM	L Company men take up skirmish line positions.			317
2:30 PM — 2:47 PM	3:27 PM — 3:44 PM	Keogh deploys his battalion, moving his horses into the swale area behind Calhoun Hill.			318
2:37 PM — 2:40 PM	3:34 PM — 3:37 PM	Lead Indians, infiltrating on foot, begin reaching a point within 100 yards of Battle Ridge/Calhoun Hill. Their arching arrows begin to threaten the troops and held horses in the swale and along the ridge.	2½ to 4½ MPH	570 yards into Calhoun Coulee (now, 1.1 miles from Ford B)	320
2:40 PM	3:37 PM	The F Company scouts, backtracking, meet Custer and Yates. The scouts inform Custer that there appears to be a crossable ford ahead, and that they can see the full extent of the Indians gathering in Squaw — Chasing Creek. A brief, but sharp exchange occurs with Indians in front on the troops, probably some warriors from the Wolf Tooth/Big Foot band.	Variously, 10 — 12 MPH	Forward and backtracking, 1 — 1½ miles	321
2:45 PM	3:42 PM	Custer arrives at Ford D.	10 MPH	2.33 miles from Calhoun Hill	254
2:45 PM	3:42 PM	Keogh, Calhoun, and Harrington discuss the threat to their horses from arching arrows falling amongst them from Indians moving up Calhoun Coulee. Keogh roders Harrington to ready his company for a charge into the coulee.			322
2:47 PM	3:44 PM	Keogh sends C Company into Calhoun Coulee to relieve pressure from Indians infiltrating up the coulee. (*This was the beginning of the general firing heard by Fred Gerard after the "scattering" shots many described as volleys.*)	(12 MPH)	(650 yards [.37 miles])	258
2:47 PM — 2:49 PM	3:44 PM — 3:46 PM	Harrington charges into Calhoun Coulee, scattering Indians all around the coulee. He moves approximately 650 yards and orders his troops to dismount and set up a skirmish line, probably anchored on the ridges to his left (Finley — Finckle Ridge) and right.	12 MPH	650 yards, total distance before dismounting	260
2:49 PM	3:46 PM	Custer begins moving away from Ford D.	12 MPH		263
2:50 PM — 2:52 PM	3:47 PM — 3:49 PM	Harrington deploys his troops, possibly spreading them too thinly for as much as 850 yards. (An alternative scenario would have been his ordering the men into squads to occupy small enclaves.)		825 — 850 yard length, ridge to ridge	323
2:51 PM	3:48 PM	Crazy Horse and his lead warriors reach the Deep Ravine crossing.	12 MPH	1.43 miles (2,500 yards) from Ford B	264
2:52 PM	3:49 PM	Crazy Horse is across the Deep Ravine crossing and starts up the ravine. He is followed by Crow King and his Hunkpapa warriors.	6 — 7 MPH	(1,200 yards from the crossing to Battle Ridge)	267
2:52 PM	3:49 PM	C Company is suddenly attacked and routed by hordes of warriors. Troops begin running for Finley — Finckle Ridge. (*It is possible this ridge is where Yellow Nose snatched the company guidon.*)	@ 6 MPH (foot) to 12 MPH (mounted)		324
2:53 PM	3:50 PM	Mark Kellogg, trailing Custer's command, is cut down and killed by trailing Indians.	7 MPH	½ mile	325

U. Keogh to Custer on Cemetery Ridge (cont.)

2:56 PM	3:53 PM	C Company breaks and makes a run—both on foot and on horseback—for Finley — Finckle Ridge.	6 MPH — 12 MPH, on foot and horse		273
2:56 PM	3:53 PM	Crazy Horse reaches the headcut of Deep Ravine.	7 MPH	675 yards from river crossing	326
2:56 PM	3:53 PM	Keogh, having realized the threat, feverishly seeks to deploy I Company to head off the Indian attack emanating from Deep Ravine.			327
2:56 PM — 3:28 PM	3:53 PM — 4:25 PM	*It is during this timeframe that the fighting on Calhoun Hill and the "Keogh Sector" becomes intense with panicked C Company troops fleeing up Finley-Finckle Ridge to Calhoun Hill; emboldened Indians beginning to storm the southern end of Calhoun Hill; and Crazy Horse assaulting I Company across Battle Ridge.*			328
2:57 PM	3:54 PM	LT Calhoun, watching the rout of C Company, quickly orders a partial shift of his skirmish line from south to west, ordering his troops to cover the retreating soldiers.			329
2:57 PM	3:54 PM	Custer reaches Cemetery Ridge.	12 MPH	1¼ — 1½ miles	275
2:57 PM — 3:02 PM	3:54 PM — 3:59 PM	Custer rapidly sets up his dispositions on Cemetery Ridge. He and Yates confer as they see masses of Indians mounting the headcut of Deep Ravine and heading up to Battle Ridge, effectively splitting the two commands.			330
2:58 PM	3:55 PM	The first Indians from the Reno fight are beginning to arrive in the vicinity of Ford D at this time.	8 MPH through the camp; 12 MPH thereafter	3.4 miles to Ford B; 2.3 miles to Ford D	277
2:58 PM	3:55 PM	LT Harrington, still mounted and trailing about eight of his retreating troopers up Finley — Finckle Ridge, kills a Cheyenne warrior, then a Sioux Indian, before he himself is cut down.			331
2:58 PM — 3 PM	3:55 PM — 3:57 PM	Lead elements of routed C Company reach Finley — Finckle Ridge, pursued mostly by Indians on foot coming up from Calhoun Coulee and the lower end of Deep Coulee.	6 — 12 MPH, on foot and horse	¼ mile (450 yards)	332
2:58 PM — 3:02 PM	3:55 PM — 3:59 PM	Crazy Horse and his warriors—unaware of Custer and Yates to their northwest—crest Battle Ridge and charge down through Keogh's men, splitting his command off from Custer and the Yates battalion. They charge through the troops and up to the ridge to the east.	10 MPH	525 yards from the Deep Ravine headcut to Battle Ridge crest; 600 yards from the crest of Battle Ridge to Crazy Horse Ridge	278
2:58 PM — 3:28 PM	3:55 PM — 4:25 PM	Fighting in the "Keogh Sector" begins to rage, ultimately with panicking troops from companies C and L intermingling with I Company men. Indians pressing from the Calhoun Hill area force troops north along Battle Ridge, some soldiers fleeing westward across the ridge.			333
2:59 PM	3:56 PM	A number of LT Calhoun's troops, having established a second skirmish line facing toward Finley Ridge, attempt to cover the withdrawal of C Company, but are faced with increasing dust and smoke making visibility difficult.			334
3:00 PM	3:57 PM	Additional elements of C Company reach Finley — Finckle Ridge as others begin running toward Calhoun Hill. Fighting is hand-to-hand and the troops are overwhelmed.	6 — 12 MPH, on foot and mounted	(670 yards to Calhoun Hill)	335
3:01 PM	3:58 PM	Indians from the Henryville area and from the ridge east of Calhoun Hill—watching as L Company troops re-deploy and hearing the action of Crazy Horse's charge through Keogh's I Company—begin to charge Calhoun's men from their close-in positions.		600 yards from the top of Battle Ridge	336

U. Keogh to Custer on Cemetery Ridge (cont.)

| 3:01 PM | 3:58 PM | Indians from the Reno fight—having been told that soldiers were spotted across Ford D—begin fording the river at "D" to chase after Custer. | Various speeds | | 337 |

V. Cemetery Ridge to the End; 3:54 p.m.–4:40 p.m.

Local Sun Time	Command's Watch Time	Event	Speed	Distance Traveled	Notes
2:57 PM	3:54 PM	Custer reaches Cemetery Ridge.	12 MPH	1¼ — 1½ miles from Ford D	275
2:57 PM — 3:02 PM	3:54 PM — 3:59 PM	Custer rapidly sets up his dispositions on Cemetery Ridge. He and Yates confer as they see masses of Indians mounting the headcut of Deep Ravine and heading up to Battle Ridge, effectively splitting the two commands.			330
2:58 PM	3:55 PM	The first Indians from the Reno fight are beginning to arrive in the vicinity of Ford D at this time.	8 MPH through the camp; 12 MPH thereafter	3.4 miles to Ford B; 2.3 miles to Ford D	277
2:58 PM — 3 PM	3:55 PM — 3:57 PM	Lead elements of routed C Company reach Finley — Finckle Ridge, pursued mostly by Indians on foot coming up from Calhoun Coulee and the lower end of Deep Coulee.	6 — 12 MPH, on foot and horse	¼ mile (450 yards)	332
2:58 PM — 3:02 PM	3:55 PM — 3:59 PM	Crazy Horse and his warriors—unaware of Custer and Yates to their northwest—crest Battle Ridge and charge down through Keogh's men, splitting his command off from Custer and the Yates battalion. They charge through the troops and up to the ridge to the east.	10 MPH	525 yards from the Deep Ravine headcut to Battle Ridge crest; 600 yards from the crest of Battle Ridge to Crazy Horse Ridge	278
2:58 PM — 3:28 PM	3:55 PM — 4:25 PM	Fighting in the "Keogh Sector" begins to rage, ultimately with panicking troops from companies C and L intermingling with I Company men. Indians pressing from the Calhoun Hill area force troops north along Battle Ridge, some soldiers fleeing westward across the ridge.			333
2:59 PM	3:56 PM	A number of LT Calhoun's troops, having established a second skirmish line facing toward Finley Ridge, attempt to cover the withdrawal of C Company, but are faced with increasing dust and smoke making visibility difficult.			334
3:00 PM	3:57 PM	Additional elements of C Company reach Finley — Finckle Ridge as others begin running toward Calhoun Hill. Fighting is hand-to-hand and the troops are overwhelmed.	6 — 12 MPH, on foot and mounted	(670 yards to Calhoun Hill)	335
3:01 PM	3:58 PM	Indians from the Henryville area and from the ridge east of Calhoun Hill—watching as L Company troops re-deploy and hearing the action of Crazy Horse's charge through Keogh's I Company — begin to charge Calhoun's men from their close-in positions.			336
3:01 PM	3:58 PM	Indians from the Reno fight—having been told that soldiers were spotted across Ford D—begin fording the river at "D" to chase after Custer.	Various speeds		337
3:02 PM	3:59 PM	Custer sends Yates (F) into "basin" area as a reserve and to try to head off the infiltration of Indians out of Deep Ravine.	8 MPH	(½ mile)	338
3:02 PM	3:59 PM	Crazy Horse reaches the ridge east of Battle Ridge. He moves down its east slope and turns to head back and resume his attack. He pauses a few minutes to gather his warriors and discuss the situation with Indians who had come up from Deep Coulee.			279
3:07 PM — 3:18 PM	4:04 PM — 4:15 PM	Crazy Horse and the Minneconjou warrior, White Bull, lead a charge from east of Battle Ridge, into the middle of panicking and re-deploying troopers, breaking the back of Keogh's command and overrunning splintering Calhoun's L Company. Gall and Indians from the Henryville/Deep Coulee area merge into the melee, preventing any southward escape.			284
Admin entry ➡ 3:08 PM	*4:05 PM*	*This is the earliest any C Company troopers on foot could have possibly reached Last Stand Hill.*	*5 MPH, average*	*1.15 miles (lower Finley Ridge to LS Hill)*	339
3:09 PM	4:06 PM	Yates and F Company arrive in the "basin" area. He deploys his men in an attempt to stem the flow of Indians from Deep Ravine.	8 MPH	½ mile (875 yards)	340

V. Cemetery Ridge to the End (cont.)

3:10 PM — 3:11 PM	4:07 PM — 4:08 PM	Indians from the Ford D area now arrive north and west of Cemetery Ridge, putting extreme pressure on Custer. The Indians were both dismounted and on horseback.	12 — 14 MPH	1 to as much as 1¾ miles	341
3:12 PM	4:09 PM	Now under increasing pressure, Custer begins moving up Cemetery Ridge to Last Stand Hill. E Company—partially dismounted—is overrun. Casualties are fairly heavy—maybe as many as 6 troops killed—and the unmounted horses are run off.	@ 6 MPH (foot), 8 MPH (mounted)	(4/10 of a mile; 700 yards)	342
3:15 PM	4:12 PM	Yates, under heavy pressure and seeing Custer moving, re-mounts his troops and heads for Last Stand Hill.	@ 8 MPH	(3/10 of a mile; 525 yards)	343
3:16 PM	4:13 PM	In a semi-controlled move protected by the mounted troops, lead elements of HQ and E Company reach Last Stand Hill.	8 MPH (mounted)	4/10 of a mile	344
3:18 PM	4:15 PM	Final stragglers of E Company reach Last Stand Hill.	6 MPH (on foot), pulling their horses with them	4/10 of a mile	345
3:18 PM	4:15 PM	Yates and F Company begin arriving at Last Stand Hill.	8 MPH	3/10 of a mile	64
3:18 PM	4:15 PM	Crazy Horse and White Bull now join in the fighting for Last Stand Hill.			346
3:18 PM — 3:28 PM	4:15 PM — 4:25 PM	The fighting intensifies around the Custer command on the ridge, up to the top of the knoll. Stragglers from the Keogh debacle—no more than about 10 men—continue arriving, Indians chasing them slowing down, keeping their distance.			347
3:18 PM — 3:43 PM	4:15 PM — 4:40 PM	Indian fire north of Custer Hill threatens troops there.			348
3:23 PM	4:20 PM	Benteen climbs highest point of Weir Peaks and is now with CPT Weir.			293
3:23 PM — 3:28 PM	4:20 PM — 4:25 PM	A cry goes up amongst the Indians that the suicide boys are arriving.			349
3:24 PM	4:21 PM	With the pressure mounting and the realization that they are surrounded, E Company men release their horses. The mounts stampede down the ridge toward the river, giving the impression of a charge.			350
3:28 PM	4:25 PM	E Company men under the command of LT Sturgis prepare to charge off Custer/Last Stand Hill down the SSL.			351
3:28 PM — 3:34 PM	4:25 PM — 4:31 PM	E Company men charge down the South Skirmish Line. Some troops are mounted, but most are on foot.	(5 to 10 MPH)	(550 — 875 yards)	352
3:30 PM — 3:34 PM	4:27 PM — 4:31 PM	E Company troopers on horseback begin arriving parallel to the top of Deep Ravine. Those on foot take a little longer and because of the distance and the heat, they begin slowing. Initially, Indians in their way separate and retreat.	5 to 10 MPH	550 — 875 yards	353
3:35 PM — 3:39 PM	4:32 PM — 4:36 PM	Led by the suicide boys, Indians on Cemetery Ridge charge off the ridge—some on horseback, many on foot—and burst in amongst the exhausted troopers along the SSL. At the same time, other Indians—including the suicide boys on Cemetery Ridge—charge up to Custer — Last Stand Hill. The final fighting becomes furious, all the more so because of the extreme dust and gunsmoke.	6 to 12 MPH	350 — 700 yards (2/10 — 4/10 of a mile)	354
3:37 PM — 3:39 PM	4:34 PM — 4:36 PM	Indians on foot and horseback overrun Custer — Last Stand Hill.	6 to 12 MPH	700 yards	355
3:43 PM	4:40 PM	The Custer battle is ending. The last of the E Company men are forced into Deep Ravine where they are slaughtered.			356

W. Warriors; 1:02 p.m.–5:14 p.m.

Local Sun Time	Command's Watch Time	Event	Speed	Distance Traveled	Notes
12:05 PM	1:02 PM	Several scouts, seeing a Hunkpapa youngster named Deeds and another warrior, chase them as they try to signal a warning to the village. The Crow scout, Goes Ahead, kills Deeds.			80
12:18 PM	1:15 PM	Gerard is informed by several of his Ree scouts that the Indians are coming back up the valley to confront the troops.			96
12:38 PM	1:35 PM	Reno orders his command to dismount.			114
12:45 PM	1:42 PM	The Hunkpapa warrior, Iron Cedar, on or near Weir Point, sees Custer's column approaching near the bluffs to the south. He turns immediately and heads down the bluffs to warn the village of more soldiers.	(5 MPH)	(2/3 of a mile across the river and into the village)	127
12:54 PM	1:51 PM	Iron Cedar, having swum the river, reaches the Hunkpapa village and seeks out Gall.	5 MPH	1,150 yards, including the river	143
1:11 PM	2:08 PM	Skirmish line begins pulling back.			164
1:13 PM	2:10 PM	Gall and Iron Cedar head off to swim the LBH and climb the bluffs to watch for the soldiers on the east bank.			168
1:14 PM	2:11 PM	Crazy Horse, followed by a considerable number of his warriors, begins arriving as M Company breaks for the timber.			172
1:26 PM	2:23 PM	Reno begins retreat.			177
1:26 PM	2:23 PM	Gall and Iron Cedar reach the top of the bluffs. Iron Cedar points toward the troops near the mouth of Cedar Coulee.	3 MPH, including swimming the LBH and climbing the bluffs	2/3 of a mile (1,150 yards)	178
1:29 PM	2:26 PM	Gall and Iron Cedar watch as Custer turns into MTC.			181
1:32 PM	2:29 PM	Gall and Iron Cedar turn to head back to the village.			181
1:39 PM — 1:49 PM	2:36 PM — 2:46 PM	DeRudio—still in the timber—watches as masses of Indians follow Reno's command to the crossing, fighting all along the way.			188
1:42 PM	2:39 PM	Gall and Iron Cedar have returned to the village and Gall seeks to rally any warriors he can find to head downstream and confront the new threat.	4 MPH including swimming the LBH	2/3 of a mile (1,150 yards)	181
1:42 PM — 1:57 PM	2:39 PM — 2:54 PM	Gall rallies some warriors and begins to move toward Ford B. They are all mounted.	(8 MPH)	Various	194
1:45 PM	2:42 PM	Other Indians—primarily Cheyenne like American Horse and Brave Wolf—leave the valley fight and head back to their village.	6 to 8 MPH		198
1:53 PM	2:50 PM	Crazy Horse, now alerted to more troops mounting the bluffs and hearing that there are additional troops farther downstream, begins to gather his warriors to head off Custer's command.			206
1:55 PM	2:52 PM	The Oglala warrior, Shave Elk, and several others begin to move up MTC. They see Smith's command and immediately turn around to head back to Ford B.			301
1:56 PM	2:53 PM	Cheyenne warriors American Horse and Brave Wolf, having left the Reno fighting, reach the Ford B area of the Cheyenne village.	8 — 10 MPH	1½ miles	208
1:58 PM	2:55 PM	Crazy Horse, with a number of his warriors, turns and heads toward the village.	(8 MPH)		209

W. Warriors (cont.)

1:58 PM	2:55 PM	Custer and Yates arrive at the bluff overlooking Ford B.	8 MPH	6/10 mile	210
2:00 PM	2:57 PM	Benteen arrives on Reno Hill.	8 MPH from meeting the Crows; 7.7 MPH, from the morass		211
2:01 PM	2:58 PM	LT Algernon Smith arrives at Ford B and proceeds to the river's edge, deploying his troops and dismounting some of his men. He sets up a screening force covering the troops on the ridge above him. (*There is some evidence from Indian interviews that a soldier wearing buckskin was wounded at this time. That could have been Smith.*)	8 MPH	1 mile	212
2:05 PM	3:02 PM	Indians still in full force in valley. Estimates ranged from 600 to 1,000 or more.			214
2:08 PM	3:05 PM	Godfrey estimates 600 to 700 Indians in the valley with more arriving. In addition, he spots quite a number in the ravines on the east side of the LBH. He also sees dust from ther packs and estimates they are some 3 to 4 miles away. In reality, the packs are within ½ mile of the lone tepee. Edgerly estimated 800 — 1,000. Benteen used a figure of 900.			218
2:08 PM	3:05 PM	His rear protected by Smith's Gray Horse Troop at the ford, Custer moves across "Custer's Bluff/Butler Ridge" and into Deep Coulee, then the "flats" beyond, heading for the northern ridgeline later named Finley — Finckle Ridge.	6 MPH		219
2:09 PM	3:06 PM	Trailed by sharp, sniping fire, Smith—his company fully remounted—begins moving away from Ford B. He heads for the Finley — Finckle Ridge area and Calhoun Hill. Yates protects his rear.	8 MPH		220
2:10 PM	3:07 PM	Keogh spots Indians coming down North MTC (the Wolf Tooth and Big Foot band), plus Indians along West Coulee's ridges and orders his troops to open fire.			221
2:10 PM	3:07 PM	Crazy Horse and his warriors—cantering back toward the village—hear the volley firing as they near the Hunkpapa circle of Sitting Bull.	8 MPH	1½ miles—to this point—from the Reno retreat crossing	224
2:12 PM	3:09 PM	Gall arrives in the vicinity of Ford B; sees Smith's command (E Company) pulling back through the Deep Coulee flats toward the Finley — Finckle Ridge and Calhoun Hill area.	6 MPH	1½ miles	304
2:13 PM	3:10 PM	Crazy Horse and some followers pick their way through the Hunkpapa circle—still in great turmoil—and head toward their own camp.	8 MPH down to 6 MPH		226
2:16 PM — 2:18 PM	3:13 PM — 3:15 PM	Some Indians—initially three Cheyenne and four Sioux warriors—cross the LBH and continue to harass Smith's men; this is the beginning of the Indian movement across Medicine Tail Ford. Wolf Tooth and Big Foot continue to engage Keogh's troops, albeit from a distance.			307
Starting @ 2:18 PM and continuing	Starting @ 3:15 PM and continuing	More Indians arrive at Medicine Tail Ford and begin crossing. Some on horseback ride up Deep Coulee for as far as 1 mile; others dismount and begin making their way on foot toward the Calhoun Coulee area.	10 — 12 MPH	650 yards to 1 mile	309
2:19 PM — (2:34 PM)	3:16 PM — (3:31 PM)	Crazy Horse reaches his camp circle and pauses to prepare for more fighting.	6 MPH	1 mile from where he heard the volley firing	233
2:20 PM	3:17 PM	More Indians begin leaving the valley and heading downstream.			234
2:21 PM	3:18 PM	Lead Indians on horseback—crossing at Ford B—dismount in Deep Coulee and begin infiltrating up the cut-bank, into the flats, and across toward Calhoun Coulee. Others continue to ride up the coulee toward Henryville.	12 MPH (mounted); 5 — 6 MPH on foot	.38 of a mile (670 yards) to 1 mile	311
2:22 PM and continuing	3:19 PM and continuing	Indians, mostly on foot and out of range of the cavalry carbines, make their way toward Greasy Grass Ridge and Calhoun Coulee.	5 — 6 MPH	¾ mile (1,350 yards)	312

W. Warriors (cont.)

2:23 PM	3:20 PM	Wolf Tooth sees Keogh's movements and begins mounting and crossing the ridges, heading toward Calhoun Hill.	10 MPH		313
2:25 PM	3:22 PM	Keogh arrives on Calhoun Hill.	8 MPH	.86 of a mile (1,500 yards) from Nye — Cartwright	64
2:28 PM — 2:46 PM	3:25 PM — 3:43 PM	Many Indians who left the Reno battlefield are arriving at Ford B. Some continue on toward Ford D. Others—who did not get into the valley fight—are arriving, as well.	8 — 10 MPH	3.42 miles	256
2:30 PM	3:27 PM	Part of Wolf Tooth's band reach upper Deep Coulee and the Henryville area. They sequester their horses in the ravine and begin infiltrating toward Calhoun Hill.	10 MPH	1.14 miles (2,000 yards)	315
2:30 PM — 2:47 PM	3:27 PM — 3:44 PM	Keogh deploys his battalion, moving his horses into the swale area behind Calhoun Hill.			318
2:32 PM	3:29 PM	Lead Indians on foot from Deep Coulee, begin reaching Calhoun Coulee, still out of effective range of the cavalry carbines atop Calhoun Hill and Battle Ridge. They begin their slower infiltration toward Calhoun Hill/Battle Ridge. Others continue up Deep Coulee into what is now called "Henryville."	5 — 6 MPH	3/4 mile (1,350 yards)	319
2:34 PM	3:31 PM	Crazy Horse and a large band of warriors leave the Oglala camp heading for the Ford B area.	@ 8 — 10 MPH		246
2:36 PM	3:33 PM	Gall, with more warriors, reaches the Henryville area.	3 MPH	1 2/10 miles from Ford B crossing	249
2:37 PM — 2:40 PM	3:34 PM — 3:37 PM	Lead Indians, infiltrating on foot, begin reaching a point within 100 yards of Battle Ridge/Calhoun Hill. Their arching arrows begin to threaten the troops and held horses in the swale and along the ridge.	2½ to 4½ MPH	570 yards into Calhoun Coulee (now, 1.1 miles from Ford B)	320
2:40 PM	3:37 PM	More and more Indians involved in the valley fighting begin to leave, heading downstream to the sound of the volley firing.	Various speeds		251
2:41 PM	3:38 PM	Crazy Horse and his band reach Ford B. They stop momentarily to see what they can from the edge of the ford.	8 — 10 MPH	1 mile from the Oglala village circle	253
2:43 PM	3:40 PM	Deciding not to cross at the Medicine Tail ford, Crazy Horse spurs his horse on and heads downriver for Deep Ravine ford.	@ 12 MPH		253
2:45 PM	3:42 PM	Custer arrives at Ford D.	10 MPH	2.33 miles from Calhoun Hill	254 & 64
2:47 PM	3:44 PM	Keogh sends C Company into Calhoun Coulee to relieve pressure from Indians infiltrating up the coulee. (*This was the beginning of the general firing heard by Fred Gerard after the "scattering" shots many described as volleys.*)	(12 MPH)	(650 yards [.37 miles])	258
2:48 PM	3:45 PM	Most of the Indians are now out of the valley, only about 100 — 150 remaining on both sides of the river.			262
2:49 PM	3:46 PM	Custer begins moving away from Ford D.	12 MPH		263
2:51 PM	3:48 PM	Crazy Horse and his lead warriors reach the Deep Ravine crossing.	12 MPH	1.43 miles (2,500 yards) from Ford B	264
2:52 PM	3:49 PM	Crazy Horse is across the Deep Ravine crossing and starts up the ravine. He is followed by Crow King and his Hunkpapa warriors.	6 — 7 MPH	(1,200 yards from the crossing to Battle Ridge)	267
2:52 PM	3:49 PM	C Company is suddenly attacked and routed by hordes of warriors. Troops begin running for Finley — Finckle Ridge. (*It is possible this ridge is where Yellow Nose snatched the company guidon.*)	@ 6 MPH (foot) to 12 MPH (mounted)		324
2:56 PM	3:53 PM	Crazy Horse reaches the headcut of Deep Ravine.	7 MPH	675 yards from river crossing	326

W. Warriors (cont.)

2:56 PM	3:53 PM	Keogh, having realized the threat, feverishly seeks to deploy I Company to head off the Indian attack emanating from Deep Ravine.			327
2:58 PM	3:55 PM	The first Indians from the Reno fight are beginning to arrive in the vicinity of Ford D at this time.	8 MPH through the camp; 12 MPH thereafter	3.4 miles to Ford B; 2.3 miles to Ford D	277
2:58 PM — 3:02 PM	3:55 PM — 3:59 PM	Crazy Horse and his warriors—unaware of Custer and Yates to their northwest—crest Battle Ridge and charge down through Keogh's men, splitting his command off from Custer and the Yates battalion. They charge through the troops and up to the ridge to the east.	10 MPH	525 yards from the Deep Ravine headcut to Battle Ridge crest; 600 yards from the crest of Battle Ridge to Crazy Horse Ridge to the east	278
2:58 PM — 3:28 PM	3:55 PM — 4:25 PM	Fighting in the "Keogh Sector" begins to rage, ultimately with panicking troops from companies C and L intermingling with I Company men. Indians pressing from the Calhoun Hill area force troops north along Battle Ridge, some soldiers fleeing westward across the ridge.			328
3:01 PM	3:58 PM	Indians from the Henryville area and from the ridge east of Calhoun Hill—watching as L Company troops re-deploy and hearing the action of Crazy Horse's charge through Keogh's I Company—begin to charge Calhoun's men from their close-in positions.			336
3:01 PM	3:58 PM	Indians from the Reno fight—having been told that soldiers were spotted across Ford D—begin fording the river at "D" to chase after Custer.	Various speeds		337
3:02 PM	3:59 PM	Crazy Horse reaches the ridge east of Battle Ridge. He moves down its east slope and turns to head back and resume his attack. He pauses a few minutes to gather his warriors and discuss the situation with Indians who had come up from Deep Coulee.			279
3:07 PM — 3:18 PM	4:04 PM — 4:15 PM	Crazy Horse and the Minneconjou warrior, White Bull, lead a charge from east of Battle Ridge, into the middle of panicking and re-deploying troops, breaking the back of Keogh's command and overrunning splintering Calhoun's L Company. Gall and Indians from the Henryville/Deep Coulee area merge into the melee, preventing any southward escape.			284
3:10 PM — 3:11 PM	4:07 PM — 4:08 PM	Indians from the Ford D area now arrive north and west of Cemetery Ridge, putting extreme pressure on Custer. The Indians were both dismounted and on horseback.	12 — 14 MPH	1 to as much as 1¾ miles	341
3:12 PM	4:09 PM	Now under increasing pressure, Custer begins moving up Cemetery Ridge to Last Stand Hill. E Company—partially dismounted—is overrun. Casualties are fairly heavy—maybe as many as 6 troops killed—and the unmounted horses are run off.	@ 6 MPH (foot), 8 MPH (mounted)	(4/10 of a mile; 700 yards)	342
3:15 PM	4:12 PM	Yates, under heavy pressure and seeing Custer moving, re-mounts his troops and heads for Last Stand Hill.	@ 8 MPH	(3/10 of a mile; 525 yards)	343
3:16 PM	4:13 PM	In a semi-controlled move protected by the mounted troops, lead elements of HQ and E Company reach Last Stand Hill.	8 MPH (mounted)	4/10 of a mile	344
3:18 PM	4:15 PM	Final stragglers of E Company reach Last Stand Hill.	6 MPH (on foot), pulling their horses with them	4/10 of a mile	345
3:18 PM	4:15 PM	Yates and F Company begin arriving at Last Stand Hill.	8 MPH	3/10 of a mile	64
3:18 PM	4:15 PM	Crazy Horse and White Bull now join in the fighting for Last Stand Hill.			346
3:18 PM — 3:28 PM	4:15 PM — 4:25 PM	The fighting intensifies around the Custer command on the ridge, up to the top of the knoll. Stragglers from the Keogh debacle—no more than about 10 men—continue arriving, Indians chasing them slowing down, keeping their distance.			347
3:18 PM — 3:43 PM	4:15 PM — 4:40 PM	Indian fire north of Custer Hill threatens troops there.			348

W. Warriors (cont.)

3:23 PM — 3:28 PM	4:20 PM — 4:25 PM	A cry goes up amongst the Indians that the suicide boys are arriving.			349
3:24 PM	4:21 PM	With the pressure mounting and the realization that they are surrounded, E Company men release their horses. The mounts stampede down the ridge toward the river, giving the impression of a charge.			350
3:28 PM	4:25 PM	E Company men under the command of LT Sturgis prepare to charge off Custer — Last Stand Hill down the SSL.			351
3:28 PM — 3:34 PM	4: 25 PM — 4:31 PM	E Company men charge down the South Skirmish Line. Some troops are mounted, but most are on foot.	(5 to 10 MPH)	(550 — 875 yards)	352
3:30 PM — 3:34 PM	4:27 PM — 4:31 PM	E Company troopers on horseback begin arriving parallel to the top of Deep Ravine. Those on foot take a little longer and because of the distance and the heat, they begin slowing. Initially, Indians in their way separate and retreat.	5 to 10 MPH	550 — 875 yards	353
3:35 PM — 3:39 PM	4:32 PM — 4:36 PM	Led by the suicide boys, Indians on Cemetery Ridge charge off the ridge—some on horseback, many on foot—and burst in amongst the exhausted troopers along the SSL. At the same time, other Indians—including the suicide boys on Cemetery Ridge—charge up to Custer — Last Stand Hill. The final fighting becomes furious, all the more so because of the extreme dust and gunsmoke.	6 to 12 MPH	350 — 700 yards (2/10 — 4/10 of a mile)	354
3:37 PM — 3:39 PM	4:34 PM — 4:36 PM	Indians on foot and horseback overrun Custer — Last Stand Hill.	6 to 12 MPH	700 yards	355
3:43 PM	4:40 PM	The Custer battle is ending. The last of the E Company men are forced into Deep Ravine where they are slaughtered.			356
3:48 PM	4:45 PM	Word begins to spread amongst the Indians in the Calhoun — Custer sectors that additional soldiers can be seen on the high bluffs upstream. Some of the Indians in the Calhoun Hill area begin moving toward Weir Peaks.			361
3:53 PM	4:50 PM	More Indians begin moving toward Weir Peaks.	8 — 10 MPH	(2 + miles)	362
3:54 PM	4:51 PM	Benteen, seeing the Indians begin to move toward the troops, hustles back to Reno to tell him this position is untenable.	8 MPH	(1± mile)	363
4:13 PM	5:10 PM	The Indians are moving toward Weir Peaks with the lead elements approaching the struggling Edgerly and SGT Harrison—no more than 150 to 200 yards away—on the Weir "sugarloaf."	12 — 14 MPH	(As much as 3½ — 4 miles)	372
4:14 PM	5:11 PM	There are now as many as 200 Indians near Weir Point, with many more closely behind. They slow, first to gather numbers, second to assess what the soldeirs are doing.	8 — 14 MPH	3½ — 4 miles	376
4:17 PM	5:14 PM	Warriors follow after LT Edgerly and SGT Harrison.	10 MPH		377

X. Weir Peaks and Return; 3:10 p.m.–5:30 p.m.

Local Sun Time	Command's Watch Time	Event	Speed	Distance Traveled	Notes
2:13 PM	3:10 PM	As Benteen orders his men to consolidate the hilltop and set up a skirmish line, LT Edgerly sees they are still coming under some fire from Indians hidden on the hilltops and behind rocks and bushes. He also sees a number of Reno's wounded. Benteen orders the Indians to be driven away.			227
2:18 PM	3:15 PM	CPT Weir discusses the situation and the firing heard downstream with his lieutenant, Win Edgerly. Edgerly assures him he would follow if Weir were to head north.			232
2:20 PM	3:17 PM	Edgerly discusses the situation with the D Company first sergeant, 1SG Michael Martin. They agree that the command should go toward the sound of the firing.			229
2:20 PM	3:17 PM	CPT Weir decides to discuss the situation with MAJ Reno.			235
2:26 PM — 2:30 PM	3:23 PM — 3:27 PM	Weir is with Reno and Benteen. Whether or not Weir seeks permission to move downstream has never been satisfactorily established, but he leaves the meeting and goes to get his striker. Edgerly claimed, "He told me later that he hadn't spoken to Reno or Benteen, but rode out on the bluff hoping to see something of Custer's command." PVT Fox claimed to have heard Weir speaking with Reno just before Weir moved out from Reno Hill. "Weir remarked, 'Custer must be around here somewhere and we ought to go to him.' Reno said 'We are surrounded by Indians and we ought to remain here.' Weir said, 'Well if no one else goes to Custer, I will go.' Reno replied, 'No you can not go. For if you try to do it you will get killed and your Company with you.'" Moylan and Benteen overheard this conversation "and talked as though to discourage him."			241
2:30 PM — 2:37 PM	3:27 PM — 3:34 PM	Weir turns and leaves, and seeking out his striker, mounts up to head downstream.			242
2:30 PM	3:27 PM	As Weir turns and leaves, Reno takes SGT Culbertson and several men and heads down the bluffs to find LT Hodgson's body.			243
2:38 PM	3:35 PM	CPT Tom Weir takes his orderly and starts downstream.			250
2:43 PM	3:40 PM	Edgerly begins moving D Company downstream.	6 MPH		250
2:52 PM	3:49 PM	CPT Weir reaches Weir Peaks and heads up its slope.	6 MPH	1½ miles from Reno Hill	268
2:53 PM	3:50 PM	Edgerly and D Company reach the head of Cedar Coulee and begin descending it.	6 MPH slowing to 4 MPH	9/10 mile	269
2:54 PM	3:51 PM	CPT Weir reaches the top of the northernmost peak.			271
2:55 PM	3:52 PM	LT Hare leaves for Weir Point to tell CPT Weir to try to contact Custer.	6 MPH		272
2:57 PM	3:54 PM	Packs seen several hundred yards off; Reno orders the command to begin moving north.			274
2:58 PM — 3:20 PM	3:55 PM — 4:17 PM	Pack train begins arriving on Reno Hill. Benteen's timing would have put the arrival of the first mules at about 4:15 PM.	2 2/3 to 4 MPH	2 miles from meeting Hare	281
3:00 PM	3:57 PM	LT Edgerly and D Company, using Cedar Coulee, reach the east side of Weir Point.	3 MPH	3/10 additional miles	268
3:03 PM	4:00 PM	The general move toward Weir Peaks begins, Benteen's command leading out. Godfrey first claimed he was 3rd in line, then told Camp the order of march was M, K, H; Wallace said H, then K led. Edgerly said H, K, and M.	5 — 7 MPH		280

X. Weir Peaks and Return (cont.)

3:03 PM	4:00 PM	As he arrives on Reno Hill, Tom McDougall sees the tail-end of Edgerly's troops in Cedar Coulee.			282
3:05 PM	4:02 PM	D Company reaches its farthest point in advance of Weir Peaks. Edgerly stops his troops and sees CPT Weir motioning for him to return and come to the high ground. He begins turning his troops toward Weir.	3 to 4 MPH	1.6 miles, total, from Reno Hill	283
3:12 PM	4:09 PM	An orderly from Reno reaches Varnum mid-way down the bluffs and tells him to return to the command. They are moving downstream.	A cautious crawl		285
3:12 PM	4:09 PM	Hare, climbing the steep peaks, reaches CPT Weir and tells him of Reno's request that he try to contact Custer.	5 — 6 MPH	1½ + miles	286
3:17 PM	4:14 PM	LT Edgerly and D Company have moved back up Cedar Coulee and climbed the slopes of the Weir loaf to get in position.	5 MPH	1 mile	287
3:17 PM	4:14 PM	Benteen, French, and Godfrey approach Weir Point, the command stretched out behind them.	Now, 4 MPH	1½ miles	288
3:18 PM	4:15 PM	Edgerly sees Benteen, French, and Godfrey nearing Weir Point.			288
3:18 PM — 3:21 PM	4:15 PM — 4:18 PM	Edgerly spreads out his troops along the north side of the "sugarloaf" of Weir Point.			289
3:20 PM	4:17 PM	The last of the pack train arrives on Reno Hill.			290
3:21 PM	4:18 PM	Edgerly orders D Company to commence firing at Indians within range. These are the remnants of the Indians left behind after the valley fighting. Both Weir and the company "had stopped back at the south end of this sugarloaf and Edgerly said he would go out to the end of the sugarloaf to look down and see if he could see Custer while they were out there."			291 & 357
3:23 PM	4:20 PM	Varnum returns to Reno Hill from his foray to try to find and bury Hodgson. Sees most of the command heading downstream.			292
3:23 PM	4:20 PM	Benteen climbs highest point of Weir Peaks and is now with CPT Weir. His first sight of the village was from "that high point." It was the only point from which the village could be seen and he estimated about 1,800 tepees. When Benteen reached Weir Peaks and saw for the first time the extent of the Indian village he realized they had bitten off too much.			293
3:23 PM — 3:38 PM	4:20 PM — 4:35 PM	Companies H, K, and M are positioning themselves alongside Company D on the Weir Point complex of hills.			294
3:23 PM — 3:38 PM	4:20 PM — 4:35 PM	LT Godfrey moves his own K Company along the edge of the bluffs, closest to the river. "Weir's and French's troops were posted on the high bluffs and to the front of them; my own troop along the crest of the bluffs next to the river…."			295
3:23 PM — 3:38 PM	4:20 PM — 4:35 PM	CPT French moves M Company all the way to "Edgerly" Peaks, where he can look down in the direction of Battle Ridge. When PVT Pigford first looked over in that direction he saw Indians firing from a large circle. It gradually closed until it "converged into a large black mass on the side hill toward the river and all along the ridge." Hare said M, K, and H "were strung out along bluffs behind Company D parallel with the river but not quite up to Company D."			296
3:23 PM — 3:38 PM	4:20 PM — 4:35 PM	Edgerly described the H Company position as occupying the two peaks—as Benteen said, in a file—and D Company deployed on the loaf at a right angle to H. Edgerly said M was a little to H's rear. Godfrey's K seemed to be adjacent to D, on a narrow spur along the bluffs adjacent to the river.			297
3:33 PM	4:30 PM	After a short delay with CPT Moylan and to help with the wounded, Varnum heads downstream to the troops on Weir Point.	@ 8 MPH		292

X. Weir Peaks and Return (cont.)

3:45 PM	4:42 PM	Varnum reaches the "sugarloaf" of Weir Point and joins Edgerly and D Company. "I went to the position of Captain Weir's company at the far point of the ridge downstream. At that time his men were firing at pretty long range—I should say seven or eight hundred yards—at Indians here and there. At that time I could see all over the plain where… the Custer battlefield had been, and it was just covered with Indians in all directions, coming back towards us."	8 MPH	1¼ miles	359
3:46 PM	4:43 PM	At some point, the heavy firing from downstream ceased and Herendeen began his move out of the timber. This is more than a 2—hour stay in the woods, though Herendeen claimed some 3 hours.			360
3:48 PM	4:45 PM	Word begins to spread amongst the Indians in the Calhoun — Custer sectors that additional soldiers can be seen on the high bluffs upstream. Some of the Indians in the Calhoun Hill area begin moving toward Weir Peaks.			361
3:54 PM	4:51 PM	Benteen, seeing the Indians begin to move toward the troops, hustles back to Reno to tell him this position is untenable.	8 MPH	(1± mile)	363
3:56 PM	4:53 PM	D Company firing eases as it becomes apparent Indians are beginning to move toward the troops at Weir Point.			364
4:00 PM	4:57 PM	Benteen reaches Reno and tells him about the approaching Indians. Reno agrees to the pull-back and orders TMP Penwell (K) to inform French, Godfrey, and Weir. Penwell leaves immediately.	8 — 10 MPH	¾ of a mile	365
4:03 PM	5:00 PM	Herendeen and the men from the timber would be arriving at Weir Peaks at this time.			366
4:06 PM	5:03 PM	TMP Penwell signals to French to begin pulling back, then reaches Godfrey and tells him of Reno's orders to withdraw.	10 MPH	¾ of a mile	365
4:06 PM	5:03 PM	French's M Company begins its withdrawal. French yells over to Edgerly ordering D Company to withdraw.	10 MPH		367
4:07 PM	5:04 PM	LT Godfrey directs LT Hare to take 10 men and occupy some high ground on the right facing the Indians. Hare had just cut the men out when orders came—through TMP Penwell—to fall back as quickly as possible. Penwell informed Hare, who then told Godfrey.			368
4:07 PM	5:04 PM	D Company begins its withdrawal. Edgerly sees everyone off before attempting to leave.	8 — 10 MPH		369
4:09 PM	5:06 PM	As Hare moves to occupy the high ground, Godfrey orders K Company to mount up and prepare to move back.			365
4:10 PM	5:07 PM	Last of D Company leaves the Weir "sugarloaf" down a draw and into Cedar Coulee. Edgerly struggles with his horse as his orderly, SGT Harrison stands nearby. Edgerly had trouble mounting and claimed Indians got within 15 feet of him and his orderly, an old veteran. The horse kept moving away from him, so Harrison moved in such a way to prevent the horse from going any farther. He smiled and told Edgerly the Indians were bad marksmen from so close.	8 — 10 MPH		370
4:12 PM	5:09 PM	Godfrey's K Company—the last one to leave the Weir Point complex—begins its move toward Reno Hill.	8 — 10 MPH		371
4:13 PM	5:10 PM	The Indians are moving toward Weir Peaks with the lead elements approaching the struggling Edgerly and SGT Harrison—no more than 150 to 200 yards away—on the Weir "sugarloaf."	12 — 14 MPH	(As much as 3½ — 4 miles)	372
4:13 PM	5:10 PM	According to Hare, it was about 1½ hours from the time Weir left Reno Hill to when the "general engagement" on Reno Hill began.			373

X. Weir Peaks and Return (cont.)

4:14 PM	5:11 PM	As D Company moves up Cedar Coulee in front of the on-coming Indians, FAR Vincent Charley is hit in the hips and falls from his horse.	10 MPH	½ of a mile off the "sugarloaf"	374
4:14 PM	5:11 PM	Finally, as Indians begin to reach the top of the "loaf," Edgerly has managed to mount his horse and he and Harrison fight their way off and down a draw toward Cedar Coulee.	10 — 12 MPH		375
4:14 PM	5:11 PM	There are now as many as 200 Indians near Weir Point, with many more closely behind. They slow, first to gather numbers, second to assess what the soldeirs are doing.	8 — 14 MPH	3¼ — 4 miles	376
4:17 PM — 4:18 PM	5:14 PM — 5:15 PM	Entering the coulee and riding hard toward its head, Edgerly and Harrison come across the injured and un-horsed Charley. Edgerly instructs him to crawl into a ravine and they would come back for him as soon as he could get reinforcements. As Edgerly and Harrison rode on and looked back they saw the Indians finishing off Charley.	12 MPH to a halt	½ of a mile off the "sugarloaf"	377
4:17 PM	5:14 PM	Warriors follow after Edgerly and Harrison.	10 MPH		377
4:20 PM	5:17 PM	As he headed back, Godfrey realized he needed to protect the rear of the retreating troops, so he halted and formed a skirmish line, sending his led – horses back. The Indians firing "was very hot," but no one was hit. Several horses were hit.	8 — 10 MPH	1 mile from its position on the Weir complex	378
4:28 PM	5:25 PM	Based on the 3:55 PM time as the beginning of the "general" move from Reno Hill to Weir Peaks, a 1¼-hour time frame would place the command back on Reno Hill at this time. This would be in general agreement with packer B. F. Churchill, who said the round trip to Weir and back took about one hour for the packs.		1 — 1½ miles	379
4:33 PM	5:30 PM	Varnum agreed with Hare, citing a 5:30 PM return to Reno Hill from Weir Peaks. Varnum's estimate was 3 hours, from Reno first reaching the hilltop at 2:30 PM. SGT Culbertson thought 1¼ hours from beginning of move to Weir to the return to Reno Hill. Herendeen and Edgerly claimed they were back on Reno Hill by 5 PM.		1 — 1½ miles	380

Y. Stragglers; 12:42 p.m.–4:30 p.m.

Local Sun Time	Command's Watch Time	Event	Speed	Distance Traveled	Notes
11:45 AM	12:42 PM	As the commands move down Reno Creek, varying speeds between rapid bursts and slower canters, a number of the Ree scouts begin to fall behind. These include Strikes The Lodge, Rushing Bull, Soldier, Bull, White Eagle, and Red Wolf.	10+ MPH down to as low as 6 MPH		70
11:48 PM	12:45 PM	The fast pace of the advancing column now begins to take its toll on some of the troops' horses. C Company trooper James Watson begins falling behind.	Declining gait, down to a walk		71
12:08 PM	1:05 PM	The Ree scouts, Soldier, Bull, and White Eagle—struggling with slower horses—catch up to the rest of the command.			85
12:16 PM	1:13 PM	Some Ree scouts, having trouble with their horses, ride with Custer's column, trying to catch up. These scouts are Soldier, Bull, and White Eagle.			92
12:17 PM	1:14 PM	The Ree scout, Stab—who had been with Benteen's column initially—rides up to Soldier and the others. He rides on ahead to follow Custer's column up the bluffs.			94
12:17 PM	1:14 PM	Two more C Company troopers—Brennan and Fitzgerald—fall out.			71
12:22 PM	1:19 PM	Custer hears Cooke's report and makes the fatal decision to try to get to the northern end of the village. He swings his command to the right and orders a gallop.	@ 9 – 10 MPH		101
12:27 PM	1:24 PM	The Ree scouts, Soldier, Bull, and White Eagle follow after Custer's command.			94
12:44 PM	1:41 PM	PVT Peter Thompson of C Company drops out of formation as his horse begins to break down. He is on the northern side of Reno Hill. The rest of the command passes him by.			124
12:44 PM	1:41 PM	As Thompson dismounts to tend to his horse, the F Company advance scouts pass him by.	10 MPH		125
12:58 PM	1:55 PM	As the leading Rees reach the hills above Reno Hill, they are fired on by some troopers lagging behind Custer's behind. The Ree scout, Stab, is amongst those shot at and he joins others with the stolen ponies.			150
1:13 PM	2:10 PM	By now, Ree scouts have captured a number of Sioux ponies—28—and have herded them across the LBH and up a small coulee coming off the bluffs. As they were doing so, they ran into the tail-end of Custer's command and were fired on by some trailing soldiers who mistook them for Sioux. The scouts now include Rees, Red Star, Strikes Two, Little Sioux, Boy Chief, One Feather, Bull-Stands-In-Water, and the Dakota, Whole Buffalo. Stab has already joined them, and they are soon joined by several others who did not cross the river with Reno, including Soldier, Bull, White Eagle, Strikes The Lodge, Billy Cross; and Dakotas, White Cloud, *Caroo*, and *Ma-tok-sha*.			167
1:13 PM	2:10 PM	Martini, in the vicinity of Reno Hill, sees stragglers from C Company. He does not stop but begins to slow. His horse has been wounded, but he is unaware of it.	6 MPH down to 5 MPH		169
1:33 PM	2:30 PM	PVT Watson of C Company is picked up by the packs; he is told to ride with McDougall's B Company when it catches up.			183

Y. Stragglers (cont.)

2:21 PM	3:18 PM	Eight to ten Rees drive about 15 stolen Sioux ponies along Reno Creek and meet the pack train west of the lone tepee. One of them was the half-breed, Billy Cross. It appears some of the others were the Ree stragglers, Bull, Red Bear, Soldier, Stab, Strikes Two, and White Eagle, along with Red Star, Red Wolf, and Strikes The Lodge. After the packs turned toward the hills, trailing Sioux retrieved their horses and the Rees returned to the hilltop. These are the same scouts who passed Benteen on his way to Reno Hill.	5 MPH	2 miles from picking up the horses in the ravine	237
3:33 PM	4:30 PM	Little Sioux and some other Rees head back to the ravine where they had sequestered the stolen Sioux ponies. There they met other stragglers, Boy Chief, Rushing Bull, Caroo, Red Bear, and Strikes Two.			298

Notes to the Timelines

1. LT Wallace, Report of the Chief of Engineers, Appendix PP, St. Paul, MN, January 27, 1877, Carroll, *General Custer abd the Battle of the Little Big Horn: The Federal View* [hereafter cited as *The Federal View*], 64–66; George Herendeen, *New York Herald*, January 4, 1878.

2. LT Mathey, Walter Camp interview, October 19, 1910; PVT DeVoto (B), letter to Camp, November 15, 1917.

3. LT Varnum, letter to his father, July 4, 1876; LT Godfrey, "Custer's Last Battle," 18.

4. George Herendeen, from Bismarck, D. T., July 7, 1876, Hutchins, *The Army and Navy Journal on the Battle of the Little Bighorn and Related Matters 1876–1881* [hereafter cited as *The Army and Navy Journal*], 40.

5. LT Godfrey, "Custer's Last Battle," 18.

6. LT Godfrey, *On the Little Bighorn with Walter Camp*, 173; LT Varnum, *I, Varnum*, 60 and 85; LT Wallace, report of the Chief of Engineers, Appendix PP, St. Paul, MN, January 27, 1877, Carroll, *The Federal View*, 64–66. Charles Kuhlman, *Legend into History*, 34.

7. LT Wallace, report of the Chief of Engineers, Appendix PP, St. Paul, MN, January 27, 1877, Carroll, *The Federal View*, 64–66; Billy Jackson; Windolph/Hunt, *I Fought with Custer*, 152.

8. Tom Heski, "'Don't Let Anything Get Away,'" *Research Review*, Summer 2007. Heski claims that around 7:00 p.m. in June, the sun is behind the Wolf Mountains, creating shadows in the valley. If there are no clouds, you can still see objects until about 10:00 p.m.

9. LT Godfrey, *Century Magazine* article, "Custer's Last Battle." Tom Heski/PVT Windolph (H), "'Don't Let Anything Get Away,'" *Research Review*, Summer 2007, 12, citing Frazier and Robert Hunt, *I Fought with Custer*, 73. LT Wallace, Report of the Chief of Engineers, Appendix PP, Report of LT G. D. Wallace, 7th Cavalry, St. Paul, MN, January 27, 1877, *The Federal View*, 64–66; LT Varnum, Walter Camp letters and interviews, Hardorff, *On the Little Bighorn with Walter Camp*, 49.

10. LT Varnum, letter to Walter Camp, April 14, 1909, Hardorff, *On the Little Bighorn with Walter Camp*, 50.

11. CPT Benteen manuscript, circa 1890–1892.

12. United States Naval Observatory: local time is from Gray, *Custer's Last Campaign*; it does not correspond exactly to the same event as shown on the U.S. Naval Observatory Website.

13. LT Varnum, letter to Walter Camp, April 14, 1909; White Man Runs Him (Crow scout) interview with General Hugh Scott, August 24, 1919.

14. LT Godfrey, *Century Magazine*, 1892, "Custer's Last Battle," 19.

15. CPT Benteen, 1890, "Benteen Manuscript," *The Custer Myth*, 165 and 179; and *The Benteen-Goldin Letters on Custer and His Last Battle* [hereafter cited as *The Benteen-Goldin Letters*], 179–180; LT Godfrey, *Century Magazine*, 1892, "Custer's Last Battle," 19; LT Edgerly, *Scalp Dance*, 24.

16. CPT Benteen, manuscript, 1890; CPT Moylan, *RCOI*, 213; LT Hare, Walter Camp interview February 7, 1910; LT Edgerly, letter to his wife, July 4, 1876; George Herendeen, *New York Herald*, July 8, 1876.

17. CPT Benteen, manuscript, 1890.

18. LT Varnum, letter to father, July 4, 1876; *RCOI*, 146; Camp interviews, 1909–1910, *On the Little Bighorn with Walter Camp*, 50; *I, Varnum*, 62.

19. LT Godfrey, *Century Magazine*, 1892, "Custer's Last Battle," 19; George Herendeen, *RCOI*, 262.

20. CPT Benteen. An hour and a half after they stopped, "daylight began to peer through..." *The Benteen-Goldin Letters*, 180.

21. LT Varnum, letters to Walter Camp, April 14 and May 5, 1909.

22. LT Varnum, letter to Walter Camp, April 14, 1909.

23. Red Star (Arikara scout), 1912 interviews, *The Arikara Narrative of Custer's Campaign and the Battle of the Little Bighorn* [hereafter cited as *The Arikara Narrative*], 89.

24. PVT Burkman (HQ/L). Primary source attribution uncertain; G. D. Wagner, *Old Neutriment*, 149, from Liddic, *Vanishing Victory*, 25.

25. PVT Burkman (HQ/L); see Source Note 24, above.

26. Fred Gerard, *RCOI*, 108; Red Star, *The Arikara Narrative*, 89.

27. LT Varnum, *RCOI*, 145.

28. PVT DeVoto (B), Hardorff, *Indian Views of the Custer Fight*, 203–209.

29. LT Varnum, 1909–1910, correspondence with Walter Camp, *Custer in '76*, 60–61.

30. CPT Moylan, *RCOI*, 214; LT Godfrey, undated Camp notes, *On the Little Bighorn with Walter Camp*, 174–175; SGT Kanipe (C), Walter Camp interview, June 16th and 17th, 1908, *Custer in '76*, 91.

31. LT Godfrey, undated Camp notes, *On the Little Bighorn with Walter Camp*, 174–175.

32. SGT Kanipe (C), Walter Camp interview, June 16th and 17th, 1908, *Custer in '76*, 91.

33. CPT Moylan, *RCOI*, 214.

34. LT Varnum, *I, Varnum*, 88; Little Sioux (Arikara scout), undated Walter Camp interview, *Custer in '76*, 180.

35. LTs Hare and DeRudio. Walter Camp mentioned to Varnum that Luther Hare told him the regiment halted around 10 a.m. about ¼ to ½ mile east of the divide and remained there until about 11:45 a.m. Camp said DeRudio told him the same thing.

36. CPT Benteen, *RCOI*, 402.

37. MAJ Reno, *RCOI*, 560; LT Edgerly, *Leavenworth Times*, August 18, 1881; LT Varnum; TMP Martini (HQ/H), *Cavalry Journal*, July, 1923; Fred Gerard, 1912 interview, *The Arikara Narrative*, 172.

38. PVT Peter Thompson (C), *Belle Fourche Bee* (South Dakota), 1922 or 1923: "The Experience of a Private Soldier in the Custer Massacre"; Young Hawk (Arikara scout), 1912 interviews, *The Arikara Narrative*, 93.

39. George Herendeen, *RCOI*, 250–251.

40. George Herendeen, from a statement made by Herendeen in Bozeman, M. T., on January 4, 1878, and published in the *New York Herald*, January 22, 1878, *The Custer Myth*, 262–263; *RCOI*, 250–251.

41. LT Edgerly, *The Custer Myth*, 219. It should be noted here that the reference pertains only to the fact Custer was aware of the Boyer/Herendeen incident, not specifically that it was Boyer or anyone else who informed him.

42. MAJ Reno, *RCOI*, 560; LT Edgerly, *Leavenworth Times*, August 18, 1881.

43. CPT McDougall, *RCOI*, 528.

44. LT DeRudio, Walter Camp interview, February 2, 1910. Camp wrote that DeRudio told him Custer went "the second time to the Crows' Nest to take a look at the valley of the Little Bighorn," and this was when Cooke borrowed DeRudio's field glasses. LT Hare, Walter Camp interview, February 7, 1910.

45. PVT Windolph (H), memoirs, 1946, *I Fought with Custer*; George Herendeen, *RCOI*, 250.

46. Vern Smalley, *More Little Bighorn Mysteries*, 1–9.

47. LT DeRudio, Walter Camp interview conducted February 2, 1910, *Custer in '76*, 84; LT Hare, Walter Camp interview conducted February 7, 1910, *Custer in '76*, 64; George Herendeen, *RCOI*, 250.

48. LT DeRudio, Walter Camp interview conducted February 2, 1910, *Custer in '76*, 84; LT Hare, Walter Camp interview conducted February 7, 1910, *Custer in '76*, 64.

49. PVT Windolph (H), memoirs, 1946, *I Fought with Custer*, 76 and 78.

50. LT Varnum, memoirs, probably early 1930s, *I, Varnum*, 64.

51. LT Wallace, report of the Chief of Engineers, Appendix PP, St. Paul, MN, January 27, 1877, Carroll, *The Federal View*, 64–66.

52. LTs Godfrey, Wallace, Mathey, PVT Windolph (H), TMP Martini (HQ/H).

53. LT Godfrey, *Century Magazine*, 1892 "Custer's Last Battle," 21; PVT Windolph (H), memoirs, 1946.

54. LT Wallace, January 27, 1877, Appendix, Official Report, Chief of Engineers.

55. CPT McDougall, undated Walter Camp interview; possibly February 26, 1909; TMP Hardy (A), undated interview with Walter Camp, but from correspondence between the two men, probably 1910; Hardorff, *Camp, Custer and the Little Bighorn*, 81. "Hardy says Boss Custer was with the five cos when Reno separated, and Boss said he was going to where the fighting would be. Haddon had Boss Custer's extra pony. Boss had two Indian ponies." Unclear about *which* separation: at the divide or near lone tepee. In addition, there was no Haddon in the Seventh Cavalry.

56. CPT McDougall, undated Walter Camp interview; possibly February 26, 1909.

57. CPT McDougall, *RCOI*, 529.

58. CPT Benteen, *RCOI*, 405.

59. LT Wallace, *RCOI*, 540–541; LT DeRudio, *RCOI*, 311.

60. CPT Benteen, *RCOI*, 403.

61. CPT Benteen, *RCOI*, 403; "Benteen Manuscript," 1890, *The Custer Myth*, 168–169; 179–180.

62. LT Godfrey, article in *Century Magazine*, 1892, "Custer's Last Battle," 22; LT Edgerly, *RCOI*, 441, 457.

63. CPT Benteen, *New York Herald*, August 8, 1876; *RCOI*, 403.

64. Simulation.

65. LT Varnum, *RCOI*, 168.

66. LT Edgerly, *Reno Court of Inquiry*, 439. Edgerly claimed about one mile, but in reality, it was closer to 1⅓ miles from the separation point just west of the divide.

67. CPT Benteen, *RCOI*, 403; "Manuscript," 1890; February 24, 1892, letter to Goldin, *The Benteen-Goldin Letters*, 213.

68. CPT Benteen, *RCOI*, 404 and 422; "Benteen Manuscript," 1890, *The Benteen-Goldin Letters*, 183; LT Edgerly, *RCOI*, 439.

69. CPT Freeman (H/7I), personal journal, June 29, 1876, 31. The Freeman reference pertains to speed only. LT DeRudio, *RCOI*, 312; SGT Kanipe (C), undated Walter Camp notes, *On the Little Bighorn with Walter Camp*, 176.

70. Soldier (Arikara scout), undated interview with Walter Camp, *Custer in '76*, 187, and *The Arikara Narrative*, 115; Bull (Arikara scout), *The Arikara Narrative*; White Eagle (Arikara scout), *The Arikara Narrative*. The Bull and White Eagle narratives are problematic in so far as attribution; their story is excerpted from Graham's, *The Custer Myth*, 44.

71. PVT Thompson (C), *Belle Fourche Bee* (South Dakota), 1922 or 1923: "The Experience of a Private Soldier in the Custer Massacre," 27.

72. LT Hare, Walter Camp interview, February 7, 1910, *Custer in '76*, 65.

73. LT Varnum, *RCOI*, 168; *I, Varnum*, 64 and 156; LT Hare, Walter Camp interview, February 7, 1910.

74. MAJ Reno, *RCOI*, 560; CPT Moylan, *RCOI*, 215; LT DeRudio, *RCOI*, 311–312; LT Wallace, January 27, 1877, Appendix, Official Report, Chief of Engineers; Little Sioux (Arikara scout), *The Arikara Narrative*, 150, confirming, "They rode at full speed...." *Et al.*

75. LT Varnum, Walter Camp interview, May 1909, *Custer in '76*, 61.

76. CPT Moylan, *RCOI*, 215. LT Godfrey, his field diary, June 24th and 25th, 1876, entry, 11. The Godfrey reference pertains only to his estimate of the tepee's distance from the main village, i. e., four miles. LT Varnum, *RCOI*, 168; LT Wallace, July 4, 1876, letter to Knoblauch, and *RCOI*, 541; LT Hare, *RCOI*, 276, and in interview with Walter Camp, February 7, 1910, *Custer in '76*, 65; 1SG Ryan (M), memoirs 1880's and between 1904–1906, *Ten Years with Custer*, 290; Dr. Henry R. Porter (HQ), *RCOI*, 198; George Herendeen, from a statement made by Herendeen in Bozeman, M. T., on January 4, 1878, and published in the *New York Herald*, January 22, 1878; Strikes Two (Arikara scout), undated interview with Walter Camp, *Custer in '76*, 183.

77. LT Hare, *RCOI*, 276; TMP Martini (HQ/H), *Cavalry Journal*, July 1923, *The Custer Myth*, 289; Curley (Crow scout), first Walter Camp interview, September 18, 1908, *Custer in '76*, 156; White Man Runs Him (Crow scout), Scott/McCoy interview, August 24, 1919, *The Custer Myth*, 23; Little Sioux (Arikara scout), *The Arikara Narrative*, 150; Red Bear (Arikara scout), *The Arikara Narrative*, 121.

78. LT Hare, *RCOI*, 276; PVT Davern (Reno's HQ/F), *RCOI*, 332; Fred Gerard, *RCOI*, 84.

79. Fred Gerard, *RCOI*, 86, 90, and 112.

80. Black Bear (Oglala Sioux), interview with Walter Camp, July 18, 1911, *Custer in '76*, 203–204; Iron Hawk (Hunkpapa Sioux), DeMallie, *The Sixth Grandfather*, 190; Standing Bear (Minneconjou Sioux), DeMallie, *The Sixth Grandfather*, 184.

81. LT Wallace, *RCOI*, 45, 76, and 544; LT Godfrey, article revision, 1921, 1920s–1930s, *The Custer Myth*, 139; LT Edgerly, undated interview with Walter Camp, *Custer in '76*, 55. Godfrey's and Edgerly's comments here would have to be considered hearsay. Fred Gerard, *RCOI*, 87–88, 90, and 116.

82. LT Hare, *RCOI*, 276.

83. MAJ Reno, after-action report, addressed to CPT E. W. Smith, ADC and AAAG to BG Terry, dated July 5, 1876, from camp on the Yellowstone River, Carroll, *The Federal View*, 103; LT Wallace, *RCOI*, 541 and 544; Dr. Henry Porter (HQ), *RCOI*, 188; PVT Davern (Reno's HQ/F), *RCOI*, 332.

84. SGT White (M), his personal diary, pre–1910, and copied by Walter Camp, Hardorff, *Indian Views of the Custer Fight*, 16.

85. Soldier (Arikara scout), *The Arikara Narrative*, 115.

86. CPT Moylan, *RCOI*, 216; LT Varnum, *RCOI*, 145; LT Wallace, *RCOI*, 541; SGT Culbertson (A), *RCOI*, 366; George Herendeen, *RCOI*, 251.

87. CPT Moylan, *RCOI*, 216; LT Varnum, *RCOI*, 139.

88. LT Varnum, letter to Camp, May 5, 1909, *On the Little Bighorn with Walter Camp*, 74.

89. TMP Martini (HQ/H), *RCOI*, 387.

90. LT Varnum, *RCOI*, 141; Fred Gerard, *RCOI*, 87.

91. Fred Gerard, *RCOI*, 86.

92. Soldier (Arikara scout), undated Camp interview, *Custer in '76*, 188, and, *The Arikara Narrative*, 115–116; White Eagle (Arikara scout), *The Custer Myth*, taken from *The Arikara Narrative*, 44.

93. Fred Gerard, *RCOI*, 111 and 113–114.

94. Soldier (Arikara scout), *The Arikara Narrative*, 116.

95. MAJ Reno, from a July 30, 1876, letter by Reno, addressed to T. L. Rosser, late MG-CSA, and published in the *New York Herald*, August 8, 1876, *The Custer Myth*, 226; LT Wallace, July 4, 1876, letter to Knoblauch; Fred Gerard, *RCOI*, 113.

96. Fred Gerard, *RCOI*, 87; George Herendeen, from Bismarck, D. T., July 7, 1876, *The Army and Navy Journal*, 40.

97. Fred Gerard, *RCOI*, 87.

98. MAJ Reno, *RCOI*, 561; LT Varnum, *RCOI*, 141 and 145; LT Wallace, *RCOI*, 44; 1SG Ryan (M), 1880's and between 1904–1906, *Ten Years with Custer*, 291; PVT Morris (M), from a letter dated November 1, 1908, to Walter Camp, Denver Public Library, Robert S. Ellison papers, WH131 File Folder, Donahue, *Drawing Battle Lines*, 128.

99. George Herendeen, from Bismarck, D. T., July 7, 1876, Hutchins, *The Army and Navy Journal*, 40.

100. Simulation, but supported by Gerard, *RCOI*, 87.

101. LT DeRudio, *RCOI*, 312; Red Bear (Arikara scout), *The Arikara Narrative*, 122.

102. MAJ Reno, *RCOI*, 561; PVT Davern (Reno's HQ/F), *RCOI*, 358. In Fred Dustin's classic work, *The Custer Tragedy* (69–70), he describes the April 3rd crossing of the Yellowstone River by CPT Henry Freeman's battalion (companies A, B, H, I, and K, 7th Infantry; LT Bradley's mounted scouts; and 10 contract wagons). Bradley's scouts found a ford to the south bank, some 300 feet across the river, and despite a rapid current, managed to ford the wagons (carrying some of the infantry), the remainder of the infantry, and the mounted scouts, and taking only 20 minutes to cross, some of the infantry doubled up on the few horses. The Little Big Horn crossing at Ford A was only some 30 feet wide and more shallow than the Yellowstone, so a four-minute crossing here is not unreasonable at all, especially considering the speed they were moving.

103. TMP Martini (HQ/H), *RCOI*, 388.

104. 1SG Ryan (M), 1880's and between 1904–1906, *Ten Years with Custer*, 291; George Herendeen, from a statement made by Herendeen in Bozeman, M. T., on January 4, 1878, and published in the *New York Herald*, January 22, 1878.

105. LT Wallace, *RCOI*, 46.

106. 1SG Ryan (M), memoirs, Barnard, *Ten Years with Custer*, 291; SGT White (M), his personal diary, pre–1910, and copied by Walter Camp, Hardorff, *Indian Views of the Custer Fight*, 16; PVT Wilber (M), undated interview with Walter Camp, Hammer, *Custer in '76*, 148; PVT Morris (M), Donahue, *Drawing Battle Lines*, 130.

107. Red Bear (Arikara scout), *The Arikara Narrative*, 122; Strikes Two (Arikara scout), Hammer, *Custer in '76*, 183.

108. PVT O'Neill (G), Walter Camp interview, probably conducted October 12, 1909, *Custer in '76*, 106; PVT Petring (G), undated Walter Camp interview, *Custer in '76*, 133.

109. CPT Benteen, official report to Major Reno, July 4, 1876, and *The Benteen-Goldin Letters*, 184; LT Godfrey, *RCOI*, 479, and "Custer's Last Battle," 22; LT Edgerly, Clark, *Scalp Dance*, 24; PVT Windolph (H), *I Fought with Custer*, 80.

110. TMP Martini (HQ/H), *RCOI*, 388; PVT O'Neill (G), Walter Camp interview conducted, October 12, 1909 (?), *Custer in '76*, 106; PVT Petring (G), undated interview with Walter Camp, *Custer in '76*, 133. *Et al.*

111. Curley (Crow scout), first interview with Walter Camp, conducted September 18, 1908, along Reno Creek and onto the Custer battlefield, *Custer in '76*, 157; Goes Ahead (Crow scout), Walter Camp interview conducted August 5, 1909, *Custer in '76*, 74; Hairy Moccasin (Crow scout), Walter Camp interview conducted February 23, 1911, *Custer in '76*, 177; White Man Runs Him (Crow scout), interview with COL Tim McCoy with GEN Scott during 1919 trip to the battlefield, *The Custer Myth*, 23.

112. Boy Chief (Arikara scout), *The Arikara Narrative*, 118; Red Bear (Arikara scout), *The Arikara Narrative*, 122; Little Sioux (Arikara scout), *Custer in '76*, 180; One Feather (Arikara scout), *Camp on Custer*, 129; Strikes Two (Arikara scout), *Custer in '76*, 183–184.

113. SGT Kanipe (C), Walter Camp interview

114. LT DeRudio, *RCOI*, 313; LT Varnum, *RCOI*, 146. Varnum used a 30-minute time span from separation to the skirmish line. 1SG Ryan (M), *Ten Years with Custer*, 291; Thunder Bear (Nakota-Yankton Sioux), a 1907 narrative, *Indian Views of the Custer Fight*, 92. The Thunder Bear reference is for the approximate time the fighting began.

115. PVT Wilber (M), undated interview with Walter Camp, *Custer in '76*, 148. One source claimed Ryan continued on into the village, but this seems to be incorrect.

116. PVT Morris (M), from a letter written by Morris to Robert Bruce, May 23, 1928, Carroll, *The Battles of the Little Big Horn*, 18.

117. CPT Moylan, *RCOI*, 241; LT DeRudio, *RCOI*, 313–314; LT Varnum, memoirs, early 1930's; *I, Varnum*, 122, and *RCOI*, 147; LT Wallace, *RCOI*, 25; LT Hare, *RCOI*, 277; CPL Roy (A), undated Walter Camp correspondence, *Custer in '76*, 112.

118. LT Varnum, from a letter he wrote to his father in Tallahassee, FL, July 4, 1876, and published in a Tallahassee newspaper, *The Custer Myth*, 342.

119. Boy Chief (Arikara scout), *The Custer Myth*, 39; Goes Ahead (Crow scout), *The Custer Myth*, 20; Hairy Moccasin (Crow scout), *Custer in '76*, 177.

120. 1SG Ryan (M), *Ten Years with Custer*, 293; SGT Culbertson (A), *RCOI*, 367; PVT Morris (M), letter dated November 1, 1908, to Walter Camp, Donahue, *Drawing Battle Lines*, 130.

121. CPT Moylan, *RCOI*, 223. Moylan's reference is to distance only. PVT Wilber (M), undated interview with Walter Camp, *Custer in '76*, 148; Kill Eagle (Blackfeet Sioux), from an interview conducted September 17, 1876, and appearing in the *New York Herald*, September 24, 1876, Hutchins, *The Army and Navy Journal*, 53; Red Horse (Minneconjou Sioux), from an extract of the report of Colonel W. H. Wood, Commanding Post Cheyenne Agency, dated February 27, 1877, giving Red Horse's account of the battle of the 'Little Horn' and Massacre of Custer and his battalion, *The Army and Navy Journal*, 136–137.

122. Red Bear (Arikara scout), *The Arikara Narrative*, 123.

123. Little Sioux (Arikara scout), *Custer in '76*, 180–181; Strikes Two (Arikara scout), *Custer in '76*, 184; Boy Chief (Arikara scout), *The Arikara Narrative*, 118–119.

124. PVT Peter Thompson (C), Walter Camp interview, January 1909; Hardorff, *On the Little Bighorn with Walter Camp*, 24; and, narrative, "The Experience of a Private Soldier in the Custer Massacre," 29–30; also contained in the *Belle Fourche Bee*, 1922 or 1923.

125. PVT Peter Thompson (C), narrative, "The Experience of a Private Soldier in the Custer Massacre," 28; also contained in the *Belle Fourche Bee*, 1922 or 1923.

126. LT Varnum, *RCOI*, 157.

127. Gall (Hunkpapa Sioux). Supported by Greg Michno, *Lakota Noon*, 68–69.

128. SGT Kanipe (C), 1903, published in the magazine of the Historical Society of Montana and written by Daniel Kanipe; also, from the Greensboro, NC, *Daily Record*, April 27, 1924.

129. SGT White (M), his personal diary, pre-1910, and copied by Walter Camp, Hardorff, *Indian Views of the Custer Fight*, 17; PVT Morris (M), from a letter written by Morris to Robert Bruce, May 23, 1928, Carroll, *The Battles of the Little Big Horn*, 18.

130. Hairy Moccasin (Crow scout), *The Custer Myth*, 25; Goes Ahead (Crow scout), *The Custer Myth*, 20.

131. PVT Wilber (M); supported by Wilber, undated interview with Walter Camp, *Custer in '76*, 148.

132. MAJ Reno, *RCOI*, 562; LT Wallace, *RCOI*, 27.

133. LT DeRudio, *RCOI*, 314.

conducted June 16th and 17th, 1908, *Custer in '76*, 92; TMP Martini (HQ/H), *RCOI*, 388.

134. SGT Kanipe (C), from the Greensboro, NC, *Daily Record*, April 27, 1924, *The Custer Myth*, 249.

135. TMP Martini (HQ/H), *RCOI*, 398.

136. LT DeRudio, *RCOI*, 314 and 337; TMP Martini (HQ/H), *RCOI*, 398.

137. LT DeRudio, *RCOI*, 314 and 337.

138. MAJ Reno, *RCOI*, 562.

139. LT Varnum, *RCOI*, 141–142.

140. LT Edgerly, Liddic, *Vanishing Victory*, 39, citing Carroll.

141. CPT Benteen, official report to MAJ Marcus Reno, dated July 4, 1876, Carroll, *The Federal View*, 105; PVT Windolph (H), Hunt, *I Fought with Custer*, 80.

142. CPT Benteen, *RCOI*, 404.

143. Gall (Hunkpapa Sioux); Greg Michno, *Lakota Noon*, 68.

144. LT Edgerly, as quoted in Liddic, *Vanishing Victory*, 39, citing Carroll, *The Gibson and Edgerly Narratives*, 5. "He (Boston) had stayed back with the pack train and was now hurrying up to join the general's immediate command. He have me a cheery salutation as he passed, and with a smile on his face, rode to his death."

145. LT Varnum, *RCOI*, 142.

146. Boy Chief (Arikara scout), *The Custer Myth*, 39; Goes Ahead (Crow scout), *The Custer Myth*, 20.

147. Goes Ahead (Crow scout), *Where Custer Fell*, 74, and in an August 5, 1909, interview with Walter Camp, *Custer in '76*, 174; Hairy Moccasin (Crow scout), *The Custer Myth*, 25.

148. LT DeRudio, *RCOI*, 337.

149. CPT Benteen, LTs Godfrey and Edgerly, PVT Windolph (H). See 1:56 PM.

150. Strikes Two (Arikara scout), undated Camp interview, *Custer in '76*, 184; Boy Chief (Arikara scout), *The Arikara Narrative*, 119.

151. CPT Benteen, from Benteen's official report to Major Marcus Reno, dated July 4, 1876, and included with BG Terry's report, Carroll, *The Federal View*, 105. LT Godfrey, his field diary, June 24th and 25th,1876, entry, 11; and in 1879, *RCOI*, 479; and January 1892, "Custer's Last Battle," *Century Magazine*, 22. LT Edgerly, *RCOI*, 439–440. PVT Windolph (H), Hunt, *I Fought with Custer*, 184.

152. Curley (Crow scout), interview with GEN Hugh Scott, August 24, 1919, *The Custer Myth*, 13: "Custer turned around as he reached the top of the ridge and waved his hat, and his men at the bottom of the hill waved their hats and shouted. Custer kept on going on the ridge and the men followed him."

153. PVT Wilber (M), undated interview with Walter Camp, *Custer in '76*, 148.

154. TMP Martini (HQ/H), *RCOI*, 390.

155. Supported by, Thompson, Walter Camp interview, January 1909, Hardorff, *On the Little Bighorn with Walter Camp*, 24–25.

156. TMP Martini (HQ/H), *RCOI*, 390–391.

157. Hairy Moccasin (Crow scout), from the June 1916, "Tepee Book," *The Custer Myth*, 25; Goes Ahead (Crow scout), *Where Custer Fell*, 74, and in a Walter Camp interview conducted August 5, 1909, *Custer in '76*, 175; White Man Runs Him (Crow scout), undated interview with Walter Camp, *Custer in '76*, 178 and FN 2, 178.

158. TMP Martini (HQ/H) claimed to be moving "at a jog trot"; *The Custer Myth*, 290.

159. Strikes Two (Arikara scout), *Custer in '76*, 184.

160. CPT Moylan, *RCOI*, 216; LT Varnum, *I, Varnum*, 112–113.

161. Goes Ahead (Crow scout) and White Man Runs Him (Crow scout), *Where Custer Fell*, 74.

162. LT Godfrey, *RCOI*, 480, *Century Magazine*, 1892, "Custer's Last Battle," 22; PVT Windolph (H), *I Fought with Custer*, 81.

163. CPT Benteen, official report to MAJ Reno, July 4, 1876, Carroll, *The Federal View*, 105; LT Godfrey, *RCOI*, 479, and *RCOI*, 480.

164. CPT Moylan, *RCOI*, 216.

165. Simulation, inference.

166. CPT Benteen, official report to MAJ Reno, July 4, 1876, *The Federal View*, 105; LT Godfrey, "Custer's Last Battle," 22; LT Edgerly, *RCOI*, 441; PVT Windolph (H), *I Fought with Custer*, 80.

167. Boy Chief (Arikara scout), *The Arikara Narrative*, 119; Strikes Two (Arikara scout), *Custer in '76*, 184; Little Sioux (Arikara scout), *Custer in '76*, 180–181.

168. Gall (Hunkpapa Sioux); supported by Greg Michno, *Lakota Noon*, 69.

169. TMP Martini (HQ/H), Walter Camp interviews, October 24, 1908, and May 4, 1910, *Custer in '76*, 104, footnote 7.

170. CPT Moylan, *RCOI*, 216; Fred Gerard, *RCOI*, 119; George Herendeen, statement made in Bozeman, M. T., January 4, 1878, published in the *New York Herald*, January 22, 1878.

171. PVT Sivertsen (M), Coffeen, *The Custer Battle Book*, 42–46; Young Hawk (Arikara scout), *The Arikara Narrative*, 97; Red Bear (Arikara scout), *The Arikara Narrative*, 125; Black Elk (Oglala Sioux), DeMallie, *The Sixth Grandfather*, 182.

172. Black Elk (Oglala Sioux), Neihardt, *Black Elk Speaks*, 110–111, and DeMallie, *The Sixth Grandfather*, 182.

173. Goes Ahead (Crow scout), *The Arikara Narrative*, 160; White Man Runs Him (Crow scout), 1919 battlefield interview with COL Tim McCoy, *The Custer Myth*, 23; Hairy Moccasin (Crow scout), from the June 1916, "Tepee Book," *The Custer Myth*, 25.

174. PVT Sivertsen (M), Coffeen, *The Custer Battle Book*, 42–46; Red Bear (Arikara scout), *The Arikara Narrative*, 125.

175. Boy Chief (Arikara scout), *The Arikara Narrative*, 119; Strikes Two (Arikara scout), *The Arikara Narrative*, 119.

176. LT Varnum, *RCOI*, 148.

177. MAJ Reno, *RCOI*, 563; CPT Moylan, *RCOI*, 217; LT Varnum, *RCOI*, 143; LT Wallace, *RCOI*, 23; LT Hare, *RCOI*, 279; 1SG Ryan (M), memoirs, 1880s, 1904–1906, *Ten Years with Custer*, 293; CPL Roy (A), undated correspondence with Walter Camp, *Custer in '76*, 112; Dr. Henry Porter (HQ), *RCOI*, 190; George Herendeen, *RCOI*, 286; Wooden Leg (Northern Cheyenne), Marquis interviews, 1922–1931, *Wooden Leg*, 220–221.

178. Gall (Hunkpapa Sioux); supported by Greg Michno, *Lakota Noon*, 68–69, 86–87, 89, 93.

179. LT Varnum, *RCOI*, 149.

180. Goes Ahead (Crow scout), interview with Walter Camp, August 5, 1909, *Custer in '76*, 175. Pretty White Buffalo (Hunkpapa Sioux): "From across the river I could hear the music of the bugle and could see the column of soldiers turn to the left, to march down to the river to where the attack was to be made"; *St. Paul Pioneer Press*, May 19, 1883, *The Custer Myth*, 86.

181. Gall (Hunkpapa Sioux); supported by Greg Michno, *Lakota Noon*, 86–87, 89, 93.

182. LT Mathey, *RCOI*, 513; One Bull (Minneconjou Sioux), 1929 interview, Hardorff, *Indian Views of the Custer Fight*, 140. The One Bull reference pertains to this entry only in so far as One Bull, chasing soldiers up toward Reno Hill during Reno's retreat, claimed to have seen pack mules along Reno Creek. This sighting is possible from some of the higher elevations and indicates the packs were already in the flats at this time.

183. PVT Slaper (M); Brininstool, *A Trooper with Custer and Other Historic Incidents of the Battle of the Little Big Horn* [hereafter cited as *A Trooper with Custer*], 17–56. Slaper claimed his friend, Watson, trailed the column and was eventually picked up by the "rear guard" and arrived on Reno Hill with the "rear guard," i. e., McDougall's B Company.

184. Boy Chief (Arikara scout), *The Arikara Narrative*, 119; Little Sioux (Arikara scout), undated interview with Walter Camp, *Custer in '76*, 181; Strikes Two (Arikara scout), *The Arikara Narrative*, 119.

185. Goes Ahead (Crow scout), interviews with Walter Camp, 1909 and 1912, *Where Custer Fell*, 74–75. Goes Ahead does not specifically state he saw the troops mounting the ridges, but that he saw troops up there. He Dog (Oglala Sioux), Camp interview, July 13, 1910, *Custer in '76*, 206.

186. Goes Ahead (Crow scout), *The Arikara Narrative*, 160; Hairy Moccasin (Crow scout), from the June 1916, "Tepee Book," *The Custer Myth*, 25.

187. CPT Benteen, excerpts from a separate, July 4, 1876, letter from Benteen to his wife. It is widely considered to be the more important of the letters Benteen wrote to his wife. It was written at the Seventh Cavalry camp on the Yellowstone River opposite the mouth of the Big Horn River; *The Custer Myth*, 298; *RCOI*, 404.

188. LT DeRudio, *RCOI*, 325.

189. 1SG Ryan (M), memoirs, 1880's and between 1904–1906, Barnard, *Ten Years with Custer*, 293; CPL Roy (A), undated Walter Camp interview may have been taken from correspondence between them, *Custer in '76*, 112–113; PVT Slaper (M), 1925, Brininstool, *A Trooper with Custer*, 17–56; PVT Rutten (M), undated Walter Camp interview may have been taken from correspondence between them, Hammer, *Custer in '76*, 119; PVT Petring (G), undated Walter Camp interview may have been taken from correspondence between them, *Custer in '76*, 134.

190. Soldier (Arikara scout), undated interview with Walter Camp, *Custer in '76*, 188, and *The Arikara Narrative*, 117.

191. SGT Kanipe (C), Walter Camp interview conducted June 16th and 17th, 1908, *Custer in '76*, 93.

192. CPT Benteen, from Benteen's official report to MAJ Marcus Reno, July 4, 1876, and included with BG Terry's report, *The Federal View*, 106; also *RCOI*, 404; SGT Kanipe (C), Walter Camp interview conducted June 16th and 17th, 1908, *Custer in '76*, 93.

193. Goes Ahead (Crow scout), *The Arikara Narrative*, 160; Two Moons (Northern Cheyenne), a 1901 interview with J. M. Thralls, Hardorff, *Cheyenne Memories of the Custer Fight*, 109. Two Moons does not mention the ridge by any name, only that this was the first the Indians saw of Custer's command.

194. Gall (Hunkpapa Sioux); supported by Michno, *Lakota Noon*, 93.

195. LT Godfrey, diary entry written several days after the battle, *The Field Diary of Lieutenant Edward Settle Godfrey* [hereafter cited as *Field Diary*], 11.

196. TMP Martini (HQ/H) saw Benteen, "was riding quite a distance in front of [his] troops, with his orderly trumpeter, at a fast trot." Graham, *The Custer Myth*, 290. From an article by Graham, published in the July 1923 edition of *The Cavalry Journal*. Graham does not say when Martini told this story, but it seems like some time in 1922.

197. CPT Benteen, *RCOI*, 405; LT Edgerly, *RCOI*, 440; TMP Martini (HQ/H), *RCOI*, 390. Martini only said Benteen read the note, put it in his pocket, then continued on toward the Little Big Horn River.

198. American Horse (Northern Cheyenne), 1895 interview with George Bird Grinnel, Hardorff, *Cheyenne Memories of the Custer Fight*, 29; Brave Wolf (Northern Cheyenne), 1895 interview with George Bird Grinnel, *Cheyenne Memories of the Custer Fight*, 35–36.

199. CPT McDougall, *RCOI*, 529; LT Mathey, *RCOI*, 513.

200. CPT McDougall, *RCOI*, 529–530.

201. LT Varnum, *RCOI*, 143 and 155.

202. CPT Benteen, *RCOI*, 405; LT Godfrey, *RCOI*, 480, and his "Field Diary," 12; LT Edgerly, *Leavenworth Times*, August 18, 1881; PVT Windolph (H), *I Fought with Custer*, 89; White Man Runs Him

(Crow scout), 1919 interview with Tim McCoy, *The Custer Myth,* 24.

203. Yellow Nose (Ute/Southern Cheyenne), *Indian School Journal,* November 1905; *Big Horn-Yellowstone Journal,* Summer 1992, Vol. 1, No. 3. Artifactual evidence supports the presence of troops on this ridge. In Michno, *Lakota Noon,* 153, all along the Nye-Cartwright/Luce Ridge complex were found upwards of 480 .45/55 cases and cartridges; several .50/70 cases; an undetermined number of additional shells; saddle and tack parts; and uniform buttons and buckles.

204. SGT Culbertson (A), *RCOI,* 370.

205. Russell White Bear, 1926, from a letter by Russell White Bear three years after Curley's death on May 21, 1923, *The Custer Myth,* 19.

206. Two Moons (Northern Cheyenne), in a series of interviews, March 3rd–5th, 1913, New Capitol Hotel, Washington City; Hardorff, *Indian Views of the Custer Fight,* 114. This sounds plausible and hints at a period of elapsed time before a fairly large number of warriors were leaving the Reno fighting.

207. PVT Windolph (H), *I Fought with Custer,* 89.

208. American Horse (Northern Cheyenne), 1895 interview with George Bird Grinnel, Hardorff, *Cheyenne Memories of the Custer Fight,* 29; Brave Wolf (Northern Cheyenne), 1895 interview with George Bird Grinnel, *Cheyenne Memories of the Custer Fight,* 35–36.

209. Kingsley Bray; supported by Bray, *Crazy Horse,* 221.

210. Pretty White Buffalo (Hunkpapa Sioux), *St. Paul Pioneer Press,* May 19, 1883, *The Custer Myth,* 86; Shave Elk (Oglala Sioux), undated interview with Walter Camp, *Camp on Custer,* 122; Feather Earring (Minneconjou Sioux), Hugh Scott interview, September 9, 1919, *The Custer Myth,* 97; Flying Hawk (Oglala Sioux), Eli Ricker interview, 1907, *Lakota Recollections,* 50; Two Eagles (Brulé Sioux), Weston interview, 1908, *Lakota Recollections,* 143, 145; Lights (Minneconjou Sioux), Weston interview, 1909, *Lakota Recollections,* 165. There is artifactual evidence, as well, that soldiers occupied this position. In Michno, *Lakota Noon,* 153, along the front side of Butler Ridge which faces the LBH, were found: ten .45/55-caliber bullets; four .45/55 cases; two unfired .45/55 cartridges; two Colt .45 bullets; one .50/70 cartridge; three .44 Henry cases; three .50 Spencer cases; four brass cavalry insignia; one arrowhead; two half horseshoes; one metal ring; brass grommets; iron snaps; and one Winchester rifle. Fox wrote this was where Custer and Yates watched the action at Ford B.

211. LTs Hare and Wallace, and SGT Culbertson (A) all figured 1½ hours from Reno-Custer separation at the lone tepee to Benteen-Reno uniting. Doc Porter's guess was "about 1 hour."

212. Standing Bear (Minneconjou Sioux), interview with Walter Camp, July 12, 1910, *Custer in '76,* 214; Shave Elk (Oglala Sioux), Walter Camp interviews, *Camp on Custer,* 122. Also supported by Pretty White Buffalo (Hunkpapa Sioux), *St. Paul Pioneer Press,* May 19, 1883, *The Custer Myth,* 86; Feather Earring (Minneconjou Sioux), Hugh Scott interview, September 9, 1919, *The Custer Myth,* 97; Flying Hawk (Oglala Sioux), Eli Ricker interview, 1907, *Lakota Recollections,* 50; Two Eagles (Brulé Sioux), Weston interview, 1908, *Lakota Recollections,* 143, 145; Lights (Minneconjou Sioux), Weston interview, 1909, *Lakota Recollections,* 165. Foolish Elk (Oglala Sioux), interview with Walter Camp, September 22, 1908, *Custer in '76,* 198. White Cow Bull (Oglala Sioux): Bobtail Horse killed one soldier who fell into the water. White Cow Bull claimed to hit another soldier who also fell into the water, from Miller, *Echoes of the Little Big Horn,* 33, and contained in *Vanishing Victory,* 108; Moving Robe Woman (Hunkpapa Sioux), in a 1936 interview, Hardorff, *Indian Views of the*

Custer Fight, 186. She claimed, "Custer's men got to the river above the beaver dam where the water was very deep. [The] soldiers dismounted and fired.... [The] soldiers got down to the river (at Medicine Tail Creek), but did not cross." Good Voiced Elk (Hunkpapa Sioux), May 21, 1909, interview with Camp, Hardorff, *Camp, Custer and the Little Bighorn,* 84.

213. LT Godfrey, *RCOI,* 481, and *Century Magazine,* 1892, "Custer's Last Battle," 25–27; LT Edgerly, *RCOI,* 442; CPL Roy (A), undated interview with Walter Camp, *Custer in '76,* 113; PVT Windolph (H), 1946, *I Fought with Custer,* 96; PVT Slaper (M), E. A. Brininstool, *A Trooper with Custer,* 17–56.

214. LT Edgerly, *RCOI,* 442; Two Moons (Northern Cheyenne), March 4, 1913, interview, Hardorff, *Indian Views of the Custer Fight,* 110. The Two Moons reference is by implication.

215. PVT Davern (F), *RCOI,* 351.

216. SGT Culbertson (A), *RCOI,* 373.

217. LT Godfrey, diary entry written several days after the battle, *Field Diary,* 12; LT Edgerly, *Leavenworth Times,* August 18, 1881, *The Custer Myth,* 219; PVT Windolph (H), Windolph/Hunt, *I Fought with Custer,* 89–90 and 96.

218. CPT Benteen, from his official report to Major Marcus Reno, dated July 4, 1876, and included with Terry's report, *The Federal View,* 106; LT Godfrey, *RCOI,* 482; LT Edgerly, *RCOI,* 442.

219. Shave Elk (Oglala Sioux); timing element supported by Shave Elk: Custer's column "came down this coulee toward the river and stopped just a little while, but not long and the Indians crossed over and attacked them. There were a few soldiers ahead of the main body"; interviews with Walter Camp, *Camp on Custer,* 122.

220. Two Eagles (Brulé Sioux), interview with Sewell B. Weston, December 1908, *Lakota Recollections,* 145.

221. Crow King (Hunkpapa Sioux), *Leavenworth Weekly Times,* August 18, 1881, possibly by Frank H. Huston, *The Custer Myth,* 77. Sitting Bull (Hunkpapa Sioux): this fits perfectly with Sitting Bull's claim the fighting began "two hours past the time when the sun is in the centre of the sky." He was referring to the start of the Custer fight; Hutchins, *The Army and Navy Journal,* 166; Moving Robe Woman (Hunkpapa Sioux), in a 1936 interview, Hardorff, *Indian Views of the Custer Fight,* 186. She said, "Long before Custer got to the river Custer began shooting to try to scare the Indians." This appears to be an allusion to the Keogh volley firing. John Two Moons (Northern Cheyenne), in a George Bird Grinnell interview, 1908, Hardorff, *Cheyenne Memories of the Custer Fight,* 65. He does not mention Wolf Tooth by name, but says Indians trailed Custer's command as it came "down the steep hill east of the battlefield." Goes Ahead (Crow scout), *The Arikara Narrative,* 160. Artifactual evidence also supports *Indians* in this area. In Michno, *Lakota Noon,* 153; found in the north fork of MTC, below and along the south and southeast face of Luce Ridge were: four .45/55 cases; three .50/70 cases; 14 .45/55 cases, plus an additional undetermined number; at least three horse skeletons, plus additional horse bones; at least three human skeletons, plus additional human bones; a saddle and bridle, saddle leather and pommel rings, and horseshoes; much of this was probably from the battle with the southern half of Wolf Tooth's band. John Stands In Timber (Cheyenne tribal historian), in a 1956 interview with Don Rickey, Hardorff, *Cheyenne Memories of the Custer Fight,* 171.

222. LT Godfrey, from a letter written by Godfrey, August 7, 1876, at the Seventh Cavalry camp on the Rosebud, to the editor of *The Army and Navy Journal,* 90; *RCOI,* 483; "Custer's Last Battle," 26; LT Edgerly, *RCOI,* 444; Clark, *Scalp Dance,* 19; LT Varnum, *RCOI,* 160; Goes Ahead (Crow scout), *The Arikara Narrative,* 160. This fits almost perfectly with Sitting

Bull's claim the fighting began "two hours past the time when the sun is in the centre of the sky." He was referring to the start of the Custer fight. Hutchins, *The Army and Navy Journal,* 166. Et al.

223. George Herendeen, *The Army and Navy Journal,* from Bismarck, D. T., July 7, 1876, 41; from a statement made by Herendeen, also published the following day, July 8, 1876, in the *New York Herald,* from *The Custer Myth,* 259; *RCOI,* 257.

224. Flying Hawk (Oglala Sioux), in an interview by Judge Eli S. Ricker, March 8, 1907, on the Pine Ridge Reservation, Hardorff, *Lakota Recollections of the Custer Fight,* 51. Supported by Bray, *Crazy Horse,* 221.

225. CPT McDougall, *RCOI,* 529, and interview or correspondence with Walter Camp, probably dated February 26, 1909, *Custer in '76,* 69; LT Mathey, *RCOI,* 513. Also see, Horn, *Fifty Years On Custer's Trail,* 21.

226. Kingsley Bray; supported by Bray, *Crazy Horse,* 221.

227. LT Godfrey, diary entry written several days after the battle, *Field Diary,* 12; LT Edgerly, *Leavenworth Times,* August 18, 1881, *The Custer Myth,* 219; PVT Windolph (H), Windolph/Hunt, *I Fought with Custer,* 89–90 and 96.

228. Goes Ahead (Crow scout), *The Arikara Narrative,* 160.

229. LT Edgerly, letter to W. A. Graham, December 5, 1923, *The Custer Myth,* 217.

230. CPL Wylie (D), Walter Camp interview conducted October 16, 1910, Junction City, KS, *Custer in '76,* 129, and, Smalley, *Little Bighorn Mysteries,* A6–6.

231. LT Mathey, *RCOI,* 513.

232. LT Edgerly, *RCOI,* 444; from the *Leavenworth Times,* a statement by Edgerly, August 18, 1881, made at Fort Yates, *The Custer Myth,* 219–220; undated Walter Camp interview: Edgerly—in a letter to W. A. Graham—stated he never met Camp and believed the "interview" must have been taken from his correspondence with Camp, *Custer in '76,* 55–56; *Scalp Dance,* 19.

233. Kingsley Bray; supported by Bray, *Crazy Horse,* 222.

234. LT Godfrey, *RCOI,* 482; Two Moons (Northern Cheyenne), March 4th and 5th, 1913 interview, Hardorff, *Indian Views of the Custer Fight,* 110 and 114. Two Moons' first reference is by implication, the second more specific though the time element is missing. Hollow Horn Bear (Cu Brulé), 1909 interview with Sewell B. Weston, *Lakota Recollections,* 179 and 181.

235. LT Edgerly, *Leavenworth Times,* August 18, 1881, *The Custer Myth,* 219–220.

236. CPT McDougall, interview or correspondence with Walter Camp, probably dated February 26, 1909, *Custer in '76,* 69; LT Mathey, *RCOI,* 513, and Walter Camp interview conducted October 19, 1910, *Custer in '76,* 78; CPL Hammon (G), 1908 interview with Walter Camp, Hardorff, *Camp, Custer, and the Little Bighorn,* 74.

237. CPT McDougall, interview or correspondence with Walter Camp, probably dated February 26, 1909, *Custer in '76,* 69; LT Mathey, *RCOI,* 513, and Walter Camp interview conducted October 19, 1910, *Custer in '76,* 78; Soldier (Arikara scout), undated interview with Walter Camp, *Custer in '76,* 188, and *The Arikara Narrative,* 117.

238. LT Godfrey, *RCOI,* 483; LT Hare, *RCOI,* 289, and Walter Camp interview conducted February 7, 1910, *Custer in '76,* 66.

239. Goes Ahead (Crow scout), Walter Camp interview, February 23, 1911, *Custer in '76,* 177.

240. PVT DeVoto (B), Hardorff, *Indian Views of the Custer Fight,* 203–209.

241. MAJ Reno, after-action report, addressed to CPT E. W. Smith, ADC and AAAG to GEN Terry,

dated July 5, 1876, from camp on the Yellowstone River, Carroll, *The Federal View,* 105, and *RCOI,* 567; CPT Benteen, *RCOI,* 408; LT Edgerly, *Scalp Dance,* 19; PVT Fox (D), Liddic/Harbaugh, *Camp On Custer,* 94–95.

242. CPT Benteen, *RCOI,* 408; LT Edgerly, *RCOI,* 444; and from a letter to W. A. Graham, dated December 5, 1923, from Cooperstown, NY, *The Custer Myth,* 217. PVT Fox (D), undated interview with Walter Mason Camp, Liddic/Harbaugh, *Camp on Custer,* 96.

243. SGT Culbertson (A), *RCOI,* 371.

244. LT Mathey, *RCOI,* 514.

245. LT Hare, *RCOI,* 289; and Walter Camp interview conducted February 7, 1910, *Custer in '76,* 66.

246. Kingsley Bray; supported by Bray, *Crazy Horse,* 222–223.

247. LT Mathey, *RCOI,* 514 and 521.

248. CPT McDougall, *RCOI,* 529; and in a 1909 letter to Walter Camp; Hammer, *Custer in '76,* 70.

249. Gall (Hunkpapa Sioux), from a June 26, 1886, Chicago newspaper, *The Custer Myth,* 88. A significant Indian presence in this area is supported by archaeological evidence; Fox, *Archaeology, History, and Custer's Last Battle,* 69, 81–86, and 88–93. Michno, *The Mystery of E Troop,* 51–52; 114 relics were found here, indicating a strong Indian position.

250. LT Edgerly, *RCOI,* 444–445.

251. LT Godfrey, *RCOI,* 482; and from the *Century Magazine,* January 1892, "Custer's Last Battle," 26; Waterman (Arapaho), *The Custer Myth,* 110. Tim McCoy interview, 1920.

252. White Man Runs Him (Crow scout), Graham, *The Custer Myth,* 23. COL Tim McCoy who had accompanied GEN Scott during their 1919 trip to the battlefield with the Crow scouts, transcribed the interview. Graham wrote this was the most definitive account by any of the Crows, despite a few "minor details." McCoy was extremely proficient in sign language. Red Star (Arikara scout), *The Arikara Narrative,* 120.

253. Kingsley Bray; supported by Bray, *Crazy Horse,* 223–224.

254. John Stands In Timber (Cheyenne tribal historian), Liberty, *Cheyenne Memories,* 199.

255. LT Hare, interview with Walter Camp, February 7, 1910, *Custer in '76,* 66.

256. PVT Davern (F), *RCOI,* 352. Benteen had already arrived. Davern saw Indians farther downstream—a good many—circling around on what appeared to be the right bank of the river, raising a lot of dust. He called CPT Weir's attention to it, saying, "'That must be General Custer fighting down in the bottom.' He asked me where and I showed him. He said, 'Yes, I believe it is.'"

257. Goes Ahead (Crow scout), *The Arikara Narrative,* 160; Red Bear (Arikara scout), *The Arikara Narrative,* 129.

258. White Bull/Ice (Northern Cheyenne), Brave Wolf (Northern Cheyenne), and Hump (Minneconjou Sioux), 1878 interviews, Hardorff, *Indian Views of the Custer Fight,* 49. While not specific to Keogh, this entry is supported further by the Cheyenne warrior, Wooden Leg; Thomas Marquis, *Wooden Leg,* 105. Fred Gerard, *RCOI,* 135.

259. Fred Gerard, *RCOI,* 135.

260. White Bull/Ice (Northern Cheyenne), Brave Wolf (Northern Cheyenne), and Hump (Minneconjou Sioux), 1878 interviews, Hardorff, *Indian Views of the Custer Fight,* 49; Wooden Leg (Northern Cheyenne), Thomas Marquis, *Wooden Leg,* 105; Yellow Nose (Ute/Southern Cheyenne), interview in 1911, *Indian Views of the Custer Fight,* 102–103.

261. LT Hare, *RCOI,* 289–290; LT Godfrey, *RCOI,* 484; PVT Windolph (H), *I Fought with Custer,* 98.

262. CPT Benteen, *RCOI,* 406 and 414; LT Hare, *RCOI,* 280 and 296.

263. John Stands In Timber (Cheyenne tribal historian), written from notes and recordings, 1957–1966; published shortly after Stands In Timber's death; Liberty, *Cheyenne Memories,* 199.

264. Flying Hawk (Oglala Sioux), Bray, *Crazy Horse,* 224.

265. LT Edgerly, *RCOI,* 458.

266. PVT DeVoto (B), Hardorff, *Indian Views of the Custer Fight,* 205.

267. Flying Hawk (Oglala Sioux), Bray, *Crazy Horse,* 224; Pretty White Buffalo (Hunkpapa Sioux), *St. Paul Pioneer Press,* May 19, 1883, *The Custer Myth,* 87.

268. LT Edgerly, *Leavenworth Times,* August 18, 1881.

269. LT Edgerly, *RCOI,* 444.

270. MAJ Reno, *RCOI,* 566; LT Wallace, *RCOI,* 37; SGT Culbertson (A), *RCOI,* 373.

271. LT Edgerly, *RCOI,* 444, and *Leavenworth Times,* August 18, 1881, *The Custer Myth,* 220.

272. LT Edgerly, undated Camp interview, *Custer in '76,* 56; LT Hare, *RCOI,* 289.

273. Wooden Leg (Northern Cheyenne), Thomas Marquis, *Wooden Leg,* 105.

274. MAJ Reno, *New York Herald,* August 8, 1876. Reno claimed as the packs closed up, the command began its move toward Weir Peaks.

275. Brave Wolf (Northern Cheyenne), Hump (Minneconjou Sioux), White Bull/Ice (Northern Cheyenne), report of LT Oscar F. Long, 5th U.S. Infantry, dated June 27, 1877, *Indian Views of the Custer Fight,* 47 and 50.

276. LT Varnum, *RCOI,* 144; memoirs, probably early 1930s, *I, Varnum,* 173–174; from the Reno Court of Inquiry (RCOI).

277. White Hair On Face (Hunkpapa Sioux), in an interview with Walter S. Campbell (aka, Stanley Vestal), June 1930, Fort Yates, ND; Hardorff, *Indian Views of the Custer Fight,* 148. While not specific to the time, this reference alludes to Indian refugees at Ford D. White Hair On Face claimed he was one of the Indians guarding these refugees.

278. Lone Bear (Oglala Sioux), interview with Sewell B. Weston in 1909, *Lakota Recollections,* 157. Lone Bear claimed there were short stands made on Finley-Finckle Ridge and Calhoun Hill, but a heavy "stand" in the Keogh Sector. Many horses were killed there. He seemed to think Keogh made a longer stand than that made on Last Stand Hill. Lone Bear does not specifically refer to Crazy Horse in this citation. He Dog (Oglala Sioux), interview with GEN Hugh Scott, August 19, 1920, *Lakota Recollections,* 75. There *is* reference to Crazy Horse in this citation.

279. White Bull (Minneconjou Sioux), interviewed by Walter S. Campbell, summer 1930, at the Cheyenne River Agency, SD; interpreter was Sam Eagle Chase, Hardorff, *Lakota Recollections of the Custer Fight,* 115. Artifactual evidence shows Indians occupied the east side of this ridge. In Michno, *Lakota Noon,* 226, all along the ridges and gullies east of Battle Ridge and the Keogh Sector, 108 Indian cartridges, including .50/70's, .44's, and .56's, were found.

280. MAJ Reno, *RCOI,* 567; CPT Benteen, *The Benteen-Goldin Letters,* 186; LT Godfrey, *RCOI,* 485, and *Custer in '76,* 76; LT Varnum, *RCOI,* 180; LT Wallace, *RCOI,* 59; LT Edgerly, *Custer in '76,* 56 and 59; LT Hare, *RCOI,* 289; SGT Culbertson (A), *RCOI,* 372.

281. CPT Benteen, *RCOI,* 406; CPT McDougall, *RCOI,* 530–531; LT Varnum, *RCOI,* 180.

282. CPT McDougall, letter to Camp, February 26, 1909, *Custer in '76,* 70; CPT Moylan, *RCOI,* 218.

283. LT Edgerly, *RCOI,* 446; *Leavenworth Times,* August 18, 1881; CPL Wylie (D), Camp interview, October 16, 1910, *Custer in '76,* 130.

284. He Dog (Oglala Sioux), Walter Camp interview conducted July 13, 1910, William Berger, interpreter; *Custer in '76,* 207; and in an interview by Gen-

eral Hugh L. Scott, August 19, 1920, at the Pine Ridge Reservation, probably translated by Baptiste Pourrier and William Garnett; Hardorff, *Lakota Recollections of the Custer Fight,* 75; White Bull (Minneconjou Sioux), interviewed by Walter S. Campbell, summer 1930, at the Cheyenne River Agency, SD; interpreter was Sam Eagle Chase, *Lakota Recollections of the Custer Fight,* 115. Artifactual evidence shows troops moved across these areas. In Michno, *Lakota Noon,* 226, across Calhoun Hill, roughly south to north five Army cartridge cases were found. Archaeological and artifactual evidence indicates a strong mixed presence; some 86 mixed relics were found in the Keogh Sector leading from Calhoun Hill. Fox, *Archaeology, History, and Custer's Last Battle,* 69, 81–86, 88–93; Michno, *The Mystery of E Troop,* 51–52.

285. PVT DeVoto (B), Hardorff, *Indian Views of the Custer Fight,* 206.

286. LTs Edgerly, undated Camp interview, *Custer in '76,* 56; LT Hare, *RCOI,* 289.

287. LT Edgerly, *RCOI,* 445–446; *Leavenworth Times,* August 18, 1881.

288. LT Edgerly, undated Camp interview, *Custer in '76,* 56.

289. SGT Harrison (D), June 11, 1911, interview with Walter Camp; Liddic and Harbaugh, *Camp on Custer,* 98.

290. CPT McDougall, from a letter written by McDougall to Walter Camp, February 26, 1909, *Custer in '76,* 70; LT Mathey, *RCOI,* 518.

291. LT Edgerly, from the *Leavenworth Times,* a statement by Edgerly, August 18, 1881, at Fort Yates, *The Custer Myth,* 220; SGT Harrison (D), interview with Walter Camp, June 11, 1911, Liddic/Harbaugh, *Camp On Custer,* 97.

292. LT Varnum, *RCOI,* 144.

293. MAJ Reno, *RCOI,* 574; CPT Benteen, *RCOI,* 408, 409, 423; "Benteen Manuscript," 1890; March 1, 1892, letter to Goldin, Carroll, *The Benteen-Goldin Letters,* 215.

294. CPT Benteen, "Benteen Manuscript," 1890, *The Benteen-Goldin Letters,* 186, and *RCOI,* 408–409; LT Godfrey, article in *Century Magazine,* 1892, "Custer's Last Battle," 27; LT Edgerly, *RCOI,* 446; LT Hare, Walter Camp interview, February 7, 1910, *Custer in '76,* 66; LT Varnum, *RCOI,* 164.

295. LT Godfrey, article in *Century Magazine,* 1892, "Custer's Last Battle," 27.

296. LT Hare, Walter Camp interview, February 7, 1910, *Custer in '76,* 66; PVT Pigford (M), undated Camp correspondence, *Custer in '76,* 143.

297. LT Godfrey, 1892 article in *Century Magazine,* "Custer's Last Battle," 27; LT Edgerly, *RCOI,* 446.

298. Little Sioux (Arikara scout), undated Walter Camp interview, *Custer in '76,* 181.

299. Little Sioux (Arikara scout), undated Camp interview, *Custer in '76,* 181, and *The Arikara Narrative,* 154.

300. Red Bear (Arikara scout), *The Arikara Narrative,* 131.

301. Shave Elk (Oglala Sioux), interviews with Walter Camp, *Camp on Custer,* 122.

302. Hairy Moccasin (Crow scout), Walter Camp interview, February 23, 1911, *Custer in '76,* 177; White Cow Bull (Oglala Sioux): Bobtail Horse killed one soldier who fell into the water. White Cow Bull claimed to hit another soldier who also fell into the water, from Miller, *Echoes of the Little Bighorn,* 33, and contained in *Vanishing Victory,* 108.

303. LT DeRudio, *RCOI,* 322; Hairy Moccasin (Crow scout), Walter Camp interview, February 23, 1911, *Custer in '76,* 177. Artifactual evidence supports troop movements from this area into Deep Coulee. In Michno, *Lakota Noon,* 153, in the lower ground, north and northwest of Butler Ridge, above the Deep Coulee ingress: two .45/55 cartridges; a horseshoe, harness buckle, and straps; a leather boot; a leather

scabbard; an arrowhead; two human skeletons; numerous horse bones. Michno felt these were, "from a combination of Yates' men moving back up Butler Ridge and from the Indians who followed Yates and Keogh." A reasonable assumption. On the June 28, CPT Benteen killed a white horse that was wounded and lying on the right bank in a pool of mud a little distance below the ford. There were the trousers of an enlisted man hanging on the branch of a log stump, *RCOI*, 419 and 424. Dose was a trumpeter and trumpeters rode white horses.

304. Simulation, though there is support in Michno, *Lakota Noon*, 168.

305. Curley (Crow scout), interview in the *Helena Herald*, July 15, 1876, *The Custer Myth*, 11. The Curley interview must be taken with a grain of salt and is probably hearsay. Furthermore, he contradicts himself in his first interview with Walter Camp, September 18, 1908, *Custer in '76*, 157. Lights (Minneconjou Sioux), Weston interview, 1909, *Lakota Recollections*, 165–166. White Bull (Minneconjou Sioux), interviewed by Walter S. Campbell (aka, Stanley Vestal), June 1932, Cheyenne River Reservation, Cherry Creek, SD; Hardorff, *Indian Views of the Custer Fight*, 155.

306. Gregory F. Michno. There is considerable artifactual evidence that troops occupied this position and the slope to it immediate front. In Michno, *Lakota Noon*, 153, on the southern slope of Nye-Cartwright Ridge, directly behind the Little Big Horn face of Butler Ridge: four .45/55 cases; four .45/55 cartridges; six .56 Spencer cases; 24 .50/70 cases; 15 .44 Henry cases; nine .44 Henry cartridges; and an Indian bridle. In addition, all along the Nye-Cartwright/Luce Ridge complex: upwards of 480 .45/55 cases and cartridges; several .50/70 cases; an undetermined number of additional shells; saddle and tack parts; and uniform buttons and buckles.

307. Wooden Leg (Northern Cheyenne), Marquis interviews, 1922–1931, *Wooden Leg*, 228. Also, see Brust, Pohanka, Barnard, *Where Custer Fell*, 79. There is artifactual evidence of an Indian presence behind troops on these ridges. In Michno, *Lakota Noon*, 153, behind Nye-Cartwright Ridge, along a dry ravine of South Branch: three .44 Henry cases. This could have been from a skirmish with the northern half of Wolf Tooth's band.

308. Two Eagles (Cu Brulé Sioux), interview with Sewell B. Weston, December 1908, *Lakota Recollections*, 145; Hollow Horn Bear (Cu Brulé Sioux), Weston interview, 1909, *Lakota Recollections*, 181–182. Hollow Horn Bear was emphatic that troops moved directly from Ford B up Finley-Finckle Ridge and did not go into the coulee toward Deep Ravine.

309. Wooden Leg (Northern Cheyenne), Thomas Marquis, *Wooden Leg*, 228.

310. Standing Bear (Minneconjou Sioux), interview with Eli Ricker, March 12, 1907, Hardorff, *Lakota Recollections*, 59.

311. Wooden Leg (Northern Cheyenne), Thomas Marquis, *Wooden Leg*, 228. In addition, there is artifactual evidence to support Indians crossing the ridges to reach these areas. In Michno, *Lakota Noon*, 153, below the western edge of Nye-Cartwright, in what appears to be a series of gullies or ravines leading to, but south of Deep Coulee, three human and three horse skeletons and various bridle and saddle parts were discovered. Thunder Bear (Nakota Yankton Sioux), in 1907 narrative, *Indian Views of the Custer Fight*, 88.

312. Wooden Leg (Northern Cheyenne), Marquis, *Wooden Leg*, 229; Turtle Rib (Minneconjou Sioux), Walter Camp interview conducted September 22, 1908, *Custer in '76*, 201; Shave Elk (Oglala Sioux), interview with Walter Camp, *Camp on Custer*, 127; Red Feather (Oglala Sioux), interviewed by GEN Hugh L. Scott, August 19, 1920, at the Pine Ridge Agency. The translators were probably Baptiste Pour-

rier and William Garnett, *Lakota Recollections*, 87; Iron Hawk (Hunkpapa Sioux), Neihardt interviews, 1931, DeMallie, *The Sixth Grandfather*, 190. Archaeological evidence shows significant Indian activity of Greasy Grass Ridge; Fox, *Archaeology, History, and Custer's Last Battle*, 69, 81–86, 88–93. Michno, *The Mystery of E Troop*, 51–52; 173 Indian artifacts were found on the southern portion; 32 on the northern. Fox claims this was a significant Indian position. PVT DeVoto (B), Hardorff, *Indian Views of the Custer Fight*, 204. The DeVoto reference pertains to his observation that there were no dead Indian ponies found on the field, leading the Reno survivors to believe the Indians fought dismounted.

313. John Stands In Timber (Cheyenne tribal historian), Liberty, *Cheyenne Memories*, 198.

314. Hollow Horn Bear (Cu Brulé Sioux), interview with Sewell Weston, 1909, Hardorff, *Lakota Recollections*, 183; White Bull (Minneconjou Sioux), interview with Walter S. Campbell (aka, Stanley Vestal), Cheyenne River Reservation, Cherry Creek, SD, June 1932, *Indian Views of the Custer Fight*, 155.

315. Gregory F. Michno; there is artifactual evidence supporting Indians in this area; Michno, *Lakota Noon*, 153. Found in the northern part of Deep Coulee on its west side, toward Calhoun Hill and the Henryville area: human bones and two horse skeletons; eight .45/55 cases; two .50/70 cases; two .50- and one .56-caliber Spencer cases; one .32 rim-fire case; two .44 Henry cases; and one Winchester rifle.

316. Two Eagles (Cu Brulé Sioux), interview with Sewell B. Weston, December 1908, *Lakota Recollections*, 145–146; Two Moons (Northern Cheyenne), interview with Dr. Joseph K. Dixon, Custer battlefield, 1909, first published in 1913; Hardorff, *Cheyenne Memories of the Custer Fight*, 130–131.

317. CPT Benteen, *RCOI*, 417–418.

318. Standing Bear (Minneconjou Sioux), interview with Eli Ricker, March 12, 1907, *Lakota Recollections*, 59; Wooden Leg (Northern Cheyenne), Marquis interviews, 1922–1931, *Wooden Leg*, 228.

319. Respects Nothing (Oglala Sioux), 1906 Eli Ricker interview, *Lakota Recollections*, 31. The Indians who attacked Finley-Finckle Ridge/Calhoun Hill, crossed the river at the mouth of Water Rat Creek (Medicine Tail Coulee or Ford B). PVT DeVoto (B), Hardorff, *Indian Views of the Custer Fight*, 204. The DeVoto reference pertains to his observation that there were no dead Indian ponies found on the field, leading the Reno survivors to believe the Indians fought dismounted.

320. Gall (Hunkpapa Sioux), from a Chicago newspaper, June 26, 1886, and an interview printed in the *St. Paul Pioneer Press*, July 18, 1886, *The Custer Myth*, 89.

321. Two Moons (Northern Cheyenne), Hardorff, *Cheyenne Memories of the Custer Fight*, 130–131. An interview of Two Moons by Dr. Joseph K. Dixon on the Custer battlefield in 1909, first published in 1913. Supported by doctors Douglas D. Scott and Peter Bleed, *A Good Walk Around the Boundary*, 42.

322. Two Moons (Northern Cheyenne), in a 1901 interview with J. M. Thralls, Hardorff, *Cheyenne Memories of the Custer Fight*, 109. The reference is to horse-holders being the first of Custer's troops killed.

323. Yellow Nose (Ute/Southern Cheyenne), interview in 1911, *Indian Views of the Custer Fight*, 102–103.

324. White Bull/Ice (Northern Cheyenne), Brave Wolf (Northern Cheyenne), Hump (Minneconjou Sioux), Hardorff, *Indian Views of the Custer Fight*, 49. Wooden Leg (Northern Cheyenne), Thomas Marquis, *Wooden Leg*, 105. Archaeological evidence supports both Indians and soldiers at this location: Richard A. Fox, Jr., *Archaeology, History, and Custer's Last Battle*, 69, 81–86, 88–93; and Gregory F. Michno, *The Mystery of E Troop*, 51–52. Evidence sup-

ports a mixed Indian/soldier presence thereby suggesting considerable intermingled activity. A total of 43 relics were found in the coulee.

325. LT Mathey, October 19, 1910, interview with Walter Camp, *Custer in '76*, 79; LT Thompson (K/6 Inf.), February 14, 1911, interview with Walter Camp, *Custer in '76*, 248; SGT M. Wilson (I/7I), undated Camp interview, Hardorff, *Camp, Custer and the Little Bighorn*, 107; PVT Glenn (H), January 22, 1914, interview with Walter Camp, *Custer in '76*, 136; John Stands In Timber (Cheyenne tribal historian), Liberty, *Cheyenne Memories*, 199.

326. Pretty White Buffalo (Hunkpapa Sioux), St. Paul *Pioneer Press*, May 19, 1883, Graham, *The Custer Myth*, 86; He Dog (Oglala Sioux), Walter Camp interview, July 13, 1910, Camp/Hammer, *Custer in '76*, 207.

327. He Dog (Oglala Sioux), GEN Hugh Scott interview, August 19, 1920, Hardorff, *Lakota Recollections*, 75. While not specific, the implication is quite clear.

328. Shoots Walking (Hunkpapa Sioux), 1935 interview, Hardorff, *Indian Views of the Custer Fight*, 169. Shoots Walking's comment that the soldiers, "did not fire their guns together and they fought without system whatsoever," is indicative of a lack of discipline and can be construed as panic. This is supported further by archaeological work. See Fox, *Archaeology, History, and Custer's Last Battle*, 145, 147, 151, 154, 158–159.

329. Supported by archaeological work. See Fox, *Archaeology, History, and Custer's Last Battle*, 145, 147, 151, 154, 158–159.

330. Crow King (Hunkpapa Sioux), interview conducted July 30, 1881, Fort Yates, D. T., and carried in the *Leavenworth Times*, August 14, 1881, Hardorff, *Indian Views of the Custer Fight*, 68; Shave Elk (Oglala Sioux), multiple interviews with Walter Camp, Liddic/Harbaugh, *Camp on Custer*, 122–123; Soldier Wolf (Northern Cheyenne), interview with George Bird Grinnell, Northern Cheyenne Indian Reservation, Montana, 1898, Hardorff, *Cheyenne Memories of the Custer Fight*, 43; John Stands In Timber (Cheyenne tribal historian), from notes and recordings, 1957–1966, and published shortly after Stands In Timber's death, Liberty, *Cheyenne Memories*, 199; and interview with Don Rickey, Jr., and Jesse W. Vaughn, Custer Battlefield, Montana, 1956, Hardorff, *Cheyenne Memories of the Custer Fight*, 169.

331. Brave Bear (Southern Cheyenne), in a March 8, 1906, letter from George Bent to George Hyde, Hardorff, *Indian Views of the Custer Fight*, 85–86, footnote 9; Little Hawk (Northern Cheyenne), in a 1908 interview by George Bird Grinnell, Hardorff, *Cheyenne Memories of the Custer Fight*, 62.

332. Tall Bull (Northern Cheyenne), interview with Walter Camp, July 22, 1910, *Custer in '76*, 213.

333. Shoots Walking (Hunkpapa Sioux), 1935 interview, Hardorff, *Indian Views of the Custer Fight*, 169. Shoots Walking's comment that the soldiers "did not fire their guns together and they fought without system whatsoever," is indicative of a lack of discipline and can be construed as panic.

334. See Richard Fox, *Archaeology, History, and Custer's Last Battle*, 145, 147, 151, 154, 158–159. Archaeological and artifactual evidence shows a strong soldier position on this hill; Fox, *Archaeology, History, and Custer's Last Battle*, 69, 81–86, 88–93; Greg Michno, *The Mystery of E Troop*, 51–52. Some 63 relics were found here, primarily military.

335. Artifactual evidence shows Indians were on this ridge. In Michno, *Lakota Noon*, 226, nine Indian bullets were found along the south side of Finley-Finckle Ridge. On the ridge itself, 23 relics were found—both Indian and soldier—indicating a strong mixed presence. Fox, *Archaeology, History, and Custer's Last Battle*, 69, 81–86, 88–93; Michno, *The Mystery of E Troop*, 51–52.

336. Lone Bear (Oglala Sioux), interview with Sewell B. Weston in 1909, *Lakota Recollections,* 157. Lone Bear claimed there were short stands made on Finley-Finckle Ridge and Calhoun Hill, but a heavy "stand" in the Keogh Sector. Many horses were killed there. He seemed to think Keogh made a longer stand than that made on Last Stand Hill. There is *no* reference in this citation to Crazy Horse, *per se.* Additional artifactual evidence supports the contention of Indians in the Henryville area attacking across Deep Coulee and onto Calhoun Hill. In Michno, *Lakota Noon,* 226: in Henryville, on the Deep Coulee side, 32 Indian cartridge cases; and on the Calhoun Hill side, 13 Indian cartridge cases were found. Also, across Calhoun Hill, roughly from west to east, nine Indian cartridge cases were found.

337. Foolish Elk (Oglala Sioux), interview with Walter Camp, September 22, 1908, *Custer in '76,* 198. The Ford D location is inferred as Foolish Elk claimed the Indians, now coming up in numbers, crossed both at Ford B and farther downriver, getting in front and to the east of "Custer," as well as behind the soldiers.

338. Turtle Rib (Minneconjou Sioux), Camp interview, September 22, 1908, Camp/Hammer, *Custer in '76,* 201; John Stands In Timber (Cheyenne tribal historian), written from notes and recordings, 1957–1966, and published shortly after Stands In Timber's death; Liberty, *Cheyenne Memories,* 200.

339. Two Eagles (Cu Brulé Sioux) is quoted here only as reference to the battle moving toward Last Stand Hill from the Keogh Sector. "It was a moving fight from [Calhoun Hill] to [Last Stand Hill]. The Indians were in the draws that were just below the crown of the ridge. There were no Indians to the northwest of [Last Stand Hill]." Interview with Sewell B. Weston, 1908, *Lakota Recollections,* 148.

340. Turtle Rib (Minneconjou Sioux), Camp interview, September 22, 1908, *Custer in '76,* 201. Archaeological evidence supports a strong Indian presence at the ravine's "bend"; Richard Fox, *Archaeology, History, and Custer's Last Battle,* 69, 81–86, 88–93; Greg Michno, *The Mystery of E Troop,* 51–52.

341. Archaeological evidence supports both Indian and soldiers at this location; Fox, *Archaeology, History, and Custer's Last Battle,* 69, 81–86, 88–93; Michno, *The Mystery of E Troop,* 51–52. Evidence supports a stronger Indian presence thereby indicating troops were forced off the ridge.

342. Turtle Rib (Minneconjou Sioux), interview with Walter Camp, September 22, 1908, *Custer in '76,* 201; Little Hawk (Northern Cheyenne), in a 1908 interview by George Bird Grinnell, Hardorff, *Cheyenne Memories of the Custer Fight,* 63; Runs The Enemy (Two Kettle Sioux), Fox, *Archaeology, History, and Custer's Last Battle,* 181, footnote 35, citing J. K. Dixon, *The Vanishing Race,* 175, and L. Tillet, *Wind on the Buffalo Grass,* 81; Fox, *Archaeology, History, and Custer's Last Battle,* 181, 353, footnote 36.

343. Waterman (Arapaho), interview with COL Tim McCoy, 1920, *The Custer Myth,* 110. This could have also been in reference to troops moving to Last Stand Hill from Cemetery Ridge.

344. White Bull/Ice (Northern Cheyenne), interview with George Bird Grinnell, Northern Cheyenne Indian Reservation, Montana, 1895, Hardorff, *Cheyenne Memories,* 39–40.

345. Archaeological and artifactual evidence shows a strong soldier position on this hill; Fox, *Archaeology, History, and Custer's Last Battle,* 69, 81–86, 88–93; Michno, *The Mystery of E Troop,* 51–52. Some 80 relics were found here, primarily military.

346. White Bull (Minneconjou Sioux), 1930 and 1932 interviews; interviewed by Walter S. Campbell,

summer, 1930, at the Cheyenne River Agency, S. D., interpreter was Sam Eagle Chase; Hardorff, *Lakota Recollections of the Custer Fight,* 115.

347. CPT French spoke with a number of Cheyenne chiefs—Two Moon (Northern Cheyenne), Brave Wolf (Northern Cheyenne), and White Bull (probably Ice; Northern Cheyenne)—and they told him the Indians swarmed over Custer's command, "so thickly that scarcely half of them could fight, for fear of killing each other." June 1880, letter from French to a Mrs. Cooke of Chicago, *Custer in '76,* 341.

348. Archaeological evidence supports a strong Indian presence at this location; Fox, *Archaeology, History, and Custer's Last Battle,* 69, 81–86, 88–93. Michno, *The Mystery of E Troop,* 51–52. Some 45 relics were discovered there.

349. John Stands In Timber (Cheyenne tribal historian), Liberty, *Cheyenne Memories,* 200–201.

350. Two Moons (Northern Cheyenne), March 5, 1913, interview, *Indian Views of the Custer Fight,* 114 and 114, FN 14. John Stands In Timber (Cheyenne tribal historian), Liberty, *Cheyenne Memories,* 201.

351. John Stands In Timber (Cheyenne tribal historian), Liberty, *Cheyenne Memories,* 201.

352. Lights (Minneconjou Sioux), 1909 interview with Sewell B. Weston, *Lakota Recollections,* 168; Iron Hawk (Hunkpapa Sioux), interview with John Neihardt, 1930, *Black Elk Speaks,* 122.

353. He Dog (Oglala Sioux), interview with Walter Camp, July 13, 1910, *Custer in '76,* 207.

354. CPT French spoke with a number of Cheyenne chiefs—Two Moon (Northern Cheyenne), Brave Wolf (Northern Cheyenne), and White Bull (probably Ice; Northern Cheyenne)—and they told him the Indians swarmed over Custer's command "so thickly that scarcely half of them could fight, for fear of killing each other." June 1880 letter from CPT French to a Mrs. Cooke of Chicago, *Custer in '76,* 341; Red Horse (Minneconjou Sioux), report of COL W. H. Wood, February 27, 1877. Archaeological and artifactual evidence indicates a strong mixed presence of troops and Indians at this location; Fox, *Archaeology, History, and Custer's Last Battle,* 69, 81–86, 88–93; Michno, *The Mystery of E Troop,* 51–52. A total of 169 mixed relics were found along this ridgeline. John Stands In Timber (Cheyenne tribal historian), Liberty, *Cheyenne Memories,* 201.

355. Red Horse (Minneconjou Sioux), report of COL W. H. Wood, February 27, 1877.

356. PVT O'Neill (G), Dustin, *The Custer Tragedy,* 122–123: "I think it was about five o'clock when we heard the last shots in Custer's direction"; Fred Gerard (interpreter), *RCOI,* 98–99, 135–136; the time reference can be traced back to Gerard's testimony. Two Eagles (Cu Brulé Sioux), interview with Sewell B. Weston, 1908, *Lakota Recollections,* 147; Flying Hawk (Oglala Sioux), 1928 interview, Hardorff, *Indian Views of the Custer Fight,* 126. The Flying Hawk reference is to the approximate duration of the fighting once the command was surrounded: about one hour. This is computed from the time the entire five companies were on Calhoun Hill: one hour, 18 minutes.

357. LT Edgerly, from the *Leavenworth Times,* a statement by Edgerly, August 18, 1881, at Fort Yates, *The Custer Myth,* 220.

358. LT DeRudio, *RCOI,* 318.

359. LT Varnum, memoirs, probably early 1930s, *I, Varnum,* 143; from the Reno Court of Inquiry. This reference does *not* relate to time.

360. George Herendeen, from Bismarck, D. T., July 7, 1876, Hutchins, *The Army and Navy Journal,* 41.

361. LT Godfrey, diary entry written several days

after the battle, *Field Diary,* 13. The reference pertains to the beginning of the Indians' movement toward Weir.

362. LT Godfrey, diary entry written several days after the battle, *Field Diary,* 13.

363. LT Hare, *RCOI,* 292.

364. LT Edgerly, from the *Leavenworth Times,* a statement by Edgerly, August 18, 1881, at Fort Yates, *The Custer Myth,* 220.

365. LT Godfrey, *RCOI,* 485.

366. George Herendeen, from Bismarck, D. T., July 7, 1876, *The Army and Navy Journal,* 41.

367. LT Godfrey, early 1900s correspondence with Walter Camp, *Custer in '76,* 76; LT Edgerly, memoirs circa 1910, Clark, *Scalp Dance,* 20.

368. LT Godfrey, *RCOI,* 485, and early 1900s correspondence with Walter Camp, *Custer in '76,* 76; article in *Century Magazine,* 1892, "Custer's Last Battle," 27–28; Godfrey letter to R. G. Carter, April 14, 1925, *The Custer Myth,* 319; LT Hare, interview with Walter Camp, February 7, 1910, *Custer in '76,* 67.

369. LT Godfrey, early 1900s correspondence with Walter Camp, *Custer in '76,* 76.

370. LT Godfrey, article in *Century Magazine,* 1892, "Custer's Last Battle," 28; LT Edgerly, undated correspondence with Walter Camp, *Custer in '76,* 57; SGT Harrison (D), interview with Walter Camp, June 11, 1911, Liddic/Harbaugh, *Camp on Custer,* 97–98.

371. LT Godfrey, *Field Diary,* 13; *RCOI,* 485.

372. CPT Benteen, letter to Theodore Goldin, March 1, 1892, *The Benteen-Goldin Letters,* 216, and the "Benteen Manuscript," circa 1890, *The Custer Myth,* 172, 181; LT Godfrey, article in *Century Magazine,* 1892, "Custer's Last Battle," 28; LT Edgerly, *RCOI,* 446; LT Wallace, *RCOI,* 60; LT Hare, interview with Walter Camp, February 7, 1910, *Custer in '76,* 67; SGT Harrison (D), interview with Walter Camp, 1911, *Camp on Custer,* 97–98; PVT Glenn (H), Walter Camp interview, January 22, 1914, *Custer in '76,* 136.

373. LT Hare, *RCOI,* 292.

374. SGT Harrison (D), June 11, 1911, interview with Walter Mason Camp, Liddic/Harbaugh, *Camp on Custer,* 97; CPL Wylie (D), Walter Camp interview, October 16, 1910, in Junction City, KS, *Custer in '76,* 130.

375. SGT Harrison (D), June 11, 1911, interview with Walter Mason Camp, *Camp on Custer,* 97–98; CPL Wylie (D), Walter Camp interview, October 16, 1910, in Junction City, KS, *Custer in '76,* 130.

376. SGT Harrison (D), interview with Walter Mason Camp, June 11, 1911, Liddic/Harbaugh, *Camp on Custer,* 98.

377. SGT Harrison (D), June 11, 1911, interview with Walter Mason Camp, *Camp on Custer,* 98; CPL Wylie (D), Walter Camp interview, October 16, 1910, in Junction City, KS, *Custer in '76,* 130.

378. LT Godfrey, *Field Diary,* 13; *RCOI,* 485; Fred Gerard, RCOI, 135–136. Gerard's comments pertain to the time of firing, from the end of firing downstream to the beginning of the fighting on Reno Hill.

379. SGT Culbertson (A), *RCOI,* 372; B. F. Churchill (packer), *RCOI,* 468.

380. MAJ Reno, LTs Varnum, Hare, Edgerly, Wallace; George Herendeen—MAJ Reno, *New York Herald,* August 8, 1876; LT Varnum, *RCOI,* 181; LT Edgerly, *Scalp Dance,* 20; LT Wallace, *RCOI,* 37; George Herendeen, Bismarck, DT, July 7, 1876, *The Army and Navy Journal,* 41; *New York Herald,* July 8, 1876.

APPENDIX A:
PLACE NAMES AND DISTANCES

NOTE—In an article by Bruce A. Trinque titled, "Elusive Ridge," January, 1995, *Research Review,* Vol. 9, No. 1, Trinque calls the traditional "Luce Ridge" referred to by John Gray, Robert Utley, and Richard Hardorff as "East Ridge," and Richard Fox' "Luce" as "West Ridge." East Ridge/traditional "Luce" Ridge plays no part in this saga and the naming of the ridge after the former superintendent of the battlefield turns out to be a misnomer.

According to Evan Connell (in 1984)—"U. S. highway 94 parallels [Custer's] route to the Yellowstone and follows it almost exactly to the junction of Rosebud Creek.... At this point Montana 447 branches south and then southwest, occasionally angling across the creek ... a brushy creek sometimes narrow enough to hop across.

"Beyond Lame Deer, near the present town of Busby ... [t]he approximate site of his final camp is marked by the Busby Post Office, G & J's store....

"[A] gas station with a *Happy Motoring* sign. Beyond this landmark General Custer angled southwest toward the divide, while the present state highway continues due west—rising gently toward the ridge."[1]

Fort Rice was located 30 miles south of Bismarck, D. T.

The Red Cloud Agency was known by the Cheyenne Indians as the White River Agency. According to Wooden Leg, the White River Agency became known as the Pine Ridge Agency.[2]

The Cheyenne called the **North Platte River** the Geese River.

Pryor Creek was known as Shooting-At-The-Bank Creek by the Cheyenne.

The Sioux, Cheyenne, and Arikara called the **Yellowstone River** the Elk River.

The **Rosebud River/Creek** was also called the Sweet Briar (by Boston Custer, in a letter to his mother).[3]

Along the Rosebud Creek the distance between Lame Deer Creek and Muddy Creek is seven miles.

Busby camp—
- Halt One was approximately 6½ miles from the Busby camp. The writer/historian, Tom Heski, says 6.7 miles (the map in his *Research Review* article shows 6.2 miles).[4]
- The Busby camp was approximately 11.5–11.9 miles from the divide.

Halt One—
- Halt One was approximately 6½ miles from the Busby camp. Heski says 6.7 miles.
- The Busby camp was approximately 11.5–11.9 miles from the divide.
- Heski puts the distance between Halt One and Halt Two at four miles.[5]
- From the Crow's Nest back to Halt One is approximately 4 ½ to 4¾ miles.

Halt Two—
- About 3½ miles from Halt One.
- Heski puts the distance between Halt One and Halt Two at four miles.[6]
- Heski's Halt Two is approximately 1.7 miles east-southeast of the divide and 1.1 miles from the foot of Crow's Nest hill.[7]
- "Officers' Call Knoll" to the area on the divide where Custer may have viewed the Little Big Horn valley using DeRudio's field glasses, i.e., Vern Smalley's "Varnum's Lookout," is about ¾ mile.
- Halt Two—map reference, Thompson Creek NW, block 27 (northern section), along the trail between elevations 3,923 and 3,893 at the confluence of Davis Creek and an intermittent rill running due north and south.

Crow's Nest—
- To the lone tepee: 9¼ miles, straight line.
- 4½ to 4¾ miles from Crow's Nest back to Halt One.
- The Crows Nest pocket is ³⁄₁₀ to ⁴⁄₁₀ mile (525–700 yards) southwest of Halt Two, depending on which site is accepted for the halt area.
- The Sioux village was about 15 to 15½ miles from the Crow's Nest.
- Crow's Nest—map reference, Thompson Creek NW, block 34 (NW corner), at elevation 4440 (unmarked).

The divide—
- The Busby camp was approximately 11.5–11.9 miles from the divide.
- The divide to the divide *halt* was about ¼ mile (440 yards).
- Divide *halt* to the mouth of No-Name Creek (at Reno Creek), approximately 6.7 miles (this is the creek Benteen moved down to return to the main trail).

- From the divide crossing to the confluence of No-Name Creek and Reno Creek is 6.9 miles.
- The divide to the morass is about 7½ miles.
- The divide crossing to Ford A is 11.81 miles along Reno Creek, almost straight-line except for one or two sharp bends in the valley.
- Divide crossing—map reference, Thompson Creek NW, block 28, along trail and between large 4,400' elevation and a smaller rise to its south.

Reno Creek—has been known also as Benteen Creek, Ash Creek, Trail Creek [Lakota], Little Wolf Creek, Medicine Dance Creek— or Great Medicine Dance Creek—and Sundance Creek. It appears the Sioux also called it Spring Creek at one time.

No-Name Creek—
- From No-Name Creek to the Little Big Horn is about 5 to 5.4 miles.
- From the divide crossing to the confluence of No-Name Creek and Reno Creek is 6.9 miles.
- Divide *halt* to the mouth of No-Name Creek (at Ash or Reno Creek), approximately 6.7 miles (this is the creek Benteen moved down to return to the main trail).
- The distance from No-Name Creek to the morass was only about ¼ mile (440 yards).

The morass—
- It is ¾ mile from the morass to the eastern "lone tepee" (according to John Gray). Roger Darling figured 1.4 to 2.4 miles from morass to the lone tepee. Vern Smalley says one mile.
- Smalley places the morass approximately 5½ miles from the Little Big Horn.
- Morass—map reference, Lodge Grass NE, block 16 (northern half), just west of the confluence of No-Name Creek and Reno Creek.

South Fork—
- South Fork is about one mile below No-Name Creek and at Reno Creek about four miles above the Little Big Horn River. My figures are 1.05 miles between where No-Name joins Reno Creek and where South Fork joins Reno Creek.
- South Fork to Gerard's Knoll is 2.62 miles.
- South Fork to Ford A is 4.32 miles.

The Reno Creek flats—
- About 2¾ miles from the eastern lone tepee.
- The North Fork—also known as Custer Creek—was another ¼ to ½ mile more.
- The "eastern lone tepee"—map reference, Lodge Grass NE, block 8 (SW corner), in the vicinity of the 3,282 elevation marker.

Varnum's lookout—[termed by Bruce Liddic and not to be confused with Smalley's "Varnum's Lookout" atop the divide]
- (South of the flats)—map reference, Lodge Grass NE, block 13 (in the middle), on the 3,405 elevation marker.

Gerard's Knoll—
- Gerard's Knoll to Middle Knoll is 1.1 miles.
- Gerard's Knoll to the Ford A crossing is 1.7 miles.

Lone tepee—
- From the divide halt to the lone tepee is 9¾ to 10 miles.
- From the lone tepee to Ford A is approximately 1.7 miles.

Custer-Reno separation in the flats—
- Reno's route to the Ford A crossing was 1.62 miles.
- From the separation point to where Lieutenant Cooke met Custer was approximately one mile.
- From the Cooke-Custer meeting to where I believe Custer may have watered, 335 yards (²⁄₁₀ of a mile).
- From the watering point to the peak on the bluffs, 670 yards (.38 of a mile). (This would have been the first "high point" on the bluffs along the river north of Reno Creek valley.)
- From the peak on the bluffs to 3,411 is 1½ miles.

"Middle Knoll"—
- Middle Knoll to Cooke's Knoll is 0.38 miles (670 yards).
- The western side of Middle Knoll to Last Stand Hill is approximately 5.71 miles.

"Cooke's Knoll"—
- Middle Knoll to Cooke's Knoll is 0.38 miles (670 yards).

North Fork—
- Also referred to as Custer Creek.
- North Fork (or Custer Creek) to Reno Hill: 1.3 to 1.5 miles.
- North Fork is about two miles from 3,411 based on an easier route, not quite straight line.

The Cheyenne name for the **Little Big Horn River** was Little Sheep Creek or the Goat River. The Sioux called it Greasy Grass Creek or *Pa-zees-la-wak-pa*. Wooden Leg referred to a Greasy Grass Creek emptying into the Little Big Horn River. It seems the Cheyenne name for Reno Creek may have been Greasy Grass Creek.

Ford A—
- Ford A crossing point approximately 102 miles from mouth of Rosebud.
- Ford A is about 4 to 4½ miles from the eastern lone tepee.
- Ford A is about 1.7 miles from the real lone, burning tepee.
- From the Ford A crossing to the open Little Big Horn valley is approximately ½ mile.
- The Indian village was approximately three miles from Ford A.
- Reno dismounted to form his skirmish line about 2½ miles from Ford A.
- Ford A to Gerard's Knoll, located in the flats, is approximately 1.7 miles.
- Ford A to Ford B is 4.3 miles, not straight line.
  Ford A ↔ *1.7 miles* ↔ Gerard's Knoll/lone tepee in the flats ↔ *2.3 miles* ↔ South Fork ↔ *1 mile* ↔ No—Name Creek ↔ *6.9 miles* ↔ divide crossing.
  Total distance: *11.9 miles.*

Reno Hill—(also referred to as the **Reno-Benteen Hill** complex)
- Reno Hill to Ford B, crossing the Little Big Horn River and going through the valley and the Indian villages is about over 3.3 miles by horseback. If the Indians crossed the Little Big Horn

going towards Reno Hill, then reversed themselves and rode to Medicine Tail Coulee, the distance would be a little over three miles.

- Weir Peak is 1¼ miles (2,200 yards) along the bluffs from Reno Hill.

3,411—

- North Fork is about two miles from 3,411 based on an easier route, not quite straight line.
- 3,411 is approximately 250 yards (.14 mile) from the summit of Sharpshooters' Ridge (to its rear).
- 3,411 is approximately 600 yards (.33 mile) from the head of Cedar Coulee.
- 3,411 is 1,260 yards (.71 mile) from the southern peak of Weir Point.

Sharpshooters' Ridge—

- Map reference, Crow Agency, block 34 (lower half of the block), just south of the south end of the 3,400'-marked elevation (Sharpshooter Ridge).

Weir Point/Peaks—

- Sioux called it Black Butte.
- Weir Peak is 1¼ miles (2,200 yards) along the bluffs from Reno Hill.
- From 3,411 to the southern peak of Weir Point is 1,260 yards (.71 mile).
- Weir Peak is 2⅓ miles—straight line—from Calhoun Hill.
- Weir Peak "rises rather steeply about a mile and a quarter from Reno Hill. The point is in effect a group of three promontories that resemble a sort of an 'L' on its side. There are two points along the river's bluffs, west of the present road and parallel with the river. The other peak lies east of the road and presents a round 'sugarloaf' appearance. At the time of the battle, the eastern and western projections were connected by gradual sloping sides that have since been graded down for the present road bed."[8]
- The distance traveled by the three Crows from Weir Peaks along the bluffs to the so-called Boyer's Bluff above Ford B was 1.3 miles (2,275 yards).

Cedar Coulee—

- Also referred to as South Coulee.
- The head of Cedar Coulee is approximately 9/10 of a mile (1,600 yards) from the center of the Reno Hill complex.
- The Cedar Coulee "bend" is about ½ mile (880 yards) from the head of the coulee.
- Cedar Coulee is about 1⅛ miles (2,000 yards) from its head to its confluence with Medicine Tail Coulee.
- From the top of Cedar Coulee to the top of Luce Ridge, following a probable route is 2.6 miles. This would be made up of a one-mile trip down Medicine Tail Coulee and .48 mile (850 yards) up the slopes to Luce added to the 1⅛ miles of Cedar Coulee.
- From where Cedar Coulee meets Medicine Tail Coulee, it is approximately 9/10 of a mile (1,600 yards) to the beginning of the slopes leading to Luce Ridge.
- The bottom of Cedar Coulee is approximately 1.4 miles (2,450–2,500 yards) from the top of Luce Ridge.

Medicine Tail Coulee—A wide, intermittent streambed that led Custer in the direction of Ford B. Indians never called it that, however. Also called Muddy Creek and referred to frequently as "the watering place" during the Reno Court of Inquiry. The Sioux and Cheyenne had several names for it:

- Muskrat Creek (referred to by Standing Bear).
- Dry Creek (Soldier Wolf).
- Water Rat Creek (Fears Nothing).

Luce Ridge—

- Luce Ridge is approximately 6/10 mile from the bluffs above Ford B.
- From where Cedar Coulee meets Medicine Tail Coulee, it is approximately 9/10 of a mile (1,600 yards) to the beginning of the slopes leading to Luce Ridge.
- The bottom of Cedar Coulee is approximately 1.4 miles (2,450–2,500 yards) from the top of Luce Ridge.
- Luce Ridge to Nye-Cartwright Ridge is ¼ mile (440 yards).

Nye-Cartwright Ridge—

- Nye-Cartwright Ridge to Ford B is .86 mile (1,500 yards), but up slopes to the ridgeline.
- Nye-Cartwright Ridge to Calhoun Hill is .86 miles (1,500 yards), down a ravine and straight across the Deep Coulee flats.
- Nye-Cartwright Ridge to "Custer Bluff" is ⅔ of a mile (1,175 yards).
- Luce Ridge to Nye-Cartwright Ridge is ¼ mile (440 yards).

"Custer Bluff"—

- The edge of this bluff is approximately .86 miles (1,500 yards) from the high point of Luce Ridge.
- 325–350 yards east of Ford B, at the edge of the ridges forming Luce and Nye-Cartwright ridges.

Ford B—

- Also referred to as Minneconjou Ford and Medicine Tail Coulee Ford.
- Ford A to Ford B is 4.3 miles, not straight-line distance.
- From Reno's retreat crossing ford around the river loops and through the village to Ford B, it is about 3.4 miles. It is another 2.48 miles to Ford D, a total of 5.88 miles from the retreat crossing to Ford D, not straight-line distance.
- Ford B to the Deep Ravine crossing is 1.43 miles (2,500 yards), not straight-line distance.
- Ford B to Ford D is 2.48 miles (4,375 yards), not straight-line distance.
- Ford B to the top of Calhoun Hill is about 1.1 miles.
- Ford B is almost ½ mile (880–900 yards) wide at its mouth.
- Ford B to Nye-Cartwright Ridge is .86 mile (1,500 yards), but up slopes to the ridgeline.
- Ford B to Custer Bluff is about 2/10 of a mile (325–350 yards).
- For Indians crossing at Ford B, then riding up Deep Coulee to hide their horses, the distance could have been as little as 650 to 670 yards. From there along an infiltration route, they would have had to move ¾ of a mile (1,340 yards) to reach a point in Calhoun Coulee. It would then be some 4/10 of a mile (670 yards) to the top of Calhoun Hill.

NOTE—In a test on a high school track, ¼ mile was completed in crouching, jumping-up, running, and dodging fashion in five to six minutes. The experiment added as much as ⅛ mile to the distance because of the way we crouched and ran in various diagonals. This would mean that an infiltrating Indian, under optimal conditions, could move at a rate of 2½ mph to 3 mph or as much as 3¾ mph to 4½ mph. For the Indians to close to within 100 yards of Calhoun Hill-Battle Ridge via Calhoun Coulee using infiltration tactics from as far out as 670 yards, it would take five to eight minutes to move the 570 yards (.324 miles).

From the North branch of Medicine Tail Coulee across the ridges and into the coulee that empties into Deep Coulee near Henryville, Indians would have traveled some 1.14 miles (2,000 yards).

Shoulder Blade or **Box Elder Creek** was also known as Big Shoulders. In *Lakota Recollections,* p. 40, footnote 9, Richard Hardorff surmises that another name for Shoulder Blade Creek was Muddy Creek.

Squaw Creek is also called Chasing Creek and Shavings Creek. Near or opposite Ford D, and is believed to be the place the Indian families were gathering as they left the village.

"Curtis Knoll"—

The southern extremity of Greasy Grass Ridge. Named for the famous photographer, Edward Sheriff Curtis, who had his own ideas of how the battle unfolded. It appears this is the knoll Yellow Nose scaled as he watched Custer's troops reach Ford B.

Deep Coulee—

- From Ford B to the mouth of Deep Coulee is approximately 420 yards (¼ mile). This measurement is from the river to the beginning of the cut-bank leading to the coulee's flats and does not consider the coulee's spillway into the ford area.
- From the mouth of Deep Coulee to the peak of Calhoun Hill is 1,600 yards (.9 mile).
- From the mouth of the coulee to the upper area of Finley-Finckle Ridge is in the vicinity of 1,350 yards (¾ mile).

Finley-Finckle Ridge—

- Also called Calhoun Ridge.
- From the mouth of Deep Coulee to the upper area of Finley-Finckle Ridge is in the vicinity of 1,350 yards (¾ mile).

Calhoun Hill—

- Calhoun Hill is approximately 1,000 yards (.57 miles) from the top of Greasy Grass Ridge.
- If the C Company men dismounted and then ran by foot from a point 650 yards deep in Calhoun Coulee to Finley-Finckle Ridge, then up onto Calhoun Hill, across into the Keogh Sector, and then onto Custer/Last Stand Hill, the distance from that point would have been approximately 9/10 to 1.15 miles (1,585–2,025 yards).
- If C Company men reached Finley-Finckle Ridge, they would have had to go 4/10 mile or 670 yards to reach Calhoun Hill.
- Calhoun Hill is approximately ⅔ mile (1,175 yards) from Last Stand Hill and the monument.

Henryville is the area in the flats of Deep Coulee near Calhoun Hill. Named for the number of Henry cartridges found within a large grouping.

Calhoun Coulee—

- The C Company charge off Battle Ridge into Calhoun Coulee may have gone for as long as 650 yards (.37 miles).

Battle Ridge, also known as **Custer Ridge—**

- The ridge runs roughly parallel to and about one mile east of the Little Big Horn, and is about 6/10–7/10 of a mile (1,050–1,225 yards) long.
- The C Company charge off Battle Ridge into Calhoun Coulee may have gone for as long as 650 yards (.37 miles).
- From the middle of the presumed dismount area in Calhoun Coulee to the lower part of Finley-Finckle Ridge is approximately ¼ mile (425 yards).
- From Battle Ridge, east, to the so-called Crazy Horse Ridge east of the Keogh Sector, is approximately ⅓ of a mile (600 yards).

Ford D—

- Ford B to Ford D is 2.48 miles (4,375 yards), not straight line.
- From Reno's retreat crossing ford around the river loops and through the village to Ford B, it is about 3.4 miles. It is another 2.48 miles to Ford D, a total of 5.88 miles from the retreat crossing to Ford D, not straight line.
- The distance from Ford D to Cemetery Ridge using the route that Custer probably followed is 1¼ to 1½ miles.

Cemetery Ridge—

- The distance from Ford D to Cemetery Ridge using the route that Custer probably followed is 1¼ to 1½ miles.

Custer Hill, also known as **Last Stand Hill—**

- Last Stand Hill is about ⅔-mile from Calhoun Hill.
- Custer Hill to Reno areas: about 4⅜ miles (all straight-line distances).
- Colonel Nelson A. Miles visited the battlefield in 1878 and measured distances and times from point to point:
    - o Reno Hill to Custer Hill measured at 4 miles.
    - o Miles took cavalry horses between the two points and found the distance could be covered in 58 minutes at a walk and 15 minutes at a variable trot and gallop.
- Custer Hill is about three miles from Weir Peak.
- On August 22, 1878, Captain J. S. Payne measured the distance from Custer Hill to Reno Hill. The straight-line distance was four miles, 160 yards.
- Calhoun Hill to Ford D is approximately 2.33 miles via the Keogh Sector, then down the coulee north of Cemetery Ridge.

The South Skirmish Line (SSL)—

- "[R]oughly 720 yards from the monument on Custer Hill to Deep Ravine following a line down from the monument to Marker 54, then along the Deep Ravine Trail, which meanders a bit, touches near most of the remaining gravemarkers, and continues to its end at the lower trail crossing near gravemarker 7."[9]
- At 720 yards, this would make it 4/10 of a mile from the top

of Custer/Last Stand Hill to Deep Ravine. This would make it a run of some 550 yards to 875 yards off the general Last Stand Hill area to the ravine.

- The actual "line" itself begins about 200 yards down from Custer Hill at Markers 52, 53, and 54 in the upper reaches of Cemetery Ravine. It wavers down the ravine and then climbs up obliquely across the ravine's south bank, following the grave markers in descending order. The Boyer cluster, Markers 33–39, is near the divide and about 180 yards from the start of the line. Markers 29–32 are the last stones on the Cemetery Ravine side of the divide and are about 200 yards from the head of the line. About 220 yards along the trail there is a soft crest where the trail begins to dip down into the upper Deep Ravine watershed. At 270 yards is another cluster, grave Markers 24–28. The South Skirmish Line has been heading roughly north to south, but at this point a branch of markers diverges to the southeast. This branch consists of seven more or less isolated stones, numbers 20–23, 255, and 1–2. The latter two are down in the upper reaches of Deep Ravine, far above the headcut.[10]

- The formal South Skirmish Line terminates just below the low divide in the 24–28 group of markers.

- Markers 7–19 are considered the "fugitive" markers.

- From markers 24–28, "the southeast branch splits off, the trail and fugitive lines follow the markers another 190 yards to stone 7 at the edge of Deep Ravine. The total length of the line—formal and fugitive ... is about 430 yards."

Deep Ravine—

- From the monument to the headcut is 640 meters, straight-line. The headcut is slightly above where the interpretive trail enters the ravine and it is slightly above that area where the bodies are believed to have been found. "Kanipe and Logan had remembered the bodies near the ravine headcut."[11]

- "Deep Ravine near the headcut ... is narrow, with high, steep walls.... Goldin, recollecting in 1928 and 1930, described the ravine that trapped the men as a cul-de-sac with high banks in front and on both sides."[12] LT Bradley also noticed a cul-de-sac.

- "[G]eomorphology has shown, despite the lack of artifactual data, that in 1876 the ravine structure near the South Skirmish Line formed a cul-de-sac. People who shortly after the fight observed the cul-de-sac saw that it contained bodies and they saw it exactly where we found it, some 2,000 feet (610) meters from the monument of Last Stand Hill."[13]

- Deep Ravine extends approximately 700 yards from the "headcut," the area where the ravine forks as it approaches the western edges of the Battle Ridge area, downstream to its mouth at the LBH. From head to mouth it measures about 1,000 yards.

- The headcut is about ½ mile from the Little Big Horn.[14]

- From the Deep Ravine ford, up the ravine to its headwall, and then on to Battle Ridge, is approximately .76 miles (1,350 yards).

- The *floor* of the ravine is from 5 to 15 yards wide, with grassy sloping banks about 3 to 6 yards high and angling up between 40° and 60°.

- The floor of the ravine below the "headcut" is practically flat.

- The ford crossing at Deep Ravine is called Cheyenne Ford.

- The drainage extends northeasterly 1,340 meters (4,397 feet) from the mouth to near the divide on Last Stand Hill.[15]

- Calhoun Coulee branches off, southeasterly, at the lower fork, 350 meters (1,148 feet) from the mouth.

- The bend occurs 550 meters (1,805 feet) above the mouth.

- A small headcut occurs 120 meters (394 feet) above the bend.

- The upper fork occurs 190 meters (624 feet) above the bend.

- The floor is 5 to 15 meters (16.4–49.2 feet) wide.

- The banks are 3 to 6 meters (9.8–19.7 feet) high.

Appendix B:
Vegetation at the
Little Big Horn

Note—It seems the vegetation at the Little Big Horn was lusher in 1876 than it was a year later when the first photographs of the battlefield were taken. This is supported by eyewitness accounts but should not be considered definitive.

- Shortgrass prairie
- Buffalo grass, spreading by aboveground roots, rooting as it spreads, with tufts of green grass. It can grow as much as an inch or two a day.
- Blue grama grass, taller than buffalo grass, 6 to 20 inches high.
  - Western wheatgrass
  - Needle-and-thread
  - Locoweed
  - Plains wallflower
  - Gumweed
  - Prairie clover
  - Sunflower
  - Sagebrush
  - Some prickly pear cactus and yucca
- Trees grow primarily in sheltered coulees and along riverbanks.
  - Mostly cottonwood
  - Aspen
  - Chokeberry
  - Western snowberry
  - Wild roses
  - Mountain muhly
  - Northern redgrass
  - Prairie junegrass
  - Rabbit grass
  - Mesquite
  - Juniper
  - Some cedar
  - Ash
- Most precipitation occurs during May through July, only 10 to 12 inches per year.

In 1876 the valley was thick with dust from a drought. In 1877, Lieutenant Colonel Michael V. Sheridan and Captain Henry J. Nowlan (Seventh Cavalry) went to the battlefield to re-bury the dead and mark the officers' graves, and found that "flowers were in abundance and luxurious grasses grew as high as the horses' stirrups."[1] Greg Michno also mentions Robert G. Rosenberg, a Wyoming historical consultant with a background in forestry and western history. The trees everyone calls cedars are actually Rocky Mountain junipers, very common in this region. They grow as tall as 40' to 55', but are more commonly 10' to 25' tall. These are the trees that line Cedar Coulee.[2]

"Coulees intervened, trees and shrubbery masked the Indians retreat along the river bank below; tall, heavy sagebrush, since cropped by sheep, covered the battlefield at a height that would conceal a lurking savage." All of which gives weight to the contention that the topography of the country in the vicinity of the hostile village had more to do with Custer's defeat than any other factor.[3]

APPENDIX C:
MARKER PLACEMENT AND
ARTIFACT ANALYSIS

In 1891 the United States Geological Survey sent a topographer, R. B. Marshall, to the Custer field to map out the marker placement. He mapped 244 markers, a discrepancy of two, only one year from when Captain Owen Sweet placed his 246 stones.[1] It also appears the marker map produced from this survey is erroneous in many areas and was incorrectly marked, bearing little correlation to the accurate work done in the 1984–1985 excavations. Then, in the 1920s, Joe Blummer found Springfield cartridge cases along a series of ridges north of Medicine Tail Coulee. In a 1928 letter, Blummer wrote,

> I found 17 shells on the east side of this small ridge ... strung out for about 150 yards and all on the east side of the ridge about 10 feet from the top. This ridge is about three-fourths of a mile southeast of the southeast corner of (the) battlefield fence."[2]

In 1938, Colonel Elwood L. Nye and R. G. Cartwright checked the same site and discovered many more cases. These locations were on Blummer/Nye-Cartwright Ridge. The proliferation of cartridge cases indicated conclusive proof that troops of the Seventh Cavalry occupied these locations. Through an analysis of the letters Superintendent Edward S. Luce wrote describing the artifacts he and others found, Bruce Trinque concluded that Richard Fox' "West Ridge" is the real Luce Ridge and it is this area—north to Nye-Cartwright—that the troops traversed. More than 100 cases were found by Luce, generally three to four yards apart, indicating dismounted skirmishers. As the trail of cases continued, the spacing changed to about nine yards indicating mounted skirmishing. The author and historian, Jerome Greene, claimed 214 empty carbine cases were found on or near Nye-Cartwright Ridge.[3]

In addition, the body of L Company first sergeant, James Butler, had been found along these ridges. Richard Hardorff wrote,

> Dr. James S. Brust rediscovered Butler's kill site, which was originally identified by Gen. Godfrey in 1916, and which location is some 125 yards southwest of the present site of the Butler marker. In years past, Godfrey's Butler site yielded a horse skeleton, several expended cartridges, a horseshoe and a shank portion of a boot, containing a decomposed foot. The rotted leather revealed some faded initials, thought to read "JD," but which may well have been the letters "JB."[4]

Greg Michno, in his work, *Lakota Noon,* outlined the artifact fields as follows[5]:

(A) Along the front side of Butler Ridge that faces the Little Big Horn, were found:

- Ten .45/55 caliber bullets.
- Four .45/55 cases
- Two unfired .45/55 cartridges
- Two Colt .45 bullets
- One .50/70 cartridge
- Three .44 Henry cases
- Three .50 Spencer cases
- Four brass cavalry insignia
- One arrowhead
- Two half horseshoes
- One metal ring
- Brass grommets
- Iron snaps
- One Winchester rifle
- Fox claimed this is where Custer himself and Yates watched the action at Ford B. Michno felt Custer remained with Keogh's battalion on East Ridge, then Luce, then Nye-Cartwright.

(B) In the north fork of Medicine Tail Coulee, below and along the south and southeast face of Luce Ridge—traditional Luce Ridge is East Ridge—roughly parallel to East Ridge:

- Four .45/55 cases
- Three .50/70 cases
- Fourteen .45/55 cases, plus an additional undetermined number
- At least three horse skeletons, plus additional horse bones
- At least three human skeletons, plus additional human bones
- A saddle and bridle, saddle leather and pommel rings, and horseshoes
- Much of this was probably from the battle with the southern half of Wolf Tooth's band.

(C) In the lower ground, north and northwest of Butler Ridge, east of Deep Coulee:

- Two .45/55 cartridges
- A horseshoe, harness buckle, and straps
- A leather boot

- A leather scabbard
- An arrowhead
- Two human skeletons
- Numerous horse bones
- Michno felt these are, "from a combination of Yates' men moving back up Butler Ridge and from the Indians who followed Yates and Keogh."[6] This is a reasonable assumption and tactically sound.

(D) On the southern slope of Nye-Cartwright Ridge, directly behind the Little Big Horn face of Butler Ridge:

- Four .45/55 cases
- Four .45/55 cartridges
- Six .56 Spencer cases
- Twenty-four .50/70 cases
- Fifteen .44 Henry cases
- Nine .44 Henry cartridges
- An Indian bridle
- Michno feels these are "from a combination of Yates' men moving back up Butler Ridge and from the Indians who followed Yates and Keogh."

(E) All along the Nye-Cartwright/"new" Luce Ridge complex. This is now behind all of the previous references, including (B):

- Upwards of *480* .45/55 cases and cartridges
- Several .50/70 cases
- An undetermined number of additional shells
- Saddle and tack parts
- Uniform buttons and buckles
- Regardless of the accuracy of various theories, no one can deny the troops moved along these ridgelines.

(F) Behind Nye-Cartwright along a dry ravine of South Branch:

- Three .44 Henry cases
- This was probably from the skirmish with the northern half of Wolf Tooth's band.

(G) Below the western edge of Nye-Cartwright, in what appear to be a series of gullies or ravines leading to, but before, Deep Coulee:

- Three human and three horse skeletons
- Various bridle and saddle parts

(H) Northern part of Deep Coulee on its west side, toward Calhoun Hill and the Henryville area:

- Human bones and two horse skeletons
- Eight .45/55 cases
- Two .50/70 cases
- Two .50-caliber and one .56-caliber Spencer cases
- One .32 rimfire case
- Two .44 Henry cases
- One Winchester rifle

Michno went on to say there were "few or no relics found along the traditional northward line directly from the ford to Greasy Grass Ridge and Calhoun Hill."[7] References "A" through "G" count eight to nine bodies; "H" counts some more. Whose? Indians or soldiers? Indians generally policed up their dead, though these may have been missed; possible single warriors, present without families. The soldiers were accounted for (lieutenants Porter,

Harrington, and Sturgis were exceptions) despite the inability to identify everyone.

Michno summarized some of the 1984–1985 archaeological data[8]:

- Henryville, on the Deep Coulee side: 32 Indian cartridge cases.
- Henryville, on the Calhoun Hill side: 13 Indian cartridge cases.
- Across Calhoun Hill, roughly from west to east: nine Indian cartridge cases.
- All along the ridges and gullies east of Battle Ridge and the Keogh Sector: 108 Indian cartridges, including .50/70's, .44's, and .56's.
- Along the south side of Finley Ridge: nine Indian bullets.
- Across Calhoun Hill, roughly north to south: 5 Army cartridge cases.

Bruce Liddic investigated this work as well:

Shell cases have been found for nearly a quarter mile along the crest [of Blummer-(Nye) Cartwright Ridge]. Hank Wiebert [*sic*] reported he found a number of shell cases along the crest of Blummer (Nye)–Cartwright Ridge. However, Joseph Blummer wrote to Robert Cartwright in a 1928 letter that he found a number of shells along the northern slope of this ridge about 10 feet from the crest.[9]

Michno broke down the 1984–1985 archeological finds into 12 main areas. Furthermore, "All areas had a mix of both Indian and army relics, while some had a predominance of one type over another to mark it as either a soldier or Indian position."[10]

- Greasy Grass Ridge, particularly in the southern portion (173 artifacts); northern portion (32 artifacts): Indian positions.
- Henryville (114): Indian.
- Today's cemetery (53): Indian.
- The "bend" of Deep Ravine (34): Indian.
- North of Custer Hill (45): Indian.
- Soldier positions were strongest at Custer Hill (80) and to a lesser extent at Calhoun Hill (63).
- Mixed areas were in Calhoun Coulee (43), Finley-Finckle Ridge (23), the Keogh Sector (86), and the South Skirmish Line (169). The latter two areas show *considerable* mixed activity.

The archeological survey conducted by Richard Fox and Douglas Scott in 1984 found that at least seven "of the Indian weapons which were used to break the soldier's line on Finley Hill were also fired against Calhoun's position from Henryville Ridge, southeast of this hill."[11] Liddic correctly suggested the reason for this was because at 700 yards away on Greasy Grass Ridge, the Indians' fire was not effective against troops on Calhoun Hill, but at the shorter distance of about 350 yards from Henryville, the Henrys and Winchesters were lethal.

Initial burials occurred on June 28, 1876. The battlefield was divided into five sectors:

1. The company commanders went over the whole field to try to identify the officers.

2. The first sergeants led the men over the sectors to try to identify the men and bury them. Company B was on the extreme

left, closest to the river. Company A was to their right. Companies G, M, and K took the central area, and companies D and H covered the right farthest back from the river. They moved north, burying and counting as they moved.

3. There were numerous accounts of bodies seen in a [D]eep [R]avine:

- 1SG Ryan (M): 18 or 20 men of E Company.
- CPT Benteen (H): 22 bodies.
- CPT Moylan (A): 20-odd bodies of E Company.
- LT Godfrey (K): 28 men of Smith's troop.
- LT Hare (K): 28 bodies of Smith's troop in a coulee in skirmish order.
- SGT Kanipe (C): rode along the edge of a deep gully and counted 28 bodies in there [Walter Camp].
- LT Richard Thompson (6th Infantry): maybe 34 bodies in a gully [Walter Camp].
- LT Edward Maguire (Engineers): drew a map showing 28 bodies in one particular ravine.
- LT Edward McClernand (2nd Cavalry): 28 bodies of Smith's troop were found at the lower end of the line in a deep coulee.
- COL John Gibbon (7th Infantry): 40 or 50 bodies were found in a valley running perpendicular to the river.
- Walter Camp interviewed two Sioux warriors, Good Voiced Elk (Hunkpapa), who claimed 25 to 30 died in a gully; and He Dog (Oglala) who corroborated the number of 28. (Of course, one would like to know how he arrived at this precise number.)
- LT/Dr. Holmes Paulding: 28 bodies found in a deep ravine by the scouts.

When the burials of Custer's men were completed late on June 28th, the re-united columns moved north. They moved only about 4½ miles, however, when the lateness of the day and the inadequacies of the transport for the wounded forced them to halt. The troops camped just below the north end of the abandoned Indian village.

In a November 6, 1920, letter from Walter Camp to Edward Godfrey, Camp discussed the marker placements.

> There are 17 or 18 too many markers in the group at the monument, too many in the group around Keogh's marker, too many between the monument and the river, and none in the big gully where about 28 ought to be. I discovered these dead in the gully with Capt. McDougall ... and he was clear that there were only 9 dead between the end of the ridge and the gully, and 28 in the gully (not counting the group that lay around the body of Gen. Custer).... As the markers now stand, there are more than 50 where there should be only 9, on that side hill, and not enough at or in the gully.[12]

In a random sampling of marker sites, however, Richard Fox estimated 91 percent of 43 "paired marker sites" showed only *one* body had been buried there. He therefore eliminated 43 of the 252 markers (209 remaining) in determining where men fell.

Douglas Scott estimated 27–44 men were killed in the area between Custer Hill and Deep Ravine. This included the South Skirmish Line. Michno as well claimed there are 44 grave markers on the main branch of the South Skirmish Line (also dubbed the "fugitive line"), seven on the southeast branch, and four more across Deep Ravine (55 total).[13]

Custer/Last Stand Hill—

Scott claimed Custer, five officers, and perhaps 40 enlisted personnel lay on Custer/Last Stand Hill.

- 28 names are documented: 14 privates
  Ygnatz Stungewitz (C)
  Willis B. Wright (C)
  Anton Dohman (F)
  Gustav Klein (F)
  William H. Lerock (F)
  Werner L. Liemann (F)
  Edward C. Driscoll (I)
  Archibald McIlhargey (I)
  John E. Mitchell (I)
  John Parker (I)
  Francis T. Hughes (L)
  Charles McCarthy (L)
  Oscar F. Pardee (L)
  Thomas S. Tweed (L)
- Two civilians
  Boston Custer (QM)
  Autie Reed
- One surgeon: Dr. George Lord (HQ)
- One trumpeter: Henry Voss (HQ)
- Four NCOs
  SGM William Sharrow (HQ)
  1SG Michael Kenney (F)
  SGT John Vickory—Groesbeck (F)
  CPL William Teeman (F)

NOTE: CPL John J. Callahan (K) was identified on Last Stand Hill by others. A body exhumed in 1877 wearing corporal's stripes could have been Callahan's. Less likely in this location would be CPL William Teeman (F), probably found a little lower on the ridgeline. This would make the identifications total 29.

- Sergeant Robert Hughes' (K) body was most likely the one found at the head of Deep Ravine, though there is a remote chance he was killed on Custer Hill. Supposedly identified by Captain McDougall.
  - Six officers:
    George Armstrong Custer (HQ)
    William Cooke (HQ)
    Tom Custer (C/HQ)
    Algernon Smith (E)
    George Yates (F)
    William Van W. Reily (F)
- Presently, 52 markers are located on Custer Hill; 42 bodies had been buried there initially.
  - Deep Ravine (eight men from Company E):
    1SG Frederick Hohmeyer
    SGT John S. Ogden
    CPL George C. Brown
    CPL Albert H. Meyer
    PVT Richard Farrell
    PVT William Huber
    PVT Andy Knecht
    PVT William H. Rees

Bruce Liddic presented his own description of where bodies were found. Grouped near Custer around the top of the knoll[14]:

    LT Cooke (HQ)
    PVT Driscoll (I)
    PVT Parker (I)
    LT Smith (E)
    SGT John Vickory-Groesbeck (F)
    TMP Voss (HQ)
    PVT McCarthy (L)

- Deep Ravine:
    SGT Hughes (K)
    PVT Tim Donnelly (F)
    PVT Andrew Knecht (E)[15]
- On a rise above Deep Ravine: CPL John Briody (F)
- Farthest north on the battlefield, opposite the present parking lot on the east side of the service entrance road: SGM Sharrow (HQ).
- Lower west side, down the slope from the monument, about 100 yards from George Custer:
    Boston Custer
    Autie Reed
- About 20 feet southeast of GAC, on a hillside: Dr. Lord (HQ)

Sergeant John Rafter (Company K) claimed the body of Private Weston Harrington (L Company) "was found between Custer and the deep gully. The body was not mutilated and a blanket was thrown over him. He was known among the Sioux before he was enlisted and it was thought that some of them recognized him and protected his body in this way."[16]

- Private John C. Creighton (also of K Company) said Sergeant Vickory-Groesbeck's body was found in a ravine between Calhoun and Keogh. He also said Lieutenant Reily was not mutilated.[17]
- Private Charles Graham of L Company was found on a line between Calhoun and Keogh.[18]

Second Lieutenant Richard Thompson, General Terry's Acting Commissary of Subsistence, said there were only nine or 10 men found between Custer and the gully (June 27, 1876).[19]

James Brust, Brian Pohanka, and Sandy Barnard wrote that on Custer/Last Stand Hill[20]:

- Lieutenant Wallace: "They had apparently tried to lead the horses in a circle on the point of the ridge and had killed them there and apparently made an effort for a final stand." [p. 127]
- Sergeant Kanipe: the horses "were 'scattered all over the hill.'" [127]
- Captain Walter Clifford (Seventh Infantry): "slain horses, placed head to tail." [128]
- Lieutenant DeRudio: "Five or six horses lay as if they had been led there and shot down for a barricade. These horses were all sorrels from Company C." [128]
- Captain Michael Sheridan: "It was a rough point or narrow ridge not wide enough to drive a wagon on. Across that ridge were five or six horses apparently in line, and looked as if they had been killed for the purpose of resistance, but the remains were found in a confused mass." [128]

- George and Tom Custer and Lieutenant "Cooke were among the dead on or just below the crest of the ridge." [128]
- Tom Custer "was found some 15–20 feet from his elder brother and somewhat higher on the ridge." [128]
- Cooke was found just below the crest.
- George Custer was actually buried on the ridge, but below the spot where his body was found. [132]
- "Post battle eyewitnesses described the top of Custer Hill as a small knoll, some 30 feet in diameter, an area roughly equivalent to the grass around the granite memorial shaft today. About 10 bodies were found there, including that of General Custer near the southwestern rim of the elevation. Six horses lay in a convex perimeter on the east side." [132]

The South Skirmish Line (SSL)—

- "[R]oughly 720 yards from the monument on Custer Hill to Deep Ravine following a line down from the monument to Marker 54, then along the Deep Ravine Trail, which meanders a bit, touches near most of the remaining grave markers, and continues to its end at the lower trail crossing near grave marker 7."[21]
- The actual "line" itself

begins about 200 yards down from Custer Hill at Markers 52, 53, and 54 in the upper reaches of Cemetery Ravine. It wavers down the ravine and then climbs up obliquely across the ravine's south bank, following the grave markers in descending order. The Boyer cluster, Markers 33–39 [*sic;* should be 33–34], is near the divide and about 180 yards from the start of the line. Markers 29–32 are the last stones on the Cemetery Ravine side of the divide and are about 200 yards from the head of the line. About 220 yards along the trail there is a soft crest where the trail begins to dip down into the upper Deep Ravine watershed. At 270 yards is another cluster, grave Markers 24–28. The South Skirmish Line has been heading roughly north to south, but at this point a branch of markers diverges to the southeast. *This branch consists of 7 more or less isolated stones, numbers 20–23, 255, and 1–2* [emphasis added]. *The latter two are down in the upper reaches of Deep Ravine, far above the headcut.*[22]

- The formal SSL terminates just below the low divide in the 24–28 group of markers.
- Markers 7–19 are considered the "fugitive" markers.
- From Markers 24–28, "the southeast branch splits off, the trail and fugitive lines follow the markers another 190 yards to stone 7 at the edge of Deep Ravine. The total length of the line—formal and fugitive ... is about 430 yards."[23]

Markers

In the 1984–1985 archaeological excavations and surveying of the battlefield, it was determined that there were 252 markers on the Custer field of battle, a mismatch of eight markers from the 1891 U.S.G.S. survey.[24]

NOTE—The marker excavation work is from, Scott, Douglas D., and Fox, Richard A., Jr., *Archaeological Insights into The Custer Battle,* University of Oklahoma Press, Norman, OK, 1987; and, Scott, Douglas D.; Fox, Richard A., Jr.; and Connor, Melissa A., *Archaeological Perspectives on the Battle of the Little Bighorn,* Norman: University of Oklahoma Press, 1989. In determining the cause of death, the most common occurrence was massive blunt-force trauma. Bullet wounds were detected with much lower frequency.

Marker 2—Southeast side of Deep Ravine. An isolated marker.
- Skull fragments showing massive blunt-force trauma; finger and toe bones.
- Single individual between 25–40 years of age.
- Three four-hole iron trouser buttons.
- Six different types of bullets: one a .50/70 fired from an old lot of Springfield ammunition; a round ball from a .50-caliber muzzle-loader; one unidentifiable bullet; one .45 Colt revolver bullet; two .45/55 Springfield carbine *bullets*.
- Because of the variety of bullets found around the site, speculation has this individual being killed very late in the fight, possibly as he attempted to get away.

Markers 5 and **6** (paired)—Isolated; on the Deep Ravine trail directly above the ravine itself.
- No material discovered.
- Bedrock was found only two inches below the surface, making it unlikely that anyone had ever been buried there. Even wooden stakes could not have been driven deeply enough into the ground to have remained for long.
- *The conclusion was reached that these markers could have been for men who died in Deep Ravine.*

Marker 7—Southern extent of the South Skirmish Line near the head of Deep Ravine and the end of the trail where it enters the ravine.
- Fourteen skull fragments, plus vertebrae fragments; rib fragments.
- Damage to the vertebrae is consistent with decapitation. Perimortem blunt—force trauma evidence.
- Single individual between 20–36 years old.
- Horseshoe nail.
- One 4-hole iron trouser button.

Markers 9 and **10** (paired)—On the South Skirmish Line.
- Largest and most nearly complete grouping of human remains found in the 1984 excavations. Fragments of skull, ribs, vertebrae, hands, a right foot, both upper arms, both lower arms.
- Appeared to be a single individual with massive head damage and severe cutting across the breastbone. The body had been placed face down. (NOTE—Cheyenne warriors generally turned their dead victims face down, fearing it was bad luck to leave an enemy facing the sky. He may have been buried as found or merely had dirt thrown on him, as found.) Bone damage indicates blunt-force trauma as well as damage by an arrow or knife and hatchet.
- .44-caliber Henry bullet found in the lower chest/upper abdominal region.
- .45-caliber Colt bullet found in the area of the head.
- Eleven buttons, including several trouser buttons; three blouse buttons, two with cloth still attached; three four-hole white-glass shirt buttons.
- An iron arrowhead.
- Several cobbles.
- White male between 30–40 years of age; about 5' 10½" tall, with a range of 5' 8¾"–6'.

o John Rauter (C)
o L. St. John (C)
o Alpheus Stewart (C)
o G. Warren (F)—most likely
o William Teeman (F)—doubtful
o F. Varden (I)—doubtful
o William Reed (I)
o W. Cashan (L)
o T. Kavanaugh (L)

Marker 17 is for Dr. Lord and is located on the lower South Skirmish Line (the so-called "fugitive line").

Markers 33 and **34** (paired)—On the trail near the middle of the South Skirmish Line.
- Skull fragments; finger; coccyx. Condition of the teeth indicated a pipe-smoker and the condition of the bones indicate a man between 35–45 years of age. Also, Caucasian-Mongoloid racial mixture. Later determined to be the bones of Mitch Boyer. Skull damage indicated blunt-force trauma.
- Single individual.
- .50/70 bullet.
- Lead-bullet fragment.
- Lead shot.
- A boot heel and boot nails.
- Rubber poncho button.
- Three, four-hole iron trouser buttons.
- Mother-of-pearl shirt button.
- Cedar stake fragment.
- Cobbles.

Marker 42—South Skirmish Line.
- Both human remains and battle related artifacts were found.
- A finger bone with a ring was found here. Four other hand bones were found, as well.
- A number of river cobbles.

Marker 48, set in Cemetery Ravine along the South Skirmish Line, is for LT Sturgis.

Markers 52 and **53** (paired)—Northern end of the South Skirmish Line, about 492 feet from the visitors center.
- Skull and rib fragments from a single individual.
- One four-hole iron trouser button.
- A Benét primer from a .45/55 cartridge.
- Lead shot.
- Bone damage is consistent with that caused by a hatchet or ax.

Markers 55 (possibly PVT Gustav Klein [F]) and **56** (CPL William Teeman [F]) are too close to Custer/Last Stand Hill to be considered part of the South Skirmish Line.

Marker 63—Last Stand Hill.
- No material recovered.

Markers 67 and **68** (paired)—Last Stand Hill near the fence enclosing the area.
- Both human remains and battle related artifacts were found.
- Cobbles.

- The bones found at this site were of one human and one horse.
  - Skull fragments.
  - Vertebrae—with a compressed fracture of lower lumbar—rib, facial bones, hand bone.
  - One of the ribs showed evidence of possible bullet damage.
  - Fragmented facial bones indicate possible postmortem blunt—force damage.
  - 35–45 years old. Five F Company troopers fit within the age parameters, being born between 1831–1841: (NOTE—*This does not mean these bones were from an F Company soldier.*)
    - o FAR Benjamin Brandon—1831.
    - o PVT Thomas Atcheson—1838.
    - o PVT Herman Knauth—1838.
    - o PVT Sebastian Omling—1838.
    - o PVT George Warren—1840—unlikely.

Marker 78—Last Stand Hill.
- Both human remains and battle related artifacts were found.
- Several cobbles.
- Four trouser buttons.
- One .45 Colt bullet.
- One wood screw.
- Wood fragments.
- Human bones consistent with those of a single individual, 18 to 30 years old: carpals, skull, a tooth, almost all the left hand bones and some of the right, three small bones of the foot, coccyx, and "the lower third of the left lower arm bone" [*Perspectives,* p. 61]. The arm bone was shattered by a gunshot, with some of the shot still embedded in the bone.
- Evidence of postmortem blunt-force trauma to the skull.

Markers 86 and **87** (paired)—Last Stand Hill at the bottom of the fenced area.
- Human remains discovered.
- Three trousers buttons.
- One square nail.
- One human bone: right kneecap from an adult.

Marker 105—(Marker inscribed, "Algernon Smith")—Last Stand Hill.
- A complete, mostly articulated left lower arm and hand.
- Numerous other bones: hands and feet; a vertebra; several ribs.
- Foot bones indicated fracture and infection prior to the battle.
- Vertebrae damage indicated wounding by stabbing or a metal-tipped arrow.
- Single individual, first thought to be between 20 and 35 years old—later changed to 30–40 years of age—and approximately 5' 3" tall, with a range of 5' 1¾" to 5' 5¼".
  - o B. Stafford (E)—unlikely.
  - o J. Carney (F)
  - o W. Liemann (F)
  - o S. Omling (F)
  - o T. Acheson (F)
  - o P. Kelly (I)—unlikely.
  - o H. Lehmann (I)—unlikely.

- o J. McGucker (I)—unlikely.
- o A. Assadaly (L)—unlikely.
- Two, four-hole iron trouser buttons, generally associated with those on army trousers to attach suspenders and to close the fly.
  - .45/55 cartridge case found beneath the arm.
  - .45/55 bullet found near the center of the excavation.
- 5 cobbles (stones) associated with those used to hold dirt thrown over the body.

Markers 112 and **113** (paired)—Isolated on the west side of the park road southeast of Last Stand Hill.
- Both human remains and battle related artifacts were found.
- Four trouser buttons and one white-glass button were found.
- One .44 or .45-caliber ball.
- Male, older than 35; age range: 35–45.
- Portion of a tooth crown; segment of tailbone; three finger bones; one toe bone.

Marker 128—Isolated; behind Greasy Grass Ridge. This is the so-called "Trooper Mike," marker, so named because of the sector where the remains were found.
- Both human remains and battle related artifacts were found.
- Almost a complete burial discovered at this site; the most complete set of human remains recovered during the 1984–1985 archaeological excavations.
- Lower right leg articulated, its foot bones encased in a cavalry boot.
- Other bones had been re-buried after the flesh had decayed.
- Male, between 19–22 years old, and approximately 5' 6¾" tall, with a range of 5' 5¾"–5' 7⅞"; or, 66.8" ± 1.18". Individual was stocky with well-developed musculature.[25] Right-handed. Because of its presence in this area, the likelihood of the remains belonging to a trooper from C Company is the highest:
  - o F. Meyer (C)
  - o J. Shea (C)
  - o J. Thadus (C)
  - o N. Short (C)
- Evidence of two gunshot wounds in the chest, one from the right, one from the left. Also, massive blunt-force trauma to the skull at about the time of death.
- Bullet fragment in lower left arm.
- Three parallel cut marks on thighbones and another on collarbone.
- Vertebrae showed congenital defect, probably causing the individual pain when he rode his horse for long periods.
- Blouse and trousers buttons found; underwear cloth; hooks and eyes, probably from his campaign hat.
- Because of the way the bones were dispersed, the individual had to have been re-buried, probably in 1877 or 1879.
- Our research names Nathan Short as the most likely candidate.

Marker 131—Marker located on Finley-Finckle Ridge adjacent to Markers 132 and 133.
- No material discovered other than four river cobbles nearby.

Markers 134 and **135** (paired)—Markers located on Finley-Finckle Ridge.

- Human remains discovered: adult hand bones and a tooth fragment.

Marker 148—(N6656-E2848)—On Calhoun Hill.
- Only human remains discovered along with post-battle metal devices used to attach floral arrangements to their bases.
- Highly deteriorated bone fragments thought to be from ribs from a single person.

Markers 152 and **155** (paired)—Calhoun Hill.
- Both human remains and battle related artifacts were found.
- A "pavement" of river cobbles.
- One finger bone and nine right foot bones and one left foot bone. Bones indicate some postmortem mutilation.
- Gold watch chain.

Marker 153—Calhoun Hill.
- No material discovered.

Near **Marker 174**—Eastern fence boundary in the Keogh Sector.
- One boot nail.
- Three .45/55 carbine cartridge cases, all fired from the same weapon.
- One Colt cartridge case.
- One .50/70 bullet.

Marker 178—Keogh Sector. Marker is inscribed as that of CPT Myles Keogh and is near several other markers including **Marker 181**.
- Both human remains and battle related artifacts were found.
- Bone fragments indicate a person about 20–40 years of age. Evidence of massive blunt-force trauma.
- Cobbles and deteriorated wood were also found.
- Small bones: skull fragment with some postmortem blunt-force trauma indications; one rib; wrist fragment; ankle fragment; one toe.
- One trouser button.

Markers 194 and **195** (paired)—Keogh Sector.
- Both human remains and battle related artifacts were found.
- 20–30 years of age; about 5' 6" tall. Skull fragments indicate massive blunt-force trauma at time of death.
- Lower arm bone, two skull fragments, a tooth, three right hand bones.
- One trouser button.

Marker 199—Keogh Sector. Photo comparisons show this could have been where the wooden marker for CPL John Wild was set. Based on the morphology, however, it appears only C Company's PVT Willis Wright fits the criteria established by the analysis of bone fragments.
- Both human remains and battle related artifacts were found.
- Several buttons found: eight trouser buttons; one white-glass button; one blouse button, all consistent with a service uniform.
- Small pieces of skull were found. Peri- and postmortem blunt-force damage indicated.
- A short distance north of the marker, the archaeologists found an articulated arm with all the bones from the shoulder down. Some 30 centimeters away were found a scattering of bones

from the opposite hand. Found between these bones were a tailbone, four buttons, and two five-cent pieces.
- Forensic analysis determined the individual to be between 15–17 years old and no older than 19; 5' 7½" tall, with a range of 5' 5½"–5' 9½". Wild was 26 at the time of his death.
  - o Autie Reed
  - o Willis Wright (C)

Marker 200—(N7126-E2760)—In the Keogh area. It is possible that the bones found at this location were from the same individual at **Markers 201** and **202**.
- Right cavalry boot, upper section cut away.
- Human bones: lower left arm; lower right leg; fingers; toes; cranial fragment.
- Single individual male; 18–22 years old; 5' 8¼" tall, with a range between 5' 6" and 5' 11" tall. The best possible candidate to meet the description is PVT Weston Harrington, Company L.
- Cranial fragment thought to be from damage to head, perimortem blunt-force trauma.

Markers 201 and **202** (paired)—Keogh Sector. It is possible that the bones found at this location were from the same individual at **Marker 200**.
- Both human remains and battle related artifacts were found.
- A number of river cobbles found.
- Thighbone; two wrist bones; one toe bone; one tooth.
- One trouser button.
- Adult male, 20–35 years old; 5' 7½" tall.
- Femur cuts suggest mutilation.

Marker 252—Isolated, at the top of a wash.
- No material discovered.

Marker 257—Isolated, between Deep Ravine and Greasy Grass Ridge.
- Human remains were found: three bone fragments from a hand and foot.
- The Walter Camp interviews maintained that CPL John Briody (F) had been found at this site with one leg cut off and placed under his head by the Indians. The placement of the discovered bones would be consistent with such an event.

Marker Placement

NOTE—Markers starred with an asterisk (*) were excavated by the Fox and Scott teams in 1984–1985. Survey map is oriented to due north and delineated by "north"—N64-N81—and "east"—E20-E30—grid squares (higher numbers being more north and more east).

Fox, Scott, and Connor list a total of 13 sets of paired markers. I have identified, as well, 23 additional pairs or groupings that could be paired markers. The remaining seven pairs are located probably on Last Stand Hill or, less likely, in the grouping around the Myles Keogh marker. Last Stand Hill makes the most sense, however. If only 42 bodies were counted there initially and there are 52 markers, we have an overage of 10. The archaeologists identified two sets of paired markers, 67–68 and 86–87, leaving eight possibles. The beta symbol—ß—below, marks possible paired markers.

1. Midway down the South Skirmish Line near Deep Ravine.

2. *South Skirmish Line near Deep Ravine: southeast side of Deep Ravine. An isolated marker. Single individual. Marker located within N72-N73 and E22-E23 grid square, approximately N7225-E2215.

3. Lower South Skirmish Line.

4. Lower South Skirmish Line.

5. *Lowest marker on South Skirmish Line, paired with Marker 6. Isolated; on the Deep Ravine trail directly above the ravine itself. Nothing found.

6. *Lowest marker on South Skirmish Line, paired with Marker 5. Isolated; on the Deep Ravine trail directly above the ravine itself. Nothing found.

7. *Lower South Skirmish Line. Southern extent of the South Skirmish Line near the head of Deep Ravine and the end of the trail where it enters the ravine. Single individual.

8. Lower South Skirmish Line.

9. *Lower South Skirmish Line, paired with 10. Single individual on the South Skirmish Line.

10. *Lower South Skirmish Line, paired with 9.

11. Lower South Skirmish Line.

12. South Skirmish Line: grouped, 12–17. ß—possibly paired with 13.

13. South Skirmish Line: grouped, 12–17. ß—possibly paired with 12.

14. South Skirmish Line: grouped, 12–17.

15. South Skirmish Line: grouped, 12–17. ß—possibly paired with 16.

16. South Skirmish Line: grouped, 12–17. ß—possibly paired with 15.

17. *South Skirmish Line: grouped, 12–17; marked for Dr. Lord. Called lower South Skirmish Line.

18. South Skirmish Line.

19. South Skirmish Line.

20. South Skirmish Line, midway down.

21. South Skirmish Line, midway down.

22. South Skirmish Line, midway down.

23. South Skirmish Line, midway down.

24. South Skirmish Line, midway down, grouped, 24–27.

25. South Skirmish Line, midway down, grouped, 24–27.

26. South Skirmish Line, midway down, grouped, 24–27.

27. South Skirmish Line, midway down, grouped, 24–27.

28. Upper South Skirmish Line, alone on its southern side.

29. Above midway point of South Skirmish Line, grouped 29–32. ß—possibly paired with 32.

30. Above midway point of South Skirmish Line, grouped 29–32. ß—possibly paired with 31.

31. Above midway point of South Skirmish Line, grouped 29–32. ß—possibly paired with 30.

32. Above midway point of South Skirmish Line, grouped 29–32. ß—possibly paired with 29.

33. *Mid- to Upper South Skirmish Line, grouped 33–39; paired with 34. Marked for Mitch Boyer. On the trail near the middle of the South Skirmish Line.

34. *Mid- to Upper South Skirmish Line, grouped 33–39; paired with 33. Marker for Mitch Boyer. On the trail near the middle of the South Skirmish Line.

35. Mid- to Upper South Skirmish Line, grouped 33–39.

36. Mid- to Upper South Skirmish Line, grouped 33–39.

37. Mid- to Upper South Skirmish Line, grouped 33–39.

38. Mid- to Upper South Skirmish Line, grouped 33–39. ß—possibly paired with Marker 39.

39. Mid- to Upper South Skirmish Line, grouped 33–39. ß—possibly paired with Marker 38.

40. Cemetery Ravine, grouped with 41.

41. Cemetery Ravine, grouped with 40.

42. *Upper South Skirmish Line, grouped with 43. Single individual. ß—possibly paired with Marker 43.

43. Upper South Skirmish Line, grouped with 42. ß—possibly paired with 42.

44. Upper South Skirmish Line.

45. Upper South Skirmish Line.

46. Upper South Skirmish Line, Cemetery Ravine side.

47. Upper South Skirmish Line, Cemetery Ravine side.

48. *Cemetery Ravine side of South Skirmish Line; marked for LT Sturgis.

49. Upper South Skirmish Line, north side; grouped 49–51.

50. Upper South Skirmish Line, north side; grouped 49–51. ß—possibly paired with 51.

51. Upper South Skirmish Line, north side; grouped 49–51. ß—possibly paired with 50.

52. *Upper Cemetery Ravine side of South Skirmish Line, paired with 53. Northern end of the South Skirmish Line, about 492 feet from the visitors' center. Single individual.

53. *Upper Cemetery Ravine side of South Skirmish Line, paired with 52.

54. Upper Cemetery Ravine side of South Skirmish Line.

55. *Close to lower Last Stand Hill; grouped with 56. Possibly PVT Gustav Klein [F]. Too close to Custer/Last Stand Hill to be considered part of the SSL.

56. *Close to lower Last Stand Hill; grouped with 55. Possibly CPL William Teeman [F]. Too close to Custer/Last Stand Hill to be considered part of the SSL.

57. North side of Last Stand Hill; grouped with 58. Approximate location, N7740-E2595. ß—possibly paired with 58.

58. North side of Last Stand Hill; grouped with 57. ß—possibly paired with 57.

59. Last Stand Hill. NOTE—Almost all the Last Stand Hill markers are located in grid square, N76-N77 and E26-E27.

60. Last Stand Hill.

61. Last Stand Hill.

62. Last Stand Hill.

63. *Last Stand Hill. Nothing found.

64. Last Stand Hill.

65. Last Stand Hill.

66. Last Stand Hill.

67. *Last Stand Hill; paired with 68. Near the fence enclosing the area. Single individual.

68. *Last Stand Hill; paired with 67. Near the fence enclosing the area.

69. Last Stand Hill.

70. Last Stand Hill; marked for Tom Custer.
71. Last Stand Hill.
72. Last Stand Hill.
73. Last Stand Hill.
74. Last Stand Hill.
75. Last Stand Hill.
76. Last Stand Hill.
77. Last Stand Hill.
78. *Last Stand Hill. Single individual.
79. Last Stand Hill.
80. Last Stand Hill.
81. Last Stand Hill.
82. Last Stand Hill; marked for Autie Reed.
83. Last Stand Hill; marked for Boston Custer.
84. Last Stand Hill.
85. Last Stand Hill.
86. *Last Stand Hill near bottom of fenced area; paired with 87. Single individual.
87. *Last Stand Hill near bottom of fenced area; paired with 86.
88. Last Stand Hill.
89. Last Stand Hill.
90. Last Stand Hill.
91. Last Stand Hill.
92. Last Stand Hill.
93. Last Stand Hill; marked for LT Harrington.
94. Last Stand Hill.
95. Last Stand Hill.
96. Last Stand Hill.
97. Last Stand Hill.
98. Last Stand Hill.
99. Last Stand Hill.
100. Last Stand Hill.
101. Last Stand Hill.
102. Last Stand Hill; marked for LT Cooke.
103. Last Stand Hill.
104. Last Stand Hill.
105. *Last Stand Hill; marked for LT Algernon Smith. Single individual.
106. Last Stand Hill.
107. Last Stand Hill.
108. Last Stand Hill; marked for CPT Yates.
109. Last Stand Hill; marked for George Custer.
110. Last Stand Hill; marked for LT Reily.
111. West side of Battle Ridge, closer to Last Stand Hill.
112. *West side of Battle Ridge, fairly close with 113–115; paired with Marker 113. Isolated on the west side of the park road southeast of Last Stand Hill. Single individual.
113. *West side of Battle Ridge, fairly close with 113–115; paired with Marker 112.
114. West side of Battle Ridge, fairly close with 113–115.
115. West side of Battle Ridge, fairly close with 113–115.
116. East side of Battle Ridge, northern end of Keogh Sector.
117. East side of Battle Ridge, northern end of Keogh Sector.
118. East side of Battle Ridge, northern end of Keogh Sector; grouped with Marker 119. ß—possibly paired with 119.

119. East side of Battle Ridge, northern end of Keogh Sector; grouped with Marker 118. ß—possibly paired with 118.
120. East side of Battle Ridge, northern end of Keogh Sector.
121. Calhoun Coulee.
122. West side of Calhoun Hill near upper Finley-Finckle Ridge; grouped with 123.
123. West side of Calhoun Hill near upper Finley-Finckle Ridge; grouped with 122.
124. Calhoun Coulee/Greasy Grass Ridge area.
125. Calhoun Coulee/Greasy Grass Ridge area.
126. Calhoun Coulee/Greasy Grass Ridge area.
127. Calhoun Coulee/Greasy Grass Ridge area.
128. *Isolated behind Greasy Grass Ridge, north of Finley-Finckle, south of Marker 127. Single individual.
129. Finley-Finckle Ridge.
130. Finley-Finckle Ridge.
131. *Finley-Finckle Ridge. Calhoun Hill or Greasy Grass Ridge; nothing found but cobbles nearby.
132. Finley-Finckle Ridge.
133. Finley-Finckle Ridge.
134. *Finley-Finckle Ridge; paired with 135. Marked as Calhoun Hill. Single individual.
135. *Finley-Finckle Ridge; paired with 134. Marked as Calhoun Hill.
136. Finley-Finckle Ridge.
137. Finley-Finckle Ridge.
138. Finley-Finckle Ridge.
139. Finley-Finckle Ridge.
140. Finley-Finckle Ridge.
141. Finley-Finckle Ridge.
142. Finley-Finckle Ridge.
143. Upper Finley-Finckle Ridge.
144. Upper Finley-Finckle Ridge.
145. Upper Finley-Finckle Ridge; paired with 146.
146. Upper Finley-Finckle Ridge; paired with 145.
147. Upper Finley-Finckle Ridge.
148. *Calhoun Hill. Single individual. ß—possibly paired with 150.
149. Calhoun Hill.
150. Calhoun Hill. ß—possibly paired with 148.
151. Calhoun Hill.
152. *Calhoun Hill; paired with 155. Single individual.
153. *Calhoun Hill. Nothing found.
154. Calhoun Hill.
155. *Calhoun Hill; paired with 152.
156. Calhoun Hill.
157. Calhoun Hill.
158. Northern end of Calhoun Hill.
159. Northern end of Calhoun Hill.
160. Swale area between Calhoun Hill and Keogh Sector. Approximate location, N6865-E2815.
161. Swale area between Calhoun Hill and Keogh Sector.
162. Swale area between Calhoun Hill and Keogh Sector.
163. Swale area between Calhoun Hill and Keogh Sector.
164. Swale area between Calhoun Hill and Keogh Sector. Approximate location, N6905-E2805.

165. South end of Keogh Sector coming off Calhoun Hill.

166. South end of Keogh Sector coming off Calhoun Hill.

167. South end of Keogh Sector coming off Calhoun Hill. Approximate location, N6970-E2800.

168. South end of Keogh Sector coming off Calhoun Hill, grouped 168–170. Approximate location, N6990-E2800.

169. South end of Keogh Sector coming off Calhoun Hill, grouped 168–170. Approximate location, N6990-E2800. ß—possibly paired with 170.

170. South end of Keogh Sector coming off Calhoun Hill, grouped 168–170. Approximate location, N6990-E2800. ß—possibly paired with 169.

171. South end of Keogh Sector coming off Calhoun Hill.

172. East end of Myles Keogh grouping.

173. East end of Myles Keogh grouping.

174. *Eastern boundary fence in the Keogh Sector. No human remains, but evidence of a single individual based on identical carbine cartridge cases.

175. Myles Keogh grouping.

176. Myles Keogh grouping, grouped with 177.

177. Myles Keogh grouping, grouped with 176.

178. *Myles Keogh grouping; marked for CPT Keogh. Single individual.

179. Myles Keogh grouping.

180. Myles Keogh grouping.

181. *Myles Keogh grouping. Single individual.

182. *No marker found.*

183. Myles Keogh grouping. ß—possibly paired with 199.

184. Myles Keogh grouping.

185. Myles Keogh grouping.

186. Myles Keogh grouping.

187. Myles Keogh grouping.

188. A. Myles Keogh grouping.
B. Myles Keogh grouping.

189. Myles Keogh grouping.

190. Myles Keogh grouping.

191. Myles Keogh grouping.

192. Myles Keogh grouping.

193. Myles Keogh grouping.

194. *Myles Keogh grouping, paired with 195. Single individual.

195. *Myles Keogh grouping, paired with 194.

196. *No marker found.*

197. Myles Keogh grouping, northern side.

198. Myles Keogh grouping, northern side.

199. *Myles Keogh grouping. Photo comparisons show this could have been where the wooden marker for Corporal John Wild was set. Based on the morphology, however, it appears only C Company's Private Willis Wright fits the criteria established by the analysis of bone fragments. Single individual. ß—possibly paired with 183.

200. *Keogh Sector. Single individual. It is possible that the bones found at this location were from the same individual at Markers 201 and 202. Located at N7126-E2760.

201. *Keogh Sector, paired with 202. Single individual. It is possible that the bones found at this location were from the same individual at Marker 200.

202. *Keogh Sector, paired with 201. It is possible that the bones found at this location were from the same individual at Marker 200.

203. Keogh Sector, grouped with 204. ß—possibly paired with 204.

204. Keogh Sector, grouped with 203. ß—possibly paired with 203.

205. Keogh Sector, grouped with 206. ß—possibly paired with 206.

206. Keogh Sector, grouped with 205. ß—possibly paired with 205.

207. Keogh Sector.

208. Keogh Sector.

209. Keogh Sector.

210. *No marker found.*

211. Keogh Sector; grouped with 211A. ß—possibly paired with 211A.

• 211A. Keogh Sector; grouped with 211. ß—possibly paired with 211.

212. Keogh Sector.

213. Keogh Sector.

214. Keogh Sector, grouped 214–216.

215. Keogh Sector, grouped 214–216.

216. Keogh Sector, grouped 214–216.

217. Eastern Keogh Sector, grouped with 218. ß—possibly paired with 218.

218. Eastern Keogh Sector, grouped with 217. ß—possibly paired with 217.

219. Keogh Sector.

220. Keogh Sector.

221. Keogh Sector, grouped 221–224.

222. Keogh Sector, grouped 221–224. ß—possibly paired with 223.

223. Keogh Sector, grouped 221–224. ß—possibly paired with 222.

224. Keogh Sector, grouped 221–224.

225. Keogh Sector.

226. Keogh Sector.

227. Keogh Sector, grouped with 228. ß—possibly paired with 228.

228. Keogh Sector, grouped with 227. ß—possibly paired with 227.

229. Keogh Sector.

230. Keogh Sector near Marker 231.

• 230A. Keogh Sector in Myles Keogh grouping.

231. Keogh Sector, grouped 231–234.

232. Keogh Sector, grouped 231–234.

233. Keogh Sector, grouped 231–234. This marker seems incorrectly noted as there is another Marker 233 on the south side of the South Skirmish Line near Deep Ravine. ß—possibly paired with 234.

234. Keogh Sector, grouped 231–234. ß—possibly paired with 233.

235. Northern Keogh Sector, paired with 236.

236. Northern Keogh Sector, paired with 235.

237. Northern Keogh Sector, grouped with 238. ß—possibly paired with 238.

238. Northern Keogh Sector, grouped with 237. ß—possibly paired with 237.

239. Northern Keogh Sector, grouped with 240. ß—possibly paired with 240.

240. Northern Keogh Sector, grouped with 239. ß—possibly paired with 239.

241. Northern Keogh Sector, grouped with 242. ß—possibly paired with 242.

242. Northern Keogh Sector, grouped with 241. ß—possibly paired with 241.

243. Northern Keogh Sector, grouped with 244. ß—possibly paired with 244.

244. Northern Keogh Sector, grouped with 243. ß—possibly paired with 243.

245. Northernmost Keogh Sector, grouped 245–247.

246. Northernmost Keogh Sector, grouped 245–247. ß—possibly paired with 247.

247. Northernmost Keogh Sector, grouped 245–247; marked for Marc Kellogg. ß—possibly paired with 246.

248. *No marker found.*

249. *No marker found.*

250. *No marker found.*

251. *No marker found.*

252. *No marker found.* The archaeologists recorded this marker as isolated, at the top of a wash; nothing discovered. There is no record of it, however, on the survey map.

253. Calhoun Coulee, vicinity of Greasy Grass Ridge, south of 257, but generally north of the other Calhoun Coulee markers and closer to Deep Ravine.

254. Calhoun Coulee, vicinity of Greasy Grass Ridge, south of 257, but generally north of the other Calhoun Coulee markers and closer to Deep Ravine.

255. South side of South Skirmish Line near Deep Ravine headwall, but below Marker 233.

256. *No marker found.*

257. South of Deep Ravine near Greasy Grass Ridge. Isolated, between Deep Ravine and Greasy Grass Ridge. Single individual. The Walter Camp interviews maintained that CPL John Briody (F) had been found at this site with one leg cut off and placed under his head by the Indians. The placement of the discovered bones would be consistent with such an event.

NOTE—A total of nine markers are missing: 182, 196, 210, 248–252, inclusive; and 256. There is one duplicate (233) and three "add-ons": 188B, 211A, and 230A. This still leaves a total of 252 markers.

Summary Analysis of Marker Placement

Assuming Lieutenant Godfrey was correct in claiming there were 42 bodies on Custer/Last Stand Hill, the maker placements should appear as follows (in order of perceived activity):

NOTE—Numbers in brackets indicate elimination of paired markers and locations where no remnants or artifacts were found. *Of necessity, the bracketed numbers equal 210.*

1. Calhoun Coulee: 9 [9]
2. Finley—Finckle Ridge: 19 [17]
3. Calhoun Hill: 14 [11]
4. Swale area: 5 [5]
5. Keogh Sector: 89 [81]
6. West Battle Ridge: 5 [4]
7. Custer/Last Stand Hill: 56 [42]
8. South Skirmish Line: 49 [36]
9. Cemetery Ravine: 6 [5]
10. Markers where nothing was found: 5 and 6 (paired); 63; 131; 153; 252 (no marker mapped on the survey).

Firearm artifact analysis indicates seven discrete Indian positions:

1. The so-called Henryville area near Calhoun Hill.
2. A small knoll some 200 meters northeast of Last Stand Hill.
3. Two positions on Greasy Grass Ridge.
4. Three positions on the lower end of Greasy Grass Ridge and the flanks of the upper portion of Deep Ravine. Government cartridge cases were found at these three positions, but it is possible these cartridges could have been retrieved from either the Rosebud fight or the Reno valley fighting. *This would give a good indication of the tribes involved. Probably Sioux at these locations, rather than Cheyenne.*
5. "For the Custer battlefield the number of Indian firearms is projected between 354 and 414. These figures suggest Custer's command was outgunned about two to one."[26]
6. "At the Reno-Benteen defense site the projected number of Indian guns ranges between 259 and 300, with the repeating guns ranging between 150 and 174."[27]

APPENDIX D:
INDIAN RECOLLECTIONS OF THE TIME THE BATTLE BEGAN

A word of caution is necessary here. The idea that the Indians of 1876 would refer to "watch" times is preposterous. All times given or alluded to by Indians are second- or third-hand translations, some more reliable than others. In some cases the translator would point to an angle of sky—or the Indian would do the same—and an estimate was then developed and turned into a watch-time. *Notoriously inaccurate!* Greater credence may be given to an allusion of, "the sun was directly overhead," or some such reference. The 23 examples here are sprinkled with each of these and should be taken with that in mind. Sometimes the extremes are best. The Flying Hawk reference of 9:00 a.m. is a perfect example. I would translate that *not* as 9:00 a.m., but as some time before the sun was directly overhead. White Bull gives times: about 11:00 a.m. when Reno was attacked, and about 1:00 p.m. by the time Custer had been killed.[1] As Richard Hardorff explained in a footnote, it is not the *absolute* time that matters—Respects Nothing, an Oglala, claimed the fight lasted from 1:00 p.m. to 4:00 p.m. and he knew this by virtue of a watch obtained from a soldier during the Crook/Rosebud fight (!)—instead, the *relative* time of a battle lasting some three hours. I agree totally with Hardorff's conclusions here.[2]

Antelope	10:00 a.m.
Beard	Noon–1:00 p.m.
Crazy Horse	11:00 a.m.
Fears Nothing	1:00 p.m.
Flying Hawk	9:00 a.m.
Four Woman	Noon
Gall	Before 2:00 p.m.
Hump	Noon
Kill Eagle	Noon
Lights	9:30 a.m.
Low Dog	Noon
One Bull	2:00 p.m.
Red Feather	Before 10:00 a.m.
Red Horse	Noon
Respects Nothing	1:00 p.m.
Runs the Enemy	10:00 a.m.
Sitting Bull	2:00 p.m. (Custer)
Standing Bear	After noon
Waterman	9:00 a.m.
White Bull (Ice)	Before noon
White Cow Bull	After mid-day
Wooden Leg	Noon–1:00 p.m.
Yellow Nose	Noon

CHAPTER NOTES

Chapter 1

1. Loyd J. Overfield, II, *The Little Big Horn, 1876: The Official Communications, Documents and Reports* [hereafter cited as *The Little Big Horn, 1876*] (Lincoln: University of Nebraska Press, 1990), 23. Brigadier General Alfred H. Terry's original orders to Lieutenant Colonel G. A. Custer, written by Captain Edward W. Smith, Acting Assistant Adjutant General.

2. James Willert, *Little Big Horn Diary* (El Segundo, CA: Upton & Sons, 1997), 146, quoting Walter Mason Camp in Kenneth Hammer, ed., *Custer in '76* (Norman: University of Oklahoma Press, 1990), 212, footnote 2. This is an interview with Tall Bull, July 22, 1910, in Lamedeer, Montana, a Mr. Thaddeus Redwater interpreting.

3. Neil C. Mangum, "The Little Bighorn Campaign," *Blue & Gray* XXIII, no. 2 (2006): 19–20.

4. Fred Dustin, *The Custer Tragedy* (El Segundo, CA: Upton & Sons, 2011), 87.

5. Edgar I. Stewart, *Custer's Luck* (Norman: University of Oklahoma Press, 1955), 289.

6. Colonel William Alexander Graham, *The Custer Myth* (Mechanicsburg, PA: Stackpole, 2000), 177. From one of Captain Frederick W. Benteen's narratives.

7. John Gibbon, *American Catholic Quarterly*, April 1877, 293.

8. John S. Gray, *Custer's Last Campaign* (Lincoln: University of Nebraska Press, 1993), 208.

9. Edward Settle Godfrey, "Custer's Last Battle," *Century Magazine*, January 1892. Reprint by Outbooks, Olympic Valley, CA, 1976, 16.

10. *Ibid.*, 17.

11. *Ibid.*

12. Willert, *Little Big Horn Diary*, 227.

13. Thomas B. Marquis, *Wooden Leg* (Lincoln: University of Nebraska Press, 1931 [1965]), 190.

14. Evan Connell, *Son of the Morning Star* (New York: HarperCollins, 1984), 267.

15. Charles A. Varnum, *I, Varnum*, ed. John M. Carroll (Mattituck, NY: J. M. Carroll, 1982), 60 and 85; also, Kenneth Hammer, ed., *Custer in '76* (Norman: University of Oklahoma Press, 1990), 59, Walter Mason Camp's notes.

16. Thomas M. Heski, "'Don't Let Anything Get Away,'" *Research Review* 21, no. 2 (Summer 2007): 10.

17. *Ibid.*; see pp. 10 and 11.

18. Charles Kuhlman, *Legend into History* (Harrisburg, PA: Stackpole, 1952), 34.

19. *Ibid.*

20. Godfrey, "Custer's Last Battle," 18.

21. Willert, *Little Big Horn Diary*, 172.

22. Stewart, *Custer's Luck*, 234.

23. Connell, *Son of the Morning Star*, 267.

24. Stewart, *Custer's Luck*, 192.

25. Gray, *Custer's Last Campaign*, 215.

26. Varnum, *I, Varnum*, 85.

27. Stewart, *Custer's Luck*, 259.

28. Godfrey, "Custer's Last Battle," 18.

29. Gray, *Custer's Last Campaign*, 217, quoting George Herendeen.

30. Kuhlman, *Legend into History*, 40.

31. Dustin, *The Custer Tragedy*, 104.

32. Willert, *Little Big Horn Diary*, 139.

33. *Ibid.*, 241.

Chapter 2

1. Gray, *Custer's Last Campaign*, 220–221.

2. *Ibid.*, 219.

3. As with everything else involving this battle, the numbers and names of people accompanying Varnum is up for grabs. See Varnum, *I, Varnum*, 87; Camp, *Custer in '76*, 60, footnote 2; and Vern Smalley, *More Little Bighorn Mysteries* (Bozeman: Little Buffalo Press, 2005), 1–8. Best guess is the party consisted of Varnum; his orderly, Private Elijah Strode; the scouts, Mitch Boyer and Charlie Reynolds; five Crows—White Man Runs Him, Curley, Goes Ahead, Hairy Moccasin, and White Swan; and six Rees—Forked Horn, Black Fox, Red Foolish Bear, Strikes the Lodge, Red Star, and Bull.

4. Bruce R. Liddic, *Vanishing Victory* (El Segundo, CA: Upton & Sons, 2004), 23.

5. *Ibid.*

6. *Ibid.*

7. *Ibid.*

8. Camp, *Custer in '76*, 229.

9. Gray, *Custer's Last Campaign*, 224.

10. *Ibid.*, 223.

11. Gregory F. Michno, *The Mystery of E Troop* (Missoula: Mountain Press, 1994), 282.

12. Heski, "'Don't Let Anything Get Away,'" 31, footnote 92.

13. Vern Smalley, *Little Bighorn Mysteries* (Bozeman: Little Buffalo Press, 2005), 2–3.

14. Heski, "'Don't Let Anything Get Away,'" 30.

15. John M. Carroll, *General Custer and the Battle of the Little Big Horn: The Federal View* [hereafter cited as *The Benteen-Goldin Letters*] (New York: Liveright, 1974), 21. A comment by former private and G Company trooper, Theodore Goldin, in a letter to Albert W. Johnson, November 18, 1928.

16. Varnum, *I, Varnum*, 118; testimony at the RCOI. Also see Ronald H. Nichols, ed., *Reno Court of Inquiry* (Hardin, MT: Custer Battlefield Historical & Museum Association, Inc., 1996), 145.

17. Godfrey, "Custer's Last Battle," 17.

18. Nichols, *Reno Court of Inquiry*, 491.

19. *Ibid.*, 74.

20. John M. Carroll, ed., *General Custer and the Battle of the Little Big Horn: The Federal View* [hereafter cited as *The Federal View*] (Mattituck, NY: J. M. Carroll, 1986), 65. The official "Report of the Chief of Engineers, Appendix PP, Report of Lieutenant George D. Wallace, Seventh Cavalry, Saint Paul, Minn., January 27, 1877."

21. *Ibid.*

22. Graham, *The Custer Myth*, 262.

23. Godfrey, "Custer's Last Battle," 18.

24. Walter M. Camp, *On the Little Bighorn with Walter Camp*, ed. Richard G. Hardorff (El Segundo, CA: Upton & Sons, 2002), 49.

25. Charles Windolph, Frazier Hunt, and Robert Hunt, eds., *I Fought with Custer* (Lincoln: University of Nebraska Press, 1947), 73.

26. John M. Carroll, ed., *The Sunshine Magazine Articles*, John P. Everett, "Bullets, Boots, and Saddles," Sioux Falls, SD, 1930 (Bryan, TX: Privately republished, 1979), 12.

27. Carroll, *The Benteen-Goldin Letters*, 179.

28. Graham, *The Custer Myth*, 164–165, 178. From a manuscript written by Benteen and loaned to Edward Godfrey by Benteen's son, Major Frederick Benteen. It was one of two manuscripts given to Godfrey and was only returned to the Benteen family after Godfrey's death. The earlier of the two—considered the more important—was returned missing its final pages; the second manuscript was not returned and is now missing. This was believed written shortly after the battle of Wounded Knee in 1890. See Graham, page 160, as well.

29. *Ibid.*, 164–165, 178.

30. Godfrey, "Custer's Last Battle," 18–19.

31. Nichols, *Reno Court of Inquiry*, 568.

32. *Ibid.*, 62.

33. George M. Clark, *Scalp Dance* (Oswego, NY: Heritage Press, 1985), 24.

34. William O. Taylor, *With Custer on the Little Bighorn*, ed. Greg Martin (New York: Viking Penguin, 1996), 24.

35. See Taylor, *With Custer on the Little Bighorn*, 23. Taylor wrote, "We reached the Powder River about 7 o'clock p.m. and went into camp.... The next day, June 10, Major Reno with six Troops of the Regiment ... left camp ... for a scout." While he got the time of day just about right, the Seventh Cavalry reached the Powder on June 7, not June 9.

36. Willert, *Little Big Horn Diary*, 243.

37. Godfrey, "Custer's Last Battle," 19.

38. Graham, *The Custer Myth*, 165 and 179. From the "Benteen Manuscript."

39. *Ibid.*, 166, 179.

Chapter 3

1. Godfrey, "Custer's Last Battle," 19.

2. See Smalley, *Little Bighorn Mysteries*, 2–4, for a good annotated breakdown.

3. Heski, "'Don't Let Anything Get Away,'" 19.

4. Nichols, *Reno Court of Inquiry*, 46. Lieutenant Wallace testified at the Reno inquiry that a column-of-twos was the usual order for crossing rough country.

5. Willert, *Little Big Horn Diary*, 216–217, quoting Fred Dustin, *The Custer Tragedy* (Glendale, CA: Arthur H. Clark, 1965), 234. Note—the Dustin book was reprinted from the original Edwards Brothers,

Inc., Ann Arbor, Michigan, 1939, printing, by Upton and Sons, in 2011, and page references throughout our work will be different from the 1965 printing.

6. Charles K. Mills, *Harvest of Barren Regrets: The Army Career of Frederick W. Benteen 1834–1898* (Glendale, CA: Arthur H. Clark, 1985), 240.

7. Carroll, *The Benteen-Goldin Letters*, 179–180.

8. Graham, *The Custer Myth,* 166. This is from the so-called "Benteen Manuscript," written by Benteen and loaned to Edward Godfrey by Benteen's son, Major Frederick Benteen. It was one of two manuscripts given to Godfrey and was only returned to the Benteen family after Godfrey's death. The earlier of the two—considered the more important—was returned missing its final pages; the second manuscript was never returned and is now missing. This was believed written shortly after the battle of Wounded Knee in 1890.

9. *Ibid.,* 179.

10. Godfrey, "Custer's Last Battle," 19.

11. Carroll, *The Benteen-Goldin Letters,* 180.

12. *Ibid.,* 166.

13. Nichols, *Reno Court of Inquiry,* 262.

14. Michno, *The Mystery of E Troop,* 18.

15. Smalley, *Little Bighorn Mysteries,* 2–4 and 2–5.

16. Nichols, *Reno Court of Inquiry,* 85.

17. *Ibid.,* 71–72.

18. Carroll, *The Benteen-Goldin Letters,* 180. From the "Benteen Manuscript."

19. Nichols, *Reno Court of Inquiry,* 219.

20. *Ibid.,* 85. Gerard's testimony.

21. This 2:00 a.m. time is verified by Reno in his report to Captain E. W. Smith, ADC and AAAG, dated July 5, 1876. See Overfield, *The Little Big Horn, 1876,* 43.

22. Varnum, *I, Varnum,* 62, 87, and 120.

23. Smalley, *More Little Bighorn Mysteries,* 1–9.

24. Willert, *Little Big Horn Diary,* footnote, 444, quoting Dustin, *The Custer Tragedy,* 101.

25. *Ibid.,* footnote, 444, quoting Stewart, *Custer's Luck,* 272.

26. *Ibid.,* 252.

27. Smalley, *Little Bighorn Mysteries,* 3–5.

28. Varnum, *I, Varnum,* 87.

29. Orin G. Libby, *The Arikara Narrative of Custer's Campaign and the Battle of the Little Bighorn* [hereafter cited as *The Arikara Narrative*] (Norman: University of Oklahoma Press, 1920 [1998]), 89.

30. Jack Pennington, *The Battle of the Little Bighorn* (El Segundo, CA: Upton & Sons, 2001), 40.

31. Willert, *Little Big Horn Diary,* 253.

32. Libby, *The Arikara Narrative,* 89.

33. *Ibid.,* 89–90.

34. James S. Hutchins, ed., *The Army and Navy Journal on the Battle of The Little Bighorn and Related Matters, 1876–1881* [hereafter cited as *The Army and Navy Journal*] (El Segundo, CA: Upton & Sons, 2003), 40. From a newspaper article by George Herendeen published July 7, 1876, Bismarck, D. T., and republished in *The Army and Navy Journal,* July 15, 1876.

35. See Stewart, *Custer's Luck,* 275, footnote 76.

36. Carroll, *The Benteen-Goldin Letters,* 180. Carroll included this in his book, calling it "very unusual." He gives no further information, but poses the question, "Is it [Benteen's] second [the missing] manuscript?" Its final pages are also missing. It could be the portion Graham alluded to when he wrote, "The substance, and most of the content of the *other and later* narrative is mosaiced into Chapter 3 of Brininstool's 'Troopers with Custer,' and constitutes about half of 'Captain Benteen's Own Story.'"

37. Libby, *The Arikara Narrative,* 90.

38. Godfrey, "Custer's Last Battle," 19.

39. Smalley, *Little Bighorn Mysteries,* 2–5.

40. Nichols, *Reno Court of Inquiry,* 137.

41. *Ibid.*

42. Willert, *Little Big Horn Diary,* 257; also, footnote, p. 444.

43. Graham, *The Custer Myth,* 323. From a letter written by Graham to both Varnum (San Francisco) and Edgerly (Cooperstown, New York), dated July 9, 1925. A similar letter was sent to Luther Hare, but he declined to answer. The letter pertains to the Walter Camp interviews.

44. Hutchins, *The Army and Navy Journal,* 59.

45. Camp, *Custer in '76,* 60–61.

46. Libby, *The Arikara Narrative,* 93.

47. Peter Thompson, "The Experience of a Private Soldier in the Custer Massacre," *Belle Fourche* (South Dakota) *Bee,* 1922 or 1923, 24 [or page 25, depending on mimeographed edition]. State Historical Society of North Dakota. Provided through the courtesy and graciousness of Mr. William W. Boyes, Jr.

48. Varnum, *I, Varnum,* 88.

49. *Ibid.,* 59.

50. Camp, *Custer in '76,* 135.

51. *Ibid.,* 222.

52. *Ibid.,* 111.

53. *Ibid.,* 193.

54. Richard G. Hardorff, *Hokahey! A Good Day to Die!* [hereafter cited as *Hokahey!*] (Lincoln: University of Nebraska Press/Bison Books, 1993 [1999]), 27–28.

55. Nichols, *Reno Court of Inquiry,* 214.

56. Heski, "'Don't Let Anything Get Away,'" 26. Sergeant Curtiss and Private Rooney were the only ones to survive the battle. Brown, Bruce, and Omling were killed on Last Stand Hill with their captain and other members of Company F.

57. Hardorff, *Hokahey!,* 28.

58. Gray, *Custer's Last Campaign,* 241.

59. Liddic, *Vanishing Victory,* 25.

60. Camp, *Custer in '76,* 230.

61. *Ibid.,* 64.

62. Varnum, *I, Varnum,* 63.

63. Heski, "'Don't Let Anything Get Away,'" 24, citing Carroll, *Three Hits and a Miss,* 71.

64. Graham, *The Custer Myth,* 219. From the *Leavenworth Times,* a statement by Edgerly, August 18, 1881, made at Fort Yates.

65. Thompson, "The Experience of a Private Soldier in the Custer Massacre," 25 [26].

66. Crow Agency Quadrangle, Montana, Big Horn County, 7.5' series; 1:24,000. Thompson Creek NW, 45107-D2-TF-024; DMA 4574 I NW—Series V894; 1967; grid square 27.

67. Smalley, *Little Bighorn Mysteries,* 11–1.

68. Camp, *Custer in '76,* 230–231.

69. Graham, *The Custer Myth,* 181. From the "Benteen Manuscript."

70. *Ibid.,* 167 and 179.

71. Liddic, *Vanishing Victory,* 26.

72. Willert, *Little Big Horn Diary,* 13.

73. Liddic, *Vanishing Victory,* 26.

74. Willert, *Little Big Horn Diary,* 259.

75. Godfrey, "Custer's Last Battle," 19.

76. Graham, *The Custer Myth,* 219.

77. Liddic, *Vanishing Victory,* 28–29. Also "interview" with Walter Mason Camp, Camp, *Custer in '76,* 64.

78. Camp, *Custer in '76,* 64.

79. Camp, *On the Little Bighorn with Walter Camp,* 100.

80. *Ibid.,* 102.

81. *Ibid.*

82. Graham, *The Custer Myth,* 219.

Chapter 4

1. Willert, *Little Big Horn Diary,* 441, in a footnote.

2. Willert, *Little Big Horn Diary,* 274.

3. *Ibid.*

4. Camp, *Custer in '76,* 228.

5. *Ibid.,* 237. This quote was drawn from the Walter Camp field notes, Folder 94, Brigham Young University Library.

6. *Ibid.,* 237, footnote.

7. Graham, *The Custer Myth,* 258. From a statement made by Herendeen in Bismarck, D. T., on July 7, 1876, and published the following day in the *New York Herald.* Graham felt this statement and the one made in January 1878 "are considered of prime importance," 257.

8. *Ibid.,* 262. From a statement made by Herendeen in Bozeman, M. T., on January 4, 1878, and published in the *New York Herald,* January 22, 1878. This is the second article Graham alluded to, above.

9. Varnum, *I, Varnum,* 63.

10. Camp/Hammer, *Custer in '76,* 60–61.

11. Nichols, *Reno Court of Inquiry,* 107.

12. *Ibid.,* 108.

13. *Ibid.*

14. *Ibid.*

15. *Ibid.,* 134.

16. Camp/ *Custer in '76,* 230.

17. Libby, *The Arikara Narrative,* 172.

Chapter 5

1. Liddic, *Vanishing Victory,* 84–86.

2. Willert, *Little Big Horn Diary,* 200.

3. Gray, *Custer's Last Campaign,* 183. A June 22, 1876, dispatch by Custer.

4. Willert, *Little Big Horn Diary,* 124.

5. Gray, *Custer's Last Campaign,* 215.

6. Willert, *Little Big Horn Diary,* 237, quoting George Herendeen.

7. Carroll, *The Benteen-Goldin Letters,* 213.

8. Edgar Stewart noted Terry never said anything about a "pincer" attack, any plan of having the two columns meet. This was probably "in accordance with Sheridan's idea that it was an absurdity to expect cooperation." *Custer's Luck,* 239.

Chapter 6

1. Nichols, *Reno Court of Inquiry,* 540.

2. *Ibid.,* 431. Benteen's testimony, Monday, February 3, 1879.

3. *Ibid.,* 528.

4. Godfrey, "Custer's Last Battle," 21.

5. Nichols, *Reno Court of Inquiry,* 514.

6. Graham, *The Custer Myth,* 289. From an article written by Graham and published in the July 1923 edition of *The Cavalry Journal.* Graham did not say when Martini told this story, but it certainly seems like it was some time in 1922.

7. Windolph, *I Fought with Custer,* 76 and 78.

8. Kenneth Hammer, *Men with Custer: Biographies of the 7th Cavalry,* ed. Ronald H. Nichols (Hardin, MT: Custer Battlefield Historical & Museum Association, Inc., 1995), 22. Like everything else associated with this battle, even the authorship of this particular book is disputed. Referring to this CBHMA edition, Vern Smalley states, "Dr. Hammer was improperly credited as the author." *Amazing!* [Smalley, *Little Bighorn Mysteries,* A3–4.]

9. Francis B. Heitman, *Historical Register and Dictionary of the United States Army* (Washington, D.C.: U.S. Government Printing Office, 1903 [Urbana: University of Illinois Press, 1965]), vol. 2, 1015.

10. Company A: Privates Franklin and Ionson; Company G: Sergeant Alexander Brown and privates Campbell and McEagan; Company H: Private Jacob Adams; Company K: Sergeant John Rafter and privates Burkhardt, Raichel, and Robers.

11. Liddic, *Vanishing Victory,* 32.

12. Pennington, *The Battle of the Little Bighorn,* 7.

13. Gray, *Custer's Last Campaign,* 359–361.

14. Gregory F. Michno, *Lakota Noon* (Missoula: Mountain Press, 1997), 121.

15. Robert J. Kershaw, *Red Sabbath* (Hersham, Surrey: Ian Allan, 2005), 141.

16. Richard Allan Fox, Jr., *Archeology, History, and Custer's Last Battle* (Norman: University of Oklahoma Press, 1993), 319–322.

17. Liddic, *Vanishing Victory*, 99.

18. Edgerly/, *Scalp Dance*, 24. Letter written July 4, 1876, from the Yellowstone Depot.

19. Nichols, *Reno Court of Inquiry*, 213.

20. Graham, *The Custer Myth*, 216. From a letter by Edgerly to Graham, dated December 5, 1923, from Cooperstown, New York.

21. Carroll, *The Benteen-Goldin Letters*, 182. Carroll included these comments in his book, calling it "very unusual." He gives no further information, but poses the question "Is it [Benteen's] second [the missing] manuscript?" Its final pages are also missing. It could be the portion Graham alluded to when he wrote, "The substance, and most of the content of the *other and later* narrative is mosaiced into Chapter 3 of Brininstool's 'Troopers with Custer,' and constitutes about half of 'Captain Benteen's Own Story.'"

22. Godfrey, "Custer's Last Battle," 21–22.

23. Roger Darling, *Benteen's Scout* (El Segundo, CA: Upton & Sons, 2000), xv, footnote 2, quoting Kuhlman, *Legend into History*, 90.

24. Kuhlman, *Legend into History*, 90. Despite Gibson's obvious support for Benteen, his comment must be treated with a grain of salt and may reflect assumptions rather than definitive orders. Benteen admitted he was to pitch into anything he came across, but *specific* orders to go into the Little Horn valley itself were never heard by anyone not named Benteen. If Benteen heard that phrase he never let on and over the years he merely used the "valley hunting *ad infinitum*" comment in describing his orders.

25. Connell, *Son of the Morning Star*, 274.

26. Everett, *The Sunshine Magazine Articles*, "Bullets, Boots, and Saddles," 20.

27. Nichols, *Reno Court of Inquiry*, 423.

28. *Ibid.*, 421.

29. *Ibid.*, 427.

30. *Ibid.*, 433.

Chapter 7

1. Nichols, *Reno Court of Inquiry*, 403.

2. *Ibid.*

3. Carroll, *The Benteen-Goldin Letters*, 213.

4. Nichols, *Reno Court of Inquiry*, 421.

5. *Ibid.*, 436.

6. *Ibid.*

7. Windolph, *I Fought with Custer*, 188. Written July 4, 1876, while in camp at the confluence of the Big Horn and Yellowstone rivers.

8. Graham, *The Custer Myth*, 187. Excerpts from a multi-part letter begun on July 2, 1876, from Benteen to his wife. Other parts of the letter were written on July 23, July 24, July 25, and July 30, 1876.

9. Nichols, *Reno Court of Inquiry*, 404.

10. *Ibid.*, 479.

11. Godfrey, "Custer's Last Battle," 22.

12. Windolph, *I Fought with Custer*, 80.

13. Graham, *The Custer Myth*, 187. From Benteen's July 2, 1876, letter to his wife.

14. Edgerly, *Scalp Dance*, 24. In a letter to his wife, July 4, 1876.

15. Nichols, *Reno Court of Inquiry*, 479.

16. *Ibid.*, 440.

17. *Ibid.*, 479.

18. Graham, *The Custer Myth*, 227. From an interview carried in the August 8, 1876, *New York Herald*.

19. Windolph, *I Fought with Custer*, 80.

Chapter 8

1. Nichols, *Reno Court of Inquiry*, 404.

2. *Ibid.*, 422.

3. *Ibid.*, 440.

4. *Ibid.*, 441.

5. *Ibid.*, 457.

6. Godfrey, "Custer's Last Battle," 22.

7. Graham, *The Custer Myth*, 248. From the Greensboro, North Carolina, *Daily Record*, April 27, 1924.

8. Daniel A. Kanipe, "A New Story of Custer's Last Battle Told by the Messenger Boy Who Survived," *Contributions to the Historical Society of Montana* IV (1903): 279.

9. E. A. Brininstool, *A Trooper with Custer and Other Historic Incidents of the Battle of the Little Big Horn* [hereafter cited as *A Trooper with Custer*] (Columbus, OH: Hunter-Trader-Trapper, 1925), 17–56.

10. Freeman was no military lightweight. For this campaign he was placed in charge of the Seventh Infantry battalion under Gibbon. By 1861, he was already an experienced NCO and enlisted in the 18th Infantry at the outbreak of the Civil War. He received two brevets and the Medal of Honor for gallantry. He was captured at Chickamauga and spent 1½ years as a prisoner of war. After three failures, he escaped in February 1865. After the war he was transferred to the 27th Infantry, and on January 7, 1870, assigned to the 7th Infantry. He retired as a brigadier general in 1901.

11. Captain Henry B. Freeman, Captain Henry B., *The Original Manuscript Journal of General Henry Freeman During the Custer Campaign Against the Sioux Indians in 1876,* March 21–October 5, 1876, 31.

12. Libby, *The Arikara Narrative*, 149–150.

13. Graham, *The Custer Myth*, 23.

14. *Ibid.*, 342. From a letter written by Varnum to his father in Tallahassee, Florida, July 4, 1876. The letter was published in a Tallahassee newspaper.

15. Gray, *Custer's Last Campaign*, 251.

16. Colonel Charles Edward Callwell, *Small Wars* (Lincoln: University of Nebraska Press, 1896 [1996]), 241.

17. From the website ultimatehorsesite.com.

18. A realistic assessment of cavalry horse speeds came in a letter dated February 26, 1953, from battlefield superintendent E. S. Luce—a retired U.S. Army veterinary officer—to Charles G. DuBois. Luce wrote, "A cavalry horse walks 4 miles per hour; trots 8 miles per hour; gallops 12 miles per hour, and the extended gallop or charge is 16 miles per hour. Normally in good weather a troop would average about 9½ miles per hour. They generally start off for the first 10 minutes, then halt about two minutes ... then trot for about 20 minutes, gallop for some 10 come down to a trot and then a walk."

19. Privates John Brennan, Morris Farrar, John Fitzgerald, Peter Thompson, and James Watson from C Company; privates William Reese and William Shields from E Company; Private John Sweeney, F Company; and Private Gustave Korn, I Company.

20. Graham, *The Custer Myth*, 249. From the Greensboro, North Carolina, *Daily Record,* April 27, 1924. Graham made a note regarding many of the inaccuracies in Kanipe's story: "The many inaccuracies in Sgt. Kanipe's story are characteristic of the accounts of most of the enlisted survivors recounted during the '20s." One would think, however, this comment would not refer to Kanipe's tale of Sergeant Finckle.

21. Marquis, *Wooden Leg*, 198.

22. Graham, *The Custer Myth*, 250–251.

23. Liddic, *Vanishing Victory*, 29, citing Charles T. Brady, *Indian Fights and Fighters* (New York: Doubleday, 1904), 383.

24. *Ibid.*, 29.

25. Nichols, *Reno Court of Inquiry*, 168.

26. Gray, *Custer's Last Campaign*, 251.

27. Darling, *Benteen's Scout*, 38.

28. Nichols, *Reno Court of Inquiry*, 276.

29. Graham, *The Custer Myth*, 298.

30. Nichols, *Reno Court of Inquiry*, 441.

31. *Ibid.*, 480.

32. Varnum, *I, Varnum*, 64.

33. Liddic, *Vanishing Victory*, 36.

34. Crow Agency Quadrangle, Montana, Big Horn County, 7.5' series; 1:24,000. Specifically: Crow Agency Montana, N4530-W10722.5/ 7.5, 1967, AMS 4575 III SW, series V894; Crow Agency SE Montana, N4530-W10715/ 7.5, 1967, AMS 4575 III SE, series V894; Benteen Quadrangle, Benteen Montana, 45107-D4-TF-024, 1967, DMA 4574 IV NW, series V894; and, Lodge Grass NE Quadrangle, Lodge Grass NE, Montana, 45107-D3-TF-024, 1967, DMA 4574 IV NE, series V894.

35. Camp, *Custer in '76*, 156 and 161.

36. Nichols, *Reno Court of Inquiry*, 276.

37. Graham, *The Custer Myth*, 293.

38. Willert, *Little Big Horn Diary*, 271.

39. W. Donald Horn, *Fifty Years on Custer's Trail* (Privately published, West Orange, NJ: David McMillin, 2010), 23.

40. Private correspondence between Don Horn and Jack Connor, undated, but sent to me by Mr. Horn in October 2012. The copied note is typewritten and signed by Mr. Connor and includes a hand-drawn sketch-map—not to scale—of the area from east of the morass to the Little Big Horn River. On the map he indicated the distance from the "bog" to the river was 4.1 miles.

41. Marquis, *Wooden Leg*, 209.

42. Richard G. Hardorff, *Indian Views of the Custer Fight* (Norman: University of Oklahoma Press, 2005), 112–113, footnote 12.

43. Marquis, *Wooden Leg*, 92.

44. Graham, *The Custer Myth*, 40.

45. Willert, *Little Big Horn Diary*, 271.

46. "However, if one assumes the 'lone tepee' to be 1 to 1¼ miles back up Reno Creek from the Little Big Horn River, there is a knoll about 20–25 feet high, 40 or 50 yards north of the tepee. From the top of this knoll, there is a view, through a geological cleft in the bluffs, of the Little Big Horn River downstream about three miles. In 1876 there were tepees in view, hence, Gerard's comments about where he 'could see the town, the Indians' tepees and ponies.'" An "editor's note" by Bill Boyes, editor-in-chief of the Little Big Horn Associate's *Research Review*, to the author's article, "Frederic Francis Gerard: A Questionable Cause and an Unforeseen Effect" (Winter 2007).

47. Crow Agency Quadrangle maps.

48. Willert, *Little Big Horn Diary*, 271.

49. Camp, *Custer in '76*, 231.

50. Nichols, *Reno Court of Inquiry*, 276.

51. Graham, *The Custer Myth*, 226.

52. Carroll, *The Federal View*, 103.

53. Nichols, *Reno Court of Inquiry*, 579.

54. *Ibid.*, 584.

55. *Ibid.*, 20.

56. *Ibid.*, 21.

57. *Ibid.*, 44.

58. *Ibid.*, 198.

59. *Ibid.*, 188.

60. Hardorff, *Indian Views of the Custer Fight*, 16. This advance scout was recorded by Sergeant Charles White (aka Weihe) in a diary he kept. Walter M. Camp copied the diary, loaned to him by White's widow, in 1909. White listed the following troopers involved in this advance: himself, Sergeant O'Harra, Corporal Scollin, Blacksmith Newell, and privates Meier, Gordon, Turley, Galenne, Braun, and Thorpe. It is thought these same men skirmished the river as Reno moved down the Little Big Horn valley, and possibly four more were involved in getting into the village, the farthest of Reno's advance.

61. Nichols, *Reno Court of Inquiry,* 139.
62. Stewart, *Custer's Luck,* 329.
63. Nichols, *Reno Court of Inquiry,* 87.
64. *Ibid.,* 113.
65. Liddic, *Vanishing Victory,* 49.
66. *Ibid.,* 50; Willert, *Little Big Horn Diary,* 273–274.
67. Nichols, *Reno Court of Inquiry,* 588.
68. Camp/Hammer, *Custer in '76,* 231.
69. Nichols, *Reno Court of Inquiry,* 90.
70. *Ibid.,* 87.
71. *Ibid.,* 116.
72. Camp, *Custer in '76,* 148.
73. *Ibid.,* 55.
74. Private correspondence from W. Donald Horn, quoting a preliminary article, "Did Custer Plan to Follow Reno into the Valley?"
75. Nichols, *Reno Court of Inquiry,* 115.
76. *Ibid.,* 87.
77. Willert, *Little Big Horn Diary,* 274.
78. Liddic, *Vanishing Victory,* 45.
79. Hardorff, *Indian Views of the Custer Fight,* 18.
80. Liddic, *Vanishing Victory,* 46.
81. *Ibid.,* 45.
82. *Ibid.,* 47.
83. *Ibid.*
84. *Ibid.,* 81, quoting Blummer.
85. *Ibid.,* 81, quoting Thomas A. Holmes.
86. Edward S. Godfrey, *The Field Diary of Lieutenant Edward Settle Godfrey (1876)* [hereafter cited as *Field Diary*], ed. Edgar I. Stewart (Portland, OR: The Champoeg Press, 1957), 32.
87. Camp, *Custer in '76,* 229.
88. Gray, *Custer's Last Campaign,* 243.
89. Liddic, *Vanishing Victory,* 28.
90. *Ibid.,* 23.
91. Stewart, *Custer's Luck,* 330.
92. *Ibid.,* 328.
93. Carroll, *The Federal View,* 105. Reno's after-action report, addressed to CPT E. W. Smith, ADC and AAAG to General Terry, dated July 5, 1876, from camp on the Yellowstone River.
94. Camp, *Custer in '76,* 54, footnote 4, Walter Camp field notes, folder 103, BYU Library.
95. Carl von Clausewitz, *On War,* trans. Michael Howard and Peter Paret (Princeton: Princeton University Press, 1976), 557–558.
96. Fox, *Archeology, History, and Custer's Last Battle,* 297.
97. James S. Robbins, "Custer: The Goat at West Point and at War," *Custer and His Times, Book Five,* ed. John P. Hart (Cordova, TN: The Little Big Horn Associates, Inc., 2008), 17.
98. *Ibid.,* 16.
99. Paul Carell, *Foxes of the Desert* (Atglen, PA: Schiffer Military History, 1994), 189.
100. Willert, *Little Big Horn Diary,* 277.
101. Camp, *Custer in '76,* 27.
102. Graham, *The Custer Myth,* 263.
103. Nichols, *Reno Court of Inquiry,* 561. Reno mentioned both men by name.
104. Jerome A. Greene, *Evidence and the Custer Enigma* (Silverthorne, CO: Vistabooks, 1995), 11.
105. Liddic, *Vanishing Victory,* 49.
106. Varnum, *I, Varnum,* 107. RCOI testimony.
107. Liddic, *Vanishing Victory,* 49.
108. Horn, "Did Custer Plan to Follow Reno into the Valley?"
109. Liddic, *Vanishing Victory,* 52, citing Graham, *The Custer Myth,* 19.
110. *Ibid.,* 53.
111. Michno, *Lakota Noon,* 137.
112. Nichols, *Reno Court of Inquiry,* 332.
113. Graham, *The Custer Myth,* 263. Graham brings this up in a footnote, saying Gerard, George Herendeen, and Lieutenant Winfield Scott Edgerly all verified that Custer issued this order to Reno.

"Other witnesses" disagreed, saying Lieutenant Cooke gave it to the major. We do know, however, Cooke gave Reno the original *attack* order, so these "other witnesses," as Graham calls them, in all likelihood got the two orders confused as one.

Chapter 9

1. Carroll, *The Federal View,* 103.
2. Nichols, *Reno Court of Inquiry,* 235.
3. *Ibid.*
4. *Ibid.,* 216.
5. *Ibid.,* 551–552.
6. *Ibid.,* 312–313.
7. Hammer, *Custer in '76,* 148. An undated James Wilber interview with Walter Camp. This "interview" may have been taken from correspondence between them.
8. Nichols, *Reno Court of Inquiry,* 366. Notice that evidence of any delay comes from people in the middle to the end of the column, a natural occurrence, as they would slow to approach a river crossing. Those at the head of the column—the first to cross—would more likely be the ones telling of watering their horses or re-cinching their saddles as the slower-moving followers would be crossing.
9. *Ibid.,* 380.
10. In January 2007, a descendant of Miles O'Harra posted a comment on what was then the Little Big Horn Associates Internet message board (http://www.lbha.proboards.com) claiming the original spelling of the name included the second "r." O'Harra's father was a private in the Civil War and the family was from Alton, Ohio. Some descendants still live on O'Harra Road. Sergeant O'Harra was the first man killed at the Little Big Horn. The poster's father dropped the second "r" in the surname. Sergeant O'Harra had six brothers and sisters.
11. Michael N. Donahue, *Drawing Battle Lines: The Map Testimony of Custer's Last Fight* (El Segundo, CA: Upton & Sons, 2008), 128. From a letter dated November 1, 1908, to Walter Camp. Denver Public Library, Robert S. Ellison papers, WH131 File Folder, "Papers-Diaries-Interviews-Comments."
12. *Ibid.,* 128.
13. Nichols, *Reno Court of Inquiry,* 189 and 193.
14. *Ibid.,* 194.
15. Graham, *The Custer Myth,* 263. Colonel Graham attached special significance to this statement by Herendeen and to another, earlier one published in Bismarck, D. T., on July 7, 1876, and published the following day in the *New York Herald.* Graham claimed they "are considered of prime importance." Many others also considered Herendeen's statements quite reliable. See page 257, as well.
16. Camp, *Custer in '76,* 106. Private O'Neill was subjected to one of the more harrowing exploits of the whole event when he and three others—including Lieutenant DeRudio and interpreter Gerard—were left behind in the timber after Reno's command "charged" out of it. Captain Frederick Benteen, hearing of O'Neill's exploits in the bottoms, considered him "a cool, level-headed fellow—and tells it plainly *and the same way all the time*—which is a big thing towards convincing one of the truth of a story." [Graham, *The Custer Myth,* 300.]
17. Graham, *The Custer Myth,* 241.
18. *Ibid.*
19. Nichols, *Reno Court of Inquiry,* 141.
20. *Ibid.,* 141 and 145.
21. *Ibid.,* 145.
22. *Ibid.,* 146.
23. *Ibid.,* 239.
24. *Ibid.,* 6. Wallace's testimony.
25. Graham, *The Custer Myth,* 241–242.
26. Liddic, *Vanishing Victory,* 62.
27. Graham, *The Custer Myth,* 263.
28. Nichols, *Reno Court of Inquiry,* 90.

29. *Ibid.,* 313.
30. *Ibid.,* 146.
31. *Ibid.,* 222.
32. *Ibid.,* 194.
33. *Ibid.,* 590.
34. *Ibid.,* 561.
35. *Ibid.,* 313.
36. *Ibid.,* 329.
37. Graham, *The Custer Myth,* 149. This includes a section from a 1908 revision Godfrey made to his 1892, *Century Magazine* article, "Custer's Last Battle." Apparently this revision was not printed until Libbie Custer had it published in 1921.
38. Nichols, *Reno Court of Inquiry,* 202–203.
39. Bruce R. Liddic and Paul Harbaugh, eds., *Camp On Custer* (Spokane: Arthur H. Clark, 1995), 128.
40. Nichols, *Reno Court of Inquiry,* 376.
41. *Ibid.*
42. *Ibid.,* 313.
43. *Ibid.,* 216.
44. *Ibid.,* 141 and 169.
45. Private Elihu F. Clear was a 33-year-old army veteran from Indiana and was subsequently killed in Reno's retreat from the timber.
46. Varnum, *I, Varnum,* 65.
47. Nichols, *Reno Court of Inquiry,* 331.
48. *Ibid.,* 561.
49. *Ibid.,* 313.
50. *Ibid.,* 202.
51. Donahue, *Drawing Battle Lines,* 130. From a letter dated November 1, 1908, to Walter Camp, Denver Public Library, Robert S. Ellison papers, WH131 File Folder, Papers-Diaries-Interviews-Comments.
52. Camp, *Custer in '76,* 148.
53. *Ibid.,* 118.
54. *Ibid.,* 232.
55. Nichols, *Reno Court of Inquiry,* 141.
56. *Ibid.*
57. *Ibid.*
58. *Ibid.,* 147.
59. *Ibid.,* 277.
60. *Ibid.*
61. *Ibid.,* 22.
62. *Ibid.,* 48.
63. *Ibid.,* 332.
64. *Ibid.,* 361.
65. *Ibid.,* 332.
66. *Ibid.,* 333.
67. *Ibid.*
68. Camp, *Custer in '76,* 180.
69. *Ibid.,* 183.
70. Libby, *The Arikara Narrative,* 118.
71. *Ibid.*
72. Nichols, *Reno Court of Inquiry,* 189.
73. *Ibid.,* 585.
74. *Ibid.,* 562.
75. Graham, *The Custer Myth,* 263.
76. Nichols, *Reno Court of Inquiry,* 252.
77. Camp, *Custer in '76,* 106.
78. *Ibid.,* 133.
79. Nichols, *Reno Court of Inquiry,* 222.
80. *Ibid.,* 367.
81. Taylor, *With Custer on the Little Bighorn,* 36.
82. *Ibid.,* 37.
83. Herbert Coffeen, *The Custer Battle Book* (New York: Carlton Press, 1964), 42–46.
84. Graham, *The Custer Myth,* 242.
85. Donahue, *Drawing Battle Lines,* 129.
86. *Ibid.*
87. Graham, *The Custer Myth,* 77; from an article in the *Leavenworth Weekly Times,* August 18, 1881, possibly by Frank H. Huston, a former Confederate soldier and sworn hater of the U.S. Army.
88. *Ibid.,* 75, quoting the same article.
89. *Ibid.,* 70, from an article in the *New York Herald,* November 16, 1877.
90. Camp, *Custer in '76,* 206, from a Camp interview, July 13, 1910.

91. Nichols, *Reno Court of Inquiry,* 561–562.
92. *Ibid.,* 590.
93. *Ibid.,* 562.
94. *Ibid.*
95. *Ibid.*
96. *Ibid.*
97. Bonafede, *Little Bighorn Battlefield Map.*
98. Graham, *The Custer Myth,* 341.
99. John Ryan, *Ten Years with Custer,* ed. Sandy Barnard (Terre Haute: AST Press, 2001), 291.
100. Graham, *The Custer Myth,* 242.
101. *Ibid.*
102. *Ibid.*
103. *Ibid.*
104. Carroll, *Battles of the Little Big Horn,* 18. From a letter written by Morris to Robert Bruce, May 23, 1928. This was from an e-mail dated January 29, 2011, and an Internet forum post, January 21, 2011, by Jose Luis Arcon-Dominguez, Ediciones SIMTAC, Valencia, Spain. Listed on Amazon.com as *Battles of the Little Bighorn: General Fry [i.e. Roe] on the Custer battle, William E. Morris, Lieutenant Roe to his wife, General Roe article.* Out of print.
105. Hardorff, *Indian Views of the Custer Fight,* 17. From White's diary, copied by Walter Camp in 1909, and loaned to him by White's widow.
106. James S. Brust, Brian C. Pohanka, and Sandy Barnard, Sandy, *Where Custer Fell* (Norman: University of Oklahoma Press, 2005), 32.
107. *Ibid.*
108. Nichols, *Reno Court of Inquiry,* 146.
109. *Ibid.,* 141.
110. *Ibid.,* 157–158.
111. *Ibid.,* 158.
112. *Ibid.,* 174.
113. *Ibid.,* 146.
114. *Ibid.,* 148.
115. *Ibid.,* 147.
116. *Ibid.,* 305.
117. *Ibid.,* 277.
118. *Ibid.*
119. Camp, *Custer in '76,* 66.
120. Nichols, *Reno Court of Inquiry,* 277 and 301.
121. *Ibid.,* 301–302.
122. *Ibid.,* 277.
123. *Ibid.*
124. *Ibid.,* 22.
125. *Ibid.,* 21.
126. *Ibid.,* 26.
127. *Ibid.,* 23.
128. *Ibid.,* 26 and 47.
129. *Ibid.,* 25.
130. *Ibid.,* 22–23.
131. *Ibid.,* 23.
132. *Ibid.,* 48.
133. *Ibid.,* 334.
134. *Ibid.*
135. *Ibid.,* 194.
136. *Ibid.*
137. *Ibid.,* 202.
138. Carroll, *The Benteen-Goldin Letters,* 33, in a letter to Albert W. Johnson, December 14, 1931.
139. Camp, *Custer in '76,* 133.
140. *Ibid.,* 112.
141. *Ibid.,* 111.
142. *Ibid.,* 61. In a letter from Varnum to Camp, dated April 14, 1909, postmarked Boise, Idaho.
143. Nichols, *Reno Court of Inquiry,* 367.
144. Hardorff, *On the Little Bighorn with Walter Camp,* 16.
145. *Ibid.,* 17.
146. Libby, *The Arikara Narrative,* 95.
147. Everett, "Bullets, Boots, and Saddles," *The Sunshine Magazine Articles,* 10.
148. Libby, *The Arikara Narrative,* 123.
149. Graham, *The Custer Myth,* 258. From a statement by Herendeen in Bismarck, D. T., on July 7,

1876, and published the following day in the *New York Herald.*
150. *Ibid.,* 263. From a statement made by Herendeen in Bozeman, Montana, on January 4, 1878, and published in the *New York Herald,* January 22, 1878.
151. Nichols, *Reno Court of Inquiry,* 252.
152. *Ibid.,* 264.
153. *Ibid.,* . 266.
154. Camp, *Custer in '76,* 222; footnote 8, from the Walter Camp field notes, folder 98, BYU Library.
155. *Ibid.,* 232.
156. Nichols, *Reno Court of Inquiry,* 93.
157. Graham, *The Custer Myth,* 251.
158. Nichols, *Reno Court of Inquiry,* 88.
159. *Ibid.*
160. *Ibid.,* 88 and 118.
161. *Ibid.,* 119.
162. *Ibid.,* 91.
163. *Ibid.,* 88.
164. *Ibid.,* 135.
165. *Ibid.,* 94.
166. *Ibid.*
167. Raymond J. DeMallie, ed., *The Sixth Grandfather* (Lincoln: University of Nebraska Press/Bison Books, 1985), 185.
168. Donahue, *Drawing Battle Lines,* 130.
169. *Ibid.*
170. *Ibid.*
171. *Ibid.*
172. Camp, *Custer in '76,* 148.
173. Graham, *The Custer Myth,* 53.
174. This is similar to an account recorded in pictographs and text at the Cheyenne River Reservation, 1881, and told to Assistant Surgeon McChesney of the Army. The full text of the statement is carried on the Website of the Public Broadcasting System at www.pbs.org/weta/thewest/resources/archives/six/bighorn.htm.
175. Hardorff, Richard G., *Cheyenne Memories of the Custer Fight* (Lincoln: University of Nebraska Press, 1998), 39. In a footnote, Hardorff expresses some doubt, mentioning the oft-told tales of First Sergeant John Ryan leading the 10-man detail into the village, a story not corroborated by Ryan himself. Hardorff speculates that panicking Indian inhabitants anxious to get away set the fires. That speculation, of course, leaves fallow Private Wilber's narrative; 39, footnote 1.
176. *Ibid.,* 42 and 46.
177. Godfrey, *Field Diary,* 23–24.
178. *Ibid.,* 69, footnote 112.
179. Hardorff, *Cheyenne Memories of the Custer Fight,* 158. Also see Hardorff, 158, footnote 14. This is the only account I have ever read of *six* Arapaho, the consensus being five: Left Hand, Waterman, Well Knowing One, Yellow Eagle, and Yellow Fly.
180. Camp, *Custer in '76,* 143.
181. *Ibid.,* 118.
182. Nichols, *Reno Court of Inquiry,* 222.
183. *Ibid.,* 241.
184. *Ibid.,* 223.
185. *Ibid.*
186. *Ibid.,* 234.
187. *Ibid.,* 216.
188. *Ibid.,* 222.
189. *Ibid.,* 230.
190. *Ibid.,* 216.
191. *Ibid.*
192. *Ibid.,* 313.
193. *Ibid.*
194. *Ibid.,* 328.
195. Camp, *Custer in '76,* 88.
196. Nichols, *Reno Court of Inquiry,* 313.
197. *Ibid.,* 314.
198. *Ibid.*
199. *Ibid.,* 347.
200. *Ibid.,* 314.
201. *Ibid.,* 316.

202. *Ibid.*
203. Camp, *Custer in '76,* 84.
204. Nichols, *Reno Court of Inquiry,* 317.
205. *Ibid.,* 314.
206. Camp, *Custer in '76,* 85.
207. Nichols, *Reno Court of Inquiry,* 325.
208. *Ibid.,* 367.
209. *Ibid.*
210. *Ibid.*
211. Camp, *Custer in '76,* 112.
212. Hardorff, *On the Little Bighorn with Walter Camp,* 38. Walter Camp letters and interviews; correspondence between Camp and Roy.
213. Camp, *Custer in '76,* 112.
214. Taylor, *With Custer on the Little Bighorn,* 37.
215. Graham, *The Custer Myth,* 344.
216. Taylor, *With Custer on the Little Bighorn,* 38.
217. *Ibid.,* 37.
218. Camp, *Custer in '76,* 106.
219. *Ibid.,* 106–107.
220. Theodore Goldin is considered one of this event's great liars and much of what he had to say is either discounted or discarded. The business about a "note from Custer" is a case in point. At best, we can use whatever the man said in a corroborative sense only. He had nothing to pat himself on the back about when describing the size of trees.
221. Graham, *The Custer Myth,* 270.
222. Nichols, *Reno Court of Inquiry,* 14.
223. Windolph, *I Fought with Custer,* 93.
224. Bonafede, Mike, *Little Bighorn Battlefield Map* (Loveland, CO: Atalissa, 1999).
225. DeMallie, *The Sixth Grandfather,* 182.
226. Richard G. Hardorff, ed., *Lakota Recollections of the Custer Fight* (Lincoln: University of Nebraska Press/Bison Books, 1997), 111.
227. Coffeen, *The Custer Battle Book,* 42–46.
228. Carroll, *The Benteen-Goldin Letters,* 74–75.
229. Nichols, *Reno Court of Inquiry,* 217.
230. *Ibid.,* 562.
231. *Ibid.*
232. *Ibid.,* 562–563.
233. *Ibid.,* 189–190.
234. *Ibid.,* 194.
235. *Ibid.,* 211.
236. *Ibid.,* 148.
237. *Ibid.,* 141–142.
238. *Ibid.,* 142.
239. *Ibid.*
240. *Ibid.*
241. *Ibid.*
242. *Ibid.,* 25.
243. *Ibid.,* 27.
244. *Ibid.,* 49.
245. *Ibid.,* 51.
246. *Ibid.,* 21.
247. *Ibid.,* 23.
248. *Ibid.,* 49.
249. *Ibid.,* 78.
250. *Ibid.,* 50.
251. *Ibid.,* 83.
252. *Ibid.,* 23.
253. *Ibid.,* 31.
254. *Ibid.,* 54.
255. Marquis, *Wooden Leg,* 219.
256. Nichols, *Reno Court of Inquiry,* 278–279.
257. *Ibid.,* 301.
258. *Ibid.,* 294.
259. *Ibid.,* 334.
260. *Ibid.,* 335.
261. *Ibid.*
262. *Ibid.*
263. Camp, *Custer in '76,* 232.
264. Nichols, *Reno Court of Inquiry,* 94.
265. Camp, *Custer in '76,* 232.
266. Nichols, *Reno Court of Inquiry,* 94.
267. Graham, *The Custer Myth,* 251.
268. Camp, *Custer in '76,* 232.

269. Nichols, *Reno Court of Inquiry,* 88.
270. Graham, *The Custer Myth,* 258.
271. Nichols, *Reno Court of Inquiry,* 265.
272. Graham, *The Custer Myth,* 263.
273. Nichols, *Reno Court of Inquiry,* 264 and 266.
274. *Ibid.,* 253.
275. *Ibid.,* 264.
276. *Ibid.,* 265.
277. Camp, *Custer in '76,* 222.
278. Graham, *The Custer Myth,* 242.
279. Brininstool, *A Trooper with Custer,* 17–56.
280. Donahue, *Drawing Battle Lines,* 130.
281. *Ibid.*
282. *Ibid.*
283. Camp, *Custer in '76,* 143.
284. Nichols, *Reno Court of Inquiry,* 216.
285. *Ibid.,* 217.
286. *Ibid.,* 224.
287. *Ibid.*
288. Graham, *The Custer Myth,* 344.
289. Taylor, *With Custer on the Little Bighorn,* 38.
290. Graham, *The Custer Myth,* 270.
291. Camp, *Custer in '76,* 107.
292. Libby, *The Arikara Narrative,* 125.
293. Nichols, *Reno Court of Inquiry,* 316.
294. *Ibid.,* 325.
295. *Ibid.,* 340.
296. *Ibid.,* 337.
297. *Ibid.,* 338.
298. *Ibid.,* 314.
299. *Ibid.,* 315.
300. *Ibid.,* 314–315.
301. *Ibid.,* 316.
302. *Ibid.,* 315.
303. Everett, "Bullets, Boots, and Saddles," *The Sunshine Magazine Articles,* 10. The Newell account.
304. *Ibid.*
305. *Ibid.*
306. Nichols, *Reno Court of Inquiry,* 142.
307. *Ibid.,* 170.
308. *Ibid.,* 142.
309. *Ibid.,* 148.
310. *Ibid.,* 143.
311. *Ibid.,* 179.
312. *Ibid.,* 168.
313. *Ibid.,* 148.
314. *Ibid.,* 149.
315. *Ibid.,* 149–150.
316. Graham, *The Custer Myth,* 226.
317. Nichols, *Reno Court of Inquiry,* 555.
318. *Ibid.,* 557.
319. *Ibid.*
320. *Ibid.*
321. *Ibid.,* 414–415.
322. *Ibid.,* 415.
323. *Ibid.,* 416.
324. Graham, *The Custer Myth,* 341.
325. Nichols, *Reno Court of Inquiry,* 234.
326. *Ibid.,* 241.
327. *Ibid.,* 246.
328. Graham, *The Custer Myth,* 319. From a letter written by Godfrey to Captain R. G. Carter, during a continuing debate between Carter and Graham regarding the performance of the Seventh Cavalry, in general, and of Reno and most of the regiment's officers in particular. It seems Carter counted Godfrey as his sole ally from the Seventh. The letter is dated April 14, 1925, from Cookstown, New Jersey.
329. Nichols, *Reno Court of Inquiry,* 10.
330. *Ibid.,* 15.
331. *Ibid.,* 339.
332. Camp, *Custer in '76,* 86.
333. Nichols, *Reno Court of Inquiry,* 318.
334. *Ibid.,* 316.
335. *Ibid.,* 156 and 179.
336. *Ibid.,* 156.
337. *Ibid.,* 157.
338. *Ibid.,* 147.

339. *Ibid.,* 52.
340. *Ibid.,* 30–31.
341. *Ibid.,* 31.
342. *Ibid.,* 282.
343. *Ibid.,* 295.
344. *Ibid.,* 296.
345. *Ibid.,* 293.
346. *Ibid.,* 294.
347. Graham, *The Custer Myth,* 242–243.
348. Carroll, *The Benteen-Goldin Letters,* 22. In a letter to Albert W. Johnson dated December 8, 1928.
349. Nichols, *Reno Court of Inquiry,* 104.
350. Camp, *Custer in '76,* 233.
351. Nichols, *Reno Court of Inquiry,* 97.
352. *Ibid.,* 262.
353. Camp, *Custer in '76,* 223.
354. Michno, *Lakota Noon,* 56–57.
355. von Clausewitz, *On War,* 452.
356. Callwell, *Small Wars,* 415.
357. One officer, 16 enlisted men, and three scouts remained trapped in the woods after Reno retreated. These were Lieutenant DeRudio and Private Holmstead from Company A; Blacksmith Taylor and privates O'Neill, McGonigle, McCormick, Moore, Johnson, Petring, Weiss, and Lattman from Company G; sergeants White and Carey, Trumpeter Weaver, and Private Sivertsen from M; the interpreter, Fred Gerard; and the scouts, George Herendeen and the half-breed, Billy Jackson. DeRudio, O'Neill, Gerard, and Jackson did not reach Reno's command until the evening of the 26th—after the Indians pulled out—while the others all followed Herendeen and made Reno Hill later in the afternoon of the 25th. Two other troopers, privates Armstrong (A) and McGinniss (G), chose to stay in the timber and were never seen alive again. Armstrong's head was discovered atop a pole in the Indian village on June 27. His headless body was reported to have been found near Isaiah Dorman's body and may have been buried there. Headless remains found on May 25, 1926, were thought to be Armstrong's and were buried at Garryowen, Montana, as an unknown soldier.
358. Donald W. Moore, *Where the Custer Fight Began* (El Segundo, CA: Upton & Sons, 2011), 16.
359. Ryan, *Ten Years with Custer,* 290.

Chapter 10

1. Camp, *Custer in '76,* 133.
2. Nichols, *Reno Court of Inquiry,* 341.
3. *Ibid.,* 314.
4. *Ibid.,* 337.
5. Michno, *Lakota Noon,* 51.
6. Nichols, *Reno Court of Inquiry,* 338 and 340.
7. *Ibid.,* 317.
8. *Ibid.,* 340.
9. *Ibid.,* 174.
10. *Ibid.,* 266 and 270.
11. *Ibid.,* 94 and 120.
12. *Ibid.,* 337.
13. *Ibid.,* 338.
14. *Ibid.*
15. Crow Agency Quadrangle maps.
16. In June 2009, I walked this area in the valley with some friends. Our guide was Steve Adelson, a historian—and currently, a National Park Service ranger at the battlefield—with a great knowledge of the area and the battle. As we reached the Reno timber area (a good deal of the timber is gone, but Gerard's "brow" is dramatic and clearly visible) we looked up at the bluffs; "3,411" jumped out at us and from the valley floor, it is so obviously DeRudio's "highest point" that little further proof need be required. Photographs do not do it justice, but when standing on the valley floor, it is stunningly obvious.
17. Nichols, *Reno Court of Inquiry,* 388.
18. Graham, *The Custer Myth,* 269–270.
19. Camp, *Custer in '76,* 94.

20. Nichols, *Reno Court of Inquiry,* 388.
21. Existence of this small village on the east side of the river has been questioned at times. There seems to be enough evidence, however, for its presence on June 25. Martini's comments tend to verify it, especially when the fighting in the valley is considered and the timing of Custer's approach to the bluffs. See Hardorff, *Indian Views of the Custer Fight,* 44–45. The narrative of White Bull, Hump, and Brave Wolf is contained in the report of Lieutenant Oscar F. Long, Fifth U.S. Infantry, dated June 27, 1877. It is found in the collection of Long papers, Collection CB 939, Box 1, University of California at Berkeley. It should be remembered this is a combined narrative and includes both Cheyenne and Minneconjou experiences. They may have been in different parts of the fighting. The three Indians related that the camp consisted of six separate tribes and a "small tribe of disaffected Indians from Spotted Tail Agency." Hardorff claims this last group—the "disaffected"—were probably Cu Brulé Lakota, 45, footnote 4. In addition, see the Hollow Horn Bear interview, Hardorff, *Lakota Recollections of the Custer Fight,* 177–178. Hollow Horn Bear was interviewed by Sewell B. Weston using a questionnaire submitted by Walter Mason Camp. The interview took place in June 1909. Hollow Horn Bear was a Cu Brulé Lakota agency Indian from Spotted Tail Agency in northwest Nebraska. Also see Scott, *Uncovering History,* 80.
22. Douglas D. Scott and Peter Bleed, *A Good Walk Around the Boundary* (Lincoln: The Nebraska Association of Professional Archaeologists and the Nebraska State Historical Society, 1997 [2006]), 35.
23. Nichols, *Reno Court of Inquiry,* 395.
24. Graham, *The Custer Myth,* 270.
25. Michno, *Lakota Noon,* 23.
26. *Ibid.,* 23–24.
27. *Ibid.,* 24.
28. *Ibid.,* 25.
29. *Ibid.,* 25–26.
30. *Ibid.,* 28–29.
31. *Ibid.,* 29–30.
32. Graham, *The Custer Myth,* 293.
33. Willert, *Little Big Horn Diary,* 291.
34. Graham, *The Custer Myth,* 23.
35. Willert, *Little Big Horn Diary,* 286; Goes Ahead, Hairy Moccasin, and Curley.
36. Nichols, *Reno Court of Inquiry,* 389.
37. *Ibid.* Elisabeth Kimber—a friend from England—was kind enough to point this out to me. In an e-mail dated September 1, 2007, Elisabeth wrote, "Graham interprets the 'hour and a half' to be either a slip of the tongue, or a mistake in the written record; he thinks what was meant was 'a mile and a half.' That would make much more sense, I think.... In which case the watering place he's referring to is presumably North Fork."
38. Nichols, *Reno Court of Inquiry,* 390.
39. *Ibid.,* 397.
40. Carroll, *The Benteen-Goldin Letters,* 48; in a letter to Albert W. Johnson dated April 21, 1934.
41. Graham, *The Custer Myth,* 270.
42. Nichols, *Reno Court of Inquiry,* 398.
43. *Ibid.,* 390.
44. *Ibid.,* 398.
45. *Ibid.,* 391.
46. *Ibid.,* 395.
47. *Ibid.,* 390.
48. *Ibid.,* 395.
49. *Ibid.,* 396.
50. *Ibid.,* 325.
51. Camp, *Custer in '76,* 100, footnote 3.
52. *Ibid.,* 100.
53. *Ibid.,* 103.
54. *Ibid..* See endnote 2.
55. *Ibid.,* 103, endnote 5.
56. Liddic, *Vanishing Victory,* 89.
57. Captain Timothy T. Lupfer, "The Dynamics

of Doctrine: The Changes in German Tactical Doctrine During the First World War," *Leavenworth Papers* 4 (Fort Leavenworth: Combat Studies Institute, U.S. Army Command and General Staff College, July 1981), vii. The quote was taken from Wilhelm Balck, *Development of Tactics—World War*, trans. Harry Bell (Fort Leavenworth, 1922), 14.

58. Nichols, *Reno Court of Inquiry,* 341.
59. *Ibid.*
60. *Ibid.,* 406.
61. *Ibid.,* 414.
62. See Hardorff, *Lakota Recollections of the Custer Fight,* 51, the Flying Hawk interview with Judge Eli S. Ricker, March 8, 1907, on the Pine Ridge Reservation. The contention that Crazy Horse left the Reno field shortly after Benteen arrived is heavily supported by the extremely fine work in Kingsley M. Bray, *Crazy Horse* (Norman: University of Oklahoma Press, 2006), 221.
63. Nichols, *Reno Court of Inquiry,* 316.
64. *Ibid.,* 318.
65. *Ibid.,* 323.
66. *Ibid.,* 342.
67. *Ibid.,* 316.
68. *Ibid.,* 351.

Chapter 11

1. Hammer/Camp, *Custer in '76,* 93. Interviews with Walter Camp conducted on June 16th and 17th, 1908.
2. The four men were Farrier John Fitzgerald, in his fourth enlistment; and privates John Brennan, Peter Thompson, and James Watson, none of whom had more than nine months service, making them three of the most inexperienced troopers at the battle. There is some evidence Fitzgerald may have fallen behind along Reno Creek, thereby putting ideas in the rookies' heads. While Thompson later distinguished himself during the Reno Hill fighting, none of the others hold claim to such distinction. In fact, for a number of months after the fighting Fitzgerald and Brennan were the recipients—*and initiators?*- of considerable barracks guffawing about avoiding any fighting on the 25th. Private John McGuire (also of C Company) went so far as to tell Walter Camp that among C troop men it was always the opinion John Brennan and John Fitzgerald fell back from Custer's five troops out of cowardice and in that way did not get into the fight. He said "they ... often joked about it afterward." (See Hammer, *Custer in '76,* pp. 123–126.) Peter Thompson went on to write one of the more outlandish memoirs of the whole affair—thereby etching his life in stone—and Brennan spent more than 500 days of the ensuing three years in confinement, finally being dishonorably booted from the service on December 4, 1879. Hardly the stuff of confidence for the veracity of their claims.
3. The note survives today in the museum at the United States Military Academy, West Point, New York.
4. Nichols, *Reno Court of Inquiry,* 390.
5. *Ibid.*
6. Martini's precise location when given the note is irrelevant. Whether at the very head of the coulee or partway down makes no difference, not even in the timing studies. A few hundred yards would only increase his rate-of-speed by one- or two-tenths of a mile and would have no bearing on other events including his meeting with Benteen. Another historical tempest in a teapot.
7. See Scott/Bleed, *A Good Walk Around the Boundary,* 29–30.
8. Camp/Hammer, *Custer in '76,* 177. February 23, 1911, interview with Walter Camp.

Chapter 12

1. Nichols, *Reno Court of Inquiry,* 87; testimony of the interpreter, Fred Gerard.
2. *Ibid.,* 116.
3. *Ibid.,* 87.
4. Camp, *Custer in '76,* 106.
5. Nichols, *Reno Court of Inquiry,* 388.
6. *Ibid.,* 397.
7. *Ibid.,* 388.
8. Crow Agency Quadrangle maps.
9. Camp, *Custer in '76,* 156.
10. *Ibid.,* 156–157.
11. Graham, *The Custer Myth,* 13.
12. Camp, *Custer in '76,* 86.
13. Graham, *The Custer Myth,* 220. From an article in the *Leavenworth Times,* a statement by Edgerly, August 18, 1881, made at Fort Yates.
14. Camp, *Custer in '76,* 56.
15. Liddic, *Vanishing Victory,* 54; citing Camp, University of Indiana, box 2, folder 8.
16. *Ibid.,* 55.
17. Willert, *Little Big Horn Diary,* 306.
18. Indians who we know by name were the Hunkpapas: Gall and Iron Cedar; Minneconjoux: Iron Thunder, Owns The Horn, Red Horse, Shoots Bear As He Runs, Standing Bear, and White Bull; the Oglala: Eagle Elk, He Dog, Kicking Bear, Red Feather, Running Eagle, White Eagle, and Young Skunk; the Cheyenne, Wooden Leg, White Shield, and Yellow Nose, and the two other, unknown Cheyenne, referred to in various writings as just that—"unknown Cheyenne."
19. Michno, *Lakota Noon,* 69.
20. Graham, *The Custer Myth,* 20, citing Goes Ahead, and 39, citing Boy Chief.
21. Everett, "Bullets, Boots, and Saddles," *The Sunshine Magazine Articles,* 11.
22. Camp, *Custer in '76,* 198. Walter Camp interview conducted September 22, 1908; interpreters, Lois Roubideaux of Rosebud and a Mr. Shaw of Valentine, Nebraska.
23. Camp, *Custer in '76,* 198.
24. Richard G. Hardoff, ed., *Camp, Custer, and the Little Big Horn* (El Segundo, CA: Upton & Sons, 1997), 81. Undated interview with Walter Mason Camp, though it probably took place in 1910. Camp MSS, field notes, Little Bighorn, Battle of 1876, II, IU Library, IN.
25. Liddic, *Vanishing Victory,* 39; quoting from Carroll, *The Gibson and Edgerly Narratives* (Bryan, TX: privately printed, undated), 5.

Chapter 13

1. Graham, *The Custer Myth,* 300.
2. *Ibid.,* 298.
3. Nichols, *Reno Court of Inquiry,* 417.
4. Carroll, *The Benteen-Goldin Letters,* 210.
5. Nichols, *Reno Court of Inquiry,* 494–495.
6. *Ibid.,* 498.
7. Godfrey, "Custer's Last Battle," 33.
8. Graham, *The Custer Myth,* 94.
9. *Ibid.* Godfrey's comments regarding Gall's story at the 1886 reunion as found in Graham, *The Custer Myth,* 93–96. This is from a revised printing of *Custer's Last Battle,* and contains some duplication from other editions, though all were slightly different. The issue is based on Godfrey's discussion with Gall in 1886, but was used to write Godfrey's 1892 article.
10. *Ibid.,* 94.
11. *Ibid.*
12. Liddic, *Camp on Custer,* 122.
13. *Ibid.*
14. *Ibid.,* 122–123.
15. Camp, *Custer in '76,* 214. Standing Bear interview with Walter Camp, July 12, 1910.
16. Hardorff, *Lakota Recollections,* 59. Standing Bear interview with Judge Eli Ricker, March 12, 1907.
17. Camp, *Custer in '76,* 214; Camp interview, July 12, 1910.
18. Hardorff, *Lakota Recollections,* 50; Ricker interview, 1907.
19. *Ibid.,* 143. Two Eagles interview with Sewell B. Weston, December 1908.
20. *Ibid.,* 145.
21. *Ibid.,* 165. Lights interview with Sewell B. Weston, spring of 1909.
22. Hardorff, *Indian Views of the Custer Fight,* 115.
23. Graham, *The Custer Myth,* 110. Waterman was interviewed by Colonel Tim McCoy in 1920. Of the five Arapaho who fought at the Little Big Horn, Waterman and Left Hand were the only ones still alive in 1920.
24. Hardorff, *Cheyenne Memories of the Custer Fight,* 35–36. An interview with George Bird Grinnell at the Northern Cheyenne Indian Reservation in Montana in 1895.
25. *Ibid.,* 39. An interview with George Bird Grinnell at the Northern Cheyenne Indian Reservation in Montana in 1895.
26. Graham, *The Custer Myth,* 85. From an article carried in the *St. Paul Pioneer Press,* May 19, 1883.
27. Hardorff, *Cheyenne Memories of the Custer Fight,* 29. An interview with George Bird Grinnell at the Northern Cheyenne Indian Reservation in Montana in 1895.
28. Hardorff, *Indian Views of the Custer Fight,* 48. The narratives of Brave Wolf, White Bull, and Hump are contained in the June 27, 1877, report of Lieutenant Oscar F. Long, Fifth U.S. Infantry.
29. Frederic C. Wagner, III, *Participants in the Battle of the Little Big Horn* [hereafter cited as *Participants*] (Jefferson, NC: McFarland, 2011), 206 and 207.
30. Hardorff, *Cheyenne Memories of the Custer Fight,* 52. An interview with George Bird Grinnell, at the Northern Cheyenne Indian Reservation in Montana, 1908.
31. Marquis, *Wooden Leg,* 206. The only creek below Medicine Tail Coulee and flowing into the Little Big Horn from the southwest is Onion Creek. On the McElfresh map this creek appears too far downstream from the indicated Cheyenne camp. On the topo map, however, it is more intermittent and cuts into the Little Big Horn valley approaching the river near Medicine Tail Coulee. In 1876, it may have flowed into the river near or at some point just below Medicine Tail Coulee. In all likelihood the northern extremity of the Cheyenne circles reached no farther than ¼ mile below Ford B.
32. Hardorff, *Camp, Custer, and The Little Bighorn,* 99. Undated interview between General Edward J. McClernand and Walter Mason Camp. Camp MSS, field notes, unclassified envelope 92, IU Library, IN.
33. *The Big Horn-Yellowstone Journal* 1, no. 5 (Summer 1992): 15. Taken from an article in the *Chicago Record-Herald.* The interview appeared originally in *The Indian School Journal,* November 1905, and probably took place where Yellow Nose—now blind—lived on the North Canadian River, near Cantonment, Oklahoma. Edward Guerriere translated.
34. *Ibid.*
35. Hardorff, *Camp, Custer, and the Little Bighorn,* 84. Interview with Walter Mason Camp, May 21, 1909, at the Standing Rock Indian Reservation. Camp papers, Ellison Collection, DPL. Harry McLaughlin was the interpreter.
36. According to the Northern Cheyenne warrior Wooden Leg, if the village were attacked, the camp guards would rally to its defense. It would therefore make sense any camp guards remaining in the Cheyenne camp would have rallied at Ford B. The Kit Fox warrior society provided the Cheyenne camp guards

on June 25. Known by name to have been in the vicinity were the Cheyenne (seven to 10; possibly a few more), Bob-tail Horse, Roan Bear, Buffalo Calf, Big Nose, Mad Wolf, White Shield (not there initially, but joining a few minutes later), Rising Sun, Hanging Wolf, Young Little Wolf (who first saw Custer in Medicine Tail Coulee, which should have put him near the ford), American Horse (the Cheyenne chief, returning early from the Reno fight where he was not one of those crossing the Little Big Horn), and possibly Pawnee, Wooden Thigh, Yellow Horse, and Horse Road, who were camp guards. In addition, there were some Sioux, maybe as many as four or five, but certainly White Cow Bull (an Oglala) and probably Shave Elk. A member of Big Road's northern band of Oglala Sioux, Shave Elk and four others were riding up Medicine Tail Coulee when they saw Custer's column coming at them. They rode back down, crossed at Ford B, and it is not unreasonable—though not certain—one or more of them stayed to help defend the ford. If they all stayed—and that is equally unlikely—then it would explain the various commentaries about four or five Sioux being at the ford. If Shave Elk's band remained at Ford B to oppose the on-coming soldiers, it could mean as many as 20 or more Indians fought Custer's column at the crossing. This, of course, would include the four Cheyenne camp guards, above. Yellow Nose, a Ute/Cheyenne, may have been another.

37. See Fox, *Archaeology, History, and Custer's Last Battle,* 275–277.

38. This unfortunate soul was in all likelihood Private William Brown from Company F. Brown's body was found on the west side of the Little Big Horn, near the mouth of Medicine Tail Coulee. Liddic wrote that his body was found 250 yards across the river from the Deep *Coulee* crossing (which is also Ford B) [*Vanishing Victory,* 164]. Private James M. Rooney (F) identified Brown's body in the village, in all likelihood making Brown the trooper whose horse bolted as Custer and Yates approached Ford B [see Hardorff, *On the Little Bighorn with Walter Camp,* p. 13, footnote 2; and Hardorff, *Camp, Custer, and the Little Bighorn,* p. 95; an undated interview between James Rooney and Walter Mason Camp. Camp MSS, field notes, box 4, BYU]. In this latter source book, Camp has written that Brown's body lay opposite Crazy Horse Gully, considered generally to be Deep *Ravine.* One does not know if this is from Rooney or part of Camp's editorial license, found throughout his note taking. Brown's body near the Deep Ravine crossing is almost impossible to fathom; not so across from Deep *Coulee.* One can also make a reasoned assumption Brown would have been part of the five- or six-man contingent of F Company "scouts" Custer had Captain Yates send out starting near the lone teepee on Reno Creek. That would account for a small F Company presence *off* the ridge and would give added plausibility and importance to the Shave Elk account claiming Custer's column "came down this coulee toward the river ... a few soldiers ahead of the main body."

39. Graham, *The Custer Myth,* 231. Rosser was a life-long friend and U.S.M.A. schoolmate of George Custer and had written a letter critical of Reno. It had been published in the St. Paul-Minneapolis *Pioneer-Press and Tribune,* on July 8, 1876, and re-printed in the *New York Herald,* July 11, 1876. Reno responded, but before Rosser could reply to Reno's letter, the *New York Herald* interviewed both Benteen and Reno. Reno's interview was carried in the August 8, 1876, edition. This is from Rosser's response, carried in the *New York Herald,* August 22, 1876.

40. Glennwood J. Swanson, *G. A. Custer, His Life and Times* (Agua Dulce, CA: Swanson, 2004), 293.

41. Bonafede, *Little Bighorn Battlefield Map.*

Chapter 14

1. Camp, *Custer in '76,* 282–288.
2. Graham, *The Custer Myth,* 27–28.
3. Roger L. Williams, *Military Register of Custer's Last Command* (Norman: Arthur H. Clark, 2009), 323–344.
4. Smalley, *Little Bighorn Mysteries,* A2-1-A2-2.
5. Gray, *Custer's Last Campaign,* 296–297.
6. Hardorff, *On the Little Bighorn with Walter Camp,* 53.
7. *Ibid.,* 54.
8. Most battle scholars leave Custer with the usual gang of four Crow scouts. In latter years, however, as they were waltzed around by so many interested parties, one of the Crows—Goes Ahead—claimed Curley rode off with the Ree, Black Fox, shortly after Custer directed the scouts to head up to Weir Peaks. See, Libby, *The Arikara Narrative,* 160. Wading through much of the Crow statements can be rather hazardous, but it is only with claims like Goes Ahead's, when compared with those of others, can any semblance of truth be derived, and while neither White Man Runs Him, nor Hairy Moccasin, mentioned Black Fox by name, they both alluded to the fact that Curley was not with them beyond the general area of "3,411."
9. Libby, *The Arikara Narrative,* 119; statements of Boy Chief.
10. Hardorff, *Camp, Custer, and the Little Bighorn,* 57. Whole Buffalo interview with Walter Mason Camp. Camp MSS, field notes, box 3, BYU. Interview conducted at the Standing Rock Indian Reservation, May 21, 1909; Harry McLaughlin, interpreter.
11. See the interviews of Strikes Two in an undated Camp interview, Camp, *Custer in '76,* 184, and Boy Chief, Libby, *The Arikara Narrative,* 119.
12. Camp, *Custer in '76,* 184; Strikes Two interview, undated.
13. Graham, *The Custer Myth,* 20 and 25.
14. *Ibid.,* 20 and 39; interviews with Goes Ahead and Boy Chief.
15. Brust, Pohanka, and Barnard, *Where Custer Fell,* 74. Edward Sheriff Curtis, the famous photographer, compiled this account during a 1907 visit to the battlefield with White Man Runs Him, Hairy Moccasin, and Goes Ahead. It is principally from White Man Runs Him's recollections. The interpreter was Alexander Upshaw.
16. Camp, *Custer in '76,* 177. Walter Camp interview conducted February 23, 1911, with Eli Black Hawk as the interpreter.
17. Brininstool, *A Trooper with Custer,* 17–56.
18. Libby, *The Arikara Narrative,* 159.
19. *Ibid.,* 160.
20. *Ibid.*
21. *Ibid.*
22. Camp, *Custer in '76,* 177; Camp interview, February 23, 1911, Eli Black Hawk interpreting.
23. *Ibid.*
24. Graham, *The Custer Myth,* 25; from the June 1916 "Tepee Book."
25. Camp, *Custer in '76,* 178, footnote 2.
26. Graham, *The Custer Myth,* 15.
27. *Ibid.,* 16.
28. *Ibid.,* 23–24.
29. Nichols, *Reno Court of Inquiry,* 405.
30. Graham, *The Custer Myth,* 219.
31. Nichols, *Reno Court of Inquiry,* 480.
32. Godfrey, "Custer's Last Battle," 25.
33. Camp, *Custer in '76,* 76.
34. Godfrey, *Field Diary,* 12.
35. *Ibid.,* 64, footnote 60.
36. Windolph, *I Fought with Custer,* 89.
37. Hardorff, *On the Little Bighorn with Walter Camp,* 55.

Chapter 15

1. Godfrey, *Field Diary,* 11. Godfrey's entries for June 24 and June 25 were clearly written several days after the battle and he confuses the sequencing of several events. In a footnote to the diary entry Stewart points out the discrepancy between various accounts mentioning that the watering was done prior to reaching the abandoned tepee; 64, footnote 56.
2. Nichols, *Reno Court of Inquiry,* 143.
3. *Ibid.,* 143–144.
4. *Ibid.,* 180.
5. *Ibid.,* 23.
6. Camp, *Custer in '76,* 120. Camp interview, October 16, 1910.
7. *Ibid.,* 80. Camp interview, December 7, 1910.
8. *Ibid.,* 66. Camp interview, February 7, 1910.
9. *Ibid.,* 113.
10. Godfrey, "Custer's Last Battle," 27.
11. Nichols, *Reno Court of Inquiry,* 392 and 396.
12. Graham, *The Custer Myth,* 291. From an interview with Martini and carried in the *Cavalry Journal,* July 1923.
13. Edgerly, *Scalp Dance,* 19.
14. Camp, *Custer in '76,* 150.
15. Godfrey, "Custer's Last Battle," 27.
16. Gray, *Custer's Last Campaign,* 272.
17. *Ibid.,* 251.
18. Graham, *The Custer Myth,* 142. Included here is a section from the 1908 revision Godfrey made to his 1892 *Century Magazine* article.
19. *Ibid.,* 170, 180. From the so-called "Benteen Manuscript," circa 1890.
20. Nichols, *Reno Court of Inquiry,* 406.
21. *Ibid.*
22. Graham, *The Custer Myth,* 172 and 181. This was also from the so-called "Benteen Manuscript," written by Benteen and loaned to Edward Godfrey by Benteen's son, Major Frederick Benteen. It was one of two manuscripts given to Godfrey and was only returned to the Benteen family after Godfrey's death. The earlier of the two—considered the more important—was returned missing its final pages; the second manuscript was not returned and is now missing. This was believed written shortly after the battle of Wounded Knee in 1890. See page 160 of *The Custer Myth.*
23. Kuhlman, *Legend into History,* 222, footnote 34. Kuhlman expresses his gratitude for viewing this letter to Captain E. S. Luce. The letter is apparently in the collection of the Little Big Horn Battlefield Museum.
24. Windolph, *I Fought with Custer,* 89–90.
25. *Ibid.,* 96.
26. Camp, *Custer in '76,* 150. An undated Camp interview.
27. Nichols, *Reno Court of Inquiry,* 184.
28. *Ibid.,* 143.
29. *Ibid.,* 171.
30. *Ibid.*
31. *Ibid.,* 336.
32. *Ibid.,* 279–280.
33. *Ibid.,* 482.
34. *Ibid.,* 197.
35. *Ibid.,* 191.
36. *Ibid.,* 206.
37. *Ibid.,* 191.
38. Edgerly, *Scalp Dance,* 19.
39. Nichols, *Reno Court of Inquiry,* 160.
40. *Ibid.,* 483.
41. *Ibid.,* 371. Culbertson's testimony.
42. *Ibid.,* 482.
43. *Ibid.,* 325 and 330.
44. *Ibid.,* 350–351.
45. *Ibid.,* 482.
46. Hardorff, *Lakota Recollections of the Custer Fight,* 51. Interviewed by Judge Eli S. Ricker, March 8, 1907, on the Pine Ridge Reservation.

47. Nichols, *Reno Court of Inquiry,* 442.

48. *Ibid.,* 280 and 296.

49. Wagner, *Participants in the Battle of the Little Big Horn,* 228–232.

50. Nichols, *Reno Court of Inquiry,* 316.

51. See Douglas D. Scott and Richard A. Fox, Jr., *Archaeological Insights into the Custer Battle* (Norman: University of Oklahoma Press, 1987), 111–113; and Douglas D. Scott, Richard A. Fox, Jr., Melissa A. Connor, and Dick Harmon, *Archaeological Perspectives on the Battle of the Little Bighorn* (Norman: University of Oklahoma Press, 1989), 103–113.

52. Horn, *Fifty Years on Custer's Trail,* 21.

53. Nichols, *Reno Court of Inquiry,* 513.

54. *Ibid.,* 529.

55. *Ibid.,* 513.

56. Camp, *Custer in '76,* 69.

57. Nichols, *Reno Court of Inquiry,* 513, and Camp, *Custer in '76,* 78.

58. Hardorff, *Camp, Custer, and the Little Bighorn,* 74. It should be noted that it has been assumed Hammon fought with his company on Reno's skirmish line. This 1908 interview calls that into question as it seems Hammon had been assigned to the pack train.

59. Edgerly, *Scalp Dance,* 19.

60. Graham, *The Custer Myth,* 217.

61. Liddic, *Camp on Custer,* 94–95. In an undated interview with Walter Mason Camp.

62. *Ibid.,* 94–96.

63. Nichols, *Reno Court of Inquiry,* 444.

64. Camp, *Custer in '76,* 56.

Chapter 16

1. Scott/Bleed, *A Good Walk Around the Boundary,* 39.

2. Hardorff, *Camp, Custer, and the Little Bighorn,* 87. Interviews by Walter Mason Camp of the Minneconjoux, One Bull and White Bull, in 1912, at the Standing Rock Indian Reservation. Camp MSS, field notes, unclassified envelope 41, IU Library, IN.

3. Hutchins, *The Army and Navy Journal,* 90. From a letter written by Godfrey, August 7, 1876, at the Seventh Cavalry camp on the Rosebud, to the editor of the *The Army and Navy Journal.*

4. Nichols, *Reno Court of Inquiry,* 316.

5. *Ibid.,* 318.

6. *Ibid.,* 323.

7. *Ibid.,* 318.

8. *Ibid.,* 327.

9. *Ibid.,* 98–99.

10. *Ibid.,* 135.

11. *Ibid.,* 99.

12. *Ibid.,* 128.

13. *Ibid.,* 135–136.

14. Hardorff, *Hokahey!,* 80.

15. Hardorff, *Camp, Custer, and the Little Bighorn,* 80, footnote 5. For a marvelous series of photos of Camp's maps, see Donahue, *Drawing Battle Lines,* 271–323, and the color plates, v–xxiii.

16. *Ibid.*

17. George W. Glenn—also known as George W. Glease—was a private in Benteen's H Company.

18. Donahue, *Drawing Battle Lines,* 133.

19. Hardorff, *Camp, Custer, and the Little Bighorn,* 79. A Camp interview with Boyle, February 5, 1913.

20. Hardorff, *Indian Views of the Custer Fight,* 206. DeVoto's narrative was appended to a letter to Walter Camp dated October 1, 1917.

21. Nichols, *Reno Court of Inquiry,* 322.

22. *Ibid.,* 419 and 424.

23. *Ibid.,* 33.

24. For the complete interview, along with one of the most rationalized tales of justification, see Pennington, *The Battle of the Little Bighorn,* 182–186.

25. Hardorff, *Indian Views of the Custer Fight,* 40–41. The statement is contained in John F. Finerty's, *War-path and Bivouac: The Bighorn and Yellowstone Expedition* (Chicago: Lakeside Press, 1955), 208–211. Taken at Camp Robinson, Nebraska, 1877, during an interview with Lieutenant William Philo Clark.

26. Hardorff, *Lakota Recollections of the Custer Fight,* 137. An interview of the Cheyenne warrior Two Moons by Richard Throssel, summer 1909, Northern Cheyenne Reservation, Lame Deer, Montana. Interpreter was an educated Cheyenne named Red Water. Interview appeared in the Billings *Daily Gazette,* 1911. Also see Hardorff, *Indian Views of the Custer Fight,* 155; an interview with the Minniconjou warrior White Bull by Walter S. Campbell (aka,Stanley Vestal) at the Cheyenne River Reservation, Cherry Creek, South Dakota, June 1932.

27. *Ibid.,* 156. A 1909 interview with Sewell B. Weston.

28. *Ibid.,* 166.

29. Graham, *The Custer Myth,* 75. From the *Leavenworth Weekly Times,* by Frank Huston, August 18, 1881.

30. Hardorff, *Lakota Recollections of the Custer Fight,* 179. A June 1909 interview with Sewell B. Weston using a Walter Camp "questionnaire."

31. Graham, *The Custer Myth,* 87; *St. Paul Pioneer Press,* May 19, 1883.

32. Hardorff, *Lakota Recollections of the Custer Fight,* 166. A spring 1909 interview with Sewell B. Weston using a Walter Camp "questionnaire."

33. Marquis, *Wooden Leg,* 230–231. Interviews conducted between 1922 and 1931.

34. Hardorff, *Lakota Recollections of the Custer Fight,* 146. An interview with Sewell B. Weston, 1908.

35. Hardorff, *Indian Views of the Custer Fight,* 166, footnote 38. This is one of the more fascinating observations of the entire Custer fight, for knowingly or unknowingly, "Dutch" Hardorff hands us the perfect answer for the ultimate deployment of Keogh's own Company I, probably answering most of the questions of why his command was found the way it was. The footnote reads in total, "This action took place on the east side of Custer [Battle] Ridge where Crazy Horse charged through Keogh's line and through a gap in Custer Ridge which brought him onto the west slope. This gap was filled in 1934 to facilitate the present blacktop." The allusion here is the east-to-west movement of Crazy Horse, but it would have worked the other way as well, especially if Horse was coming up Deep Ravine.

36. Graham, *The Custer Myth,* 97. An interview with General Hugh Scott, September 9, 1919.

37. Hardorff, *Cheyenne Memories of the Custer Fight,* 57. In an interview with George Bird Grinnell in 1908, at the Northern Cheyenne Reservation in Montana.

38. Hardorff, *Indian Views of the Custer Fight,* 155. In an interview with Walter S. Campbell (aka Stanley Vestal), June 1932, at the Cheyenne River Reservation, Cherry Creek, South Dakota.

39. *Ibid.*

40. *Ibid.,* 88. Narrative contained in the Edward Curtis papers, Natural History Museum of Los Angeles County, California. Interviewed on a Sioux reservation, 1907.

41. *Ibid.,* 132. Interview at Fort Yates, North Dakota, September 2, 1929. From an interview by Walter S. Campbell, aka Stanley Vestal.

42. Hardorff, *Cheyenne Memories of the Custer Fight,* 62. An interview with George Bird Grinnell at the Northern Cheyenne Indian Reservation in Montana, 1908.

43. Graham, *The Custer Myth,* 89. From a Chicago newspaper, June 26, 1886.

44. Hardorff, *Cheyenne Memories of the Custer Fight,* 130–131. An interview of Two Moons by Dr. Joseph K. Dixon on the Custer battlefield in 1909. It was first published in 1913.

45. Scott/Bleed, *A Good Walk Around the Boundary,* 42.

46. *Ibid.,* 43.

47. Margot Liberty and John Stands in Timber, *Cheyenne Memories* (New Haven: Yale University Press, 1967 [1998]), 199. The sequencing of Stands in Timber's narrative makes this appear to be near the Ford D area. Written by Liberty from notes and recordings taken over a period of several years. The book was published shortly after Stands in Timber's death.

48. Hardorff, *Indian Views of the Custer Fight,* 148. Interview between White Hair on Face and Walter S. Campbell (aka Stanley Vestal), at Fort Yates, North Dakota, June 1930.

49. Hardorff, *Lakota Recollections,* 52. In an interview with Judge Eli Ricker, March 8, 1907.

50. Liberty, *Cheyenne Memories,* 199. This sounds like it could have referred as well to the fighting at Ford B, but because of the sequencing of events and Stands in Timber's narrative, it becomes clear he was referring to activity farther downstream.

Chapter 17

1. Marquis, *Wooden Leg,* 229.

2. *Ibid.,* 228, 230–231.

3. Hardorff, *Lakota Recollections of the Custer Fight,* 59. Interview with Judge Eli Ricker, March 12, 1907.

4. Hardorff, *Cheyenne Memories of the Custer Fight,* 168. An interview of John Stands in Timber with Don Rickey, Jr., and Jesse W. Vaughn at the Custer Battlefield in Montana, 1956. Also see Liberty and John Stands in Timber, *Cheyenne Memories,* 197–198.

5. Marquis, *Wooden Leg,* 228.

6. See Fox, *Archaeology, History, and Custer's Last Battle,* 139–142.

7. *Ibid.,* 140. Citing C. G. du Bois, *The Custer Mystery* (El Segundo, CA: Upton & Sons, 1986), 103.

8. Marquis, *Wooden Leg,* 231.

9. *Ibid.,* footnote, 231.

10. Graham, *The Custer Myth,* 110; interview in 1920 with Colonel Tim McCoy.

11. Marquis, *Wooden Leg,* 380.

12. Scott, Fox, et al., *Archaeological Perspectives on the Battle of the Little Bighorn,* 268. While not certain, the evidence found at Marker 128 indicates the remains were *probably* that of a C Company trooper. The following men fit the profile: F. Meyer (C), J. Shea (C), J. Thadus (C), N. Short (C), G. Moonie (E), W. Huber (E; highly doubtful), T. Donnelly (F; highly doubtful), E. Babcock (L), F. Hughes (L; highly doubtful). No other E, F, or L Company remains were found anywhere near this area. If we stick to our contention of the remains being from a C Company trooper, we could probably eliminate Meyer (a tailor in civilian life). Shea and Short were laborers and Thadus was a farmer, all three better fitting the "muscular" description of the remains. And Short came within ¼ inch of the height parameter, a bit closer than Shea and Thadus.

13. Fox, *Archaeology, History, and Custer's Last Battle,* 149. Footnote 70 cites Thomas Marquis, *Keep the Last Bullet for Yourself: The True Story of Custer's Last Stand* (Algonac, MI: Reference, 1976), 159.

14. *Ibid.,* 151.

15. Camp, *Custer in '76,* 212.

16. Hardorff, *Lakota Recollections of the Custer Fight,* 31. Interview with Judge Eli Ricker, 1906.

17. Hardorff, *Indian Views of the Custer Fight,* 49. June 27, 1877, report of Lieutenant Oscar F. Long, Fifth U.S. Infantry.

18. Camp, *Custer in '76,* 207. In an interview with Walter Camp, July 13, 1910.

19. *Ibid.,* 213. Camp interview, July 22, 1910.

20. *Ibid.*

21. Hardorff, *Cheyenne Memories of the Custer Fight,* 90. From an interview with Walter Camp at

the Northern Cheyenne Indian Reservation in Montana, 1918.

22. Fox, *Archaeology, History, and Custer's Last Battle,* 155.

23. Hardorff, *Lakota Recollections of the Custer Fight,* 146. Weston interview, 1908.

24. *Ibid.,* 157. Weston interview, 1909.

25. Hardorff, *Camp, Custer, and the Little Bighorn,* 100.

26. Hardorff, *Lakota Recollections of the Custer Fight,* 167. Weston interview, 1909.

27. *Ibid.,* 157.

28. *Ibid.,* 146–147.

29. Wagner, *Participants,* 228–230.

30. Hardorff, *Indian Views of the Custer Fight,* 155. An interview of the Minneconjou White Bull by Walter S. Campbell, Cheyenne River Reservation, Cherry Creek, South Dakota, June 1932.

31. Fox, *Archaeology, History, and Custer's Last Battle,* 154; see also Figure 7–1, 95.

32. Knife sticks were a particularly brutal weapon. They consisted of a long shaft with three blades set into slots, protruding about three or four inches. For a good picture of this dreadful thing, see Scott, et al., *Archaelogical Perspectives on the Battle of the Little Bighorn,* 103.

33. *Ibid.,* 101.

34. Richard G. Hardorff, *The Custer Battle Casualties* (El Segundo, CA: Upton & Sons, 2002), 112. Citing Walter Mason Camp notes, Indiana University, transcript page 42.

35. Hardorff, *Cheyenne Memories of the Custer Fight,* 62–63. From an interview with George Bird Grinnell at the Northern Cheyenne Indian Reservation in Montana, 1908.

36. Wagner, *Participants,* 223.

37. Hardorff, *Indian Views of the Custer Fight,* 85. This appears to be from a letter written by George Bent (an educated mixed-blood Indian married to a Southern Cheyenne woman) and addressed to George Hyde, an anthropologist and historian. The letter is dated March 8, 1906, from Colony, Oklahoma.

38. *Ibid.,* 85–86, footnote 9.

39. *Ibid.,* 86, footnote 9.

40. *Ibid.,* 85.

41. Hardorff, *Lakota Recollections,* 123, footnote 38. See also Wagner, *Participants,* 128.

42. Wagner, *Participants,* 157.

43. Stephen W. Myers, "Roster of Known Hostile Indians at the Battle of the Little Big Horn," *Research Review* 5, no. 2 (June 1991).

44. Wagner, *Participants,* 157.

45. Cross, Walt, *Custer's Lost Officer* (Stillwater, OK: Cross, 2006), 139.

46. Hardorff, *Indian Views of the Custer Fight,* 65. From an interview conducted at Fort Yates, July 30, 1881, and carried in the August 14, 1881, *Leavenworth Times.*

47. *Ibid.,* 111. From a series of interviews held from March 3 to March 5, 1913, at the New Capitol Hotel, Washington City.

48. Hardorff, *Lakota Recollections,* 157. Interview with Sewell Weston, 1909.

49. Hardorff, 43. In an interview by Eli Ricker with Red Hawk and Nicholas Ruleau, 1906.

50. Graham, *The Custer Myth,* 88–89. From a June 26, 1886, Chicago newspaper.

51. *Ibid.,* 346. Letter by Godfrey to E. S. Paxson, January 16, 1896.

52. Liddic, *Vanishing Victory,* 156, footnote 171. Citing Dale T. Schoenberger, *End of Custer* (Blaine, WA: Hancock House, 1995), 199.

53. Hardorff, *Indian Views of the Custer Fight,* 126. Hardorff writes that this interview was contained in M. I. McCreight's, *Firewater and Forked Tongues* (Pasadena: Trail's End, 1947), 111–115. It was conducted at DuBois, Pennsylvania, in 1928.

54. Richard G. Hardorff, *The Custer Battle Casu-*

alties, *II* (El Segundo, CA: Upton & Sons, 1999), 131.

55. *Ibid.,* 130.

56. Wagner, *Participants,* 229 and 230.

57. Hardorff, *Indian Views of the Custer Fight,* 188. This interview appeared in an unidentified newspaper forwarded in a field dispatch, September 25, 1936. Apparently, it was conducted at the Pine Ridge Reservation, the interpreter being a woman whose only name was known to be "Josephine."

58. Graham, *The Custer Myth,* 87. From an article appearing in the St. Paul, Minnesota, *Pioneer Press,* May 19, 1883.

59. Camp, *Custer in '76,* 207. An interview conducted on July 13, 1910.

60. Hardorff, *Lakota Recollections,* 75. An interview with General Hugh Scott, August 19, 1920.

61. These soldiers were Ygnatz Stungewitz and Willis B. Wright (C Company); Edward C. Driscoll, Archibald McIlhargey, John E. Mitchell, and John Parker (I); and Francis T. Hughes, Charles McCarthy, Oscar F. Pardee, and Thomas S. Tweed (L). It is unknown if the two Reno orderlies—McIlhargey and Mitchell—sent back from Ford A as messengers, remained with Custer or were relegated to their unit, but their presence in the Last Stand Hill area seems to favor the former choice, the coincidence of their remaining together as "refugees" from one killing zone to another rather mind-bending.

62. Scott, *Uncovering History* (Norman: University of Oklahoma Press, 2013), 110. Both Douglas Scott and Jerome Greene (*Evidence and the Custer Enigma,* 39–40) speak of a body found in Deep Coulee: "A soldier's skeleton was found by Frank Bethune in the Deep Coulee area in 1928. [P.] Willey examined that skeleton ... and found it to be that of a 35-year-old white male about 68 inches tall. He had a gunshot wound to the head, evidence of blunt force trauma, and at least 98 cut marks on his bones, indicating that the victorious Lakota and Cheyenne mutilated him.... No identity has been established for this man." This is in all likelihood the same area where Joseph Blummer in 1904, found a boot with bones in it and equipment bearing the initials, "J. D." or "R. D." At the time, the boot was thought to be from John Duggan (L). Duggan was 5' 9½" tall and 27 years old, making him a little too tall and a little too young for the 1928 discovery. There are a number of other Keogh troopers fitting this description: CPL William H. Harrison (L), 67¾" tall and 31 years old; BSM Charles Siemon (L), 67½" tall and 33 years old; PVT David J. O'Connell (L), 67½" tall and 33 years old; and PVT James Farrand (C), 68" tall and 37 years old. Jerome Greene wrote, "During the years after the battle, Frank Bethune found several skeletons in the area of Deep Coulee, and in 1928 found one with an arrowhead fixed in its spine" (*Evidence...* p. 39). Greene was alluding to the four run-aways Wooden Leg spoke of, another possibility, especially since the Greene artifact map shows the bones found well above where the E and F Company troopers would have cut across the flats of Deep Coulee. Privates O'Connell and Siemon best fit the description.

63. Marquis, *Wooden Leg,* 229. From the Wooden Leg interviews, 1922–1931.

64. Hardorff, *Lakota Recollections,* 182. In an interview with Sewell Weston, 1909.

65. Graham, *The Custer Myth,* 88–89. Citing an article from an unnamed Chicago newspaper, June 26, 1886.

66. *Ibid.,* 89.

67. Camp, *Custer in '76,* 201. An interview with Walter Camp, September 22, 1908.

68. Graham, *The Custer Myth,* 85. From the St. Paul *Pioneer Press,* May 19, 1883.

69. Hardorff, *Indian Views of the Custer Fight,* 155. In an interview with Walter S. Campbell at the

Cheyenne River Indian Reservation, Cherry Creek, SD, in June 1932.

70. *Ibid,* 124. In an interview conducted in Du Bois, PA, 1928.

71. Hardorff, *Lakota Recollections,* 148–149.

Chapter 18

1. Hardorff, *Cheyenne Memories of the Custer Fight,* 169. From an interview with Don Rickey, Jr., and Jesse W. Vaughn at the Custer Battlefield, 1956.

2. Liberty, *Cheyenne Memories,* 199–200. Written from notes and recordings, 1957–1966, and published shortly after Stands in Timber's death.

3. Hardorff, *Indian Views of the Custer Fight,* 68. From an interview conducted at Fort Yates on July 30, 1881, and carried in the *Leavenworth Times,* August 14, 1881.

4. Fox, *Archaeology, History, and Custer's Last Battle,* 181–182.

5. Scott/Bleed, *A Good Walk Around the Boundary,* 43–44.

6. Hardorff, *Cheyenne Memories of the Custer Fight,* 43. From an interview with George Bird Grinnell on the Northern Cheyenne Indian Reservation, Montana, 1898.

7. *Ibid.*

8. *Ibid.,* 63. From an interview with George Bird Grinnell on the Northern Cheyenne Indian Reservation, Montana, 1908.

9. Fox, *Archaeology, History, and Custer's Last Battle,* 181 and 353, footnote 36.

10. *Ibid.,* 353, footnote 36.

11. Camp, *Custer in '76,* 72. Undated interview with Walter Camp. This "interview" may have been taken from correspondence between them, primarily from a letter written by McDougall, dated February 26, 1909, a few months before he died.

12. *Ibid.,* 248. Walter Camp interview, February 14, 1911, probably conducted at Fort Snelling, Minnesota.

13. Graham, *The Custer Myth,* 110. From an interview with Colonel Tim McCoy, 1920.

14. Camp, *Custer in '76,* 213.

15. Hardorff, *Lakota Recollections,* 147. An interview with Sewell Weston, 1908.

16. *Ibid.,* 168. An interview with Sewell Weston, 1909.

17. *Ibid.,* 184. An interview with Sewell Weston, 1909.

18. *Ibid.,* 189. An interview with Sewell Weston, 1909.

19. Camp, *Custer in '76,* 199. An interview with Walter Mason Camp, September 22, 1908.

20. Hardorff, *Cheyenne Memories of the Custer Fight,* 43–44. From an interview with George Bird Grinnell at the Northern Cheyenne Indian Reservation, Montana, 1898.

21. John G. Neihardt, *Black Elk Speaks* (Lincoln: University of Nebraska Press, 1932 [1988]), 115–116. A 1930 interview.

22. Hardorff, *Cheyenne Memories of the Custer Fight,* 67. Interview with George Bird Grinnell at the Northern Cheyenne Indian Reservation, Montana, 1908.

23. Hardorff, *Indian Views of the Custer Fight,* 89–90. From a narrative contained in the Edward Curtis papers, Natural History Museum of Los Angeles County, California. The interview took place on a Sioux reservation in 1907.

24. Hardorff, *Cheyenne Memories of the Custer Fight,* 63. From an interview with George Bird Grinnell at the Northern Cheyenne Indian Reservation, Montana, 1908.

25. Hardorff, *Indian Views of the Custer Fight,* 157. From an interview with Walter S. Campbell at the Cheyenne River Reservation, Cherry Creek, South Dakota, June 1932.

26. Hardorff, *Lakota Recollections,* 167. Sewell Weston interview, 1909.

27. *Ibid.,* 162. Weston interview, 1909.

28. Camp, *Custer in '76,* 210. Interview with Walter Mason Camp, May 21, 1907.

29. *Ibid.,* 199. Interview with Walter Mason Camp, September 22, 1908.

30. *Ibid.,* 201. Interview with Walter Mason Camp, September 22, 1908.

31. Hardorff, *Lakota Recollections,* 149. Interview with Sewell Weston, 1908.

32. *Ibid.,* 159. Interview with Sewell Weston, 1909.

33. Scott/Bleed, *A Good Walk Around the Boundary,* 13.

34. Willert, *Little Big Horn Diary,* 451, footnote 6. Willert added, "This map of Benteen's was discovered in May 1954, in an old trunk on the Benteen estate."

35. Graham, *The Custer Myth,* 220. From the *Leavenworth Times,* August 18, 1881.

36. Nichols, *Reno Court of Inquiry,* 454.

37. *Ibid.,* 68.

38. Camp, *Custer in '76,* 179. Interviews with Walter Camp, October 1908, and February 8, 1909.

39. Liddic, *Camp on Custer,* 73. Undated interview.

40. Hardorff, *The Custer Battle Casualties, II,* 81, from the *Pacific Monthly,* July 1908, and Hardorff, *On the Little Bighorn with Walter Camp,* 186, Camp's notes, October 13, 1912.

41. Camp, *Custer in '76,* 215. From an interview, July 12, 1910.

42. Graham, *The Custer Myth,* 78 and 81. From the *Leavenworth Weekly Times,* August 18, 1881, possibly by Frank Huston.

43. DeMallie, *The Sixth Grandfather,* 186. From an interview with John Neihardt, 1931.

44. Hutchins, *The Army and Navy Journal,* 106. From the report of Agent Mitchell, Fort Peck, September 25, 1876.

45. Hardorff, *Lakota Recollections,* 147. Sewell Weston interview, 1908.

46. *Ibid.,* 157. Sewell Weston interview, 1909.

47. *Ibid.,* 167. Sewell Weston interview, 1909.

48. Camp, *Custer in '76,* 213. Interviewed July 22, 1910.

Chapter 19

1. Camp, *Custer in '76,* 66. From an interview with Camp, February 7, 1910.

2. Nichols, *Reno Court of Inquiry,* 408.

3. Graham, *The Custer Myth,* 172 and 181. From "The Benteen Manuscript," written by Benteen and loaned to Edward Godfrey by Benteen's son, Major Frederick Benteen. It was one of two manuscripts given to Godfrey and was only returned to the Benteen family after Godfrey's death. The earlier of the two—considered the more important—was returned missing its final pages; the second manuscript was not returned and is now missing. This was believed written shortly after the battle of Wounded Knee in 1890. See Graham, 160.

4. Camp, *Custer in '76,* 177. Camp interview, February 23, 1911.

5. Libby, *The Arikara Narrative,* 129 and 160.

6. Nichols, *Reno Court of Inquiry,* Benteen's testimony, 406 and 414, and Hare's, 280 and 296.

7. *Ibid.,* 484.

8. *Ibid.*

9. Richard G. Hardorff, *Indian Views of the Custer Fight,* 205. From a letter by former B Company private, August DeVoto, to Walter Mason Camp, October 1, 1917.

10. Nichols, *Reno Court of Inquiry,* 567.

11. *Ibid.,* 144.

12. *Ibid.,* 529.

13. Camp, *Custer in '76,* 70. Undated Walter Camp interview. This "interview" may have been taken from correspondence between Camp and McDougall, primarily from a letter written by McDougall, dated February 26, 1909.

14. Nichols, *Reno Court of Inquiry,* 529.

15. Carroll, *The Benteen-Goldin Letters,* 186. From the so-called "Benteen Manuscript," 1890.

16. Hutchins, *The Army and Navy Journal,* 90. A letter from Godfrey, dated August 7, 1876, from the camp of the Seventh Cavalry, "Rose Bud, M. T."

17. Godfrey, *Field Diary,* 36–37. Godfrey's field diary, starting from May 17, 1876, to September 24, 1876—in this case, August 15, 1876. In the introduction Stewart points out that some diary entries were probably written several days after the event, but no more than four or five days after the actual date. This would be true certainly during the days of the battle. The late entries were probably done all at once.

18. Nichols, *Reno Court of Inquiry,* 289.

19. Camp, *Custer in '76,* 66. Interview with Walter Camp, February 7, 1910.

20. Varnum, *I, Varnum,* 174, quoting his Reno inquiry testimony. See also Nichols, *Reno Court of Inquiry,* 180.

21. Graham, *The Custer Myth,* 343. From Varnum's letter to his father dated July 4, 1876.

22. Nichols, *Reno Court of Inquiry,* 374.

23. Godfrey, "Custer's Last Battle," 27.

24. Godfrey, *Field Diary,* 12–13. Stewart pointed out that some diary entries were probably written after the event, but no more than four or five days after the actual date.

25. Camp, *Custer in '76,* 70. In a letter from McDougall to Walter Camp, dated February 26, 1909.

26. Nichols, *Reno Court of Inquiry,* 353.

27. *Ibid.,* 392.

28. Windolph, *I Fought with Custer,* 98–99. Windolph's memoirs, 1946.

29. Nichols, *Reno Court of Inquiry,* 144.

30. Varnum, *I, Varnum,* 92. From Varnum's memoirs, probably written in the early 1930s.

31. Nichols, *Reno Court of Inquiry,* 218.

32. *Ibid.,* 529 and 532.

33. *Ibid.,* 144.

34. *Ibid.,* 444.

35. Graham, *The Custer Myth,* 220. From an article in the *Leavenworth Times,* August 18, 1881.

36. Liddic, *Camp on Custer,* 97. Thomas Harrison interview with Walter Camp, 1911.

37. Nichols, *Reno Court of Inquiry,* 485.

38. Graham, *The Custer Myth,* 142. From the 1921 revision of Godfrey's 1892 *Century Magazine* article.

39. Ryan, *Ten Years with Custer,* 297. From Ryan's memoirs, probably written in the 1880s and between 1904 and 1906.

40. Windolph, *I Fought with Custer,* 99. Windolph's memoirs, 1946.

41. Nichols, *Reno Court of Inquiry,* 144.

42. *Ibid.,* 161.

43. *Ibid.,* 145 and 161.

44. *Ibid.,* 292.

45. Graham, *The Custer Myth,* 259. From an article appearing in the *New York Herald,* July 8, 1876. It was obviously from an interview with Herendeen.

46. Nichols, *Reno Court of Inquiry,* 219.

47. Carroll, *The Benteen-Goldin Letters,* 216. From a March 1, 1892, letter, Benteen to Goldin.

48. Graham, *The Custer Myth,* 172 and 181. From the so-called "Benteen Manuscript," probably written around 1890.

49. Camp, *Custer in '76,* 57. Walter Camp interview, undated but probably in the early 1900s. Edgerly—in a letter to W. A. Graham—stated he never met Camp and believed the "interview" must have been taken from his correspondence with Camp.

50. Godfrey, "Custer's Last Battle," 28.

51. Liddic, *Camp on Custer,* 97. From an interview with Walter Camp, 1911.

52. Camp, *Custer in '76,* 130. From an interview with Walter Camp, October 16, 1910.

53. Hardorff, *Camp, Custer, and the Little Bighorn,* 63, footnote 3.

54. Liddic, *Camp on Custer,* 98. From an interview with Walter Camp, 1911.

55. Hardorff, *Camp, Custer, and the Little Bighorn,* 63–64, footnote 3. Undated interview between former D Company sergeant, Thomas W. Harrison, and Walter Mason Camp. Camp MSS, field notes, box 3, BYU.

56. *Ibid.,* 64, footnote 4. It is unclear here if this was *said* by Edgerly or *written* by Camp, i.e., Camp's opinion, though it certainly reflects Edgerly's opinion. The Charley incident haunted Edgerly for the rest of his life and it is clear it changed his relationship with Weir.

57. Camp, *Custer in '76,* 76. From correspondence with Walter Camp, early 1900s.

58. Graham, *The Custer Myth,* 319. Godfrey's letter to R. G. Carter, April 14, 1925.

59. Ryan, *Ten Years with Custer,* 298. Ryan's memoirs, 1880s, 1904–1906.

60. Godfrey, *Field Diary,* 14.

Chapter 20

1. Shelby Foote, *The Civil War: A Narrative* (New York: Random House, 1958), Vol. 1, 611.

2. Godfrey, "Custer's Last Battle," 38.

3. Graham, *The Custer Myth,* 147. This includes a section from Godfrey's 1908 revision. Apparently the revision was not printed until Libbie Custer had it published in 1921.

4. *Ibid.,* 147.

5. *Ibid.*

6. Carroll, *The Benteen-Goldin Letters,* 213–214. Written between 1891 and 1896. It is important to understand that Benteen—in the writing of these letters—believed Theodore Goldin had served at least a full five-year term of enlistment with the Seventh Cavalry and Goldin did nothing to dissuade Benteen from that belief. In actuality, Goldin served only 19 months (April 8, 1876 to November 13, 1877), being discharged "without honor." In future years, Goldin led people to believe he had served from 1875 to 1879, being discharged because of disability suffered from wounds received in the Little Big Horn battle. Of course, that was another Goldin lie: he suffered no wound there. These letters also give us a tremendous insight into the personalities of many military men of the time, not the least of whom were the Custer brothers, and Sturgis, Merrill, Reno, *et al.* Benteen shows his colors here. He was a strong-willed, uncompromising man, who refused to take the easy way and unsuffering of fools. He was extremely opinionated and while one may be a bit more compassionate, he saw life for what it really was.

7. von Clausewitz, *On War,* 546–547.

8. Graham, *The Custer Myth,* 116. Quoting from a letter issued by Lieutenant General P. H. Sheridan in response to Captain Philo Clark's report of his 1877 battlefield survey.

9. Graham, *The Custer Myth,* 154. Graham quotes Fry's article from *Century Magazine* XLIII, no. 3 (January 1892).

10. Stewart, *Custer's Luck,* 29.

11. *Ibid.,* 53, footnote 2, *Report of the Secretary of War, 1876,* 27 and 499. Recent studies contend these numbers are greatly inflated. Like the Pinkerton estimates of the Army of Northern Virginia troop strength—both during the Peninsula Campaign and at Antietam—factors other than direct head-count raised estimates to hopelessly wild numbers. A more realistic figure for the Lakota population in 1876 is some 14,500 to 16,500 souls. An extended study in the methodology behind these figures was provided me by Stephen Krzyk, a fine student of the battle, though the main analysis is contained in Kingsley M.

Bray, "Teton Sioux: Population History, 1644–1881" (*Nebraska History,* Vol. 75, 1994), 165–188, Krzyk providing insight and clarification.

12. Bray, "Teton Sioux: Population History, 1644–1881," 165–188.

13. *The Frank L. Anders-R. G. Cartwright Correspondence,* Volume 1, 95–96. Anders letter to Cartwright, February 7, 1948.

Appendix A

1. Connell, *Son of the Morning Star,* 401 and 402.
2. Marquis, *Wooden Leg,* 324.
3. Willert, *Little Big Horn Diary,* 201.
4. Heski, "Don't Let Anything Get Away," 16–17.
5. *Ibid.,* 25.
6. *Ibid.*
7. *Ibid.,* 31, footnote 147.
8. Liddic, *Vanishing Victory,* 131.
9. Michno, *The Mystery of E Troop,* 234.
10. *Ibid.,* 234–235.
11. Scott, Fox, Connor, and Harmon, *Archaeological Perspectives on the Battle of the Little Bighorn,* 42.
12. *Ibid.,* 42, citing Goldin, *The Benteen-Goldin Letters,* 19 and 27.
13. *Ibid.,* 47.
14. *Ibid.,* 43.
15. *Ibid.,* 226.

Appendix B

1. Michno, *The Mystery of E Troop,* 188.
2. *Ibid.,* 197.
3. Stewart, *Custer's Luck,* 436–437, citing Edna L. Waldo, *Dakota,* 197, in footnote 22, and Burdick, *Last Battle of the Sioux Nation,* 40, in footnote 23.

Appendix C

1. Scott, *et al., Archaeological Perspectives,* 51.
2. Trinque, "Elusive Ridge," *Research Review* 9, no. 1 (January 1995): 3.
3. Greene, *Evidence and the Custer Enigma,* 45, and Smalley, *More Little Big Horn Mysteries,* 16–14, footnote 29.
4. Hardorff, *On the Little Bighorn with Walter Camp,* 6, footnote 2.
5. Michno, *Lakota Noon,* 153, including his map.
6. *Ibid.*
7. *Ibid.*
8. *Ibid.,* 226, map.
9. Liddic, *Vanishing Victory,* 116.
10. Michno, *The Mystery of E Troop,* 51–52.
11. Liddic, *Vanishing Victory,* 151.
12. Hardorff, *On the Little Bighorn with Walter Camp,* 155.
13. Michno, *The Mystery of E Troop,* 218.
14. Liddic, *Vanishing Victory,* 164.

15. Hardorff, *On the Little Bighorn with Walter Camp,* 132, footnote 5.
16. Hardorff, *Camp, Custer, and the Little Bighorn,* 64–65. An undated interview between Rafter and Walter Mason Camp.
17. *Ibid.,* 71.
18. *Ibid.*
19. Camp, *Custer in '76,* 248.
20. Brust, Pohanka, Barnard, *Where Custer Fell,* 127–132.
21. Michno, *The Mystery of E Troop,* 234.
22. *Ibid.,* 234–235.
23. *Ibid.,* 235.
24. Scott, et al., *Archaeological Perspectives,* 51.
25. *Ibid.,* 268.
26. *Ibid.,* 118.
27. *Ibid.*

Appendix D

1. Hardorff, *Cheyenne Memories of the Custer Fight,* 40. An interview with George Bird Grinnell, at the Northern Cheyenne Indian Reservation in Montana, 1895.
2. *Ibid.,* 40, footnote 3.

BIBLIOGRAPHY

Books

Balck, Wilhelm. *Development of Tactics—World War.* Harry Bell, trans. Fort Leavenworth, 1922.

Barnard, Sandy, ed. *Ten Years with Custer.* Terre Haute: AST Press, 2001.

Bradley, Lieutenant James H. *The March of the Montana Column.* Edgar I. Stewart, ed. Norman: University of Oklahoma Press, 2001.

Brady, Charles T. *Indian Fights and Fighters.* New York: Doubleday, 1904.

Bray, Kingsley M. *Crazy Horse.* Norman: University of Oklahoma Press, 2006.

Brininstool, E. A. *A Trooper with Custer and Other Historic Incidents of the Battle of the Little Big Horn.* Columbus, OH: Hunter-Trader-Trapper, 1925.

Brust, James S., Brian C. Pohanka, and Sandy Barnard. *Where Custer Fell.* Norman: University of Oklahoma Press, 2005.

Callwell, Colonel C. E. *Small Wars.* Lincoln: University of Nebraska Press, 1996.

Carell, Paul. *Foxes of the Desert.* Atglen, PA: Schiffer Military History, 1994.

Carroll, John. *The Gibson and Edgerly Narratives.* Bryan, TX: privately printed, undated.

Carroll, John M., ed. *The Benteen-Goldin Letters on Custer and His Last Battle.* New York: Liveright, 1974.

_____. *General Custer and the Battle of the Little Big Horn: The Federal View.* Mattituck, NY: J. M. Carroll, 1986.

Chorne, Laudie J. *Following the Custer Trail of 1876.* Bismarck: Printing Plus, 1997.

Clark, George M. *Scalp Dance.* Oswego, NY: Heritage Press, 1985.

Coffeen, Herbert. *The Custer Battle Book.* New York: A Reflection Book, Carlton Press, 1964.

Connell, Evan. *Son of the Morning Star.* New York: HarperCollins, 1984.

Cooke, Philip St. George. *The 1862 U.S. Cavalry Tactics.* Mechanicsburg, PA: Stackpole, 2004.

Cross, Walt. *Custer's Lost Officer.* Stillwater, OK: Cross, 2006.

Curtis, Edward Sheriff. *Visions of a Vanishing Race.* Edison, NJ: Promontory Press, 1974–1976 (1994).

Darling, Roger. *Benteen's Scout.* El Segundo, CA: Upton, 2000.

_____. *A Sad and Terrible Blunder.* Vienna, VA: Potomac-Western Press, 1990.

DeMallie, Raymond J., ed. *The Sixth Grandfather.* Lincoln: University of Nebraska Press/Bison Books, 1985.

DePuy, General William E. *Selected Papers of General William E. DePuy.* Richard M. Swain, Donald L. Gilmore, and Carolyn D. Conway, comp. and eds. Fort Leavenworth: Combat Studies Institute, U.S. Army Command and General Staff College, 1994.

Dickson, Ephriam D., III. *The Sitting Bull Surrender Census.* Pierre: South Dakota State Historical Society Press, 2010.

Dixon, Joseph Kossuth. *The Vanishing Race.* Garden City, NY: Doubleday, Page, 1913.

Donahue, Michael N. *Drawing Battle Lines.* El Segundo, CA: Upton, 2008.

Donovan, James. *Custer and the Little Bighorn.* Stillwater, MN: Voyageur Press, 2001.

_____. *A Terrible Glory.* New York: Little, Brown, 2008.

Doran, Robert E. *Horsemanship at Little Big Horn.* West Conshohocken, PA: Infinity, 2007.

Du Bois, Charles G. *The Custer Mystery.* El Segundo, CA: Upton, 1986.

Dustin, Fred. *The Custer Tragedy.* El Segundo, CA: Upton, 2011 (Ann Arbor: Edwards Brothers, 1939 [1965]).

Finerty, John F. *War-Path and Bivouac: The Bighorn and Yellowstone Expedition.* Chicago: Lakeside Press, 1955.

Foote, Shelby. *The Civil War: A Narrative.* Volumes 1–3. New York: Random House, 1958, 1963, 1974.

Fox, Richard Allan, Jr. *Archaeology, History, and Custer's Last Battle.* Norman: University of Oklahoma Press, 1993.

Godfrey, Edward S. *The Field Diary of Lieutenant Edward Settle Godfrey (1876).* Edgar I. Stewart, ed. Portland, OR: Champoeg Press, 1957.

Graham, Colonel William A. *The Custer Myth.* Mechanicsburg, PA: Stackpole, 2000.

Gray, John S. *Custer's Last Campaign.* Lincoln: University of Nebraska Press, 1993.

Greene, Jerome A. *Evidence and the Custer Enigma.* Silverthorne, CO: Vistabooks, 1995.

Hammer, Kenneth. *Men with Custer: Biographies of the 7th Cavalry.* Ronald H. Nichols, ed. Hardin, MT: Custer Battlefield Historical & Museum Association, 1995.

Hammer, Kenneth, ed. *Custer in '76.* Norman: University of Oklahoma Press, 1990.

Hardorff, Richard G. *Hokahey! A Good Day to Die!* Lincoln: University of Nebraska Press/Bison Books, 1999.

_____. *The Custer Battle Casualties.* El Segundo, CA: Upton, 2002.

Hardorff, Richard G., ed. *Camp, Custer and the Little Bighorn.* El Segundo, CA: Upton, 1997.

_____, ed. *Cheyenne Memories of the Custer Fight.* Lincoln: University of Nebraska Press, 1998.

_____, ed. *The Custer Battle Casualties, II.* El Segundo, CA: Upton,

_____, ed. *Indian Views of the Custer Fight.* Norman: University of Oklahoma Press, 2005.

_____, ed. *Lakota Recollections of the Custer Fight.* Lincoln: University of Nebraska Press/Bison Books, 1997.

_____, ed. *On the Little Bighorn with Walter Camp.* El Segundo, CA: Upton, 2002.

Hart, John P., ed. *Custer and His Times.* Cordova, TN: Little Big Horn Associates, 2008. Book Five.

Heitman, Francis B. *Historical Register and Dictionary of the United States Army.* Washington, D.C.: U.S. Government Printing Office, 1903 (Urbana: University of Illinois Press, 1965). Vol. 2.

Horn, W. Donald. *Fifty Years on Custer's Trail.* Privately published, West Orange, NJ: David McMillin, 2010.

Hutchins, James S., ed. *The Army and Navy Journal on the Battle of The Little Bighorn and Related Matters, 1876–1881.* El Segundo, CA: Upton, 2003.

Johnson, Barry C. *Case of Marcus A. Reno.* London: English Westerners' Society, 1969.

Kershaw, Robert J. *Red Sabbath.* Hersham, Surrey, England: Ian Allan, 2005.

King, W. Kent. *Massacre: The Custer Cover-Up.* El Segundo, CA: Upton, 1989.

Klokner, James B. *The Officer Corps of Custer's Seventh Cavalry: 1866–1876.* Atglen, PA: Schiffer Military History, 2007.

Kuhlman, Charles. *Legend into History.* Harrisburg, PA: Stackpole, 1952.

Libby, Orin G., ed. *The Arikara Narrative of Custer's Campaign and the Battle of the Little Bighorn.* Norman: University of Oklahoma Press, 1920 [1998].

Liberty, Margot, and John Stands in Timber. *Cheyenne Memories.* New Haven: Yale University Press, 1967 (1998).

Liddell Hart, B. H. *Strategy.* New York: Meridian/Henry Holt, 1991.

Liddic, Bruce R. *Vanishing Victory.* El Segundo, CA: Upton, 2004.

Liddic, Bruce R., and Paul Harbaugh. *Camp on Custer.* Spokane: Arthur H. Clark, 1995.

Mackintosh, John D. *Custer's Southern Officer.* Lexington, SC: Cloud Creek Press, 2002.

Marquis, Thomas B. *Keep the Last Bullet for Yourself: The True Story of Custer's Last Stand.* Algonac, MI: Reference, 1976.

_____. *Wooden Leg.* Lincoln: University of Nebraska Press, 1931 [1965].

Martinez, David. *The Legends & Lands of Native North Americans.* New York: Sterling, 2003.

McChristian, Douglas C. *The U.S. Army in the West, 1870–1880.* Norman: University of Oklahoma Press, 1995.

McCreight, M. I. *Firewater and Forked Tongues.* Pasadena: Trail's End, 1947.

Michno, Gregory F. *Lakota Noon.* Missoula: Mountain Press, 1997.

_____. *The Mystery of E Troop.* Missoula: Mountain Press, 1994.

Miller, David Humphreys. *Echoes of the Little Bighorn.* Rockville, MD: American Heritage, 1971.

Mills, Charles K. *Harvest of Barren Regrets.* Glendale, CA: Arthur H. Clark, 1985.

Moore, Donald W. *Where the Custer Fight Began.* El Segundo, CA: Upton, 2011.

Neihardt, John G. *Black Elk Speaks.* Lincoln: University of Nebraska Press, 1932 (1988).

Nichols, Ronald H., ed. *Men with Custer.* Hardin, MT: Custer Battlefield Historical & Museum Association, 2000.

_____, ed. *Reno Court of Inquiry.* Hardin, MT: Custer Battlefield Historical & Museum Association, 1996.

O'Neil, Tom, comp. *The Field Diary and Official Report of General Alfred H. Terry.* Brooklyn: Arrow and Trooper, date unknown.

Overfield, Loyd J., II. *The Little Big Horn, 1876: The Official Communications, Documents and Reports.* Lincoln: University of Nebraska Press, 1990.

Panzeri, Peter. *Little Big Horn 1876.* Oxford: Osprey, 1995.

Pennington, Jack. *The Battle of the Little Bighorn.* El Segundo, CA: Upton, 2001.

Scott, Douglas D. *Uncovering History.* Norman: University of Oklahoma Press, 2013.

Scott, Douglas D., and Richard A. Fox, Jr. *Archaeological Insights into the Custer Battle.* Norman: University of Oklahoma Press, 1987.

Scott, Douglas D., Richard A. Fox, Jr., Melissa A. Connor, and Dick Harmon. *Archaeological Perspectives on the Battle of the Little Bighorn.* Norman: University of Oklahoma Press, 1989.

Scott, Douglas D., P. Willey, and Melissa A. Connor. *They Died with Custer.* Norman: University of Oklahoma Press, 1998.

Scudder, Ralph E. *Custer Country.* Portland, OR: Binfords & Mort, 1963.

Smalley, Vern. *Little Bighorn Mysteries.* Bozeman: Little Buffalo Press, 2005.

_____. *More Little Bighorn Mysteries.* Bozeman, MT: Little Buffalo Press, 2005.

Stewart, Edgar I. *Custer's Luck.* Norman: University of Oklahoma Press, 1955.

Sun Tzu. *The Art of War.* London: Oxford University Press, 1963.

Swanson, Glenwood J. *G. A. Custer, His Life and Times.* Agua Dulce, CA: Swanson, 2004.

Taylor, William O. *With Custer on the Little Bighorn.* Greg Martin, ed. New York: Viking Penguin, 1996.

Tillett, Leslie. *Wind on the Buffalo Grass.* New York: Crowell, 1976.

Upton, Richard, comp. and introd. *Custer Catastrophe at the Little Big Horn, 1876.* El Segundo, CA: Upton, 2012.

Varnum, Charles A. *I, Varnum.* John M. Carroll, ed. Mattituck, NY: J. M. Carroll, 1982.

Viola, Herman J. *Little Bighorn Remembered.* New York: Times Books/Random House, 1999.

von Clausewitz, Carl. *On War.* Michael Howard and Peter Paret, trans. Princeton: Princeton University Press, 1989.

Wagner, Frederic C., III. *Participants in the Battle of the Little Big Horn.* Jefferson, NC: McFarland, 2011.

Wagner, Glendolin Damon. *Old Neitriment.* Lynden, WA: Sol Lewis, 1973

Willert, James. *Little Big Horn Diary.* El Segundo, CA: Upton, 1997.

_____. *To the Edge of Darkness.* El Segundo, CA: Upton, 1998.

Williams, Roger L. *Military Register of Custer's Last Command.* Norman: Arthur H. Clark, 2009.

Windolph, Charles. *I Fought with Custer.* Frazier Hunt and Robert Hunt, eds. Lincoln: University of Nebraska Press, 1947.

Articles, Broadcast Media, Journals, Maps, Newspapers, Pamphlets, Periodicals, Organizations, Miscellaneous

Abrams, Marc H., ed. *Newspaper Chronicle of* the Indian Wars 5, *January 1, 1876—July 12, 1876.* Brooklyn: Abrams, 2010.

Bates, Colonel Charles Francis. *Custer's Indian Battles.* Bronxville, NY, 1936.

Belle Fourche Bee, 1922 and 1923.

Bighorn-Yellowstone Journal 1, no. 3 (Summer 1992).

Bonafede, Mike. *Little Bighorn Battlefield Map.* Loveland, CO: Atalissa, 1999.

Bray, Kingsley M. "Teton Sioux: Population History, 1655–1881." *Nebraska History* 75 (1994).

Brininstool, E. A, et al. "Chief Crazy Horse, His Career and Death." *Nebraska History Magazine* XII, no. 1 (January-March 1926). Lincoln: Nebraska State Historical Society.

Camp, Walter Mason. Field Notes, Folder 94, Brigham Young University Library.

Carroll, John M. *Battles of the Little Big Horn.* From a letter written by Morris to Robert Bruce, May 23, 1928. From an e-mail dated January 29, 2011, by Jose Luis Arcon-Dominguez, Ediciones SIMTAC, Valencia, Spain. Listed on Amazon.com as *Battles of the Little Bighorn: General Fry [i.e. Roe] on the Custer battle, William E. Morris to Robert Bruce, Lieutenant Roe to his wife, General Roe article.* Out of print.

Carroll, John M., ed. *The Sunshine Magazine Articles.* John P. Everett, "Bullets, Boots, and Saddles," Sioux Falls, SD, 1930. Privately republished, Bryan, TX, 1979.

Cavalry Journal, Fort Riley, KS: July 1923.

Crow Agency Quadrangle, Montana, Big Horn County, 7.5' series; 1:24,000. Specifically: Crow Agency Montana, N4530-W10722.5/7.5, 1967, AMS 4575 III SW, series V894; Crow Agency SE Montana, N4530-W10715/7.5, 1967, AMS 4575 III SE, series V894; Benteen Quadrangle, Benteen Montana, 45107-D4-TF-024, 1967, DMA 4574 IV NW, series V894; and, Lodge Grass NE Quadrangle, Lodge Grass NE, Montana, 45107-D3-TF-024, 1967, DMA 4574 IV NE, series V894.

Daily Record, Greensboro, NC, April 27, 1924.

Dickson, Ephriam D., III. "The Big Road Roster." 21st Annual Symposium, Custer Battlefield Historical & Museum Association, Inc., Hardin, MT, June 22, 2007.

_____. "The Sitting Bull Surrender Census." 21st Annual Symposium, Custer Battlefield Historical & Museum Association, Inc., Hardin, MT, June 22, 2007.

Du Bois, Charles G. *Kick the Dead Lion.* Billing: Reporter Printing & Supply, 1961.

The Editors of Time-Life Books. *Echoes of Glory: Arms and Equipment of the Union.* Alexandria, VA: Time-Life, 1996.

Ellison, Douglas W. *Mystery of the Rosebud.* Medora, ND: Western Edge Book Distributing, 2002.

Fox, Richard A., Jr. "West River History." Charles E. Rankin, ed. *Legacy,* Helena: Montana Historical Society Press, 1996.

Frank L. Anders-R. G. Cartwright Correspon-

dence, Volume 1, 95–96; Anders letter to Cartwright, February 7, 1948.

Freeman, Captain Henry B. *The Original Manuscript Journal of General Henry Freeman During the Custer Campaign Against the Sioux Indians in 1876*. March 21–October 5, 1876.

Gibbon, Colonel John. "Gibbon on the Sioux Campaign of 1876." *American Catholic Quarterly*, April and October 1877, Old Army Press, Bellevue, NE, 1969.

Godfrey, E. S. "Custer's Last Battle." *Century Magazine,* January 1892. Reprint by Outbooks, Olympic Valley, CA, 1976.

Helena Herald, Helena, MT, July 15, 1876.

Heski, Thomas M. "'Don't Let Anything Get Away.'" *Research Review* 21, no. 2 (Summer 2007).

Hinman, Eleanor H. "Oglala Sources on the Life of Crazy Horse, Interviews Given to Eleanor H. Hinman." *Nebraska History* 57 (1976).

Horn, W. Donald. "Did Custer Plan to Follow Reno into the Valley?" Unpublished article, 2012.

Indian School Journal, Oklahoma, November 1905.

Kanipe, Daniel A. "A New Story of Custer's Last Battle Told by the Messenger Boy Who Survived," *Contributions to the Historical Society of Montana* IV (1903).

Leavenworth Times, Leavenworth, KS, August 18, 1881.

Little Big Horn Battlefield, Montana Territory, June 1876. Olean, NY: McElfresh Map, 1996.

Luce, Lieutenant Colonel Edward S. Letter to Charles G. Du Bois, dated February 26, 1953.

Charles G. Du Bois Historical Collection. Provided through the courtesy of Bruce R. Liddic.

Lupfer, Captain Timothy T. "The Dynamics of Doctrine: The Changes in German Tactical Doctrine During the First World War." *Leavenworth Papers,* No. 4. Fort Leavenworth: Combat Studies Institute, U.S. Army Command and General Staff College, July 1981.

Mangum, Neil C. "The Little Bighorn Campaign." *Blue & Gray* XXIII, no. 2 (2006).

Marquis, Thomas B. *Custer Soldiers Not Buried.* Privately published, 1933.

_____. *Which Indian Killed Custer?* Privately published, 1933.

Myers, Stephen W. "Roster of Known Hostile Indians at the Battle of the Little Big Horn," *Research Review* 5, no. 2 (June 1991).

New York Herald, July 8, 1876.

New York Herald, August 8, 1876.

New York Herald, September 24, 1876.

New York Herald, January 4, 1878.

New York Herald, January 22, 1878.

Pioneer Press, St. Paul, MN, May 19, 1883.

Pioneer Press, St. Paul, MN, July 18, 1886.

Public Broadcasting System, www.pbs.org/weta/thewest/resources/archives/six/bighorn.htm.

Robbins, James S. "Custer: The Goat at West Point and at War." John P. Hart, ed. *Custer and His Times, Book Five.* Cordova, TN: Little Big Horn Associates, 2008.

Scott, Douglas D., and Charles E. Rankin, ed. "Archaeological Perspectives on the Battle of the Little Bighorn," *Legacy,* Helena: Montana Historical Society Press, 1996.

Scott, Douglas D., and Peter Bleed. *A Good*

Walk Around the Boundary. Lincoln: A Special Publication of the Nebraska Association of Professional Archaeologists and the Nebraska State Historical Society, 1997 (2006).

Sheridan, Lieutenant General P. H., and Marc Abrams, ed. *Record of Engagements with Hostile Indians Within the Military Division of the Missouri from 1868–1882.* Chicago: Headquarters Military Division of the Missouri, 1882.

Sklenar, Larry. "Too Soon Discredited?" *Research Review,* January 1995, Vol. 9, No. 1.

Sundstrom, Linea. *The Thin Elk/Steamboat Winter Count: A Study in Lakota Pictography.* Privately published by Linea Sundstrom, 2003.

Taunton, Francis B. *Sufficient Reason?* London: English Westerners' Society, 1977.

Tepee Book, June 1916.

Thompson, Peter. "The Experience of a Private Soldier in the Custer Massacre," *Belle Fourche* (South Dakota) *Bee,* 1922 or 1923. State Historical Society of North Dakota.

Trinque, Bruce A. "Elusive Ridge," *Research Review,* January 1995, Vol. 9, No. 1.

United States Naval Observatory, Washington, D. C.

Wagner, Frederic C., III. "Frederic Francis Gerard: A Questionable Cause and an Unforeseen Effect," *Research Review,* Winter 2007, Vol. 21, No. 1.

Yellow Nose; Guerriere, Edward, trans. *The Big Horn-Yellowstone Journal,* Summer, 1992, Vol. 1, No. 3, 15. Article in the *Chicago Record-Herald.* Originally appeared in *The Indian School Journal,* November 1905.

Index

Page numbers in ***bold italics*** indicate pages with illustrations.